BLUE GUIDE

VENICE

Alta Macadam

Somerset Books • London
WW Norton • New York

4

pp. 400-01

S. Alvise

Madonna dell' Orto

CANAL

Jewish Mus.

CANNAREGIO

I Gesuiti

pp. 410-11

GRAND

S. Stae

Ca' d'Oro

Santa Lucia Station

SANTA CROCE

Ca' Pesaro

S. Maria d. Miracc

S. Giacomo dell'Orio

CANAL

Rialto Bridge

SAN POLO

pp. 408-09

S. Polo

Santa Maria Gloriosa dei Frari

CANAL

S. Salvatore

GRAND

St Mark Basilic

Ca' Rezzonico

SAN MARCO

GRAND

S. Stefano

La Fenice

Museo Correr

Carmini

DORSODURO

CANAL

Gallerie dell' Accademia

Peggy Guggenheim Collection

Salute

Gesuati

CANALE

pp. 406-07

Mulino Stucky

GIUDECCA

DELLA

Zitel

Redentore

GIUDECCA

pp. 412-13

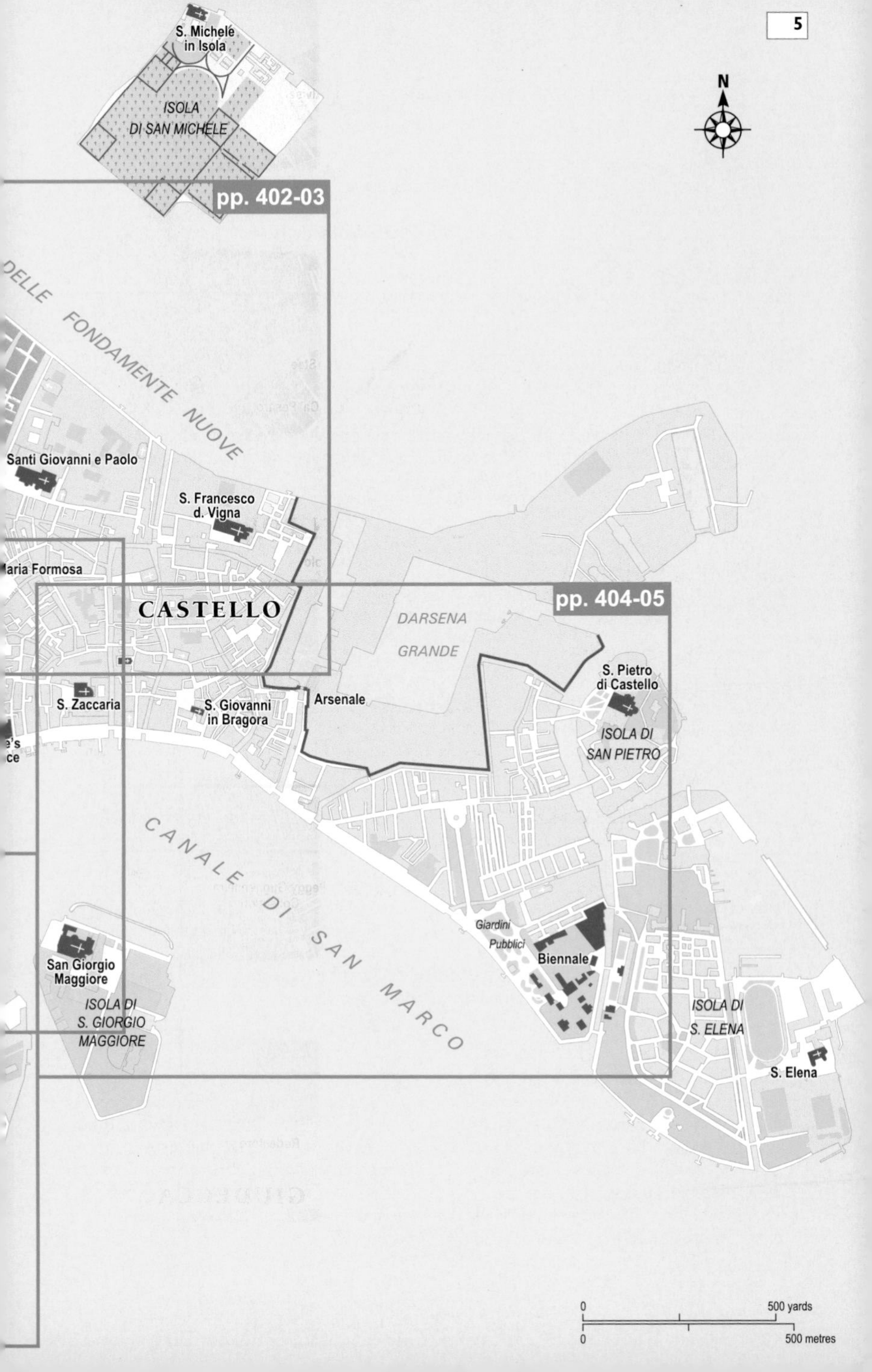

N

S. Michele
in Isola

ISOLA
DI SAN MICHELE

pp. 402-03

DELLE FONDAMENTE NUOVE

Santi Giovanni e Paolo

S. Francesco
d. Vigna

aria Formosa

CASTELLO

pp. 404-05

DARSENA
GRANDE

S. Pietro
di Castello

ISOLA DI
SAN PIETRO

S. Zaccaria

S. Giovanni
in Bragora

Arsenale

e's
ce

CANALE DI SAN MARCO

Giardini
Pubblici

Biennale

San Giorgio
Maggiore

ISOLA DI
S. GIORGIO
MAGGIORE

ISOLA DI
S. ELENA

S. Elena

0   500 yards
0   500 metres

Eighth edition 2007

Published by Blue Guides Limited, a Somerset Books Company
49–51 Causton St, London SW1P 4AT
www.blueguides.com
'Blue Guide' is a registered trademark

ISBN 978–1–905131–17–4

A CIP catalogue record of this book is available from the British Library.

Published in the United States of America by
WW Norton and Company, Inc
500 Fifth Avenue, New York, NY 10110
USA ISBN 978–0–393–33007–6

The author and the publishers have made reasonable efforts to ensure the accuracy of all the
information in *Blue Guide Venice*; however, they can accept no responsibility for any loss, injury or
inconvenience sustained by any traveller as a result of information
or advice contained in the guide.

Statement of editorial independence: Blue Guides, their authors and editors, are prohibited from
accepting any payment from any restaurant, hotel, gallery or other establishment for its inclusion in
this guide, or for a more favourable mention than would otherwise have been made.

Your views on this book would be much appreciated. We welcome not only specific
comments, suggestions or corrections, but any more general views you may have: how this
book enhanced your visit, how it could have been more helpful. Blue Guides authors and
editorial and production team work hard to bring you what we hope are the best-researched
and best-presented cultural guide books in the English language. Please write to us by email
(editorial@blueguides.com), via the comments page on our website (www.blueguides.com)
or at the address given above. We will be happy to acknowledge useful contributions in the
next edition, and to offer a free copy of one of our titles.

CONTENTS

Historical sketch 8
The art of Venice 18
Venice in Peril 30

Topography of Venice 32
Highlights of Venice 38

THE GUIDE

The *sestieri* & Grand Canal

San Marco 41
The Grand Canal 127
Dorsoduro 143
San Polo 191
Santa Croce 214
Cannaregio 225
Castello 255

San Michele 311
Murano 313
Burano and Torcello 320
The Lido and Pellestrina 328
Chioggia 336
The minor islands 338

Guided walks

Dorsoduro 185
Cannaregio 246
Castello 296

Practical information

Arriving in Venice 345
Getting around 346
Accommodation 350
Food and drink 357
Further reading 374
Glossary of special terms 377
Doges of Venice 380
Index 382

The islands & lagoon

San Giorgio Maggiore 302
The Giudecca 306

MAPS

Overview of Venice 4–5
Murano 314
Burano and Torcello 322

Atlas of the city 400–413
Vaporetto routes 414–415
The Venetian lagoon Inside back cover

About the author

Alta Macadam has been a writer of Blue Guides since 1970. She lives with her Italian family in Florence, where she has been associated with the Bargello museum, the Alinari photo archive, Harvard University at Villa I Tatti, and New York University at Villa La Pietra. Her *Americans in Florence* was published in 2003 (Giunti, Florence). As author of the Blue Guides to Florence, Rome, Tuscany, Umbria and Central Italy, she travels extensively every year to revise new editions of the books.

HISTORICAL SKETCH

by Charles Freeman

> This race did not seek refuge in these islands for fun, nor were those who joined later moved by chance; necessity taught them to find safety in the most unfavourable location. Later, however, this turned out to their greatest advantage and made them wise at a time when the whole northern world still lay in darkness; their increasing population and wealth were a logical consequence. Houses were crowded closer and closer together, sand and swamp transformed into solid pavement… The place of street and square and promenade was taken by water. In consequence, the Venetian was bound to develop into a new kind of creature, and that is why too, Venice can only be compared to itself.
>
> *Goethe, Italian Journey, 1786–88.*

Venice is a city of ambiguities, not least in the way it presents its past. Stung by accusations that it never had a Classical heritage, the city created a legend that it had been founded by refugees from Troy, long before Rome had even been heard of. A more enduring foundation myth is that it began life under the protection of the Virgin Mary, precisely at midday on the Feast of the Annunciation, 25th March 421, and this is celebrated by reliefs of the Angel Gabriel and Mary both on the façades of St Mark's and on the Rialto Bridge.

In truth, it was probably not until the 6th century that Lombard invaders sweeping down through the northeast of Italy forced refugees out onto the scattered islands of the lagoon. There is evidence of settlement on the island of Torcello by 600. In these early years the Byzantine Empire kept control of this corner of Italy, and the population was ruled from Ravenna by an appointed military official, the *dux*. The islanders gradually consolidated their identity: by the 7th century they had their own bishopric (on Torcello), and when Ravenna itself was overrun by the Lombards in 751, the *dux* became the city's doge, a ruler now chosen from within the emerging merchant families.

It was trade with the Islamic East which stimulated the wealth of early Venice. Documents and archaeological evidence (in coins) show increasing numbers of Venetian ships heading east as early as the 8th century to the stable and expanding economies of the Arab world. Slaves from northern Europe appear to have been one export, and gold, spices and relics from the Holy Land the return. The early Venetians, then, were focused on the two great civilizations of the Near East: their Byzantine overlords in Constantinople, and the world of Islam. Wealth grew steadily. The cathedral at Torcello is a lone foundation of the 7th century, but there are 12 new churches in the 8th century and 23 in the 9th. In this century too the original patron saint of the city, the Byzantine Theodore, was replaced by the Evangelist St Mark, whose body was reputedly smuggled out from Alexandria in 828 and placed in what was the doge's private chapel; now St Mark's basilica. The centre of power in Venice began to shift from the islands to the area around St Mark's, and in the 11th century the basilica was rebuilt with domes which echoed the (now vanished) church of the Holy Apostles in Constantinople. Despite the transfer of the city's allegiance to St Mark, the links with the Byzantine Empire remained close, and in 992 Venetians were given special trading privileges in Constantinople in return for recognising continuing Byzantine sovereignty.

Venice was too remote from the East to be truly controlled, however, and by 1082 its independence was recognised. After this, in return for naval help they had given to the Byzantines, the Venetians were allowed to trade freely throughout the Empire. The city vigorously developed its own identity as a stable and effective trading community. The doge had originally been an absolute ruler, but after the year 1000 documents suggest that he was aided by officials, the forerunners of the interlocking councils which were later to run the Republic. In 1144 there is the first mention of Venice as a *comune* (the word used to describe the self-ruled cities of northern Italy), and communal activity was reinforced by the need to defend and sustain Venice's precarious position in the lagoon. The city's government took a leading role in regulating water supplies, reclaiming land and setting out communal space. St Mark's Square, modelled on an imperial forum in Constantinople or the great squares of an Islamic city such as Damascus, showed the ability of the Venetian government to preserve space in a crowded city from the incursions of the wealthy merchant families (no other Italian city of the period had such a large open space). Under the patronage of Doge Sebastiano Ziani (1172–78), the square was extended westwards to reach its present size. The procurators, responsible for the fabric of the basilica and the square itself, were among the most prestigious officials of the city, and they took on added functions in overseeing the welfare of patrician families. Some even used the position as a stepping stone to the dogeship. Meanwhile merchants' palaces were beginning to spread along the Grand Canal. 'While the burghers and barons of the north were building their dark streets and grisly castles of oak and sandstone, the merchants of Venice were covering their palaces with porphyry and gold', as John Ruskin put it. It was this combination of public and private display along the waterfronts which was to make the city appear so glittering to outsiders.

The Fourth Crusade and emerging patterns of power

The 12th century was a time of increasing tension as disputes between Venice and Constantinople erupted in self-defeating trade wars. Nothing, however, could have prepared the city for the events of the Fourth Crusade (*see also p. 60*), when under the energetic leadership of Doge Enrico Dandolo, Constantinople was sacked by the crusaders and the Byzantine emperor deposed. Venice trumpeted herself as 'lord of a quarter plus half a quarter of the Roman [i.e. Byzantine] empire'. Large sections of Constantinople, Thrace, the coast of Greece and Crete now passed to Venice, giving her trading posts all the way to the East, with control too of the entrance to the Adriatic. Back in the city, the doges took on the trappings of a Byzantine emperor, appearing to their subjects on the loggia of St Mark's as if they were in the imperial hippodrome of Constantinople. In the reign of Doge Ranier Zeno (1253–68), opulence reached its zenith. St Mark's Square was paved and the doge himself would process around it in rich cloth and jewels. The grand ceremony of the *Sensa*, when the doge went out into the lagoon in the *Bucintoro*, the state barge, and threw a gold ring into the sea to symbolise Venice's 'marriage' to the waters, reached its most elaborate form.

Abroad, however, the newly acquired empire was less stable. Genoa, Venice's most powerful trading rival, allied with Michael Palaeologus, and restored him to the Byzantine throne (1261). The Venetian quarter in Constantinople went up in flames. For the next century Venice and Genoa were engaged in a series of deadly wars which only ended in 1380, when Venice drove off a Genoese force at Chioggia. There were years of unrest and hunger as other cities disputed Venice's trading routes. In 1310 there was an assassination attempt on Doge Pietro Gradenigo after he had failed in a war against Ferrara. He survived, but a Council of Ten was set up to oversee internal security. Its secretive work and readiness to intrude into every aspect of political and social life gave it an unwholesome reputation. In 1355 Doge Marin Falier even tried to seize power and establish a dictatorship (much as nobles in the mainland cities were doing at the same time). He was overcome, deposed and executed.

These troubles masked a steady consolidation of power in the hands of the nobility at the expense of the doge. The *Serrata* of 1297 restricted government to the noble class and they, sitting on the Grand Council, elected the bodies which ruled Venice (*see pp. 96–97*). The consolidation was marked by the rebuilding from 1340 of the private house of the doge, the seat of justice and the meeting halls of the councils into one building, the Doge's Palace, the highest achievement of the Venetian Gothic, the style which was now flamboyantly decorating the palaces of the nobility. Venice's confidence is shown in the openness of these buildings to the sun and the sea, a vivid contrast to the enclosed, fortress-like buildings found, for instance, in Florence at this period. The arrival of the mendicant orders, notably the Dominicans and the Franciscans, saw the fine Gothic churches of Santi Giovanni e Paolo and the Frari (both begun in the 14th century and finished in the 15th) bring a new dimension to the city's religious life, which up to now had centred either on St Mark's or on small parish churches (of which San Giacomo di Rialto is the sole survivor).

The communal identity of the city was strengthened by its use of space, notably St Mark's Square, for ceremonial rituals which displayed the doge, his councillors and its citizens to each other. The anniversary of the arrival of the body of St Mark was celebrated on 31st January. The saint's own feast day was 25th April; and the miraculous recovery of his intact body after a fire destroyed the basilica in the 11th century was commemorated on 25th June. The anniversary of the dedication of the basilica itself followed on 8th October. Gentile Bellini's *Procession in Piazza San Marco* (1496; *see pp. 68–69*) shows how the procession on a ceremonial occasion was arranged, so that each participant could look round to see the officials preceding or following him.

For those excluded from political power—all those outside the four or five per cent of the population which belonged to noble families—the *Scuole Grandi* provided an alternative source of influence. The *scuole* were in fact charitable institutions, but their officials were given high status within the city. Each year on 26th April, for instance, they paraded their relics (the School of St John the Evangelist had a relic of the True Cross, the centrepiece of the procession shown in Bellini's painting), and then presented candles to the doge, as well as to his leading councillors, to foreign ambassadors and senior members of the clergy. The Venetian statesman Gasparo Contarini, writing in the mid-16th century, argued that such rituals satisfied these men's ambition and cooled any resentment they might feel towards the nobility. Certain non-noble families, making up perhaps another seven per cent of the population, were also granted the status of *cittadino originario*, which allowed privileged access to administrative posts.

All this display and stability depended on commercial prosperity. The Rialto was like a permanent trade fair, where goods were brought from all over the Mediterranean. Spices and precious stuffs, furs, jewels and raw materials for cloth, often from as far afield as India and China, all came through the Byzantine or Islamic states. Metals, finished cloth and, it appears, slaves, were brought from Europe by merchants over the Alps. Venice acted as the entrepôt. Once customs fees had been paid, goods could be reshipped either by Venetian vessels (who were also heading west by the 1320s) or by those merchants, mostly Italian and German, who had been given special trading privileges. The Germans had their own great storehouse and meeting house, the Fondaco dei Tedeschi, across the Rialto Bridge from the main markets; the Turks later had another. There were many more smaller communities— Florentines, Luccans, Slavs, Armenians—who would have their own areas of town and places of worship. The Venetians proved adept at working out credit arrangements, dues and storage facilities, all of which accrued further wealth for the city.

Mainland expansion and the fall of Constantinople

Up to now Venice's possessions had all been in the East, but in the 14th century it was hotly debated whether she should expand onto the mainland, to secure her own supplies of grain and gain more effective control of the Alpine passes. The Hundred Years War between England and France (1337–1453) heightened the city's insecurity, and the expansionist party gained strength. The city of Treviso, just inland, was, in fact, taken in 1339, but it was not until 1404–05 that a power vacuum left by the fall of the aggressive Gian Galeazzo Visconti in Milan allowed Venice to seize Vicenza, Verona and Padua. In 1420 the acquisition of the Friuli and Udine brought Venetian territory, the *terraferma*, up to the foot of the Alps. Then a famous debate broke out between Doge Tommaso Mocenigo who, as spokesman for 'the party of the sea', presented an idealised version of Venice as a city purely focused on maritime trade, and Francesco Foscari, who succeeded Mocenigo as doge in 1423, and who stood for expansion on land. The wars with rival mainland cities that broke out under Foscari showed just how intractable the mainland was to prove, and it was not until 1454 that a peace treaty with Milan recognised Venice's new Italian possessions.

The immediate effect of the expansion was an economic boom, and the years 1420–50 could be seen as the highest point of Venice's power. Her trade routes were extensive and well policed; she had defeated her rivals. Her wealth was being ploughed into such opulent palaces as the Ca' d'Oro on the Grand Canal, and the façades of the Ca' Foscari and the palaces of the Giustinian family near the Rialto Bridge reflect the confidence of the age. Venice's population, which like that of the rest of Europe had been devastated by the Black Death in 1349, had recovered to some 100,000 by 1400, and grew steadily to 140,000 by 1500.

Yet, just as she seemed more secure, the news came through in 1453 that Constantinople had fallen to the Ottoman Turks. From now on Venice was to be on the defensive in the East. Although Cyprus, a vital staging post for Eastern trade, was taken by Venice in 1489, the Ottomans began to nibble away at other Venetian outposts in the Aegean. In one war Ottoman raids even reached the Adriatic, and the clouds of smoke from the destruction could be seen from the campanile of St Mark's. Meanwhile, in 1498, Portuguese traders had rounded the Cape of Good Hope and reached India, showing that the riches of the East no longer had to come overland, to be sent onwards through the entrepôt of Venice. It was a presage of future economic decline.

Sixteenth-century Venice

Just at the same time Venice attempted to exploit unrest in northern Italy, caused by a French invasion in 1494, by expanding further on the mainland. It was a misguided strategy which succeeded only in uniting the powers of Europe against her. The pope organised the League of Cambrai in opposition, and there followed a humiliating defeat at Agnadello, near Milan, in 1509. Even Venice's 'own' cities closed their gates against her fleeing troops. 'In one battle', wrote Niccolò Machiavelli, 'the Venetians lost what in eight hundred years they had gained with so much effort.' Although the land was regained, Venice's power and image was irreparably damaged, and when Pope Clement VII presided over a reorganisation of the Italian states in 1530, Venice was not even consulted. Despite the odd success in the next century, notably the Battle of Lepanto in 1571, when Venetian galleys routed the Turkish fleet, there was little to celebrate. Cyprus, in fact, had been lost to the Turks just before Lepanto.

The Venetians were always adept at manipulating their image, and they concealed their humiliation by presenting themselves as the ideal republic in which everyone lived in harmony. The propagandist for the city was Gasparo Contarini in his *De magistratibus et republica Venetorum* (written in the 1520s but published in 1543). 'Such moderation and proportions characterise this Republic,' he wrote, 'that this city by itself incorporates at once a princely sovereignty, a governance of the nobility, and a rule of citizens so that all appear as equal weights.' Contarini even compared the Venetians with the Greeks under the Roman Empire: defeated perhaps, but still the arbiters of all that was culturally best. There was now some truth in this. While the merchant families of the early 15th century had shown little interest in art, the late 15th and 16th centuries produced Giovanni and Gentile Bellini, Giorgione, Tintoretto, Veronese, and the first artist to achieve a quasi-aristocratic status for his profession, Titian.

Though Contarini's depiction was largely a myth, the endless interaction of foreign merchants made Venice a much more fluid society than most in Europe. Her wealth was also too great to be easily dissipated, and she showed some resilience in creating her own industries. The city had produced only 2,000 lengths of wool in 1500; by the end of the 16th century she was manufacturing between 20,000 and 26,000 lengths annually. After having imported silk workers from Lucca in the 14th century, the industry grew in the 16th century to employ thousands of weavers. Standards, set by the government, were very high, ensuring that Venice's European reputation rested heavily on the quality of its luxury goods. Glass-making, based then as now in Murano, where fires from the furnaces could not spread far, dominated the international market for the whole of the 16th century. Mirrors were a great speciality. Printing was another important industry. The great printer Aldus Manutius had, by his death in 1515, published 55 texts in Greek and 67 in Latin (as against only six in Italian). Thirty-one of the Greek texts were the first printed editions anywhere, and confirmed Venice's status as the leading Greek cultural centre in Italy. The major library of Greek manuscripts donated by Cardinal Bessarion in 1468 is still part of the Libreria Marciana (*see p. 82*).

To the outside world, therefore, Venice still appeared a prosperous city, and no expense was spared in further glorifying her surroundings. In 1490, the Torre dell'Orologio, the clock-tower, was built in St Mark's Square, facing directly towards the water so that it would provide a backdrop for important visitors as they landed. The Procuratie, the arcaded buildings on either side of the Piazza, were rebuilt during the 16th century. Most magnificently of all, the architect Jacopo Sansovino was commissioned to design a mint (the Zecca) on the waterfront and a grand library along the western side of the Piazzetta, with its northern facade in St Mark's Square itself. At the base of the Campanile, the city's bell-tower, he built the exquisite Loggetta, where nobles met for discussion before entering the Doge's Palace for formal debate. Likewise, when a fire destroyed much of the Rialto in 1505, it was rebuilt in a programme which culminated in Sansovino's Fabbriche Nuove, the warehouses to the north (started in 1554), and the Rialto Bridge, built in the 1590s to a design by Antonio da Ponte. The *scuole* played their own part, as shown in the great upper chamber of the Scuola Grande di San Rocco, built between 1515 and 1560 and sumptuously decorated by Jacopo Tintoretto. Andrea Palladio's great church of San Giorgio Maggiore was begun in 1566. 'We have always,' proclaimed the Senate in 1535—with justification—'striven to provide this city with most beautiful temples, private buildings and spacious squares, so that from a wild and uncultivated refuge it has grown, been ornamented and constructed so as to become the most beautiful and illustrious city which at present exists in the world.'

Venice in decline

Venice's relationship with the Church was always ambiguous, as is perhaps symbolised by the fact that the city's cathedral was not St Mark's (until 1807), nor any major building in the centre of the city, but San Pietro di Castello, out of the way at its eastern extremity. The Church was not allowed to intrude on the city's economic or political independence. Whatever the Church said about usury, the Venetians justified their high interest rates as 'a Venetian custom', and when the pope forbade any trade with Muslim states in the 1340s it was said that the Venetians complied but placed Islamic-style cresting on the Doge's Palace in protest. In the early 17th century Venice came into direct conflict with the Church. The head of the Servite Order in the city, Pietro Sarpi, a man who was both intellectually brilliant and devout, had criticised the way in which the papacy put its territorial ambitions before the spiritual welfare of its flock. At the same time Venice had shown its supremacy over the Church by trying clerics in secular rather than Church courts. The pope, Paul V, was outraged, and in 1606 he placed Venice under papal interdict. It was a misjudged strategy. The Venetians, urged on by Sarpi, stood firm and expelled the Jesuits, who sided with the papacy. To his embarrassment, Paul found that no one in Europe was willing to support this outdated exercise of papal power, and he had to withdraw his interdict. It was an important moment in the reassertion of secular against religious power in Europe.

Nevertheless, from the 17th century onwards, Venice was entering what one of its leading historians, Pompeo Molmenti, called the *decadimento*, the years of decline, which were to end with the extinction of the republic in 1797. The economic vitality of the city was being eroded by the consolidation of the French, English and Dutch mercantile relationships in the Levant and by the rise of Atlantic trade. Even within the Adriatic, Venice faced competition from the expanding Austrian port of Trieste, and she had to endure Austria's tightening grip on the land around the *terraferma*. A series of debilitating wars with the Turks saw the loss of Crete, Venice's last major possession in the Mediterranean, in the 1660s. Even though Venice did regain some territory in the Peloponnese in 1680, the increasingly debt-ridden city could not hold it, and it was surrendered back to the Turks in 1718.

By the 18th century Venice was living off its past. It was a city that visitors now came to view, rather than admire for its achievements. 'The English use their powder for their cannon, the French for their mortars, in Venice its is usually damp and if it is dry they use it for fireworks', one visitor remarked. Another, William Beckford, complained how the Venetians 'pass their lives in one perpetual doze'. The playwright Carlo Goldoni's satires on the Venetian aristocracy making fools of themselves in front of their canny servants in their villas on the mainland sum up an age of frivolity and lack of purpose. Coffee house activity became more prominent—in St Mark's Square Florian was founded in 1720, Quadri in 1775. Venice's courtesans were renowned throughout Europe, and Casanova became a symbol of sexual decadence. Outsiders such as the patrician Lombard family of the Rezzonico could now buy their way into the city. (Their palace and its collections give a vivid impression of 18th-century Venice.)

Napoleon and the extinction of the Republic

For the sober observer of Enlightenment Europe, Venice was viewed with some derision as a corrupt, and—through the continuing activities of the Council of Ten—despotic state. The radical philosopher Jean-Jacques Rousseau, who spent some time in the city as Secretary to the French Ambassador, called the Council 'a tribunal of blood'. 'Venice sacrifices everything with the single object of giving no offence to other states,' was another scathing observation. The city was no match for the dynamism of the revolutionary French general Napoleon, who swept through Italy in 1796 and 1797. Venice, with no forces with which to confront the invader, grovelled in negotiations and finally succumbed to an ultimatum to install a 'democratic government' or submit to a French assault. The Great Council was summoned for the last time on 12th May 1797, but not even the required quorum of 600 members was reached. Those who did attend voted to replace themselves by a democratic government in the hope of 'preserving the religion, life and property of all these most beloved inhabitants'. Lodovico Manin, the 118th doge, acquiesced in the capitulation, handing his robes to his manservant with the tired words, 'I shall not be needing these again'. Thus, wrote Pierre Daru in his *History of the Venetian Republic* in 1819, 'a republic, famous, long powerful, remarkable for the singularity of its origin, of its site and institutions, has disappeared in our time, under our eyes, in a moment.'

French and Austrian rule

French talk of democracy proved hollow. The only immediate beneficiaries of the capitulation were the Jews, who were released from their ghetto. A 'Festival of Liberty' was held in St Mark's Square, at which the doge's regalia and the *Libro d'Oro*, the book which contained the official list of nobles, were burned. Napoleon, who did not visit the city himself until 1807, then ordered the burning of the *Bucintoro* and a choice of plunder for himself. The famous horses above St Mark's were taken to Paris, along with some of the city's finest paintings and most precious manuscripts. The new ruler's pragmatism was then shown by the transferral of Venice to Austria in the Treaty of Campo Formio in October 1797.

In 1805, when the French defeated the Austrians at Austerlitz, Venice came back under French control, and was incorporated into Napoleon's Kingdom of Italy. Some improvements were made, including the Giardini Pubblici, reclaimed from swampland in the east of the city, and the setting up of a cemetery outside the city on the island of San Michele; but the French treatment of Church property was more ruthless. The creation of a palace wing, complete with ballroom, at the western end of St Mark's Square, involved the demolition of one of Venice's most treasured churches, San Gemignano, whose façade by Jacopo Sansovino was a Venetian favourite. Altogether some 50 religious buildings and 40 palaces vanished in these years.

When Napoleon fell in 1815, the persistent efforts of the great Venetian sculptor Canova at the peace negotiations in Paris led to the return of the horses and some of Venice's other treasures, but the European powers once again placed Venice under direct Austrian rule. The Austrians proved less destructive than the French, but they presided over a city whose spirit had been destroyed. Over 90 per cent of the servants employed in the Venetian palaces lost their jobs, and Venice's decline was hastened by the continuing growth of the port of Trieste. It was not until the 1830s that a Venetian bourgeoisie began to re-emerge. In 1846, for the first time in her history, Venice was connected to the mainland, by a railway bridge. While romantics like Gustav von Aschenbach, the narrator of Thomas Mann's *Death in Venice*, might well complain that entering Venice through a station is like entering a palace by the back door, this was the first time the city was truly accessible to a wider public. In the late 1840s the annual number of tourists exceeded the total number of inhabitants (some 120,000) for the first time.

Austrian rule had its advantages (the education system was probably the best in Italy), but no one could deny that the Austrians exploited the Veneto for men and taxes, or that their police became increasingly obsessive about the growth of the 'secret societies' which planned to unite Venice to an Italian nation. With growing economic discontent in the 1840s, and the spread of revolutionary fervour throughout Europe in the spring of 1848, Venice was bound to be affected. The hero of the revolution which followed was Daniele Manin, a lawyer imbued with the ideals of the Enlightenment, who declared a new Venetian republic in a speech from a coffee table at Florian's on 24th March. It was a heroic gesture, and the Austrians were forced by rioting crowds to withdraw from the city. For 17 months Venice held out while the Austrian troops took advantage of the failed revolutions elsewhere in Italy to regroup their forces. By the summer of 1849, a bombardment of the city began and famine led to cholera. In August 1849, Manin made a last defiant speech to the Venetians and then fled into exile as the Austrians arrived to reoccupy the city. It is good to note that when Venice eventually became part of the Kingdom of Italy in 1866, Manin's body was brought up the Grand Canal in a procession made up of thousands of gondolas to be buried in the northern arcade of St Mark's.

Questions for the future

In the 19th century Venice appeared to be a city in decay, its palaces sliding into the lagoon. The predatory Lord Byron helped to give the city—as Casanova had done before him—a reputation for sexual adventure. Certainly homosexuals were able to live more freely in Venice than in England, and some employed gondoliers who doubled as their lovers. There were many visitors who indulged in the nostalgia of vanished greatness. Writers and composers found solace in the city and even relished the sense of decay. When there was talk of widening or filling in canals for sanitary reasons, it was John Ruskin who pleaded that 'the voice of poetry should be sought in the gloomy canals and picturesque alleys.' Yet the damp and crumbling buildings which he had come to muse over could hardly be left suspended picturesquely on the water's edge, and so a debate began over whether Venice should be preserved and its palaces restored as a museum, or whether it should be modernised in the interests of its permanent inhabitants. The debate over restoration crystallised in the 1860s when the Fondaco dei Turchi (the former storehouse for Turkish merchants), which even Ruskin admitted was 'a ghastly ruin', was rebuilt in an unrecognisable form to save it. Such *lucidatura*, as it was known, was deeply offensive to romantics such as Ruskin, who wished for the preservation even of ancient dirt. 'Off go all the glorious old weather stains, the rich hues of the marble which nature, mighty as she is, has taken ten centuries to bestow,' he complained to his father as he observed a cleaning of St Mark's. He opposed every attempt to create new iron bridges, install gas lighting or make the city more habitable for its citizens. Venice risked becoming the public property of a foreign intelligentsia, who would define it as they wished it to be. Local architects such as Camillo Boito (1836–1914), who actually worked to recreate the essence of an ancient building, sometimes by removing later accretions, became furious at the way outsiders portrayed him and others like him as 'barbarians'. When the Campanile collapsed in 1902, there were some—the Futurists, for instance—who argued that now was the time to let Venice sink forever below the lagoon. This time the conservatives triumphed. *Dov'era, com'era* ('Where it was, how it was') was the cry which successfully led to the replacement of the tower exactly as it had been, even if new materials had to be used. It was compromise of a sort which has enabled Venice to continue to present a façade of superb churches and great galleries against a backdrop of upmarket boutiques and opulent hotels for visitors, while its own citizens become strangers in their own town. A population of 184,000 in 1950 has fallen to some 64,000 today, with a comparative collapse in local services.

Yet there are far greater dangers to Venice. In November 1966, a massive flood left the city under two metres of water for several days, causing an estimated six billion dollars' worth of damage. It was a dramatic reminder of how vulnerable Venice has become to the very environment which in previous centuries it had used to its advantage.

Today's visitor can still enjoy Venice as a fantasy, even though the ever increasing numbers of tourists make the core of the city less and less comfortable to visit. And behind the fantasy lie highly challenging conservation issues. What is being preserved and for whom? Have the citizens been sacrificed for the preservation of a tourist playground? Is there a realistic chance of saving the city in any case? If so, is this an Italian or an international problem? It is perhaps unfortunate that an early morning walk through the narrow *calli*, when the light is clear on the lagoon, and some of the ancient churches are beginning to open alongside canals where the fruit barges are bringing up their wares, all too easily dispels the fears one must hold in more realistic moments.

THE ART OF VENICE

by Nigel McGilchrist

A first sight of Venice is one of the revelations of a lifetime. However much we may know about its construction, it still seems wholly improbable that a city can really be suspended on the water. The water is everywhere, and it has conditioned not only Venice's attitude to the world outside, but also the themes and nature of its paintings. Most important of all has been the determining influence of the water on the materials with which artists could work. Everywhere else in medieval Italy and southern Europe, wall painting was the principal mode of expression in figurative art; but in Venice, the walls of the churches and public buildings, whose foundations stood under water, were unusable for fresco work, since the paintings rapidly perished from salt and damp. Venetian art could only ever truly flourish by the development of new kinds of materials and techniques and supports. And as it turned out, these essentially Venetian developments were to change the course of Western art.

A crucial example of this was the adoption, in the 15th century, of canvas as a support for painting. It happened in Venice not just because its atmosphere was inimical to fresco painting, but because, in the Arsenale, there was the largest manufactory of sailcloth in the world, for fitting out the military and merchant navies of a city who depended entirely on ships for her survival and defence. Though a simple idea, when combined with the revolutionary new techniques of painting in oil which were arriving in Venice at the same time, its consequences were far-reaching.

Venetian painting owes its influence and much of its character to these material considerations. But none of this explains its genius: it owes that principally to two giants of the history of art, Giovanni Bellini and Titian. Neither was a thinker or scientist in the way that, in Florence, Brunelleschi, Leonardo or Michelangelo had been. They were simply master painters; and for this reason the Renaissance in Venice, which comes a whole generation later than it does to Florence, has a completely different nature: not primarily theoretical or intellectual, but practical and visual. As a result, its artistic influence across Europe was greater and more compelling: in fact it all but eclipsed the memory of Florence.

The origins of Venetian art

From its earliest examples, there is a richness at the core of Venetian art, which arises from an intrinsic delight in beautiful materials. Nowhere exemplifies this better than the Basilica of St Mark. It is here, in this extraordinary building, that the story of Venetian art begins. Already by the 12th century, St Mark's had one of the most richly decorated interiors in the Christian world: its floors were made up of hundreds of thousands of cut pieces of precious ancient marble; its walls, inside and out, were clad in ancient jaspers, porphyries, alabasters and polychrome marbles, which the moisture often made more brilliant and translucent; and then there were the mosaic ceilings of coloured glass-flux, and glass with gold leaf overhead. All this was consciously created to vie with the greatest churches of Constantinople. When the passage from Revelation was read, those listening inside the basilica knew that what they saw around them was a glimpse of the New Jerusalem, a deliberate evocation of John's vision of the walls and pavements of heaven (*Revelation 21, 18–21*).

In this same period of the 11th and 12th centuries, the Pala d'Oro, a Byzantine masterpiece of cloisonné enamel, was put up on the main altar of St Mark's. This was one of the defining moments of Venice's early artistic history. Its tiny, icon-like panels, framed in jewels and gold, are certainly a long way from a painting by Bellini; but he and the other great painters of the Venetian Renaissance cannot be properly understood without looking at the Pala d'Oro, because it is here that that same love of the depth and translucence of colour first becomes fully evident.

In the early Middle Ages, the workshops of St Mark's dominated the art of the city: no patrons other than the Church counted for much. The only place in the Venetian lagoon where there was an independent and more commercial flourishing of art, was on the island of Murano, where secret techniques for making glass were being perfected. Glass is a versatile medium, which performs remarkable tricks with colour and light. When we look at the works of Bellini and Giorgione and Titian, we should not forget that these artists were working in what was Europe's foremost centre for glass production. Its translucence is there in their works, and it was there in material form also, at the heart of their painting.

In addition to this, and in ever richer variety, were the commodities of Venice's expanding commercial empire. Like Ancient Rome before her, Venice looked east for trade, and dominated the market in luxury goods, nearly all of which came from the Middle East, Persia and India: spices, textiles, dyes, precious stones, metals, and—of greatest importance for the history of art—pigments, colours and resins. On these, Venice soon gained the European monopoly, reserving those of the best quality for herself.

Painting in the 14th and 15th centuries

Early Venetian art was the child of Byzantium. A picture was a sacred object similar to an icon, a focus of devotion, whose painstaking creation by a team of craftsmen partook of the nature of a spiritual exercise. We know the master artists of the mid-14th century often only by their first name: Paolo or Lorenzo, called 'Veneziano', 'from Venice'. At first sight, these early works can seem like many others of the same epoch produced elsewhere; but there is a technical mastery and a management of colour in them that goes beyond that of their contemporaries. There is a deliberate play on different kinds of surface—shiny and opaque, metallic and enamel-like—which would have appeared highly compelling in the low candle-light and wide spaces of a Venetian church interior. Their elaborate Gothic decoration is courtly and refined, quite in contrast to the style of the early Tuscan painters. Vasari had delighted in telling how Giotto was just a country shepherd boy when Cimabue found him doodling on a rock in the Mugello valley: that is very Florentine—a pride in humble, amateur genius. Venice had no fields or shepherds or rocks: it was all city. Artists were formed in urban workshops of considerable sophistication, often with Greek Constantinopolitan masters teaching a method and style of painting whose roots lay in the Hellenistic traditions of the late Roman Empire of the East. This tradition produced devotional paintings in the 14th century, all of which aspired, to a greater or lesser degree, to emulate the exquisite richness of the Pala d'Oro.

The wealth of technical know-how involved in these intricate creations was jealously guarded: it naturally tended to be kept within families, and we therefore see a handful of family workshops emerge in Venice during the 1400s: the Crivelli, the Vivarini and the Bellini. The paintings of all three of these workshops show, in different ways, a new concentration on volume and the sculptural qualities of figures. This is initiated by the first generation, Jacopo Bellini (c. 1400–70/71) and Antonio and Bartolomeo Vivarini. The elegant patterned design, the enamel-like paint surface, and the rich colour are all still there; but the new interest in the solidity of the figures reveals something unusual and important for Venice—that she was, for once, looking over her shoulder at what was happening in the nearby mainland centres of Ferrara and Padua. During the 1440s the great Florentine sculptor Donatello was working in Padua: his powerful influence must have been impossible to ignore. In 1442, Andrea del Castagno, one of the brightest and most modern painters from Florence, came briefly to decorate the church of San Zaccaria in Venice. Their influence is not immediately obvious; it is subtle and cautious, as befitted the natural conservatism of the city. Slowly the soft Gothic flow of early Venetian painting acquires backbone and anatomy, and its figures begin to inhabit a world that has spatial order and coherence.

Notwithstanding the perfect craftsmanship of their work, the Crivelli and Vivarini remain imaginatively in the Gothic world. The works of Carlo Crivelli (1430–1500), in particular, have an arresting and unforgettable personality—an exhilarating combination of purely decorative fantasy and yet a naturalism that takes us completely by surprise. A Madonna and Child, who almost seem carved in stone, stare from their niche at a startlingly realistic horsefly or bluebottle that appears to have alighted on the surface of the painting. This is not mere play, however; Crivelli's masterful paintings, with their wealth of fruit, flowers and fauna, are woven from an intricate web of allegorical allusions, in which the cucumber is made to symbolise the Resurrection of Christ, and the infamous bluebottle represents the presence both of evil and, more specifically, the plague. A highly accomplished but very eccentric painter, Crivelli left Venice early, after a period in prison for adultery, and worked for most of his life further south, in the Marche. He always proudly signed himself 'Venetus' nonetheless.

Jacopo Bellini appears instinctively to have looked beyond the imaginative world of this beautiful but old-fashioned style. On his death, he left two sketchbooks containing over 230 drawings, which include fascinating experiments in spatial composition, perspective and architectural design. They are a unique legacy; nothing like them exists for any other Italian artist of the early 15th century. We do not know enough about Jacopo to say where the stimulus for these innovations came from; but their importance, especially for his family, was immense. Jacopo had two sons who were painters, Gentile (named after Gentile da Fabriano, who came to Venice in 1408 to decorate the Doge's Palace) and Giovanni; he also had a daughter, who married the most talented artist in northern Italy at the time, Andrea Mantegna. The Bellini dynasty was to have a defining influence over the evolution of Venetian art for the next hundred years.

The two brothers had quite different vocations: Giovanni was to develop an art of wide, international appeal, while Gentile created a genre which was deeply and uniquely Venetian. Something in the solipsistic nature of being an island-city meant that Venice appears never to have tired of celebrating itself, its beauty and its pageantry. Gentile has left us a remarkable documentation of the appearance of the 15th-century city. In 1496, for the Scuola di San Giovanni Evangelista, he contributed the finest paintings to the cycle depicting the *Story of the Relic of the True Cross* (now in the Accademia; *see p. 154*); they are simultaneously full of space and detail, of narrative interest and architectural documentation. A decade later, and similar in conception, *The Preaching of St Mark* and *Martyrdom of St Mark in Alexandria* (left unfinished at the time of his death, and now in the Brera Gallery in Milan) both contain fascinating passages of orientalising fantasy— the minarets and turbans and giraffes of an imagined Alexandria—based on drawings made when Gentile worked at the court in Constantinople between 1479 and 1481. Something of Gentile's renown can be gauged by the fact that the Ottoman sultan should have called him there all the way from Italy. It was at this period that he executed his brilliant portrait of the conqueror, Mehmet II, now in the National Gallery, London.

Architecture and sculpture in the 14th and 15th centuries

This orientalism in Gentile Bellini reflects how much of an eastern taste and aesthetic had already been absorbed by Venice. Domes become moulded and stylised with an oriental profile; the runs of arches and finials along the front of the Doge's Palace or Ca' d'Oro (which was further gilded and coloured) have more in common with the Alhambra than with contemporary architecture in Florence or Rome; the slender *campanili* seem at times like minarets; and the colours and abstract designs of some of the façades would not be out of place in Isfahan or Jaipur. It is in its architecture, more than anything else, that Venice goes so entirely its own way. Once again the water is fundamental to this development, because the delicately varying colours of marble and stone used in a Venetian façade make sense with the rippling surface of the water in front. Furthermore, these elegant façades, which emphasised beauty over fortification, were possible in Venice in a way that was unimaginable in the turbulent world of Florence: the rigorous constitution of the Serene Republic discouraged the interfamily mob rivalries which were a common feature of Florentine history and necessitated the construction of residences as impregnable as the Strozzi and Medici palaces. Nor had Venice any need for defensive walls. The lagoon, with its maze of invisible underwater channels, was the city's perfect defence: in times of danger it was sufficient to pull up the posts that marked these channels and leave the waters to confound any invader. Its unique geography once again allowed Venice to develop architecturally in a way quite different from the other cities of Europe.

The elegant Venetian façade replaced the windowless, fortified exterior necessary in other cities, at the same time dispensing with the interior courtyard, which was necessary as a well of light elsewhere. This saved precious space, and for the palaces themselves it meant that the *piano nobile* could now occupy the whole extent of the building's plan. These grand rooms possessed much greater areas of window than elsewhere, made from the special, clear glass that Venice, alone in Italy, produced. The resulting interiors were light, unencumbered and resplendent. There was no horse-drawn traffic below, and none of the accompanying smells and noise that went with it. The tide washed the lagoon daily; mosquitoes were unable to cover the distance from the mainland out to the islands; in short, Venice became just about the most salubrious city in Europe.

Nor could any city come close to Venice in the calculated grandness of its main approach from the sea. To arrive slowly by ship at the city's ceremonial entrance, the Piazzetta of San Marco, passing the sweep of palaces culminating in the Doge's Palace and the entrance to the Grand Canal, was to be subjected to one of the clearest—and most excitingly beautiful—programmes of aesthetic propaganda anywhere. There was to be no doubt that you were entering one of the world's richest imperial capitals. The south and west fronts of St Mark's which greeted you as you stepped ashore were decorated with marble and sculptural trophies from Rome, from Constantinople, and from many parts of the Mediterranean, mostly captured from Venice's aspiring rivals.

The early architecture of Venice is shrouded in anonymity, but by the 15th century two architects stand out. They were contemporaries, relations and rivals: Mauro Codussi (c. 1440–1504) and Pietro Solari, called 'Lombardo' (c. 1438–1515). Codussi changed the external appearance of Venetian mansions with a new use of materials. He showed how effective the white, Istrian stone, which had previously only been used for details on brick housefronts, could be when used for covering the whole façade, especially if combined with a lower area of rustication, as in his refined Palazzo Corner-Spinelli of 1480—one of Venice's first truly 'Renaissance' palaces. An unforgettable characteristic of his work, which was copied all over the city, was the introduction of a type of marble tracery window, created by surmounting a pair of round-arched windows, with an oculus, all within a larger round-arched frame; but a more general love of the rhythmic combination of semi-circles with rectangles lies behind all his creations, recognisable in the upper façade of the church of San Zaccaria (1483), and in the little-visited, but perfect, funerary church of San Michele (1469–78). This was Codussi's first—and perhaps his purest and best—architectural essay: it shows his thoughtful study of Alberti's Malatesta temple at Rimini.

A number of strikingly similar elements are found in one of the loveliest of all Venetian buildings, the church of Santa Maria dei Miracoli (1481–89), whose appearance, as you approach from around the corner of a narrow calle, is itself a sort of miracle. It was designed by Pietro Lombardo, who had worked as both sculptor and architect in Padua before settling in Venice. The church has the appearance of a treasure-chest. Both on the outside and the inside, the complex and ingenious architectural details in Istrian stone frame precious marbles and porphyry insets. Yet the form of the building could hardly be simpler. This again invites contrast with Florence, where often complex abstract forms in architecture were paramount, and decoration was reduced to the minimum. In Santa Maria dei Miracoli, Lombardo has transfigured a perfectly elementary form with dignified and beguiling decoration.

Pietro Lombardo had two sons, Tullio (1455–1532) and Antonio (c. 1458–1516); together they formed a family *bottega*. Venice's sculptural tradition had mostly been a decorative adjunct of architecture up until the late 15th century; its outstanding examples were the scenes, carved by Giovanni and Bartolomeo Bon, on the corners of the south and west façades of the Doge's Palace, depicting stories from the Book of Genesis: *Adam and Eve*, and a beautifully concise and unforgettable *Drunkenness of Noah*. The same sculptors had been responsible for the design and sculpture of the magnificent Porta della Carta (1438–43). With the Lombardo family, however, sculpture acquires the status of an independent artform, unfettered from architectural decoration. Tullio in particular was a deeply attentive student of Classical originals; but it takes time in his development for the Classicism to become absorbed into a coherent, Renaissance sculptural language of truly Venetian character. Once it does, the results are of a rare beauty: the delicate portrait relief of two heads, like a piece of Roman funerary sculpture, in the Ca' d'Oro Museum, and the monuments to Doge Andrea Vendramin (d. 1478) and to Doge Giovanni Mocenigo (d. 1485), in the church of Santi Giovanni e Paolo, are exquisite and poised essays in Classicism. Their figures beautifully typify the humanity and freshness of the early Renaissance in Venice.

Carpaccio and Giovanni Bellini

Nobody looked more carefully at Venice's array of architecture or at the big narrative paintings of Gentile Bellini than Vittore Carpaccio (c. 1460–1525/26). He watched intently the grand ceremony and pageantry of Venice, as well as its domestic life and interiors. He appropriated them all and fused them into what have become some of the most delightful narrative tableaux in the history of painting. He has the Venetian love of rich textile; the Venetian love of crowds and special occasions; above all the Venetian love of Venice.

Just as with Gentile's paintings, Carpaccio's were largely commissioned for the Venetian *scuole*. These *scuole*, or self-governing lay confraternities, were a particularly Venetian phenomenon: they united groups of men of similar profession or craft (surgeons, painters) or ethnic origin (Slavs, Greeks), and their object was to provide material and spiritual succour to their members, as well as to the poor and indigent more generally, in times of need. They were a middle-class phenomenon, from which patricians were excluded. The surplus of their revenues was used to decorate their meeting houses, which were generally small but fine buildings. Carpaccio's two great painting cycles, the *Lives of St George, St Tryphon and St Augustine* (in the Scuola di San Giorgio degli Schiavoni) and the *Legend of St Ursula* (now in the Accademia; *see p. 155*), have a wide and inexhaustible appeal for their clarity and narrative interest. Carpaccio's scenes have a tendency towards the static; even the *Massacre of the Eleven Thousand Virgins* from the *Legend of St Ursula* is a curiously un-dramatic scene; he is more in his element with the graceful details of the interior of St Ursula's bedroom or of St Augustine's study, where the tiny, seated dog is a quite unforgettable presence. In both of these interiors there is an unusual, and masterfully evoked, Venetian light, which shows the influence of Giovanni Bellini, Carpaccio's greatest Venetian contemporary.

In Giovanni Bellini we witness the imaginative discovery of light in Italian painting. Where other painters had dallied with it, Bellini firmly grasped its primary importance. No painter in Italy before him was so sensitive to its inflections, or understood so well its expressive potential. The only problem for Bellini was how to transfer that sensitivity into paint, because, like his father, he grew up in a world in which painting was done in egg-tempera on a gessoed, wooden panel. As a technique this offered little flexibility: tempera colours are bright and opaque, dry almost instantaneously, and give no possibility for correction or alteration. Bellini fared well in such a milieu nonetheless, because he was instinctively such a master of line, of detail and of the creation of volumes by shade. But during his lifetime—and it may have been through his brother-in-law, Mantegna—he came in contact with the new, Flemish method of mixing pigment with walnut oil and a siccative resin, to create hitherto unimagined effects of translucency, depth of colour, and delicacy of shadow. At first hesitant—perhaps just laying transparent oil glazes over dry tempera colour—it is not long before Bellini begins to expand the possibilities of the new medium, always working, however, in the manner in which he had been trained, with precision and in superimposed layers. To look at his exquisite early Madonnas is to realise that the new technique was perfectly adapted for his particular sensibility.

Then in 1475, at the height of Bellini's maturity as a painter, a little-known genius by the name of Antonello da Messina visited Venice for a year, collaborated with Bellini, and left behind him works which made a deep and lasting impression. Antonello had understood and mastered the Flemish technique of painting in translucent glazes of pigment and varnish, loosened with oil—a method initiated and perfected almost half a century earlier by van Eyck. The greatest painting Antonello left behind in Venice—the San Cassiano altarpiece, of which only central fragments remain today in the Vienna Kunsthistorisches Museum—found echo for long to come in Bellini's work, and in the works of other contemporaries, Cima da Conegliano and Marco Basaiti, whose great altarpieces are now in the Accademia.

Giovanni Bellini's works are to be found in many churches around the city: there are early, slightly stiff, pieces such as his *Polyptych of St Vincent Ferrer* (1460) in the church of Santi Giovanni e Paolo, and later masterpieces such as the Frari triptych of 1488. Last of all, is his sublime *Virgin with Saints*, signed and dated 1505, on the north wall of the church of San Zaccaria, painted in oil. In 1500, Leonardo da Vinci had visited Venice, and it is not wholly fanciful to see some lessons learnt from the Florentine master in this extraordinary picture. As in Bellini's magnificent earlier portrait of Doge Leonardo Loredan (National Gallery, London), this picture represents a mastery of oil technique. It has the stillness and transparency of deep water; the warm colours of Venice, reminiscent of its enamels and its glass; and it shares the almost palpable light of the lagoon. It represents the summit of Venetian art, before the genius of Bellini's pupils was to turn everything on its head.

Giorgione, Titian and Tintoretto

The thunder of Giorgione's famous *Tempesta* announces the coming of a new season in Venetian painting. This tiny and enigmatic picture (now in the Accademia; *see p. 147*) was not a large, public or religious work like nearly all Venetian painting before: it was a private commission, for a select and intellectual group, for whom the discussion and debate of its deliberately recondite allegory provided erudite entertainment. Small and intimate though it is, the painting breaks entirely fresh ground: in it, landscape is no longer just a background, it is the emotive purpose of the picture.

Giorgione (c. 1476–1510) was around 40 years younger than Giovanni Bellini, and his life was to be tragically cut short—possibly by the plague—at the age of thirty-five. He instinctively understood the potential of Bellini's achievement with the softer medium of oil, but he did not wish to be bound by Bellini's rather geometric ideas of composition, his patterning of colour, or his adherence to the primacy of line. Giorgione begins to dissolve line in shadow, and to replace pattern with a tonal unity of colour and mood. Slowly and unobtrusively, landscape and its expressive power elbows everything else out of the way: in his *Adoration of the Shepherds* (now in Washington), it is not the miraculous birth, which occupies just one corner of the picture, but the receding landscape all around, which commands our attention. Brilliant colour is vanishing and is replaced by an ever more expressive depth of shadow, as for example in his moving study of the face of an elderly lady (sometimes thought to be his mother), bearing the inscription '*Col Tempo*' ('in time, it shall come to us all'), in the Accademia. How were such rich depths of paint achieved? Not by the addition of more varnish and oil to the pigment, which would risk deadening the colour. Giorgione was adding ground glass (available to him from the factories in Murano) to his pigment preparation—a brilliant development, because it simultaneously did three things. It hastened the drying time of the paint; it gave bulk to the glazes while reducing the amount of oil necessary, thereby cutting the risk of yellowing with time; and it imparted an inner brilliance and depth.

Watching intently all these trials and experiments from the wings, was a young apprentice, Tiziano Vecellio (c. 1485–1576), from the mountains of Cadore above Venice, who was scarcely even in his adolescence. Giovanni Bellini's studio was the Rutherford Laboratory of Venetian painting: Alvise Vivarini, Antonello da Messina, Carpaccio, Sebastiano del Piombo, Lorenzo Catena, Lorenzo Lotto, Marco Basaiti, Giorgione, Titian—virtually every name in Venetian painting of the period passed through it in one capacity or another, and was affected by what was happening there. But it was the last and youngest of these, Titian, who was to transform the nature of painting completely, and in the process turn Venetian art in his age from a local phenomenon into the most influential force in European painting. He was the friend and assistant of Giorgione, and on the latter's death was his artistic heir, completing a number of his unfinished works. But what Titian was to do with the technique of painting makes even Giorgione seem old-fashioned. Every painter mentioned so far was taught to paint—whether in oil or tempera—with what we might call the 'tempera mentality'. This means painting in layers of colour, following a carefully drawn design, on a solid, smooth white gesso base. In the early painters such as Lorenzo

Veneziano or Jacopo Bellini, the thin layers of colour were in opaque egg-tempera, while in Giovanni Bellini and Giorgione they were often transparent layers, or 'glazes'. Whatever the medium, though, the process was the same: a bright white base plus drawing plus thin layers of colour, added successively so that they subtly interacted with and modified the layers below, to create exactly the desired effect. A painting was therefore a complex stratified creation: in optical terms, its reflective white gesso base was a mirror which sent the light back to the eye through the layers of interposed colour. Their pictures therefore were back-lit; and the surface smooth and flat.

Titian, although trained in exactly this manner by Giovanni Bellini, dispensed with it almost immediately. He saw that oil paint could have a quite different effect if it did not *refract* the light from its depth, but *reflected* it from its surface. He also saw that the surface of a painting had far greater life if it was not flat, but broken and agitated, like the surface of the water on the lagoon—playing with the light rather than absorbing it. Lastly, he abandoned the wooden panel for the ease and texture of stretched canvas, learning to exalt its weave as a living element of the painting. His example was so completely compelling that fresco and egg-tempera painting died an almost immediate death: canvas was adopted all over Europe as a support, and the method of painting with dissolved contours and broken surfaces, using varying heights of *impasto* (thickness of paint strokes) spread to the corners of the continent. Velázquez, Rubens, Delacroix, Constable, Rembrandt, even the French Impressionists and Cézanne, are heirs in different ways, to Titian's emancipation of painting. Furthermore, with pre-prepared oils and lightweight canvas, the artist could sketch in front of nature, giving scope and possibility to a new artform: landscape painting. With the disappearance of the primacy of drawing, and the new living texture of the broken surface instead, the potential for drama and pathos was increased. And, thanks to the ease with which light, rollable canvas could travel, the exchange of images around the continent was a development of comparable importance to the invention of printing.

Titian's active painting career may have spanned over 80 years—more even than his long-lived contemporary Michelangelo. Of the many examples of his work in Venice, two highlight different ends of the fascinating spectrum of his development: his *Assumption of the Virgin* of 1518 in the church of the Frari, and his last work, the unfinished *Pietà* of 1573–75, intended for his own tomb and now in the Accademia. It is a rare joy when a great painting is seen in the place for which it was created. Titian's *Assumption* still occupies the centre of the 14th-century Gothic interior of the Frari like a vision of intense, liquid colour—an unforgettable ruby red, which has the shimmering effect of glass. Only in a painting as great as this is the exhilaration of the miraculous event itself matched by the picture's chromatic vigour and sweeping design. It belongs to another imaginative world from the Pala d'Oro; but its intensity of colour and texture and the play on surface and depth are both similar to it in effect, and quintessentially Venetian. In the same church, by rights, should hang Titian's *Pietà*, painted 60 years later and left unfinished at his death. Here the colour has leached out of Titian's vision, except for a few sickly hues. The weave of the canvas breaks the surface of the paint and the febrile brush-strokes dissolve the contours of everything. Titian's assistant, Palma Giovane, who 'finished' this work after his master's death, described the way Titian worked: 'the last retouching involved his moderating here and there the brightest highlights by rubbing them with his fingers.... And so he would proceed... in the last stages... painting more with his fingers than his brushes'.

When rules are abolished, anarchy can swiftly follow. Titian had, in effect, spirited away the design, the reassuring line, and the familiar compactness of a picture's surface. The old certainties of painting were now gone. And into the vacuum, rushed that dynamic painter, and curious counterpart to everything Titian stood for, 'Tintoretto' (1519–94). After the sheer technical mastery of Bellini, Giorgione and Titian, it takes time to adjust to the apparent haste of Tintoretto. Where Titian had altered the physical surface of a painting for good, Tintoretto revolutionised its imaginative space. Venetian painting had, up until now, generally disposed the figures of a composition across the vertical plane of the picture: in Tintoretto, that plane swings inwards and back, often diagonally, and we find ourselves watching a drama which takes places in a daringly receding space, as, for example, in the early *Miracle of the Slave* in the Accademia, or the late dramatic *Last Supper* (1594) in the chancel of San Giorgio Maggiore. Tintoretto, according to Boschini, was mostly self-taught, and he learned to achieve these effects by studying foreshortening and the effects of light and shade produced by suspending wax models in specially constructed boxes, which were illuminated from different angles. Sometimes these special effects can disturb with their artificiality, and give rise to the over-rhetorical poses of some of his figures. But in his maturity, as in the famous cycles of the *Life of Christ* (1576–81) and the *Life of the Virgin* (1582–87) for the Scuola di San Rocco, his designs acquire a new and mystical power which goes beyond rhetoric. In the latter cycle, his *Flight into Egypt* depicts the Holy Family head-on, as they come forwards out of the picture towards us: it is in this simple, but complete, originality of concept that his greatness lies. There is nothing traditionally Venetian in Tintoretto's light effects. The actual light of this world interested him less than the unworldly luminosity he creates instead. This very unusual illumination, and the broken surface of his paint, were to be important influences on El Greco, when he stayed in Venice in the 1560s. The rapid darkening of the oils and varnishes since Tintoretto's time has inevitably altered our perception of his desired effects, and we can only guess at how delicate and dramatic they may have appeared at the time—or even to Ruskin, 300 years later, who was so profoundly moved by them.

From Palladio to Guardi

It is strange that, in this city of ornate and colourful façades, the distilled Classicism of Palladio's architecture should have become so memorable an ingredient of the scene. Facing back across the water to the Gothic fantasy of the Doge's Palace, is Palladio's serene San Giorgio Maggiore, whose façade, made up of interlocking temple fronts in white stone, is everything which the Doge's Palace is not. Still, reposed, unshowy, cerebral and utterly international, it throws into relief everything that came before: it is the perfect counterpoint which the city needed. Andrea Palladio (1508–1580) was from Padua, and he only properly settled in Venice in his 63rd year. By rights he does not belong in this survey; and yet his architecture is such an integral part of the city's whole, that it is not possible to omit him. The serenely measured, yet luminous, interiors of San Giorgio Maggiore (begun 1565) and of the church of the Redentore (begun 1577) are amongst the great achievements of Renaissance architecture. They use that same combination of white walls with stone details which had embodied and enhanced the interiors of buildings by Brunelleschi and Michelangelo: yet Palladio's designs appear at once simpler and more universal. His first work in Venice, the refectory of San Giorgio Maggiore (1560), is already the product of accumulated experience and maturity. The proportions of its spaces have a perceptible, physical effect on the visitor passing through the cadenced progression of ante-rooms and majestic doorways. His is an architecture which profoundly quells human anxiety.

Where Palladio calms, Baldassare Longhena (1604–82), who was much indebted to Palladio's legacy, exhilarates and surprises; where Palladio's idiom was international, Longhena's is, once more, idiosyncratically Venetian. His church of Santa Maria della Salute is Venice's greatest creation of the Baroque era. Like the outlines of St Mark's and the Doge's Palace, its profile stays in the memory long after everything else has receded. Its position at the entrance to the Grand Canal, its unusual octagonal plan, the reassuring weight of its monumental entrance set back from the waterfront, the form of its ballooning domes like wind-filled spinnakers over the prow of the Dogana, and, above all, the unforgettable and luxuriant scrolls of its buttresses with the crown of sculptural figures above them, combine in a piece of consummate architectural theatre. It is the first large-scale octagonal building since Romanesque times—a period when spiritual numerology saw in the number eight a symbol of new life and rebirth. This building was a votive offering, dedicated to the Virgin by the city of Venice in gratitude for salvation after the terrible plague-year of 1630: in its unusual eight-sided design, Longhena brilliantly echoes this ancient symbol.

Longhena's work itself marks a moment of renewal for Venetian art. Far from being a period of retreat, the final century of the life of the Republic, before its extinction in 1797, brings an unexpected burst of creativity. Just at the point when it appeared that fresco painting had been dealt a terminal blow by Titian's perfection of oil-on-canvas, and just as it seemed that the city's great 17th-century decorative works, such as those in the Doge's Palace, had lost their way and become irremediably clogged, an artist emerges in Venice who is one of history's greatest ever practitioners of fresco, and who conceives designs for large-scale decorative programmes of a lightness which is positively uplifting. Giambattista Tiepolo (1696–1770) is a phenomenon difficult to account for. Just as the Venetian palette seemed to be getting darker and darker, Tiepolo works exclusively with bright and sunlit colours; just as decorative schemes were becoming more artificial and more crowded with rhetorical figures, Tiepolo purges the situation with his insistence on large areas of space and sky, and the seemingly unaffected naturalness of his narratives. Few other painters embody 'brilliance' better. His mastery of *quadratura* and of complex perspective and foreshortening had no peer in his age: nor had the sheer *élan* of his imaginative ideas, and his simultaneous grasp of every detail within the context of the whole. His ceilings never overwhelm or tire or confuse; they always succeed and they always delight. And for this reason his services were widely sought on the Italian mainland, in Spain and in Germany, to produce works that have since remained among the greatest examples of decorative art in Europe. Many of his finest works are outside Venice; but in Palazzo Labia on the Cannaregio canal, his visual narrative of *Antony and Cleopatra*—a subject perfectly suited to his imagination—is one of the city's greatest joys.

His exact contemporary, Canaletto (Antonio del Canale, 1697–1768), reached international fame from Venice by a technical mastery of a wholly different kind. In him, as also in the works of his contemporaries Pietro Longhi (1701–85) and Francesco Guardi (1712–93), Venice returned to one of her oldest habits: the description and celebration of her own beauty. This time, however, in these last decades before the end of the Serene Republic, it was to be a description without the glorification of earlier times. Longhi's humorous and delicately painted vignettes of Venetian life were to have little influence outside Venice; but Canaletto's views of the city and its buildings were exported widely, especially to England through the agency of the British Consul, Joseph Smith. Their popularity depended on the outstandingly rendered light and shadow which suffused the ordered spaces he described. He gives remarkable delight to the eye both from a distance and close to. Canaletto came to London between 1746 and 1754: in his views of the city, he performed the remarkable feat of making the banks of the River Thames look as serene and beautiful as the Bacino di San Marco. Stillness is all in Canaletto. The coruscations of light and vibrancy of atmosphere in Guardi's views of the city reveal a diametrically different response to its beauty, a response which was only appreciated many generations later, once European sensibilities had been educated to see things differently by the Impressionists. For Canaletto, the light is the vehicle of his passion for the architecture: for Guardi the architecture is a necessary receptacle for his passion for the light.

The works of Canaletto and Guardi remind us that so much of Venetian art, indeed so much of the fascination of the city, has always depended upon its unique light—immediately, tangibly different from anywhere else in Italy because of the surrounding water which constantly modifies it. It is this that explains the primacy of the the the visual sensibility in Venice: we look in vain for internationally great writers, poets, thinkers or scientists. Venice has no Dante or Leonardo or Alberti or Machiavelli; but it produced painters whose universal influence has been incomparable, because of one fundamental lesson they imbibed from the endless modulations of their native light. They instinctively understood how light in painting is the vehicle of human empathy. Bellini and Titian, and the painters who worked near to them, showed for the first time how feeling is evoked and expressed not by idea or narrative or description, but by the drama of light and colour; and Titian above all, with his new and dramatic use of the oil and canvas medium, evolved the technical tools for this revolutionary way of painting. Venice may not have altered the course of intellectual history as Florence so notably did; but there are few painters in 17th-, 18th- and 19th-century Europe who were not profoundly touched by her far-reaching influence.

VENICE IN PERIL

The 8th edition of the Blue Guide to Venice issues at a critical point in the fortunes of the city: 4th November 2006 marked the 40th anniversary of the great floods which spectacularly devastated Florence, but at the same time Venice and its hinterland. It was in response to the appeal made by the Italian government to the world through UNESCO in November 1966 that the British Italian Art and Archives Rescue Fund was set up, to be transformed into the Venice in Peril Fund in 1971. A member of the international association of Private Committees for the Safeguarding of Venice, a non-governmental organisation recognised by UNESCO, the Fund's trust deed enjoins it 'to rescue and restore all antiquities, ancient buildings, monuments, archives and works of art situated in Venice and on the islands of the Venetian lagoon, recognising that the same represent a vital element in the history of European culture and the heritage of mankind'. Funds are allocated over a wide programme, ranging from monumental and pictorial conservation to academic research, bursaries, collaboration with the city, the universities and other institutions.

On 22nd November 2006, the crucial decision was taken by the inter-ministerial committee in Rome to go ahead with the second phase of the Mo.S.E. project for mobile flood barriers at the three entrances to the Venetian Lagoon, despite opposition by the city council, who maintain that the environmental impact has not been rigorously assessed, that Mo.S.E. will be obsolete by 2050, and that funds allocated annually to the city under the special law for maintenance of its fabric are being reduced to meet the cost of Mo.S.E., estimated at €4.2million. The second phase of construction, due to terminate in 2012, will be monitored by the city council: their declared priorities are the physical conservation of the fabric and its native population, now reduced to some 64,000 in the historic centre as the escalation in house prices and the costs of maintenance drives people to Mestre and the *terraferma*, leaving the city increasingly occupied by the owners of second homes. Flooding—*acque alte*—is not a priority for the city council, but this is contested by the regional government, and now two successive national governments of diverse political affiliations have confirmed their commitment to protecting the city against the waters.

The diminishing population concerns not only the civic authorities but also the Curia and diocesan administration, whose patrimony includes a number of historic churches no longer parochial, sometimes closed but not de-consecrated, and in varying degrees of preservation. At the annual general meeting of the International Association of Private Committees, appeals for funding according to location, with priorities and estimated cost, are presented by the Superintendency for Architecture, Environment and Historic Patrimony for Venice and the Lagoon (Ministry of Cultural Heritage). The statutory vigilance of the Superintendency and the parallel office of the Polo Museale (responsible for State Museums) puts their staff under great pressure; we are privileged to work with them on all the projects which the Fund has been able to finance over the past 40 years.

Since the last edition of the Blue Guide a number of Venice in Peril's long-term projects have been completed, such as the monumental Cappella Emiliani attached to the church of San Michele in Isola, a complex project because of its unique cupola construction and vulnerability to excessive wash from passing boats, which has caused continuous erosion to the foundations. The cemetery island belongs to the city, since under the Napoleonic regime burial grounds attached to parish churches were suppressed and the islands of San Michele and San Cristoforo were joined to create the municipal cemetery for Catholic residents, encompassing also the historic Protestant Reparto Evangelico, where many of the graves with monumental commemorative stonework are badly in need of attention.

Across the water, the soaring bell tower of the Madonna dell'Orto, a landmark on the Cannaregio waterfront, was Venice in Peril's first conservation project in 1968. Greatly admired by Ruskin, Tintoretto's parish church has been revived by the Fund's repairs to the entire fabric, the cycle of paintings and the fine Bazzani organ. Eastwards from Cannaregio into Castello, the Arsenale remains state property, divided between civil and military administration. As Ancona has now the operational naval command for the Adriatic, the post of Admiral-in-Command in Venice derives from the Institute for Strategic Studies within the military area. Part of the Arsenale, including the great Corderia (rope-walk) is ceded to the Biennale of Visual Art alternating with Architecture. The quay of the basin is dominated by the massive Armstrong Mitchell hydraulic crane no. 2919, built in Newcastle-upon-Tyne in 1883 to the order of the Arsenale. Threatened with demolition in 1966, it is now the only one of its type surviving. This is Venice in Peril's latest project, a novel experience for the Superintendency, who have drawn up the initial project to make the huge structure safe before tackling the main problem of preserving the ironwork, badly rusted and corroded, also with its hydraulic machinery housed in the octagonal brick and stone base construction.

Three new requests to which the Fund has agreed to respond demonstrate the variety of problems posed: the Chinese 12-fold screen in the Museum of Oriental Art; the inscriptions dating from the 14th century in the quarantine warehouse on the island of the Lazzaretto Nuovo; and a bursary for research into the collection of antiquities made by Cardinal Giovanni Grimani, housed in his palazzo in Ruga Giuffa near Santa Maria Formosa. The palazzo, with its remarkable frescoes, marbles and statuary *tribuna*, is now the property of the state, and once restoration is finished will open—with luck before the next edition of this book—an important addition to the number of Venetian palaces revealing their treasures to the inquisitive visitor guided so meticulously by Alta Macadam. Venice in Peril is immensely grateful to her and to the publishers of Blue Guides for giving us this opportunity to reach their readers. Venice is unfortunately ever more dependent on tourism for its economic viability, but if the visitor comes prepared to explore with Blue Guidance, both they and the city will benefit.

Frances Clarke
Venice in Peril Fund
www.veniceinperil.org

THE TOPOGRAPHY OF VENICE

Venice stands in a unique position, built on an archipelago of islets or shoals, a few kilometres from the mainland, in a lagoon protected from the open sea by the natural breakwater of the Lido. The seawater enters the lagoon through three channels. The city is supported on piles of pine, driven down about 7.5m to a solid bed of compressed sand and clay, and many of the buildings are built above a foundation course of Istrian limestone which withstands the corrosion of the sea. As long as it is protected from the air, pine is the only wood which hardens with time when exposed to water, becoming almost fossilised.

The irregular plan of the city is crossed by some 170 canals, the broadest of which, the Grand Canal, divides the city into two unequal parts. The other canals, called *rii* (*rio* in the singular), with the exception of the wider and straighter Cannaregio canal, have an average breadth of 3–4m. They are spanned by about 430 bridges, mostly built out of Istrian stone, but some in iron or wood.

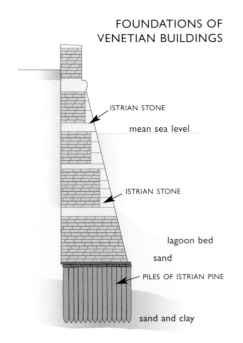

FOUNDATIONS OF VENETIAN BUILDINGS

ISTRIAN STONE

mean sea level

ISTRIAN STONE

lagoon bed

sand

PILES OF ISTRIAN PINE

sand and clay

The only *piazza* is that of St Mark: there are two *piazzette*, one in front of the Doge's Palace, the other, the Piazzetta Giovanni XXIII, by the north flank of the Basilica of St Mark. Any other square in Venice is called a *campo* (or, if very small, *campiello* or *corte*). The streets, nearly all narrow, are called *calli*; the more important thoroughfares, usually shopping streets, are known as *calle larga*, *ruga* or *salizzada* (the name given to the first paved streets in 1676). A smaller alley is called *caletta* or *ramo*. A street alongside a canal is called a *fondamenta*: a *rio terrà* is a street along the course of a filled-in rio. A *riva* is a wharf. A *sottoportego* (or *sottoportico*) passes beneath the overhanging upper floor of a building. A *piscina* is a place where a basin of water (*bacino*) connected to a canal formerly existed; and a *sacca* a stretch of water where canals meet. A *lista* is a lane which led up to an ambassador's palace.

The buildings of Venice

A Venetian palace or important residence is sometimes called *Ca'* (or *Casa*) instead of *Palazzo*. The ground floor of a typical palace has an *androne*, with a water-gate and sometimes a portico and a courtyard, often with a well. The main rooms are on the first floor or *piano nobile*, arranged on either side of the *portego*, a large central oblong hall which often extends for the whole depth of the building (and is usually lit by tall windows on the façade). On the upper floors palaces sometimes have a protruding loggia (*liagò*), and, on the roof, characteristic open wooden balconies called *altane*. Venetian chimneys have a particularly charming shape. In front of the most important palaces, and in particular those on the Grand Canal, wooden *pali* or mooring posts are traditionally painted with the striped livery colours of their proprietors.

CA' REZZONICO: A TYPICAL PALAZZO

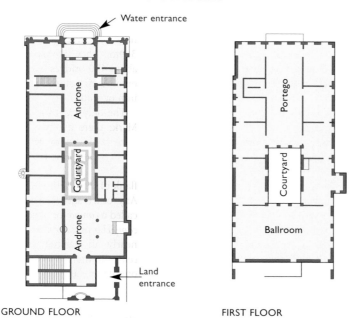

GROUND FLOOR　　　　　　　　FIRST FLOOR

Other important buildings in the city include *scuole*—a *scuola* is a lay confraternity dedicated to charitable works (and also the name of the building which serves as its headquarters). A *fondaco* (or *fontego*) was a trading-post, and a *magazzino* (or *magazen*) a warehouse.

　Beneath many of the *campi* are cisterns which received the rain-water which was collected through grilles in the pavement. Below ground level the water filtered through sand before reaching the central well-shaft which is crowned with a *vera da pozzo*, or well-head, usually circular and built in Istrian stone.

Almost all the bridges remained without parapets up until the 19th century, when numerous elegant wrought-iron balustrades were added. Also at this time many bridges were rebuilt in iron or cast-iron. The bridges are also used to carry gas and water pipes and electricity cables through-out the city.

Names of the streets and canals are often written (in the form of painted signs) in a simplified Venetian dialect and changed when the paint is renewed.

Houses are numbered con-secutively throughout each of

THE VENETIAN WELL

grille

well-head

sand acting as filter

the six *sestieri* the districts into which the city was divided in the 12th century (San Marco, Castello, Dorsoduro, San Polo, Santa Croce and Cannaregio).

The Venetian Lagoon

The hauntingly beautiful Venetian Lagoon is separated from the open sea by the low, narrow sandbars of the Lido and Pellestrina, which are pierced by three channels: the Porto di Lido, the Porto di Malamocco, and the Porto di Chioggia. A shallow expanse of water, with an average depth of only about a metre, and an area of 544km square, it is the largest coastal lagoon in the Mediterranean, and the only one in the world which supports a large town in its centre. On some of the islands townships and monasteries were established in the Middle Ages, most of which have now diminished in impor-tance, except for Murano, with its glass manufactories. On others, isolation hospitals were built, and after a fire in the Arsenale in 1569, many of the smaller islands were used as forts or stores for gunpowder. The Lido became a famous resort in the early 20th century. The future of some of the islands, abandoned in the 1960s and '70s, is uncer-tain. There is an excellent service of public *vaporetti* to all the inhabited islands.

The ecology of the lagoon

The survival of the lagoon and Venice itself depends on an extremely delicate ecolog-ical balance between the open sea and the enclosed lagoon, and from as early as the 12th century work was being carried out to preserve it. Canals were dug between the early 16th and the 18th centuries to divert the silt-bearing rivers (notably the Brenta and Bacchiglione, the Piave and Sile) away from the area so that they could flow directly into the sea to the north and south of the lagoon. In the 18th century a great sea wall (the *murazzi*) was constructed at Pellestrina out of *pozzolana* and Istrian stone to control the eroding waters of the Adriatic, and in the 19th and early 20th centuries outer breakwaters were built up at the three entrances. The salt marshes, the extent of which has dramatically diminished in this century, still protect a great number of aquatic species, although marine life is threatened by the increase in seaweed.

Since the early years of the 16th century, the lagoon has been protected by a board presided over by the Magistrato alle Acque. In 1987 this board, which has become the local office of the Italian Ministry of Public Works, granted a licence to a private consortium of firms (the Consorzio Venezia Nuova) to undertake studies and carry out work to safeguard the lagoon and the city. The division of responsibility between the municipality and the regional and central governments continues to cause problems and delays. However, a great deal of valuable scientific research has been carried out in the last few decades.

It is now known that much damage was caused in the 1920s and '30s by the growth of the port of Marghera, and by the decision in the 1950s to set up the second largest oil refinery in Italy inside the lagoon itself, only a short distance from Venice. The three sea entrances were deepened to allow tankers into the lagoon, and a channel 12m deep was excavated in the 1960s so that these ships could cross the lagoon from Malamocco, actions which accelerated the process of erosion. The discharge of nitrogen and the creation of dump sites inside the lagoon also caused serious problems. It is widely recognised today that the passage of oil tankers represents a very real hazard: urgent measures have been called for to eliminate this traffic by the installation of pipelines, and in 2001 ships without a double hull and carrying dangerous cargo were banned from the lagoon. Further damage was caused when the natural process of subsidence in the lagoon was increased by the construction of artesian wells for industrial use (drilling has officially been prohibited since the 1970s, but the extraction of liquids or gas in the Adriatic and the lagoon area has still not been totally halted). There is a suggestion that a buffer zone of artificial wetlands should be created in order to preserve the lagoon from pollution from the *terraferma*.

The navigable channels in the lagoon are marked by piles (*bricole*) in the water, and the only way to see the remote parts of the lagoon is to hire a private boat. However, much of it can also be seen from the ACTV (Venice Navigation Company) public transport service of *vaporetti*. A particularly good view of the lagoon can be had from the walk around the outside of the walls of the island of the Lazzaretto Nuovo (*see p. 343*; there is also a little observation post here in one of the towers), and from the top of the bell-tower of Torcello cathedral.

The Consorzio Venezia Nuova offices in Venice are in Palazzo Morosini, 2803 San Marco (*Campo Santo Stefano; T: 041 529 3511*). The WWF (World Wide Fund for Nature) has a reserve in the southern part of the lagoon at Valle Averto (*T: 041 538 2820 or 041 518 5068*).

The conservation of Venice

At present the greatest problem facing Venice is the notable increase in the number of days when the city suffers from *acqua alta* (a flood tide over 110cm above mean sea level). One day in 2000 there was an exceptionally high tide of 144cm, which meant that over 90 per cent of the city was under water for a few hours; in the winter of 2004 tide levels reached 137cm. *Acqua alta* is caused not only by subsidence (there has been a diminution in the height of the land in the lagoon in respect of sea level of about 23cm since the beginning of the 20th century) but also by the gradual rise in the mean sea level and climate change in general.

A project first mooted in 1970, and finalised in 1984, planned to regulate tides of over 1m by the installation of moveable barriers at the three lagoon entrances, using a system similar to those already functioning in the Netherlands and Britain. These sluice gates are designed to lie on the seabed, and be raised only when a particularly high tide is expected (it was originally estimated that this would happen only about seven times a year). Each barrier measures some 20m across, and is 18–30m high, and 4–5m thick: to close all three entrances to the lagoon, some 128 of these will be needed. At the widest Lido entrance an artificial island will have to be built in mid-channel to facilitate construction work. The barriers will be able to be activated in about 30mins once a high tide is forecast, and will probably remain raised for anything between two and five hours. All three entrances will have locks for use by shipping when the barriers are closed. Although a prototype (known as Mo.S.E.; *modulo sperimentale elettromeccanico*) was installed at the Porto di Lido entrance to the lagoon in 1988, and exhaustive scientific experiments were carried out, this project—seen by many engineers to be the only possible solution to the problem of *acqua alta*—was halted in 1995 to be re-examined by an Italian government committee. In 1998 a commission of five international experts reported in favour of the project, giving it their conditional approval and stating that in their opinion the barriers would not adversely effect the ecology of the lagoon. In the same year, a commission appointed by the Italian Ministry of the Environment pronounced a negative verdict.

In 2000 the Comitatone, an inter-ministerial working group under the chairmanship of the Magistrato alle Acque, was unable to take a decision on Mo.S.E. owing to the irreconcilable opinions of the Minister for Public Works and the Minister for the Environment, and they passed responsibility to the Cabinet of Ministers in Rome. Finally in 2003 the last three (out of a total of 42) inter-ministerial meetings unanimously agreed that the executive phase of the project should proceed, provided that certain conditions imposed by the City Council concerning the environment and morphology of the lagoon were observed. This decision was reconfirmed in 2006, and the second phase of the project is now underway, due to be operational in around 2012. The Consorzio Venezia Nuova has started work on the breakwaters designed to protect the three entrances to the lagoon, and reduce the depth of the channel at Malamocco by two metres in order to inhibit excessive tidal surge.

There is opposition from environmentalists, who are worried about the project's impact on the lagoon ecology. It has also now been recognised that the sea level is rising due to global warming (it is estimated that by 2200 there will be a rise of 100cm in the mean sea level), so the barriers might no longer be adequate. There is also an urgent need to find a more reliable method for forecasting exceptionally high tides.

In the meantime, detailed scientific studies of the lagoon continue, the sea defences are being strengthened, the beaches on the sea at Pellestrina and Cavallino reclaimed, some of the grass-grown shoals which emerge from the lagoon and the mud banks normally awash at high tide reconstructed, the polluted waters cleaned, and the fish-farms in the marshes (where eels, mullet and sea bream are raised) reopened to tidal flow. Additional operations are to be carried out to guarantee the hydro-dynamics necessary to maintain water quality and the ecosystem.

Since 1997, in the centre of Venice itself, Insula, a consortium for urban mainte-nance under the direction of the municipality, has been carrying out an excellent pro-gramme of dredging and cleaning canals and, where possible, raising the level of the lower-lying *fondamente* to 1.2m above mean sea level. A long-term project by the Magistrato alle Acque (through Consorzio Venezia Nuova) is being undertaken to pro-tect Piazza San Marco and the basilica from high tides of up to 110cm (at present the Piazza is flooded about 250 times a year). The first stage is underway on the Molo, where the quayside along the Bacino di San Marco will be slightly raised, and work will then start in the Piazza itself, where the underground drainage system is to be restored. This project is not expected to be completed before 2011, and studies are still underway to decide whether the foundations of the pavement in the Piazza should be waterproofed as well.

The foundations of all Venetian buildings and the quays on the main canals are being eroded by the wash or wave damage (*moto ondoso*) caused by motorboats which continue to exceed the speed limits imposed by the city council.

A conference on the lagoon, the flooding risks, and the barrier system was held in 2003 in Cambridge, England, with the collaboration of the Venice-based Consortium for the Coordination of Research into the Lagoon, with contributions from leading fig-ures in the international scientific community; their papers were published by Cambridge University Press in 2005 (*Flooding and Environmental Challenges for Venice and its Lagoon: State of Knowledge*). The findings were summarised for the layman in the same year by the Venice in Peril Fund in both Italian and English (*The Science of Saving Venice* by Caroline Fletcher and Jane da Mosto).

However, despite these few encouraging signs it is generally recognised that all nec-essary action has not yet been taken, even though ever since 1973 a series of Special Laws for Venice have been passed by the Italian government, all of which have stipu-lated the urgent need to deal with the pollution and ecology of the lagoon and to pro-tect her buildings from flooding.

HIGHLIGHTS OF VENICE

The most famous sights in Venice—the Basilica of St Mark, Doge's Palace, Grand Canal and Rialto Bridge—are, not surprisingly, also the most visited. During daylight hours, except in the depths of winter, these areas can become dramatically overcrowded.

But Venice is one of the most beautiful and best preserved cities in the world, and a walk through any of its narrow streets or quiet squares or along the picturesque canals can be as rewarding as a visit to its greatest monuments. The secluded district of Dorsoduro, for example, is one of the most delightful parts of the city. The island of the Giudecca, with the church of the Redentore, a masterpiece of Palladio, is also a peaceful district seldom visited by tourist groups. On the next-door island of San Giorgio Maggiore is another church by Palladio, with a superb view from its bell-tower.

Other churches of particular interest include the huge Dominican church of Santi Giovanni e Paolo, with numerous funerary monuments to doges, some of them Renaissance masterpieces; and the Franciscan church of the Frari, which has more good funerary monuments and paintings by Giovanni Bellini and Titian. San Giovanni in Bragora is interesting for its paintings; San Zaccaria and Santa Maria Formosa for their paintings and architecture alike. Santa Maria della Salute is the masterpiece of Baldassare Longhena, in a splendid position at the beginning of the Grand Canal. San Sebastiano is decorated with superb paintings by Veronese; Santa Maria dei Miracoli has exquisite Renaissance carvings by Pietro Lombardo. The Madonna dell'Orto, in a lovely quiet area of the city, contains important works by Tintoretto. La Pietà has a fine 18th–century interior, and San Stae has 18th-century paintings.

The best buildings which belonged to the *scuole*, or lay confraternities dedicated to charitable works during the Republic, include the Scuola Grande di San Rocco, with over 50 paintings by Tintoretto, one of the most remarkable pictorial cycles in existence; the Scuola Grande dei Carmini, with beautiful ceiling paintings by Tiepolo; and the Scuola di San Giorgio degli Schiavoni, charmingly decorated with paintings by Vittore Carpaccio.

Museums of great interest include the famous Gallerie dell'Accademia, home to the most important collection of Venetian paintings in existence, with Giovanni Bellini, Titian, Tintoretto and Veronese all well represented. Museo Correr is the city museum, with historical collections and some important paintings. The Ca' d'Oro has some fine Venetian sculptures; the Museo Querini-Stampalia has Venetian paintings; and Ca' Rezzonico on the Grand Canal has splendid 18th–century decorations including frescoes by Tiepolo. The Museo Archeologico has ancient Greek and Roman sculpture. The Peggy Guggenheim collection contains one of the most representative displays of 20th–century art in Europe.

Of all the islands in the beautiful Venetian lagoon, the most evocative is Torcello, with its ancient cathedral. Murano is interesting for its glass-works and glass museum, and its Veneto-Byzantine basilica.

ART IN SITU

Though much Venetian painting has now found its way into museums, the churches and *palazzi* of the city still provide an unparalleled opportunity to appreciate works of art in the kind of context and atmosphere for which they were intended. Below is a list of where paintings by some of the city's major artists can still be found *in situ*.

Giovanni Bellini (c. 1433–1516)
S. Francesco della Vigna
S. Giovanni Crisostomo
SS. Giovanni e Paolo
S. Maria Gloriosa dei Frari
S. Pietro Martire (Murano)
S. Zaccaria

Vittore Carpaccio (c. 1460–1525/26)
Doge's Palace
S. Domenico (Chioggia)
S. Vitale
Scuola di San Giorgio degli Schiavoni

Cima da Conegliano (c. 1459–1518)
Madonna dell'Orto
Giovanni in Bragora
S. Maria dei Carmini

Lorenzo Lotto (1480–1556)
S. Giacomo dell'Orio
SS. Giovanni e Paolo
S. Maria dei Carmini

Palma Giovane (1548–1628)
Doge's Palace
Gesuiti
Madonna dell'Orto
Oratorio dei Crociferi
Redentore
S. Francesco da Paola
S. Francesco della Vigna
S. Giacomo dell'Orio
S. Giovanni in Bragora
S. Giovanni Elemosinario
SS. Giovanni e Paolo
S. Giuliano
S. Lazzaro degli Armeni
S. Lio
S. Maria dei Carmini

S. Maria Gloriosa dei Frari
S. Martino
S. Nicola da Tolentino
S. Pietro Martire (Murano)
S. Polo
S. Simeone Grande
S. Trovaso
Scuola Grande S. Giovanni Evangelista
Spirito Santo
Zitelle

Palma Vecchio (c. 1480–1528)
S. Maria Formosa

Giovanni Battista Piazzetta (1683–1754)
Gesuati
La Pietà
SS. Giovanni e Paolo
S. Maria della Fava
S. Stae
S. Vitale
Scuola Grande dei Carmini

Sebastiano Ricci (1659–1734)
Gesuati
Palazzo Querini-Stampalia
S. Giorgio Maggiore
S. Marciliano
S. Maria dei Carmini
S. Rocco
S. Stae
S. Vitale
Seminario Patriarcale

Giambattista Tiepolo (1696–1770)
Ca'Rezzonico
Doge's Palace
Duomo (Chioggia)
Gesuati

Ospedaletto
Palazzo Labia
La Pietà
S. Alvise
SS. Apostoli
S. Benedetto
S. Francesco della Vigna
S. Lazzaro degli Armeni
S. Maria della Fava
S. Martino (Burano)
S. Polo
S. Stae
Scalzi
Scuola Grande dei Carmini

**Giovanni Domenico Tiepolo
(1727–1804)**
S. Francesco da Paola
S. Lio
S. Polo
S. Zaccaria
Scuola Grande S. Giovanni Evangelista

Jacopo Tintoretto (1519–94)
Doge's Palace
Gesuati
Gesuiti
Libreria Marciana
Madonna dell'Orto
S. Cassiano
S. Felice
S. Giorgio Maggiore
S. Lazzaro dei Mendicanti
S. Marciliano
S. Marcuola
S. Maria del Giglio
S. Maria Mater Domini
S. Maria della Salute
S. Polo
S. Rocco (church and *scuola*)
S. Silvestro
S. Simeone Grande
S. Stefano
S. Trovaso
S. Zaccaria

Titian (c. 1488–1576)
Doge's Palace
Gesuiti
Libreria Marciana
S. Giovanni Elemosinario
S. Lio
S. Maria Gloriosa dei Frari
S. Maria della Salute
S. Salvatore
S. Sebastiano

Paolo Veneziano (active 1335–60)
S. Maria Gloriosa dei Frari
S. Pantalon
S. Samuele

Paolo Veronese (1528–88)
Doge's Palace
Libreria Marciana
Palazzo Trevisan (Murano)
Scuola di S. Fantin
S. Francesco della Vigna
SS. Giovanni e Paolo
S. Giuliano
S. Giuseppe di Castello
S. Lazzaro dei Mendicanti
S. Luca
S. Pantalon
S. Pietro di Castello
S. Pietro Martire (Murano)
S. Polo
S. Sebastiano

**The Vivarini: Alvise (1445/6–1503/4),
Antonio (c. 1415–84), Bartolomeo
(active 1450–99)**
Redentore
S. Eufemia
S. Giobbe
S. Giovanni in Bragora
SS. Giovanni e Paolo
S. Maria Formosa
S. Maria Gloriosa dei Frari
S. Pantalon
S. Stefano
S. Zaccaria

SAN MARCO

The small *sestiere* of San Marco is very much at the heart of Venice: it stretches from Piazza San Marco to the Rialto Bridge, cradled in the curve of the Grand Canal and bounded by the narrow calle known as the Merceria. The Rialto (*riva alta*) was probably the first area to be settled because of its slightly higher position, although the *sestiere* is in fact in the lowest part of the city and therefore always particularly liable to flood. In the Middle Ages it developed as the administrative, financial, commercial, political and cultural centre of Venice. Little has changed: this *sestiere* remains the seat of local government, it has the greatest number of hotels and the most expensive restaurants and shops. It is the backdrop for the defining and enduring symbols of the *Serenissima*—its magnificent Gothic, Renaissance and Baroque churches, its imposing *palazzi* and above all, the Basilica of St Mark and the Doge's Palace. For centuries, this *sestiere* was the first place any visitor to Venice would set foot, and while today far fewer people arrive by water, it is still the district to which most are first drawn.

THE BASILICA OF ST MARK
Map p. 407, E2

The Basilica of St Mark is the most important church in Venice and its most splendid building, with superb Byzantine mosaics. It stands high in importance among the churches of Christendom. Founded in 832, its sumptuous architecture retains the original Greek-cross plan derived from the great churches of Constantinople, in particular from the (destroyed) 6th-century Justinian church of the Holy Apostles. Its five onion-shaped domes are Islamic in inspiration. This famous shrine has been embellished over the centuries by splendid mosaics, marbles, and carvings. It contains outstanding art treasures, the origins of some of which are still uncertain (including the gilded horses and the columns which support the baldacchino in the sanctuary). Numerous different styles and traditions have been blended in a unique combination of Byzantine and Western art. The basilica was formerly the private chapel of the doges, and was used throughout the Republic's history for state ceremonies. It replaced San Pietro di Castello (*see p. 299*) as the cathedral of Venice only in 1807.

Opening times

The basilica is open to visitors daily 9.45–4.30 or 5; Sun and holidays 2–4.30 or 5. However, the mosaics are only lit for one hour on weekdays, 11.30–12.30, and on Sundays and holidays from 2–5. The Treasury and Pala d'Oro (the gilded and enamelled high altarpiece) can be seen from 10–4 or 6; Sun and holidays 3–6 (both with an extra admission charge). The north transept is usually reserved for prayer (entrance by the north door); and services are frequently held in the sanctuary on Sundays (on other days Eucharist is celebrated here at

9am), when many of the basilica's treasures and mosaics can be seen to full advantage; attending a service gives an incomparable sense of St Mark's as a functioning place of worship.

The Museo di San Marco, which houses the original gilded horses, also includes access to the loggia on the façade and two balconies in the interior of the basilica. It is open 10–4.30 (admission charge). Other areas of the basilica, including the crypt, baptistery, and Cappella Zen, normally kept locked or reserved for prayer, can usually be seen by special request at the offices of the Proto of San Marco (the architects in charge of the fabric of the building) inside the basilica; enquire about procedure from one of the uniformed guards.

Visiting the basilica

The basilica must be the most visited building in Venice, and unfortunately the authorities have not yet found a way of coping satisfactorily with the incessant crowds. There are postcard shops in inappropriate places within the basilica itself, which sometimes has a rather shabby atmosphere, and the attendants are not always as friendly as they might be. Most of the atrium, which has some of the most important mosaics, is inaccessible, and in the interior you are restricted to a 'one-way' route. It is only by attending one of the numerous services which take place here that you can fully appreciate the special atmosphere of this deeply holy place.

Building history

The first church, built on a Greek-cross plan by Doge Giustiniano Particiaco, was consecrated in 832. Recent investigations of the foundations seem to confirm that this is the very church which stands today. It has been discovered that the building rests on a wooden platform supported by wooden piles, 50–80cm long, driven down through the sand into the solid lagoon bed of sand and clay some 2.5–3.5m below the present pavement. The church was damaged by fire in a popular rising in 976 against Doge Pietro Candiano IV and restored by Doge Pietro Orseolo I. In 1063, when Doge Domenico Contarini carried out important work to consolidate the building, which had been damaged by movement in the foundations, he decided to add the narthex. At this time he may also have blocked up a number of apertures which had provided light in the interior when he commissioned the first mosaics. Work was continued by Doge Domenico Selvo (1071–84). The church was reconsecrated in 1094 when the relics of St Mark were refound (*see box opposite*) by Doge Vitale Falier. The original brick vaults were at a later stage surmounted on the exterior by false domes built in wood and covered with lead and each topped with an onion-shaped crown.

The mosaic decoration, begun at the end of the 11th century, is the work of centuries. After 1159 the walls were faced with marble from Ravenna, Sicily, Byzantium and the East. During the Fourth Crusade and sack of Constantinople (1204) many of the greatest treasures which now adorn the basilica (including the four horses) were transported to Venice. The sculptural decoration of the upper façade dates from the end of the 14th and beginning of the 15th centuries. For some 40 years in the 16th century Jacopo Sansovino was *proto* of San Marco, and during this time he carried out important work to consolidate the structure of the building; a task which continues to this day.

THE LEGEND OF ST MARK

According to legend, St Mark the Evangelist anchored off the islands of the Rialto while on a voyage from Aquileia to Rome. While he was there he had a vision of an angel who greeted him with the words *Pax tibi, Marce, evangelista meus. Hic requiescet corpus tuum.* ('Peace be with you, Mark my evangelist. Here will be your resting place.'). This portent was supposed to have been fulfilled in 828, when two Venetian merchants brought the body of St Mark from the Arab port of Alexandria and placed it in charge of Doge Giustiniano Particiaco, who ordered the first church on this site to be built. When this church was damaged by fire in the 10th century the body of St Mark was lost, only to be miraculously 'rediscovered' by Doge Vitale Falier in 1094. The basilica has numerous depictions in mosaic (both on the façade and in the interior) of the various adventures of the body of St Mark, and it was a favourite subject with Venetian painters, notably Tintoretto (*see p. 150*). The name and symbol of St Mark (a winged lion) have been emblematic of Venice since the 9th century. There are numerous stone lions all over the city, and the lion of St Mark can also still be seen on columns, in *piazze*, or decorating public buildings in many towns which were once subject to the *Serenissima*, in the Veneto and further afield. The saint was invoked as a battle cry ('Viva San Marco!') during the Republic, and again in the 19th century during the Venetian struggle against Austrian rule.

EXTERIOR OF THE BASILICA

Plans of the basilica are given on pp. 50–51.

Main façade

NB: The lower order of the façade is described here. The upper order, better seen from the balcony reached from the Museo di San Marco, is described with that museum (see p. 63).
The sumptuous main façade of St Mark's is in two orders, each of five arches, those below supported by clusters of columns and those above crowned by elaborate Gothic tracery, pinnacles, sculptures and tabernacles. A balcony with water-spouts separates the two orders, and copies of the famous horses stand here. The columns are of different kinds of marble, many from older buildings, and most of them have fine capitals. At the left end of the façade, a huge single column with a fine capital supports three porphyry columns. Between the arches are six bas-reliefs. From left to right: *Hercules carrying the Erymanthean Boar*, *St George*, *St Demetrius*, the *Virgin Orans*, the *Archangel Gabriel* and *Hercules and the Hydra*. The first is a Roman work; the third was made by a Byzantine craftsman in the late 12th century, and the others are all 13th-century works in the Veneto-Byzantine style. Below the reliefs at either end of the façade, between the columns, are statuettes of water-carriers.

The doors

(1) Door of Sant'Alipio: In the arch above the door is a beautiful mosaic of the *Translation of the Body of St Mark to the Basilica* (1260–70). This is the only original mosaic to have survived on the façade, and is the earliest representation known of the exterior of the basilica (you can see that the horses are already in place). Beneath it is a fine arched lunette with early 14th-century bas-reliefs of the symbols of the Evangelists and five pretty arches decorated with fretwork, Islamic in style. The architrave above the door is formed by a long 13th-century Venetian bas-relief in the early Christian style. Superb capitals surmount the columns on either side of the door, which is the work of an otherwise unknown master who signs himself 'Magister Bertuccio' and records the date 1300 (he also made the second doors).

(2) Second doorway: The mosaic of *Venice Venerating the Relics of St Mark* dates from 1718 (from a cartoon by Sebastiano Ricci). Above the door is a window with Gothic tracery surrounded by fine carvings of Christ and two prophets on a mosaic ground.

(3) Central doorway: This is crowned by a mosaic of the *Last Judgement* (1836). Among the columns flanking the doorway eight are in red porphyry. The three arches have beautiful carvings dating from c. 1240 (first inner arch) to c. 1265 (third outer arch). These constitute one of the most important examples of Romanesque carving in Italy, showing the influence of Benedetto Antelami, the greatest sculptor of 12th-century Italy. The main outer arch surrounding the mosaic has, on its underside, carvings showing Venetian trades (such as boat-building and fishing), and, on the outer face, *Christ and the Prophets*. The middle arch depicts the months and signs of the zodiac on the soffit and the Virtues and Beatitudes on the outer face. The smallest arch shows the Earth, the Ocean, and seven pairs of animals on the soffit, and, on the outer face, scenes of daily life from youth to old age. The very ancient doors, dating from the 6th century, are wonderful Byzantine works. In the lunette is a marble carving of the *Dream of St Mark* by the school of Antelami.

(4) Fourth doorway: The mosaic, made in the early 18th century by the Roman mosaicist Leopoldo dal Pozzo (again based on a cartoon by Sebastiano Ricci), shows *Venice Welcoming the Arrival of the Body of St Mark*. There are 13th-century reliefs above a Gothic window.

(5) Fifth doorway: Above the door is a mosaic showing the *Removal of the Body of St Mark from Alexandria*, also by dal Pozzo. The Moorish window has Byzantine reliefs and mosaics.

Detail of the Door of Sant'Alipio, showing the *Translation of the Body of St Mark to the Basilica*. Note the four horses in mosaic above the central lunette of Christ.

South façade (towards the Doge's Palace)

This continues the design of the west façade. The first doorway **(6)**, which was blocked by the construction of the Cappella Zen (*see p. 62 below*), was formerly one of the main entrances to the basilica and the first to be seen from the waterfront. The columns are surmounted by two marble griffins (12th–13th century). The second arch **(7)** contains the 14th-century bronze doors of the Baptistery and a Gothic window. The two upper arches are finely decorated; between them and above a small 10th-century door, is a Byzantine mosaic of the *Madonna in Prayer* (13th century), in front of which two lamps are lit every night in fulfilment of the vow made by a sea-captain after he had survived a storm at sea. The Gothic sculpture which crowns the arches is partly the work of the Florentine sculptor Niccolò di Pietro Lamberti, who came to work in the city in 1416. The two rectangular walls of the Treasury **(8)** stand beside the Porta della Carta of the Doge's Palace. These are richly adorned with splendid marbles and fragments of ambones and *plutei* (9th–11th century). The front of the bench at the foot of the wall bears an inscription of the late 13th century—one of the earliest examples of the Venetian dialect.

At the southwest corner of the façade is the Pietra del Bando **(9)**, a stump of a porphyry column thought to come from Acre, from which decrees of the Venetian government were proclaimed from 1256 onwards. It was hit when the Campanile collapsed in 1902 (*see p. 66*), but at least it saved the corner of the church from serious damage.

Two of the four porphyry *Tetrarchs*, probably Egyptian works of the 4th century.

On the corner are two delightful sculptured groups in porphyry known as the *Tetrarchs* **(10)**, thought by some scholars to represent Diocletian and three other emperors, and by others the four sons of Constantine. Their symbolic embrace apparently was meant to represent political harmony. Probably Egyptian works of the 4th century, they may come from Constantinople.

In front of the baptistery door are two isolated pillars **(11)**, beautifully carved in the 6th century, and traditionally thought to have been brought by Lorenzo Tiepolo (later doge) from the church of St Saba in Acre (now part of Israel) after his victory there over the Genoese in 1256. Recent excavations in Istanbul have, however, confirmed that they came instead from the palace church of St Polyeuctus there, built in AD 524. The pillars would therefore have been seized during the Fourth Crusade in 1204 (*see p. 60*), and brought back to Venice at that time.

North façade (facing Piazzetta Giovanni XXIII)

This was probably the last to be finished, and was splendidly restored in 2005. Between the arches and in the upper bays are interesting bas-reliefs, including one (between the first two arches) showing the *Flight of Alexander the Great*. He is shown in triumph and as a Byzantine emperor: the curious iconography includes two skewered pieces of meat which Alexander holds above the griffins' noses to egg them on in their flight to Heaven (as in donkey and carrot). The last of the four arches, the Porta dei Fiori **(12)** has beautifully carved 13th-century arches enclosing a Nativity scene. The upper part of the façade (as on the south front) has more early 15th-century statues by the Tuscan sculptor Niccolò di Pietro Lamberti, and more fine water-carriers thought to be by his son Pietro di Niccolò Lamberti, although these have also been attributed to Jacopo della Quercia (*see p. 64*). Beyond the Porta dei Fiori the projecting walls of the Mascoli and St Isidore chapels bear Byzantine bas-reliefs. The marble sarcophagus **(13)** contains the body of Daniele Manin, who proclaimed the city's independence from Austrian rule in 1848 (*see p. 124*). Manin died in Paris in 1857, and his body was returned to Venice 20 years later. After lying in state at the foot of the Campanile, his sarcophagus (designed by Luigi Borro) was installed here, even though the Church authorities refused his burial inside the basilica.

THE NARTHEX

The west narthex was probably built around 1063–72, and it seems that the north side was added at least 100 years later (certainly before 1253), but scholars still discuss the exact date of construction. It provides a fitting vestibule to the basilica (although it is often now sadly cluttered with barriers and notices). It could once have been approached also from the south side before the construction of the Cappella Zen. The slightly pointed arches, probably the earliest of their kind in Italy, support six small domes. The fine columns of the inner façade were either brought from the East or are fragments of the first basilica. The lower part of the walls is encased in marble; the upper part and the pavement are mosaic. The superb mosaics of the domes and arches represent stories from the Old Testament, and are mainly original works of the 13th century.

(14) First bay: Mosaics (1200–10) of the *Story of Genesis* to the *Death of Abel*. The mosaics are in poor condition and have suffered from earlier restorations. The carefully worked-out iconographical scheme is thought to have been inspired by the Cotton Bible miniatures (probably late 5th century), once in the collection of Sir Robert Bruce Cotton (1571–1631), whose library is now in the British Museum. The 24 episodes are divided into three bands: in the centre of the dome, *Creation of the Sky, Earth and Firmament*; in the middle band, *Creation of the Sun, Moon, Animals and Man*; third band, *Stories of Adam and Eve*. In the pendentives are four winged Seraphs. The door of San Clemente (protected by outer doors), cast in the East, is traditionally supposed to be a gift from the Byzantine Emperor Alexius Comnenus. It is decorated with figures of saints (their names in Greek). The Byzantine capitals of the columns flanking it are beautifully decorated with birds.

(15) First arch: The mosaics show the *Story of Noah and the Flood*. Here lies Doge Vitale Falier (d. 1096) who consecrated the basilica in 1094, and who was responsible for much of its most beautiful decoration. The tomb, made up of Byzantine fragments, is the oldest surviving funerary monument in the entire city.

(16) Second bay: In front of the main door two tiers of niches contain the earliest mosaics in the basilica (c. 1063);

they are doubly precious since they have never had to be restored. They represent the Madonna with the Apostles Peter, Paul, James, Andrew, Simon, Thomas, Philip and Bartholomew, with the four Evangelists beneath. The *St Mark in Ecstasy* in the semi-dome was added centuries later in 1545 (on a cartoon attributed to Lorenzo Lotto). Two Byzantine angels stand on the columns flanking the arch. We know that the great door (between two wooden doors) was commissioned in 1113 by Leone da Molino, who was a procurator of St Mark's: it is modelled on the Byzantine door of San Clemente.

The slab of red Verona marble with a white marble lozenge in the pavement traditionally marks the spot where the Emperor Frederick Barbarossa was forced to kneel before Pope Alexander III in 1177. This marked a significant moment in the history of Venice's rise to power, since the city had been chosen as the scene for the reconciliation between the Papacy and the Empire (despite the fact that it had at first, under the dogeship of Sebastiano Ziani, joined the Lombard League against Barbarossa). The little door on the right leads up to the Museo di San Marco and the loggia (*described on p. 63*).

(17) Second arch: The mosaics show the *Death of Noah* and the *Tower of Babel*. The tomb of the wife of Doge Vitale Michiel (d. 1101) is decorated with *plutei* and *transennae* which were carved in the previous century.

(18) Third bay: In the dome and the arch above the door, the *Story of Abraham* mosaics date from c. 1230. In the pendentives are four *tondi* with prophets. In the lunette above the door there is a Byzantine mosaic of St Peter.

(19) Third arch: Mosaics of St Alipio and St Simon, and, in the centre, a tondo with *Justice* (c. 1230).

(20) Fourth bay: The tomb of Doge Bartolomeo Gradenigo (d. 1342) is by a Pisan sculptor. The reign of this doge, which only lasted three years since he was already an old man when elected, but which saw the beginning of the reconstruction of the Doge's Palace, is remembered particularly since it coincided with a terrible flood, the consequences of which were thought to have been ameliorated by the intervention of St Mark, together with St Nicholas and St George (the famous tale of the fisherman and the ring is illustrated in Paris Bordone's painting now in the Galleria dell'Accademia; *see p. 152*). The mosaics along this side of the narthex were partly re-made in the 19th century; they portray the *Story of Joseph*, and, in the pendentives, the prophets.

(21) Fifth bay: Here is the tomb of Doge Marin Morosini (who died, otherwise forgotten, in 1253): this has been recomposed, but includes a 13th-century relief.

(22) Seventh bay: The mosaics show the *Story of Moses*. The bust of 'Papa Giovanni' (who was Venetian Patriarch when elected Pope John XXIII in 1958; *see p. 86*) is by Giacomo Manzù, a sculptor well known for his religious subjects.

THE INTERIOR

Monuments and mosaics are labelled on the plans overleaf.
The glimmering interior of St Mark's is one of the great sights of the Christian world. Five great domes cover the Greek cross, alternating with barrel vaults; each of the four arms has vaulted aisles in which the numerous columns with exquisite foliated capitals support a gallery (formerly the matroneum), fronted by a parapet of ancient *plutei* (dating from the 6th–11th centuries). The sanctuary, where the religious and political ceremonies of the Republic were held, is raised above the crypt, and separated from the rest of the church by a rood screen. The whole building is encased by Eastern marbles below, and splendid mosaics on a gold ground above, illuminated high up by small windows (the rose window in the south transept and the arch opened at the west end are later additions which alter the delicate effect of dim lighting). At the centre of the nave hangs a huge Byzantine chandelier, while red lamps decorate the side chapels.

The splendid 12th-century pavement, which has subsided in places, has a geometric mosaic of antique marble with representations of beasts and birds. Part of it is covered with unattractive protective matting. The light in the interior of the church changes constantly; ideally it should be visited at different times of the day, though in high season the crowds make this impossible.

BASILICA OF ST MARK
(MONUMENTS)

A   West end
B   South aisle
C   South transept
D   Crossing
E   North transept
F   North aisle
G   Sanctuary
H   Pala d'Oro
I   Treasury
J   Baptistery
K   Cappella Zen

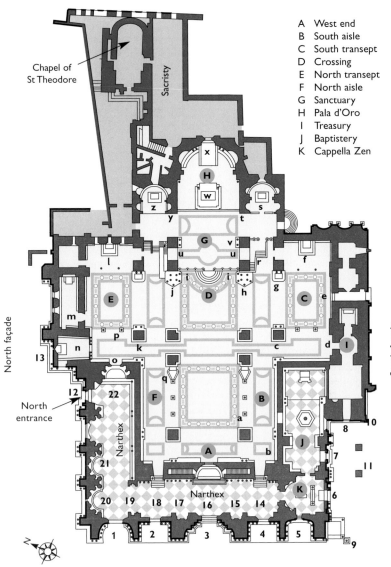

Chapel of
St Theodore

Sacristy

North façade

South façade

North
entrance

Narthex

Narthex

Main façade

BASILICA OF ST MARK
(MOSAICS)

PRINCIPAL MOSAICS

I	Pentecost
III	St Leonard
VII	Ascension
IX	St John
XIV	Religion of Christ
XVI	Christ Pantocrator

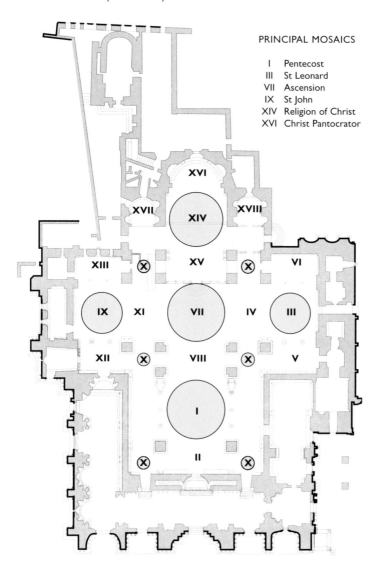

THE MOSAICS OF ST MARK'S

The mosaics (only lit at certain times; see p. 41), which cover a huge area of the basilica, were begun after 1063. They were badly damaged by fire in 1106, and work continued on them right up until the 20th century, although the original medieval iconographical scheme was largely preserved. Over the centuries some of the mosaics have had to be repaired or renewed. In the 12th and 13th centuries the Venetian school of mosaicists flourished, much influenced by Byzantine prototypes, and the decoration of the interior was largely completed by 1277. In the 14th and 15th centuries mosaics were added to the baptistery and other chapels, with the help of Tuscan artists including Paolo Uccello and Andrea del Castagno. In the early 16th century many well-known Venetian painters (such as Titian, Giuseppe Salviati, Tintoretto and Palma Giovane) provided cartoons for the mosaicists, including the Zuccato brothers, and the partial replacement of the mosaics took place. From 1715–45 Leopoldo dal Pozzo carried out restoration work and added new mosaics. In 1881 a mosaic laboratory was set up for the restoration of the mosaics. Many of them were cleaned in the 1970s, when a remarkable survey of them was undertaken by Otto Demus. The Museo di San Marco has a small display illustrating mosaic technique and restoration.

Mosaics are composed of *tesserae*, individual cubes of coloured glass, stone, and enamel set in a plaster bed. The pictorial design for a mosaic was sketched onto the wall beforehand. Early mosaic technique had a limited range of colours, which encouraged a rather non-naturalistic style with attention focused on line and simplified colour definition. Blue was made by adding cobalt; green with copper oxide; and red with copper. Gold and silver were obtained by overlaying the *tesserae* with a thin layer of glazed metal. In more opulent mosaics, mother-of-pearl was also used, as well as white and grey marble. The earliest mosaics in St Mark's date from the 11th century, and in terms of style they cling quite strongly to their Byzantine cousins. Here the *tesserae* were set into the plaster at different depths and angles, in order to catch as much light as possible and create a brilliant, sparkling glow. With the arrival of the Tuscan painters, who designed mosaics with *tesserae* laid as smoothly as possible, surface irregularity was minimised and the fantastic light effects eliminated. These artists also developed a range of colours that could produce delicate tonal gradations. With these innovations, mosaics lost the stylisation of earlier works and gained a painterly naturalism in the depiction of form, becoming, in essence, 'paintings in stone'.

Tour of the basilica

A **The west end:** Over the nave rises the great **Dome of the Pentecost (1)**, dating from the early 12th century and probably the first of the five domes to be

View down the nave towards the east end of St Mark's basilica.

decorated with mosaics. The fine composition shows the *Descent of the Holy
Spirit*; between the windows, the
Converted Nations; in the pendentives,
four huge figures of angels. Lower down
above the main door into the narthex, is
a brightly coloured lunette **(II)** of *Christ
Enthroned between the Madonna and St
Mark* (a very fine restored 13th-century
work). In the barrel vault stretching to
the façade (better seen from the gallery
in the Museo di San Marco) are scenes
of the *Last Judgement*, *Paradise*, the
Apocalypse and *Vision of St John* dating
from the 16th–17th centuries and partly
restored in the 19th.

B **South aisle:** Here is a superb frieze
of five mosaic rectangles with the elegant single figures of the Madonna and
the prophets Isaiah, David, Solomon
and Ezekiel (c. 1230; well restored in
the 19th century). On the wall above,
the splendid large composition of the
Agony in the Garden is the earliest 13th-
century mosaic in the basilica. On either
side of the windows, and in the arch
above, are scenes from the lives of the
Apostles (dated to the end of the 12th
and beginning of the 13th century). The
stoup **(a)** is of Oriental porphyry (the
carved base is now in the Museo di San
Marco). On the south wall **(b)** is a

Byzantine relief (12th century) of Christ between Mary and St John the Baptist.

c **South transept:** The **Dome of St Leonard (III)** has just four lone figures of male saints: St Nicholas, St Clement, St Blaise and St Leonard (early 13th century); in the spandrels are four female saints: St Dorothea (13th century), Sts Erasma and Euphemia (both 15th century), and St Thecla (early 16th century). In the arch towards the nave **(IV)** are very fine mosaic scenes from the life of Christ (early 12th century): the *Entry into Jerusalem*, *Temptations of Christ*, *Last Supper* and *Washing of the Feet*. The first narrow arch in front of the rose window is decorated with Sts Anthony Abbot, Bernardino of Siena, Vincent Ferrer and Paul the Hermit, good works dating from 1458 (showing Tuscan influence).

On the right wall **(V)** the mosaic shows prayers for, and the miraculous rediscovery of, the body of St Mark, with interesting details of the interior of the basilica. Made in the 13th century (although later restored), it includes a supposed portrait of Doge Vitale Falier, the doge who was present when the body was found in 1094, and a portrait of the mosaicists' contemporary Doge Ranier Zeno, who reigned from 1253–68. In the vault (difficult to see), there are 17th-century scenes from the life of the Virgin. The mosaics on the arch above the Altar of the Sacrament **(VI)** show the parables and miracles of Christ (late 12th or early 13th century; restored); those on the end wall (scenes from the life of St Leonard) were renewed in the early 17th century from cartoons by Pietro Muttoni.

On one of the corner piers **(c)** is a bas-relief of the Madonna and Child (known as the *Madonna of the Kiss* since it has been worn away by the kisses of the faithful), thought to date from the 12th century. A small door **(d)** leads into the treasury (*see p. 59 below*). Above a door **(e)** which is now kept closed but which was once the main entrance to the church from the Doge's Palace, is a 13th-century mosaic lunette of St Mark. Early 14th-century fresco fragments (including the *Marys at the Tomb*) have been uncovered in the passageway, which is, however, closed to the public. The huge Gothic rose window was inserted in the 15th century. The altar in this transept **(f)** has a tabernacle borne by columns of porphyry and *pavonazzetto*. It is flanked by two bronze candelabra dating from 1527. On the two pilasters are rectangles of fine marble inlay; the one on the left marks the place where St Mark's body was miraculously rediscovered on 24th June 1094 (illustrated in the mosaic on the opposite wall). On the wall to the right of the altar is a relief of St Peter enthroned (and two bishop saints in mosaic beneath the arch); to the left of the altar, a Byzantine relief of the Madonna and Child. The mosaic pavement here bears early Christian motifs. On the nave pier is the **Altar of St James (g)**, a charming work with beautiful decorative details by Antonio Rizzo. Here is the entrance to the sanctuary and Pala d'Oro (*see p. 59 below*).

D **Crossing:** The central **Dome of the Ascension (VII)** shows Christ seated on a rainbow, with the symbols of the Evangelists, the man, the lion, the bull and the eagle below Him, above four figures representing the rivers of Paradise, as described in the Vision of

Ezekiel. It is a brilliant work of Venetian masters of the late 12th century. Around the Ascension in the centre are the Virgin and two angels and the twelve Apostles; between the windows, the 16 Virtues of Christ. The exquisite mosaics on the arch towards the nave **(VIII)** also date from the late 12th century and portray scenes of the Passion: the *Kiss of Judas, Crucifixion, Marys at the Tomb* (15th-century copy), *Descent into Limbo*, and the *Incredulity of St Thomas*.

After his coronation in the sanctuary the doge traditionally showed himself to the people from the **polygonal pulpit (h)**. Above the pulpit is a 15th-century statue of the Madonna and Child, attributed to Giovanni Bon, father of the more famous sculptor Bartolomeo. The presbytery is raised above the crypt on a stylobate of 16 little marble arches at the foot of the rood screen. The **rood screen (i)**, with eight columns of dark marble, bears the great Cross (or rood), a work in silver and bronze by the otherwise unknown Venetian Jacopo di Marco Benato (1394). The very fine marble statues of the Virgin, St Mark the Evangelist, and the Apostles, of the same date, are signed by the brothers Jacobello and Pier Paolo dalle Masegne, and are usually considered their best works (their workshop in Venice was the most productive in the 14th and 15th centuries).

The **second pulpit (j)** is really two pulpits one above the other, supported by precious marble columns and surrounded by parapets of *verde antico*. It is crowned by a little oriental cupola. The fine stairway can be seen from the left transept. At the spring of the pendentives of the central cupola are four lovely gilded marble angels (Romanesque works showing the influence of Antelami). In the pavement is a large rectangle of veined Greek marble on the site of the old choir (11th–12th century).

E **North transept:** The beautiful **Dome of St John (IX)** was decorated in the first half of the 12th century. The Greek cross in the centre is surrounded by stories from the life of St John the Evangelist. On the arch towards the nave **(XI)** are 16th-century mosaics of the miracles of Christ (on cartoons by Jacopo Tintoretto, Giuseppe Salviati and Veronese). On the left wall **(XII)** the arch has scenes from the life of the Virgin and the Infant Christ (end of the 12th, beginning of the 13th century). The cycle was continued with the *Story of Susanna* on the west wall in the 16th century (from cartoons by Palma Giovane and Tintoretto).

In the archivolt (difficult to see above the marble wall of the Chapel of St Isidore, but well seen from the Museo di San Marco), *Miracles of Christ* (end of the 12th, beginning of 13th century; restored), and, on the end wall, the huge *Tree of Jesse* (from a cartoon by Giuseppe Salviati, 1542). The east wall of the transept has the *Communion of the Apostles*, and *Christ at Emmaus* from cartoons by Aliense and Leandro Bassano (1611–17).

On the nave pier is the **Altar of St Paul (k)** by Antonio Rizzo, which matches that of St James (*see p. 54 above*). The **Chapel of the Madonna of Nicopeia (l)** contains a precious icon, the *Virgin Nikopoios*, representing the Virgin enthroned with the blessing Christ Child. This type of icon, with a frontal view of the Child as Redeemer, was known as the 'Victory-maker', since it would often be carried by the Byzantine emperor into battle at the head of his army. A similar icon is known to have hung in the apse of Haghia Sophia in Constantinople in 843. The St Mark's work, stolen by the Venetians from Constantinople in 1204, was traditionally considered to be the original icon, and became the protectress of Venice. It remains the most venerated image in the basilica to this day. Most scholars now consider it to date from the 12th century. It is surrounded by a fine enamelled frame encrusted with jewels. Candelabra dating from 1520 and Byzantine bas-reliefs flank the altar. The arch over the altar **(XIII)** has Baroque mosaics of the miracles of Christ.

A door to the left leads to the **Chapel of St Isidore (m)** (*officially reserved for prayer, so usually difficult to visit*) constructed by Doge Andrea Dandolo in 1354–55 (note the charming stoup near the door). Behind the altar, in a niche, a sarcophagus bears a reclining 14th-century statue of the saint, with an angel bearing a censer. The arch is richly carved; on the outside are statuettes of the *Annunciation*. The upper part of the walls and the barrel vault of the chapel are completely covered by mosaics in a beautiful decorative scheme depicting the history of the saint.

The adjacent **Chapel of the Madonna dei Mascoli (n)** (*closed by a screen but easy to view*) is so named because it became the chapel of a confraternity of male worshippers (*maschi*) in 1618. Set into the end wall encased in splendid marbles is a carved Gothic altar (1430), with 15th-century statues of the Madonna and Child between Sts

Mark and John, by the Venetian sculptor Bartolomeo Bon. The mosaics (1430–50) on the barrel vault, which depict the life of the Virgin, are one of the most important mosaic cycles of this time. They were carried out under the direction of Michele Giambono, whose style is usually considered to be typical of the International Gothic. Here, however, using cartoons by the famous Tuscan artist Andrea del Castagno and probably also Venice's Jacopo Bellini, he produced one of the earliest examples of Renaissance art in Venice. The *Birth and Presentation of the Virgin* (left wall) bear his signature; on the right wall are the *Visitation* and *Dormition of the Virgin*. On the wall outside the chapel (right) is a Byzantine relief of the *Virgin Orans*.

Above the door leading out to the narthex **(o)** is a pretty carved ogee arch with a late 13th-century mosaic. The Greek marble stoup **(p)** has Romanesque carvings. On the nave piers are a Byzantine *Virgin Orans*, and a large bas-relief of the Madonna and Child known as the *Madonna 'dello schioppo'* ('of the explosion') because of the gun placed here as an ex-voto.

F **North aisle:** Here is a memorable frieze of five mosaic rectangles with the single figures of a beardless Christ and the prophets Hosea, Joel, Micah and Jeremiah. On the wall and arch above is a depiction of the life of Christ and the Apostles, replaced in 1619–24 from cartoons by Padovanino, Aliense and Palma Giovane. The lovely little Chapel of the Crucifix **(q)** has a pyramidal marble roof surmounted by a huge oriental agate and supported by six columns of precious marble with gilded Byzantine capitals. It contains a painted wood Crucifix thought to have been brought from the East in 1205. Nearer the west door is a stoup made of *bardiglio* marble, streaked with blue and white.

THE MUSIC SCHOOL OF ST MARK'S

The music school of the Doge's Chapel of St Mark, founded in 1403, became famous towards the end of the 15th century, when the first Maestro di Cappella was appointed. These distinguished *maestri* were usually well known composers who acted as directors of religious music. Music was performed on all state occasions and every day at Vespers. The Flemish choir-master Adrian Willaert (c. 1490–1562) was appointed Maestro di Cappella in 1527, and remained here until the end of his life. Using the two organs, he experimented with double choirs, and totally changed the performance of music in the basilica. The composer Andrea Gabrieli first became organist in 1564, and then Maestro di Cappella; his more famous nephew Giovanni, also a composer, succeeded him in 1585. Much of their choral and organ music was composed for the basilica, with its unique acoustics and divided choirs (using the two pulpits): for example, *Selva morale* (1641), and *Messa a quattro voci et salmi* (1650). Giovanni's fame attracted the German composer Heinrich Schütz as a pupil in 1609. Claudio Monteverdi directed the music at St Mark's from 1613 until his death in 1643, and wrote some beautiful church music during this period for small groups of solo voices and instruments, to be sung at Vespers. He was followed by Giovanni Rovetta (1596–1668). Monteverdi's pupil Pier Francesco Cavalli (1602–76), who came to Venice from Crema as a chorister, became organist at St Mark's, and later followed his master's operatic lead, becoming Maestro di Cappella for the last nine years of his life. From 1748 until 1785 the position was held by Baldassare Galuppi (*see p. 321*). In the late 18th century Domenico Dragonetti, famous as a double bass player, was a member of the orchestra, and the Procurators of St Mark's presented him with a precious double bass, made by Gasparo da Salò two centuries earlier, and which can be seen today in the Museo di San Marco.

G **Sanctuary:** The entrance to the sanctuary **(r)** is from the south transept beneath a transenna bearing Gothic statues of the Madonna and four female saints. Ahead is the Chapel of St Clement **(s)** with sculptures by the dalle Masegne brothers. The upper part of the altar is by Antonio Rizzo. Below is a votive relief of saints with the 16th-century doge Andrea Gritti in adoration. Tickets for admission to the sanctuary and Pala d'Oro can be bought here (*for times, see p. 41*). On the side pier is a fine Gothic tabernacle **(t)**. The singing galleries **(u)** have reliefs of the martyrdom and miracles of St Mark, made in 1537–44 by Jacopo Sansovino, who is buried in the church (*see p. 62*). The other works in bronze he made for the sanctuary of the basilica include the four Evangelists on the marble balustrades (c. 1552); the gilded door of the tabernacle in the apse; and the very fine reliefs of the *Entombment* and *Resurrection* on the sacristy door, in the frame of which he included a self-portrait, as well as portraits of Pietro Aretino and Titian.

The **sanctuary dome (XIV)** is a superb work of the 12th century showing the Religion of Christ as foretold by the prophets with the bust of Christ Emmanuel holding a half-revealed scroll (re-made around 1500), surrounded by the Virgin between Isaiah and Daniel and eleven other Prophets. In the spandrels are symbols of the Evangelists. In the arch above the rood-screen **(XV)** are 16th-century mosaics of the life of Christ (on cartoons by Tintoretto). The mosaic in the apse at the east end **(XVI)** is *Christ Pantocrator*, the ruler of the universe, signed 'Petrus F.' and dated 1506, but copied from its 12th-century prototype. Below, between the windows, are the four patron saints of Venice: St Nicholas, St Peter, St Mark and St Hermagorus, among the earliest mosaics of the basilica (probably completed before 1100). The figures of St Peter and St Mark are particularly beautiful, and on the arches above the singing galleries to the left and right (**XVII** and **XVIII**) are mosaic scenes from their lives (beginning of the 12th century, some of them restored). The mosaics on the end walls are partly hidden by the organs; they represent more scenes from the lives of these saints, and also of St Clement.

The little domes and arches at the piers forming the side aisles here and in the rest of the church (marked **X** on the plan) are also beautifully decorated with 13th-century mosaics (mostly of saints), many of them restored or re-worked.

The small marble **chair of St Mark (v)** is on the right, set up on a high podium. This was a gift from the emperor Heraclius to the patriarch of Grado in 630, and was traditionally held to be the throne used by the Evangelist during his preachings in Alexandria. In fact it is a symbolic Egyptian throne made in Alexandria probably in the early 7th century and subsequently decorated by Venetian craftsmen. The organ (1767), made by the famous Venetian organ-maker Gaetano Callido, has been reconstructed.

The **baldacchino (w)** of the high altar is borne by four beautiful columns of eastern alabaster sculpted with New Testament scenes which are extremely interesting both from an artistic and from a historical point of view. Incredibly enough, it is still uncertain whether these are Byzantine works of the early 6th or even 5th century, or Venetian works of around 1250. On the side walls are six Gothic statues of saints. The **sarcophagus of St Mark** is preserved beneath the altar. An altarpiece attributed to Michele Giambono has been placed over the altar (covering the back of the Pala d'Oro).

In the central niche of the **apse (x)** are two fine gilded capitals from Orseolo's basilica, and an altar with six precious columns, including two of unusually transparent alabaster, and statues of St Francis and St Bernardino by Lorenzo Bregno, who was Antonio Rizzo's nephew and was active in the city at the beginning of the 16th century.

Beyond a Gothic pier tabernacle **(y)**, with more sculptures by the dalle Masegne, is the Chapel of St Peter **(z)**, with a large 14th-century relief of St Peter with two small kneeling procurators. The two columns have superb Byzantine capitals.

H **The Pala d'Oro:** Behind the high altar is the Pala d'Oro, an altarpiece glowing with gemstones, enamel and old gold, the most precious work of art in the basilica. This is one of the most remarkable works ever produced by medieval goldsmiths, and incorporates some of the finest Byzantine enamels known. The first Pala was ordered in Constantinople by Doge Pietro Orseolo I. Embellished in 1105 (in Constantinople) for Doge Ordelafo Falier, it was enlarged by order of Doge Pietro Ziani in 1209, and finally re-set in 1345 by Gian Paolo Boninsegna, with a new gilded silver frame decorated with busts and embossed patterns.

In the upper part, the Archangel Michael is surrounded by roundels with the busts of 16 saints; on either side are six exquisite enamel scenes: *Entry into Jerusalem*, *Descent into Limbo*, *Crucifixion*, *Ascension*, *Pentecost*, and *Dormition of the Virgin* (these last perhaps from the church of the Pantocrator in Constantinople). In the centre of the lower part, the Pantocrator (thought to be a 12th-century work also from Constantinople) is surrounded by 14th-century Venetian panels, with the four Evangelists in the *tondi*. Above are two rectangles with angels, on either side of a lozenge depicting the empty throne prepared for the Last Judgement.

Below the Pantocrator are three niches with the Virgin in prayer flanked by the empress Irene of Byzantium and Doge Ordelafo Falier. In this central lower section there are also two inscriptions on gilded plaques recording the work on the Pala carried out by the Falier doges in the 12th and 13th centuries and by Andrea Dandolo in the 14th century. The other 39 niches in three rows show the standing figures of Prophets, Apostles and angels with enamels from Constantinople.

In the border, the 27 rectangular scenes from the lives of Christ (at the top) and of St Mark (at the two sides), are thought to survive from the Pala of Doge Falier. The precious stones used to decorate the work include pearls, sapphires, emeralds, amethysts, rubies and topaz. The enamels have been worked using the cloisonné technique, divided by narrow strips of metal. This is considered one of the most exquisite examples of this art, typical of Byzantine craftsmanship.

I **Treasury:** The little door **(d)** which leads into the treasury from the south transept has a pretty ogee arch with a 13th-century mosaic of two angels holding a reliquary of the True Cross, and a 14th-century statuette of the *Risen Christ*.

The treasury (*for admission see p. 41*) contains a rich store of booty from the sack of Constantinople in 1204 (*see box overleaf*). Even though many of its most precious possessions were melted down in 1797 on the fall of the Republic, it still retains one of the most important collections of Byzantine goldsmiths' work of the 12th century in existence.

THE FOURTH CRUSADE

In 1201, a band of Frankish knights, led by Geoffrey de Villehardouin, arrived in Venice seeking men and ships to transport them on crusade to the Holy Land. The Great Council acceded to the demand: ships were made ready, and the aged doge, Enrico Dandolo, was to accompany the crusaders as the leader of the Venetian contingent. But Villehardouin and his men found themselves unable to pay Venice the amount they had agreed. Venice refused to accept any reduction, and the crusaders remained stranded in the Adriatic. Two years passed; and then something occurred to make Dandolo change his mind. Envoys arrived from Constantinople, asking for help in ousting the usurping emperor, Alexius III, from the throne. In return the lawful claimant, Alexius Angelus, son of the deposed emperor Isaac, promised that the money owed to Venice would be paid off in full, that once he was placed upon his rightful throne the crusaders' passage to the Holy Land would be financed, and—more important still—that he would unite the churches of East and West, placing himself and his bishops at the disposal of the pope. The chance to become the saviour of Christendom was too tempting to resist, and the fleet set sail for Byzantium. It was a city completely unprepared for war, and Alexius III fled. The city elders then freed the deposed Isaac, restoring him to the throne. With the aim of their siege—deposing the usurper—achieved, the crusaders had no further reason to attack. Hostilities ceased, and Alexius Angelus was crowned Alexius IV, as co-emperor. But he could not fulfil the promises he had so rashly made: the imperial coffers were empty, and Isaac had no intention of abjuring his religion. Alexius was also unpopular with his own people. At length a plot by the son-in-law of Alexius III to regain the throne succeeded: Alexius IV was strangled, and a new emperor, Alexius V Ducas, took his place. For Venice this represented a reason to resume the siege, to depose the usurper and murderer, and place a Latin emperor of her own choosing on the throne instead, thus uniting the churches of East and West. Not only this, but Venice would be assured of trade privileges in a Latin Constantinople such as she had never known under the Byzantines. In vain Alexius V sued for peace: in April 1204 the city was besieged and fell, and then was cruelly sacked. Baldwin of Flanders was proclaimed emperor, and Venice apportioned to herself half of the city itself, as well as other strategic territories in the western Aegean and Peloponnese. Many of the priceless treasures of Byzantium were removed to Venice, to adorn St Mark's basilica. For over 50 years, until 1261 when Michael Palaeologus recaptured the eastern throne, there was no Byzantine emperor of the East. Even after the reconquest, the Byzantine empire was much weakened. When it fell to the Ottomans in 1453, Venice struggled to retain her lands in Greece, which eventually also fell to Turkey. She was ultimately the victim of her own success.

In the anteroom is a fine silver statuette of St Mark made in 1804 by a little-known artist, Francesco Francesconi. On the left is the sanctuary, with many precious reliquaries, mostly Byzantine. Above the altar frontal made of oriental alabaster is a relief of *Christ Among the Apostles*, and, even higher, a tondo of *Christ Between Two Angels* (13th century).

On the right is the treasury proper, in a room with exceptionally thick walls thought once to have been a 9th-century tower of the Doge's Palace. Left wall: two elaborate silver-gilt altar frontals (13th and 14th century), and two silver-gilt 15th-century candelabra. Central case: Egyptian alabaster vase (500–300 BC), Roman ampulla in onyx, and a Roman lamp in rock crystal. Four exquisite Byzantine icons (11th–13th century), with gilding and enamels, two of them depicting St Michael Archangel, and two of them the *Crucifixion*. Beautiful Byzantine chalices and patens (10th–11th century) in onyx, agate, alabaster and other precious materials. The remarkable incense burner or coffer in the shape of a Byzantine garden pavilion with five domes is a Romanesque-Byzantine work from southern Italy (12th–13th century).

Also displayed here are reliquary caskets; bowls made of precious stones including one in turquoise (a gift in 1472 from the Shah of Persia), one in alabaster, and one in rock crystal and enamel, decorated with Classical figures, which may be a Corinthian work; glass phial with incised decoration (Saracen, 10th century); oriental vases; red onyx chalice with enamel panels (10th century, Byzantine); and two Roman *situlae*. The exquisite paten with Christ blessing, a Byzantine work thought to date from the 11th century, is richly decorated in oriental alabaster, cloisonné enamel, gold, silver gilt, rock crystal and pearls. A rare chalice is known to have belonged to the 10th-century Byzantine Emperor Romanos, since his name is inscribed in blue enamel letters on the base. Made of sardonyx, it is possibly a reused Roman work of the 1st century AD in agate-onyx, with a Byzantine silver gilt mount and cloisonné enamels, and gold. The chalice with a Eucharistic inscription made of sardonyx is also a Byzantine work of the 10th–11th century in imitation of a Classical work. On either side of the window: a marble monstrance (6th–7th century) and the sword of Doge Francesco Morosini (*see p. 75*)—a gift from Pope Alexander VIII. In the right wall-cases: reliquary caskets, including a Gothic one which belonged to Charles VIII of France; a lovely gospel cover in gilded silver (12th century, from Aquileia); 16th-century paxes; and huge precious gems.

Other chapels of the basilica

The areas described below are closed to regular visitors. Applications to view them must be made to the office of the Proto of San Marco; see p. 42.

Baptistery and Cappella Zen

In the Baptistery **J** is a font designed by Jacopo Sansovino (c. 1545), with a lid with bronze reliefs by his pupils Tiziano Minio and Desiderio da Firenze; the statue of St

John the Baptist was executed by Francesco Segala (1575). The fine Gothic sarcophagus of Doge Andrea Dandolo (d. 1354) is by Giovanni de' Santi. This doge, a friend of Petrarch, took a degree at Padua University and was a famous man of letters. He was the last doge to be buried in St Mark's. To the right, near a 13th-century relief of an angel, is the sarcophagus of Doge Giovanni Soranzo (d. 1328). A slab in the pavement marks the resting place of Jacopo Sansovino (*see p. 84*), who was not only one of the most prominent architects in Venice, but also, as *proto* of St Mark's, looked after the basilica for many years (and carried out a number of sculptural works for the sanctuary). The huge block of granite (with an ancient inscription) is said to have been brought from Tyre in 1126. It has been raised to reveal traces (discovered at the end of the 20th century) of a rectangular font, for total immersion, with fresco fragments, thought to have survived from the earliest church. On the wall are three reliefs of the *Baptism of Christ*, and Sts George and Theodore on horseback (13th–14th century). On the left wall are fresco fragments dating from the 13th century. The baptistery mosaics, carried out for Doge Andrea Dandolo (c. 1343–54), are extremely fine. They illustrate the life of St John the Baptist and the early life of Christ. The delightful scene of the *Banquet of Herod*, above the door into the church, shows the influence of the greatest Venetian painter of the time, Paolo Veneziano.

The adjoining **Cappella Zen** Ⓚ was built largely by Tullio Lombardo in 1504–22, in honour of Cardinal Giovanni Battista Zen, who had left his patrimony to the Republic on the condition that he was buried in the basilica (he died in 1501). Unfortunately, the construction of the chapel blocked up the original entrance to the narthex from the Piazzetta. The very fine doorway into the narthex remains: beneath a mosaic of the Madonna between two archangels (the Madonna dates from the 19th century, but the two angels are 12th century) are niches with mosaics (early 14th century) alternating with fine statuettes of prophets (by the school of Antelami). The mosaics in the barrel vault dating from the late 13th century (but restored) relate to the life of St Mark. There are some interesting bas-reliefs (11th–13th century), and two red marble Romanesque lions which were probably once outside the entrance to the basilica. But the chapel is especially remarkable for its bronze sculptures, which include the Cardinal's tomb and the altar: these were begun by Alessandro Leopardi and Antonio Lombardo. In 1506 Antonio also made the classical statue of the *Madonna 'of the Shoe'* (so called because when a poor man offered a shoe to the statue, the shoe miraculously turned to gold).

Crypt, sacristy and Chapel of St Theodore
The crypt of St Mark's, restored and water-proofed in 1995, may date in part from the 9th century (although it has recently been suggested that it post-dates the original church). It has an interesting plan with 50 ancient columns. The body of St Mark was placed here in 1094. The pavement dates from the 19th century.

The Renaissance sacristy by Giorgio Spavento, and the Chapel of St Theodore, with organ shutters painted and signed by Gentile Bellini (with Sts Mark, Theodore, Jerome and Francis), are rarely open to the public.

MUSEO DI SAN MARCO

From a small door to the right of the main west door, steep narrow stairs lead to the Museo di San Marco and the loggia (*for admission see p. 42*).

Beyond models of the basilica at various stages of its construction, there is a display on the technique of mosaic decoration, together with some fragments of the original mosaics detached during restoration work in the 19th century. A model illustrates the technique, used since the 20th century, of restoring the mosaics from the wall behind. The gallery above the narthex provides a splendid view of the interior of the basilica and its mosaics. The mosaics directly above include a *Last Judgement* from a cartoon by Tintoretto, Aliense and Maffeo da Verona (1557–1619; restored in the 19th century), and *Paradise*, a Mannerist work of 1628–31, and, on the arch, the *Apocalypse and Vision of St John*, by the Zuccato brothers (1570–89; also restored).

In the area beyond, some of the original 13th- and 14th-century mosaics from the Baptistery and Cappella Zen, detached in 1865, are displayed. The double bass which belonged to Domenico Dragonetti (*see p. 57*) is also displayed here. Beyond two short flights of steps is a *Madonna and Child* in gilded terracotta. This was made by Jacopo Sansovino for the Loggetta at the foot of the Campanile, but it was broken when the tower collapsed in 1902. A charming work, it has recently been recomposed from the shattered fragments, although the young St John, to whom the attention of both the Madonna and Child is specially drawn, was lost irreparably.

Visitors are now directed out onto one of the walkways which encircle the upper part of the basilica, where Jacopo Sansovino inserted iron girders to consolidate the structure of the church. From here, above the north transept, can be seen the wonderful mosaic domes at the east end of the church. The nearest is the Dome of St John, which was made in the first half of the 12th century and illustrates the life of the Evangelist. Dating from the end of that century (and subsequently restored) are the four charming scenes of miracles of Christ, including the miraculous draught of fishes, in the archivolt immediately above. On the end wall is a huge mosaic *Tree of Jesse*, made in the 16th century from a cartoon by Giuseppe Salviati. Stairs lead up to a room which displays watercolours and drawings made in the 1880s when it was realised (partly as a result of Ruskin's objections) that restoration work needed to be more carefully monitored and the original appearance of the building carefully documented.

Sala dei Banchetti

This huge room, once used for state banquets, was purpose-built in 1623 by Bartolomeo Monopola as an annexe to the doge's apartments. The ceiling was frescoed by Jacopo Guarana and Francesco Zanchi. After the fall of the Republic the room was incorporated into the Palazzo Patriarcale. Now filled with an overcrowded display of precious fabrics, it is difficult to appreciate the grandeur of the room. A group of late 15th-century Flemish tapestries which belonged to Cardinal Zen are displayed near some exquisite lace vestments. The magnificent series of ten tapestries depicting the *Passion of Christ*, made around 1420 to cartoons attributed to the Venetian painter

Niccolò di Pietro, is the oldest complete series of tapestries to have survived in Italy. Two very early Byzantine embroidered fabrics are also displayed here, one with the *Lamentation over the Dead Christ*, and another with two archangels, probably made in Venice in the early 13th century. The magnificent cover for the Pala d'Oro was painted in 1345 by Paolo Veneziano and his sons Luca and Giovanni. The lion of St Mark was carved in the late 15th century, and used to watch over the organ in the basilica. Four tapestries made for the Medici by Giovanni Rost in 1531 have scenes from the life of St Mark. The five Persian (Isfahan) carpets date from the early 17th century, and were formerly used to adorn (and protect) the pavement of the basilica.

The Horses of St Mark's
Visitors are now directed back on themselves and into a room with sculptural fragments including five large 13th-century reliefs, which were once on the north façade of the basilica. Here, in a sadly cramped corner, are the four magnificent gilded copper horses of St Mark's. After their restoration in 1979, the controversial decision was taken to exhibit them here and place replicas on the façade of the basilica.

The loggia
As well as the replicas of the horses and a spectacular view of the piazza, the loggia also offers a good view of the Gothic sculpture on the upper part of the façade. The central window is flanked by arches filled in the 17th century with mosaics (*Descent from the Cross*, *Descent into Hell*, *Resurrection* and *Ascension*) designed by Maffeo da Verona. The façade is crowned by fine Gothic sculpture, begun in the early 15th century by the dalle Masegne brothers and continued by Lombard and Tuscan artists (including Pietro di Niccolò Lamberti, who worked on the central arch, which has the gilded lion of St Mark and is crowned by a statue of the saint). Between the arches are figures of water-carriers by a Lombard master of the 15th century, and the two outer tabernacles contain the *Annunciatory Angel* and the *Virgin Annunciate*, attributed to Jacopo della Quercia. A few other sculptures in Venice, including one on a corner of the Doge's Palace, are sometimes attributed to this great Tuscan sculptor, but there is no work in the city documented by him and we do not even know if he ever came to Venice.

The south-facing loggia overlooks the Piazzetta. Here, at the angle of the balcony (hidden behind the flagstaff), is a red porphyry head—an unexpected 'trophy' to find decorating a sacred place. For long thought to be a contemporary portrait of Justinian II (d. 711), it is now dated even earlier and taken to be a portrait of Justinian I (527–65), the last Roman emperor of the East. Like the Tetrarchs (*see p. 47*), it was probably carried back from Constantinople after the Fourth Crusade in 1204. It still retains an air of mystery and it is fascinating to be able to get face to face with this ancient work of art which portrays a man of great character. For centuries the Venetians knew it by the name of '*Carmagnola*', as they liked to identify it with an unfortunate sea captain called Francesco Bussone, who was thus nicknamed, and whose head had been exposed on the Pietra del Bando below for three days after he was unjustly condemned to death as a traitor in 1432.

THE HORSES OF ST MARK'S

In 1549, Anton Doni, a Florentine living in Venice, noted that, of all the many treasures of the city, the finest were the four gilded horses which stood aloft on the loggia of St Mark's. Four horses, always stallions, were in Antiquity a sign of triumph and splendour. From the 7th century BC, the four-horse chariot race was the most prestigious in the Olympics, and such racing eventually became the most exciting spectator sport of the Roman empire. Yet it was also in a four-horse chariot, a quadriga, that an emperor would parade in a Roman triumph.

The four horses of St Mark's are the only team to survive from the ancient world. They are beautifully crafted; even the 'chestnut', the horny lump on the inner side of the back leg is cast, as are muscles and veins. They arrived in Venice as part of the plunder of the Fourth Crusade of 1204, and were placed on the log-gia some time before 1267, as shown in the mosaic of that date above the Door of Sant'Alipio. The site was a prestigious one. Their position might symbolise the triumph of Venice but it has also been argued, by the art historian Michael Jacoff, that they were intended to represent the Evangelists, who were seen as drawing the chariot of Christ. It is also possible that the horses symbolise a hippodrome, as the doges in the 13th century used the loggia as a platform to show themselves to the people, just as emperors did in the hippodrome in Constantinople.

The horses quickly endeared themselves to the Venetian population as a sym-bol of the freedom of their city. When the Genoese threatened Venice from Chioggia in 1379, the Genoese commander promised he would put 'bridles on those unreined horses of yours'. It was perhaps inevitable that Napoleon would include them among the plunder he took from Venice in 1797. In Paris, they were placed on the triumphal Arc du Carrousel, probably precisely the sort of setting for which they had been designed.

The origins of the horses remains mysterious. They have been attributed to almost every great sculptor of the past, including Pheidias and Lysippus. Yet it is their casting in copper which has helped towards a solution. Even though copper, with its high melting point, is more difficult to mould than bronze, it is now known that any sculpture which was to be gilded had to be cast in copper, as bronze reacted badly to the mercury-based gilding method and became blem-ished. This method of gilding (highly effective, as can be seen by its survival) appeared in the 2nd century AD. By this time no one but an emperor would have commissioned such a symbol of triumph. The most likely candidate is Septimius Severus, who conquered Byzantium in AD 195. It is known that he celebrated his triumphs with arches surmounted by *quadrigae* and that Constantine pre-served Septimius' city when he rebuilt it as Constantinople in 330. This may well account for the horses' presence in Constantinople in 1204. For a fuller account see Charles Freeman, *The Horses of St Mark's*, Little Brown, 2004.   C.F.

THE LOGGETTA & CAMPANILE OF ST MARK'S

At the base of the campanile is the Loggetta, in red Verona marble, Jacopo Sansovino's first work to be completed in Venice (1537–46). It was originally a meeting-place of the *nobili*, or patricians, during sessions of the Great Council (*Maggior Consiglio*) in the Doge's Palace. After 1569, owing to its strategic position, a military guard was posted here when the Council was sitting.

Since it was crushed by the fall of the Campanile in 1902, it had to be restored. Its form is derived from the Roman triumphal arch and its sculptures celebrate the glory of the Republic. Three arches, flanked by twin columns, are surmounted by an ornate attic. White Carrara marble, Istrian stone, and a dark green marble have been used for the decorative details. Between the columns are niches with bronze statues of Pallas, Apollo, Mercury and Peace, also the work of Jacopo Sansovino. The three reliefs in the attic show Venice (represented by the figure of Justice), Crete (represented by Jupiter) and Cyprus (represented by Venus). The two fine little bronze gates by Antonio Gai were added in 1734. The sculpture from inside of the Madonna and Child, also by Sansovino, is now displayed in the Museo di San Marco.

Campanile of St Mark's

Normally open daily 9 or 9.30–dusk (4.45 in winter, 7 in spring, 9 in summer). The bell-chamber is reached by a lift from the Loggetta.

Over 98.5m high, the campanile was first built in 888–912, and completed in 1156–73. It was later restored, the last time by Bartolomeo Bon the Younger in 1511–14. In 1609 Galileo demonstrated his latest invention, the telescope, to Doge Leonardo Donà, a friend and supporter, from the top of the tower, and even dedicated the instrument to the doge. Repeatedly struck by lightning, in 1793 the campanile was fitted with a lightning conductor, one of the first in Europe. On 14th July 1902, it collapsed without warning causing little damage (except to the Loggetta; *see above*) and no human casualties. From the proceeds of a world-wide subscription, an exact reproduction of the original was immediately begun, *'Dov' era e com' era'*—'where it was and as it was'—and opened on 25th April 1912, St Mark's feast day, 1,000 years after it was first completed. At its base instruments record the level of the tides in the lagoon.

The brick tower of the Campanile is surmounted by a bell-chamber with four-light windows of Istrian stone, and a square storey decorated with two winged lions and two figures of Venice beneath the symbol of Justice; the spire at the top is crowned by a golden Archangel Gabriel. Only one of the original five bells (the *marangona; see below*) survived the collapse of the tower; the others were presented by Pius X. The five bells during the time of the Republic were as follows: the *marangona* rang to signify the start and end of the working day, the *nona* was tolled at noon, the *mezza terza* called the senators to the Doge's Palace, the *trottiera* signalled that the Great Council was in session, and the *maleficio* rang at the time of an execution.

From the top of the Campanile there is a magnificent view of Venice and the lagoon, and (on clear days) of the Euganean hills and the Alps.

PIAZZA SAN MARCO & ITS MUSEUMS
Map p. 407, D2–E2

Piazza San Marco

Piazza San Marco is one of the most famous and beautiful squares in the world. Laid out around the two most important buildings in Venice, the Basilica of St Mark and the Doges' Palace, it had more or less reached its present vast dimensions by the 12th century, although it was partly redesigned in the 16th century, when it was enclosed on three sides by the porticoes of the uniform façades of stately palaces, built as the residence of the Procurators of St Mark's, who looked after the ducal basilica of St Mark. The colonnades open out towards the east end of the piazza and the fantastic façade of the basilica. On the left the decorative clock-tower (Torre dell' Orologio) provides an entrance from the piazza to the Merceria, the main pedestrian thoroughfare of the city, which leads to the Rialto. Opposite is the tall isolated Campanile of St Mark's.

Called by the Venetians simply 'the Piazza', it is the only square in Venice to be so named, since all the others are termed *campi*. It retains the character Henry James gave it over a century ago: 'It is in the wide vestibule of the square that the polyglot pilgrims gather most densely: Piazza San Marco is the lobby of the opera in the intervals of the performance'. In the arcades (hung with draped curtains on sunny days) the elegant cafés have tables outside grouped around their orchestra podiums. To the despair of those in charge of the conservation of Venice's buildings, the famous pigeons of St Mark still flock to the square to be fed and photographed.

In front of the basilica are three tall flagstaffs which, during the great days of the Venetian Republic, bore the red-and-gold standard with the winged lion of St Mark. Nowadays, on Sundays and holidays, the standard is still flown, but beside the Italian tricolour and the flag of the European Union (and there is a solemn little military ceremony at 9am and at sunset when they are hoisted and lowered). The elaborate bronze pedestals were added in 1505. The pavement of the piazza survives from 1722.

The two most famous cafés in the square are Florian and the Caffè Quadri (*both described on p. 70*). They both have orchestra podiums, and concerts are provided for clients at the tables outside. The orchestra battles between the two were famous in their day.

On days when there is an *acqua alta*, the piazza is one of the first places in the city to be flooded; the duck-boards used on these occasions are usually stacked in readiness (the water first reaches the atrium of the basilica). The problem of flooding in the piazza is known to have existed since at least the 13th century, and there has been a drainage system beneath the pavement for centuries, which helps in part to channel the water away. However, since the frequency of the *acque alte* has increased dramatically in the last few years, there is now a Consorzio Venezia Nuova project to renew this drainage system and possibly introduce a waterproof lining beneath the layer of sand on which the pavement rests. Work is at present concentrated on the Molo, the waterfront in the Piazzetta.

Gentile Bellini: *Procession of the Relic of the True Cross* (1496).

PUBLIC CEREMONIES IN PIAZZA SAN MARCO

The Piazza provided a magnificent setting for the sumptuous public ceremonies held throughout Venice's history, the form of which often echoed Byzantine spectacles. These were staged to impress her inhabitants as well as the foreign ambassadors and merchants from overseas, and splendid long processions lasting many hours would give a visual sense to the dignified order within the Venetian State. These took place on religious festivals (including the Feast of St

Mark, Palm Sunday and Corpus Christi), as well as on important occasions such as the arrival of a foreign dignitary. The officials who processed would include the Canons of St Mark's, the Doge, the Council of Ten, the Procurators, and representatives of the *scuole* and religious orders, and they would be accompanied by the musicians and choir of St Mark's. Gentile Bellini's celebrated painting of the *Procession of the Relic of the True Cross* here in 1496 (in the Gallerie dell'Accademia; *pictured above*) provides us with one of the most accurate representations of such a ceremony.

Procuratie Vecchie

Along the entire north side of the Piazza run the stately arcades, with three open galleries, of the Procuratie Vecchie, reconstructed after a fire in 1512, probably to a design by the great Renaissance architect Mauro Codussi, who had died a few years earlier, having built numerous important churches and palaces in the city (*see p. 243*). Work was continued under the direction of Bartolomeo Bon and another local architect, Guglielmo dei Grigi, before Jacopo Sansovino added an upper storey, with a hundred arches, in 1532. The building served as the residence and offices of the Procurators of St Mark's who, after the doge, were considered the highest officials in the Republic, and were in charge of the building and conservation of the basilica. They were the only patrician officers of the Republic (besides the doge) who were elected for life. By the 13th century they had taken on a role of fundamental importance not only as guardians of the basilica but also as administrators of the conspicuous sums of money given by noble families to St Mark's.

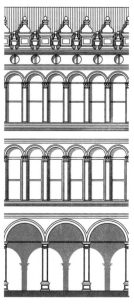

PROCURATIE VECCHIE

Beneath the portico is the famous **Caffè Quadri**, which, together with the even more famous Florian opposite, is considered the most elegant café in Venice. It was opened in 1775 by Giorgio and Naxina Quadri, and is mentioned countless times in descriptions of the city. It also gained a reputation as the 'Austrian café' during the time when Venice was under Austrian rule. Quadri has pretty Venetian-style decorations in its little rooms, and a tiny bar where you can stand at the counter for a drink. The restaurant, in two lovely rooms upstairs overlooking the Piazza, was opened in 1844 (*see p. 364*).

Also beneath the portico, at no. 101, an art gallery occupies the showrooms designed by Carlo Scarpa for Olivetti in 1958. Both interior and exterior illustrate Scarpa's innovative style and use of different materials.

Procuratie Nuove

The Procuratie Nuove, on the south side of the square, were planned by Jacopo Sansovino to continue the design of his Libreria (*see p. 82*) which faces the Doge's Palace. Up to the tenth arch from the left they are the work of Vincenzo Scamozzi (1582–86); they were completed by his more famous pupil Baldassare Longhena around 1640. Like the Procuratie Vecchie, they were also a (later) residence of the Procurators, but became a royal palace under Napoleon.

In the portico beneath is one of the city's most celebrated cafés, the **Caffè Florian**, named after its first proprietor in 1720, Floriano Francesconi. It retains its comfortable old leather-seated benches and chairs around the columns and a charming old-

PROCURATIE NUOVE

fashioned interior with an intimate atmosphere, decorated in 1858 by the little-known artist Lodovico Cadorin. There is a little bar at the back where you can sit at the counter; light lunches and afternoon tea are also served. It has been famous for over a century as a place where all the illustrious visitors to the city come to enjoy the scene. Even if you don't intend to sit and take a coffee you are made to feel welcome, and can look at the book which tells its history on the stand at the entrance. Florian's was the meeting place of Italian patriots during Austrian rule; during the 1848 uprising in the Piazza the wounded were brought here. Balzac is said to have likened it to a stock exchange, a theatre foyer, a reading room, a club and a confessional.

Ala Napoleonica

The west end of the piazza, between the two Procuratie, was once occupied by the small, centrally-planned church of San Gemignano, with a very fine Istrian stone façade by Jacopo Sansovino. Napoleon (who apparently remained

ALA NAPOLEONICA

unimpressed by Venice on his one visit in 1807, when he spent only slightly over a week here) had it pulled down in the same year to make space for a suite of grand reception rooms, including a ballroom. As a wing of the royal palace in the Procuratie Nuove (*see below*), it came to be known as the Ala Napoleonica (now open as part of the Museo Correr), and was used by both the French and Austrian courts during their occupation of the city before Unification in 1866. It is the best-known work of Giuseppe Soli, who, in the two lower floors, copied the style of the Procuratie Nuove, but appropriately added a row of Roman emperors, who look down from the top storey.

Torre dell'Orologio

Daily visits by appointment at the Museo Correr or Doge's Palace, or T: 041 520 9070. Ticket includes admission to Museo Correr. During the tour, along a series of very narrow stairs, you can see the various clock mechanisms, as well as the fine view from the terrace.
The Torre dell'Orologio was designed by Mauro Codussi, although the two wings, added in 1505 perhaps by Pietro Lombardo, were heightened in the mid-18th century. The tower was built to house a remarkable clock constructed in 1499 by the celebrated Rainieri clockmakers from Reggio Emilia, and which was acclaimed at the time as the most complex astronomical clock in existence. It was modified in 1757 by the famous clockmaker Bartolomeo Ferracina (who also supplied the Doge's Palace with three clocks). The great clock-face shows the hours in Roman numerals (the hand of the clock is in the form of the sun); a moveable inner ring, brightly decorated with gilding and blue enamel, shows the signs of the zodiac and their constellations, and in the centre, on a dark blue sky filled with stars, is the earth with the moon, half gilded and half dark: as the moon turns, its various phases are recorded. Above the clock is a tabernacle with the figure of the Madonna. Originally, every hour, figures of the Magi, accompanied by an angel, came out of the side doors and processed and bowed before her. This now only happens during Ascension week and at Epiphany, because in 1858 two small drums which display the hour in Roman numerals and the minutes in Arabic numerals were inserted into the little doors (and lit from behind by gas lamps), to make the time easier to read from the Piazza below, especially at night (these have to be removed temporarily when the 'procession' is reactivated).

Above the lion of St Mark, against an enamelled bronze background, hangs a great bell cast in 1497, which is struck every hour by two giant mechanical figures in bronze, made at the same time. Because of their colour, they have always been known as the *Mori* (Moors), but were in fact probably intended to represent Cain and Abel. In addition, another mechanism with two hammers strikes the bell 132 times at midday and midnight (the number represents the sum of the preceding eleven hours).

There is another, simpler, clock-face on the other side of the tower overlooking the Merceria, where the hours are shown in Roman numerals and the hand is in the form of the sun fixed to a central 'sun' decorated with the lion of St Mark.

The complicated mechanism of the entire clock was modified in 1753 (when the wooden processional figures were remade) and again in 1866. Its various parts were dismantled in 1999 and restoration of the entire building was finally completed in 2006.

MUSEO CORRER
Map p. 407, D2

Open 9–5 or 7. Entrance beneath the Ala Napoleonica. The Torre dell'Orologio, Museo Archeologico (and Libreria Marciana) can be visited with the same ticket. The Correr Library, with a fine collection of prints and drawings (including many by Pietro Longhi and Palma Giovane) and a photo archive, is only open to scholars.
Having been used, since the days of Napoleon, as a royal palace, in 1920 the

Procuratie Nuove were presented to the city by the Savoy royal family, and since 1923 they have been occupied by the Museo Correr, the city museum which illustrates the history of Venice, and includes a picture gallery. Also in the Procuratie Nuove, and now entered directly from the Museo Correr, is the Museo Archeologico, which has some masterpieces of Greek and Roman sculpture. From this museum visitors can also visit the Libreria Marciana, which preserves its 16th-century painted decorations, and houses the city's precious collection of books.

The nucleus of the Correr collection was left to Venice by the wealthy citizen Teodoro Correr (1750–1830), who spent his life collecting works of art that illustrate Venetian history. It was first opened to the public in 1836 in Correr's house on the Grand Canal, but moved here in 1922. Some of the exhibition space was designed in 1952–60 by Carlo Scarpa, who also redesigned part of the interior of the Gallerie dell'Accademia, but is best remembered for his work at the Palazzo Querini-Stampalia (*see p. 273*).

The Throne Room and Ballroom

The rooms in the Ala Napoleonica and the first rooms in the royal palace retain their delightful Neoclassical decorations (1806–17) by little-known artists including Giuseppe Borsato and Giovanni Carlo Bevilacqua (beside the latter's particularly lovely detached frescoes in the Throne Room **(4)**, hang panels with mythological scenes and dancers, early works by the most famous Italian painter of this period, Francesco Hayez). The Ballroom **(2)**, designed by Lorenzo Santi in 1822, is usually visited just before the exit from the museum.

These rooms also provide an appropriate setting for some important works by Antonio Canova, Italy's greatest Neoclassical sculptor: exquisite small models for a funerary monument (never realised) for Francesco Pesaro, and that of Titian (adapted for use as the sculptor's own tomb in the Frari; *see p. 206*); marble statues of Daedalus and Icarus, a winged Cupid, Eurydice and Orpheus (these last two usually displayed in the Ballroom); a painting of *Eros and Psyche*, and an unfinished portrait of a portly Venetian antiquarian called Amedeo Svajer, which recalls English paintings of the period. The contemporary furniture includes a French circular table with mythological scenes in Sèvres porcelain.

The historical collections

These rooms display paintings and objects illustrating the history of Venice with particular reference to the doge and officials of the Republic. Only a very few of the most significant possessions are mentioned below.

Room 6: Formal hats worn by the doges are displayed here beside a portrait in profile of Doge Francesco Foscari, by the Venetian painter Lazzaro Bastiani, who worked with Gentile Bellini (and must have been influenced by Gentile's portrait of Doge Giovanni Mocenigo, exhibited in the Picture Gallery; *see pp. 77–78 below*). The doge is shown wearing his brocaded *cornu*

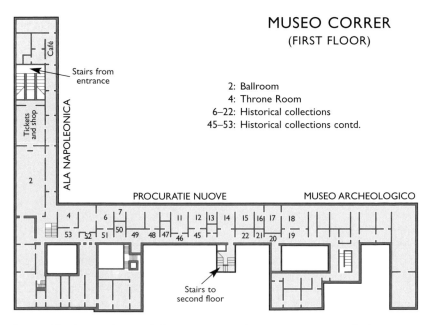

MUSEO CORRER
(FIRST FLOOR)

2: Ballroom
4: Throne Room
6–22: Historical collections
45–53: Historical collections contd.

Café

Stairs from entrance

Tickets and shop

ALA NAPOLEONICA

PROCURATIE NUOVE

MUSEO ARCHEOLOGICO

Stairs to second floor

hat, and his benign features belie an iron character which resulted in numerous military victories (with the help of famous *condottieri* such as Gattamelata and Colleoni) on the Italian mainland over the Visconti of Milan; victories which saw a spectacular expansion of the power of the Republic. This was painted around the time that the Council of Ten decided that Foscari, at the grand old age of 84, should abdicate (1457): as it turned out, an unnecessary step: he died just a week later.

Room 7: A wood engraving by Matteo Pagan of a procession in Piazza San Marco (1559) has been carefully studied by scholars and historians for its illustration of the hierarchy at the doge's court and for the costumes worn by the officials and onlookers. A display, including ballot boxes and instruments used to count votes, records the complicated procedures during the election of the doge. Examples of the *promissione ducale* (*see p. 96*) made by the doge as he took office are also exhibited.

Room 11: Contains a very complete collection of coins minted in Venice, from the 9th century to the fall of the Republic (1797), and the huge standard which the 17th-century doge Domenico Contarini flew from his galley when he defended Crete for the Republic. The painting of St Justina with Venetian officials, including treasurers, is a late work by Jacopo Tintoretto, with the help of his son Domenico.

Rooms 12–13: These rooms illustrate the maritime history of Venice, with models of galleys, navigational instruments, ships' lanterns, plans of the

Arsenale, and a portrait painted in 1769 by Alessandro Longhi of a 'Capitano da Mar', the Captain General of the Venetian fleet.

Room 14: Displays an inscribed edict warning against the misuse of the city's waterways, a reminder of the importance of the 'Magistrato alle Acque', which to this day takes care of Venice's public waters. Also here are two globes made in the late 17th century by the Venetian cartographer Vincenzo Coronelli.

Rooms 15–16: The armoury, with armour made in the 16th and 17th centuries and arms dating from the 14th–16th centuries.

Rooms 17–18: Two rooms devoted to Francesco Morosini who, as Captain General of the Venetian fleet, had many victories—most famously his conquest of the Peloponnese (although during the siege of Athens in 1687 he all but reduced the Parthenon to ruins). After such success he was unanimously elected doge in 1688. The finely carved triple lantern and the standard from his galley, Turkish banners and Persian shields he captured during his campaigns, his sword and prayer book (with a hidden dagger), and the *cornu* hat he wore as doge, are all preserved here.

Rooms 19–22: Small Renaissance bronzes from the late 15th–17th centuries by Paduan and Venetian sculptors, including Bartolomeo Bellano, Il Riccio, Jacopo Sansovino and Alessandro Vittoria. At the foot of the stairs is a quaint gilt-wood statue of a seated man in a top hat, a 19th-century copy of one venerated in a temple in Canton (and thought to be an effigy of Marco Polo).

From Room 18 or 19 there is access (with the same ticket) to the Museo Archeologico Nazionale and the Libreria Marciana. If you decide to visit them now, they are described on pp. 80–83; otherwise you can complete the visit to the Correr Museum, and then return to visit the others. The Correr itinerary takes you upstairs to the Picture Gallery at this point, returning to complete the historical collections afterwards.

The Picture Gallery

The Picture Gallery, or Quadreria, on the second floor (the rooms are now a little shabby) follows a strictly chronological arrangement and provides a good idea of art in Venice up to the late 15th century. Highlights are given here.

Rooms 25–26: Works by Paolo Veneziano, considered the founder of the Venetian school, and his successor as the leading artist of his day, Lorenzo Veneziano (no relation).

Room 27: Here are a few detached frescoes, interesting as rare examples of the Gothic period in Venice. There is also a charming little statue of Doge Antonio Venier, a portrait carried out during his dogeship in the 1380s or '90s by his contemporary Jacobello dalle Masegne, whom the doge had asked to work on the sculpture for the Basilica of St Mark (including the rood screen). The doge is

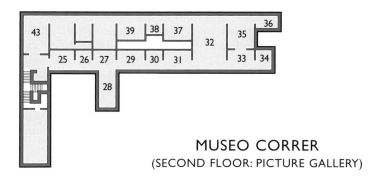

MUSEO CORRER
(SECOND FLOOR: PICTURE GALLERY)

shown kneeling, and was made to hold a standard—this was probably once part of a statuary group including the lion of St Mark which may have decorated a lintel in the Doge's Palace.

Rooms 28–29: More Gothic works, with the International Gothic school represented with *Madonnas* by Michele Giambono and Jacobello del Fiore.

Rooms 30–31: Room 30 has an exquisite little *Pietà* by Cosmè Tura, who was the most important painter from Ferrara in the Renaissance. This is one of his masterpieces, showing not only his entirely original style, but also the influence of painters from Tuscany and northern Europe. The *Profile of a Man* exhibited beside it is also by a Ferrarese painter of the same period, and there are more works by painters from the same school in the next room (Room 31), including another charming portrait of a man in profile by Baldassare Estense, who was court painter in Ferrara. Also displayed in this room is a beautiful *Madonna and Child*, an early work (c. 1460) signed by the Venetian artist Bartolomeo Vivarini.

Room 32: This is one of the few rooms on this floor of the Procuratie Nuove to have survived from the late 16th century. The wonderful wood engraving of Venice in 1500 by Jacopo de' Barbari is displayed here: it is doubly precious since the six original wood blocks (made out of pear wood) have survived in excellent condition. De' Barbari invented the idea of the perspective view of a city, as seen from above: his work was to influence the long series of maps and views of cities which were produced right up until the 18th century. Very few representations of Venice had been made before this time, and this bird's-eye view, showing in detail how the city appeared in 1500, is of fundamental importance to historians of Venice. It was originally attributed to Dürer, but in the 19th century was recognised as the work of the otherwise little-known de' Barbari, who left Venice for the court of the Habsburg emperor Maximilian I. The engraving survives in three states and was first printed by a German merchant, Anton Kolb (the last time prints were made from these blocks was in the 19th century).

Rooms 33–35: A collection of works by Flemish and German painters, including religious scenes by Pieter Brueghel, Hugo van der Goes and Dieric Bouts. Displayed with them is Antonello da Messina's *Pietà*—a very ruined painting (*see box*).

A MASTERPIECE AT THE CORRER

Perhaps the most influential and important painting of the Correr collection is Antonello da Messina's *Pietà* (*pictured overleaf*). Antonello can be seen as the godfather of all subsequent Venetian painting. He came from Messina in Sicily: Giorgio Vasari says that he travelled to Flanders to study with Jan van Eyck. This is almost certainly not accurate, but what is true is that Antonello brilliantly absorbed and understood the technical revolution initiated by Flemish painting under the van Eycks, and was profoundly influenced by its subtle delicacy. In 1474/5 he came to Venice. Though he stayed only a year, he produced a number of works that changed the course of painting in Venice forever, finally wrenching it out of its rich, but backward-looking, Gothic tradition. It was Antonello—either in person or by example—who taught Bellini and his contemporaries a new technique: no longer to paint in tempera (in other words with a fast-drying and opaque mixture of egg-yolk, water and pigment), but to experiment with the new Flemish technique of painting in thin, translucent veils of pigment in an oil and varnish mix. This allowed the bright white preparation of the panel to illuminate the colours from behind, giving an astonishing brilliance to both the strong and the delicate tints. Venetian painting was never to be the same again. And even though this *Pietà* has suffered terribly from overcleaning in past centuries, you can still unmistakably pick out the changing gradations of colour and the naturalism of the light.   N.McG.

Room 36: Important works by the most famous Venetian painter of all: Giovanni Bellini. The *Transfiguration* is a remarkable early work painted around 1460, which shows Christ between Moses and Elijah on Mount Tabor, with the Apostles Peter, James and John below. The subject matter is particularly interesting as this is probably the first altarpiece of the Transfiguration to have been painted, as the religious festival celebrating the event was only introduced (by Pope Calixtus III) in 1457. The influence of Mantegna and Flemish painters such as Jan van Eyck can be seen here. The *Crucifixion* probably dates from about the same time (the landscape has remarkable depth). Other works by Bellini are a *Pietà* (the two angels as well as Christ have their mouths memorably open in horrified pain), the *Madonna Frizzoni*, damaged when it was transferred from panel to canvas, and a portrait of a young saint crowned with laurel leaves. The other *Crucifixion* is attributed by some scholars to Giovanni's father Jacopo. The portrait of Doge Giovanni Mocenigo in

profile is by Giovanni's brother Gentile: the doge appears as a homely old man, and he was in fact known for his gentle character. Gentile is thought to have left the portrait unfinished when he was called to Constantinople in 1479 to paint the Sultan's portrait (now in the National Gallery in London). He executed a number of other portraits of the rulers of his day, but is best remembered for his huge historical works which decorated two of Venice's *scuole* (*see p. 287*).

Room 37: Here, in its fine original frame, is displayed *St Anthony of Padua*, a delicately painted work showing the emaciated saint 'in the clouds', by Alvise Vivarini, member of the famous family of painters from Murano. Other painters from Venice and the Veneto represented here include Bartolomeo Montagna, whose painting of *St Justina* shows the saint in the guise of a pretty Venetian girl, and Lorenzo Lotto whose *Madonna*, crowned by two angels, includes a lovely landscape.

Room 38: Here is Vittore Carpaccio's famous painting of *Two Venetian Ladies*, probably painted around 1495 or later. For long thought to represent two courtesans, other critics, including Ruskin, thought it was simply the portrait of a mother and daughter with their pets. It is known to be the lower half of a painting; the other half, depicting hunting scenes in the lagoon, is now owned by the J. Paul Getty Museum in California. Some scholars think the panels decorated two doors of a cupboard. The two patrician ladies, dressed in high fashion, with the bleached blonde hair that was all the rage in their day, are shown deep in contemplation, seated on a roof terrace, a feature of many contemporary Venetian houses. Various symbols may represent allegories of Love (the dove and the orange) and Maternity (the lily and myrtle plants). Carpaccio was one of Venice's greatest painters (*see p. 265*), and another painting by him (*St Peter Martyr*) is also displayed here.

Room 39: The delightful portrait of a *Young Man in a Red Hat*, formerly attributed to Carpaccio, is now thought to be by an unknown Ferrarese artist and dated around 1490. However, the *Madonna and Child and Young St John* here, dating from around 1495, has been attributed to Carpaccio since its restoration in 2001.

Room 43: Here is a bust of Tommaso Rangone, a rich and learned physician, one of several portraits of him in Venice by Alessandro Vittoria.

The Picture Gallery ends here, and stairs lead down to the continuation of the historical collections (shown on the plan on p. 74 above).

Room 45: The display commemorates the *Bucintoro* (*Bucentaur*), the gala ship used to transport the doge from his palace to the entrance to the lagoon

Antonello da Messina: *Pietà* (1474/5).

near San Nicolò al Lido for the ceremonial marriage of Venice with the sea on the Festa della Sensa (Ascension Day; *see p. 332*). The lanterns and gilded wood fragments which decorated the last ship were carved in 1729 by the successful Rococo sculptor Antonio Corradini.

Rooms 46–53: The displays in these rooms illustrate daily life in the Venetian Republic over the centuries. Rooms 46 and 47 contain 17th-century paintings of festivals. In Rooms 48–50 there is a charming display illustrating the trades and crafts of Venice (shop signboards, household objects, lace-making equipment and ladies' apparel, including platform shoes), and 17th–18th-century lace, tapestries, embroideries and altar-frontals. Room 51 has two 15th- and 16th-century sculptured reliefs from islands in the lagoon, and the last two rooms (52 and 53) illustrate typical entertainments and games which used to be held in Venice.

MUSEO ARCHEOLOGICO NAZIONALE & THE LIBRERIA MARCIANA
Map p. 407, E2

The usual entrance to the Museo Archeologico is from Room 18 or 19 of the Correr. However, since it has longer opening hours, from 8.15am–9am and from 5pm–7pm (or when it is opened specially on summer evenings), it can also be entered from the Piazzetta, through its original main entrance at no. 17 in the portico of the Libreria Marciana. The use of the Correr entrance means that the museum now normally has to be visited in reverse order. Room numbers have not been changed, and those found in situ are used in the following description (the reverse order of the numbers reflects the way they are visited). However, the room numbers and arrangement will probably be changed in the next few years, and some of the pieces moved to Palazzo Grimani (see p. 272) when it is opened to the public after restoration. The Libreria Marciana is entered directly from the Museo Archeologico.

This museum was founded in 1523 from a bequest of Greek and Roman sculptures made by Cardinal Domenico Grimani to the Republic; in 1593 his nephew Giovanni Grimani, Patriarch of Aquileia, donated his collection from Palazzo Grimani. It is especially remarkable for its very fine pieces of ancient Greek sculpture.

Rooms X–IX: Roman busts, including, in Room X, a famous bust thought to be of the Emperor Vitellius, a particularly fine Roman portrait of the early 2nd century AD.

Room VIII: Three Gallic warriors found on Grimani property in Rome near the Quirinal Hill, copies of a group presented by Attalus of Pergamon to Athens, are displayed here, along with a fragment of a Hellenistic Greek statue with good drapery; heads of satyrs; and a statuary group of *Leda and the Swan*.

Room VII: Two cases with precious small objects of varying date and provenance. In the left case: a 5th-century

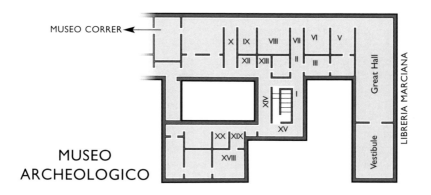

Byzantine reliquary casket in ivory found near Pola (modern Pula, Istria) with Christian motifs, restored in Vienna in the early 19th century; 11th-century Byzantine ivory plaque of Sts John the Theologian and Paul; gems and cameos including the so-called *Zulian Cameo* of Jupiter, from Ephesus, which is variously dated to two centuries before Christ or two centuries after; the head of a Hellenistic princess in rock crystal; and two heads of Jupiter, one of them the *Chalcedon Cameo* (Pergamene art, 3rd century BC). An engraved cornelian, and a gem showing the Dioscuri from the Quirinal Hill in Rome, a Neoclassical work signed by Nathaniel Merchant, are also displayed here.

In the right case: early bronzes, some dating from 1700 BC, and other Etruscan and Roman works, including the two most recent acquisitions, which are two Roman bronze statuettes dating from the 1st–3rd centuries AD, found in the 20th century in the lagoon near Malamocco.

Room VI: The precious Grimani Altar with Bacchic scenes (1st century BC) is

displayed here, as well as heads of satyrs, and the head of an athlete.

Room V: Contains a series of heads and busts of Athena; funerary reliefs; and a Roman copy of the *Apollo Lycius*, perhaps after Praxiteles. (Here is the entrance to the great hall of the Libreria Marciana; *see below*).

Room III: Roman copies of Greek works including the *kore* known as the *Abbondanza Grimani*, an Attic original of c. 420 BC, and a fine series of female statues of 5th and 4th centuries BC, including *Hera* and *Athena* (modelled on the famous Parthenon *Athena* by Pheidias).

Room II: Houses a well-arranged numismatic collection, showing coins from the Roman to Byzantine periods.

Room I: The display includes an original Greek inscription from Crete, and four busts, two of which are Roman and the other two date from the 16th century.

Room XII: Material from Zara (modern Zadar, Croatia), and Greek and Roman coins and gems.

Room XIII: Reliefs, busts and statues related to Roman religious cults.

Room XIV: This room, the loggia, has a late 16th-century relief of vintage scenes and centaurs by Tiziano Aspetti (once thought to be a Roman work).

Rooms XVIII–XX: The Correr Collection, including Greek and Roman heads and torsos; a black Romano-Egyptian head; a small Roman mosaic of a harbour scene (4th century AD); the head of a boy of the Julio-Claudian dynasty (1st century AD); a statuette of Isis; and a mummy.

Room XV: Pre-Roman material, including Villanovan and Corinthian vases.

Libreria Marciana

The famous Library of St Mark is also known as the Libreria Sansoviniana, after Jacopo Sansovino, who designed it in 1537 and provided it with a splendid façade on the Piazzetta (*described overleaf*).

Petrarch gave his books to Venice in 1362, but it was not until Cardinal Bessarion presented his extremely important collection of Greek and Latin manuscripts in 1468 that the library was formally founded. Bessarion (1389–1472), an Armenian born in Trebizond (in modern Turkey), accompanied Emperor John VII Palaeologus to the Council of Florence in 1439 as the Orthodox Archbishop of Nicaea. The council failed to unite the churches of East and West, but Bessarion remained in Italy and made his mark both as a Humanist scholar and a churchman (his fame was such that he was even considered seriously as a candidate to succeed Nicholas V as pope in 1455). When Pietro Bembo the Venetian humanist (famous as one of the speakers in Castiglione's *Courtier*) became the official historian of the Venetian Republic in 1530, Bessarion was appointed librarian. It was Bembo who was instrumental in finally persuading the doge to commission a fitting building for the Bessarion collection from his friend Sansovino. Today the library contains about one million volumes and 13,500 manuscripts (many of them Greek). It is also housed in the adjoining building of the Zecca, again designed by Sansovino.

The Great Hall

The walls and ceiling of the Great Hall (the reading room) are magnificently decorated. The 21 ceiling medallions with allegorical paintings (completed in 1557) are the work of seven Venetian Mannerist artists, who each painted three *tondi*. Both Sansovino and Titian advised the procurators on the choice of artists, but Paolo Veronese is today by far the most famous of the group. Above the desk at the window end are three works by Lo Schiavone; the next three are by Veronese; then come two by Giovanni Battista Zelotti (the third one by him was damaged and substituted in 1635 by Padovanino); then two by Giulio Licinio (the third one by him was damaged and substituted by Bernardo Strozzi also in 1635); the next three are by Battista Franco; then three by Giuseppe Salviati; and the three at the far end (nearest to the door into the library vestibule) are by Giovanni de Mio (called 'Fratina'; a painter represented nowhere else in Venice). The painted architectural perspectives are by Battista Franco.

In 1562–72 these artists then went on to decorate the walls with paintings of philosophers: on the end wall by the desk are two by Jacopo Tintoretto; on the right wall are four more by Tintoretto and two by Lo Schiavone; on the far wall, on either side of the door into the vestibule, are two by Paolo Veronese, and on the last wall are works by his brother Benedetto Caliari, by Giuseppe Salviati, Battista Franco and an artist from the Netherlands, Lambert Sustris (only the last two formed part of the original decoration on this wall).

The floor was moved here from the Scuola Grande della Misericordia in 1815. The cases usually display photocopies of some of the library's holdings. The most precious works include a late 14th-century *Divina Commedia* with illuminations; evangelistaries dating back to the 9th century; a Byzantine book cover with *Christ Pantocrator* and the *Virgin Orans*, dating from the late 10th or early 11th century and decorated with silver-gilt, gold cloisonné enamel, gems and pearls; the exquisite *Grimani Breviary*, illuminated by Flemish artists of c. 1500; Fra' Mauro's celebrated world map of 1459, drawn on the island of San Michele; a map of Tunis by Hadji Mehemed (c. 1560); Marco Polo's will; navigational charts; and a manuscript in Petrarch's hand.

Vestibule

The vestibule or anteroom, connected to the Great Hall by a monumental doorway, has a ceiling decorated in the 16th century with remarkable *quadratura* by the little-known Cristoforo Rosa, who had also been commissioned to paint the central panel of the *Allegory of Wisdom*; this was instead executed by the great Venetian artist Titian (although one of his least known works, it is painted with a delightful freshness of touch). In 1587 Grimani arranged a public gallery of some 150 pieces of statuary on the walls of this room. In recent years this has been partially reconstructed, although some of the masterpieces which were moved to the Museo Archeologico in 1922 are substituted with casts. It is a fascinating illustration of how great archaeological collections used to be displayed. The monumental staircase (which leads down to the original entrance) has a splendid stuccoed vault by Alessandro Vittoria.

PIAZZETTA DI SAN MARCO
Map p. 407, E2

The Piazzetta, with the Doge's Palace on the left and the Library on the right, is an extension of Piazza San Marco from St Mark's to the waterfront on the Bacino di San Marco: this was the entrance to the city in the days of the Republic, when the ships carrying ambassadors and foreign dignitaries would dock here and the visitor would at once be confronted with Venice's most magnificent buildings.

Near the water's edge are two huge monolithic granite columns brought back to Venice from the ill-fated expedition to Constantinople by Doge Vitale Michiel II (*see p. 255*), and erected here at the end of the 12th century. One bears a winged lion, adapted as the symbol of St Mark. It is thought to be a Hellenistic work (4th–3rd century BC) and may have come from a tomb in Cilicia or Tarsus.

The other column is crowned with a copy of a statue of the first patron saint of Venice, St Theodore, and his dragon. The torso is a fragment of a Roman statue of the time of Hadrian, and the head a fine Greek portrait in Parian marble (the original is now in the courtyard of the Doge's Palace).

A scaffold used to be set up between the columns for executions; and as paintings by Canaletto and others show, there used to be numerous market stalls and booths here until they were ordered to be removed by Jacopo Sansovino when, as a procurator of St Mark's, he became the chief architect (*see box below*).

Façade of the Libreria Marciana

The façade of the Libreria Marciana (Library of St Mark), opposite the Doge's Palace, is the masterpiece of Jacopo Sansovino, hence its other name, Libreria Sansoviniana.

Jacopo Sansovino (1486–1570)

The Tuscan architect and sculptor Jacopo Sansovino left Rome for Venice in 1527 at the age of 41. Rome had just suffered its infamous sack by the troops of the Holy Roman Emperor Charles V; Sansovino's invitation came from Doge Andrea Gritti, who later became a close friend. He was appointed *proto*, or chief architect in charge of the fabric of St Mark's and the Piazza in the 1530s, and redesigned the Piazzetta, isolating the Campanile (and designing the Loggetta at its foot) and building the library. He helped to introduce a new Classical style of architecture into the city, based on his knowledge of Roman buildings; his library was considered by Palladio to be the most beautiful building since the days of Antiquity.

By the time of Sansovino's death at the age of 84 he had built the Zecca (mint), the Fabbriche Nuove at the Rialto on the Grand Canal, the churches of San Francesco della Vigna, San Martino and San Giuliano, and Palazzo Dolfin and Palazzo Corner, both on the Grand Canal. His son Francesco wrote a remarkable guide to the city in 1581 called *Venetia città nobilissima et singolare.*

Begun in 1537, the library is built of Istrian stone, its ornate design derived from Classical Roman architecture, with a Doric ground floor, and an Ionic *piano nobile* with an elaborate frieze beneath a balustrade crowned by obelisks and statues of gods and heroes, executed by Sansovino's collaborators including Alessandro Vittoria, Tiziano Minio, Tommaso Lombardo and Danese Cattaneo, as well as the Florentine Bartolomeo Ammannati, who came to Venice to work with Sansovino early in his career, before he became famous as an architect and sculptor in his native city. After Sansovino's death in 1570 it fell to Vincenzo Scamozzi to finish the building (between 1588 and 1591), having already successfully completed the Procuratie Nuove (*see p.*

70 above) to Sansovino's design. A versatile architect born in Vicenza, Scamozzi is known for his numerous fine buildings in the Veneto. He also collaborated with Palladio, wrote a treatise on architecture, and even planned the cathedral of Salzburg. In the first years of the 17th century he was still at work in Venice, at the churches of San Lazzaro dei Mendicanti, San Salvatore and the Tolentini, and he built Palazzo Contarini degli Scrigni on the Grand Canal. He is also remembered as the master of the most famous Venetian architect of the 17th century, Baldassare Longhena.

The great hall, vestibule and staircase are now open to the public, with access from the Museo Correr and Museo Archeologico (*see pp. 72 and 80 above*).

The waterfront

The quay on the busy waterfront is called the **Molo**. Until 1846, when the railway line connected the mainland to Venice, this would have been visitors' first view of the city—and it must have created an amazing impression indeed. Opposite it stands the island of San Giorgio Maggiore, divided from the long Giudecca island by a narrow channel. On the Giudecca the Palladian façades of the Zitelle and Redentore churches can be seen. Nearer at hand is the promontory known as the Punta della Dogana with the church of the Salute. In the other direction (left) the quay extends along Riva degli Schiavoni to the public gardens. Major work is underway here by the Consorzio Venezia Nuova in an attempt to protect the Piazzetta and Piazza San Marco from flooding (*for details see p. 37*).

To the right, beyond the end of the Libreria Marciana, is the severe façade of the old **Zecca** or Mint (now part of the Libreria). This rusticated Doric building was finished in 1547 by Jacopo Sansovino on the site of the 13th-century mint. The first golden ducat was issued in 1284, and at the height of the Republic the Venetian *zecchini* were used as currency throughout the world.

The **public gardens**, which take their name from the former Palazzo Reale in the Procuratie Nuove which backs onto them, were laid out c. 1814 after the demolition of a huge Gothic building which contained the Republican granaries. They are decorated with two small Neoclassical buildings designed by Lorenzo Santi, one of which, formerly a coffee-house, is now used as a tourist information office. Across the bridge is the building which was once the seat of the Magistrato della Farina, the magistrates in charge of the distribution of bread and flour to the citizens of the Republic from the granaries (it is now the Port Authority office). By the San Marco landing-stage is **Harry's Bar**, which, since it was opened in the 1920s by Giuseppe Cipriani, has been famous for its international clientèle. All the notable, wealthy visitors to Venice in the 20th century came here to be seen and talked about—and it is perhaps particularly associated with the flamboyant figures of Ernest Hemingway, Orson Welles and Truman Capote. Inside, the bar was intentionally placed right at the entrance so that more timid clients could immediately find a place to 'lean on'. It continues to flourish, under the direction of Giuseppe's son Arrigo, as the city's most celebrated restaurant and cocktail bar. It has an inconspicuous entrance on Calle Vallaresso, and a few years ago it became a 'national monument', meaning that its original furnishings will be preserved intact.

Piazzetta Giovanni XXIII and the Museum of Diocesan Art

To the left of St Mark's is the **Piazzetta Giovanni XXIII**, named after Angelo Roncalli, a native of the Veneto, who was Patriarch of Venice when elected to the Holy See in 1958. Greatly loved and respected (and always known simply as 'Papa Giovanni'), he was beatified in the year 2000. The centre of the little square was designed by Andrea Tirali in 1724, when he installed the well-head and the two chubby little lion cubs (carved out of red Verona marble around this time by Giovanni Bonazza), which are now rather worn since they are just the right size to be ridden by children. Palazzo Patriarcale was built in 1834–43 by Lorenzo Santi, Venice's most successful Neoclassical architect. The façade of the church of San Basso, by Longhena, dates from 1675. Devoid of all internal decoration, the church is at present ignominiously used as a cloakroom deposit for visitors to St Mark's.

Calle di Canonica leads to Rio di Palazzo, across which rises the façade of the 16th-century Palazzo Trevisan-Cappello, with good marble inlay. On the other side of the rio, at the end of the short fondamenta, is the entrance (at no. 4312) to the **Museum of Diocesan Art** (*map p. 407, E2; closed at the time of writing*) and the tiny Cloister of Sant'Apollonia. Dating from the early 14th century, it is the only Romanesque cloister in the city, and it retains its original brick paving. Sculptural fragments from the basilica (some dating from the 9th–11th centuries) are displayed here. The museum contains a collection of vestments, missals, church plate, Crucifixes and reliquaries, as well as paintings and sculpture from Venetian churches either closed permanently or unable to provide safe-keeping for their treasures.

THE DOGE'S PALACE
Map p. 407, E2

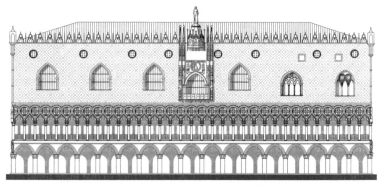

DOGE'S PALACE: WATERFRONT FAÇADE

This magnificent palace, built for the doges, which stands just out of Piazza San Marco, is one of Venice's most famous buildings, with a remarkable Gothic exterior. Formerly the official residence of the doges and the chief magistrates, it was founded on this site in the 9th century, when they moved from Malamocco (*see p. 333*). The present building dates from the 14th century, and the two façades overlooking the Bacino di San Marco and the Piazzetta are wonderful examples of florid Gothic architecture. In the vast interior, the decoration of the numerous rooms used by the governing bodies of the Republic, by Venetian painters of the 16th–17th centuries (after fires in 1574 and 1577), survives intact. To study with care the pictorial and historical significance of these paintings, which cover both the walls and ceilings, requires several hours, but they give a vivid idea of the glory of Venice at the height of her power.

Visiting the palace

Open 1 April–31 Oct 9–5.30 (the palace closes at 7); 1 Nov–31 March 9–3.30 (the palace closes at 5). The building can be extremely cold in winter. Although the palace is very well kept, it is often crowded with tour groups (except for the Museo dell'Opera on the ground floor). The fascinating 'Itinerari Segreti', tours of the 'secret' rooms in the building used by the administrators of the Republic, take place daily in English at 9.45, 10.45, 11.35 and 12.50, by appointment at the ticket office; you can also book in advance. Only 25 people are allowed on each tour. For information, T: 041 522 4951.

History of the building

The palace was begun in the 9th century and was rebuilt in the 12th under Doge Sebastiano Ziani, but was then almost totally destroyed by fire. In 1340 a large sum of money was voted by the Great Council to build a room big enough to contain its 1,212 members. Inaugurated in 1419, it overlooked the Bacino di San Marco and extended as far as the seventh column of the portico on the Piazzetta. Shortly afterwards, in 1422, with the financial aid of Doge Tommaso Mocenigo, the Great Council decided to demolish part of the 12th-century law courts on this site in order to extend the façade in exactly the same style towards the Basilica of St Mark. It is thought that the building was constructed under the direction of officials of the Republic by a group of master masons, including Filippo Calendario, but the exact role of this obscure figure (whose name is not connected with certainty to any other building work) in the design of the palace is still not clear. All that is known is that he was beheaded in 1355, together with Doge Marin Falier, because he had supported the Doge in his treacherous conspiracy against the state, but sources as early as the 15th century connect his name to the Doge's Palace.

After another conflagration in 1483, Antonio Rizzo began the main interior façade and the Scala dei Giganti, and the work was continued by Pietro Lombardo, Giorgio Spavento and Scarpagnino. Although it was again twice damaged by fire in the 1570s, it was decided to restore rather than rebuild it, under the direction of Antonio da Ponte. Paintings glorifying Venetian history were commissioned for the ceilings and walls of the main rooms. The courtyard and façade overlooking the Rio di Palazzo were then completed in the 17th century (following Rizzo's original design) by Bartolomeo Monopola.

EXTERIOR OF THE DOGE'S PALACE

The waterfront façade

The main façade overlooking the Bacino di San Marco is a superb Gothic work. Each arcade of the portico supports two arches of the loggia decorated with quatrefoil roundels. This in turn is surmounted by a massive wall 12.5m high lightened by a delicate pattern of white Istrian stone and pink Verona marble. Marble ornamental crenellations crown the façade. The windows along this side belong to the immense Sala del Maggior Consiglio. In the centre is a balconied window built in 1404 by Pier Paolo di Jacopo dalle Masegne, crowned with a statue of *Justice*. The sculptors Pier Paolo and Jacobello ran the most important workshop in Venice in the last decades of the 14th and the beginning of the 15th century. The work of these two brothers is often indistinguishable (and in fact they often signed their sculptures together). Their most impressive works are the statues on the rood screen of the Basilica of St Mark, but their sculptures also decorate numerous other churches in Venice.

A few decades later the high reliefs, inspired by Old Testament subjects, were carved on the three external corners of the building. They would have been seen by the Venetians as statements of the importance of the Christian faith. On the corner nearest to the Ponte della Paglia the relief depicts the *Drunkenness of Noah*, and, in the loggia above, the Archangel Raphael. On the corner nearest the Piazzetta are Adam and Eve, plucking figs from a tree which sprouts leaves to cover their nakedness, with the Archangel Michael above. (The third corner relief, near the Porta della Carta, shows the *Judgement of Solomon*; *see below.*) The level of the pavement used to be two steps lower so that the bases of the columns of the portico were exposed, altering the proportion of the lower façade (the columns now seem somewhat stumpy).

The beautiful capitals of the portico are superb examples of medieval carving dating from 1340–55. It is well worth taking time to study them on the comfortable benches beneath the porticoes. In a complicated series of allegories (mostly explained by inscriptions), they represent the virtues of wise government and the importance of justice (the subjects include scenes of childhood, birds, heads of men and women from various countries, emperors, Vices and Virtues, myths, animals, courtly love and famous men). The capital on the corner nearest to the Piazzetta has particularly fine carvings of the signs of the zodiac. This, together with seven others capitals on this side of the building, were replaced by excellent copies in 1884–87, and the originals are now displayed in the Museo dell'Opera inside the palace (*see p. 91 below*).

The Piazzetta façade

The original 14th-century building reached as far as the seventh column of the portico, above which is a tondo of *Justice* on the loggia. This shows the crowned figure of Justice (the personification of Venice) sitting on a throne guarded by two lions with two Vices trampled underfoot and the sea full of fish below. In 1424 the palace was extended in the same style using the same building materials as far as the basilica, and the Porta della Carta was added in 1438. In the centre is a balconied window (1538), similar to that on the front of the building. During restoration work, necessitated by the deterioration of the Istrian stone and polychrome brick, and which was completed in 1999, traces of colour were found, particularly on the earlier masonry and on the frames of the 14th-century windows.

In the ground-level portico the first six capitals towards the lagoon, as on the main façade, were superbly carved in 1340–55 (three of them replaced by excellent copies in 1876–84). They represent sculptors, animals with their prey, craftsmen, astrology and foreign nations. The seventh one beneath the tondo of *Justice*, which is slightly bigger than the others, has scenes of death and courtly love. The last twelve capitals (two replaced in the 19th century) were carved when the palace was enlarged in 1424 and are mostly copies of the earlier ones on the main façade. The most interesting is the last one, nearest the basilica, showing Justice surrounded by famous legislators and wise men. This bears the signature of two Florentine sculptors, Pietro di Niccolò Lamberti and Giovanni di Martino da Fiesole, who also worked together on the tomb of Doge Tommaso Mocenigo in Santi Giovanni e Paolo (and Lamberti had worked with his father Niccolò on the sculpture on the façade of the Basilica of St Mark). On the corner above is a high relief illustrating the *Judgement of Solomon*, with the Archangel Gabriel in the loggia above, beautiful works attributed by some scholars to the famous Tuscan sculptor Jacopo della Quercia (c. 1410; *but see p. 64*).

The **Porta della Carta** (1438–43) is an extremely graceful gateway in the florid Gothic style, one of the most important works by Bartolomeo Bon and his family workshop, which was extremely active in Venice in the mid-15th century. Bartolomeo was born in Venice and in his architecture and sculpture successfully combines elements from northern sculptors with the influence of the more classical Tuscan Renaissance. He worked on the Ca d'Oro (and carved the magnificent well-head there), and produced sculptures for the exteriors and portals of a number of churches in the city (including Santi Giovanni e Paolo and the Frari).

It is thought that the Porta della Carta owes its name to the state archives or *cartae* (papers) which used to be kept near here. The gateway, which is signed by Bon on the architrave (the original of which has been removed to the Museo dell'Opera; *see below*), is crowned by a figure of *Venice*, symbolised by Justice, attributed to Bartolomeo himself, and he also probably carved the original statues of Doge Francesco Foscari kneeling before the lion of St Mark, which were destroyed by Napoleon's troops in 1797 but were replaced here with excellent reproductions in 1885 (the head of the doge survived French mutilation and can be seen in the Museo dell'Opera). The name of the sculptor who carved the very fine statues of *Temperance*, *Fortitude*, *Prudence* and *Charity* is unknown.

The rio façade

The fine Renaissance east façade on Rio di Palazzo, built of Istrian stone, can be seen from Ponte della Paglia or Ponte della Canonica. Begun by Antonio Rizzo (*see p. 94 below*), it was continued by the Lombardo family, by Scarpagnino, and finally completed in the 17th century by Bartolomeo Monopola.

DOGE'S PALACE
(GROUND FLOOR)

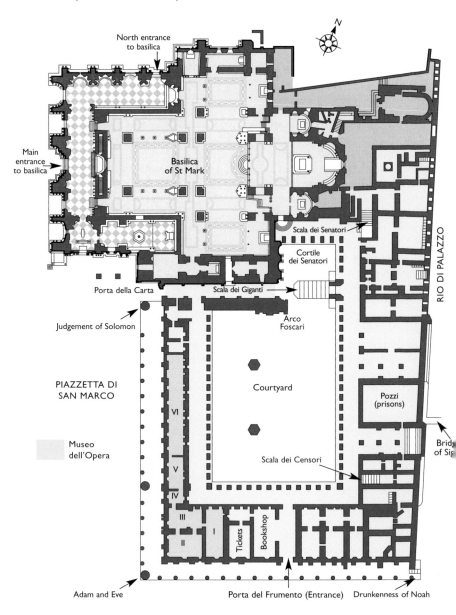

North entrance to basilica

Main entrance to basilica

Basilica of St Mark

Scala dei Senatori

Cortile dei Senatori

Porta della Carta

Scala dei Giganti

Judgement of Solomon

Arco Foscari

PIAZZETTA DI SAN MARCO

Courtyard

Pozzi (prisons)

VI

Museo dell'Opera

V

IV

Scala dei Censori

Bridge of Sighs

III

II

I

Tickets

Bookshop

RIO DI PALAZZO

Adam and Eve

Porta del Frumento (Entrance)

Drunkenness of Noah

The quay extends in front of the Doge's Palace as far as the Ponte della Paglia, a bridge of Istrian stone, first constructed in 1360 across Rio di Palazzo. It was widened in 1844 when the pretty balustrade of little columns with sculpted pine cones was added. Low down on the arch (only visible from the waterfront) is a tabernacle with a relief of the Madonna and two gondolas, dating from 1583. Here can be seen the famous **Bridge of Sighs** (or Ponte dei Sospiri), an elegant little flying bridge in Istrian stone, one of very few works by Antonio Contino (1600). It was constructed for the passage of the Inquisitors of State between the prisons and the law courts, and only received its popular name in the 19th century when the idea of the 'sighing' prisoners on their way to trial fired the imagination of the Romantics.

GROUND FLOOR OF THE DOGE'S PALACE

The entrance to the palace is through the Porta del Frumento at the centre of the main façade overlooking the Bacino di San Marco. The door gets its name *frumento* (wheat) from the offices here which used to be occupied by the government officials responsible for the distribution of grain.

Museo dell'Opera

On the ground floor, in rooms which were once used as prisons, the Museo dell'Opera displays the original capitals and columns (mostly dating from 1340–55; restored) from the exterior portico, where they were replaced by fine copies in 1876–87. These six rooms are hardly ever visited by groups, so they are one of the most peaceful areas of the palace. Diagrams in each room show where each capital was on the façade.

Room I: Displayed here are six capitals from the main waterfront façade, dating from the 14th century. They show Solomon and wise men (personifying the Liberal Arts); birds with their prey; heads of men from different latitudes (each is shown with markedly different features and hats, but since the capital is without inscriptions it is difficult to identify them: one apparently represents a Tartar and another, with a turban, a Moor); kings of the ancient world and Roman emperors: Titus, Trajan, King Priam of Troy, Nebuchadnezzar, Alexander the Great, King Darius of the Persians, Julius Caesar and Augustus (holding a globe with the inscription *Mondo di pace*); female heads (representing Latin women of various ages in different costumes and head-dresses); and heads of Latin people, including a soldier in armour decorated with two Crosses, and so usually identified as a crusader, women of various ages, and children (this capital is sometimes thought to represent a crusader's family). The scaffolding model displayed here shows how the capitals were removed during the 19th century.

Room II: The famous capital from the corner of the palace between the Piazzetta and the Bacino, which depicts the *Creation of Adam*, with the planets and signs of the zodiac, is displayed here. This is perhaps the most beautiful of all of them, greatly admired by

Ruskin. Larger than the other capitals, it represents the focal point of the carefully worked-out narrative scheme which involved each capital as it introduces the history of the universe and the history of man. The *Creation of Adam* shows God the Father seated on a throne and Adam as a boy. Saturn, depicted as an old man with a beard is shown sitting on Capricorn (a goat) holding Aquarius (a jug). Jupiter, wearing a doctorial head-dress, is seated on Sagittarius (a centaur with a bow and arrow) and he indicates the sign of Pisces. Mars, a warrior in armour is seated on Aries, with Scorpio on his left. The Sun, personified by a young boy with rays around his head, is seated on Leo and he holds a disc carved with a face. Venus, holding a mirror, is seated on Taurus and holds the sign of Libra (the scales). Mercury, in a toga holding an open book, is shown between Virgo and Gemini (the twins). On the last side, the Moon, represented by a girl in a boat holding a crescent moon, is shown with Cancer. The movement in the sea and the girl's clothes symbolise the influence the moon has on tides and winds.

Also here are two 14th-century capitals, one decorated with baskets of fruit, and the other with allegories of the Seven Deadly Sins and Vanity (the deadly sins—Lust, Greed, Pride, Anger, Avarice, Envy, and Sloth—are all represented by female figures except for Pride).

Room III: Four 14th-century capitals from the Piazzetta façade are shown here. One of them illustrates the months of the year: March is represent-

Detail from the famous *Creation of Adam* capital, showing Jupiter seated on Sagittarius, with Pisces on his other side.

Aged Saturn, seated on Capricorn, holds the sign of Aquarius.

ed by a figure playing a musical instrument; June is shown with cherries; September is represented by a young man crushing grapes, and December is represented by the butchering of a pig. The other months are shown in pairs. There is also a capital with the heads of animals with their prey. Another capital shows sculptors, all of them intent on carving blocks of stone or sculpting figures, including the four patron saints (identified by their haloes and crowns) of the Scuola dei Tagliapietra or stonemasons, and their four disciples. The fourth capital shows craftsmen at work (a stonemason, a blacksmith, a notary, a peasant, a surveyor, a carpenter, a cobbler and a goldsmith).

Rooms IV–V: The massive wall of the old palace can be seen in Room IV, and in Room V stonework from the tracery on the upper loggia.

Room VI: The last room, a long gallery, has a splendid display of 14th–15th-century capitals from the upper portico, some of them with traces of gilding and paint. They are decorated with a great variety of motifs including foliage, acanthus leaves, flowers, shells, musicians, nuns, female heads, the lion of St Mark, animals, children, griffins, eagles and warriors. The marble head of Doge Francesco Foscari is the only part of the original relief of the doge kneeling in front of the lion of St Mark on the Porta della Carta to have survived destruction in 1797. It is attributed to Antonio Bregno or Bartolomeo Bon; the original architrave of this door is preserved at the end of the room, with Bartolomeo Bon's signature. The bust of Doge Cristoforo Moro used to be part of a group in the courtyard, also destroyed in 1797.

The courtyard and Scala dei Giganti

Three sides of the courtyard belong to the Doge's Palace, while the flank of St Mark's (the Chapel of the Doge) rises above the fourth. After the fire in 1483, it was Antonio Rizzo who designed the magnificent east façade, which has four storeys with a double row of porticoes and numerous windows. The carved decoration is extremely beautiful and is partly the work of the Lombardo family of sculptors (*see p. 279*). At this time Doge Marco Barbarigo also commissioned Rizzo to design the ceremonial Scala dei Giganti, as a setting for the doge's coronation ceremony (which up to then had not been held in public). Built of Istrian limestone, it is famous for its exquisitely-carved reliefs. On the wide landing at the top, the doge was crowned (over a white skull cap) with the jewelled and peaked *cornu*, modelled on a Byzantine head-dress and always an important symbol of his position (an example can be seen in the Museo Correr; *see p. 75*). The giant statues of Neptune and Mars (the *giganti* of the stairway's name) symbolise the maritime and terrestrial might of the Republic. They are late works (c. 1554) by Jacopo Sansovino, added in order to diminish the figure of the doge during his coronation.

The right-hand end of the façade was finished by Scarpagnino in the following century, when the two splendid bronze well-heads were made. The lower storeys of the other two sides of the courtyard were completed in Rizzo's style by Bartolomeo Monopola in the 17th century.

Antonio Rizzo (c. 1430–99)

Not much is known about Rizzo's early life, although his presence is documented in Venice from 1457. His first works include the sculpted altars of St James and St Paul in St Mark's; but it is in the courtyard of the Doge's Palace that we see his extraordinary skills both as architect and sculptor. From 1483 he was appointed chief architect of the palace, and not only did he design the exterior of its eastern wing (both the courtyard and canal façades), but he also built the Scala dei Giganti, which is recognised as a masterpiece of delicate carving. On another side of the courtyard he worked on the Arco Foscari and carved for it two marble statues of Adam and Eve (replaced by copies; the originals are in the palace; *see p. 105*), which are his most beautiful works. His contribution to the diffusion of the classical Renaissance style in Venice was fundamental, and in these two figures we also see the influence of northern European art, in particular (in the figure of Eve) of Dürer, who was in Venice at the time they were made. The classical figure of Adam is one of the most remarkable nude figures produced in Renaissance Venice. Rizzo also designed and carved the tomb of Doge Niccolò Tron in the Frari (*see p. 203*), one of the very best Renaissance tombs in the city. There are others sculptures attributed to him on the exterior or inside Venetian churches (the Madonna dell'Orto, Sant'Elena, the Salute), but these are undocumented works, and some scholars believe them to be by his more famous contemporary Pietro Lombardo. Rizzo remains a somewhat shadowy figure, perhaps less famous than he deserves to be.

On the last side of the courtyard, towards the basilica, is a Baroque façade by Bartolomeo Monopola incorporating a clock, and the side of the Arco Foscari which faces the Scala dei Giganti. This triumphal arch was begun in the 15th century by the Bon family and completed by Antonio Bregno and Antonio Rizzo. On the side facing the main courtyard is a statue of the *condottiere* Francesco Maria I della Rovere, Duke of Urbino (1490–1538), the only work in Venice by the Florentine sculptor Giovanni Bandini (1587), and (right) a page-boy attributed to Antonio Rizzo (both now replaced by copies; originals inside the palace; *see p. 105*). The main front of the arch bears statues of the mid-15th century, and bronze copies of two fine marble statues of Adam and Eve by Rizzo (*see opposite*).

PRIMO PIANO NOBILE

The Doge's Apartments (Rooms 5–13)

From the other end of the courtyard, the Scala dei Censori leads up to the inner loggia. From here the Scala d'Oro **(1)**, built in 1558–59, to Sansovino's design, and decorated with gilded stuccoes by Alessandro Vittoria, continues up to the first floor (or *primo piano nobile*) and the Doge's Apartments, reconstructed after a fire in 1483.

Room 5 (Sala degli Scarlatti): This first room was the Robing Room (it takes its name from the scarlet robes worn by the ducal counsellors). It was decorated in the first years of the 16th century with a beautiful gilded ceiling, and boasts a fine chimneypiece by Tullio and Antonio Lombardo. Over the door is an interesting bas-relief by their father, Pietro, of *Doge Leonardo Loredan at the Feet of the Virgin*. Many scholars consider this one of Pietro's very best reliefs. Opposite is a *Madonna* in coloured stucco (attributed to Antonio Rizzo).

Room 6 (Sala dello Scudo): This was where the doge's guards were stationed, and it is named from the shield which was displayed here showing the arms of the doge who was in office. The walls are covered with maps and charts (16th century, but repainted in 1762), and two globes are kept here. There is a wonderful view of St Mark's from the window.

Room 7 (Sala Grimani): This has another chimneypiece by Tullio and Antonio Lombardo. The ceiling (which bears the arms of Marino Grimani, doge from 1595–1605) is decorated with rosettes, above a frieze by Andrea Vicentino. Four charming paintings of the winged lion of St Mark, the famous symbol of Venice, are displayed here. The two opposite the fireplace are the earliest—the work of Donato Veneziano (with two saints and a view of Venice). The lion by Jacobello del Fiore dates from 1435. Vittore Carpaccio's painting of 1516 shows the lion between the sea and the *terraferma*, and has a very accurate view of the Doge's Palace and the Campanile and domes of St Mark's in the background, as well as a group of galleons setting sail from the Arsenale.

DOGES & THEIR COUNCILS

'Though in appearance he seemeth of great estate, yet indeed his power is but small. He keepeth no house, liveth privately, and is in so much servitude that I have heard some of the Venetians themselves call him an honourable slave.' This is how a 16th-century English visitor saw the Doge of Venice. Yet, to the outside world, the doge personified the grandeur of the Republic. On great ceremonial occasions, such as the feast of the Marriage to the Sea every Ascension Day, he would process in splendour across the lagoon in the *Bucintoro*. He was the focus of every major ritual, whether this was the reception of a foreign ambassador or visiting royalty, or the ancient religious celebrations in St Mark's and the square outside it.

Yet, remarkably for Europe at this time, the doges could for centuries only be appointed through election. In the 13th century the pretence was that the appointment was by popular acclaim. 'This is your doge if it pleases you' was the ritual formula by which a new incumbent was presented to the citizens from the loggia of St Mark's. After 1268, the election was through an intricate procedure conducted by the nobility, and certainly from then on the doge's powers became increasingly restricted. On assuming office, he had to make a *promissione ducale*, which was a solemn vow that he would obey certain rules which constrained his authority. He could not leave Venice without authorisation, nor could he open state letters in private or meet foreign ambassadors unless councillors were present. Much of government took place outside his control, and was conducted by the Great Council, or Maggior Consiglio. The *Serrata del Maggior Consiglio*, literally the 'locking' of the Great Council, in 1297, restricted membership to those families who had already sat on the council. These 'patricians' included both nobles and merchants, and they inherited the right to sit on the council for life on reaching the age of 25. This signified the introduction of an oligarchic form of government. At the beginning of the 16th century the members were formally registered at their baptism in the *Libro d'Oro* ('Golden Book'). The size of the council varied over the years; the greatest number it reached was 1,700. Clearly such a large body was too cumbersome to conduct power on a day-to-day basis, but it met once a week, on Sundays, and appointed many of the city's magistrates. Increasingly its power was delegated to a Senate, of which the leading state magistrates were members *ex officio*. The Senate, which met three or four times a week, expanded its original duties of jurisdiction in commerce and navigation to include all matters of international affairs, diplomacy and defence. Eventually it had 230 members. The Senate in its turn appointed (for the first time in 1380) a smaller committee, the Collegio, a group of 26 counsellors presided over by the doge, which met almost every day to deal with everyday affairs. Major executive decisions were taken by a still smaller council, the Signoria of ten members, all of whom were also members of the Collegio. Separate from all these organs was the Council of Ten, set up in 1310, at first as a temporary measure, but then permanently, which was given the task of supervising internal security. It soon became notorious for its secret operations and its readiness to intrude into all matters of business. All these councils met in the Doge's Palace.

It is just this proliferation of councils that helps explain the power the doge might exercise. Invariably by the time of his election he was a man of great experience. Giacomo Tiepolo, elected doge in 1229, for instance, had been governor of Crete and had served as the *podestà* (chief magistrate) in Constantinople after the Fourth Crusade, so he knew Venice's international concerns as few others. One of the objections made against the candidate Francesco Foscari, successful in the election of 1423, was that he was only fifty years old. Furthermore, a doge remained in power until death—unless forced to abdicate—while most other posts lasted only a year. Behind the façade of oligarchical rule, a shrewd doge could manipulate his smaller councils with their changing membership to his advantage. Leonardo Loredan (immortalised in Giovanni Bellini's famous portrait), doge between 1501 and 1521, and Andrea Gritti, doge between 1523 and 1538, make the point. It is noted that it was in Loredan and Gritti's reign that the major rebuilding around St. Mark's Square took place, and this suggests a consistent guiding hand behind the scenes.

Although the government of Venice appeared undemocratic, it proved impressively stable in comparison to the faction-ridden cities of the rest of northern Italy. The gradual loss of colonies to the Ottoman empire, wars on the *terraferma*, and the long economic decline were all absorbed without revolution. Yet by the 18th century the system appeared increasingly archaic and lacking in inner vitality. The Council of Ten was seen as repressive, and it was this image of decay from the centre that Napoleon was able to exploit when he forced the Republic to dissolve itself in 1797. Even so, the readiness with which it caved in to his demands made an ignominious end of so many centuries of greatness.

The election of a doge

The procedure given below is that as established in 1268, in order to prevent manipulation and pre-determination of the result by the more powerful candidates and their families.

1) Thirty men are chosen by lot from the Great Council;
2) Nine of the thirty are selected, again by lot;
3) These nine nominate forty electors, reduced by further lots to nine;
4) This second group of nine chooses forty-one electors;
5) Eleven of the forty-one are chosen by lot and and select a further forty-one;
6) These forty-one electors make the final decision.   C.F.

DOGE'S PALACE
(PRIMO PIANO NOBILE)

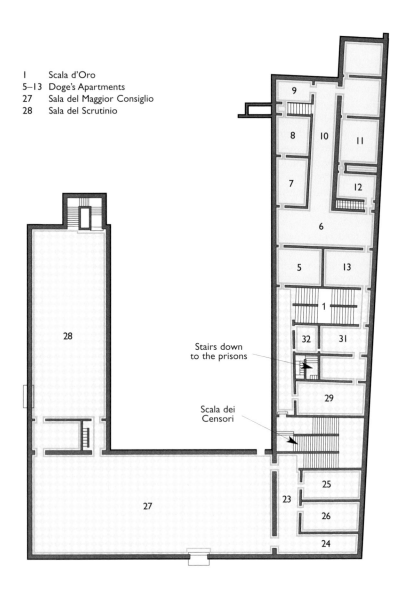

1   Scala d'Oro
5–13 Doge's Apartments
27   Sala del Maggior Consiglio
28   Sala del Scrutinio

Room 8 (Sala Erizzo): The room has a good ceiling and a fine chimneypiece (with the arms of Doge Francesco Erizzo, 1631–46). Three paintings attributed to Girolamo Bassano (son of the more famous painter Jacopo) are hung here.

Rooms 9–10: A passage leads to the **Sala degli Stucchi** (Room 9), named after its stuccoes carried out in the late 16th and early 17th centuries. The apse of the basilica can be seen from here. The gallery (Room 10) is known as the **Sala dei Filosofi**, since for a time it housed the paintings of philosophers by Tintoretto and Veronese now in the Libreria Marciana (*see p. 83*). Above the door on the right, which leads to the staircase which the doge used to reach the state council rooms directly from his living quarters, is a fresco of St Christopher, painted in three days in 1524 by Titian. There is a view of the Bacino di San Marco at his feet.

Rooms 11–13: The rooms off the other side of the Sala dei Filosofi were the private rooms of the doge. Beyond the **Sala Corner** (Room 11), with a fine gilded ceiling (and a view across the rooftops towards San Zaccaria), is the **Sala dei Ritratti** (Room 12), with a good fireplace by Antonio and Tullio Lombardo. The painted lunette displayed here of the *Dead Christ between the Madonna and St John the Evangelist* (and two kneeling saints) is almost certainly by the great Venetian painter Giovanni Bellini. Beyond the Sala dello Scudo (*see above*) is the **Sala degli Scudieri** (Room 13; named after the doge's private guards). Its two 16th-century portals have two large paintings of doges by Domenico Tintoretto, son of the great Jacopo.

SECONDO PIANO NOBILE

The Scala d'Oro continues up to the *secondo piano nobile*. The grand state rooms on this floor were restored after they were seriously damaged in fires in 1574 and 1577, and a new series of paintings glorifying Venice and her history was commissioned from the leading artists of the day on a scheme carefully worked out to include the most important military and naval victories of the Republic, as well as allegories of wise government, and scenes of the most significant events in the reigns of certain doges.

Room 15 (Atrio Quadrato): At the top of the stairs is the vestibule, where the fine wooden ceiling has a painting by Jacopo Tintoretto with *Justice presenting the Sword and the Scales to Doge Girolamo Priuli*.

Room 16 (Sala delle Quattro Porte): Named after its four doors (*quattro porte*), this was the magnificent waiting-room where ambassadors and heads of state would attend their turn to be received by officials of the Republic or by the doge himself. It was also the room through which the Venetian patricians would pass to and fro on their way to meetings of the most powerful organs of the Venetian State (the Collegio, Senate and Council of Ten) and so its grandeur and allegorical decorations

DOGE'S PALACE
(SECONDO PIANO NOBILE)

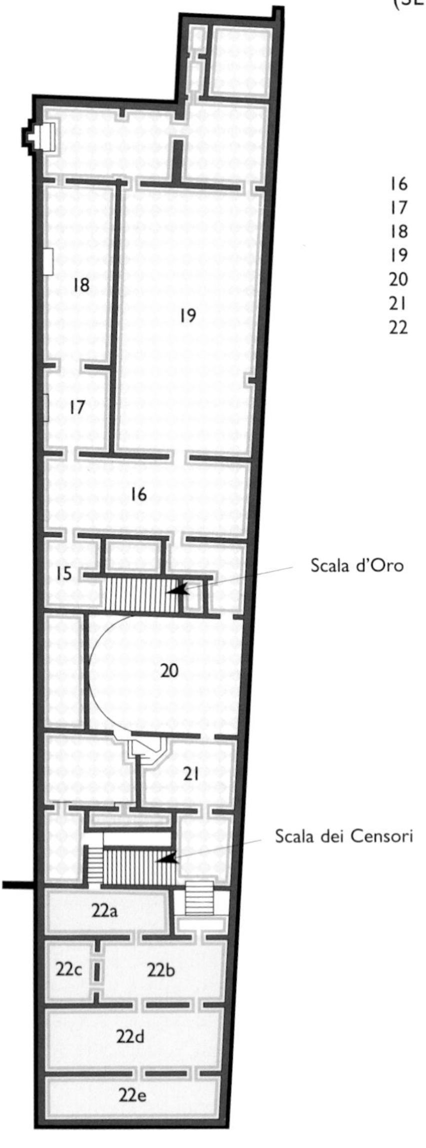

16	Sala delle Quattro Porte
17	Anticollegio
18	Sala del Collegio
19	Sala del Senato
20	Sala del Consiglio dei Dieci
21	Sala della Bussola
22	Sale d'Armi

18

19

17

16

15

Scala d'Oro

20

21

Scala dei Censori

22a

22c   22b

22d

22e

exulting the power of the Republic took on special significance. It was designed after the 1574 fire by no less an architect than Palladio, although the building work was carried out under the direction of the *proto* in charge of the palace at the time, Giovanni Antonio Rusconi. The very fine stucco work is by a little-known artist from Cremona, Giovanni Cambi, his only work in the city. The four doors are elaborately decorated with allegorical statues, some by Alessandro Vittoria.

The frescoes on the ceiling by Jacopo Tintoretto have unfortunately been spoilt over the centuries by restoration: the central rectangle depicts Jupiter presenting the territories on the Adriatic to Venice, and the two *tondi* show Venice surrounded by the Virtues, and Juno offering Venice a peacock and a shaft of lightning symbolising her grandeur. In the ovals are illustrations of Venetian territories on the Italian mainland. On the entrance wall (by the window) Giovanni Contarini painted *Doge Marino Grimani before the Madonna and Saints*: Grimani was the doge in office from 1595–1605, at the time this room was decorated. On the long wall is a painting commissioned earlier by Francesco Venier from Titian, in 1555: it apparently escaped damage in the fire since it had not yet been completed and was still in the painter's studio. It represents *Antonio Grimani Kneeling before the Faith* (Antonio was a predecessor of Marino Grimani, and a member of the same family; he was doge from 1521–23). The painting was completed around 1600 by Titian's nephew Marco Vecellio, but the parts attributed to Titian's own hand are the figure of St Mark, the helmeted warrior, and the

view of the Bacino. On the opposite wall are two paintings—one by the Caliari brothers Carletto and Gabriele (Paolo Veronese's sons), and the other by their contemporary Andrea Vicentino. (The important paintings at the other end of the room are described below since they cannot be seen from here.)

Room 17 (Anticollegio): This, another waiting-room which served as a vestibule to the Sala del Collegio, has a good 16th-century ceiling with a ruined fresco by Veronese, but it is the paintings on the walls which are of the greatest interest. Opposite the window is Veronese's very fine *Rape of Europa* next to *Jacob's Return to Canaan* by Jacopo Bassano. On the other walls are four splendid paintings by Jacopo Tintoretto, among his best works in the palace: *Vulcan's Forge*, *Mercury and the Graces*, *Bacchus and Ariadne* and *Minerva Dismissing Mars*. The fireplace by Vincenzo Scamozzi has a relief of the *Forge of Vulcan*, an early work by Tiziano Aspetti and Girolamo Campagna.

Room 18 (Sala del Collegio): It was here that the doge and the Collegio, or cabinet, deliberated and received ambassadors. The Collegio, whose 26 members were known as *savii* (from 'wise'), included the doge himself, six councillors (one for each *sestiere* of the city) and the three judges of the criminal tribunals. The room is a treasure house of art, and its decorations, carried out from 1575–81, survive almost intact, including the original rostrum and benches. The ceiling, by the little-known Francesco Bello, the finest in the palace, is doubly precious because of its wonderful paintings by Veronese. The most remarkable is that in the centre at the farther end: *Justice and Peace Offering the Sword, the Scales and the Olive-branch to Triumphant Venice*. The other panels have allegorical figures of Mars and Neptune, Faith and Religion.

The painting over the entrance, showing *Doge Andrea Gritti before the Virgin*, is by Jacopo Tintoretto, while above the throne Veronese painted *Doge Sebastiano Venier Offering Thanks to Christ for the Victory of Lepanto*. Facing the fireplace (another work by Campagna) are three more magnificent paintings by Jacopo Tintoretto: *Marriage of St Catherine*, *Doge Niccolò da Ponte Invoking the Virgin*, and *Doge Alvise Mocenigo Adoring Christ*.

Room 19 (Sala del Senato): This was where the Senate, or legislative body of the Republic, sat. The senators were also called *pregadi* because, when elected, they were formally 'begged' or 'invited' by the doge to take up their role. Their number was increased from 60 to 120, and they were elected from among the patricians by the Great Council, holding office for just one year. At the centre of the political life of the Republic, they also nominated magistrates, ambassadors, bishops and the patriarch. They treated with foreign courts, and only they could take the grave decision to declare war.

Designed by Antonio da Ponte, the room has a fine ceiling (1581), with *Venice Exalted among the Gods*, by Jacopo Tintoretto, in the central panel. Tintoretto also painted the *Descent from the Cross*, with doges Pietro Lando and Marcantonio Trevisan in adoration, over

the throne. The prolific painter Palma Giovane, who was overshadowed by his contemporaries Veronese and Tintoretto, but who carried out some of his best works for the Doge's Palace, painted the three works on the left wall: *Venice Receiving the Homage of Subject Cities Presented by Doge Francesco Venier*, *Doge Pasquale Cicogna in Prayer*, and an *Allegory of the League of Cambrai*, as well as *Doges Lorenzo and Girolamo Priuli Praying to Christ* on the end wall. Tintoretto painted *Doge Pietro Loredan Praying to the Virgin*, also on the left wall.

Room 16, further end (Sala delle Quattro Porte): Here is exhibited (on an easel) Giambattista Tiepolo's great painting of *Venice Receiving the Homage of Neptune* (it has been removed from above the windows so that it is easier to see, and replaced there by a photograph). This is the only painting by Tiepolo in the palace, and it was commissioned around 1756 to substitute a painting by Tintoretto which had deteriorated. An allegory of the Venetian state, it shows a splendid female figure personifying Venice, wearing the ducal ermine robe and dominating both the submissive figure of Neptune, who offers her a cornucopia full of gold, pearls and coral, and the tame lion of St Mark. Painted only 40 years before the fall of the Republic, this is Tiepolo's only painting which alludes directly to the glory of the Venetian state, although the air of slightly decadent opulence portrayed seems perhaps to foreshadow the end.

The paintings on the walls include *Venice under Gattamelata Conquering Verona* by Giovanni Contarini, and *Doge*

Marino Grimani Receiving Gifts from Persian Ambassadors by Veronese's son Gabriele Caliari. This last records the visit of a delegation headed by Fethi Bey from Shah 'Abbas the Great of Persia in 1603, which remained memorable because of the richness of the fabrics and carpets (clearly depicted here) presented to the doge.

Room 20 (Sala del Consiglio dei Dieci): A corridor (with a view of the upper façade of San Zaccaria) leads into the seat of the Council of Ten. This body was appointed after the rebellion in 1310 of Bajamonte Tiepolo against Doge Pietro Gradenigo (*see box*). As a court which tried political crimes, the *consiglio* became a notoriously severe organ of government, particularly efficient in times of crisis. It was this council which ordered the execution of Doge Marin Falier in 1355, because he had tried to turn his elective office into a despotic seigniory. Judges held office for one year only, and were ineligible for re-election in the succeeding year.

BAJAMONTE TIEPOLO'S CONSPIRACY

After the famous *Serrata del Maggior Consiglio* (*see p. 96*) in 1297, which restricted those eligible for election to the Great Council and effectively changed the nature of the government of the Republic from a 'democracy' to an oligarchy, a serious rebellion was organised, in 1310, against the doge responsible (Pietro Gradenigo). This was led by Bajamonte Tiepolo with the aid of some members of the wealthy Querini family and Badoero Badoer, at the head of a fleet in the lagoon. They planned to join forces in Piazza San Marco to storm the Doge's Palace from three directions, and the story is told that as Tiepolo and his horsemen rode from the Rialto into the piazza, his standard-bearer was killed by a mortar (as in pestle and mortar) which an old lady who was watching the scene let fall (apparently by accident) from a window-sill (*see also p. 110*). This contretemps discouraged the conspirators from proceeding, although unlike Querini, who was killed in a street battle, and Badoer, who was captured and condemned to death, Tiepolo managed to escape and take refuge in his house across the Grand Canal, holding out until he had won the concession of an unusually brief exile of just four years as punishment for his misconduct. Although the uprising was quickly put down, the Great Council set up a special tribunal to investigate the conspiracy, and this body survived as the dreaded Council of Ten, which from that time onwards was on the look out to try offenders of similar crimes against the state. To this day historians discuss the significance of the Tiepolo rebellion, uncertain if the motives behind it were, indeed, to save the government of the Republic from becoming too remote from the people, or whether merely personal interests were at stake, since it is probably significant that all the leaders were from important Venetian families.

The ceiling contains more paintings by Veronese, notably, in the far right-hand corner (as you stand with your back to the windows), an *Old Man in Eastern Costume with a Young Woman*. The panel by him in the centre of the left-hand side, showing *Juno Offering Gifts to Venice*, was seized by Napoleon and taken to Brussels in 1797, and only returned to Venice in 1920—the original of the oval ceiling painting (*Jupiter Fulminating the Vices*), which was removed to Paris by Napoleon in the same year, was never returned (it is now in the Louvre). On the right wall (facing the entrance): *The Meeting between Pope Alexander III and Doge Ziani*, by the brothers Francesco and Leandro Bassano; on the end wall: *Adoration of the Magi*, by Aliense; and on the left wall: *Pope Clement VII and the Emperor Charles V*, by Marco Vecellio, painted in 1529 to celebrate the peace declared between pope and emperor at Bologna.

Rom 21 (Sala della Bussola): The room takes its name from the walnut-wood screen which gives access to the Sala dei Tre Capi and the prisons. The original ceiling painting by Veronese of *St Mark in Glory Crowning the Theological Virtues* was also stolen by Napoleon and is now in the Louvre. On the right of the farther door is a *Bocca di Leone* (or 'mouth of truth'), a box in which secret denunciations were placed (posted from the outside). From the end of the 16th or beginning of the 17th century a number of these were installed in various rooms of the palace (before then the practice had been to drop notes on the floor or to give them to foreigners to deliver). The box could only be opened in the pres-

ence of all three head magistrates (*tre capi*) of the Council of Ten. There were notoriously severe punishments for false denunciations, and they were disregarded if anonymous. There are more wall paintings here by Vecellio and Aliense. On the right is the Sala dei Tre Capi del Consiglio dei Dieci, only open on the guided *Itinerari Segreti* (*see p. 108*).

Room 22 (Sale d'Armi del Consiglio dei Dieci): From the landing outside the Sala della Bussola is the approach upstairs (right) to the Sale d'Armi del Consiglio dei Dieci, the Council of Ten's private armoury, in which the state arms and armour were stored until the fall of the Republic. **Room 22a** displays various suits of armour, including one traditionally supposed to have belonged to the *condottiere* and protector of the Venetian Republic, Gattamelata; and one belonging to a page, found on the field of Marignano (1515). In a case is a display of 16th–17th-century helmets (northern Italian); a unique visored helmet of the 14th century, shaped like a bird's beak and made of a single piece; and tournament armour (c. 1510–20). A long case contains swords (the earliest dating from the 15th century), and halberds made by Giovanni Maria Bergamini (Venice, c. 1620–25). Crossbows are hung on the walls.

The huge Turkish standard on the ceiling of **Room 22b** (removed for restoration) is a trophy from the Battle of Lepanto. In a niche is a suit of armour which belonged to Henri IV of France, presented by him to the *Serenissima* in 1603. This was apparently a gift to Venice in gratitude for her support of the king in his far-sighted plan (after he had issued the Edict of Nantes in 1598 in an attempt to end the civil wars of religion in France) to establish some sort of universal Christian republic in Europe. However, hopes of this vanished when he was assassinated in 1610. Displayed here are lances, swords, falchions (short, sickle-shaped swords), suits of armour, Persian arms, horses' battle frontlets (15th–16th century) and painted shields.

Room 22c was formerly a prison reserved for important prisoners. It has another fine display of shields and swords. **Room 22d**, with the bust of Doge Morosini, has a superb collection of swords, lances and shields beautifully displayed in old show-cases. In the centre are two early quick-firing guns, one with 20 barrels, the other with a revolver mechanism, a fuse-case holding 106 fuses made of perforated and embossed copper, signed by Giovanni Antonio Comino, and a culverin (an early type of cannon) complete with its carriage and fittings (?German, 16th century). The lantern belonged to a dismantled Turkish galleon. **Room 22e** has a superb view of the Bacino and island of San Giorgio Maggiore. In the cases are 16th–17th-century pistols; muskets and arquebuses; various instruments of torture and a 16th-century cuirass (breastplate).

PRIMO PIANO NOBILE

South and west wings (Rooms 23–28)

Steps descend from the Sala d'Armi to the Scala dei Censori, which takes you back to the first floor.

Room 23 (Andito del Maggior Consiglio): This is the corridor where the patricians would gather during intervals in the session of the Great Council. It has a good 16th-century ceiling and works by Tintoretto's son, Domenico.

Room 25 (Sala della Quarantia Civil Vecchia): The tribunal of 40 members met here to try civil cases. A fragment of mural painting has been revealed behind the panelling.

Room 26 (Sala del Guariento): This room contains the remains of a huge fresco of the *Coronation of the Virgin* by Guariento (1365–67), which used to adorn the Sala del Maggior Consiglio. Guariento had been chosen for this exceptionally important commission since he was considered the best artist at work in the Veneto at the time, but he is today known almost exclusively for his works in Padua. This famous fresco, ruined by the fire of 1577, was discovered in 1903 beneath Tintoretto's painting. Today it is one of the very earliest painted works to have survived in the palace.

Room 24 (Liagò): In this veranda are exhibited three statues removed from the Arco Foscari in the courtyard (*described on p. 94*): *Adam* and *Eve*, the masterpieces of Antonio Rizzo (c. 1470), and *Francesco Maria I della Rovere*, Duke of Urbino and a *condottiere* who served the Venetian Republic, by Giovanni Bandini.

Room 27 (Sala del Maggior Consiglio): This vast hall was the seat of the governing body of the Republic. It was first built on this scale in 1340, and was large enough to hold the entire assembly of Venetian patricians. Here laws were ratified and the highest officials of the Republic were elected.

The size of the hall is exceptional: it is 52m long, 24m wide and 11m high. There is a fine view from the balcony over the Bacino di San Marco. The 14th–15th-century frescoes by leading artists of the time and the magnificent ceiling were all destroyed in the disastrous fire of 1577, but the following year the best known Venetian artists of the day were commissioned to begin the work of replacing them with painted panels—a task which was only completed in 1595. On the entrance wall is Domenico Tintoretto's *Paradise*, carried out with the help of assistants between 1588 and 1592. It is a painting crowded with figures on a huge scale (7m by 24m), and is Domenico's most important work. The commission originally went to his father, the celebrated Jacopo, but because of his advanced age, was executed by Domenico.

The magnificent ceiling is divided into 35 compartments, but the most important paintings are in the three central panels. Nearest the throne is *Venice Surrounded by Gods and Crowned by Victory* (*Apotheosis of Venice*), a masterpiece of light and colour by Veronese (painted just before he died in 1588). The central panel, *Venice Surrounded by Gods Gives an Olive-branch to Doge Niccolò da Ponte*, is by Jacopo Tintoretto. At the far end is *Venice Welcoming the Conquered Nations around her Throne* by Palma Giovane, who here takes a worthy place beside his two far more famous and skilled contemporaries.

These three artists also worked on some of the large historical canvases around the walls, recording important events in the history of the Republic: on the wall facing the courtyard the 12th-century battles between Church and Empire, culminating in peace proclaimed by Venice in 1175, are commemorated. A notable example is the *Meeting in Venice between Barbarossa and Pope Alexander III in 1177*. On the wall towards the Bacino are the events of the Fourth Crusade of 1204, including Domenico Tintoretto's *Capture and Sack of Constantinople*. On the wall opposite the throne, Veronese's *Triumph of Doge Contarini after the Battle of Chioggia*, commemorating Venetian victory over the Genoese in 1379. Other Venetian artists who had also worked in other rooms of the palace (including the Caliari brothers, the Bassano, Andrea Vicentino, Federico Zuccari, Giulio del Moro and Aliense) collaborated on these series.

The frieze of the first 76 doges (from Obelario degli Antenori, c. 804, to Francesco Venier, d. 1556) begins in the middle of the wall overlooking the courtyard and runs left to right. It is also the work of Domenico Tintoretto and assistants. The space blacked in on the wall overlooking the Piazzetta takes the place of the portrait of Marin Falier: an inscription records his execution for treason in 1355 after his famous conspiracy against the state. The frieze is continued in the Sala dello Scrutinio.

Room 28 (Sala dello Scrutinio): The last door on the right admits to the **Sala**

della Quarantia Civil Nuova, used by the high court of 40 magistrates, set up in 1492 to act in civil cases for Venetian citizens in the new territories on the *terraferma*. The **Sala dello Scrutinio** itself was used after 1532 to record the votes cast in the Sala del Maggior Consiglio for the new doge and other officials of the Republic. On the walls are paintings carried out between 1578 and 1615 of victorious Venetian battles throughout the history of the Republic, including the *Battle of Lepanto* by Andrea Vicentino. The *Last Judgement* is by Palma Giovane. The triumphal arch was erected by Antonio Gaspari in 1694, in honour of Francesco Morosini. In the corridor outside there are two plaques: one records Daniele Manin's resistance to the Austrians in 1849, and the other the plebiscite of 1866 when the inhabitants of Venice (together with those of the Veneto and Mantua) voted overwhelmingly in favour of joining the Kingdom of Italy.

Rooms 29–31: A small door to the left of the throne in the Sala del Maggior Consiglio leads out to the Scala dei Censori and a loggia overlooking the courtyard and into the **Sala del Quarantia Criminale** (Room 29), seat of a criminal tribunal. The **Sala al Magistrato alle Legge** (Room 31) contains important Flemish works in a totally different style from the paintings in the rest of the palace. The famous painter Hieronymus Bosch is represented with *Paradise* and *Hell* (which formerly flanked a *Last Judgement* which has been lost) and a triptych of hermits, with a superb landscape. These were probably acquired in Antwerp in Bosch's lifetime by Cardinal Domenico Grimani, since they are documented in his collection by 1521. There is also a painting here by Bosch's contemporary and fellow-countryman Herri met de Bles, who was known in Italy—where he worked at the end of his life—as 'Il Civetta', since his works always include an owl (*civetta*). The painting by another Flemish artist of this time, Quentin Metsys, of the *Derision of Christ* (or *Ecce Homo*) may also have belonged to Cardinal Grimani. It is known to have been in Venice by the end of the 16th century and has been kept in the palace since 1664. From the adjoining room (Room 32) stairs lead down.

The prisons

The stairs from the first floor bring you out to a prison corridor and the passage across the Bridge of Sighs, a flying bridge built across the Rio di Palazzo to allow the Inquisitors of State direct access to the new prisons on the other side of the canal from the palace law courts. At the end of the corridor beyond the bridge there is a choice of two itineraries: the one on the right is shorter and passes a few prison cells before returning across the Bridge of Sighs.

Otherwise you can continue downstairs to visit the 'new' prisons, built between 1560 and 1614 to replace the old ones (known as the '*Pozzi*'), 18 dark dungeons on the two lowest storeys of the palace (*not at present open to the public*), which were reserved for the most dangerous criminals. Even the lowest of them, however, was above ground level and they were less terrible than many other medieval prisons.

The new prisons were begun by Giovanni Antonio Rusconi (1560), continued by Antonio da Ponte (1589), and completed by Antonio and Tommaso Contino (1614). Their façade overlooks the Riva degli Schiavoni. A labyrinth of corridors passes numerous prison cells to emerge in a grim courtyard with a well surrounded by barred windows. On the opposite side of the courtyard, stairs lead back up to a room with a display of Venetian ceramics found in the 20th century (many of them during excavations in the 1990s) from various periods (those from San Lorenzo date from the 9th century; those from San Francesco del Deserto from the 14th century, and those found when the Campanile of St Mark's collapsed from the 15th century). Beyond a series of more corridors and cells (some with graffiti made by the prisoners) the Bridge of Sighs is recrossed.

Rooms used by minor officials

The exit from the Doge's Palace is through some rooms of the **Avogaria** on the mezzanine floor, used by a branch of the judiciary elected as public prosecutors in criminal trials, and who functioned as supervisors during council meetings to safeguard the principle of legality. There is a good view of the side of the new prisons on the canal. The **Sala dei Censori** (Room 35) has portraits by Domenico Tintoretto of censors (an office instituted in 1517 to protect the state's public institutions and control electoral procedures). The **Sala dei Notai** (Room 36) has similar portraits of advocates and notaries by Leandro Bassano.

The **Sala dello Scrigno** (Room 37) was where the 'Golden Book' (*Libro d'Oro*) was kept which registered the baptism of all patricians to give a record of those eligible as members of the Great Council. The officials who were responsible for recruiting the oarsmen needed to man Venice's warships deliberated in the **Sala della Milizia da Mar** (Room 38). They were first called to office in 1571 to fit out the great fleet which set sail for the Battle of Lepanto. As it turned out, this great sea battle was the last in history to be fought with galleys manned by oarsmen.

The exit is along the loggia past the top of the Scala dei Giganti to the Scala dei Senatori, which descends to the Cortile dei Senatori, a charming Renaissance work by Spavento and Scarpagnino. From here there is a fine view of the exterior of St Mark's, with the old brickwork visible. The original statue of St Theodore with his dragon, which was set up on one of the columns in the Piazzetta in 1329, is kept beneath the portico. The head is a Hellenistic portrait, the torso is Roman and dates from the period of Hadrian, and the arms, legs, shield and dragon were made by an early 14th-century Venetian sculptor.

The *Itinerari Segreti*

The *Itinerari Segreti*, literally 'secret tours', are guided tours of the lesser-known parts of the palace. The guide is particularly well informed, and the tour lasts about an hour and a half. It is highly recommended, as it gives a unique insight into the way the Republic was run. The rooms have been well restored where necessary and furnished with period furniture (*for admission, see p. 87*).

From the Atrio Quadrato (Room 29) a door gives access to the tiny administrative offices used by the bureaucrats of the Republic. These were constructed in wood, making optimum use of the space available. Often two floors have been created in one storey of the building.

The **Ducal Chancellery** is particularly well lit since this was where documents were transcribed. It retains its original 18th-century furnishings and is decorated with the coats of arms of all the Chancellors from 1268 onwards. The Grand Chancellor was responsible for keeping all the government records and registering the decisions made by the various councils of state. He was elected for life from the middle classes (he could not be a patrician) and he held an extremely important position within the hierarchy of state officials.

The area of the law courts and judiciary offices of the Council of Ten includes the macabre **Torture Room** (with the four cells for prisoners who had to wait their turn). The room reserved for the three leading magistrates of the Council of Ten (the **Sala dei Tre Capi del Consiglio dei Dieci**) is, instead, highly decorated. The chimney-piece is by Jacopo Sansovino with statues by Danese Cattaneo and Pietro da Salò, and the ceiling paintings by Paolo Veronese and Giovanni Battista Zelotti. It also has a lovely floor. The *Descent from the Cross*, derived from Antonello da Messina's *Pietà* in the Museo Correr (*see p. 78*), is by the great painter's nephew Antonello da Saliba. The little **Sala dei Tre Inquisitori** was used by the three members of the special commission of enquiry used by the Council of Ten. These officials also examined the conduct of each doge after his death. The ceiling has a painting (in excellent condition) of the *Return of the Prodigal Son* by Jacopo Tintoretto. A *Madonna and Child* by Boccaccio Boccaccino has been hung here.

From the Sala dei Tre Capi del Consiglio dei Dieci a staircase leads up to the top floor and the seven prison cells called the **Piombi**, so named because of their position beneath the leaden roof. They were built in wood, and have been reconstructed. Prisoners were only kept here for brief periods. One of them was Casanova, and his cell is shown. Giacomo Casanova was arrested in 1755 and sentenced to five years' imprisonment. The charges against him concerned his lifestyle: he was accused of being a mason, a gambler and a cheat, of frequenting people from every walk of life, of practising alchemy and magic, of showing little respect for Christians, and of writing irreverent and satirical verse and reading it in public. He escaped in 1756, with his fellow inmate, Father Marino Balbi, via the roof. His colourful description of the miseries he suffered here and his courageous escape in *Storia della mia fuga dalle prigioni della Repubblica di Venezia che si chiamono Piombi* ('Story of my Flight from the Prisons of the Venetian Republic which are called the Piombi') was published in 1788 and widely acclaimed throughout Europe. Silvio Pellico later described his much grimmer experiences, during his imprisonment here by the Austrians in 1822, in *Le Mie Prigioni*.

The remarkable structure of the great **roof of the Sala del Maggior Consiglio**, built with huge wooden beams in 1577, can also be seen here. A small collection of sculptural fragments includes a *Bocca di Leone* for posting denunciations (*see p. 104*), found in the palace. At the end of the tour the kitchens are sometimes shown.

THE MERCERIA

Map p. 407, E2–D1

The Merceria, a narrow calle, sometimes also called in Venetian dialect *Marziaria*, is the shortest route from Piazza San Marco to the Rialto. Its name comes from *merce* (goods), since from earliest days most of the shops in the city were concentrated here. As the busiest thoroughfare of the city, it is always crowded with both Venetians and tourists. On its winding course it changes name five times: Merceria dell'Orologio, Merceria di San Zulian, Merceria del Capitello, Merceria di San Salvador, and Merceria Due Aprile; and passes some interesting churches, notably San Giuliano, with a fine 16th-century façade and interior (*see below*) and San Salvatore, with a Renaissance interior and two paintings by Titian (*see p. 112*).

A passage leads out of Piazza San Marco under the Torre dell'Orologio. Just beyond the arch of the clock tower, above the Sottoportego del Cappello on the left, a relief of an old woman at a window was set up in 1841 to record a fatal incident during Bajamonte Tiepolo's rebellion against the Venetian Republic (*see p. 103*).

San Giuliano

Map p. 407, E1. Open 8.45–12 & 4–6.30.
At the first bend in the Merceria stands the church of San Giuliano (San Zulian), a church rebuilt in 1553 by Jacopo Sansovino (and completed after his death by Alessandro Vittoria). A careful restoration programme was carried out in 1990–98, financed by the Venice in Peril Fund. The dedication to Julian the Hospitaller, a legendary saint popular in the Middle Ages, remains something of a mystery, even though he was the patron of boatmen. The façade, well-suited to this unusually cramped site, bears a seated bronze statue, attributed to Vittoria, of Tommaso Rangone, the wealthy physician and scholar from Ravenna who paid for the rebuilding of the church, and who is buried in the chancel. Between the columns on the façade are inscriptions in Greek and Hebrew praising Rangone's munificence and learning.

The charming interior has a simple rectangular plan with two side chapels flanking the sanctuary. The statues of St Catherine of Alexandria and Daniel on the third south altar are also by Alessandro Vittoria. In 1582 a much less well-known contemporary of Vittoria's, Francesco Smeraldi, carried out the good stuccoes in the vault of the chapel of the Scuola del Santissimo Sacramento (left of the sanctuary)—this belonged to the confraternity whose main concern was the burial of the dead. On the altar is a relief of the *Pietà* by Girolamo Campagna, who was active in Venice at the same time as Vittoria. The high altar was erected in 1667 by Giuseppe Sardi: it encloses a *Coronation of the Virgin with three Saints* by Girolamo da Santacroce, painted more than a century earlier. On the sanctuary walls hang two huge paintings by Antonio Zanchi, who died in the early 18th century. The ceiling (1585) has a painting of *St Julian in Glory* by Palma Giovane and assistants: he also painted the *Assumption* on the second south altar.

Other paintings in the church include a *Pietà*, with three saints below, by Paolo Veronese (first south altar); *St Jerome* by Leandro Bassano (second south altar); and a

Madonna Enthroned with Saints by Boccaccio Boccaccino (first north altar). The painting on the west wall by Sante Peranda shows St Roch curing the plague-stricken in one of the isolation hospitals (*lazzaretti*) which existed in the Venetian lagoon. The organ is one of the first works by the great organ-maker from the Veneto, Gaetano Callido (1764).

The Armenian district

From the Merceria in front of the church a short detour can be made down Calle Fiubera which leads across a bridge: the first calle on the right, Calle dei Armeni, leads to the lovely old Sottoportico degli Armeni, where there is the entrance to the incon-spicuous little church of **Santa Croce degli Armeni** (*open Sun and holidays at 11 for a service in Armenian*). The church dates from 1496 and was rebuilt in the 17th century, and the little cupola with a lantern and small bell-tower can be seen on the rio. It con-tains 17th-century paintings by Andrea Celesti, Gregorio Lazzarini, Alberto Calvetti and Pietro Liberi. The Armenian community in Venice (*see also p. 339*) lived in this charming district from the late 12th century onwards, and they were allowed to build a small *fondaco* on the Rio dei Ferai. The calle ends on Rio Terrà de le Colonne, named after its portico with wooden eaves and stone columns. In the courtyard of the nearby police station there is a delightful well-head in imitation basket-work.

Ridotto Venier

The Merceria continues from San Giuliano (signposted for the Rialto) across Ponte dei Barettari, one of the widest in the city, rebuilt in 1771 with an Istrian stone balustrade. To the right beneath the portico (no. 4939) is the entrance to the Ridotto Venier, famous in the 18th century as the meeting place of elegant Venetian society, when it was the home of Elena, wife of the Procurator Federico Venier. The delightful small rooms preserve their original stuccoes and frescoes intact. Now the seat of the Associazione Italo-Francese, it is sometimes open for exhibitions.

SAN SALVATORE
Map p. 407, D1

Open 9–12 & 3 or 4–7; Sun and holidays 9–12.30 & 5–7.30.

Campo San Salvatore was laid out in the mid-17th century, when the former Scuola di San Teodoro was given its façade by Giuseppe Sardi. The column outside the church commemorates Daniele Manin's defence of Venice against Austrian rule in 1848–49 (*see p. 124*). The church (also called San Salvador) was rebuilt in the early 16th century, and the Baroque façade was added in 1663, also following a design by Giuseppe Sardi. The plan of the interior, with its five domes and barrel vaults, is one of the best examples in Venice of the way in which the problems of light and con-struction were solved at the height of the Renaissance. It is the combined work of Giorgio Spavento, also known for his work on the Doge's Palace and the Fondaco dei Tedeschi, and Tullio Lombardo, who took over after Spavento's death in 1509. Vincenzo Scamozzi carefully completed the building at the end of the century.

The church contains two splendid works by the great Venetian artist Titian—probably both painted in the 1560s—a beautiful *Annunciation* on the third south altar, and a *Transfiguration* over the high altar. In the former, the Madonna's unusual gesture is apparently derived from a Greek relief which Titian had seen in Venice in the Grimani collection (*see p. 80*), but it is the majestic figure of the annunciatory angel which dominates the scene. The silver reredos which formerly covered Titian's *Transfiguration* is only shown on special religious festivals; it is a masterpiece of Venetian goldsmiths' work of the 14th century. To make it easy to transport, it was made so that the silver gilt panels could be folded up; the upper and lower rows of sculpture are later additions.

Beneath the floor here is the tomb of a merchant with worn frescoes attributed to Francesco Vecellio, Titian's brother: he also painted the doors of the church organ, one of which has another representation of the *Transfiguration*, a great deal less dramatic than the scene painted by his more skilful brother. But it was probably Francesco who had the original idea of decorating the sacristy (*shown on request*) with a delicate pattern of flowers and birds, very unusual for Venice (recently restored).

Jacopo Sansovino carried out a number of works in the church: he designed the organ and several of the side altars (including that which bears Titian's *Annunciation*), and, when nearly 80 years old, he sculpted the two statues of *Charity* and *Hope* for the funerary monument in the south aisle of Doge Francesco Venier, who died in 1556. The figure of *Hope* is particularly beautiful. The doge is shown lying in gilded robes beneath a lunette of the *Pietà* (where he is also present). The grand monument is resplendent with coloured marbles, and even a mottled slab was chosen to bear the inscription. This doge, although apparantly a learned man, is chiefly remembered for his tomb here, since he had an uneventful reign of just two years.

The tomb of his successors, the brothers Lorenzo and Girolamo Priuli, is also in the nave—a dark classical monument by the little-known architect Cesare Franco. The other huge monument in the nave is that of Andrea Dolfin, who was a procurator of St Mark's. It is the work of Giulio del Moro (1602), and has busts of Dolfin and his wife by Girolamo Campagna, who also sculpted the *Madonna and Child* on the adjacent altar.

In the south transept, by another little-known architect, Bernardino Contino, is the tomb of Caterina Cornaro (or Corner), who died in 1510. Born in Venice, she was married to the king of Cyprus, and as his widow she inherited the island in 1474. The Republic persuaded Caterina to cede her kingdom to Venice in 1489, and in return they presented her with the town of Asolo in the Veneto, where she presided over a court frequented by artists and men of learning, including Pietro Bembo (*see p. 196*).

The third altar in the north aisle was designed by Alessandro Vittoria, with statues of St Roch and St Sebastian. The work of two of Sansovino's collaborators can be seen close by—the statuette of St Jerome (beneath the organ) by Danese Cattaneo (1530), and the statue of St Jerome on the second altar by Tommaso Lombardo.

In the chapel to the left of the sanctuary the painting of the *Supper at Emmaus* has had various attributions, including Carpaccio. It was commissioned by Girolamo

Priuli, who is buried in the church, and whose portrait is included (shown in black sitting next to Christ). It is now thought that the drawing is by Giovanni Bellini (who made another painting of the same subject) but it was probably painted by his workshop.

The **former monastery** with its two cloisters (entered from the campo outside) was used as a barracks until it was acquired by Italy's telephone company in 1925. They have restored it and installed computers in the two cloisters, which have displays on Venetian history (there is also a free internet café off the second cloister). On request visitors are also shown the splendid large refectory (used for conferences), entered through a marble portal which has a very fine, if damaged, vault decorated by Fermo Ghisoni, a pupil of Giulio Romano, in the early 16th century.

CAMPO SAN BARTOLOMEO
Map p. 402, B4–B3

Campo San Bartolomeo, the crowded business centre of Venice, stands at the crossroads of the city. The church of **San Bartolomeo** (*open Tues, Thur, Sat 10–12, and Wed and Fri pm for services*), usually now called San Bortolo, in the Venetian dialect, stands on the San Marco side of the Rialto Bridge (*for a description of the Rialto, see p. 191*). Its inconspicuous entrance is on Salizzada Pio X. This was formerly the church of the German community in Venice (whose warehouses were the great Fondaco dei Tedeschi), and Dürer painted his famous *Madonna of the Rosary* (now in Prague) for the church when he was in the city in 1506. He made two visits to Venice, the first in 1494–95 and the second in 1505–07, and from his letters we know that he was struck by the great respect shown to him and other artists at work here at that time. His works of the period clearly show the influence of Paolo Veneziano and Giovanni Bellini. The dark little church, rebuilt in 1723 by Giovanni Scalfarotto, is currently being restored. It contains an organ made by Callido in 1775 and (on the first south altar) a Crucifix attributed to Andrea Brustolon flanked by mourning figures by Meyring. At the foot of the campanile outside, the grotesque mask is perhaps the most amusing of all of such faces to be found in Venice, mostly on *campanili*.

Fondaco dei Tedeschi
In the centre of Campo San Bartolomeo stands a statue of Goldoni, the dramatist of Venetian life, in a tricorn hat and flowing frock coat looking as though he himself is on his way to the theatre. It is the work of Antonio dal Zotto (1883). The salizzada behind the statue skirts the back of the huge Fondaco dei Tedeschi, with its barred first-floor windows. This was the most important of the trading centres on the Grand Canal, leased by the Venetians to foreign (literally, 'German') merchants. By the mid-13th century the Germans, Austrians, Bohemians and Hungarians had their warehouses, shops, offices and lodgings here. The severe commercial building, devoid of marble or carved decorations, was reconstructed after the fire of 1505 by Giorgio

Spavento and completed by Scarpagnino from the designs of Girolamo Tedesco (himself a German). Giorgione was commissioned to fresco the main façade, and Titian the side façade (on Calle del Fontego): the frescoes have entirely disappeared, although fragments survive in the Ca' d'Oro and Gallerie dell'Accademia. The building now serves as Venice's central post office.

The Ponte dell'Olio (rebuilt in 1899), with its marble columns and iron balustrade, marks the boundary between the *sestiere* of San Marco and that of Cannaregio (*described on p. 225ff*). From the bridge there are views (left), across the Grand Canal, to the corner of Palazzo dei Camerlenghi, the brick tower of San Giacomo, and the beginning of the Rialto markets, all in the *sestiere* of San Polo (*described on p. 191ff*).

THE FENICE & SANTA MARIA DEL GIGLIO
Map p. 406, C2–C3

Calle dell'Ascension

Beyond the colonnade at the end of Piazza San Marco, beneath the Ala Napoleonica, is a wide calle. Turning right, you come, at the end, to Calle Salvadego, which leads to the **Bacino Orseolo**, an unexpected sight since this is a circular pool and is usually filled with moored gondolas. The Hotel Cavalletto e Doge Orseolo here is on the site of the Ospizio delle Orsoline, founded as a hospice for pilgrims in 977 by Doge Pietro Orseolo II.

Calle Seconda dell'Ascension (straight ahead as you come through the arch under the Ala Napoleonica) continues past Calle Vallaresso, which leads down (past Harry's Bar; *see p. 364*) to the San Marco landing-stage on the Grand Canal. At no. 1332, with tall windows on the *piano nobile*, is the **Ridotto**. Now part of the Hotel Monaco Grand Canal, the building was once a famous gambling house opened with the approval of the Council of Ten in 1638, where ladies were also welcome. It was in an annexe (or *ridotto*) of Marco Dandolo's house, attached to the private theatre of San Moisè. There were two 'sitting out' rooms where savouries and wine as well as coffee, hot chocolate and tea were served, and ten gaming rooms where the croupier was always a patrician. If you were not a nobleman you had to be masked. Francesco Guardi's painting, which shows the crowded interior around 1745, is preserved in Room XVI of the Ca' Rezzonico (*see p. 182*). Although the Ridotto was enlarged in 1768 and another gambling house opened next to the San Cassian theatre, both were closed by order of the Great Council in 1774 in an attempt to heal the decadence in Venetian society. Nevertheless, gambling continued in private houses throughout the city (such as the Ridotto Venier; *see p. 111*), and Venice today has one of the few official casinos in Italy.

San Moisè

Map p. 407, D2. Open 9.30–12 & 3–6.30.

The Salizzada San Moisè leads to the campo and church of the same name. Built by the brother of the priest of the church, Alessandro Tremignon (1668), the Baroque façade has good relief sculpture (the camels are particularly striking) but the design is over-elaborate and the overall effect unpleasing.

One of the white marble paving stones just inside the entrance of the church has an inscription which marks the grave—transferred from the church of San Gemignano in 1808—of the Scottish financier John Law (*see box*).

JOHN LAW & HIS 'BUBBLE'

John Law (1671–1729) was a speculator who recognised the advantages in credit operations and paper currency, and had the idea of a national bank. After capturing the imagination of Philip, Duke of Orléans, the ineffectual regent of France, he opened a private bank in Paris in 1716. His famous 'Mississippi Scheme' to reclaim and settle Louisiana in the lower Mississippi valley was at first a spectacular success, but soon suffered all the usual defects of a boom economy, since the rise in the value of the company stocks led to inflation, panic, and its sudden collapse in 1720. This phenomenon of the 'bursting of the bubble' (which also hit the similar, more famous 'South Sea Bubble' scheme in the same decade), has ever since been the characteristic of certain speculative financial operations. However, some economists consider Law's pioneering financial operation to have had important consequences (apart from the increase in the private fortunes of those who managed to sell out in time), such as the development of shipping and the beginning of the colonisation of Louisiana. For Law, however, the bankruptcy he caused to numerous investors meant he had to flee France and England and—having also lost all his own money—he ended his life in Venice.

The interior of the church is interesting for its 17th- and 18th-century paintings. On either side of the organ by Gaetano Callido (1801) are two dramatic 18th-century works: a *Crucifixion* by Girolamo Brusaferro, and the *Stoning of St Stephen* by Sante Piatti. The altarpieces on the south side date from the 17th century: the *Adoration of the Magi* is by Giuseppe Diamantini and the *Invention of the True Cross* by Pietro Liberi. An extraordinary sculpted altarpiece fills the apse: this was installed in the early 18th century by Heinrich Meyring, and shows *Moses Receiving the Tablets of the Law*. The numerous huge figures are arranged in front of a brown rock symbolising Mount Sinai. Below, the altar has a more successful marble relief of the *Worship of the Golden Calf*, also attributed to Meyring.

There is another particularly interesting relief in the sacristy: this is the bronze altar frontal of the *Deposition*, a very crowded composition but technically extremely fine, by Niccolò and Sebastiano Roccatagliata (1633). The prettily-framed small 18th-century paintings here include works by Morleiter, Giuseppe Angeli, Giambattista Canal and Vincenzo Guarana.

The charming Rio San Moisè is used as a mooring for gondolas. The Bauer Hotel on the San Moisè side was built in 1949–54. Across the bridge is the broad **Calle Larga XXII Marzo**, whose name records the date of Manin's rebellion in 1848 (*see p. 124*). It was widened in 1880 and so is out of proportion with the rest of the city's thoroughfares; it is one of the city's most important shopping streets, but one of its least attractive. Halfway along on the left, Calle e Corte del Teatro San Moisè recalls the name of a theatre where Claudio Monteverdi's *Arianna* was performed at the inauguration in 1639, and where in 1810 the young Rossini produced his first opera (*Cambiale di Matrimonio*). It later became the Teatro Minerva. Here in 1896 the Lumière brothers gave their first film projection, using the cine camera they had invented in 1893: the theatre was demolished after 1906.

On the other side of Calle Larga XXII Marzo, Calle del Sartor da Veste diverges right and crosses a canal before reaching Campo San Fantin and the Fenice.

The Fenice

Map p. 406, C2. For daytime guided tours (also in English), book directly at the box office or T: 041 2424.

La Fenice is one of the most important opera houses in Italy. It received its name, meaning 'Phoenix' (the mythical bird which rose from the flames), when it was first built to replace a theatre destroyed by fire in 1773—the theatre of San Benedetto, then one of seven theatres in Venice. The fine Neoclassical building was commissioned by the Venier family from Giovanni Antonio Selva in 1786 and inaugurated in 1792 with *I Giuochi d'Agrigento* by Giovanni Paisiello. It was the first theatre in the city to be provided with a small campo, since the others were more or less hidden away so as not to attract the attention of the authorities. It was also given a water-gate on a canal to allow easy access for the scenery, performers and the public. When the theatre had to be rebuilt after a fire in 1836, it was designed on the same lines by Giambattista Meduna, and was again restored in 1854.

The fire of 1996 was caused by arson, and the two electricians responsible have been given prison sentences. Their intention had been to cause only slight damage to justify a delay in their work (by which they were in breach of a contract), but the fire got out of hand and the firemen were unable to get up close to the building, since the canal was temporarily dry, having been drained for cleaning. Eighty per cent of the building was destroyed, leaving only the walls of the auditorium itself and part of the foyer standing. The immediate decision was taken to rebuild a replica, which opened in 2004. Most Venetians see the new building as fulfilling its purpose, even if it is still perhaps slightly lacking in atmosphere. The only modifications made were the pastel green colour (instead of beige) of the walls of the boxes, the wooden floor in the stalls (beneath which an up-to-date air conditioning and heating system was installed), the moveable orchestra podium, and an electronic system for scene changes. There are also three new rehearsal rooms (posthumous works by the architect Aldo Rossi, who died in 1997), one of which has a reproduction of the Palladian Basilica in Vicenza, and more off-stage space for the performers. The theatre today has a seating capacity of 1,076.

Opera at the Fenice

The Fenice is famous in the history of operatic art. Domenico Cimarosa's *Gli Orazi e i Curiazi* was performed here in 1796 (the composer died in exile in Venice in 1801). The première of Rossini's *Tancredi* took place here in 1813, and many of Verdi's operas had their opening nights at the Fenice: *Rigoletto* was received with great enthusiasm in 1851, but *La Traviata*, which was written for the Fenice, had a disastrous reception in 1853. Verdi subsequently altered its happy ending to a tragic one, but it was the original opera (in the Venetian version) that was chosen to be performed in November 2004 at the reopening of the theatre. Other historic performances included Bellini's *I Capuleti e i Montecchi* (1830), and works by Donizetti and Wagner (including *Rienzi* in 1874).

In the 20th century Stravinsky's *The Rake's Progress* (1951) and Benjamin Britten's *The Turn of the Screw* both had their first nights here. Britten also composed *Curlew River* (1964) and much of *The Prodigal Son* (1968) during stays in Venice. The first Italian performance of *Intolleranza*, by the Venetian composer Luigi Nono (1924–90), was given here in 1961. Other composers whose works had first performances here in the 20th century include Gian Francesco Malipiero, Alban Berg, Sergej Prokofiev, Luciano Berio and Paul Hindemith. Maria Callas sang here between 1947 and 1954, and has recently been honoured in the naming of a bridge and fondamenta outside.

The Fenice also became the centre of the political life of the city after the fall of the Republic in 1797. Verdi became a symbol in the struggle against the Austrians, who in 1851 attempted to censor his *Rigoletto*. From 1859–66 the theatre was closed by popular request, as a demonstration of the gloom felt under foreign dominion. When Verdi's name was acclaimed at performances, it was understood to signify support for the Italian king: the letters of his name were an acronym for 'Vittorio Emanuele Re d'Italia'. The theatre was privately owned up until 1935, and in order to make ends meet, it was also used for balls or for the game of *tombola* (it was for this reason that the clock was installed above the stage). The reception rooms still include a billiard room and the ballroom and café (also open to visitors on the daytime tour).

Tour of the theatre

Tours last about an hour, and begin in the foyer, where the reconstruction work has been carefully integrated (in a slightly different colour) with the decorations which survived the fire. Upstairs, in the corridor outside the boxes, you can see the interesting original wooden model of the theatre made by Selva himself. Visitors then enter the grand Royal Box with its elaborate gilding and mirrors. When it was first built, for Napoleon in 1807, six boxes had to be destroyed to make way for it. Throughout the 19th century it suffered various vicissitudes (in the brief period when Manin's revolutionary forces took over it was hastily demolished). It is now used by the President of the Republic or other distinguished guests. The tour also includes a visit to the stalls and the reception rooms.

San Fantin

The charming Renaissance church of San Fantin (*map p. 406, C2*), probably by

Scarpagnino (1507–49) almost fills its campo in front of the Fenice. It has a beautiful domed sanctuary and apse, attributed to Jacopo Sansovino (1549–63). A 16th-century polychrome wood Crucifix belongs to the church. The Scuola di San Fantin (the seat of the Ateneo Veneto since 1811), with an Istrian stone façade by collaborators of Alessandro Vittoria (*admission sometimes granted; ring at the entrance in the calle to the left*), contains paintings by Paolo Veronese and his school, and a bronze portrait bust of Tommaso Rangone by Alessandro Vittoria. Members of this confraternity comforted those condemned to death and accompanied them in black hoods in a solemn procession to the scaffold.

Santa Maria del Giglio

Map p. 406, C3. Open Mon–Sat 10–5; Chorus Pass.

The church of Santa Maria del Giglio (or Santa Maria Zobenigo) is dedicated to the Madonna of the Lily; its second name comes from Jubanico, the name of a family who lived in this district before the 12th century. The fine façade, one of the best examples of the Venetian Baroque style, was built in Istrian stone and Carrara marble by Giuseppe Sardi in 1678–81 as a monument to the Barbaro family who paid for the rebuilding of the church. It bears portraits of them by Juste le Court; and plans of Zara (Zadar), Crete, Padua, Rome, Corfu and Spalato (Split) record the victories of various members of the family in the service of the Republic. In its unceasing battle against

Portrait statue by Juste le Court (his last work) of Antonio Barbaro, captain of the Venetian fleet, on the façade of Santa Maria del Giglio.

self-aggrandisement and the cult of heroes, the Republic didn't allow public statues to be erected, so wealthy families would donate money to churches and have statues of themselves installed as donors (as can also been seen at San Moisè and San Giuliano).

Giuseppe Sardi (1624–99)

Sardi was born in northern Italy and came to live in Venice, where his father Antonio was recognised as a skilled stonemason. Father and son worked together in the 1650s and 1660s on the façades of the Scuola di San Teodoro and San Salvatore, and the oval spiral staircase in the Ospedaletto. Giuseppe became a friend of the great Venetian architect Baldassare Longhena, and in 1683 he succeeded him as a procurator of St Mark's. Apart from the façade of Santa Maria del Giglio, usually considered his best work, he also built that of the Scalzi and San Lazzaro dei Mendicanti (following a design by his father). Baroque monuments by him are to be found in San Lazzaro dei Mendicanti and the Madonna dell'Orto, and he built the high altar for San Pantalon.

In the light interior, the 17th–18th-century paintings above the cornice of the nave and on the ceiling are by Antonio Zanchi and others. The 18th-century *Stations of the Cross* include paintings by Francesco Fontebasso, Jacopo Marieschi and Gaspare Diziani. The 16th-century paintings on the west wall include a *Last Supper* by Giulio del Moro, and four Sibyls by Giuseppe Salviati.

Beneath the organ in the sanctuary are two paintings of the four Evangelists, early works by Jacopo Tintoretto made for the organ doors of the previous church and paid for by the procurator Giulio Contarini. Tintoretto also painted the altarpiece (unfortunately damaged during restoration) in the third chapel on the north side showing *Christ with Sts Justina and Francesco da Paola*. This is an ex-voto commissioned by Francesco Duodo, commander of the Venetian fleet at the Battle of Lepanto in 1571, who was buried here in 1592. The fine 18th-century high altar has sculptures by Heinrich Meyring.

The delightful Cappella Molin, which displays the contents of the treasury, is especially interesting for the beautiful painting of the *Madonna and Child with the Young St John*. This is attributed by some scholars to Rubens, and certainly shows his influence (the great Flemish painter is known to have stopped in Venice in 1600 on his way to the court of Vincenzo Gonzaga in Mantua on the first of many trips to Italy).

The sacristy is a little 17th-century room with good works of art (*only open on weekdays 10–11.30*). It contains a Tuscan sculpted head of the young St John the Baptist, a small *Annunciation* by Andrea Schiavone, and *Abraham* by Antonio Zanchi. Above the altar are two angels in adoration by Giulio del Moro, and below it, a bas-relief with the head of St John the Baptist. The *Adoration of the Magi* is by Pietro Muttoni.

The second chapels on the north and south sides have statues by Giovanni Maria Morleiter and the first altarpiece on the south side is a painting by Johann Carl Loth.

San Maurizio

From Santa Maria del Giglio a calle (signposted Accademia) leads across two bridges, the first one in the form of a particularly high semi-arch in order that boats can pass beneath it. There is a view from the second bridge to the right of the pretty Ponte de la Malvasia Vecchia, with a wrought-iron parapet decorated with marine monsters (1858), and to the left of the side façade of Palazzo Corner, now the Prefecture (*see p. 130*). The calle ends in Campo San Maurizio. The church (*closed to worship, used by a society which gives concerts*) was begun in 1806 by Giovanni Antonio Selva and Antonio Diedo. The attractive well-proportioned interior has a fine domed tabernacle and two angels on the high altar. The leaning brick campanile which can be seen behind belongs to Santo Stefano (*see p. 122 below*).

Calle del Piovan leads out past the left flank of San Maurizio, passing immediately on the right the little building which used to house the Scuola degli Albanesi (1531), the meeting-place of the Albanian community established in this area by the end of the 15th century. There are Lombardesque reliefs on the façade. A bridge crosses the Rio Santissimo, named after the Host because it runs right past the east end of Santo Stefano. To the right can be seen a low bridge surmounted by two windows which once connected two wings of the convent of Santo Stefano; a few metres beyond (only visible from a boat) is another large low arch, c. 15m wide, which supports the apse of Santo Stefano.

CAMPO SANTO STEFANO & DISTRICT
Map p. 406, B2–B3

The huge Campo Santo Stefano (or Campo Morosini) is one of the pleasantest squares in the city. The statue of a hero of the Risorgimento, Niccolò Tommaseo (1802–74) was erected shortly after his death by Francesco Barzaghi. Tommaseo, an eminent man of letters, led a protest against the Austrians in Venice when he attacked their censorship laws and was arrested by them, together with Daniele Manin, in 1848. He was forced to follow Manin into exile the following year. To the left, the 17th-century Palazzo Morosini (no. 2802–3), home of Francesco Morosini, the admiral famous for his victory over the Turks in the Peloponnese (*see p. 75*) and who served as doge from 1688–94, faces the long Palazzo Loredan (no. 2945). Its Gothic structure was remodelled after 1536 by Scarpagnino, and the Palladian façade on the north end added by Giovanni Grapiglia. It is now occupied by the Istituto Veneto di Scienze, Lettere ed Arti, an academy of arts and sciences founded by Ferdinand I of Austria in 1838, and which has an important library. It also owns Palazzo Franchetti nearby (*see below*).

San Vitale

Map p. 406, B3. Open 9.30–6; used for concerts.
At the other end of the campo is the church of San Vitale (or San Vidal), founded in the 11th century and rebuilt in the 12th: the characteristic campanile, which incor-

porates an antique Roman inscription, survives from this time. The monumental façade by Andrea Tirali dates from 1734–37. The interior, decorated in 1696, preserves the painting of San Vitale on a splendid grey charger, painted by Carpaccio for the high altar, signed and dated 1514. Vitale (or Vitalis of Milan) is shown here with Sts James, John the Baptist and George, and a female saint thought to represent his wife, St Valeria. On the balcony above are St Andrew and St Peter with Vitale and Valeria's children Gervase and Protase (*see p. 166*) being entertained by a little nude putto. Despite his triumphant appearance here, Vitale, once thought to have been a soldier in the army of Nero, is now thought never to have existed and his cultus was suppressed in 1969. The altarpiece of the *Archangel Raphael, St Louis Gonzaga and St Anthony of Padua* on the third south altar is by

Carpaccio's *San Vitale* (1514), in the church of the same name.

Giovanni Battista Piazzetta, and that on the second north altar (the *Crucifix and Apostles*) by a pupil of his, Giulia Lama, one of the few women painters known to have worked in Venice. The *Immacolata*, with a dragon at her feet, on the third north altar, is by Sebastiano Ricci.

Opposite the church is **Palazzo Cavalli-Franchetti**, remodelled in the 17th century. It was owned by Archduke Frederick of Austria in 1840, and after his death in 1847 by the Comte de Chambord (heir to Charles X), who lived here until 1866. He entrusted Giambattista Meduna to restore it and create the garden on the Grand Canal (on the site of a *squero*). In 1878 the palace was acquired by Baron Raimondo Franchetti, and it remained in the Franchetti family until 1922. In this period it was remodelled in the neo-Medieval style by Camillo Boito, including the Gothic façade and new wing and interior staircase. It is now the property of the Istituto Veneto di Scienze, Lettere ed Arti, and is sometimes open for exhibitions and lectures.

Canaletto's famous painting *The Stonemason's Yard* dating from around 1727 (now in the National Gallery in London) depicts the view from Campo San Vidal—includ-

The Archangel Raphael with St Louis Gonzaga and St Anthony of Padua: characteristic brown-toned work by Piazzetta in the church of San Vitale.

ing the well-head which is still here—looking across the Grand Canal to the buildings of Santa Maria della Carità (now the Gallerie dell'Accademia).

The corner of the campo behind Palazzo Cavalli-Franchetti is filled by the imposing **Palazzo Pisani** which, since the beginning of the 20th century, has housed the Conservatory of Music, named after the composer Benedetto Marcello (1686–1739; *see p. 136*). This remarkable building, one of the largest private palaces in Venice, was begun by Bartolomeo Monopola (1614) and continued in 1728 by Girolamo Frigimelica, a little-known architect from Padua (1728). The two interior courtyards are divided by a huge open-arched loggia.

The church of Santo Stefano

Open Mon–Sat 10–5; Chorus Pass.

The early Gothic church of Santo Stefano was rebuilt in the 14th century and altered in the 15th. The fine brick façade bears a portal in the florid Gothic style. The Gothic interior, with three apses, has tall pillars alternately of Greek and red Veronese marble. The wonderful tricuspid wooden roof is thought to have been built by Fra' Giovanni, known as 'degli Eremitani', since he was the architect of the church of the Eremitani in Padua. It is in the form of a ship's keel and is a vivid demonstration of the skill of Venetian carpenters, who for centuries supplied the Republic with seaworthy ships for its great fleet.

In the pavement at the beginning of the nave is the imposing sepulchral seal, the largest in Venice, of Francesco Morosini (whose house stands in the square outside; *see p. 120 above*): this was cast by Filippo Parodi, who had also made the bust for the triumphal arch erected in his honour in the Doge's Palace. Above the west door is the funerary monument of a general, Domenico Contarini (not the doge of the same name), erected in 1650 and including an anachronistic wooden equestrian statue which makes Contarini look slightly ridiculous. The tomb of Giacomo Surian, a physician and philosopher, erected in 1493 on the west wall of the church, has fine Renaissance elements derived from Pietro Lombardo.

The most interesting paintings and sculptures are kept in the sacristy and adjacent cloister (entered off the south aisle). Here are four paintings by Jacopo Tintoretto: the *Last Supper* and a small *Resurrection* on the left wall, and the *Washing of the Feet* and *Prayer in the Garden* on the right wall. Here his chiaroscuro effects are dramatically seen: light glimmers only on the bald heads of the disciples, and on the edges of the leaves and grass stems ethereally illuminated in the Garden. The other artists from the 15th–18th centuries well represented here are Bartolomeo Vivarini (with two small paintings of saints), Bonifacio Veronese (*Holy Family with Saints*), Sante Peranda (a large unfinished *Martyrdom of St Stephen* painted around 1630), Antonio Triva, Gaspare Diziani and Giuseppe Angeli (the *Crucifixion* above the altar).

In the tiny cloister are some beautiful sculptures. The earliest are those by Jacobello and Pier Paolo dalle Masegne (statuettes of St John the Baptist and St Anthony of Padua). The sculptures by Pietro Lombardo and assistants include *St Andrew* and *St Jerome* from the Corbelli altar in the church, where the statue of St Nicholas of Tolentino by him is still *in situ*. There are also two very fine high reliefs (one of a young saint and the other the head of St Sebastian) by Pietro's son Tullio. The two statuettes from the stoups of the church are also kept here: *St John the Baptist* by Giovanni Maria Mosca, and an allegorical statue of *Wisdom* attributed to Giovanni Buora. The funerary stele of Giovanni Falier is by Antonio Canova (1808)—Falier was the artist's first patron. A beautiful Byzantine icon of the *Madonna* dating from the 12th century, with a contemporary frame (and another one made for it in 1541 by Venetian craftsmen) is kept here although it belongs to the church of San Samuele.

On the walls of the sanctuary are two 15th-century carved marble screens, fine Renaissance works, and in the choir in the apse are elaborate wooden stalls dating from the end of the same century by Marco and Francesco Cozzi and others.

There are two 18th-century altarpieces on the south side of the church—the *Birth of the Virgin* by Niccolò Bambini, and the *Immaculate Conception* by Jacopo Marieschi.

Campo Sant'Angelo

Campo Sant'Angelo (*map p. 406, B2*), which adjoins Campo Santo Stefano, is reached from the church of Santo Stefano across a wide bridge with a beautiful wrought-iron balustrade (beside another fine bridge in Istrian stone). The former convent of Santo Stefano fills one side of the campo, its door surmounted by a lunette with a 15th-century relief of St Augustine and monks. Here there is a view of the fine tower of Santo Stefano—the most oblique of the many leaning towers of Venice—and the vault supporting the east end of the church of Santo Stefano can also be seen here above a canal. The little oratory contains a large wooden Crucifix (16th century), surrounded with ex-votos, and an *Annunciation* attributed to Antonio Triva (1626–99; formerly thought to be by Palma Giovane). Among the fine palaces here is the Gothic Palazzo Duodo (no. 3584), once the Tre Stelle inn, in which the composer Domenico Cimarosa died in 1801. It faces the Gothic Palazzo Gritti (no. 3832). Calle del Spezier (probably named from the spices which used to be sold here), signposted for the Rialto, is a busy shopping street which leads out of the campo.

CAMPO MANIN & DISTRICT
Map p. 406, C2–C1

Campo Manin was created in 1870 on the site of a campo in front of a church (San Paternian, which had been suppressed by Napoleon) to commemorate Daniele Manin, whose family house is here (the red palace on the rio, which bears a plaque). At the same time the monument to him (by Luigi Borro) was set up in the centre. However, the campo is now dominated by a disappointing bank building erected in 1964 by Angelo Scattolin (who also built the Palazzo del Cinema on the Lido) with the help of the more famous architect Pier Luigi Nervi.

DANIELE MANIN & HIS REVOLUTION

Daniele Manin was a Venetian lawyer, Jewish by descent on his father's side. When his paternal grandparents converted to Catholicism, they had assumed the name of their sponsor, a brother of Lodovico Manin, who was later to become Venice's last doge. Daniele is remembered as leader of a glorious, if short-lived, republic after his successful rebellion against the Austrians, who had ruled Venice since 1815. Fearing his popularity, the Austrians had him imprisoned in 1848, but the same year, after an almost bloodless revolution, he became president of a new provisional government. Through his prudent leadership and his insistence on order he managed to remain in power for almost a year, holding out against a ruthless Austrian siege, during which the city was subjected to the first air-raid in history when bombs were dropped from balloons by means of pre-set fuses (they luckily caused very little damage as they either burst or were blown away by the wind). Manin was forced to surrender to the Habsburg power in August 1849, and was sent with his family into exile: he died in poverty in Paris in 1857 aged 53. Perhaps because of his lack of charisma—small of stature as he was, often suffering from poor health, and devoted above all to his family—he and his revolution immediately went down in history as of little significance to the Italian Risorgimento compared with the exploits of his more famous contemporaries Mazzini and Garibaldi. It is only recently that his role is beginning to be recognised. He was a particularly courageous and upright figure, dedicated to a cause which he believed to be noble and right. The Venetians themselves saw to it that he had a fitting tomb at St Mark's (*see p. 47*), and, besides the campo that bears his name, he is also commemorated in the name of the Calle Larga XXII Marzo, the date of his revolution.

Palazzo Contarini del Bovolo

Palazzo Contarini del Bovolo (*map p. 406, C2; open daily April–Oct 10–6; in winter only on Sat and Sun*) is celebrated for its loggia and graceful spiral staircase (hence its name, *bovolo* meaning 'snail'). They were designed by a local master mason called Giovanni Candi (c. 1499), otherwise unknown. The picturesque little garden has seven well-heads, one of them Byzantine. There are traces of painted decoration on the stairs, and a wooden dome over the circular loggia at the top, from which there is a delightful view over the rooftops of Venice, taking in most of her bell-towers. Even though the lagoon and the city's numerous canals are invisible from here, the Fenice theatre, the church of the Salute, and the basilica and campanile of St Mark's are particularly prominent.

San Luca

The church of San Luca (*map p. 406, C1*) contains a damaged high altarpiece by Veronese, and (on the first south altar) a 15th-century high relief of the *Madonna and Child Enthroned*, in terracotta. The famous writer Pietro Aretino was buried here in 1556. Known as 'the scourge of princes', he enjoyed poking fun at the rulers of his day, who came to fear his sharp tongue and outspoken manner. He also had a scurrilous reputation, and, self-styled 'a gift to courtesans', he is said to have lived in Venice with numerous concubines. He is also remembered as the great friend and protector of Titian, who painted the writer's portrait several times (the most famous of which is now in the Uffizi in Florence). Edward Hutton, in his 1922 biography of Aretino, declared: 'He was a monster, it is true: to deny that is to belittle him: but above all he was a man of his day, perhaps the most free and complete expression of the age in which he lived—the sixteenth century. That, and his enormous ability, together with the fact that he founded the modern Press and used the hitherto unsuspected weapon of publicity with an incomparable appreciation of its power, are his chief claims upon our notice.'

Museo Fortuny

Map p. 406, C2–B2. Open Tues–Sun 10–6; T: 041 520 0995. Exhibitions are frequently held on the ground floor.

The grand 15th-century Palazzo Pesaro degli Orfei, with its interesting Gothic exterior, was given its additional name, 'degli Orfei', in 1786 when it became the seat of a Philharmonic Society called 'L'Apollinea'. From 1930 this was the home of the Spanish painter Mariano Fortuny (1871–1949), who designed the famous Fortuny fabrics here. His gorgeous silks and velvets were derived from ancient Venetian designs, and he set up a factory on the Giudecca (near the Mulino Stucky; *see p. 310*), which is still in operation. He was also a pioneer in costume design, stage sets and lighting for the theatre. The house was left to the city in 1956 by Fortuny's widow, and preserves a fine old wooden staircase and loggia in the picturesque courtyard. His atelier on the first floor has a remarkable *fin de siècle* atmosphere, and it is filled with curios. The walls are lined with the beautiful fabrics he designed and the lamps he invented for stage lighting are still here. Paintings include a self-portrait of 1890 and portraits of Henriette Nigrin, whom he married in 1924, painted between 1909 and 1930. A series of photographs taken by Fortuny in 1907 with an Eastman Kodak panoramic camera are sometimes on display here, as well as photos of the palace in the 1890s (the museum owns some 11,000 negatives). A case displays portrait busts of his family by the Neapolitan sculptor Vincenzo Gemito. There are also paintings by Fortuny's father (including a copy from Goya).

The splendid main façade of the palace faces the small Campo San Benedetto, where the church of **San Benedetto**, or San Beneto (*closed to worship*) contains works by Bernardo Strozzi, Carlo Maratta and Giambattista Tiepolo.

Palazzo Grassi

From Campo Santo Stefano, Calle Botteghe leads to Salizzada San Samuele. At the end to the right is the curiously shaped Piscina San Samuele, its wide, oblong space unique in Venice. In the other direction, towards the Grand Canal, no. 3338 is the house where Veronese died. Calle Carrozze leads down to **Palazzo Grassi** (*map p. 406, A2*), built by Giorgio Massari in 1748 for Angelo Grassi, son of Paolo, who had contributed a huge sum of money to support the Venetian war against the Turks in the Peloponnese. The family was one of the richest in Venice by the end of the century. When it was bought in 1984 by the Fiat organisation, it was radically restored (partly by Gae Aulenti) as a cultural centre, and important exhibitions were held here in the 1980s and 1990s. It was then sold to François Pinault, a wealthy French collector (and owner, among other businesses, of Christie's, and the fashion houses of Gucci and Yves Saint Laurent), who had the Japanese architect Tadao Ando redesign the interior before it was re-opened in 2006 to exhibit part of Pinault's huge collection of contemporary art. The interior contains a staircase frescoed with carnival scenes, attributed to Alessandro Longhi. The small theatre in the garden is to be restored.

Campo San Samuele (*map p. 406, A2*) opens onto the Grand Canal (and has a landing-stage and a gondola ferry). There is a good view of Ca' Rezzonico across the canal. The ancient church of San Samuele (*closed to worship; sometimes used for concerts and lectures*) preserves its quaint 12th-century campanile, and contains frescoes by the 15th-century Paduan school and a painted Crucifix by Paolo Veneziano.

THE GRAND CANAL

The Grand Canal, over 3km long, is the main thoroughfare of Venice. This splendid waterway, winding like an inverted S through the city, is filled with every kind of boat, from water-buses (*vaporetti*) to motorboats, barges and gondolas. It is lined on either side with a continuous row of beautiful old buildings, including more than 100 palaces, mostly dating from the 14th–18th centuries, though a few survive from the 12th. The canal follows the old course of a branch of the Brenta as far as the Rialto, and is 30–70m wide, with an average depth of five metres. The coloured posts or *pali* in front of the palaces show the livery or *divisa* of their proprietors.

This chapter describes the Grand Canal as it is seen and appreciated from the water: the right bank is followed from San Marco to the station, and the opposite bank from the station back to San Marco. The comfortable vaporetto no. 1 travels slowly along the canal, giving time to enjoy the scene. Sights are described from landing-stage to landing-stage.

FROM SAN MARCO TO THE STATION
(THE RIGHT BANK)

San Zaccaria landing-stage

From Riva degli Schiavoni the *vaporetti* always steer right out into the Bacino di San Marco to avoid disturbing the gondolas moored at the water's edge. As they do so, they provide a wonderful view of the city's most famous stretch of waterfront: beyond the *Prigioni*, the rio crossed by the Bridge of Sighs, the Doge's Palace, the Piazzetta with its two columns and the Libreria Sansoviniana, the Zecca and the Giardinetti can be seen. Across Rio della Luna is the low Capitaneria di Porto (Port Authority office).

San Marco landing-stage

Behind the landing-stage of San Marco (also called Vallaresso, after the name of the calle here) is the building (with blue awnings) which houses Harry's Bar. Between the Hotel Monaco and the Hotel Bauer (with its modern extension) is the 15th-century Gothic **Palazzo Giustinian**, which now houses the municipal tourist offices. In the 19th century this was the noted Hotel Europa, and among its illustrious guests were Verdi, Ruskin and Proust. Turner stayed here on his last two visits to the city in 1833 and 1840. He saw Venice for the first time in 1819, but even though none of his stays exceeded more than a few weeks he made hundreds of paintings, watercolours and sketches (many of which he reworked when he returned to England). His portrayal of the water and light of this city, infused with a unique sense of irreality, informed people's image of Venice for generations. It is perhaps above all his watercolours which provide the most accurate and sensitive picture of his time here.

The narrow Palazzo Contarini-Fasan, once a tower from which a protective chain stretched across the Grand Canal mouth.

Across Rio di San Moisè is the plain Classical façade of the 17th-century **Palazzo Treves de' Bonfili**, attributed to Bartolomeo Monopola. **Palazzo Tiepolo** (also 17th century) is now occupied by the Europa and Regina Hotel. There follows **Palazzo Gaggia** with its tall chimney-pots. This was once Ca' Giustiniani, but was called Ca' Alvisi when it became the residence of Mrs Katharine de Kay Bronson and her daughter Edith in 1876. Mrs Bronson was famous in Venice for her generous hospitality to visitors from England and America. After Elizabeth Barrett's death in 1878, Robert Browning and his sister would come to stay at Ca' Alvisi (or at the Bronson's guest-house, which adjoined the palace) almost every year, and he also greatly enjoyed visiting Mrs Bronson at the little town of Asolo in the Veneto (his *Asolando* is dedicated to her). Another illustrious guest (in 1887) was Henry James. When Edith later married Cosimo Rucellai she went to live in Florence in the Palazzo Rucellai (famous for its architecture by Leon Battista Alberti), still owned by her descendants.

Next to the 15th-century Palazzo Contarini is the tiny **Palazzo Contarini-Fasan**, with just three windows on the *piano nobile* and two on the floor above. The charming 15th-century decoration includes a balcony with wheel tracery. It was traditionally called the House of Desdemona because it was believed Shakespeare's tragic heroine had lived there. Its unusual form is explained by the fact that it was once a tower, and a chain used to be suspended from the building and stretched across to the opposite bank of the canal in order to 'close' it in times of danger. **Palazzo Manolesso-Ferro** (15th-century Gothic) has been converted into offices for the regional administration. **Palazzo Flangini-Fini** is attributed to Alessandro Tremignon (1688). Beyond the rio is the 15th-century Palazzo Pisani, now the **Gritti Palace Hotel**, with a delightful terrace restaurant on the canal. John and Effie Ruskin stayed here in 1851, the year that *The Stones of Venice* was published.

RUSKIN IN VENICE

The art critic John Ruskin (1819–1900) visited Venice for the first time in 1835. He had been inspired by the poems of Samuel Rogers, who had recreated the dramatic story of Enrico Dandolo and the Fourth Crusade in verse. Venice gave Ruskin a cause, an outlet for his aesthetic yearnings. Exploring the mass of surviving architecture, much of it in decay in what was by then an impoverished city, he was drawn irresistibly to the glories of the Venetian Gothic. While his wife Effie enjoyed tea parties and the attentions of Austrian officers, he spent hour after hour copying ornaments and tracery, in what became an obsession to record the city before, as he believed must happen, it vanished for ever.

For Ruskin, Gothic art was not enjoyable for itself; it was important because it brought out the creativity of the individual artisan, who had the freedom to create his own interpretations of style. 'As long as the Gothic and other fine architecture existed, the love of Nature, which was an essential and peculiar feature of Christianity, found expression and food….' For Ruskin the Venetian Gothic and Venice's greatness as a Republic were inseparable. He argued that Venice's decline had begun in the 1420s (a view which there is some historical evidence to support), precisely as its art began to abandon the Gothic for the Renaissance.

The Stones of Venice was published between 1851 and 1853. The first volume deals with what Ruskin saw as the role of Christianity in 'colouring and spiritualising Roman or Heathen architecture'. It is also remarkable for its recognition of the important influence of the Arab world on early Venetian architecture. ('The Venetians deserve especial note as the only European people who appear to have sympathised fully with the great instinct of the Eastern Races.') The second and third volumes are full of the drawings of arches and windows that he used to make his argument for the superiority of the style. He deplored the coming of the Renaissance: while 'the Gothic architecture of Venice had arisen out of, and indicated in all its features, a state of pure national faith, and of domestic virtue,' Venice's Renaissance architecture 'had arisen out of, and in all its features indicated, a state of concealed national infidelity, and of domestic corruption.' In his Index of Venetian buildings he did not even include Sansovino's Loggetta, seen by most as one of the most charming pieces of Venetian architecture. Palladio aroused particular scorn for his cold formality.

Ruskin can be criticised for an obsessively romantic view, and for wanting to preserve Venice as if in aspic, even down to the marks on ancient marble (as he said of Palazzo Foscari, 'the beauty of it is in the cracks and the stains'); but no one did more to revive serious study in the Gothic. When the young Marcel Proust came across Ruskin's works on the French Gothic, it set him off to Venice to see 'the embodiment of Ruskin's ideas of domestic architecture in palaces that are crumbling, but which are still rose-coloured and still standing.'   C.F.

Santa Maria del Giglio landing-stage

The 17th-century **Palazzo Venier-Contarini** is by the landing-stage. Across the rio, another 17th-century palace, the **Palazzo Barbarigo**, adjoins the 15th-century Gothic **Palazzo Minotto**, which has a delightful medley of balconies and a little wooden terrace. Next rises the huge Palazzo Corner, called **Ca' Grande**, a dignified edifice in the full Renaissance style by Jacopo Sansovino (begun after 1545). Above the rusticated ground floor are the Ionic and Corinthian upper storeys. It is now occupied by the Prefecture. Behind the little garden can be glimpsed the **Casetta delle Rose**, where Canova had his studio, and where the martial poet Gabriele d'Annunzio lived during the First World War.

Beyond a narrow rio are the two **Palazzi Barbaro**, one 17th-century, the other, on Rio dell'Orso, 15th-century Gothic decorated with marbles and carvings. This is still partly owned by the Curtis family (their historic family library on the top floor was carefully restored a few years ago): it was purchased in 1885 by the wealthy Bostonians Daniel and Ariana Curtis, and here they lived a life of luxury, entertaining on a grand scale. Henry James clearly took the palace as a model for the Palazzo Leporelli, where Milly Theale stayed in *The Wings of the Dove*. In 1892 the collector Isabella Stewart Gardner (who set herself the goal of amassing works of great art to exhibit in her native America, to educate the tastes of her young country) rented the palace from the Curtises and also had James to stay. He was to return in 1899 and again in 1907.

ARTISTS AT PALAZZO BARBARO

James McNeill Whistler was in Venice between 1879 and 1880, and was a frequent guest here when he had a studio on the upper floor of the Ca' Rezzonico. The famous set of etchings he produced while in the city provide a wonderful document of the atmosphere of Venice, both by day and by night: he described it as an 'amazing city of palaces ... really a fairy land—created one would think especially for the painter'. As in his works depicting Paris and London, he ignored the best-known buildings and typical views made popular by his predecessors, and concentrated his attention instead on the texture of the marble and brick surfaces, the ever-changing light, and the distinctive 'floating' quality of the city, which he sought in the remoter districts and smaller canals crossed by their little bridges.

The Curtis family also offered hospitality to John Singer Sargent, who also had a studio at Ca' Rezzonico, and whose work in Venice was clearly influenced by Whistler. While staying with the Curtises in 1899 he painted their group portrait in the drawing room (now at the Royal Academy in London). In 1908 the elderly Claude Monet came to Venice for the first time on the invitation of the Curtises. He remained many months, finding the atmosphere of the city 'Impressionism in stone'. He returned the following year, and his exhibition of Venetian works in 1912 enjoyed enormous success.

Across the rio is **Palazzo Cavalli-Franchetti**, a sumptuous building, restored (and a wing added) in 1878–1922 in neo-Medieval style. It is adjoined by its garden (which was a *squero*, or boat-building yard, up until the 19th century), behind which rises the brick campanile of San Vitale.

The wooden **Ponte dell'Accademia** was built in 1932–33 by Eugenio Miozzi to replace an elaborate 19th-century iron bridge. The present structure, partly in iron, is an exact replica made in 1986 of Miozzi's bridge. Beyond Casa Civran-Badoer, with a small garden, stands **Palazzo Giustiniani-Lolin** (marked by its two pinnacles), an early work by Longhena (1623). It is now owned by the Fondazione Levi, a music study centre. Next comes the 15th-century Gothic **Palazzetto Falier**, with two protruding *logge* (or *liagò*), rare survivals of what used to be a characteristic feature of Venetian houses. Across the rio is a palace which incorporates the rusticated corner in Istrian stone of the **Ca' del Duca**, a remarkable building begun by Bartolomeo Bon in the mid-15th century, but never completed. It takes its name from Francesco Sforza, Duke of Milan, who bought it in 1461 from Andrea Corner. Steps lead down to the water from the adjoining campo. Beyond is the garden, with statuary, of **Palazzo Cappello-Malipiero**, rebuilt in 1622. In the Campo di San Samuele the 12th-century campanile of the church can be seen (*NB: The San Samuele landing-stage is not used by vaporetto no. 1*).

The vast **Palazzo Grassi** (*see p. 126*) was begun in 1748 by Giorgio Massari. It was purchased by François Pinault and opened in 2006 to exhibit part of his huge collection of contemporary art. Beyond a narrow calle is the 17th-century **Palazzo Moro-Lin**, with a long balcony above the portico on the waterfront. The Palazzi da Lezze and Erizzo-Nani-Mocenigo, on the bend of the canal, have been altered from their original Gothic form. **Palazzo Contarini delle Figure** is a graceful 16th-century Lombardesque building (in poor condition) by Scarpagnino, decorated with heraldic trophies and marbles. It is thought to have been named after the two figures (difficult to see) beneath the balcony.

There is now a wonderful view, after the sharp bend of the *Volta del Canal*, as the waterway straightens out for the last 800m or so all the way up to the Rialto Bridge. This stretch of the canal provided the setting for the regattas held at Carnival time during the days of the Republic, and Canaletto painted this view several times (but from the other side of the Canal). The four **Palazzi Mocenigo** (with blue and white *pali* in the water, and some blue awnings) consist of two palaces on either side of a long double façade. This was where Giordano Bruno, the Neoplatonist philosopher, who as a Dominican and ordained priest came into conflict with the Church authorities in 1592, was betrayed by his hosts the Mocenigo to the Inquisition. He was sent under escort to Rome, where he was forced to endure a trial which lasted seven long years before being burned alive as a heretic. A plaque on the third palace records Lord Byron's residence here from 1816–19, when he lived in grand style with a staff of 14, as well as a menagerie of two monkeys, a fox and two mastiffs. During this time he began *Don Juan* and wrote *Beppo*, a work in Italian prose style about Venetian life and manners.

Palazzo Mocenigo is adjoined by the 16th-century **Palazzo Corner-Gheltof**. By the San Tomà ferry stands an old one-storeyed house, just restored. Next comes the 15th-century **Palazzo Garzoni** (now owned by Venice University), with two putti high up on the façade.

Sant'Angelo landing-stage

As the boat pulls out, **Palazzo Lando-Corner-Spinelli** can be seen (now owned by the Lorenzo Rubelli fabric company). By Mauro Codussi (1490–1510), it is a particularly successful Renaissance palace, with a rusticated ground floor and attractive balconies. Beyond two more *rii* is the buff-coloured **Palazzo Benzon**, which in the time of the Countess Marina Benzon in the early 19th century was the rendezvous of Venetian fashionable society: Byron, Thomas Moore and Canova all came here to pay their respects to the hostess. Next to the 16th-century **Palazzo Martinengo**, with two coats of arms (the façade once had frescoes by Pordenone), are Palazzo and Palazzetto Tron (15th century, but later restored). On Rio di San Luca stands **Palazzo Corner-Contarini dei Cavalli**, an elegant Gothic work of c. 1450 with two coats of arms and a fine central six-light window.

Across the rio rises **Palazzo Grimani**, a masterpiece designed by Sanmicheli just before his death in 1559 and built by Gian Giacomo dei Grigi. Still in very good condition, it has a balcony across the whole length of the façade, beneath which are tall Corinthian pilasters. The two upper stories also have very refined decoration. It is now the seat of the Court of Appeal. Next to the rust-coloured façade decorated with marbles of the Casa Corner-Valmarana, is the **Casa Corner-Martinengo-Ravà**. It was owned by the Morosini family, who received distinguished visitors here in the 16th–17th century, including Paolo Sarpi (a fierce opponent of Church involvement in politics; *see p. 232*), the astronomer Galileo, and the philosopher and scientist Giordano Bruno. In the 19th century it was a well-known hotel, and the novelist James Fenimore Cooper stayed here in 1838.

The 13th-century Veneto-Byzantine Palazzi Farsetti and Loredan are occupied by the town hall. **Palazzo Farsetti**, built by Doge Enrico Dandolo (who sanctioned the sack of Constantinople in 1204; *see p. 60*), was over-restored in the 19th century. **Palazzo Loredan** has a double row of arches and reliefs of *Venice* and *Justice* beneath Gothic canopies, and bears the arms of the distinguished Corner family. Elena Corner Piscopia (1646–84), who lived here, was the first woman to receive a degree (in philosophy from Padua University in 1678). In the middle of the next group of houses is the tiny Gothic **Palazzetto Dandolo**, with a double row of four-light windows.

Just beyond the landing-stage is Ponte Manin (on the site of a bridge built in stone before the 15th century by the Dolfin family) across Rio di San Salvador. The large rust-coloured **Palazzo Bembo** was the probable birthplace of the scholar Pietro Bembo (1470–1547; *see p. 196*). Across the rio stands the white façade of **Palazzo Dolfin-Manin**, by Jacopo Sansovino, begun in 1538 for a Venetian merchant, Zuanne Dolfin. It is now an office of the Banca d'Italia. The portico on the ground floor extends over the fondamenta.

Rialto landing-stage

The **Rialto Bridge** is a famous Venetian landmark, and was the only bridge across the Grand Canal throughout the long history of the Republic. There was a bridge of boats at this point from the earliest days of the city's history. This was replaced by a wooden bridge in the mid-13th century, destroyed in 1310 by supporters of Bajamonte Tiepolo after their retreat from Piazza San Marco and the failure of their rebellion against the Venetian state (*see p. 103*). After the restored bridge collapsed in 1444 under the weight of a large crowd, it was rebuilt on a larger scale and as a drawbridge. We have a detailed picture of this bridge in Carpaccio's painting of the *Cure of a Lunatic by the Patriarch of Grado*, commissioned by the Scuola di San Giovanni Evangelista, and now in the Gallerie dell'Accademia (*see p. 155*). Antonio da Ponte won the commission to rebuild the bridge in stone in 1588: other contenders whose designs were rejected included Palladio, Sansovino, Vignola, and possibly also Michelangelo. Its single arch, 48m in span and 7.5m high, carries a thoroughfare divided into three lanes by two rows of shops. It bears 16th-century high reliefs of the *Annunciation* by Agostino Rubini, and of the patron saints Mark and Theodore on the other side.

Just beyond the bridge is the **Fondaco dei Tedeschi**, the German trading-centre from the mid-13th century onwards (*see p. 113*). In the next group of houses are **Palazzo Civran** with a mask over the door (*covered for restoration*), and the 19th-century **Palazzo Sernagiotto**, with a columned portico. In the pretty Campiello del Remer can be seen the external staircase of the 13th-century **Ca' Lioni** (or Palazzo Lion-Morosini), once a typical feature of merchants' houses—the storehouses on the ground floor would open onto the courtyard and the residence would be on the floor above.

Beyond Rio San Giovanni Crisostomo are three small palaces. Next comes **Ca' da Mosto**, a 13th-century Veneto-Byzantine building decorated with *paterae* above the windows. It is in dramatically poor condition and urgently needs restoration—luckily nowadays it is rare to see a building in Venice in such a state of neglect. It was the birthplace of Alvise da Mosto (1432–88), discoverer of the Cape Verde Islands, and from the later 15th century right up until the 18th it was a famous inn, called the Albergo del Leon Bianco.

Across Rio dei Santi Apostoli stands **Palazzo Mangilli-Valmarana**, which was restored in Classical style by Antonio Visentini for his friend Joseph Smith (*see box overleaf*), who purchased it in 1740. The name of the adjoining **Palazzo Michiel dal Brusà** is a reminder of the great fire of 1774 (*brusà* meaning burnt) which destroyed the previous Gothic palace on this site. The **Palazzo Michiel dalle Colonne** has a tall columned portico (remodelled by Antonio Gaspari in the 17th century).

Just before the busy *traghetto* station (which serves the Rialto markets), in Campo Santa Sofia, is **Palazzo Foscari** (a fine 15th-century window has colourful marble columns). On the other side of the campo is the 14th-century red-painted **Palazzo Morosini-Sagredo** with a pretty balconied Gothic window and a variety of windows on its partly Byzantine façade. It is adjoined by the 15th-century Gothic brick **Palazzo Pesaro-Ravà**.

VENICE'S CONSUL SMITH

Joseph Smith (c. 1674–1770) first came to Venice around 1700 and remained here for the rest of his life. Antonio Visentini, architect, painter and engraver, carried out renovations for him at his palace on the Grand Canal and also at the villa he purchased in 1731 on the *terraferma*. The two men collaborated on a 'guide' to Venice's most important buildings (entitled *Admiranda Urbis Venetae* and now preserved in the British Museum in London), with 488 plans and architectural elevations. After Smith's appointment as British Consul in the early 1740s, he was always known in the city as Consul Smith. He was the devoted patron of Canaletto, and through the good offices of Smith this great Venetian painter enjoyed a thriving market in Britain. In the mid-1720s Smith commissioned six important paintings of Piazza San Marco and the Piazzetta from Canaletto, and the artist's only set of published engravings was dedicated to the Consul. The business arrangement between the two endured throughout Canaletto's life, and on his first trip to London in 1746 he carried with him a precious letter of introduction from Smith. Smith also promoted other Venetian artists, including his friends Sebastiano Ricci and his nephew Marco, and Rosalba Carriera. In the 1730s Smith set up as a publisher in Venice: his Pasquali Press became one of the most important in the city, and his bookshop in Campo San Bartolomeo was a place where foreign works could also be found. He is also known to have befriended the playwright Carlo Goldoni, who dedicated to him *Il Filosofo Inglese*, written for the Carnival of 1754.

But Smith is best remembered as a brilliant collector: apart from his outstanding collection of works by contemporary artists, his interests ranged from paintings by Giovanni Bellini to the Dutch and Flemish schools including Vermeer and Rembrandt, and he acquired several hundred drawings (many of them from the great Venetian collector Zaccaria Sagredo), including works by Raphael and the Carracci, and watercolours. Other highlights of his collection were the books, Renaissance illuminated manuscripts, coins and medals. When he retired from the Consulship and found himself in financial straits, in the decade before his death, he sold his collections to the young King George III: they are preserved today in the British Royal Collections and in the British Library, and constitute some of their most precious holdings.

In 1717, Smith married the beautiful Catherine Tofts, who had become famous as a singer in the Drury Lane and Haymarket theatres before coming to Venice in 1711. Their son died as a child and she predeceased Smith in 1756 and is buried in the Protestant cemetery on the Lido. The following year Smith, already aged 80, married Elizabeth Murray, sister of the collector and art dealer John Murray. After the death of both Smith and her brother, Elizabeth sold the palace on the Grand Canal and returned to England in 1777. Smith was buried next to Catherine on the Lido, but his tomb slab was moved to the Anglican church of St George in 1974.

Ca' d'Oro landing-stage

The **Ca' d'Oro**, home to the Galleria Franchetti, has the most elaborate Gothic façade in Venice (1425–c. 1440; *see p. 225*). Beyond the green façade of the 18th-century **Palazzo Duodo** (with two statues at water-level and two busts higher up on the façade), now also part of the Galleria Franchetti, is the 16th-century **Palazzo Fontana**, where in 1693 Carlo Rezzonico was born: he was elected Pope Clement XIII in 1758. Across Rio di San Felice is a house with a garden, then **Palazzo Contarini-Pisani**, with a plain 17th-century façade above a portico; **Palazzo Boldù** (also 17th century, with a rusticated ground floor) and **Palazzo da Lezze**, with its little court on the canal. Across the rio stands the handsome **Palazzo Gussoni-Grimani della Vida**, attributed to Sanmicheli (1548–56), formerly decorated with frescoes by Tintoretto. Sir Henry Wotton, three times sent as English ambassador to Venice by James I (*see box below*), lived here during his second embassy (1619–21). Rawdon Brown (*see p. 206*) took up residence in an apartment here in 1852 and remained in it until his death in 1883.

Sir Henry Wotton (1568–1639)

Sir Henry Wotton was a poet and art collector (with a particular interest in drawings by Palladio), and one of the most cultivated Englishmen of his time. He had a profound knowledge of Italy and the Italian language, and his famous letters provide a vivid picture of 17th-century Venetian society.

In a letter dated 1622 from Venice ('this watery seat'), he remarks: 'We are newly here out of our Carnival. Never was there in the licensing of public masks a more indulgent decemvirate [Council of Ten], never fewer mischiefs and acts of private revenge; as if restrained passions were indeed the most dangerous. Now, after these anniversary follies have had their course and perhaps their use likewise, in diverting men from talking of greater matters, we begin to discourse in every corner of our new league ... '

For a time he was dismissed by James I for his contention that an ambassador was an honest man sent to lie abroad for the good of his country. He was a friend of Fra' Paolo Sarpi, and gave Venice the support of the English king in the Republic's famous quarrel with the pope in 1606 (*see p. 14*). At the end of his life he was Provost of Eton and went fishing with Izaak Walton. He was probably the first person to recognise great qualities in the writings of Milton, and the poet asked him for his advice before starting out on a journey to Italy.

There follow two 17th-century palaces, and, on Rio della Maddalena, the 16th-century **Palazzo Barbarigo**, which has almost lost the 16th-century frescoes on its façade. Across the rio are the 17th-century Palazzi Molin (*being restored*) and Emo on the bend of the canal, and then **Palazzo Soranzo**, with a fine façade probably by Tullio Lombardo's son Sante. **Palazzo Erizzo alla Maddalena** is a red 15th-century Gothic building with a good window. This is adjoined by **Palazzo Marcello** (rebuilt in the 18th century), which was acquired by the state in 1981. There are long-term plans to use it to house the Oriental Museum (at present in the Ca' Pesaro; *see p. 217*). It was the birthplace of Benedetto Marcello.

Benedetto Marcello (1686–1739)

Marcello was a composer (and rival of Vivaldi). He studied in Venice under Francesco Antonio Calegari and Francesco Gasparini. He wrote numerous compositions for the church of Santa Sofia, but his most famous work is *L'estro poetico armonico* (1724–27), based on the liturgical music he had heard in the Ghetto. He also wrote some 500 secular vocal works, and music for recorders, keyboard, cello and violin. In 1720 he published anonymously the *Teatro alla Moda*, a satire on Venetian opera at the Teatro di Sant'Angelo, where Vivaldi was director of music. As a patrician, he became a member of the Great Council in 1707, and was elected to the Quarantia tribunal in 1716. When standing at a window of this palace he heard the wonderful voice of a young girl, Rosanna Scalfi, as she sat singing in a gondola. He went down to meet her and they fell in love; she became his pupil and secret wife (since noblemen were forbidden to marry beneath their class).

The imposing building (*partly in restoration*) in Istrian stone beyond its garden (and later wing) is **Palazzo Vendramin-Calergi**, probably Mauro Codussi's last work, and regarded by many as his finest, built in the first decade of the 16th century for Andrea Loredan. The façade is a masterpiece of Renaissance architecture, in Istrian stone and marble with Corinthian columns and pilasters dividing the three storeys beneath a Classical cornice with a finely carved frieze. In 1599 the palace passed to the Calergi family (who called in Vincenzo Scamozzi to enlarge it with a wing on the garden side), and in 1738 it came into the possession of the Vendramin. It was purchased by Maria Carolina, Duchess of Berry, in 1844, who had Giambattista Meduna restore it and install heating. Her nephew Count Bardi took up residence here (and his important collection of Oriental art was sold on his death in 1906 to the Museum of Oriental Art), and it was from him that Wagner rented the large apartment on the mezzanine floor (*which can be visited; see p. 233*) and the rooms in the wing overlooking the garden, where he died in 1883 (the marble plaque on the water-front records him with a profile and inscription supplied by Gabriele d'Annunzio). Purchased in 1949 by the municipality, the palace has been the winter home of the Casinò Municipale since 1970: play (including roulette and chemin de fer) begins at 3pm and continues until about 4.30am. In summer the Casinò operates at the Lido.

Beyond the rio, **Casa Gatti-Casazza**, with a roof garden (the typical Venetian *altana*), was restored in the 18th-century style.

San Marcuola landing-stage

This landing stage is in front of the unfinished façade of the church of the same name.

On the other side of a garden is **Palazzo Martinengo-Mandelli**, reconstructed in the 18th century. There follow several 17th-century palaces, including **Palazzo Correr-Contarini**. Shortly after the Campiello del Remer, the Cannaregio canal, the second largest in Venice, diverges right. Palazzo Labia (*see p. 235*) can be seen on the canal next to the church of San Geremia. Beyond the church, on the Grand Canal, is the little Scuola dei Morti (rebuilt after 1849), and the stone façade of **Palazzo Flangini**, left unfinished by Giuseppe Sardi (c. 1682). After a group of modern houses, and just before the bridge, is the long **Palazzo Soranzo-Calbo-Crotta**, a 15th-century building enlarged and altered in later centuries. The bridge which serves the railway station was built in 1932–34 by Eugenio Miozzi (who also designed the Accademia Bridge).

Ferrovia landing-stage

Just before the landing-stage is the Baroque façade of the church of the **Scalzi** by Giuseppe Sardi (*see p. 119*). The harmony of the Grand Canal was left undisturbed when the railway station was built in 1955: the simple long, low building in Istrian stone is sensibly set back from the waterfront. Beyond it rise the huge offices of the state railways, built around the same time, but rather more obtrusive. A new bridge is under construction here, which will join the two banks of the Grand Canal between the railway station and Piazzale Roma. It is the work of Spanish architect Santiago Calatrava. The last landing-stage is at Piazzale Roma, the terminus of the road from the mainland (with a multi-storey garage, another work by Eugenio Miozzi, dating from the 1930s).

FROM PIAZZALE ROMA TO SAN MARCO
(THE RIGHT BANK)

Piazzale Roma landing-stage

From here the boat steers out into the Grand Canal and soon passes the mouth of the Rio Nuovo, a canal cut in 1933 as a short route from the station to Piazza San Marco. Beyond the Giardino Papadopoli (public gardens) a bridge crosses Rio della Croce (at the end of which stands the campanile of the church of San Nicola da Tolentino). The next important building on this side of the canal is the 18th-century church of **San Simeone Piccolo**, with a lofty green dome and Corinthian portico. Just before the station bridge is **Palazzo Foscari-Contarini**, a Renaissance building. Beyond Rio Marin and a pretty garden opens Campo San Simeone Grande with trees and a well. At the far end is a portico along the flank of the church. There follow a group of simple palaces before the landing-stage of Riva di Biasio.

Riva di Biasio landing-stage

On the corner of the next rio, just beyond another garden, stands the 15th-century Gothic **Palazzo Giovannelli**. Beyond are two little houses, one of which, called the 'Casa della Laguna', is used by the municipality for meetings on the lagoon ecology. The **Casa Correr**, which has a plain façade, was the home of Teodoro Correr, whose collection forms part of the Museo Correr. The **Fondaco dei Turchi** is an impressive Veneto-Byzantine building, insensitively over-restored in the 19th century. It was the Turkish warehouse from 1621–1838, and is now the Natural History Museum. Beneath the portico are several sarcophagi; one is that of Doge Marin Falier, beheaded for treason in 1355 (*see p. 10*). Across the rio is the plain brick façade of the **Granaries of the Republic**. This 15th-century battlemented edifice bears a relief of the lion of St Mark (a modern replacement of one destroyed at the fall of the Republic). **Palazzo Belloni-Battagià** was built by Baldassare Longhena in 1647–63 for Girolamo Belloni, whose coat of arms, with a star and crescent motif, appears on the façade. In the late 17th century ownership passed to the Battagià family, one of whom was an admiral. The fine water-gate is flanked by iron grilles. Across the rio stand Palazzo Tron (1590) and Palazzo Duodo (Gothic). Beyond a garden is **Palazzo Priuli-Bon**, with 13th-century Veneto-Byzantine traces on the ground floor.

San Stae landing-stage

The boat stops in front of the church of San Stae, whose rich Baroque façade (c. 1709) is by Domenico Rossi (*see p. 214*). It is adjoined by the charming little **Scuola dei Battiloro e Tiraoro** (goldsmiths), attributed to Giacomo Gaspari (1711). Next comes **Palazzo Foscarini-Giovannelli** (17th century), where Doge Marco Foscarini was born in 1695. He possessed the most important private library in Venice, confiscated from his descendants by the Austrian government in 1799, and most of it taken to the Imperial Library in Vienna. Across the rio stands the bright façade of **Ca' Pesaro**, a grand Baroque palace by Baldassare Longhena decorated with grotesque masks. It was completed after Longhena's death in 1682 by Antonio Gaspari, who was responsible for the façade on the rio. It now contains the Museum of Modern Art and the Oriental Museum (*see p. 217*). Beyond two smaller palaces rises **Palazzo Corner della Regina**, by Domenico Rossi (1724), which stands on the site of the birthplace of Caterina Cornaro, queen of Cyprus (1454–1510; *see p. 112*). The lower part of the façade is rusticated and bears masks. A plaque on **Casa Bragadin-Favretto** records the studio here of the painter Giacomo Favretto, who died in 1887, and some of whose typical Venetian scenes can be seen in the Ca' Pesaro. Beyond two more palaces is the Gothic **Palazzo Morosini-Brandolin**. A bridge connects Fondamenta dell'Olio with the **Pescheria**, a graceful neo-Gothic market hall built in 1907 on the site of the 14th-century fish-market. It is hung with red awnings when the sun is up to protect the day's catch from the heat.

Here begin the **Rialto markets** (*see p. 191*), the busy wholesale markets of the city, the buildings of which continue right up to the Rialto Bridge. The waterfront is colourful in the early morning when boats put in laden with fruit and vegetables. A gondola ferry is particularly active here. On the other side of the campo is the long arcaded **Fabbriche Nuove di Rialto**, a serviceable market building which follows the curve of the Grand Canal, begun by Jacopo Sansovino in 1554. It is now the seat of the Assize Court. Behind the Erberia, the fruit and vegetable market, can be seen the **Fabbriche Vecchie di Rialto**, by Scarpagnino. The building at the foot of the Rialto Bridge is **Palazzo dei Camerlenghi**, restored by Guglielmo dei Grigi (Il Bergamasco) in 1523–25.

The ornate Renaissance façade is curiously angled. This was once the seat of the Lords of the Exchequer; the name of the fondamenta here—Fondamenta dei Prigioni—is a reminder that the ground floor of the palace was conveniently used as a prison.

The boat passes beneath the Rialto Bridge (*described on p. 133 above*). The reliefs of St Mark and St Theodore on this side of the bridge are by Tiziano Aspetti. At its foot (and partly concealed by it) is **Palazzo dei Dieci Savi**, a building of the early 16th-century by Scarpagnino, used by the financial ministers of the Republic. A tondo bears a modern lion, and on the corner stands a figure of *Justice* (late 16th century). The view down the Grand Canal is closed in the distance by Ca' Foscari and Palazzo Balbi with its prominent obelisks. Fondamenta del Vin runs in front of a modest row of houses. At the end, behind a garden with two tall cypresses, is the rust-coloured façade of **Palazzo Ravà**, a successful neo-Gothic building (1906), thought to occupy the site of the palace of the patriarchs of Grado.

San Silvestro landing-stage

Beside the San Silvestro landing-stage is **Palazzo Barzizza**, which bears remarkable traces of 12th-century Veneto-Byzantine carvings on its façade. **Palazzo Businello** (formerly Giustinian), on the corner of Rio dei Meloni, was rebuilt in the 17th-century but preserves some Veneto-Byzantine elements. On the opposite corner stands **Palazzo Coccina-Tiepolo-Papadopoli**, with its two obelisks. This is a work built in the best Renaissance tradition by Gian Giacomo dei Grigi in the early 1560s. Beyond the garden is **Palazzo Donà**, with a fine 12th–13th-century window. This is adjoined by the smaller **Palazzo Donà della Madonnetta**, named after a 15th-century relief of the Madonna and Child set into the façade. It has an interesting arched window with good capitals and *paterae*. Across the rio stands **Palazzo Bernardo**, with a lovely Gothic façade (c. 1442) especially notable for the tracery on the upper *piano nobile*. **Palazzo Grimani** (now Sorlini) has an Istrian stone façade decorated with marbles. It is an elegant Lombardesque building of the early 16th century.

Beyond is the plain façade of **Palazzo Cappello-Layard**, on the corner of Rio San Polo, which from 1883 was the residence of the Englishman Austen Henry Layard. By the time he came to live in Venice, Sir Henry Layard (1817–94) was already famous as an archaeologist, having discovered Nineveh in the 1840s during eleven years' residence in the Middle East, from where he sent back to the British Museum the great bas-reliefs which are still the main treasures of their Assyrian department. When he returned to England he entered politics as a Liberal MP. In 1877 Disraeli appointed him ambassador to Constantinople, and he was knighted for his diplomatic skills. In 1869 he married Enid Guest, then only 25 years old, and they moved to Venice in 1883 having purchased the Palazzo Cappello through Rawdon Brown. Here Layard helped Antonio Salviati revive the Venetian art of glass and mosaic and became the principal shareholder of the Venice & Murano Glass and Mosaic Co. Ltd. This firm, apart from carrying out important repair and maintenance work on the mosaics of St Mark's, also made the mosaics for the Wolsey chapel at Windsor, and decorations for the Albert Memorial and Westminster Abbey in London. When the English community needed premises for an Anglican church, Layard donated a warehouse which had been used by the firm, and it was dedicated to St George (it still operates as the Anglican church in Venice; *see opposite*). Layard was also a scholar of Italian art, and an astute collector: visitors to the Ca' Cappello were shown his paintings by Carpaccio, Cima da Conegliano and Giovanni Bellini, as well as Gentile Bellini's famous *Portrait of the Sultan Mehmet II*, and these, together with a bequest of some 70 other paintings, were left by him to the National Gallery of London. Enid helped him entertain lavishly here and all the illustrious visitors to Venice in their time would be invited to the palace, including the crowned heads of Europe. Enid, who outlived Henry, continued to preside over the Anglo-American community at the turn of the century, and is also remembered for the hospital for foreign sailors she founded on the Giudecca, and for her performances on the guitar.

Across the rio stands **Palazzo Barbarigo della Terrazza**, dating from 1569, which is named after its balconied terrace on the Grand Canal (now used by the German Institute). Next comes **Palazzo Pisani della Moretta**, with graceful Gothic tracery of the second half of the 15th century. Beyond the 16th-century **Palazzo Tiepolo** is the smaller 15th-century **Palazzo Tiepoletto**. There follow two smaller houses and the rust-coloured **Palazzo Giustinian-Persico**, a 16th-century building. **Palazzo Civran-Grimani**, on the corner of the rio, dates from the 17th century.

San Tomà landing-stage

Just before the Rio di Ca' Foscari rises the grand **Palazzo Balbi**, with its two obelisks, probably by Alessandro Vittoria (1582–90); this is the seat of the regional government of the Veneto. Next to it, on the rio, is the plain brick façade (and handsome large chimneys) of the **Fondazione Angelo Masieri**, for which Frank Lloyd Wright designed a small palace in the 1950s; it was never built since planning permission was refused. At the *Volta del Canal* stands the beautifully proportioned **Ca' Foscari** (1428–37), a grand residence built for Francesco Foscari, doge for 34 years. It has notable tracery, fine marble columns, and a frieze of putti bearing the Foscari arms. It is now the seat of the University Institute of Economics and Commerce. Canaletto painted several views of the Grand Canal from this point, looking back towards the Rialto. There follows the double façade of the **Palazzi Giustinian**, begun c. 1452 by Bartolomeo Bon. Wagner wrote the second act of *Tristan* here in 1858–59.

After two small palaces rises **Ca' Rezzonico** by Longhena (begun c. 1667), with a storey added by Giorgio Massari in 1745. It now houses the city's collection of 18th-century works of art (*see p. 178*). The lowest window on the corner by the pretty little modern wooden bridge to the left of the façade was part of the mezzanine floor occupied by Robert Browning in 1889, when he stayed here as an old man and widower with his son Pen. With the money of his wife, Fanny Coddington, a wealthy heiress, Pen had purchased the entire palace a few years earlier. The great poet died here in the same year, and his coffin lay in state in the *portego* (just inside the watergate, well seen from here) before being taken by gondola to the cemetery of San Michele to await his ceremonial burial in Poets' Corner in Westminster Abbey.

Ca' Rezzonico landing-stage

Behind the landing-stage is the 17th-century Lombardesque **Palazzo Contarini-Michiel**. **Palazzetto di Madame Stern** (*covered for restoration*) is a reproduction of a Venetian Gothic palace, built in 1909–12 with a garden on the canal. Beyond the plain façade of Palazzo Moro stands **Palazzo dell'Ambasciatore**, so named because it was the Austrian embassy in the 18th century. It is a Gothic building of the 15th century with two shield-bearing pages, fine Lombard works by the school of Antonio Rizzo.

Beyond Rio San Trovaso is **Palazzo Contarini-Corfù**, a 15th-century Gothic building with varicoloured marbles, and, next to it, **Palazzo Contarini degli Scrigni**, built in 1609 by Vincenzo Scamozzi, with a huge mask above its water-gate.

Accademia landing-stage

Just before the Accademia landing-stage is **Palazzo Querini**, occupied up until a few years ago by the British Vice-Consulate (Venice no longer has a British Consulate; the nearest is in Milan). Across the campo can be seen the 18th-century façade (by Giorgio Massari) of the **Scuola della Carità**, and the bare flank (with Gothic windows) of the former church of **Santa Maria della Carità**, both now housing the famous Accademia picture gallery, and in the process of radical restoration.

Beyond the Accademia Bridge (*described on p. 131 above*), is **Palazzo Contarini dal Zaffo** (Polignac), a graceful Lombardesque building with fine marble roundels (*currently being restored*) and a garden. **Palazzo Molin-Balbi-Valier** has a handsome ground floor. The 16th-century **Palazzo Loredan**, on Rio San Vio, was the home of Vittorio Cini (1884–1977), patron of the arts, collector, philanthropist and politician. It now houses the very fine Vittorio Cini Collection of Tuscan paintings and decorative arts, only open at certain times of the year (*described on p. 158*).

Beyond is the pretty **Campo San Vio**, planted with trees, named after a church demolished in 1813. The showroom of the Venice & Murano Glass and Mosaic Company here was given to the English community in Venice in 1892 by Sir Henry Layard (*see p. 139 above*). Here they founded the Anglican church of St George (*normally open for services on Sun*), which contains the tombstone of Consul Smith (*see p. 134*).

Beyond the campo, **Palazzo Barbarigo** can be seen, with a harshly-coloured 19th-century mosaic façade by Giulio Carlini. Next door is the 15th-century Gothic **Palazzo da Mula**, painted by Claude Monet in 1908–9 (his painting is now in the National Gallery of Washington). The portrait painter and miniaturist Rosalba Carriera died in 1757 in the red **Casa Biondetti**.

Palazzo Venier dei Leoni, only the ground floor of which was ever built, houses the Peggy Guggenheim Collection of Modern Art (*see p. 159*). Beyond is **Ca' Dario**, whose outside walls incline noticeably. This is a charming Lombardesque building of 1487 in varicoloured marble, highly decorated with motifs taken from Classical, Byzantine and Gothic architecture, and with numerous delightful chimney-pots. It is an interesting example of a palace built not by a nobleman, but by a successful civil servant, Giovanni Dario, who served the Republic as Secretary to the Senate in Albania and Constantinople, negotiating peace with Sultan Mehmet II (whose portrait Gentile Bellini

The marble-fronted, Lombardesque Ca' Dario (1487), said to be the unluckiest house in Venice.

painted) in 1479, and retiring permanently to Venice only at the age of 75. Despite its exceptionally pretty exterior, over the centuries the house has come to have a reputation for bringing bad luck to its owners, since a number of them have died here in unusual circumstances, including Dario's own daughter, Marietta. It was owned by the historian Rawdon Brown (*see p. 206*) from 1838 to 1842. Next to it is the 15th-century Palazzo Barbaro (Wolkoff). **Palazzo Salviati**, with an overbright mosaic on its façade, was built in 1924 by Giovanni dall'Olivo. It is the headquarters of the Salviati glasshouse, founded in 1866, and still one of the leading Venetian glass companies. **Palazzo Orio-Semitecolo** has fine Gothic windows. This was where Henry James' close friend, the writer Constance Fenimore Woolson, committed suicide in 1894. James (who is thought to have taken her as a model for his 'Miss Tita' in *The Aspern Papers*) came here after the tragedy to sort out her belongings, and, at her express wish, attempted to sink her clothes in the lagoon.

A gondola ferry operates from the end of a calle here to Campo Santa Maria del Giglio. The last big palace on this side of the Canal is **Palazzo Genovese**, a successful imitation of the Gothic style built in 1892 (*covered for restoration at the time of writing*). Beside it are the low buildings of the ex-abbey of San Gregorio (*see p. 185*), with a delightful water-gate crowned by a large relief of the saint (which gives onto the cloister). Behind (on the rio) the fine apse of San Gregorio can be seen.

Salute landing-stage

A marble pavement opens out before the grandiose church of **Santa Maria della Salute** (*see p. 162*), a masterpiece of Baroque architecture by Longhena. The **Dogana di Mare**, the ex-customs house, is a Doric construction by Giuseppe Benoni (1676–82), extending to the end of the promontory. The picturesque turret has two telamones supporting a golden globe on which is balanced a weather-vane depicting Fortune.

DORSODURO

Dorsoduro is the district on the 'quiet side' of the Grand Canal, well away from the confusion around Piazza San Marco. Indeed, even if only separated by a few metres of water, it has a totally different atmosphere, and its quiet *campi* and little canals, often with a fondamenta on each side, are amongst the most picturesque in the city. It is principally a residential area, with shops concentrated only in certain small parts. To the south it looks over the Giudecca canal, and here the wide and sunny Zattere promenade is one of the most congenial spots in Venice. In the remotest parts of the *sestiere*, around the charming church of San Nicolò dei Mendicoli, are other lovely small churches; and since part of the university is here, there is also a lively student atmosphere. All areas of Dorsoduro lend themselves to exploration, and some of the best and most reasonably priced restaurants, cafés and hotels are to be found here. There are also two great museums: Venice's most important gallery of paintings, the Gallerie dell'Accademia, and its 18th-century museum, in the splendid Ca' Rezzonico. The Peggy Guggenheim collection of modern art claims to be the most visited museum in the city. The great church of the Salute crowns Dorsoduro's easternmost tip.

THE GALLERIE DELL' ACCADEMIA
Map p. 409, E3

Open 8.15–7.15, Mon 8.15–2. As the paintings are well labelled and all the works are of the highest quality, only a selection is given below. Some rooms are kept closed when there is a shortage of custodians (especially on Sun and Mon). Because of restricted space, less than half the collection is at present on view, but work is underway to expand the exhibition space since the Accademia di Belle Arti, which occupied part of the building, has been moved to the Zattere (see p. 188). The display was being altered at the time of writing; alterations are expected. The works are arranged chronologically, and numbering follows the status quo at the time of writing. The arrangement was designed by Carlo Scarpa in 1950. The Quadreria (reserve collection) is open by appointment on Tues 3–5.30; T: 041 522 2247.

At the foot of the Accademia Bridge, Campo della Carità is dominated by the flank of the former church and ex-convent of Santa Maria della Carità, its Gothic doorway surrounded by large reliefs dating from 1377. This and the Scuola Grande della Carità (with a Baroque façade by Giorgio Massari) are now occupied by the Gallerie dell'Accademia, one of the most important art galleries in Italy, which contains paintings from all periods of Venetian art from the 14th century, through the 15th with masterpieces by Giovanni Bellini, and the wonderful era of Titian, Jacopo Tintoretto and Veronese, down to Giambattista Tiepolo and the 18th century.

The Scuola Grande della Carità, founded in 1260, was the oldest of the six *scuole grandi* (*see p. 287*) in Venice, and two of its rooms survive with some of their original decorations inside the gallery. The collection was first opened to the public in 1817, and includes numerous works from suppressed or demolished churches.

Room 1: This room, the former chapter house of the Scuola della Carità, has a superb gilded wooden ceiling carved in 1461–84 by Marco Cozzi, otherwise known for his skill in producing choir stalls (which are to be seen in the Frari and some other Venetian churches). It has a painting of the *Holy Father* attributed to Pier Maria Pennacchi.

The earliest works in the collection are exhibited here, including two by **Paolo Veneziano**: a splendid polyptych of the *Coronation of the Virgin* flanked by stories from the lives of Christ and St Francis, and a *Virgin and Child with Donors*. Born in the last years of the 13th century, Paolo was the first truly Venetian painter: though his works show the influence of Byzantine art (it is thought that he may even have visited Constantinople), they also provide a prelude to the great Venetian school of painting.

Lorenzo Veneziano, who was no relation to Paolo, but succeeded him as an important artistic personality in Venice in the mid-14th century, is also well represented here by a large polyptych with the *Annunciation* in the central panel and the tiny kneeling figure of the donor, Domenico Lion, surrounded by saints and prophets. His masterly use of colour is also evident in the later *Annunciation with Saints*, signed and dated 1371.

Another important artist who was at work later in the century is **Niccolò di Pietro**, whose *Virgin Enthroned with Donor* exhibited here is signed and dated 1394 (with the addition of the

address of his studio at the foot of Ponte del Paradiso; *map p. 402, C4*).

Venetian art of the early 15th century is also well illustrated in this room, by artists working in the International Gothic style. At the top of the stairs is a triptych by **Jacobello del Fiore**: *Justice and the Archangels*, a work commissioned for a law court in the Doge's Palace, showing Venice personified as Justice. At the other end of the room is his *Coronation of the Virgin*, showing the Madonna in Paradise surrounded by a huge crowd of saints and angels. The *Madonna della Misericordia with St John the Baptist and St John the Evangelist* is also by Jacobello, and St James the Great between four other saints (the '*St James Altarpiece*') is a late work (c. 1450) by **Giambono**. There is also a *Coronation of the Virgin* by him.

Also here are late 14th-century works by **Jacobello Alberegno**, including his unusual *Polyptych of the Apocalypse*, particularly interesting for its iconography; and early 15th-century works by **Antonio Vivarini**. In the centre of the room is displayed the 15th-century Cross of St Theodore, made from rock crystal and gilded silver by Venetian goldsmiths.

Room 2: The room boasts a superb group of large altarpieces by leading artists of the Venetian school painted for churches in the city (three of them for San Giobbe), mostly dating from the early 16th century. The *Ten Thousand*

Martyrs on Mount Ararat (also interesting for its complex iconography) and *Presentation of Christ in the Temple*, with three charming little angels, by **Vittore Carpaccio**, were both painted in the second decade of the 16th century. The *Agony in the Garden* and *Calling of the Sons of Zebedee* (1510) are by **Marco Basaiti**. The latter has a remarkably intense atmosphere and the two brothers, the apostles James and John, indicate clearly their willingness to devote their lives to Christ; the scene is filled with men fishing. The *San Giobbe Altarpiece*, which depicts the Madonna enthroned with St Job and other saints, is a very beautiful work by **Giovanni Bellini**, with the magisterial figure of the Madonna holding the Child looking towards the future, beneath a golden apse decorated with a mosaic of six-winged seraphim, which recalls the Basilica of St Mark. The Classical details of the throne and architecture are also exquisitely painted and were repeated in the architecture of the altar itself in San Giobbe (*see p. 237*). The St Sebastian is a superb nude figure study, and at the foot of the throne are three delightful angels playing musical instruments. The Latin inscription reads: 'Hail Virgin, flower of undefiled modesty'. Probably painted in 1478, it had a profound influence on Bellini's contemporaries as can be seen from the altarpieces in this room by Carpaccio and **Cima da Conegliano**, particularly Cima's *Madonna and Child*. There are three works by Cima: a *Madonna and Child with Saints* (restored in 2006), the *Incredulity of St Thomas*, and the *Madonna of the Orange Tree*, a lovely painting with delightful botanical details.

Room 3: Displayed here are the painted organ doors from San Bartolomeo and Santa Maria dei Miracoli: those with four saints are early works by **Sebastiano del Piombo**, and those with the *Annunciation*, are by **Giovanni Bellini**. A painting of *St Peter* is also attributed to Giovanni. The two small works are by **Cima da Conegliano**. Also here is a fresco by **Giorgione** of a female nude dating from 1508, detached from the Fondaco dei Tedeschi (*see p. 114*).

Room 4: This room, and the one that follows, with its exquisite small paintings, provides one of the most vivid insights into Venetian art at its height. Here is a remarkable group of deeply religious paintings by **Giovanni Bellini**, the greatest Venetian master of the 15th century. Son of the painter Jacopo Bellini, he was born around 1433 and throughout his long life (he lived to be over 80) he had a profound influence on Venetian painting. He was an innovator whose works reveal all the qualities of the Venetian Renaissance, and in 1482 he was made official painter of the Republic. He is especially noted for his beautiful paintings of Madonnas, more than 80 of which survive by his hand or by one of the many pupils who worked in his important *bottega*. His brother Gentile was also a very good painter. Some of Giovanni's most delightful small paintings can be seen here: the *Madonna and Child between Sts Paul and George* (possibly with the help of assistants), the *Madonna and Child between Sts Catherine and Mary Magdalene*, against a dark background with remarkable light effects on the head of each figure, and the *Virgin and Child*, an early work with the half-length figure of the Madonna with exquisitely painted hands, holding the standing Child who is playing with his Mother's left thumb, and holding up his right hand in a gesture of benediction. The *Madonna Enthroned with the Sleeping Child* is one of Bellini's most moving works: the Virgin's hands are clasped in prayer, and the abandoned figure of the Child, with one arm hanging limply down, has echoes of the figure of the dead Christ in a *Pietà*. Also here are two Madonnas by Giovanni's father Jacopo. *St George*, with the dragon slumped at his feet, is a beautifully painted work by **Andrea Mantegna**, Giovanni's brother-in-law. The other small works in this room are by non-Venetian artists: an exquisite *Portrait of a Young Man* by Hans Memling, painted around 1480 but of unknown provenance; a *Madonna and Child* by the Ferrarese painter **Cosmè Tura** (also named the *Virgin of the Zodiac*, from the astrological symbols to left and right of the Virgin, though largely faded on the right). The two goldfinches perched on bunches of grapes above are prophetic symbols of the Passion. *St Jerome in the Desert* is by **Piero della Francesca**, with a kneeling donor and a view of Borgo San Sepolcro, the painter's Tuscan birthplace, in the background. Piero's signature is on the tree trunk which supports the Crucifix, but this exquisite little painting is damaged since the green pigment has turned brown.

Room 5: Here are more lovely works by **Giovanni Bellini**: another *Madonna and Child*, with the blessing Child standing, and the *Madonna degli Alberetti*, named after the two unusual trees in the painting. This is arguably the most beautiful

of all the Madonnas in these two rooms, with an extraordinary expressive energy in the movement of the Madonna's head with her eyes downcast, but turned towards the Child. The *Madonna of the Red Cherubs* receives its name from the red cherubim in the sky (painted thus to symbolise ardent love; the Virgin and Child gaze adoringly into one another's eyes). Again the Virgin's hands are superbly painted and the tender beauty of the Madonna contrasts with the chubby, curly-haired Child, who is shown in a far from idealised portrait. There is also a Madonna and Child between St John the Baptist and a female saint, and a Pietà (*Pietà Donà delle Rose*), in a landscape with depictions of Vicenza and Ravenna in the background. In these works Giovanni was apparently influenced by German Gothic sculptures of the same subject. The *Head of the Redeemer* is a fragment, and the five allegories were probably made for the doors of a cupboard.

Also here are two famous paintings by **Giorgione**: *La Tempesta*, and *Old Woman*. Giorgio da Castelfranco became known as Giorgione ('great George') as his fame as a painter increased. He was born around 1476, and despite the fact that very little is known about his life and very few paintings can be attributed with certainty to his hand, he has always been one of the best known Venetian painters. A pupil of Giovanni Bellini and influenced by Flemish and Dutch masters, he had an innovative technique of painting on canvas, applying a rich impasto and a broad range of colours. He was particularly interested in landscape as can be seen in his late masterpiece *La Tempesta* (*see box opposite*) and in the other paintings he produced for his private patrons in Venice, which are diffused with an air of mystery and an atmosphere derived from the spirit of Venetian Humanism.

LA TEMPESTA

The famous *Tempesta* is thought to date from around 1506, and is known to have been the property of the patrician Gabriele Vendramin by 1530. Even though it is one of the few paintings attributed with certainty to Giorgione, it is a painting which scholars still have difficulty in interpreting: it is not known whether the subject is meant to be an allegory, or the depiction of a legend or biblical story. In this work the influence of northern painters as well as Carpaccio can be detected. It was greatly admired by Byron when he saw it in the Manfrin collection, and it was acquired by the Italian state in 1932. The atmosphere of the painting is immediately comprehensible: an impending storm—in fact, this is one of the first 'mood' paintings in Western art. But who is the young man with the wooden staff? Or the half-naked woman breast-feeding a child? Why are the broken columns positioned where they are, as if centre-stage? The explanations are many and often unconvincing, and the matter is further complicated by the fact that X-ray examination reveals that Giorgione also changed the picture's plan and altered the *dramatis personae*. The key to the work may in fact be Francesco Colonna's poem *The Dream of Polyphilus*, published by the famous Venetian printer Aldus Manutius (*see p. 195*) in 1499, which contains a description of Venus feeding Love while the poet-shepherd Polyphilus looks on and the sky becomes heavy with thunderclouds. Whatever the correct reading—and some have argued there is no reading at all—*La Tempesta* remains one of the most forceful images in the history of painting. The air of mystery in the picture is underscored by the colours—from the soft greens of the grass, to the pale nude against the white cloak and the silvery light of the towers and city walls, which seem to glow beneath the dark sky. A dramatic and visionary scene, in poetic contrast with the apparent indifference of the figures occupying it.

Landscape, which was once no more than a decorative motif in the back corner of a painting, has suddenly stepped out of the shadows and become the protagonist. *La Tempesta* is not figures in a landscape, it is a landscape with figures: the first modern landscape painting.

Giorgione died young (of the plague) in 1510, and some of his works have also been attributed to Titian, including, in the past, the famous *Old Woman*, which is now dated a few years after the *Tempesta* and probably preserves its original frame. Like the *Tempesta* it also once belonged to Gabriele Vendramin. It seems to be an allegory of old age rather than a real portrait (it was for long taken to be Giorgione's mother), although again it has received various interpretations. It was damaged in 1881 when it was transferred to a new canvas sup-

Veronese: *Christ in the House of Levi* (1573).

port. Scholars have recognised the influence of Dürer, as well as Carpaccio and Leonardo da Vinci in this work. The woman's scroll reads '*Col Tempo*'—'with time', though her eyes still burn bright and penetrating in her wizened face.

Room 6: This room displays *St John the Baptist* by **Titian**; the *Creation of the Animals* (the seas teem with fish and the sky is full of birds), the *Temptation of Adam and Eve*, and *Cain and Abel*, all by

Jacopo Tintoretto, and *Venice Receiving the Homage of Hercules and Ceres* (from a ceiling in the Doge's Palace) and *St Francis Receiving the Stigmata* (from a church ceiling), both by **Veronese**.

Room 7: This room contains some remarkable portraits including two female portraits by Bernardino Licinio, and a male portrait by Giovanni Cariani. **Lorenzo Lotto**'s *Gentleman in his Study* is one of his best portraits,

painted around 1530. The sitter has a striking pallor, as if he were not well, and the lizard, rose petals and book all have symbolic meaning (fleeting life, disappointed love).

Room 8: The *Visitation* is a fine 16th-century Venetian painting which has received many attributions in the past but whose author remains unknown. The two works by Bonifacio de' Pitati (also known as Bonifacio Veronese; *see* Room 11 below), a follower of Titian, are interesting for their Venetian associations: *God the Father above Piazza San Marco* provides a detailed documentation of the Piazza in the 1540s, including Sansovino's recently completed Loggetta at the foot of the Campanile, and the *Madonna 'dei Sartori'* (the *Virgin with Sts Omobono and Barbara*), painted for the tailors' confraternity, shows their patron saint in Venetian garb and the scissors, symbol of the *scuola*, at the foot of the throne. This is the only work known to be signed and dated (1533) by this artist. The *Archangel Raphael with Tobias* is now generally considered to be the work of Titian. The two works by **Palma Vecchio** depict the *Assumption*, and the *Holy Family with Saints*. The latter is one of his best works, left unfinished at his death in 1528. It is now thought that Titian completed the head of St Catherine and the landscape in the background.

Room 10: This room is dominated by **Paolo Veronese**'s huge painting of *Christ in the House of Levi* (1573; *pictured on previous page*), a splendid Venetian banquet scene framed in a Palladian loggia; the man in the foreground against the pillar on the left is said to be the painter himself. Some 50 figures animate the scene, with everyone busy enjoying themselves, dressed in splendid, colourful costumes, and including servants, clowns and dogs. In the background are extravagant buildings against a twilight sky. It was the secular character of this painting that brought Veronese into conflict with the Inquisition, and the name had to be changed from 'The Last Supper' to 'Christ in the House of Levi' before it was allowed to be hung in the refectory of Santi Giovanni e Paolo.

There are five other works in this room by Veronese: a *Madonna and Child with Saints*, painted around 1564 for the church of San Zaccaria; the *Battle of Lepanto*, which he painted shortly after the battle in 1571 probably as an ex-voto for a Venetian who had taken part in this celebrated defeat of the Turks at the hand of a Christian fleet; the *Mystic Marriage of St Catherine* (c. 1575); an *Annunciation*, with beautiful architectural details; and a late *Crucifixion*.

Also in this room are four masterpieces by **Jacopo Tintoretto**, painted for the chapter hall of the Scuola Grande di San Marco (1562–66) illustrating miracles related to St Mark, all of which show the painter's remarkable imagination. The *Transport of the Body of St Mark* illustrates the story of the Venetian merchants who stole the body of St Mark from Alexandria in 828 and had it taken to Venice. The splendid camel adds an exotic Arab element to the setting, and the extraordinary ephemeral ghost-like figures and spectral buildings in the background conjure up a miraculous atmosphere. The nude figure of St Mark is painted with great skill. The *Miracle of the Slave* is another dramatic scene, in which the saint descends in flight from above our heads while the astonished crowd observes the nude figure of the slave who has just been freed from his shackles. The painter's remarkable technique can be examined in the few brushstrokes, which indicate with an extraordinary freshness of touch the details of the hatchet and splinters of wood and severed ropes in the foreground. These two works were paid for by the wealthy scholar Tommaso Rangone (*see p. 110*), whose portrait can be seen at the extreme left, and, in the first work, beside the camel. In *St Mark Saves the Saracen*, a tempest at sea rages while the saint effortlessly lifts the handsome figure of the Saracen out of a sinking boat to safety. The *Dream of St Mark* shows a night scene on board ship with St Mark (who dreams of the angel in the sky; *for the story, see p. 43*) and his three companions warmly wrapped up in blankets. The spreading, luminous wings of the angel light up a busy quayside scene in the background. This is arguably one of his most innovative works.

The moving *Pietà* is one of the last works by **Titian**, painted for his burial chapel in the Frari the year before his death in 1576, when Venice was devastated by a plague. The muted tones produce a strikingly dramatic and tragic effect, and the kneeling figure of the old man is a self-portrait.

Room 11: This displays more frescoes and ceiling paintings by **Giambattista Tiepolo**, including a ruined frieze with the *Miracle of the Brazen Serpent*, fresco fragments from the Scalzi, and the circular *Exaltation of the True Cross*. *Dives and Lazarus the Beggar* is probably the best work of **Bonifacio de' Pitati**: the scene is set in a villa in the Veneto. Sometimes called Bonifacio Veronese, because he was probably born in Verona, Bonifacio came to Venice around 1515 and enjoyed great success in the city, at the head of a productive workshop. Although there are a number of works by him in this gallery, only a few other works by him are left in Venice (in the churches of Santo Stefano, the Angelo Raffaele, Santa Maria Mater Domini, and Sant'Alvise) and most of his works are now to be found outside Venice and in museums in Europe and America. He was greatly influenced by Palma Vecchio and Titian, but then developed a Mannerist style of his own, using vibrant colours and monumental compositions for his numerous narrative paintings which, however, never reach the level of the greatest Venetian masters.

Artists from the Veneto and Liguria, born outside Venice but with strong connections with the Venetian school, are also represented in this room, including Leandro Bassano (*Resurrection of Lazarus*), Bernardo Strozzi (*Portrait of the Procurator Grimani*, and *Supper in the House of Simon*), and Pordenone (*St Lorenzo Giustinian and Saints*). There are two more works by Tintoretto here: a *Crucifixion*, and the *Madonna dei Camerlenghi*, commissioned by the treasurers of the Republic, who are shown here dominating the scene, magnificently robed, followed by their secretaries bearing gifts for the Madonna against the setting sun. It is obvious that the artist paid much less attention to the Madonna and Child than to the crowded scene around her throne.

Room 12: This corridor exhibits 18th-century landscapes, bacchanals and hunting scenes by Francesco Zuccarelli, Giuseppe Zais and Marco Ricci, nephew of the more famous painter Sebastiano Ricci.

Rooms 13–14: Room 13 contains works by Jacopo Bassano, portraits by Jacopo Tintoretto, including one of Doge Alvise Mocenigo (the victor of Lepanto), and a *Madonna and Child* by Titian. Room 14 contains late 16th- and early 17th-century works including paintings by Domenico Fetti (notably *David* and *Meditation*), Annibale Carracci, and Johann Liss.

Room 16: This has amusing mythological scenes by Giambattista Tiepolo and Sebastiano Ricci. Room 16a exhibits a well-known work, the *Fortune-teller*, by

Giovanni Battista Piazzetta (*pictured opposite*), an ambiguous piece, notable for the knowing, worldly expression of the blowsy central figure. There are also works by Giuseppe Nogari (*Head of an Old Woman*), portraits by Alessandro Longhi, and *Portrait of Count Vailetti* by Vittore Ghislandi (Fra' Galgario).

Rooms 17–18: *Capricci* by **Canaletto** and **Francesco Guardi**, and a view of Venice (*Rio dei Mendicanti and the Scuola di San Marco*) by Canaletto's brilliant nephew **Bernardo Bellotto**. In the other part of the room are paintings by Giovanni Battista Pittoni, more works by Sebastiano Ricci and Giambattista Tiepolo, portraits in pastel by Rosalba Carriera and typical Venetian interior scenes by Pietro Longhi. Room 18 contains more 18th-century works by members of Venice's Accademia di Belle Arti.

Room 23 (Church of the Carità): This large church was built in 1441–52, with a fine wooden roof, but was divided into two floors in 1811 by Giovanni Antonio Selva. Room 23 constitutes the upper floor. In the central polygonal apse are displayed four early triptychs painted for this church attributed to Giovanni Bellini and his *bottega*. The four kneeling sculptured angels date from the 15th century. In the left apse is the *Blessed Lorenzo Giustinian*, signed by **Gentile Bellini** (restored in 2006). It was painted in '*tempera magra*' on very thin canvas as it was designed as a processional standard and was already damaged by water in the 18th century. The hooded eyes and beaky nose of the protagonist (*see p. 299*) are instantly recognisable (compare Pordenone's portrait in Room 11). The

panels of *St Matthew* and *John the Baptist* are by Alvise Vivarini. On the window wall is a carved and gilded Gothic wooden 15th-century *ancona* by Bartolomeo Giolfino; a polyptych of the *Nativity*, flanked by eight saints by **Bartolomeo Vivarini**, *St Clare* by **Alvise Vivarini**, a superb work, portraying the saint as a stern, uncompromising, highly intelligent woman, and *Sts Jerome and Augustine* and *Sts Peter and Paul* by Carlo Crivelli.

At the end of the room are large canvases from the Sala dell'Albergo of the Scuola Grande di San Marco, with scenes from the life of St Mark. The works were commissioned in 1492 first from Gentile and Giovanni Bellini and then after their death from Giovanni Mansueti (who had worked in Gentile's studio). When he died in about 1527, Paris Bordone and Palma Vecchio were chosen to complete the cycle. The *Martyrdom of St Mark* (the saint is shown at the bottom of the painting, but in an insignificant scene in comparison with the splendid crowd) is by **Giovanni Bellini** (finished after his death in 1516 by Vittore Belliniano), and the *Miracle of St Mark Healing the Cobbler Anianus* is by Giovanni Mansueti, who also painted the *Episodes from the Life of St Mark*. The two later works are *St Mark in a Storm at Sea* by Palma Vecchio, with the help of Paris Bordone, who painted *The Fisherman Presents St Mark's Ring to the Doge*, which has a fine architectural background. This illustrates the popular legend that Venice was saved from a terrible flood in 1340 by the intervention of St Mark, St Nicholas and St George. The three saints asked a fisherman to transport them across the lagoon, for which St Mark thanked him by presenting him with a

Giovanni Battista Piazzetta: *Fortune-teller* (1740).

ring which he told him to give to Doge Gradenigo as proof of their presence.

On the wall opposite the windows is a triptych from the church of San Pietro Martire in Murano by a little-known painter called Andrea, who worked in Murano.

Room 19: In this corridor are small 15th-century works: Marco Marziale, *Supper at Emmaus*; Bartolomeo Montagna, *St Peter and a Donor*; Marco Basaiti, *Dead Christ*; Pietro da Saliba (attrib.), *Christ at the Column*; Antonello da Saliba, *Virgin Annunciate* (copy of the celebrated work by his uncle Antonello da Messina, now in Palermo).

Room 20: This room has charming **paintings from the Scuola di San Giovanni Evangelista** (end of the 15th and beginning of the 16th centuries), relating especially to miracles associated with a relic of the True Cross, which was given to the *scuola* in 1369 by Filippo de' Masseri on his return from Jerusalem and is still preserved there today (*see p. 213*). The paintings are particularly remarkable for their depiction of Venice, including the old Rialto Bridge and the brightly-painted Gothic palace façades, and also give a vivid picture of 16th-century Venetian dress. Originally there were nine canvases, but today only eight remain:

(1) *Offering of the Relic to the Members of the Scuola di San Giovanni Evangelista.* The relic had been a gift from the patriarch of Constantinople to Filippo de' Masseri, an officer of state in Cyprus. In this painting Lazzaro Bastiani shows de' Masseri formally handing the relic to the chief guardian of the *scuola*.

(2) *Healing of Pietro de' Ludovici*, by Gentile Bellini. In a richly-marbled chapel, Pietro is seen receiving a candle which has been kept close to the sacred relic, the touch of which heals him.

(3) *Healing of the Daughter of Benvegnudo.* The miraculous healing powers of the relic are again shown, this time by Giovanni Mansueti. He depicts a Venetian palazzo of the greatest wealth, filled with richly-dressed citizens, all celebrating the miracle of the relic.

(4) *Miracle of the Cross at San Lio.* Mansueti shows the moment when the relic, which was being carried at the funeral of a member of the *scuola* who disparaged it during his lifetime, had become too heavy to carry and could not be got across the bridge. Mansueti not only shows us the moment of the miracle with the funeral procession, with the attendant brothers of the confraternity in great detail, but also the women and children of Venice, drawn to the windows and balconies. Life also goes on, with a man carrying produce on his head, while another appears to chase a cat across the rooftops.

(5) *Procession of the Relic in Piazza San Marco.* The brothers of the confraternity are bearing the relic around Piazza San Marco, when a merchant, whose son is dying at home in Brescia, falls to his knees in veneration of it. Miraculously, his son immediately recovers. Gentile Bellini shows the Piazza in great detail. St Mark's is immediately recognisable, its mosaics glittering in the sunshine, with the Porta della Carta and the Doge's Palace on its right. To the left of the painting we can still recognise the Procuratie Vecchie as a one-storey building, though the Torre dell'Orologio

has yet to be built. On the right of the painting, at the base of the Campanile, we can see the buildings which preceded Sansovino's Procuratie Nuove. Bellini also documents the brick paving of the square, which remained until Andrea Tirali repaved it in 1722.

(6) *Miraculous Saving of a Child Fallen from a Roof*. Benedetto Diana portrays the story of the recovery of a young boy who had fallen from the top storey of a house. He shows the typical interior courtyard of a 15th-century Venetian palazzo, with its stone staircase; the fall from a great height onto the stone flags chillingly easy to imagine.

(7) *Miracle of the Relic at San Lorenzo*. While being carried in procession to the church of San Lorenzo, the relic fell into the canal as the bridge was crossed. The inevitable Venetian onlookers dived into the murky waters to rescue it; we can see people floating face down, trying to locate it underwater, and a Moor is seen standing on a wooden platform on the right of the painting, ready to throw himself into the canal. It evaded the grasp of everyone except for Andrea Vendramin, the chief guardian of the *scuola*. Gentile Bellini also incorporated contemporary characters in the scene— Caterina Cornaro, Queen of Cyprus, for example, is seen kneeling on the stage on the left, while Gentile and his brother Giovanni are portrayed kneeling on the right.

(8) *Cure of a Lunatic by the Patriarch of Grado*. Carpaccio depicts Francesco Querini, Patriarch of Grado, performing a miracle with the aid of the relic. The miracle takes place quite discreetly on the loggia of the house on the left, but we can clearly see the old wooden Rialto Bridge. Carpaccio's eye catches everyday details: thickets of chimney pots, fluttering washing and the ever-curious Venetian onlookers.

Room 21: This room contains the famous ***Legend of St Ursula* by Carpaccio**, painted for the Scuola di Sant'Orsola (1490–96). It is a delightful cycle of nine paintings, with charming details and a remarkably Venetian atmosphere. The story is told as follows:

(1) *The Ambassadors from England Arrive at the Court of King Maurus of Brittany*, to ask for the hand of his daughter, Ursula, in marriage to the son (Hereus) of their king, Conon. Ursula is shown on the right of the painting counting out on her fingers the conditions of her agreement to the proposal (a delay of three years for her and 10 maids of honour, each with 1,000 companions, to make a pilgrimage to Rome; and the conversion of Hereus to Christianity).

(2) *Dismissal of the Ambassadors*. The envoys return with Ursula's answer.

(3) *Return of the Ambassadors*. King Conon looks less than happy with the stipulated conditions.

(4) *Hereus meets Ursula, and Ursula leaves for Rome*. Everyone is wearing their finest clothes, sitting on sumptuous carpets, while banners and flags fly and trumpeters play, but Ursula's mother is seen weeping at her departure. We can see Carpaccio's signature on the central flagpole, while the golden-haired nobleman on the left holds a scroll identifying Nicolò Loredan as one of the probable donors of the cycle. This scene, as the previous one, appears to be set in Venice, with people looking on from windows, balconies and

bridges. Throughout the cycle there are hints at the architecture of Venetian buildings such as the Arsenale.

(5) *Dream of St Ursula*. An angel foretells her martyrdom, signified by the dark-coloured palm leaf he holds. In the room where Ursula sleeps in a double bed, the bridegroom's side as yet untouched, we can see from the golden light accompanying the angel, charming domestic details such as her three-legged stool and travelling bookcase, her book still open on the table along with an hourglass, her slippers neatly by the bed and her little dog curled up at its foot.

(6) *Ursula, with Hereus and the Eleven Thousand Virgins, meets Pope Cyriac at Rome*. The official in red is thought to be Ermolao Barbaro, Venetian ambassador to the Vatican and who wrote a book on diplomacy. There is a prominent view of Castel Sant'Angelo.

(7) *The Pilgrims and the Pope reach Cologne*. They find the city besieged by the Huns—the pope and Ursula can be seen leaning out of the boat to talk to the man on shore.

Titian: *Presentation of the Virgin* (1534–39).

(8) *Martyrdom of the Pilgrims*. Ursula, refusing to marry a Hun, calmly waits for the arrow of the central archer, while behind her all is chaos and bloodshed. On the right, separated by a column again bearing what is thought to be the Loredan arms, the funeral of St Ursula takes place.

(9) *Apotheosis of St Ursula and her Eleven Thousand Virgins*. God the Father looks down in benediction on St Ursula, mounted on a podium of palms of martyrdom, and surrounded by the eleven thousand.

Room 24: This is the former Sala dell'Albergo of the Scuola della Carità (with benches and a fine 15th-century ceiling). Here is **Titian**'s wonderful *Presentation of the Virgin*, painted in 1534–39 for its present position. The solitary figure of the child Mary is charmingly graceful, and the distant view of the mountains is a reminder of the artist's alpine home. The details such as the man dressed in red above at the window, and the old woman seated at the foot of the steps beside her basket of eggs, are particularly beautiful, as

well as the two splendid female figures in the centre of the picture observing Mary.

The large triptych of the *Madonna Enthroned between Doctors of the Church* by Antonio Vivarini and his brother-in-law Giovanni d'Alemagna was also painted (in 1446) for this room, although it was formerly on the wall in front of the *Presentation* (it was moved when the door was opened and steps installed in 1811 by Giovanni Antonio Selva). It is a magnificent work and one of the first in Venice to be painted on canvas.

The exquisite Byzantine reliquary of Cardinal Bessarion was made in the 14th–15th century (nearby is displayed a painting of c. 1540 showing the cardinal holding this very reliquary).

The Reserve Collection (Quadreria)

Admission by appointment only, Tues 3–5.30; T: 041 522 2247. A handlist is lent to visitors.
Part of the Quadreria, or reserve collection of the Accademia, is kept in the buildings which belonged to Santa Maria della Carità, some of which were begun by Palladio, but mostly later destroyed by fire. His fine oval spiral staircase survives, as well as the long corridor in which the paintings are hung. Highlights are given here.

Left wall: Marco Zoppo (attributed), *Christ and Four Saints*; Bartolomeo Montagna, *Madonna Enthroned with Sts Sebastian and Jerome*; Giovanni Buonconsiglio ('Il Marescalco'), *Three Saints*; Giovanni Mansueti, *Five Saints*; Marco Basaiti (attributed), *Portrait of a Man*; Francesco Bissolo, *Presentation of Christ with Saints and Donor*; Pier Maria Pennacchi, *Death of the Virgin*; Vittore Carpaccio, *Meeting of Joachim and Anne*; Cima da Conegliano, *Archangel Raphael with Tobias and Saints*; Marco Basaiti, *St George and the Princess*; Titian and his workshop, symbols of the Evangelists, cherubs, and other fragments from the ceiling of the Sala dell'Albergo in the Scuola di San Giovanni Evangelista; Paris Bordone, a small panel with winged putti; two small panels with *Sts Peter and Paul* by Jacopo Tintoretto; and another small work (*Christ on the Cross between the Two Thieves*) by Giovanni Battista Piazzetta; Gian Domenico Tiepolo, *Institution of the Eucharist*; Michele Marieschi, *Capriccio*.

Right wall: Padovanino, frieze with putti; Pietro da Cortona, *Daniel in the Lions' Den*; Luca Giordano, *Deposition*; Jacopo Tintoretto, *Deposition*; a copy of Carpaccio's *Ten Thousand Martyrs on Mount Ararat*, and *Presentation of Christ at the Temple*; Niccolò di Pietro, *Madonna and Child with Two Saints*; Lazzaro Bastiani, *St Anthony of Padua in a Walnut Tree*.

CINI COLLECTION
Map p. 409, E3

Entrance on Piscina del Forner. Usually open Sept–Oct and March–June 10–1 & 2–6 except Mon, but opening times vary according to exhibitions; T: 041 521 0755.
In 1984 Vittorio Cini's daughter Yana (1924–89) donated two floors of the Palazzo Cini on the Grand Canal to the Fondazione Giorgio Cini. It now houses the Vittorio Cini Collection of Tuscan paintings and decorative arts. Thirteenth and early 14th-

century artists are represented, including Giunta Pisano, Bernardo Daddi, Taddeo Gaddi and Guariento. Amongst the early masterpieces are a *Maestà* of c. 1315 by the Maestro di Badia a Isola, and a *Madonna Enthroned with Two Saints* by the Master of the Horne Triptych. There are 15th-century works by the Sienese school, including Sassetta, the Maestro dell'Osservanza, and Vecchietta.

Florentine paintings include the *Judgement of Paris* by Botticelli and pupils; a *Madonna and Child with Two Angels*, a beautiful composition, perhaps the masterpiece of Piero di Cosimo; an unfinished double portrait of two friends by Pontormo; and a small painting in an interesting setting of a *Madonna and Child with Saints, Angels and a Donor* by Filippo Lippi. A *Madonna and Child* is attributed to Piero della Francesca.

The collection also includes important Renaissance paintings by the Ferrara school (Ercole de' Roberti, Cosmè Tura, Ludovico Mazzolino, Battista and Dosso Dossi, and Baldassare d'Este). There are very fine 13th- and 14th-century ivories, 15th–18th-century Venetian ceramics and porcelain, illuminated manuscripts, miniatures, books, Venetian and Bolognese drawings, and prints.

PEGGY GUGGENHEIM COLLECTION
Map p. 409, F3

Open daily except Tues 10–6. Entrance at no. 704 on Fondamenta Venier or no. 701 Calle San Cristoforo. Café-restaurant. Shop.

The collection provides one of the most representative displays of modern art (after 1910) in Europe. It is housed in Palazzo Venier dei Leoni on the Grand Canal which was owned by Mrs Peggy Guggenheim from 1949 until her death in 1979. The palace was begun in 1749, but only the ground floor was completed. The building is surrounded by a luxuriant garden, in which are some exhibition pavilions.

A new wing, opened in 1993, includes a sculpture garden and galleries for temporary exhibitions. The exhibits are very well labelled, also in English.

The Nasher Sculpture Garden

Here there is a Byzantine-style bishop's throne, and sculptures by Arp, Moore, Giacometti and Max Ernst, as well as works loaned from the Nasher Sculpture Center, Dallas. In the corner, beyond the gazebo, an inscription on the wall marks the place where Peggy Guggenheim's ashes are preserved, next to the place where her pet dogs were buried. The entrance hall of the palazzo leads straight out onto the terrace fronting the Grand Canal with Marino Marini's equestrian statue *Angel of the City*. Here the wall of the palazzo has a frieze of colossal lions' heads at water level.

The paintings

Important Cubist paintings include works by Picasso (*The Poet*, *The Studio*), Braque (*The Clarinet*), Léger (*Men in the City*), Duchamp, Gris, Gleizes, Metzinger and Delaunay. Early Italian Modernism is represented by Futurist paintings by Giacomo

Balla and Severini, as well as a sculpture by Umberto Boccioni (*Dynamism of a Speeding Horse* and *Houses*), and Metaphysical paintings by Giorgio de Chirico (*The Red Tower*, a typical work, with a darkened, threatening foreground. The equestrian statue on the right of the canvas throws another sinister shadow in front of the mysterious red tower). Works by Kupka, Kandinsky (*Landscape with Red Spot*), Mondrian, van Doesburg, Malevich, Pevsner, Lissitzky and Hélion represent European Abstraction and non-Objective art in the period from 1910 to the 1930s. Works by Arp, Picabia, Schwitters and Ernst belong to the Dada movement, while elements of fantasy in works by Chagall (*Rain*) and Klee (*Magic Garden*) relate these artists to Surrealism, which is particularly well represented: Ernst (*The Kiss, Attirement of the Bride* and *Anti-Pope*), Miró (*Dutch Interior II* and *Seated Woman II*), Magritte (*Empire of Light*), Delvaux, Dalí (*Birth of Liquid Desires*), Tanguy, Cornell, Brauner, Matta and others. Peggy Guggenheim's support of young American artists in the 1940s is manifest in the paintings by Jackson Pollock (*Moon Woman, Circumcision* and *Alchemy*, among others) and early works by Motherwell, Still,

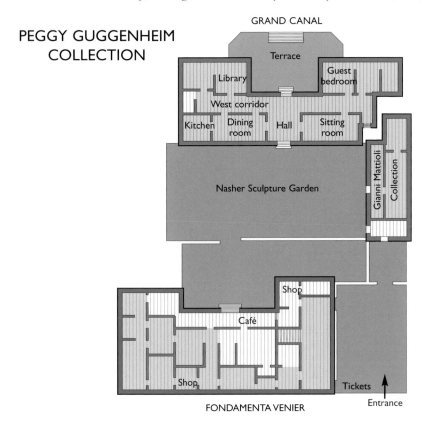

PEGGY GUGGENHEIM
COLLECTION

Rothko and Baziotes. There is also an important painting by Gorky. Post-war European art is represented by Dubuffet, Vedova, Appel, Jorn, Alechinsky, Bacon, Davie, Fontana, Nicholson, Tancredi and Bacci.

Peggy Guggenheim (1898–1979)

Peggy Guggenheim at home, with her Alexander Calder bedhead.

Peggy Guggenheim was the flamboyant daughter of one of the seven Guggenheim brothers who became rich at the end of the 19th century: their fortune came from copper mines. Peggy's father, Benjamin Guggenheim, was drowned on the *SS Titanic* in April 1912. Though born in New York, Peggy spent most of her life in Europe. In 1939 she decided to create a contemporary art museum in London with the help of the art critic Herbert Read. Her plans were frustrated by the Second World War, and she returned to New York to open (in 1942) a sensational museum-gallery called *Art of This Century*. Here, up until 1947, she exhibited European works from her own collection as well as giving exhibitions to then-unknown American artists—Jackson Pollock among them. Her patronage helped to launch the careers of several of the artists who were later to form the New York school of Abstract Expressionism. Her first husband was the American collage artist Laurence Vail, and her second the Surrealist Max Ernst.

Her own collection made its European début at the first post-war Venice Biennale (1948) in the otherwise empty Greek pavilion. In 1949 she bought Palazzo Venier dei Leoni (from the heirs of Doris, Viscountess Castlerosse) where she lived for the rest of her life. Here, in 1951, she founded her contemporary art museum, and opened it every summer to visitors. Today the collection is owned and operated by the New York Foundation named after one of her uncles, Solomon R. Guggenheim, who founded the famous museum in New York.

The sculptures

The sculpture collection includes two bronzes by Brancusi (*Maiastra* and *Bird in Space*). Alberto Giacometti is represented by early Surrealist works (*Woman with her Throat Cut* and *Walking Woman*) as well as later works (*Piazza* and *'Leoni' Woman*). There are also works by Pevsner and González (*Cactus Man*). Two mobiles and a silver bedhead (made on commission for Peggy Guggenheim) are by Alexander Calder.

The Gianni Mattioli Collection

This, one of the last great private collections of early 20th-century Italian art, is exhibited here on long-term loan. Six early paintings by Giorgio Morandi include his first masterpiece, *Bottles and a Fruit Bowl*. There are paintings by Modigliani (*Frank Haviland*) and exponents of the Metaphysical school (Carlo Carrà and Mario Sironi). The collection is dominated by Italian Futurism, with works by Boccioni (*Materia* and *Dynamism of a Cyclist*), Gino Severini (*Blue Dancer*), Balla (*Mercury Passing before the Sun*), Carrà (*Interventionist Demonstration*), Luigi Russolo, Ardengo Soffici, and Fortunato Depero.

SANTA MARIA DELLA SALUTE
Map p. 406, C3

Open 9–12 & 3–5.30 (6.30 in summer). The sacristy is open 3–5.30 and when possible also 10.30–12 (unless Mass is being held).

At the easternmost tip of Dorsoduro, and at the beginning of the Grand Canal stands the famous church of Santa Maria della Salute. It was built in 1631–81 in thanksgiving for the deliverance of Venice from the plague of 1630–31, which had left some thirty per cent of the city's entire population dead (46,000). It is a beautiful octagonal church, the masterpiece of Baldassare Longhena, and the most important edifice built in Venice in the 17th century. The water is reflected on its bright surface, built partly of Istrian stone and partly of *marmorino* (brick covered with marble dust). It rests on more than a million piles of oak, larch and elm. A unique building, and particularly well-adapted to its impressive site at the entrance to the city, it dominates the view of the Grand Canal from the lagoon. A wooden model of the dome which may have been begun by Longhena himself is preserved in the Seminary next door.

The church was built next to the older church of the Trinità, which is at present entered through the cloister of the Seminario Patriarcale (*see below*), and which contains two very fine reliefs by Tullio Lombardo. The doge visited the Salute annually on 21st November in a procession across a pontoon of boats from San Marco: this Venetian festival is still celebrated every year on the same date. Crowds throng to the church to receive a votive candle. On this occasion a *Madonna and Child* attributed to Gentile Bellini is exhibited behind the high altar.

The church is built on a central plan with six lateral façades; you enter by a monumental flight of steps. Huge volutes surmounted by statues support the drum of the fine dome (to be restored) crowned by a lantern; a smaller cupola covers the east end.

The sculptural decoration is attributed to Juste le Court (who also carried out important work in the interior) and other, less well known sculptors of the time including Michele Ongaro and Tommaso Ruer.

SANTA MARIA DELLA SALUTE

The interior

The high dome, its drum pierced by large windows, sheds a beautiful light on the central area of the church, which has a circular aisle (enhanced when the central door is open onto the Grand Canal). The polychrome marble floor is extremely fine. The large sanctuary, with the high altar beneath a second dome is, in contrast, dimly lit. In the chapels to the right are three fine altarpieces of the life of the Virgin by Luca Giordano, and on the left side, the first altar has an *Annunciation* by another 17th-century painter, Pietro Liberi. The *Pentecost* on the third left altar is by Titian: it was painted, like the more important altarpiece by him now in the sacristy (*see below*) for the church of Santo Spirito in Isola. It is usually dated around 1555 (but the two apostles in the foreground may be by assistants). In the sanctuary designed by Longhena, the arch has four ancient Roman columns. On the high altar is a 12th–13th-century Byzantine icon of the *Madonna and Child* (the *Mesopanditissa*) brought from the cathedral of Herakleion in Crete by Francesco Morosini in 1669. The altar is crowned with a remarkable sculptural group (1670) of the Virgin casting out the plague by Juste le Court, unfortunately rather too small for its setting. It shows a kneeling figure representing Venice interceding with the Virgin and Child, and the ugly female figure, an allegory of the plague, being frightened away with the help of cherubim. Also part of the group are the statues at the sides of St Mark and St Lorenzo Giustinian (see p. 299), both patron saints of Venice. The superb bronze paschal candelabrum was made in 1570 by the little-known artist Andrea Bresciano, a friend of Alessandro Vittoria. The roundels in the ceiling behind the altar by Giuseppe Salviati date from around the same time.

The sacristies

The Great Sacristy (for opening times, see above) has an important collection of works of art. It is entered either by a little door on the left of the high altar or from the chapel which has Titian's Pentecost. Over the altar is hung an early work by Titian showing St Mark Enthroned between Sts Cosmas and Damian and Sts Roch and Sebastian. This was a votive painting for the liberation of Venice from the plague (probably that of 1510), and was commissioned by the monastery of Santo Spirito in Isola and moved to the Salute by the order of the Senate in 1656. It shows St Mark (representing Venice) enthroned above and between the two doctor saints (Cosmas and Damian) and the two saints traditionally associated with the plague, St Roch and St Sebastian. Also by Titian and also from Santo Spirito are the eight tondi of the Evangelists and Doctors of the Church, and the three very fine canvases in the ceiling (Cain and Abel, Sacrifice of Isaac, David and Goliath), in remarkable perspective. On the altar frontal is a 15th-century tapestry, with charming landscapes of exquisite workmanship. To the right of the altar is a votive painting by Padovanino of the Madonna with angels holding a model of the Salute.

On the wall opposite the entrance, the Wedding at Cana is a splendid work by Jacopo Tintoretto, with very beautiful light effects. The sacristy also has works by Pier Maria Pennacchi (Madonna and Child in Clouds), Girolamo da Treviso (St Roch between Sts Sebastian and Jerome), and Sassoferrato (four Madonnas).

The Small Sacristy (usually kept locked) contains a kneeling figure of Doge Agostino Barbarigo, from the family tomb in the church of the Carità, attributed to Antonio Rizzo; and a frieze of Patriarchs by the school of Carpaccio.

Seminario Patriarcale and Manfrediniana Picture Gallery

By the church is the **Seminario Patriarcale** (admission only by appointment; T: 041 274 3911). Extensive renovations and the rehousing of the library and art gallery are planned. The interior has a grand staircase by Longhena and ceiling painting by Antonio Zanchi, Sebastiano Ricci and Niccolò Bambini. It overlooks a charming garden on the Giudecca canal with some fine old trees. The library has some 100,000 volumes. In the refectory is a Last Supper by Giovanni Laudis, and two paintings by Aliense.

A huge hall formerly used as a gymnasium is to be modified to display the contents of the **Manfrediniana Picture Gallery**, left to the seminary by Federico Manfredini of Rovigo (1743–1829), and other works of art owned by the Seminary.

The sculpture includes a very fine Greek head of a poet (1st century AD); a crèche group dating from around 1250; works by the dalle Masegne, Pietro Lombardo, and Antonio Rossellino; five splendid terracotta busts by Alessandro Vittoria, including a portrait of Girolamo Grimani; busts of two Valier cardinals which are early works by Gian Lorenzo Bernini; and a terracotta bust of Gian Matteo Amadei by Antonio Canova.

The paintings include a *Holy Family* by a follower of Leonardo, perhaps Giovanni Antonio Boltraffio (harshly restored in 1999) and a triptych which is one of the very few works known by Temporello, who was a follower of Giovanni Bellini. Other 15th-century artists represented include Antonio Vivarini, Filippino Lippi, Mariotto Albertinelli, Gerard David and Cima da Conegliano. A profile of St Lorenzo Giustinian is thought to be by Gentile Bellini (or his *bottega*) and a *Madonna and Child Crowning St Eulalia* (in need of restoration) is by Juan Matas of the late 14th-century Catalan school.

Later works include a detached fresco by Paolo Veronese; *Apollo and Daphne* (in very poor condition) by Titian; an exquisite small *Deposition* attributed to Bachiacca; and *Penelope* by Beccafumi. A mosaic Madonna, a rare Byzantine work made for Haghia Sophia in Constantinople in 1115, also belongs to the Seminary.

Punta della Dogana

NB: Restoration work at present means that the fondamenta which continues round to the Zattere on the Giudecca canal has been closed.

The Punta della Dogana is the point which divides the Grand Canal from the Giudecca canal. The **Dogana di Mare** itself is the ex-customs house, which was given its attractive low Doric façade in 1682 by Giuseppe Benoni (the only work in Venice by this little-known architect). Now usually known as the Punta della Dogana, it was acquired by the *comune* a few years ago and there are plans to turn it into a centre for contemporary art; there is talk of its possible acquisition by Francois Pinault, who owns Palazzo Grassi (*see p. 126*). At the extreme end of the promontory is a delightful little turret surmounted by a golden ball with a weather-vane supported by two telamones. The superb view embraces the whole Bacino di San Marco.

West of the Salute, the wide Rio Terrà dei Catecumeni opens out onto a characteristic Venetian court with a single row of trees and two houses above a low portico. The school here succeeds an institution founded in 1571 for the conversion of slaves and prisoners of war to Christianity. Work is in progress to raise the pavement by a few centimetres (one of the many 'Insula' projects being carried out in places where the pavement level is below 120cm) to help solve the problem of flooding during the frequent *acque alte*.

At the foot of the last bridge (the Ponte del'Umiltà) on the Zattere, in a particularly peaceful spot, is a pleasant little restaurant called Lineadombra (*see p. 363*). Across the bridge, the Zattere follows the garden wall of the Seminario Patriarcale and passes more boathouses owned by the Bucintoro society of rowers (founded in 1882) before reaching the Punta della Dogana, where a little wooden hut on the water's edge has gauges for measuring the tides.

SAN TROVASO & OGNISSANTI
Map p. 409, D3–p. 408, C3

San Trovaso

Open 8.30–11 & 3.30–6.
The church of San Trovaso, founded before 1000 (in 731 or 931) was once one of the most important churches in Venice. It was dedicated to Sts Gervase and Protase (Santi Gervasio e Protasio), but its name is always concatenated to San Trovaso. The relics of St Chrysogonus were preserved here: after his beheading in Aquileia under Diocletian, these were taken to Zara (modern Zadar) in Dalmatia, but during the Fourth Crusade in 1204 they were seized by the Venetians. However, in 1240 they were given back to Zara and only returned to Italy in the 16th century, not to Venice but to the church of San Crisogono in Rome. San Trovaso had to be reconstructed the year after it collapsed in 1584, and the architect appears to have been a pupil of Palladio. It is unusual in having two similar façades. The peaceful campo in front of the main façade is occupied by a raised cistern around its well-head. You can perfectly see the four drains for rainwater, situated slightly lower than the well-head, so that water runs into them. (*See p. 34 for a diagram of a Venetian well.*)

The interior

In the interior the altarpieces in the chapels on the north side are by Palma Giovane, including (third altar) *Birth of the Virgin*, a very well composed painting. The two paintings in the choir (*Adoration of the Magi* and *Expulsion from the Temple*) are by Domenico Tintoretto. In the chapel to the left of the sanctuary, the *Temptation of St Anthony*, by Jacopo Tintoretto (c. 1577), was commissioned by Antonio Milledonne, a wealthy citizen who took an active part in government administration and who is shown here in the guise of the saint. The charming decorative painting of St Chrysogonus on horseback, by Michele Giambono (in a 17th-century frame), comes from the earlier church. Although painted in the 15th century, it shows a flowery archaic Gothic style.

The adjacent chapel of the Scuola del Santissimo Sacramento (which survived when the rest of the church collapsed in 1584) preserves its furnishing including four little lamps (kept permanently alight), a gilded tabernacle, and an altar of Carrara marble. It contains a *Last Supper* by Jacopo Tintoretto, one of a number of paintings of this subject by him still in Venice. In this version, there is a sense of ambiguity: it is not obvious who Judas is, but there are hints. There is an urgency to the scene, with the chair knocked over, disciples leaning towards Jesus wanting to know who is to betray Him, and one member of the party grabbing more wine. As in so many of Tintoretto's canvases, ethereal, wraith-like figures populate the background; but in this work it is the details that fascinate the most. The painting of the *Washing of the Feet* opposite is

View down the picturesque Rio degli Eremite.

a copy of a painting by Tintoretto formerly here but bought by the National Gallery in London in 1882. This is one of many such chapels in Venetian parish churches founded during the Counter-Reformation and dedicated to the Eucharist, and often decorated with paintings by Tintoretto. Their members tended to be from the lower artisan classes, and their activities were controlled by the Church rather than the Council of Ten (who, instead, oversaw the building activities of the other *scuole* in the city).

Over the south door is the *Wedding at Cana*, signed by Andrea Vicentino. In the Cappella Clary, to the right of the door, the altar bears a lovely, very low bas-relief in Greek marble of angels holding signs of the Passion or playing musical instruments. One of the most interesting products of the Venetian Renaissance, it is thought to date from c. 1470, but is of unknown provenance and by an unknown master, named the Maestro di San Trovaso after this relief (he is sometimes identified by scholars with Antonio Rizzo, Pietro Lombardo, Agostino di Duccio or even Donatello). The organ is by Callido (1765).

In the sacristy is a *Madonna in Adoration*, which has been attributed to Jacobello del Fiore. The church also owns a Madonna donated to the church by Rosalba Carriera, who lived in the parish. It is probably, in fact, a self-portrait or portrait of a Venetian lady.

Ognissanti

From the campo outside San Trovaso, Rio di Ognissanti, crossed by two handsome 18th-century bridges, leads right. On the left rises **Ca' Michiel**, unusual in its design since it has two protruding wings: it was famous for its garden in the 16th century. Ponte Trevisan (1772, redesigned in 1861) crosses the particularly pretty Rio degli Eremite, where small boats are usually moored, lined on either side by *fondamente*. The little **church of the Eremite** here dates from 1694 (*admission on request at the convent of the Canossian nuns next door, who also run a simple hotel here*). It contains two marble altars with 17th-century sculptures by Tommaso Ruer and Antonio Corradini (the ceiling paintings by Niccolò Bambini have been removed for restoration). Behind the altar is an unusual early 15th-century polychrome wood relief of the *Madonna della Misericordia*. On the opposite side of the little canal is Montin (*see p. 363*), a restaurant with a lovely garden. Fondamenta Ognissanti continues through a very peaceful district. Several *calli* on the other side of the canal end at the water's edge: only one of them emerges on the Zattere, which is reached from here by a bridge. There is a good view back of the dome and twin towers of the Gesuati. The hospital of Ognissanti has an attractive cloister, from which the **church of Ognissanti** can sometimes be entered. It was founded in the 15th century, but rebuilt in the 16th, when the campanile was built with its onion-shaped dome. A house on the opposite side of the canal is decorated with sculpted heads, and another has a characteristic Venetian wooden roof-terrace (*altana*), and a relief of the lion of St Mark and more lions' heads supporting the balcony (as well as an ancient carved human head). The boatyard (*squero*) on Rio della Avogaria has belonged to the Tramontin, a family of boat-builders, since 1809.

Calle della Chiesa continues to the Rio di San Basegio (a corruption of Basilio, but also called Rio di San Sebastiano). The fondamenta here has a little group of shops, including a good greengrocer, and a trattoria, and a plaque marks the place where the painter Modigliani stayed in 1905.

In Campo San Basegio, a very simple little corner bar (Suzie) caters for the numerous university students who study close by. Even if quite without distinction, it is a pleasant place to sit outside and have a very reasonably priced coffee or sandwich and enjoy this quiet corner of the city. The restaurant Riviera (*see p. 363*) is on the Zattere.

SAN SEBASTIANO & WESTERN DORSODURO
Map p. 408, B2–A2

San Sebastiano
Open Mon–Sat 10–5; Chorus Pass.
The church of San Sebastiano was rebuilt after 1506 by Scarpagnino. The interior was decorated in 1555–70 by the great Venetian painter Paolo Veronese. He lived in the neighbouring salizzada, so this was his parish church (where he is also buried), and it is perhaps here that his great artistic skill can best be understood. Together with Fra' Bernardo Torlioni, the cultivated prior of the church, who was, like Veronese, from Verona, he worked out the complicated iconographical scheme which includes allegories of the *Triumph of Faith over Heresy*, with frequent references also to the plague and to the life of the titular saint, Sebastian.

Paolo Veronese (1528–88)
Paolo Veronese, born in Verona, was one of the great painters of the 16th century, famous for decorating numerous villas in the Veneto. He moved to Venice in 1555 where, besides his splendid works in San Sebastiano, he carried out many works for the Doge's Palace. Beautiful paintings by him are also to be seen in churches and museums all over the city. Although a devout Catholic, he was particularly interested in secular subjects, and his elegant, colourful figures are often sumptuously dressed. The atmosphere in his works is usually serene, in contrast to the more dramatic scenes produced by his contemporary Tintoretto. He influenced a great many artists, including Giambattista Tiepolo.

In the three central panels of the beautiful **ceiling**, Veronese painted scenes from the life of Esther, the 'fair and beautiful' orphan who 'obtained favour in the sight of all them that looked upon her', so much so that King Ahasuerus, after banishing his wife Vashti, decided to make her his queen. Esther's subsequent famous defence of the Jewish people, saving them from massacre ('For how can I endure to see the evil that shall come unto my people?'), and Mordecai the Jew's unselfish protection of the king from danger, are described in the Old Testament Book of Esther. The scene nearest the door depicts the grim expulsion of Vashti; the central scene the joyful crowning of the beautiful Esther by Ahasuerus (with a conspicuous white dog seated beneath the throne); and the far scene, the triumph of Mordecai, whom the grateful king ordered to be honoured with a procession through the streets of the city, dressed in royal apparel wearing the king's own crown, and mounted on horseback. This scene is dominated by Mordecai's splendid grey charger next to a dark horse in attendance—both of them with their hooves raised as they seem to prance down to us out of the ceiling, while the crowds wave him on from the top of a huge marble palace. The smaller panels have angels, flowers and fruit, and four roundels with *Hope*, *Charity*, *Faith* and *Justice*.

In the **spandrels above the nave arches** Veronese frescoed the Apostles. Around the very top of the nave are the Prophets and Sibyls, between twisted columns. On the sanctuary arch are more Prophets and Sibyls, and, at the very top, the *Annunciation*. Veronese also painted the three works in the **sanctuary**: the *Madonna and Child with St Sebastian* over the altar (also designed by him), and *St Sebastian Encourages Sts Mark and Marcellian to Martyrdom*, and the *Second Martyrdom of St Sebastian*. Above the two side paintings, flanking the round windows, are the Evangelists. The two altarpieces in the **third south and north chapels** are also by Veronese. One depicts the *Crucifixion* and the other, a small painting, the Madonna, St Catherine and the friar Michele Spaventi (who lived in the convent). This latter chapel also has fine sculpture by Alessandro Vittoria (including a bust of Marcantonio Grimani, and statuettes of St Mark and St Anthony Abbot).

The two doors of the **organ** (constructed in 1558) were also painted (inside and out) by Veronese—the outer doors show the *Presentation of Christ in the Temple* in a grand architectural setting. Beneath the organ is the door into the **sacristy**, where the recently restored panelled and painted ceiling is one of Veronese's earliest works in all Venice (1555). Since the ceiling is so low, his skill can be studied in greater detail here. The central scene of the *Coronation of the Virgin* shows the Madonna, as little more than a young girl, beside the handsome young Christ (offering support to the elderly God the Father) revealed by two cherubs who hold back the clouds. The ovals with the four Evangelists (identified by their symbols) are depicted with ingenious perspective, but the artist's immaturity is perhaps revealed here as it is not clear to us just where each of the saints is directing his gaze. The other tiny scenes have stories from the Old Testament. The sacristy is a very well preserved room, with its lovely old marble floor and wooden benches and paintings round the walls, the best of which is perhaps the *Resurrection* by Veronese's much less well-known contemporary Antonio Palma.

Veronese's brother Benedetto Caliari helped him in the frescoed decoration on the smaller panels in the church ceiling. He died ten years after Paolo, and both of them are buried in a pavement tomb at the entrance to the Lando Chapel to the left of the choir (*closed at the time of writing; its rare majolica faïence pavement, with no less than 384 tiles thought to date from around 1510, has been removed for restoration since 2001*). Paolo was simply commemorated in the 17th century with a bust on the wall close by, beside the organ.

Other works of interest in the church include *St Nicholas of Bari*, painted for the altar beneath the gallery in 1563 by Titian when he was in his mid-seventies—one wonders if the great artist may have felt like or even resembled the genial elderly saint he depicted here. The huge tomb of archbishop Livio Podocattaro of Cyprus, d. 1555, is by Jacopo Sansovino.

Behind the church are two *campi*, one of which has a well-head in Istrian stone dated 1349. A merchant called Marco Arian left funds in his will for its erection to provide fresh water for the district. He had died the previous year of the plague, believing that the outbreak of the epidemic could have been caused by contaminated water.

The church of the Angelo Raffaele

Map p. 408, B2. Open 9–12 & 3–5, Sun 11–12.

Tucked away in Campo dell'Angelo Raffaele, in a very quiet corner of the city rarely visited by tourists, is a good little restaurant (Pane e Vino; *see p. 366*), which has become popular in recent years with Venetians. Here also is the church of the Angelo Raffaele, dedicated to the Archangel Raphael, who has always been particularly venerated (together with the Archangel Gabriel) in Eastern liturgy, and whose name means 'God heals'. He is one of just three named archangels in scripture (the other being Michael). The church has numerous depictions, in both sculpture and painting, of the archangel accompanying Tobias (usually seen holding a fish and with a little dog trotting behind him, as seen on the old well-head outside the south façade), whose story is told in the Apocrypha in the Book of Tobias (or Tobit). Tobias was sent on a journey to recover a debt and was accompanied by a fellow traveller, whose real identity as the Archangel Raphael was only revealed to him after the successful outcome of his mission. The fish turned out to be miraculous, and its entrails helped cure an old man of his blindness. Interestingly enough, the dog who accompanies Tobias is considered a positive attribute, whereas all the other dogs mentioned in the Old Testament represent Evil.

Over the main door is a 16th-century sculptured Archangel Raphael with Tobias and his dog, and there are statues of the Redeemer with saints and angels on the tympanum. On the east end is another relief of Raphael, which also records the date of the church's consecration (1193).

The interior, designed on a Greek-cross plan when it was reconstructed in 1618 by Francesco Contino, has recently been carefully restored. The organ bears a series of little paintings by Francesco Guardi's brother, Giovanni Antonio (coin-operated light essential) relating the story of Tobias and the archangel set in 18th-century Venice: the elegantly-dressed figures seem to have very little to do with the religious atmosphere of a church. On the west wall are two paintings of the *Last Supper*, one by Bonifacio de' Pitati (Bonifacio Veronese) to the left of the door as you face it, and the other, painted about a century later, by Alvise dal Friso (right of the door). The altar on the north side dedicated to the archangel has a lovely wooden statue of Raphael with Tobias, and 18th-century gilded wood candelabra. Above the side door there is an unusual high relief dating from the late 16th century of a female figure holding a staff, with kneeling figures and a dragon. This is usually thought to represent St Martha (with her distaff), although it may simply be the portrait of a mother abbess symbolically overcoming the devil, shown surrounded by her nuns. There is a pretty marble tabernacle in the chapel of the sacrament, to the left of the sanctuary; the carved and gilded wood ensigns preserved here were made in the 18th and 19th centuries to be carried in procession by members of the Scuola del Santissimo. There is another pretty little tabernacle in the sanctuary (unfortunately radically restored in 1772 by the Foscarini), and on the wall behind yet another painting of Raphael and Tobias, this one, dating from 1772, by Michelangelo Morleiter. The fresco of the other famous archangel, Michael, overcoming the Devil on the ceiling of the nave, is by Francesco Fontebasso, who also frescoed the baptistery off the sanctuary (*shown on request*). The pulpit was made in 1687, but its carvings and reliefs in medieval style appear to be a replica of a 14th-century work.

San Nicolò dei Mendicoli

A bridge leads over the rio, where a 19th-century tabernacle houses a wooden Crucifix which may date from the 14th century (restored in 2005 by the British Venice in Peril Fund). Fondamenta Barbarigo now leads through an area traditionally inhabited by fish-

ermen and sailors towards the lovely little church of **San Nicolò dei Mendicoli** (*map p. 408, A2. Open 10–12 & 4–6*). Founded in the 7th century, it was subsequently rebuilt and restored. It has a well-preserved detached 12th-century campanile, and a little 15th-century porch (entrance on the north side). The charming interior retains its 12th-century Veneto-Byzantine plan, with fine columns (the capitals were replaced in the 14th century). It is rather dark, and the coin-operated light is helpful. In the nave, the interesting gilded wooden sculptural decoration of the Apostles (similar to that in the Carmini; *see opposite*) was added in the late 16th century, and the fine series of paintings was commissioned in 1553 from Alvise dal Friso and other pupils of Paolo Veronese. In the apse is a delightful wooden statue of the titular saint, by an

The Apostle Philip, one of twelve carved and gilded figures in the nave of San Nicolò dei Mendicoli.

unknown sculptor influenced by Bartolomeo Bon. The tondo of *St Nicholas in Glory* in the ceiling was painted in the late 16th century by Francesco Montemezzano: the *Miracles of St Nicholas*, on either side, are by his contemporary, Leonardo Corona. The first north chapel has a statue of St Martha with a snarling mastiff-dragon beside her. The organ loft is decorated with scenes from her life.

On the other side of the canal, a former cotton factory has been converted into lecture halls by the department of architecture at Venice University (IUAV). On its roof, conspicuous from the Giudecca canal, is a sculpture (huge wooden wings) by Massimo Scolari (1991).

From San Nicolò, the Fondamenta delle Terese leads past the disused church of **Le Terese**, completed in 1688 to a design by Andrea Cominelli, and its ex-convent, recently restored for the University. On the opposite side of the rio is the Casa dei Sette Camini (named after its seven chimney-pots): during its recent restoration by the Venice municipality, the foundations were carefully raised and it now provides housing for several Venetian families. Close by, at the corner of Calle Riello, is an attractive small palace which was beautifully converted in 2004 into a comfortable little family-run hotel called Tiziano (*see p. 353*)—one of the most successful of numerous such conversions which have taken place in the past few years. The pretty canal now bends north.

Corte Maggiore leads into Fondamenta Barbarigo, which continues left into Fondamenta Briati. Nearly opposite the end of Rio di San Sebastiano is the Gothic **Palazzo Arian-Cicogna** (no. 2376; now a school), with a very beautiful six-light window decorated above with a double row of superimposed quatrefoils with fine tracery showing the influence of Eastern architecture. This is particularly interesting since it is known to pre-date the Gothic decoration on the exterior of Doge's Palace. The fine courtyard has an outside stair. Beyond are two handsome old palaces, one (no. 2535) with rounded windows, propped up with scaffolding, and the other, next door, with trefoil windows, just restored. The building crowned with busts and set back from the fondamenta is now part of the faculty of letters of Venice University. An ancient statue, now headless, and a fat little lion of St Mark perched on a Doric column can be seen in the garden. On the opposite side of the canal is the huge **Palazzo Zenobio**, owned by the Armenian community in Venice (*admission sometimes granted on request*). Built at the end of the 17th century to a design by Antonio Gaspari, it contains a fine ballroom.

SANTA MARIA DEI CARMINI & DISTRICT
Map p. 408, C2

Santa Maria dei Carmini
Open 7.30–12 & 2.30–7.

The church of Santa Maria dei Carmini (or del Carmelo) has a 16th-century brick façade attributed to Sebastiano Mariani da Lugano, with statues by Giovanni Buora.

The most striking feature of the spacious basilican interior is the gilded wooden sculptural decoration in the nave, similar, though on a larger scale, to that in San

Nicolò dei Mendicoli (*see p. 172 above*). Above it runs a frieze of 17th–18th-century paintings. On the west wall is a monument to Jacopo Foscarini (d. 1602) by the school of Sansovino. Foscarini was a procurator of St Mark's and took an active part in the government of the Republic, but just failed to become doge.

On the second south altar is a beautiful painting of the *Nativity*, by Cima da Conegliano (c. 1509). The vault above the third altar is frescoed by Sebastiano Ricci: the two bronze angel-candelabra on the balustrade are by Girolamo Campagna, and on either side of the altar are statues by (right) Antonio Corradini, and (left) Giuseppe Torretti. In the baptist chapel to the right of the main altar, a small bronze plaque (c. 1474) with an exquisite relief of the *Deposition* is the only work in Venice by the great Sienese artist of the Renaissance (sculptor, architect and painter) Francesco di Giorgio Martini. It includes portraits (right) of his famous patron Federico da Montefeltro, for whom he worked in Urbino, and his duchess Battista Sforza. Also here is a charming small painting of the *Holy Family* by Paolo Veronese, from the church of San Barnaba.

The singing-galleries before the sanctuary are decorated with paintings by Andrea Schiavone. The sanctuary walls are covered with four large paintings by Palma Giovane (1613), Gaspare Diziani (1749) and Marco Vicentino (1613). Above the sanctuary entrance hangs a 14th-century gilded wood Crucifix.

On the second altar in the north aisle the painting of *St Nicholas in Glory, with St John the Baptist and St Lucy*, by Lorenzo Lotto, was commissioned for the church in 1529 (and is still in its original Istrian stone frame). This is one of Lotto's masterpieces, with a remarkable coastal landscape beneath, showing the influence of northern painters. Using a bird's eye perspective, it illustrates St Nicholas' protection of navigators and his help in times of famine and pestilence. On the north wall near the west door is a vast canvas by Padovanino. The side door of the church has a fine Romanesque exterior porch decorated on one side with Byzantine *paterae*. The door leads out to a calle in front of the Scuola Grande dei Carmini.

Scuola Grande dei Carmini

Open every day 10–5 or 6.

The *scuola*, facing the left flank of the church, was founded in 1597. The building, of 1668, is attributed to Baldassare Longhena. In the delightful interior the 18th-century decoration of the chapel, on the ground floor, includes monochrome paintings by Niccolò Bambini and an altarpiece by Sante Piatti. An elaborate double staircase, to a design by Longhena, with early 18th-century stucco decoration, leads to the upper floor.

The *salone* was also probably designed by Longhena and built by his pupil Antonio Gaspari. The nine superb paintings in the ceiling are by Giambattista Tiepolo (1739–49), with allegories of the Virtues around the central *Virgin in Glory* (the *Apparition of the Madonna del Carmelo to the Blessed Simon Stock*). Beautifully restored in the last few years, they are among his masterpieces. They illustrate the legend of the English hermit Simon, who is supposed to have lived in the hollow trunk of an oak tree (hence, perhaps, his name 'stock', meaning 'stump'), before becoming the sixth general of the Carmelite order in 1247. The frescoes were apparently carried out to celebrate the popular credence of the time that the Madonna herself had presented him with the scapular (the two small squares of woven cloth fastened together by strings which were worn over the shoulder by the Carmelites), which then became his attribute. Though picturesque, this legend is now recognised as a 17th-century invention. Nevertheless, Tiepolo skilfully incorporates the saint's attribute numerous times in the ceiling—mostly as a plaything for the host of delightful *putti* and angels.

Giambattista Tiepolo (1696–1770)
Tiepolo was the most important fresco painter in Venice in the 18th century. He received many important commissions from the Venetian aristocracy and the Church, and was famous both in Italy and abroad during his lifetime. His Rococo decorative style, with numerous charming details, was particularly well suited to ceilings, and had a great influence on European painting, making Venice a centre of European art. A follower of Veronese, he worked in numerous palaces and churches in Venice, and in villas in the Veneto, as well as in Germany and Madrid (where he died). The huge fresco on the staircase of the Residenz of Würzburg (1753) is considered his masterpiece. In 1719 he married Cecilia Guardi, sister of the painter Francesco. Tiepolo's son, Gian Domenico worked with him, and later developed his own style to depict delightful scenes of Venetian social life, many of which can also be seen in Venice.

On the walls are works by Antonio Zanchi and Gregorio Lazzarini. In the Sala dell'Albergo is a good ceiling painting of the *Assumption* by Padovanino, and around the walls, 17th-century paintings including works by Antonio Balestra. The Sala dell'Archivio was decorated in 1748 by Giustino Menescardi. By the door into the Sala dell'Albergo, the painting of *Judith and Holofernes* was added by Giovanni Battista Piazzetta. The contents of the treasury are also sometimes displayed, including a statute book of 1611, and an 18th-century cope.

Campo Santa Margherita and San Pantalon

Rio Terrà della Scoazzera leads to the unexpectedly spacious Campo di Santa Margherita (*map p. 408, C2–C1*) surrounded by simple low houses, some of them dating from the 14th–15th centuries. This is one of the most pleasant squares in the city, always full of local families and their children, who come here to pass the time of day or visit the little daily market (which also has three fish stalls). It has a miscellany of shops and simple cafés with tables outside—perhaps the most pleasant of which is the one called simply Caffè in the middle of the west side, painted bright red, and still retaining its charming interior with a piano. Delightfully old-fashioned, with cordial proprietors, it is one of the cheapest places to sit and have a coffee in all Venice. At the north end of the campo, an old house and the stump of a campanile bear interesting sculptural fragments from the former church of Santa Margherita, whose decayed façade is nearby. From here the domed bell-tower of San Pantalon (*see below*) can be seen, and the square tower of the Frari. The little building isolated in the middle of the campo is the Scuola dei Varotari, where the tanners met: it bears a worn relief dating from 1501, of the Virgin amidst the brothers of the *scuola*.

Beyond the campanile a bridge (redesigned by Eugenio Miozzi in 1932) leads into Campo San Pantalon, with the bare unfinished façade of the church of **San Pantalon** (*map p. 409, D1. Open 8–10 & 4–6 except Sun*). In the interior, the nave roof is covered by a huge painting (1680–1704) on canvas by Gian Antonio Fumiani (he also decorated some of the vaults in the side chapels and the painting on the east wall of the church). He was killed in a fall from the scaffolding at the end of the work and is buried in the church. It describes, in remarkable perspective, events in the life of the titular saint, and his martyrdom under Diocletian. It is a spectacular feat of *trompe l'oeil*; the eye is drawn up into the seemingly endless heavens, where flailing limbs and clashing wings accompany the martyrdom and apotheosis of the saint. The treasures of the church are kept in the chapel to the left of the high altar (seen through a grille; *usually unlocked on request*). Here there is an elaborately carved Gothic tabernacle, and paintings of the Madonna and Child and four stories from the life of the Virgin by Paolo Veneziano, and a *Coronation of the Virgin*, crowded with saints and prophets, by Giovanni d'Alemagna and Antonio Vivarini (1444). The statuettes date from the late 14th century.

San Pantaleone is also depicted (healing a child) in the altarpiece by Veronese in the second south chapel. It was originally commissioned, by the parish priest in 1587, for the high altar. The current high altar and tabernacle were designed by Giuseppe Sardi in 1668–71. On a pedestal on the north side (beneath the pulpit) there is an early 16th-century marble bust of the *Redeemer*, attributed to Cristoforo Solari. Most of the sculptures and paintings in the side chapels date from the 18th century (and include works by Pietro Baratta, Gregorio Lazzarini, Alessandro Longhi, Jacopo and Vincenzo Guarana, Niccolò Bambini and Giovanni Bonazza).

On the right of the façade, the Campiello de Ca'Angaran has a remarkable large sculpted roundel of a Byzantine emperor, dating from the late 12th century.

Ponte dei Pugni and San Barnaba

From the south side of Campo Santa Margherita, the wide Rio Terrà Canal leads past a (well-hidden) supermarket to the peaceful Rio di San Barnaba, crossed by the **Ponte dei Pugni** (*map p. 408, C2*). The bridge was rebuilt in the mid-19th century. Its white marble footprints recall the traditional fist-fights which took place in the 14th–18th centuries (when the bridge was without a parapet) between two rival factions of the city, the *Nicolotti* from San Nicolò dei Mendicoli in Dorsoduro, and the *Castellani* from San Pietro di Castello. On the near fondamenta a plaque marks the house where the composer Ermanno Wolf-Ferrari (1876–1948) was born. From the bridge the 17th-century campanile of the church of the Carmini is conspicuous to the right, and that of San Barnaba to the left. Across the bridge, a picturesque greengrocer's barge is always moored, from which you can buy good fruit and vegetables. One of the two brothers who own it can often be seen sitting at the water's edge cleaning large fresh

artichokes, discarding all but the *fondi* or hearts, which throughout Venice are always sold in tubs, floating in water, with a leaf of parsley.

Turn left to reach Campo San Barnaba, where Ponte San Barnaba (reconstructed in 1873) has an elegant iron balustrade (it leads to Ca' Rezzonico; *see below*). **San Barnaba** (*map p. 409, D2. Open mornings until 12.30*), which has a 14th-century campanile, was rebuilt in 1749–76, and the ceiling fresco dates from that time. Calle del Traghetto leads out of the campo to a vaporetto stop on the Grand Canal, passing the charming, family-run hotel Locanda San Barnaba (*see p. 353*) opened in 2000 in a small palazzo with a delightful garden. In the other direction Calle Lunga San Barnaba passes the Quattro Ferri (*see p. 366*), one of the best *bacari* in Venice (it also operates as a simple restaurant in the evenings). Some way further on, on the right, is Codussi, where excellent cakes and biscuits are sold, still made on the premises (*very irregular opening hours*).

CA' REZZONICO
Map p. 409, D2

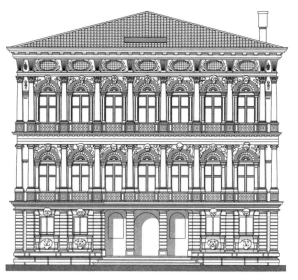

CA' REZZONICO

Open 10–5, except Tues. Off the fine androne and courtyard is the entrance to the Browning Rooms and Mestrovich Collection. The palace has a landing-stage on the Grand Canal (vaporetto no. 1), from which a bridge leads directly to its water entrance. Its land entrance is reached by Fondamenta Rezzonico along Rio San Barnaba. Near the land entrance is a pretty fountain (enjoyed by some huge goldfish) and the garden, with lots of benches which are pleasant places to rest. The collection is extremely well labelled, also in English.

The Ca' Rezzonico is one of the most important 17th–18th-century palaces in Venice, with a monumental façade on the Grand Canal. It was begun by Baldassare Longhena c. 1667, and then modified (and the upper storey added) by Giorgio Massari for the Rezzonico family soon after they bought it in 1751, a few years before Carlo Rezzonico became Pope Clement XIII. They also commissioned its splendid frescoed ceilings from Giambattista Tiepolo, Giovanni Battista Crosato and Jacopo Guarana. The last member of the Rezzonico family died in 1810, and the palace changed hands frequently in the 19th century. Both Whistler and Sargent had studios here in the late 19th century. In 1888 it was purchased by Robert Browning's son, Pen, and the great poet died here on 12th December 1889 (in a small apartment on a mezzanine floor reached from the atrium now partly occupied by the Mestrovich collection). On the side of the palace which overlooks Rio di San Barnaba, by a window of this apartment decorated with a lion and mask, a plaque records 'Roberto's' death with the famous lines from his 'De Gustibus':

> Open my heart and you will see
> Graved inside of it, 'Italy'.

The palace has been owned by the *comune* since 1934, and was first opened to the public in 1936. It contains the Museo del Settecento Veneziano, the city's collection of 18th-century art, displayed in rooms decorated in the most sumptuous 18th-century style with superb views over the Grand Canal.

First floor

On the grand staircase (by Giorgio Massari) one of the putti (*Winter*) on the banister is signed by Juste le Court.

Room I (Ballroom): The chandeliers are 18th century, and the sumptuous frescoes are by Giovanni Battista Crosato and Pietro Visconti. There are some vase-stands and sculpted figures by Andrea Brustolon, a cabinet-maker from Belluno.

Room II: The splendid ceiling fresco is the *Allegory of the Marriage of Ludovico Rezzonico*, one of the last works painted in Venice by Giambattista Tiepolo (1758), with the help of his son Gian Domenico (the *quadratura* is by Gerolamo Mengozzi-Colonna).

Room III: Pastels and miniatures by Rosalba Carriera, and a portrait of Cecilia Guardi, Giambattista Tiepolo's wife, painted by their son Lorenzo in 1757. When she sat for this portrait she was already an elderly woman, but she is bedecked with magnificent jewels.

Room IV: The room has an 18th-century lacquer-work door and 17th-century Flemish tapestries. The *Allegory of Virtue* on the ceiling is by Jacopo Guarana.

Room V (Throne Room): This sumptuous apartment overlooks the Grand Canal. The ceiling painting of the *Allegory of Merit* is by Giambattista Tiepolo. An elaborate frame (c. 1730) surrounds the portrait of Pietro Barbarigo by Bernardino Castelli. The furniture is attributed to Antonio Corradini.

CA' REZZONICO
(FIRST FLOOR)

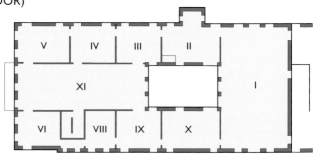

Room VI: Here is another very fine ceiling fresco (*Strength and Wisdom*) by Giambattista Tiepolo.

Room VIII (Library): Here is a bust of a veiled lady by Antonio Corradini (1668–1752) and the Casazza collection of glass displayed in 17th-century bookcases. The grandfather clock was made in London by the firm of Williamson.

Room IX: Here is a large painting by Gregorio Lazzarini, and one by Antonio Molinari. On the ceiling are five paintings in pretty oval frames by Francesco Maffei from Vicenza.

Room X: More ceiling paintings by Maffei, and a remarkable set of furniture, carved in the early 18th-century by Andrea Brustolon. These ceremonial pieces include a vase-stand with Hercules and Moors, an extraordinarily elaborate Baroque work. Made for the Venier family before 1706, out of ebony and boxwood, they resemble sculpture rather than furniture. The beautiful Murano chandelier was made c. 1730.

Room XI (Portego): The *portego* is decorated with 18th-century busts, and has two *atlantes* by Alessandro Vittoria.

Second floor

Room XII (Portego): Arranged as a picture gallery, this displays the most important paintings in the collection: a contrived landscape incorporating some Roman monuments by Luca Carnevalis; a large historical canvas with the *Death of Darius* by Giovanni Battista Piazzetta (and works by his pupil Giuseppe Angeli); landscapes by Giuseppe Zais, and works by Giovanni Antonio Guardi and Gian Antonio Pellegrini. The two Venetian views by Canaletto are early works dating from the 1720s: they were acquired in 1983 and are the only views of Venice by Canaletto owned by the city (although there are also a few of his paintings in the Gallerie dell'Accademia).

CANALETTO & THE VEDUTISTI

Giovanni Antonio Canal, always known as Canaletto, was born into an old Venetian family in 1697. His fame in England is due to Consul Smith (*see p. 134*), who acted as his agent and became his most important patron: he purchased no fewer than 50 of Canaletto's paintings (as well as 143 drawings), all of which he sold to George III, so that today the best collection of Canaletto's work is in the British royal collections. The artist also worked in London for around ten years, producing many splendid views of the city and the Thames. Influenced by the views and *capricci*, or imaginary scenes, invented by Luca Carnevalis, he produced many *vedute* of his native city, which came to symbolise its appearance for decades (and are still considered by many to represent the essence of present-day Venice). He was to influence generations of British landscape painters and water-colourists and, through his nephew and most brilliant pupil, Bernardo Bellotto (who worked as court painter in Dresden), his influence extended to the northern European schools as well. A Venetian view by Bellotto can be seen in the Gallerie dell'Accademia (*see p. 152*). Canaletto was an excellent draughtsman and may have used a *camera obscura* as an aid to accuracy (his only complete sketchbook survives in the Accademia, although it is not usually on view). He also made a set of very fine etchings and dedicated them to Consul Smith.

Francesco Guardi, born in Venice in 1712, took over from Canaletto as a highly successful painter of Venetian *vedute*, although there is no evidence that he was actually trained in Canaletto's workshop. Guardi's work is better represented in his native city than that of Canaletto.

Room XIII: This charming series of rooms was created in 1936 in an attempt to reconstruct the frescoed rooms of the simple little Villa di Zianigo, near Mira in the Veneto. This had been purchased by Giambattista Tiepolo in the 1750s, and decorated with frescoes by his son, Gian Domenico, who inherited the property. In 1906 the frescoes were detached and sold to a Venetian antiquarian and then purchased by the state. Known as the 'New World' series, they depict satyrs and fauns and Pulcinella, as well as scenes of everyday life with masqueraders, and country idylls. In the first room there is a scene from Tasso's *Gerusalemme Liberata*, with Rinaldo taking leave of Armida in her enchanted garden. The oval in the ceiling has a hawk swooping on a flock of sparrows. A tiny room has a brightly painted parrot and a frescoed statue of *Abundance* in a niche. Beyond is a room with a delightful scene called the *New World*, one of the last of the series to be carried out in 1791. It shows a crowd of onlookers, with a splendid miscellany of hats: seen exclusively from behind (with none of their faces visible), they are waiting to see a magic lantern show at a fair-

CA' REZZONICO
(SECOND FLOOR)

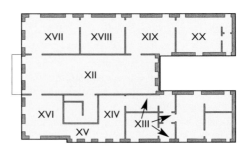

ground. Opposite are two satirical scenes of court life (*The Promenade à Trois*, showing a lady out walking with her husband and lover; and the *Minuet*). Other rooms have carnival scenes with Pulcinella (the Punch of 17th-century Neapolitan comedy), and acrobats (also on the ceiling). The chapel has suitable *grisaille* frescoes. The last two rooms, also in *grisaille*, have amusing satyrs.

Room XIV: An 18th-century interior is reproduced here, with an early-18th-century spinet and painted cupboards.

Rooms XV–XVI: A passageway (Room XV), with a rosary-maker's signboard attributed to Francesco Guardi, small paintings by Guardi, Pietro Longhi and Giuseppe Zais, as well as an elaborate torch holder in Murano glass, leads down to Room XVI, which has two well-known paintings by Francesco Guardi: the *Sala del Ridotto* and the *Parlatorio delle Monache*, delightful Venetian interior scenes. The first shows the famous gambling house called the Ridotto (*see p. 114*), and the second the visitors' room at the Convent of San Zaccaria, famous for its laxity and for the high living of its high-born inmates.

Room XVII (Longhi Room): The ceiling here is also by Giambattista Tiepolo (*Zephyr and Flora*, an early work). The room is especially interesting for its series of 34 small genre paintings by Pietro Longhi, with contemporary scenes of Venetian life (including one with a rhinoceros). To the right of the door, *The Painter's Studio* shows Longhi at work. The life-size portrait of Francesco Guardi is also by Longhi.

Room XVIII (Green Drawing Room): The room has fine lacquer furniture, views of Venice, and a ceiling fresco by Gian Antonio Guardi.

Rooms XIX–XX: Room XIX has more frescoes by Gian Antonio Guardi. Room XX is a charming (reconstructed) bedroom with the bed in an alcove (with a *Madonna* by Rosalba Carriera above it), and a fine bureau. It has an adjoining closet and boudoir, with graceful 18th-century stucco decoration, and a ceiling fresco by Jacopo Guarana.

Gian Domenico Tiepolo: *The Promenade à Trois* (1770s).

Third floor

This is really an attic, with low ceilings, and its 13 rooms are used to display the huge collection of Egidio Martini, which was left to the city in the 20th century and covers all periods from the 15th–early 20th centuries. It is displayed more or less chronologically and is well labelled.

Some of the most important works are displayed in the first room (round to the left), with Bonifacio Veronese (Bonifacio de' Pitati), Bachiacca, Alvise Vivarini (the *Redeemer*) and Benedetto Licinio (portrait of a lady with her son) well represented.

The large works upstairs in Room 3 include the *Preaching of Christ* by Jacopo Tintoretto. In Room 6 is Guercino's *Philosopher*, with other late 17th-century paintings. Room 8 contains landscapes by Marco Ricci. Room 9 has lovely landscapes of Venice, Rome and Nice by Ippolito Caffi (*see p. 218*), and Venetian views by Emma Ciardi and Antonio Mancini. Room 10 has mid-18th-century works by Rosalba Carriera and *Boy with a Flute* by Giovanni Battista Piazzetta. In Room 11 the charming Farmacia ai do San Marchi, an 18th-century pharmacy and laboratory, with its original panelling, furniture and pharmacy jars, has been carefully reconstructed.

Mestrovich Collection and the Browning rooms

On the ground floor, off the *androne*, a short flight of stairs leads up to the little mezzanine apartment, occupied at the end of his life by Robert Browning. The choice little collection, in just two rooms, of the art historian Ferruccio Mestrovich has been displayed here since 2001. The Mestrovich family escaped to Venice in 1945, together with some 340,000 other refugees from Zara (Zadar) in Dalmatia, after it was destroyed by Allied bombs in support of Tito in the Second World War. In gratitude to the city of Venice, Mestrovich bequeathed his collection to the museum. It is well labelled, also in English. In the first room there is a tiny *Ecce Homo*, signed and dated 1499 by Cima da Conegliano; a lovely *Madonna and Child with Four Saints* (and a seascape in the background) by Bonifacio Veronese, a *Deposition* (in the presence of the two donors) by Jacopo Tintoretto, and two spandrels with the *Annunciation* by Carpaccio's son Benedetto. In the second room there is a very striking painting of the *Redeemer* by Benedetto Diana (there is a similar work by him in the National Gallery in London). In quite a different spirit is Francesco Guardi's delightful *Madonna and Child*, showing them both fully dressed for carnival, complete with crowns and hung with pearls: this very unusual painting was clearly inspired by the numerous popular statues of Madonnas dressed in Venetian costume in the city's churches. The portraits (in fine frames) include works by Jacopo Amigoni, Alessandro Longhi and Jacopo Tintoretto. *St Jerome Meditating on the Crucifix* is by the Bolognese painter Ubaldo Gandolfi (1728–81). The charming painted gameboard dates from the 18th century and was used for gambling, in a game similar to the present-day roulette.

The corner room on this mezzanine floor, which has a window on the Grand Canal and one on Rio San Barnaba, retains its decorations from Browning's time.

A WALK THROUGH DORSODURO

This walk covers the small area of Dorsoduro at its easternmost tip near the great Salute church, exploring a few of its quietest and most picturesque canals and campi before emerging on the Fondamenta delle Zattere, with its wonderful views of the wide Giudecca canal, and its interesting churches. It ends at the Squero di San Trovaso, where gondolas are still repaired, close to one of Venice's best-known bacari.

The walk begins outside the Salute church. Along the Rio della Salute you will see the fine triple apse of **San Gregorio**, built in 1342. Take the first bridge over the canal (signposted to the Guggenheim) into the calle which tunnels beneath the former monastic buildings of San Gregorio (with the entrance at no. 172 to the charming cloister on the right, now part of a private house) into a campo with a huge well-head decorated with roses, dominated by the Gothic façade of the church (*closed*).

Calle del Bastion continues straight on (passing a calle on the right which leads to a gondola ferry across the Grand Canal) past a number of small art galleries opened here in recent years (because of the vicinity of the Peggy Guggenheim Collection; *see p. 159*), and emerges on **Rio delle Fornace**, which connects the Grand Canal with the canal of the Giudecca. It is particularly charming since it has *fondamente* on either side of the water. Its name recalls the brick ovens which were formerly here.

Before following the little rio left out to the Giudecca canal it is well worth making a short detour here. Across Ponte San Gregorio, dating from 1772 and with its 19th-century iron balustrade equipped with an iron flagstaff holder, Ramo and Calle Barbaro continue to the attractive little **Campiello Barbaro** with its three trees and a little garden beside a fountain with running water, and a little old-world antique shop. Turn right along the tiny rio which curves round to the Fondamenta Ospedaletto, one of the most picturesque spots in the entire city. Halfway along on the left is an archway which has a marble tympanum with a relief of the Madonna protecting two members of a confraternity. It leads into a peaceful small *corte*, as do other entranceways further on: the courtyards have typical little Venetian houses, some walled gardens, and wells. At the end of the fondamenta is a simple little old-style restaurant (Ai Gondolieri; *see p. 363*).

Return to Rio della Fornace and follow it along its left hand side towards the wide Giudecca canal. In the secluded **Calle Querini**, the last opening on the left, a plaque at no. 252 records Ezra Pound ('titano della poesia') on the little house where he died in 1972. The famous poet (b. 1885) published his first book of verse in Venice in 1908 at his own expense: *A Lume Spento* (at the Antonini printing press in Cannaregio, with a print run of just 100 copies). But in May 1945 he was seized by Partisans in southern Italy at a villa in Rapallo owned by his companion, the violinist Olga Rudge, and he was handed over to the American command who accused him of treason for his Fascist sympathies and his wartime broadcasts to America in favour of Mussolini. He was imprisoned in solitary confinement in Pisa, and in the same year transferred to America where he was interned in a psychiatric hospital in Washington from which he was only released in 1958. He lived the last years of his life in Venice with Olga Rudge in this little house (the 'Hidden Nest'), and she lived on here after Pound's death, dying at the age of 101 in 1996 (the bell still bears her family name). Next door is the English Chaplain's house.

The simple house at the end of the rio on the right has a little hanging garden with a statue of the Madonna holding the Child out to greet us (protected by a green 'umbrella'), and the wall is decorated with Byzantine relief panels of animals and birds.

The fondamenta emerges on the **Fondamenta delle Zattere**, which skirts the wide Giudecca canal, busy with boats of all shapes and sizes, including cruise ships, and the car ferries which ply to and from the Lido. First paved in 1520, the Zattere is named after the cargo boats (*zattere*, literally 'rafts'), which used to pull in here and unload into the warehouses along the quay. In centuries past there were also brickworks and boat-building yards in the area. On the island of the Giudecca directly opposite is Palladio's splendid façade of the Redentore.

On the left are the huge **Magazzini del Sale**, which were the salt warehouses when the salt monopoly was one of the richest resources of the Republic from the 11th–15th centuries. The exterior was reconstructed in a Neoclassical style around 1835. Part of the splendid 15th-century interior is sometimes opened for exhibitions in connection with the Biennale, and boat-houses occupy the rest of the building.

Follow the Zattere right past the church of the **Spirito Santo** (*usually open 3–6, Sun 9–11*), founded in 1483, with a Renaissance façade. The interior, remodelled in the 18th century, contains a painting of the *Redeemer and Saints* (first south altar) by Giovanni Buonconsiglio, and (third north altar), *Marriage of the Virgin* by Palma Giovane. The upper nuns' chapel (*opened on request*) contains an 18th-century cycle of paintings of the *Mysteries of the Rosary*, including an *Assumption* by Francesco Fontebasso. On either side of the church are the former Scuola del Spirito Santo, founded in 1506, with a façade by Alessandro Tremignon (1680); and a (disappointing) residential building of 1958 by the Italian architect Ignazio Gardella (d. 1999). This is perhaps the best known 20th-century building in the historic centre of Venice, and has been both strongly criticised and highly praised. From here there is a distant view, beyond the conspicuous 19th-century Mulino Stucky (*see p. 310*), of the industrial port of Marghera.

The huge Classical building by Antonio da Ponte (with a fine colossal stone head on either end of its façade) was once one of the four main hospitals of the city, that of the **Incurabili**. It was opened in 1522 by Gaetano da Thiene, and in 1537 the founder of the Jesuit order, Ignatius Loyola, was a visitor here. At the end of the 16th century the orphanage attached to the hospital became famous for its girls' choir (along the lines of the Pietà and the Ospedaletto; *see p. 289*); in 1567 Jacopo

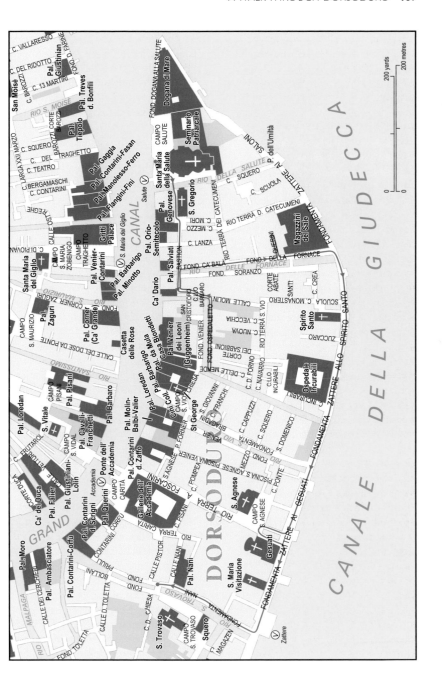

A map of the Dorsoduro area of Venice, showing the Grand Canal (CANAL GRANDE) and the Canale della Giudecca, with numerous labelled palazzi, churches, and waterways.

Labelled features on the map include:

C. VALLARESSO · C. DEL RIDOTTO · Pal. Giustinian · FOND. D. FARINE · C. BAROZZI · San Moisè · RIO S. MOISÈ · C. 13 MARTIRI · Pal. Treves d. Bonfili · FOND. DOGANA ALLA SALUTE · Dogana di Mare · Seminario Patriarcale · CAMPO SALUTE · C. LARGA XXII MARZO · C. SQUERO · C. DEL TEATRO · BAROZZI · Pal. Tiepolo · CAMPO TRAGHETTO · Pal. Gaggia · Pal. Contarini-Fasan · Pal. Manolesso-Ferro · Pal. Flangini-Fini · Santa Maria della Salute · P. DELL'UMILTÀ · SALONI · SALUTE · C. SCUOLA · ZATTERE · GIUDECCA · C. BERGAMASCHI · C. CONTARINI · REGHE · C. DEL TRAGHETTO · Gritti Palace · Salute · S. Maria del Giglio · CANAL GRANDE · Pal. Genovese · S. Gregorio · C. SQUERO · FONDAMENTA · Santa Maria del Giglio · C. DI PIOVAN · S. MARIA ZOBENIGO · Pal. Venier-Contarini · Pal. Orio-Semitecolo · RIO DELLA SALUTE · C. MORI · RIO TERRÀ DEI CATECUMENI · Magazzini del Sale · C. MAURIZIO · CORNER ZAGURI · FOND. · CAMPO TRAGHETTO · Pal. Barbarigo · Pal. Minotto · Pal. Salviati · C. MEZZO · RIO TERRÀ D. CATECUMENI · S. MAURIZIO · Pal. Zaguri · CAMPO · RIO S. MAURIZIO · Ca' Dario · BASTION · FOND. CA' BALÀ · C. LANZA · QUERINI · FORNACE · C. CREA · C. CHIESA · SANTISSIMO · RIO · Pal. Corner (Ca' Grande) · Casetta delle Rose · RIO DELLE FORNACE · FOND. SORANZO · CORTE ABATE · C. MONASTERO · SCUOLA · SANTI · C. CREA · Pal. Loredan · CAMPO PISANI · Pal. Pisani · S. Vitale · CALLE DEL DOSE DA PONTE · Pal. Barbaro · Pal. Loredan · Pal. Barbarigo · Casa Biondetti · Pal. Venier dei Leoni (Guggenheim) · SAN CRISTOFORO · C. MOLIN · CALLE MOLIN · C. D. FORNO · C. NUOVA · C. VECCHIA · RIO TERRÀ S. VIO · Spirito Santo · ZUCCARO · SCUOLA ALLO SPIRITO SANTO · C. FRUTAROL · Ca' del Duca · Pal. Falier · Pal. Giustiniani-Lolin · Pal. Cavalli-Franchetti · S. VIDAL · CAMPO S. VIDAL · Pal. Molin-Balbi-Valier · Gini Col. · CAMPO S. VIO · S. CHIESA · St George · FOND. VENIER · CORTE DEI SABBIONI · C. NAVARO · CLIO INCURABILI · Ospedale Incurabili · ZATTERE ALLO SPIRITO SANTO · C. INCURABILI · CORTE DUCA · CALLE VETTURI · Pal. Contarini d. Scrigni · Pal. Querini · Ponte dell' Accademia · CAMPO CARITÀ · Pal. Contarini d. Zaffo · Gallerie dell' Accademia · FOSCARINI · RIO TERRÀ A. FOSCARINI · P. FORNER · VENIER · P. POMPEA · S. VIO · S. GIOVANNI · C. CAPPUZZI · C. SQUERO · FONDAMENTA · S. DOMENICO · FONDAMENTA · Pal. Moro · Pal. Ambasciatore · Pal. Contarini-Corfù · CALLE DEI CERCHIERI · CONTARINI-CORFÙ · PRIULI · FOND. BOLLANI · S. AGNESE · RIO TERRÀ · CALLE PISTOR · CALLE NANI · S. Agnese · CAMPO S. AGNESE · PISCINA S. AGNESE PISONA VENIER · C. MEZZO · RIO · C. PONTE · DELLA · DORSODURO · MALPAGA · FOND. DEI CERCHIERI · RIO · FOND. TOLETTA · CALLE D. TOLETTA · FOND. D. CHIESA · S. Trovaso · CAMPO S. TROVASO · Squero · RIO S. TROVASO · Pal. Nani · CALLE NANI · S. Maria Visitazione · FONDAMENTA · Gesuati · Zattere · CANALE DELLA GIUDECCA · C. MAGAZEN

Scale: 0 — 200 yards · 0 — 200 metres

Sansovino designed an oval church in the courtyard, particularly adapted to concerts (but this was demolished in 1831). It later became an institute for children, and has recently been restored as the seat of the Accademia di Belle Arti, which has moved here from the ex-Scuola della Carità, to allow its famous galleries (Gallerie dell'Accademia) to expand and display more works. Founded in 1750, the Accademia's first director was Giovanni Battista Piazzetta; he was succeeded by Giambattista Tiepolo. The door is usually open so that you can see the cloister, but otherwise the entire building has been radically restored as classrooms and administrative offices.

On the corner of Campiello Incurabili, the green house (no. 560) with a good 19th-century *St George and the Dragon* relief was purchased in 1883 by Horatio Brown, who lived here for the rest of his life (he died in 1926). Brown was the best known British resident in Venice of his day, and continued Rawdon Brown's remarkable work in the State Archives (*see p. 206*), bringing out five more volumes of the *Calendar* on Anglo-Venetian relations. (Although they share a name, the two Browns were not related.) Horatio's *Life on the Lagoons*, written here, is dedicated to 'my gondolier' Antonio Salin, and contains an interesting history of the gondola, 'the most perfect carriage in the world'. He admired the quiet, deliberate, and unhurried motions of the gondolier, and notes how curious it is that he stands behind the passenger, hence always out of sight. He records that passengers deposit their payment on the gunwale of the boat on the gondola fer-

ries across the Grand Canal (just as they do today). He points out that the form of the gondola has remained unchanged since the 18th century, so that the ones painted by Guardi are identical to the ones still to be seen in modern Venice (*for more on the gondola, see p. 294*). He later wrote the two-volume *Studies in Venetian History* while living here, which provides a fascinating survey of the Republic. He notes that, 'In no other state have we so little about personal details of its great men: Venice demanded and secured the effacement of the individual … the state was everything, the individual nothing'. He produced a detailed analysis of the 'government machinery' of 'one of the most rigid and enduring constitutions that the world has ever seen'. He is also extremely perceptive about the Byzantine influence on Venice, and he identified what he felt to be the most important characteristic of the famous Venetian merchants, who were known throughout the world: that they were usually both the owner and the carrier of their goods, while the commercial policy of the Republic was to accumulate merchandise in the city for distribution so that foreign traders were forced to come to the city to carry out their business activities.

Beyond a bridge the fondamenta now follows a garden wall decorated with statues (behind which can be seen a large pine tree and group of ilexes) as far as another bridge across the lovely **Rio San Vio**, which has double fondamenta. Here the Zattere becomes suddenly more animated. The two, very well-known hotels right next to each other here have always been favourite places to stay,

Detail from the portal of Santa Maria della Visitazione.

especially for British visitors. The charming Seguso (*see p. 353*) is still family-run and preserves its lovely old-fashioned interior. The slightly smarter Calcina (*see p. 353*) is where Ruskin stayed in 1877, on almost the last of his many visits to the city while he was at work on *St Mark's Rest*. It has recently been renovated and a new restaurant, Piscina, opened on the ground floor (with tables on the water in fine weather) Beyond a pizzeria and a mooring for barges is the campo with the church of **Sant'Agnese** (*usually only open for Sunday services*). Founded in the 10th century, it is interesting for its simple basilican plan. It contains paintings by the little-known Venetian artist Lattanzio Querena (d. 1853).

On the Zattere the church of the **Gesuati** (Santa Maria del Rosario; *open Mon–Sat 10–5; Chorus Pass*) is a fine building by Giorgio Massari (1726–43). The steps are a popular place for people to sit and enjoy the last of the sun. The Rococo interior has a remarkably successful design, with the dark high altar lit from behind. It has two very fine works by Giambattista Tiepolo: the *Institution of the Rosary* frescoed on the ceiling in 1737–39, and the *Virgin in Glory with Sts Rosa, Catherine of Siena, and Agnes of Montepulciano* (1739) on the first south altar. Two other 18th-century altarpieces in the church also have trios of saints: that on the first north altar by Sebastiano Ricci, and that on the third south altar by Giovanni Battista Piazzetta. The *Crucifixion* is by Jacopo Tintoretto (c. 1570). The statues and reliefs in the nave are by Giovanni Maria Morleiter. The elaborate tabernacle on the high altar is encased in lapis lazuli and has precious marble columns.

The Zattere is now busy with several vaporetto stops. At the side entrance to the Centro Culturale Don Orione Artigianelli, a former convent with two cloisters, which has recently become a very simple but pleasant hotel (main entrance on Campo Sant'Agnese), you will see a worried face carved in marble with its mouth open ready to receive complaints about the local health service. It dates from the days of the Republic. Next door is the Renaissance church of **Santa Maria della Visitazione** (1494–1524) with a handsome Lombardesque façade and portal. It contains a charming wooden roof filled with 58 panels of saints and prophets, and a central tondo of the *Visitation* painted in the 16th century by a Tuscan or northern Italian artist. In the pretty sanctuary are four large painted *tondi* of the Evangelists (showing the influence of the Florentine art of Andrea del Castagno) and two 16th-century monochrome figures of bishops. In the choir hangs a *Pentecost* by Padovanino (a 15th-century bas-relief of the *Trinity* is at present hidden from view).

Beyond a well-known ice-cream bar (Nico) is Rio San Trovaso. Go up the right-hand fondamenta. On your left you will see a picturesque boat-building yard, the **Squero di San Trovaso**, which dates from the 17th century, even though it has been restored. The living quarters above have a long wooden balcony usually decorated with plants. It was in yards such as this (another survives nearby in Rio della Avogaria) that the great Venetian fleet of warships and merchant ships was built before the end of the 15th century; after that date boat-building was concentrated in the Arsenale. This *squero* now specialises in the construction and repair of gondolas. The church of San Trovaso stands next door (*see p. 166*).

At the foot of the first bridge, by the 15th-century Palazzo Nani, is one of the most popular *bacari* in this area, officially named Schiavi after the friendly proprietor and his family, but known to Venetians as the *Bottegon* (the shop). It has a delightful Venetian atmosphere: there is no seating, but when it is sunny clients stand on the pavement outside and balance their glasses on the wall of the canal. It is also a good place to buy a bottle of wine, and is especially good for its great variety of delicious *cicchetti*, made and served by the owner's wife.

SAN POLO

The *sestiere* of San Polo takes its name from the church of San Polo, which sits in one of the largest—and most 'Venetian'—*campi* in Venice, far away from the crowds, and used by local children as a playground. Goldoni lived close by, and his charming little house can be visited. The *sestiere* also includes the lively area at the western foot of the Rialto Bridge, with its busy markets where Venetians still come to do their food shopping. There are numerous grocer's shops and bakeries in the *calli* close by, as well as some of the best *bacari* in town. This area must have been just as crowded in the days of the Republic, when it was the commercial centre of the city, attracting merchants, bankers, brokers and traders of all kinds. Close together at the western limit of the *sestiere* are the famous church of the Frari, filled with Venetian masterpieces of sculpture and painting, and the Scuola Grande di San Rocco, where the walls and ceilings are covered with superb works by Tintoretto.

THE RIALTO & ITS DISTRICT
Map p. 411, F2–E2

The Rialto Bridge

This famous bridge stands at the topographical centre of the city, linking the *sestieri* of San Polo and San Marco. A bridge has existed at this point since earliest times, and it remained the only bridge across the Grand Canal throughout the Republic. The area known as the Rialto (*rivo alto*, high bank) is thought to have been one of the first places to be settled by the earliest inhabitants of the lagoon because it was one of the highest points and the best protected. Since the beginning of the Republic it has been the commercial and economic centre of Venice. The markets, established here as early as 1097, were reconstructed by Scarpagnino along the lines of the medieval buildings, after a disastrous fire in 1514. Remains of the quay of the 14th-century market were discovered beneath the present markets during maintenance work in 1999 (since covered over).

The right-hand outer walkway of the Rialto Bridge descends past the 16th-century Palazzo dei Camerlenghi, formerly the seat of the Exchequer (*see p. 138*) to the busy Ruga degli Orefici, where the goldsmiths had their workshops. It leads through the colourful market in front of the porticoed Fabbriche Vecchie, by Scarpagnino. These buildings also extend around the Campo San Giacomo. Here, amidst the stalls and barrows, is the little church of San Giacomo di Rialto. On the exterior of its apse is a 12th-century inscription exhorting merchants to honesty.

Two churches of the Rialto

San Giacomo di Rialto (San Giacometto; *map p. 411, F2. Open 9.30–12 & 4–6, except Sun afternoon*) was once thought to have been founded in the year 421 and so considered to be the oldest church in Venice. It is, instead, first documented in 1152 and so probably dates from that century. It is preceded by a Gothic entrance portico; above is a large clock of 1410. The domed Greek-cross plan on a tiny scale, derived from Byzantine models, was faithfully preserved in the rebuilding of 1601. The interior retains its six reused ancient Greek marble columns with finely carved 11th-century Corinthian capitals and pulvins, also in Greek marble. Over the high altar are statues of St James and angels by Alessandro Vittoria (1602), and on the right an *Annunciation*, by Titian's nephew, Marco Vecellio.

Across the campo is a crouching figure known as the ***Gobbo di Rialto***, made in the 16th century by Pietro da Salò: it supports a flight of steps leading to a rostrum of Egyptian granite from which the laws of the Republic were proclaimed. From here the Erberia, the wholesale market for fruit and vegetables, opens onto the Grand Canal, adjoined by Sansovino's Fabbriche Nuove (begun in 1554) and the markets which extend along the canal to the Pescheria or fish market (*see below*).

At the end of Ruga degli Orefici, in the broad Ruga Vecchia San Giovanni (left), an archway on the left forms the inconspicuous entrance to **San Giovanni Elemosinario** (*open Mon–Sat 10–5; Chorus Pass; map p. 411, F2*), the first church to be built in the Rialto area (mentioned as early as 1051), which still has its campanile of 1398–1410. After the Rialto fire of 1514 it was rebuilt by Scarpagnino in 1527–29. In the interior, on a Greek-cross plan, the high altarpiece of *St John the Almsgiver* was painted for the church by Titian (c. 1545). On the left wall there is a painting by the great painter's nephew, Marco Vecellio, which shows the interior of the church in a scene of Doge Leonardo Donà receiving the Holy Water from the parish priest. In the chapel to the right of the sanctuary there is an altarpiece of *Sts Catherine, Sebastian and Roch*, by Pordenone, who also carried out the frescoes on the dome of the church, although these were only discovered, under a thin layer of plaster, in 1985. The church also contains various late 16th-century works by Leonardo Corona, whose crowded compositions show the influence of Tintoretto, even though he never reached the heights of his master: his works produce an effect which is nearly always over-dramatic, with fussy details detracting from the central theme. However, Corona still had a successful career in Venice and was even invited to take part in the vast decorative scheme to glorify the Republic in the Sala del Maggior Consiglio in the Doge's Palace. Some of his works are also derived from Palma Giovane, who is well represented here in a lunette of *St Roch Healing the Plague-stricken*. Another lunette (attributed to Domenico Tintoretto) on the west wall (right of the door) shows God the Father and Doge Marino Grimani and Dogaressa Morosina Morosini with members of a confraternity. The organ was made by Pietro Nacchini in 1749.

Ruga dei Spezieri (where spices were sold) continues the line of Ruga degli Orefici into Campo delle Beccarie with the arcaded hall of the neo-Gothic **Pescheria**, scene of the busy daily fish market, which is well worth a visit just to see the great variety of fresh fish for sale. Notice the tops of the columns in the hall on the Grand Canal, carved with all sorts of fish, sea creatures and fishing boats. The present market was built in 1907, but there has been a fish market on this site since the 14th century. On the exterior towards the Grand Canal there is a tondo with a painted terracotta relief of Pietro Aretino, who lived nearby (*see p. 125*).

San Cassiano

Map p. 411, E2. Open Tues–Sat 9–12.

Beyond the wide Calle dei Botteri is the church of San Cassiano, thought to have been founded as early as the 10th century, but rebuilt (except for the 13th-century campanile) in the 17th century.

The interior has recently been restored. In the sanctuary are three remarkable **paintings by Jacopo Tintoretto**: the *Crucifixion*, the *Resurrection*, and the *Descent into Limbo*. All three paintings are extremely unusual for their iconography: the *Crucifixion* is particularly memorable, and unlike any other painting of this subject. The tragic atmosphere of the picture is heightened by the menacing sky and line of soldiers with their spears on the low horizon, and the abandoned pink robe at the foot of the Cross. The dramatic scene of the *Descent into Limbo* includes the nude figure of Eve and a splendid angel flying away. In the *Resurrection*, the figures of the patron saints of the church, St Cassian and St Cecilia appear, as well as charming putti, two of them holding wreaths of lilies. The altar front was carved by Heinrich Meyring in 1696.

On the first altar in the south aisle, *St John the Baptist between Saints* is attributed to Rocco Marconi. In the chapel to the right of the high altar, the *Visitation* (with a portrait in a tondo beneath of a member of the confraternity of the Scuola della Visitazione), the *Annunciation to St Zacharias*, and the *Birth of St John* are all by Leandro Bassano. Next to the sacristy in the north aisle is a charming chapel (automatic light) which preserves its decorations of 1746, with an altarpiece (*Madonna and Child with St Charles Borromeo and St Philip Neri*) signed by Giovanni Battista Pittoni (1763), and *Christ in the Garden* by Leandro Bassano. The second altarpiece in this aisle is by Matteo Ponzone.

Calle del Campanile ('del Campaniel') leads from the church down to the Fondamenta Riva d'Olio on the Grand Canal, from where it is a short walk back to the Rialto markets and bridge.

San Silvestro

From the foot of the Rialto Bridge, Fondamenta del Vin (*map p. 411, F3*) skirts the Grand Canal as far as Rio Terrà San Silvestro, which leads away from the waterfront. It passes a column with an 11th-century capital (set into the wall of a house) before reaching (left) the **church of San Silvestro** (*map p. 411, E3; open 8–11.30 & 3.30–6.30*), with a façade completed in 1909. The Neoclassical interior is by Lorenzo Santi. The apse (with the organ on the east wall) is divided from the nave by Corinthian columns. On the right side, the first altar has a *Baptism of Christ* by Jacopo Tintoretto, and the second altar a *Holy Family* by Johann Carl Loth. On the first altar on the left side is a good painting by Girolamo da Santacroce, particularly interesting since it shows the English martyr St Thomas Becket enthroned. On the left wall near the west end is a Gothic polyptych in an elaborate 14th-century frame.

Opposite the church is **Palazzo Valier** (no. 1022), with a Doric doorway, where the great painter Giorgione died in 1510. In the peaceful Campo San Silvestro, the fine brick campanile has a stone bas-relief. Calle del Luganegher leads from here to the busy **Campo Sant'Aponal** (*map p. 411, E3*) with eight *calli* leading into it. Here is the deconsecrated church of Sant'Aponal (Sant'Apollinare). Founded in the 11th century, it was rebuilt in the 15th. On the Gothic façade, above a round window, is a badly worn relief of the Crucifix (14th century); below, in a tabernacle, are reliefs of the *Crucifixion* and episodes from the life of Christ (1294). It has been closed to worship since 1970 and the interior is used as an archive. To the left, in Calle del Campanile, is the Romanesque bell-tower.

Calle del Ponte Storto leads to the bridge of the same name; on the right (no. 1280) is the birthplace of Bianca Cappello (c. 1560–87), the beautiful 'daughter of the Republic', who fled to Florence at the age of 15 and after a long liaison with Grand Duke Francesco I de' Medici, married him in 1578, just two months after the death of his unloved first wife. Across the canal, the *sottoportico* continues past an unusually narrow calle to the next bridge which re-crosses the canal. Calle Cavalli soon diverges right and over another bridge, emerging in Campo San Polo.

CAMPO SAN POLO
Map p. 411, D3

The large and peaceful Campo San Polo is one of the largest and most attractive squares in the city and its shape makes it a favourite playground for children. The church is especially noted for its painting of the *Last Supper* by Jacopo Tintoretto and the works by Gian Domenico Tiepolo in the Oratory of the Crucifix. Among the interesting palaces which follow the curved side of the campo (once bordered by a canal) are (no. 1957) the well-proportioned Baroque Palazzo Tiepolo, attributed to Giorgio Massari, and next to it (no. 2169) Palazzo Soranzo, with its marble windows with good capitals.

The church of San Polo
Open Mon–Sat 10–5; Chorus Pass.

The church of San Polo bears interesting reliefs (the earliest dating from the 13th century) on the exterior of the east end. The south doorway is a fine Gothic work attributed to Bartolomeo Bon, with two angels holding an inscription and crowned by the half-figure of St Paul. Outside, the isolated campanile (1362) has two fine Romanesque lions carved at its base.

The interior, with a ship's keel roof, was altered in 1804 by Davide Rossi and given a Neoclassical arcade. On the left of the west door, **Jacopo Tintoretto's** *Last Supper* is one of the best of his many paintings of this subject (see also San Giorgio Maggiore; *p. 304*). On the left side of the south entrance door is an interesting sculptural fragment of the *Nativity*. Above the high altar is a fragment of an early 15th-century

Venetian Crucifix, and in the sanctuary are paintings by Palma Giovane. In the left apse chapel, the *Marriage of the Virgin* is by Paolo Veronese. On the left side, the third altarpiece of the *Preaching of St Paul* is by Paolo Piazza, and the second altarpiece, the *Virgin Appearing to a Saint*, is by Giambattista Tiepolo (1754).

At the west end, beneath the organ by Gaetano Callido (1763), is the entrance to the **Oratory of the Crucifix**, recently restored. The chapel, with an attractive east end, lit by a dome with four columns, has a wonderful series of paintings carried out in 1749 by Giambattista Tiepolo's son Gian Domenico, illustrating the 14 Stations of the Cross. They are all the same size, relatively small and rectangular, and they portray Christ's Passion in a superb Venetian setting: the religious figures are accompanied by turbanned orientals in brightly-coloured robes, and elegantly-dressed ladies, probably including portraits of some of Gian Domenico's contemporaries. The sequence begins on the right wall with Christ condemned to death—as in the subsequent scenes, the diminutive figure of Christ on the balcony, exposed to the crowd, takes second place to the colourful scene below. In the third scene there is an elderly and portly Arab in a turban, splendidly dressed in yellow (the colour chosen for many of the main protagonists in the later scenes), who looks on as Christ falls beneath the weight of the Cross. In Christ's encounter with the Holy women (the eighth panel), the ladies have gorgeous damascened costumes and have even brought along their well-dressed children to be 'presented'. These are thought to be portraits of the painter's own family. The eleventh scene showing Christ being nailed to the Cross is one of the most beautiful, and the artist's attention is at last on the very finely drawn nude figure of Christ, although here again a splendidly-attired old man dominates the scene. The last scene, showing Christ placed in the tomb, provides a final dramatic note, as it is dominated by the white sarcophagus and winding sheet stained with blood with the head of the Dead Christ only just visible. Gian Domenico also painted the four paintings of scenes from the lives of saints in the sanctuary, and the glory of angels and *Resurrection* in the ceiling.

The Aldine Press

From the north side of the campo (beyond Palazzo Soranzo), Rio Terrà Sant'Antonio and Calle Bernardo lead across a bridge—where the Da Fiore restaurant (*see p. 364*) has its one tiny outdoor terrace on the water—to Rio Terrà Secondo, where a small Gothic palace (no. 2311) is the traditional **site of the Aldine Press** (*map p. 411, D2*) set up in 1490 by the Roman scholar and celebrated printer Aldus Manutius (1450–1516) on his arrival in Venice in the same year. In 1494 the first dated book issued from the press, which became famous for its publication of the Greek classics. Manutius designed the Italic type in 1501, and took advice from his friend Erasmus, as well as from the Venetian scholar Pietro Bembo (*see box overleaf*). Numerous other presses were set up in the city in quick succession, and about a quarter of the 1,821 books published in the whole of Europe between 1495–97 were produced in Venice; it has been estimated that during the 16th century three new books were printed in Venice every week. Manutius' work was carried on by his son and grandson.

Pietro Bembo (1470–1547)

The Venetian humanist Pietro Bembo worked closely with Manutius, suggesting the texts he should publish and acting as his editor (and his own *De Aetna dialogus* appeared with the Press's famous anchor and dolphin colophon mark in 1495). The edition of Petrarch's *Le cose volgari*, published by Manutius with the collaboration of Bembo in 1501, was the first book in the vernacular to be printed as an octavo volume. The following year the *Divine Comedy* issued from the press under the title of *Le terze rime di Dante* and it, too, was edited by Bembo: this edition, which marked a linguistic and literary milestone, remained the *textus receptus* for all subsequent editions right up to the end of the 16th century.

Bembo was appointed librarian of the Libreria Marciana (*see p. 82*) and official historian of the Republic in 1530. He acted as secretary to Leo X and was then created a cardinal in 1539 by Paul III. He frequented Queen Caterina Cornaro's court at Asolo (*see p. 112*), and coined the term *asolare*, meaning to amuse oneself in amiable aimlessness. He used both Latin and Italian in his writings, and was a great scholar of Greek philosophy.

Casa Goldoni and San Tomà

The salizzada past the south door of San Polo leads to the pretty Ponte San Polo (1775), from where Sanmicheli's main façade of **Palazzo Corner-Mocenigo** (begun after 1545) can be seen on the canal (right). In an apartment here the scurrilous Frederick Rolfe spent the last years of his life. Having already published his best-known novel, *Hadrian VII*, he arrived in Venice in 1908 and, calling himself Baron Corvo, came to be known and feared as an outspoken eccentric. In his autobiographical *The Desire and Pursuit of the Whole*—not published until 1934, long after his death, to avoid libel actions—he took a keen delight in insulting his contemporaries. His conduct earned him a terrible reputation, and he was many times reduced to near destitution. A.J.A. Symons attempted to solve the mystery of his life in *The Quest for Corvo*, published in the same year.

Calle dei Saoneri continues to Rio Terrà dei Nomboli. At the end on the left, the dark and narrow Ramo Pisani diverges towards the Grand Canal and Palazzo Pisani della Moretta, which has a fine 18th-century interior, beautifully restored (but not normally open to the public). Calle dei Nomboli continues to (no. 2793) Palazzo Centani (15th century), known as the **Casa Goldoni** (*map p. 411, D3; open 10–4 except Sun*), where the playwright Carlo Goldoni (1707–93) was born. His comedies give a vivid idea of social life in 18th-century Venice. Not only did he satirise the old Venetian aristocracy, but he described with brilliance the ordinary people of the city. He marked an important stage in the development of theatrical production, which hitherto had been dominated by improvised drama by professional masked actors, known as the *Commedia dell'Arte*. The house has a picturesque Gothic courtyard with a charming staircase and a pretty well-head. In the interior you can visit just three rooms. One has an 18th-century puppet theatre. Another, with a good Murano chandelier, has a display on Goldoni himself. The last room illustrates the history of Venetian theatres, and exhibits some editions of Goldoni's works and two portraits of him thought to be by Antonio Longhi. On the upper floor there is an important library and archive open to students.

Beyond Campiello San Tomà, **Campo di San Tomà** (*map p. 410, C3*) is soon reached. The church has been closed for restoration for many years. The 15th-century Scuola dei Calegheri (now used as a library) once belonged to the city's cobblers and shoemakers. The exterior bears a *Madonna della Misericordia* and a charming relief of *St Mark Healing the Cobbler Anianus*, attributed to Pietro Lombardo or Antonio Rizzo (1478), and decorated at the bottom with stylised shoes. Legend tells that when St Mark arrived in Alexandria, one of his shoes needed mending and the cobbler Anianus was called in to help. While the shoemaker was at work with his awl, he cut his hand with the blade, and swore to the 'only God'. Mark interpreted this as a miraculous sign, and healed the cut (by mixing a little of his saliva with the earth) declaring 'let him be healed in the name of God'. When Anianus saw the power of Mark's faith, he was converted to Christianity, receiving his baptism from Mark himself. As the first Christian in Alexandria, he succeeded Mark as bishop of the city. Anianus is always portrayed in a turban to denote his 'heathen' origins, and as a reminder that the episode takes place in Alexandria. At his death he was buried in a church named after him in Alexandria, but like St Mark, his body was brought to Venice in 1288, and he also became a saint.

St Mark Heals the Cobbler Anianus, relief above the door of the former shoemakers' guildhall.

SANTA MARIA GLORIOSA DEI FRARI
Map p. 410, C3

Open Mon–Sat 10–6, Sun 1–6; Chorus Pass.

Santa Maria Gloriosa dei Frari, commonly known as 'the Frari', is dedicated to the Assumption of the Virgin. It is the church of the mendicant order of Friars Minor, or Franciscans, and in size rivals that of the other mendicant order, the Dominican church of Santi Giovanni e Paolo. It contains numerous masterpieces of painting and sculpture, including Titian's huge *Assumption*, as well as his *Pala Pesaro*, and, in the sacristy, one of Giovanni Bellini's most beautiful works. The church also has numerous important doges' tombs, a statue by Donatello, and a 15th-century choir.

The exterior

The original Franciscan church was founded c. 1250, and the present brick Gothic church was begun c. 1330 but not finished until after 1443. The majestic campanile (the tallest in the city after St Mark's) dates from the second half of the 14th century, but in 2006 it was being monitored as there were signs that it was unstable. On the severe west front, the Gothic doorway has sculptures attributed to Alessandro Vittoria (the *Risen Christ*), and the workshop of Bartolomeo Bon. The other doorways have sculptures of St Peter and a fine 15th-century relief of the Madonna and Child with angels.

The interior

The huge interior, some 90m long, is cruciform with an aisled nave of eight bays joined by wooden tie-beams. Titian's magnificent *Assumption* in the apse, at its most impressive when seen from the main west door, is framed by the arch of the monks' choir. Many of the most interesting monuments in the church are high up and difficult to see, but most of them have been cleaned in recent years. Although the church faces southwest, it is described here as though it had the altar at the east end.

A **West wall:** The tomb of the senator Pietro Bernardo **(1)**, d. 1538, is thought to be a late work by Tullio Lombardo; the monument to the procurator Alvise Pasqualigo **(2)**, who died ten years earlier, is attributed to Lorenzo Bregno.

B **South aisle:** The holy-water stoup **(3)** has a bronze statuette of St Agnes by Girolamo Campagna, forming a pair with the one opposite, bearing a statuette of St Anthony of Padua (1609). The huge Carrara marble **monument to Titian (4)** is raised above the place where Venice's greatest painter is traditionally believed to have been buried. The (somewhat ponderous) monument, bearing a relief of Titian's own high altarpiece of the *Assumption*, was commissioned by the Austrian emperor Ferdinand I from Luigi Zandomeneghi and his son Pietro in 1843, and completed in 1852. The second altarpiece of the *Purification of the Virgin* **(5)** was painted in 1548 by Giuseppe Salviati. On the third altar the statue of St Jerome **(6)** is one of Alessandro Vittoria's best works. The fourth altar

has a *Martyrdom of St Catherine* **(7)** by Palma Giovane; 1590–95). Beyond is a monument to Marco Zen **(8)**, Bishop of Torcello, who died in 1641.

C **South transept:** The monument to Jacopo Marcello **(9)**, who was killed in battle in 1484 at the head of the Venetian fleet during an encounter with the Turks at Gallipoli, does not follow the usual form of niches and statues but has an oval frame and three free-standing statues at the top of a double sarcophagus. Formerly thought to be the work of Pietro Lombardo, it has recently been attributed to his contemporary, also from Lombardy, Giovanni Buora. The worn fresco high up of the hero's triumph is by a 15th-century artist of the school of Mantegna. The sarcophagus of 'Beato Pacifico' **(10)** (Scipione Bon, a friar of the church who is thought to have supervised part of the building work), beneath an elaborate canopy, in a florid Gothic style of 1437, is ascribed to the Tuscan artists Nanni di Bartolo and Michele da Firenze, who also worked in Venice on the exterior sculpture of St Mark's and the Doge's Palace. Over the door to the sacristy is the fine tomb of Admiral Benedetto Pesaro (**11**), by Lorenzo Bregno. Pesaro died in Corfu in 1503. His tomb has interesting reliefs with battleships and fortresses illustrating his victories over the Turks. The statue of Mars is by Baccio da Montelupo (1537), and is the only work in Venice by this Tuscan artist, who was both a sculptor and architect. The tomb of Paolo Savelli (**12**), a Roman *condottiere*, dates from around 1406, and was the first in Venice to include an equestrian statue. It is also thought to be a Tuscan work, and shows both Gothic and Renaissance elements. The statues on the marble sarcophagus have been attributed to the great Sienese master Jacopo della Quercia.

D **Sacristy:** This is a delightful, peaceful room with a miscellany of works of art, filled with the gentle tick of an old clock, its face adorned with the crossed hands and stigmata of St Francis. On the opposite side is an exquisitely carved wooden clock-face (**13**) with allegories of Time, the work of Francesco Pianta (17th century). In the apse, still in the original frame made for it by Jacopo da Faenza, is the splendid **triptych by Giovanni Bellini (14)**, painted for the chapel in 1488. It shows the Madonna and Child between Sts Nicholas of Bari, Peter, Mark and Benedict. 'Jewel-like' is an over-used phrase to describe Bellini's Madonnas, but it can aptly be used here. Seeing it is like looking into a shrine. The Virgin, dressed in a glorious blue robe, sits beneath a golden dome, perhaps a reference to the gold-ground mosaics in

the Basilica of St Mark. Ruskin justly considered this the greatest work in Venice by Bellini: 'the only artist who appears to me to have united, in equal and magnificent measures, justness of drawing, nobleness of colouring, and perfect manliness of treatment with the purest religious feeling'. It was commissioned in memory of Franceschina Pesaro, who died in 1478 and is buried here, by her three sons (one of them, Benedetto, is buried in the church, see **11**, above). The four saints (*Benedict and Mark are illustrated on p. 205*) were chosen since they bear the names of Franceschina's husband and sons.

The late 16th-century painting of the *Deposition* (**15**) is by Niccolò Frangipane. The Lombardesque lavabo (**16**) has two sphinxes and a classical frieze with lovely coloured marble inlay. Tullio Lombardo made the exquisite little marble tabernacle (**17**). Numerous reliquaries are kept in the incredibly elaborate 17th-century showcase (**18**) by Cabianca and Brustolon.

E **Chapter house:** A small display of vestments and church silver is kept here. The attractive Palladian cloister with its elaborate well-head can be seen outside the windows. Opposite the windows is the sarcophagus (with a relief of the *Death of the Virgin*) of Doge Francesco Dandolo, and above it a precious lunette, signed and dated 1339 by the first great Venetian painter, **Paolo Veneziano**. It shows Doge Francesco Dandolo and his wife Elizabeth being presented to the Virgin by Sts Francis and Elizabeth. It is thought to be the earliest doge's portrait drawn from life to have survived.

Lunette by Paolo Veneziano, an artist whose work is grounded in the traditions of Byzantium, but who can also be seen as the forerunner of the Venetian School.

F **South choir chapels:** The Bernardo Chapel **(19)** has a brightly-painted altarpiece by Bartolomeo Vivarini (1482), still in its magnificent original frame. In the Chapel of the Sacrament **(20)** are two Gothic funerary monuments, one of which commemorates the Florentine ambassador Duccio degli Uberti (d. 1336). The Chapel of St John the Baptist **(21)** contains an altar erected in 1436 by Florentines resident in the city. They commissioned for it a statue of their patron saint, John the Baptist, by no less a sculptor than **Donatello**. The first documented work in the Veneto by the greatest sculptor of the Florentine Renaissance, signed and dated 1438, it still stands here—easy to miss at the centre of a tabernacle decorated with

other gilded polychrome wood statues by unknown minor artists. It was Donatello's first statue to be made in wood (he may also have chosen this medium knowing that it would make it easier to transport it here from Florence), and is a superb work which has similarities with his later and much more famous *Mary Magdalene*, now in the Museo dell'Opera del Duomo in Florence.

G **Sanctuary:** The apse is lit by fine stained glass windows and is filled with **Titian's** *Assumption* (1518), the largest altarpiece in Venice, celebrated among his masterpieces for its dramatic movement and its amazing colouring.

SANTA MARIA GLORIOSA DEI FRARI

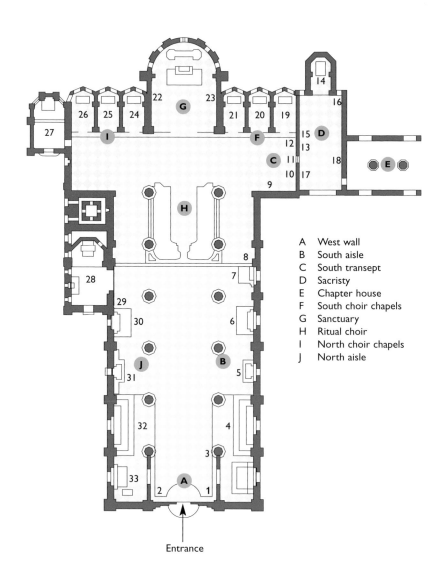

A   West wall
B   South aisle
C   South transept
D   Sacristy
E   Chapter house
F   South choir chapels
G   Sanctuary
H   Ritual choir
I   North choir chapels
J   North aisle

Entrance

Titian (Tiziano Vecellio; 1488–1576)
Titian succeeded Giovanni Bellini as the most important painter in Venice, and was one of the greatest Italian painters of all time. He was painting at a time when Venice flourished and was at the height of her power. The *Assumption*, commissioned by the Franciscans in 1516, is an early work showing the influence of Raphael and Michelangelo. It had such success with the Venetians that Titian very soon became the favourite portrait painter of the nobility; he was appointed official painter of the Republic in 1517. This meant that, among other duties, he had to paint the portrait of every doge on taking office (since he lived so long, this meant that he painted all the doges from Antonio Grimani in 1523 to Francesco Venier in 1554; a total of six). His other masterpiece in the Frari, the *Pala Pesaro* (1526; *see overleaf*), includes excellent portraits of the Pesaro family. Although there are numerous paintings by Titian in Venice, he also worked for the most important Italian courts, as well as for the papacy, the Habsburg emperors, and Philip II of Spain.

The high altar dates from 1516. The **tomb of Doge Niccolò Tron** (d. 1473) **(22)** is a masterpiece by Antonio Rizzo, even though the doge's short term of office of just two years failed to make much impression on subsequent historians of the Republic. Rizzo, who also worked in the courtyard of the Doge's Palace (*see p. 94*), here produces a perfectly proportioned monument. The doge, who is known to have been exceptionally tall and who always wore a beard, is first shown (on the lowest level) in a life-like portrait standing between two beautiful statues of *Faith* and *Charity*. Above is an inscription recounting his exploits and then his effigy on a sarcophagus held aloft by figures of the Virtues. At the top are five niches with more allegorical figures, and these also appear in the frame amongst pages holding the doge's emblem. It is less easy to make out the religious elements: the lone figure of the Risen Christ in the lunette at the very top with the annunciatory angel and Virgin on either side. The great variety of precious marbles and the gilding on the details adds to the splendour of this great tomb, recognised as one of the most sublime examples of Renaissance funerary art in Venice.

Opposite is the fine **tomb of Francesco Foscari (23)**, who died in 1457 after 34 years as doge (*see pp. 73–74*). He is shown beneath a beautifully-executed canopy, with statues representing Power, Wisdom and Justice—the virtues of a pious ruler. The late Gothic mausoleum may be the work of Niccolò di Giovanni Fiorentino. The painted 13th-century Crucifix is attributed to an artist named from this work the 'Maestro del Crocifisso dei Frari', probably of the Tuscan school.

H **Ritual choir:** The ritual choir extends into the nave as in many cathedrals in England and France, but it is rare to see this in Italian churches. It contains three tiers of magnificent choir stalls carved by Marco Cozzi (1468), with beautifully-detailed intarsia decoration by Lorenzo and Cristoforo Canozzi. The lovely choir-screen (1475) by Bartolomeo Bon and Pietro Lombardo is faced with Carrara marble and decorated with Istrian stone figures of saints and prophets in relief; above are ten apostles and a *Crucifixion* between the Virgin and St John the Evangelist, with angels as lecterns. The organs are by Gaetano Callido (1795) and Giovanni Battista Piaggia (1732).

I **North choir chapels:** The Chapel of the Franciscan Saints **(24)** has a *Madonna and Saints* by Bernardino Licinio. In the Chapel of St Michael **(25)**, on the right wall, is the tomb (perhaps by Lorenzo Bregno) of Melchiorre Trevisan (d. 1500) a Venetian commander who donated the reliquary of the Holy Blood to the church (which had been taken from Constantinople in 1480). The altarpiece of *St Ambrose and Eight Saints* in the Milanesi Chapel **(26)** was begun by Alvise Vivarini (1503) and finished by Marco Basaiti. A plain slab on the floor here marks the grave of the great composer Claudio Monteverdi, who directed the music at St Mark's for the last 30 years of his life (he died in 1643). The date of birth given here is incorrect: we know that he was in fact born in 1567.

The **Corner Chapel (27)** contains the tomb of Federico Corner, an unusual but graceful work (of Tuscan provenance) with an angel in a niche holding an inscription recording Corner's generosity in paying for the war against the Genoese at Chioggia. The font bears a marble statue of St John, exquisitely carved by Jacopo Sansovino (1554). On the altar, in a fine frame, is another painting with superb colouring by Bartolomeo Vivarini (1474) representing St Mark enthroned with four other saints. The stained glass dates from the 15th century. In 1990 some interesting and rare frescoes dating from around 1361 were discovered between the vault of the chapel and the roof, as illustrated on panels displayed here.

J **North aisle:** The Emiliani Chapel **(28)** has a marble altarpiece with ten statues in niches by the school of Jacobello dalle Masegne (15th century), and the tomb of Bishop Miani, with five similar statues. Near the monument to Bishop Jacopo Pesaro **(29)**, who died in 1547, with a fine effigy, is **Titian's** *Madonna di Ca' Pesaro* **(30)** (the *Pala Pesaro*). It was commissioned by Bishop Jacopo in 1519, but only completed in 1526. A marvel of composition and colour, it shows the Madonna and Child with saints above members of the Pesaro family (the boy looking directly out at the viewer is Jacopo's nephew and heir, Leonardo). The Bishop is to the left, and his brother to the right, both kneeling in rather static poses. Pesaro led the Venetian fleet in a victory against the Turks in 1502, when he reconquered the Greek island of Santa Maura (now Lefkas): he was in the service of the Borgia pope Alexander VI, whose arms are shown on the magnificent crimson standard held up by a soldier who turns to his captive Turk. The Bishop had already commissioned another kneeling portrait of himself from Titian (now in Antwerp), where he is shown being presented by the pope to St Peter, and the magnificent figure of St Peter also takes pride of place in the *Pala Pesaro*. Titian's great and daring invention here of placing the Madonna at one side of the painting rather than in the traditional central position adds a triangular form to the composition, and the scene is overshadowed by two mighty columns rising to the sky. The Madonna herself is particularly beautiful, and the Christ Child almost steps off her lap as He plays with her veil. The two putti above the cloud, mischievously playing with a Cross, are painted with the same extraordinary freedom of touch.

The huge mausoleum of Doge Giovanni Pesaro **(31)**, who died in 1659, is a bizarre Baroque work, and one of the most elaborate funerary monuments in Venice. It is attributed to Baldassare Longhena, with sculptures by the German artist Melchior Berthel. By any standards it is an extraordinary piece of funerary sculpture. The colossal Moors, by Berthel, are said to represent prisoners taken during struggles against the Ottomans in Crete. Pesaro himself sits high up, seeming to address anyone who will listen, beneath a tasselled baldacchino of red marble, while two long-necked monsters support his sarcophagus. The inscriptions read: Vixit anno LXX (Lived 70

St Mark and St Benedict: detail from Giovanni Bellini's altarpiece of the *Madonna and Saints* (1488).

years), Devixit anno MDCLIX (Died in the year 1659); Hic revixit anno MDCLXIX (Here he lived again in the year 1669; the year the monument was erected).

The **mausoleum of Canova (32)**, the great Neoclassical sculptor, was erected by his pupils (including Luigi Zandomeneghi) in 1827, and reproduces Canova's own design for monuments to Titian (never realised because of lack of funds; the model is preserved in the Museo Correr) and to Maria Christina, Archduchess of Austria, in the Augustinerkirche in Vienna. It adopts the most ancient form of sepulchral monument, the pyramid, also used in numerous other funerary chapels, including that of the Chigi in Santa Maria del Popolo in Rome. The weeping lion of St Mark beside a winged figure representing the Genius of Canova guards the half-open door of the pyramid in which the artist's heart lies on an urn; his body was buried in his home town, Possagno. On the other side female mourners representing the Arts approach the tomb in a funerary procession. Above the entrance two angels hold up a profile of Canova framed by a snake eating its tail—a symbol of immortality.

The **altar of the Crucifix (33)**, designed by Longhena, has sculptures by Juste le Court.

Archivio di Stato

The adjoining conventual buildings, with the Palladian cloister and another in the style of Sansovino, contain the Archivio di Stato (State Archives) restructured c. 1815–20 by Lorenzo Santi. The 15th-century summer refectory is used as a reading room. Among the most famous state archives in the world, they fill some 300 rooms, and provide a remarkable documentary of the Venetian Republic. Throughout the history of the *Serenissima*, the dispatches sent home from Venetian ambassadors and their final reports at the end of their terms of office offer extraordinary insights into the life of the times.

It was here that the English scholar and historian Rawdon Brown spent many years of research, his particular area of study being the documentation which related to England: in 1862 the Master of the Rolls, on behalf of the British government, formally appointed him to carry out this task. He published the reports made by the Great Council from 1496 to 1533, and nine volumes of a *Calendar*, being a record of the papers he found tracing Anglo-Venetian relations in the period from 1202 to 1509 (31 more were to be published over a period of more than 50 years after his death). A plaque in the building records the meticulous work of this 'English gentleman', but it is only recently that the value of the contribution he made to the history of Venice and England has been fully recognised. He saw much of John and Effie Ruskin on their visits to Venice, and Ruskin came to depend on Brown's deep knowledge of Venice and all things Venetian. Brown was also a collector and enjoyed rowing his *sandalo* out to the Lido every day for a swim. He died while still at work and is buried in the cemetery of San Michele.

THE CHURCH & SCUOLA OF SAN ROCCO
Map p. 410, C3

Close to the Frari are the church and *scuola* dedicated to San Rocco, famous for their remarkable paintings by Jacopo Tintoretto which cover the walls and ceilings. San Rocco (St Roch) was born in Montpellier in 1295. He caught the plague when he came to Italy to help cure victims of this contagious disease, but he retired alone to a wood where he was miraculously saved by an angel. He was particularly venerated in Venice in the 15th century when the Scuola di San Rocco was founded and his relics were brought to the church. Members of the confraternity offered their services especially during the frequent plagues which broke out in the city, the worst of which (after the Black Death of 1348) occurred in 1575–77 and 1630. After the plague of 1576, St Roch was declared a patron saint of the city and the doge made a pilgrimage to the church and *scuola* every year on his feast day (16th August). Canaletto was the first painter to record this event in a splendid large painting carried out around 1735 (now in the National Gallery in London). The feast is still celebrated here (when the treasury of the *scuola* is exhibited). There are paintings of St Roch and plague victims in the church and the *scuola* (St Roch is usually depicted as a young man with a sore on his leg).

Jacopo Tintoretto: *The Pool of Bethesda* (detail).

The church of San Rocco

Open 7.30–12.30; Sat, Sun 8–12.30 & 2–4.

The church was designed by Bartolomeo Bon in 1489, but almost entirely rebuilt in 1725. The late Baroque façade was added in 1765–71, and is the best known work of Bernardino Maccaruzzi. The church contains a number of **paintings by Jacopo Tintoretto**, carried out before he began work on one of the most spectacular cycles of paintings ever produced in western art in the *scuola* next door. The earliest of these, and the finest, is on the right wall of the sanctuary, and it shows *St Roch Curing Victims of the Plague*. Painted in 1549 when Tintoretto was 31 years old, it was the first Venetian painting to show the saint inside an isolation hospital such as those which operated in the lagoon during the dreaded outbreaks of pestilence. The other three paintings on the sanctuary walls by Tintoretto illustrate episodes in the saint's life. The two paintings on the west wall (including an *Annunciation*) and the two larger paintings on the south side (including the *Pool of Bethesda; pictured above*) are also by Tintoretto.

It is evident that the young Tintoretto was influenced by Pordenone, who came to the city in 1528 and frescoed the *putti* in the sanctuary to flank the marble high altar of this church. He also carried out the powerful painting, in a dynamic Mannerist style, of St Martin (on horseback) and St Christopher (once a cupboard door but now on the upper wall of the north side). Pordenone's name comes from his birthplace in the Friuli, where he painted most of his works, although others are to be seen in the Veneto. In Venice itself he frescoed some palace façades as well as the cupola of San Giovanni Elemosinario near the Rialto. Sebastiano Ricci, another successful artist from the Veneto, who spent his last years in Venice in the early 18th century (*see p. 215*) painted the *Miracle of San Francesco da Paola* for the first altar on the south side (and also the altarpiece on the opposite altar on the north side).

The lovely high altar is in the form of an arch decorated with early 16th-century statues of saints (including *St Roch* on the sarcophagus) by Giovanni Maria Mosca and the *Virgin and Annunciatory Angel* by Bartolomeo di Francesco Bergamasco. The carved dossals are attributed to Giovanni Marchiori, who also carved the statues flanking the west door (*David with the Head of Goliath*, and *St Cecilia*) in 1743.

SCUOLA GRANDE DI SAN ROCCO

Open April–Oct 9–5.30; Nov–March 10–4. Concerts of Baroque music are usually given here on Tues and Sat throughout the year.

Beside the church is the Scuola Grande di San Rocco. It was begun in 1515 by Bartolomeo Bon for the important confraternity of St Roch (founded in 1478), and finished by Scarpagnino (1549), who added the elegant main façade, which is usually considered his masterpiece. The less imposing canal façade is also by him. The interior is famous for its paintings by Jacopo Tintoretto, who produced over 50 works here; it is one of the most remarkable pictorial cycles in existence.

In 1564 a competition was held for the decoration of Scarpagnino's recently-completed building. Jacopo Tintoretto was the winner, having entered a finished work (rather than a preparatory sketch) of *St Roch in Glory*, which he had already installed in the Sala dell'Albergo. A year later he was elected a brother of the confraternity, and spent the next 23 years working on the paintings (largely without the help of collaborators). In return he received a modest pension from the brotherhood. When Ruskin saw the *scuola* in 1845 he commented, 'As for painting, I think I didn't know what it was until today', and his visit inspired him to pursue his study of the city and her art.

Ground floor

The columned hall, where religious ceremonies were held, was the last to be painted in the *scuola* by Tintoretto (1582–87). The superb cycle of paintings illustrates the life of the Virgin Mary and the individual works are on a more intimate scale than those on the floor above, with charming details and splendid landscapes. The *Circumcision* (7) appears to have been painted partly by the *bottega* of Tintoretto and by his son Domenico. The last painting, the *Assumption* (8), has suffered from poor restorations in the past. The statue of St Roch on the altar is by Girolamo Campagna (1587).

Part of a collection of Islamic, Hispano-Moresque, and European majolica and porcelain, left to the *scuola* in the 1960s, is also displayed here. The precious treasury of the confraternity is only exhibited on 16th August, the Feast of San Rocco. In the entrance passageway is a statue of St Roch by Giovanni Buora (c. 1494).

SCUOLA GRANDE DI SAN ROCCO
(GROUND FLOOR)

1 Annunciation
2 Adoration of the Magi
3 Flight into Egypt
4 Massacre of the Innocents
5 Mary Magdalene
6 St Mary of Egypt
7 Circumcision
8 Assumption

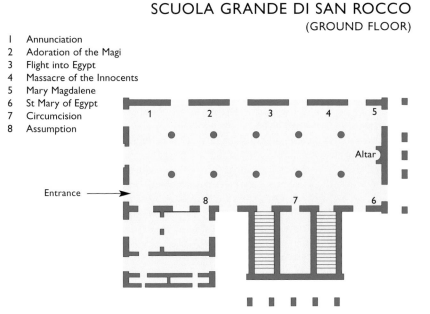

The grand staircase is by Scarpagnino (1544–46). Its two huge paintings by Antonio Zanchi (right; 1666) and Pietro Negri (left; 1673) commemorate the end of the plague of 1630. The horror of the suffering it caused is depicted with great realism.

Upper floor

Chapter house

The huge chapter house is a splendid hall by Scarpagnino, still dimly lit by the processional lanterns which were used by the *scuola* in the 18th century. It is entirely covered by wonderful paintings by Tintoretto, carried out between 1576 and 1581, with Old Testament subjects on the ceiling, and New Testament subjects on the walls. They were chosen in a careful iconographical scheme related to the teaching of St Roch and his efforts to relieve thirst, hunger and sickness. The huge central painting on the ceiling shows Moses erecting the brazen serpent to save those bitten by fiery snakes sent by God as a punishment. The subjects of the other remarkable paintings are shown on the plan. The eight smaller panels in chiaroscuro are replacements by Giuseppe Angeli (1777) of works by Tintoretto. Angeli also restored the painting of *Elisha's Miracle* (19).

On the altar is the *Vision of St Roch*, painted by Tintoretto with the help of his son Domenico. The late 17th-century carved wooden benches around the great hall, by Francesco Pianta il Giovane, incorporate bizarre figures including (near the altar) a caricature of Tintoretto and a self-portrait.

Tintoretto (c. 1519–94)
Jacopo Robusti, born in Venice, was called Tintoretto because his family were *tintori* (dyers). Throughout his long life (he died at the age of about 75) he worked exclusively in Venice, producing a remarkable number of superb paintings in the *scuole* and churches, commissioned from him by the Venetian middle classes, as well as official works for the Doge's Palace. He was one of the most daring painters who ever lived, and his creative fervour was without parallel. His output was enormous, and evidently he had an extraordinary capacity for work. Unlike Titian, he seems to have given little consideration to his earnings, but was instead intent on grasping every possible occasion to exert his skills as a painter. A member of several *scuole*, he married Faustina Episcopi, the daughter of the *guardian grande* of the Scuola di San Marco; they had eight children. Tintoretto was deeply religious, and his highly dramatic scenes, often in humble settings and always infused with a spiritual content, were given added intensity by his wonderful use of light, producing intense contrasts between the illuminated areas and those in shadow. Although he worked for a brief period with Titian, little is known about where he learnt his skills: he was already well established as an artist by the age of 20. His style of painting was transmitted to his large *bottega* as well as to his son Domenico, who also produced a great many paintings for Venetian buildings.

SCUOLA GRANDE DI SAN ROCCO
(CHAPTER HOUSE)

CEILING (OLD TESTAMENT)

9   Moses erecting the serpent of brass
10 Moses striking water from the rock
11 The Fall of Manna
12 Adam and Eve (the Fall of Man)
13 God appearing to Moses
14 Moses and the Pillar of Fire
15 Jonah issuing from the belly of the whale
16 Vision of Ezekiel of the Resurrection
17 Jacob's Ladder
18 Sacrifice of Isaac
19 Elisha's miracle of the loaves of bread
20 Elijah fed by an angel
21 The Jewish Passover

WALLS (NEW TESTAMENT)

22 Adoration of the Shepherds
23 Baptism of Christ
24 Resurrection of Christ
25 Agony in the Garden
26 The Last Supper
27 Miracle of the Loaves and Fishes
28 Resurrection of Lazarus
29 Ascension
30 Miracle of Christ at the Pool of Bethesda
    (damaged by poor restorations)
31 Temptation of Christ
32 St Roch
33 St Sebastian

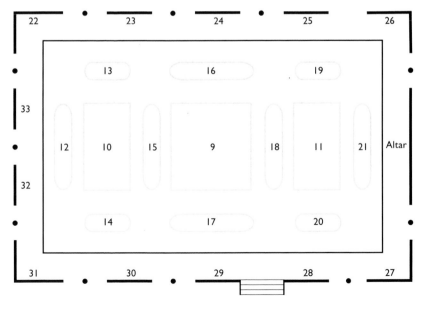

Presbytery

The walls of the presbytery have carved wooden reliefs of the life of St Roch by Giovanni Marchiori. The two statues on the altar, of St John the Baptist and St Sebastian, are late works by Girolamo Campagna. The *Annunciation* by Titian was acquired by the *scuola* in 1555 and the *Visitation* is by Tintoretto. *Christ Carrying the Cross* is a greatly venerated painting, considered to be miraculous, which hung in the church of San Rocco from about 1510 until 1955. Painted around 1508, and now in poor condition, its attribution has been discussed interminably by art historians, who have vacillated over the decades between Titian and Giorgione: today most of them seem to agree that it is the work of Giorgione rather than a late work by Titian. The *Christ in Pietà*, formerly thought to be an early work by Titian, is also now generally attributed to the circle of Giorgione. The *Portrait of a Man* by Tintoretto was once considered to be a self-portrait. The charming little Sala della Cancelleria preserves its original 18th-century furnishings.

Sala dell'Albergo

Outside the entrance to the Sala dell'Albergo are two easel paintings by Giambattista Tiepolo, acquired by the *scuola* in 1785: *Hagar and Ishmael Comforted by an Angel*, and *Abraham Visited by an Angel*.

The Sala dell' Albergo was the first room to be decorated by Tintoretto (1564–67). On the carved and gilded ceiling is *St Roch in Glory* (clearly painted in a hurry) and 20 smaller panels with heads of putti, the four seasons, allegories of the Scuole Grande of Venice, and the Cardinal Virtues. The vast *Crucifixion* is generally considered to be the painter's masterpiece. On the opposite wall are *Christ before Pilate*, *The Crowning with Thorns*, and *The Way to Calvary*. Here also is displayed a fragment of a frieze from the ceiling of three apples, showing Tintoretto's remarkable painting technique.

SCUOLA GRANDE DI SAN GIOVANNI EVANGELISTA
Map p. 410, C2

In front of the church of the Frari (*see p. 198*), Ponte dei Frari, with a marble balustrade of 1858, crosses a rio, and Fondamenta dei Frari lead left to another bridge and (left) Rio Terrà San Tomà. Calle del Magazen and its continuation leads to the fine courtyard (left) in front of the Scuola Grande di San Giovanni Evangelista, one of the six chief confraternities in Venice, founded in 1261. As early as 1301 the *scuola* had a chapel in San Giovanni Evangelista under the protection of the Badoer family, but in 1349 it was able to move to its own premises on the site of the present building. The eagle, symbol of St John the Evangelist, recurs frequently in its sculptural decoration.

The first court has a beautiful marble screen and portal by Pietro Lombardo (1481). In the second court is the wall of the *scuola* (right), with Gothic windows, dating from 1454. The relief shows the brothers of the confraternity kneeling in front of St John the Evangelist, and the inscription below (a copy of the original is preserved inside) records the acquisition of this site in 1349 for the *scuola*. Ahead is the former entrance (1512, by Mauro Codussi); the double windows above are typical of the work of this architect.

The scuola

Not at present open regularly. For information, T: 041 718 234. Concerts and lectures are often held here.

In the entrance hall is a relief of the *Resurrection of Christ*, by the workshop of Antonio Rizzo. The handsome hall has a fine row of columns with Gothic capitals (decorated with the kneeling figures of members of the confraternity) and sculpture, including a 14th-century relief of St Martin with Doge Andrea Contarini and a monk.

The double staircase, a work of great skill and elegance by Mauro Codussi (1498), leads up to the **Salone**, transformed in 1727–57 by Giorgio Massari. On the walls is a 16th-century cycle of scenes from the lives of Christ and St John the Evangelist by Domenico Tintoretto, Sante Peranda and Andrea Vicentino (and one by Giovanni Battista Cignaroli added in the 18th century). On the altar wall are *tondi* by Jacopo Guarana and paintings by Jacopo Marieschi. The ceiling (1760) has scenes from the Apocalypse: the central painting is by Giuseppe Angeli; it is surrounded by four works by Gaspare Diziani. The three paintings towards the altar are by Jacopo Marieschi, and at the opposite end of the ceiling is a painting by Jacopo Guarana flanked by two interesting smaller works by Gian Domenico Tiepolo. On the altar is a statue of St John and above the door into the oratory is a relief showing the donation of the relic of the Holy Cross, both attributed to Giovanni Maria Morleiter.

The **Oratorio della Croce** houses an exquisite gilded silver reliquary made by Venetian goldsmiths in 1379 to preserve a relic of the True Cross brought from Cyprus and donated to the school in the 14th-century (it is kept locked away, and only shown in a procession on 14th December). The famous cycle of paintings illustrating the miracle of this relic, by Giovanni Bellini, Vittore Carpaccio and others (now in the Accademia; *see p. 154*) was painted for this room. The **Sala dell'Albergo Nuovo**, now used as an office by the confraternity, contains four paintings by Palma Giovane. The 14th-century Venetian icon of the *Madonna and Saints* was formerly in the church.

The church

At present open 10–12 & 3–5, except Wed.

Opposite the *scuola* stands the church. It contains an organ built by Giovanni Battista Piaggia (1760) in an organ case designed by Giorgio Massari, and paintings in the sanctuary by Jacopo Marieschi (*Last Supper*) and Domenico Tintoretto (*Crucifixion*). The good woodwork in the church has been restored. The room with columns and a wood ceiling was the mortuary chapel, used as a burial place.

SANTA CROCE

The *sestiere* of Santa Croce grew up around a monastery and church dedicated to the Holy Cross in what was once a quiet and remote part of the city. It retains its name despite the fact that the huge monastery was demolished in 1810 and only a single column remains (*see p. 223*). These days this *sestiere* is an area of tiny, quiet back-streets and 19th- and 20th-century housing; the most interesting buildings are on, or close to, the Grand Canal: both the elaborate Baroque church of San Stae and the little-visited San Simeone Grande have *campi* on the water. Between them, in a particularly quiet area, is the little church of San Giovanni Decollato, with early frescoes in a lovely 12th-century interior. The splendid Ca' Pesaro on the Grand Canal houses the Galleria Internazionale d'Arte Moderna, and Palazzo Mocenigo, a late 17th-century patrician residence, is also open to the public.

THE SAN STAE DISTRICT
Map p. 411, D1

The little Campo San Stae opens onto the Grand Canal. Across the water to the left stands Codussi's magnificent 16th-century Palazzo Vendramin-Calergi (*see p. 233*), and on this side, just by the landing-stage, is Palazzo Priuli-Bon with Veneto-Byzantine details.

The **church of San Stae** (Sant'Eustachio; *open Mon–Sat 10–5; Chorus Pass*) presents a splendid Baroque façade to the waterfront. It is the work of Domenico Rossi, who began his career as a designer of pyrotechnical extravaganzas. He later turned to architecture, with considerable success. The church was financed in 1710 by Doge Alvise II Mocenigo, a descendant of the doge who presided over the victory of Lepanto (since that time, all Mocenigo doges have been named Alvise); the Mocenigo family vault is in the floor of the church, and their family palace is just around the corner (*see overleaf*). Concerts and exhibitions are sometimes held in the church.

The bright white and grey interior is interesting for its large collection of 18th-century paintings. These include Sebastiano Ricci's *St Peter Freed from Prison* on the wall of the sanctuary. The other scenes of martyrdom in the sanctuary are also by well-known painters of the 18th century. The artists include Antonio Balestra, Angelo Trevisani, Giovanni Antonio Pellegrini, Giovanni Battista Piazzetta and Giambattista Tiepolo. Tiepolo's *Martyrdom of St Bartholomew* is remarkable for the perspective of the saint's hands, the right one almost reaching out of the painting. Tiepolo, at 26, was one of the youngest of these painters, and here he creates a scene of intense drama, with skilful use of colour (notice the red of the executioner's trousers and the white of the saint's loincloth) and the struggles of the saint vividly portrayed, as one man holds his legs fast and the other menacingly grasps the flaying knife. Also here are works by

Gregorio Lazzarini and Niccolò Bambini, both born in the 1650s (Bambini also painted the *Madonna in Glory and Saints* in the first chapel on the right side); and by Giovanni Battista Pittoni and Giovanni Battista Mariotti, born in the 1680s. Giuseppe Angeli is also well represented: the central painting on either side is his (the *Fall of Manna* and the *Sacrifice of Melchisedech*).

Sebastiano Ricci (1659–1734)
Born in Belluno, in the Veneto, Ricci was considered the most important Venetian artist of his day. During his long career, he worked all over Italy, and travelled widely to commissions abroad, including Vienna (Karlskirche, Schönbrunn) and London, where he narrowly lost a competition to fresco the dome of St Paul's, and where his patrons included Lord Burlington (works by Ricci are still to be seen in the earl's London residence, now the Royal Academy). Ricci was also a brilliant draughtsman, and in Venice enjoyed the patronage of Consul Smith (*see p. 134*): the series of biblical scenes he made for him is now in Hampton Court, London.

But Ricci is famous as much for the scandals in his private life as for his art. He had a great appetite for other men's wives, and his liaisons often brought him into trouble. All this tends to obscure his value as an artist. And because he often finished his paintings in a hurry, his style is sometimes too dashing, and he has been accused of superficiality. But Ricci was a virtuoso talent. And the helter-skelter energy which compelled him to rush his works to completion translates into nervous brushwork which gives them an amazing lightness of touch. Ricci studied the work of Veronese, and reinterpreted him in a dazzling, colourful style which was to lift early 18th-century Venetian painting out of its doldrums and steer it on a new course, towards the brilliance of Tiepolo.

There are still a number of ceiling paintings by Ricci in Venice (in the Palazzo Querini-Stampalia, the Seminario Patriarcale and San Marciliano) and altarpieces in San Vitale, the Gesuati, San Rocco and San Giorgio Maggiore. He was devoted to his nephew Marco, another very skilled painter, who produced many landscapes and *capricci*, and the two of them often collaborated. Marco, who was also promoted by Consul Smith, is also well known for his works in tempera, his etchings, and his designs for scenery (including sets for the London opera). Sebastiano and Marco shared an apartment in the Procuratie Vecchie in Piazza San Marco, although Marco predeceased his uncle by four years. Sebastiano's intemperate eating, drinking and womanising eventually took their toll. He suffered acutely from gallstones, and died on the operating table in 1734.

In the sacristy is a Crucifix by Maffeo da Verona and (opposite) the *Dead Christ* by Pietro Muttoni, and a scene by Pittoni showing Trajan ordering St Eustace (Sant'Eustachio; San Stae) to worship the pagan idols. The third chapel on the left side of the nave has a sculpted Crucifix and funerary monuments of the Foscarini family by Giuseppe Torretti (to whose nephew Canova was apprenticed), with the help of his contemporaries Antonio Tarsia and Pietro Baratta. The early 18th-century altarpieces in the first two chapels on this side are by Francesco Migliori and Jacopo Amigoni. The organ above the west door is by Gaetano Callido (1772).

Beside the church is the charming little **Scuola dei Battiloro e Tiraoro** (goldsmiths), built in 1711.

PALAZZO MOCENIGO
Map p. 411, D1

Open April–Oct 10–5, except Mon; Nov–March 10–4, except Mon.
The Salizzada di San Stae leads away from the Grand Canal on the right of the façade of the church, passing the brick campanile with a 13th-century stone angel at its base. Calle Tron diverges right for Palazzo Tron (now owned by the University), which contains frescoes by Jacopo Guarana (*admission sometimes granted*). The salizzada continues past several fine (but dilapidated) palaces, including (no. 1988) a 13th-century building. Palazzo Mocenigo a San Stae (no. 1992) was left to the city of Venice in 1954 by the last descendant of this branch of the distinguished Mocenigo family (who provided the Republic with no fewer than seven doges). It now houses the Museo di Palazzo Mocenigo.

Interior of the palace
From the atrium, with 18th-century benches and busts, the staircase leads up to the *primo piano nobile* of the palace, which is an interesting example of a late 17th-century patrician Venetian residence, with good furniture (17th–19th centuries), including chandeliers from Murano and Venetian mirrors. Some of the 18th-century ceiling frescoes are attributed to Jacopo Guarana and others to Giambattista Canal. In most of the rooms there are now also charming displays of 18th-century costumes.

The *portego* has a fine double doorway dating from the early 18th century, and the most famous members of the Mocenigo family are depicted in the frieze and paintings above the doors. The five larger portraits between the doors include one of Charles II of England. A small sitting-room has delicate stucco decoration. In the red drawing-room the portrait of a Contarini procurator has a remarkable carved frame with elaborate allegories of the Contarini family, attributed to Antonio Corradini. The green sitting room has interesting historical scenes of events in Mocenigo history, attributed to Antonio Stom. The pink dining room has three pastels (sometimes attributed to Rosalba Carriera). In the bedroom there is a *Madonna and Child with Sts John the Baptist and Peter* by the school of Giovanni Bellini.

On the other side of the *portego* is the Room of the Four Seasons, named after four monochrome allegories by Giambattista Canal, and which also has two huge historical canvases by Stom. The library is now used to display a very fine collection of 16th–19th-century lace.

Theatre performances are sometimes held in the palace, which houses the Centro Studi di Storia del Tessuto e del Costume, with a remarkably complete documentation of costumes and fabrics from the 16th century up to the 1950s.

Santa Maria Mater Domini

Map p. 411, D2. Open Tues and Fri 11–12.30 & 3.30–6, Wed 3.30–6; closed Sat, Sun and Mon.

Beyond Palazzo Mocenigo, Ramo della Rioda diverges left across two canals for the lovely, peaceful church of Santa Maria Mater Domini, a Renaissance building probably from a design by Giovanni Buora (1502–40), with an Istrian stone façade. The pretty domed interior, where the clean lines of the architectural features are emphasised in dark grey stone, has intimate proportions with Diocletian windows, and an uncluttered sanctuary. The very fine works by Lorenzo Bregno include the lovely first south altar (1524), which bears three marble figures of saints in a niche designed in perfect perspective, and a relief of *God the Father* in the lunette above. It is thought that Antonio Minello may have helped him in this work. Bregno is also thought to have carved the pretty altar on the right of the sanctuary, and the two statuettes of St Mark and St John on the altar to the left of the sanctuary are certainly by his hand. Other interesting sculptures in the church are the 13th-century Byzantine marble basrelief of the *Virgin Orans* in the left aisle, and the Tuscan high relief in gilded terracotta of the *Madonna and Child* in the apse. The richly-coloured painting of the *Martyrdom of St Christina* (second south altar; 1520), with a charming group of angels holding onto the millstone tied around Christina's neck, is by Vincenzo Catena, a follower of Bellini, and the *Transfiguration* (first north chapel) by his contemporary, Francesco Bissolo. The copy of a *Last Supper* by Bonifacio Veronese dates from around the same time and forms a pair (in their original frames) with Jacopo Tintoretto's very fine *Invention of the Cross*.

The campo, with a fine well-head, has several good palaces. At the end opposite the rio Palazzetto Viaro (no. 2120) has a distinguished row of tall trefoil windows (14th century) and a relief of a lion (almost obliterated). Number 2173 has ogee windows with, above, a frieze of Byzantine crosses and *paterae*. Opposite, no. 2177 has a quatrefoil decoration (almost completely ruined).

CA' PESARO
Map p. 411, E1

The palace and its two museums are open 10–5. Joint ticket available.

This great Baroque palace, with a splendid façade on the Grand Canal, was built by Baldassare Longhena. It was completed after Longhena's death in 1682 by his pupil Antonio Gaspari. It is the grandest of the palaces built in the city for the famous Venetian Pesaro family, and was begun in 1658 by Giovanni when he was elected doge (he died the following year and is buried in an elaborate tomb in the Frari; *see p. 205*).

The impressive courtyard has an elaborate Renaissance well-head, with an *Apollo* by Danese Cattaneo, moved here from the Zecca when that building was altered.

The palace is Venice's museum of modern art, founded in 1897 and now officially called the Galleria Internazionale d'Arte Moderna. It has been formed over the years through the financial help of associations and private citizens in Venice, as well as from donations by the artists themselves. Many of the works purchased were first exhibited at the Biennale. The top floor houses the Museo Orientale, although for years there have been plans to move it to another palace on the Grand Canal.

Ground floor

In the huge *androne*, which stretches to the water-gate on the Grand Canal, 20th-century Italian sculpture is exhibited including a bronze *Eve* by Francesco Messina, and a *Cardinal* by Giacomo Manzù. The prelate sits, swathed in his huge cope, one hand just visible through the opening. The *Nude* by Alberto Viani joined the collection in 1952, and Emilio Vedova donated his work exhibited here in the following decade.

First floor

Room I: Venetian works of the 19th century, notably views of Venice and Rome (as well as Athens and Cairo) by Ippolito Caffi, who studied at the Venice Academy and was the last of the great Venetian *vedutisti* (*see p. 181*). He was in Venice during the revolutionary period in 1849, and took up the role of official artist to record the events. He later enlisted as a sailor in the Italian navy, and drowned while in service when his ship was sunk off the Dalmatian coast in 1866. His atmospheric paintings *Snow and Fog on the Grand Canal* and *Fair on the Quayside near San Marco* marked a renewed interest in Venetian scenes. Other typical Venetian scenes are the work of Guglielmo Ciardi and his contemporary Giacomo Favretto (his portrait of the Guidini family dates from 1873). Dramatic scenes documenting Venetian life include Luigi Nono's two abandoned orphans at a Venetian church door (*Abbandonati*; 1903).

Room II: Non-Venetian works. The Macchiaioli School, active in Tuscany before 1864, whose members took their inspiration directly from nature, is well represented in Telemaco Signorini's famous *Asylum Interior*, painted in Florence, and in his landscape entitled *November*. The scene showing a dramatic accident during a battle is by the best-known painter of this school, Giovanni Fattori. Giuseppe de Nittis lived in Paris (where, in 1874, he participated in an exhibition of the Impressionists), and his pastel portrait of a lady shows how much he was influenced by his French contemporaries. Giacomo Balla, better known in his later period as a Futurist, painted the portrait of a member of the Pesaro family in 1901. The sculptures by Medardo Rosso constitute the most important collection of his work in Italy: they were donated to the gallery in 1914. His original style, immediately recognisable, produces a fusion of the figure with the atmosphere in an attempt to abolish borders. He was especially skilled in modelling wax, and spent long periods in both Venice and Paris.

Salone: Works by Italian and foreign artists which were exhibited at the earliest Biennale art exhibitions (from 1895 up to the 1930s) are shown here. The two most important works are *Salome* (or *Judith II*) by the great Viennese Secessionist Gustav Klimt, painted in 1909 (and acquired by the gallery soon afterwards), and *Rabbi* by Marc Chagall, one of a number of his explicitly Jewish paintings, and which was exhibited in his Russian homeland when he returned there from Paris in 1914. It entered this collection in the late 1920s.

Room III: The display is devoted to the Italian sculptor Adolfo Wildt (1868–1931), whose Symbolist works are always characterised by smooth and shiny marble surfaces. The works here were donated to the museum by his descendants in 1990.

Room IV: The de Lisi bequest includes many painters (such as Felice Casorati, Mario Sironi, Giorgio Morandi, Filippo de Pisis, Giorgio de Chirico) who were members of the Novecento artistic movement, which had one of its very first joint exhibitions at the Venice Biennale of 1924. Generally in opposition to the avant-garde movements of the time, the Novecento artists promoted the values of form, and studied with renewed interest the great art produced in Italy in the 14th and 15th centuries, in particular that of Piero della Francesca. They were unanimous in their admiration of Cézanne. There are also paintings by Carlo Carrà, who went through a Futurist and Metaphysical period, and works by 20th-century foreign artists including Tanguy and Kandinsky.

Rooms V–VI: Works produced between 1908 and 1920, including paintings by Umberto Boccioni, pupil of the great Futurist Balla, sculptures by Arturo Martini, and paintings (*Le Signorine*) by Felice Casorati.

Room VII: A representative display of international art produced in the 1950s (Jean Arp, Max Ernst, Raoul Dufy, Henri Matisse, Georges Rouault, Ben Nicholson, Henry Moore and Alexander Calder), much of which was donated to the museum by the artists themselves.

Room VIII: Italian art of the 1950s, both abstract and figurative, including works by Filippo de Pisis, in his characteristic light, sketchy style.

Room IX: Venetian art of the 20th century, notably works by Virgilio Guidi, who enjoyed great success at the Biennale of 1924, and his contemporary Bruno Saetti.

Museo Orientale

The rooms on the top floor are crammed full of paintings, sculpture, arms and armour, lacquer-work, bronzes, jade, musical instruments, decorative arts, fabrics and costumes, producing a remarkable atmosphere. Prince Enrico di Borbone, Conte di

Bardi, collected these objects and artworks (numbering some 30,000) during a journey through China, Indonesia and Japan in 1887–89. Acquired by the Italian government at the end of the First World War, they have been housed here since 1925, but there are long-term plans to move them to Palazzo Marcello on the Grand Canal. The museum includes one of the most important collections in Europe of Japanese art of the Edo period (1600–1868), especially interesting for its paintings. Chinese, Siamese and Javanese art are also well represented, and there is a fine Khmer figure of Buddha from Cambodia, dating from the 12th century.

FROM SAN GIACOMO DELL'ORIO TO THE GRAND CANAL
Map p. 410, C2–p. 411, D1

San Giacomo dell'Orio

Map p. 410, C2. Open Mon–Sat 10–5; Chorus Pass.
Of ancient foundation, the church was rebuilt in 1225 (the tall campanile survives from this time), and altered in 1532. The interior, recently restored, contains massive low Byzantine columns (12th–13th century), one (in the south transept) of *verde antico*, and one (behind the pulpit) with a pretty flowered capital. There is a beautiful 14th-century wooden ship's keel roof. Around the west door (beneath the organ) are paintings attributed to Andrea Schiavone, including two prophets flanking the door. The huge stoup in Greek marble was probably used as a font.

In the south aisle, beyond a 16th-century painting of the *Last Supper*, the first altar has a Tuscan wooden statue of the Madonna and Child. In the south transept the old wall of the church has been exposed with interesting fragments embedded in it (the *Virgin Orans* dates from the 13th century). Above the sacristy door is an early 16th-century painting of the *Supper at Emmaus*. In the new sacristy is a ceiling painting of the *Allegory of Faith*, by the workshop of Veronese (restored), and four Doctors of the Church. The paintings include *Madonna in Glory with Sts John and Nicholas*, and (opposite, above a fine carved fragment) *St John the Baptist Preaching*, both by Francesco Bassano. The latter incorporates portraits of Bassano's family and Titian (on the extreme left wearing a red hat).

In the pretty domed chapel to the right of the high altar are vault frescoes by Jacopo Guarana, and paintings by Padovanino and Palma Giovane. In the sanctuary the *Madonna and Four Saints* is by Lorenzo Lotto (1546). Beneath it is a relief from the old high altar, with the *Martyrdom of St James the Apostle* (1704). In the apse hangs a Crucifix attributed to Paolo Veneziano. On the walls are two large marble crosses, fine Lombardesque works. On the left pier, the charming Byzantine statuette of the *Virgin Annunciate* was formerly over the door of Santa Maria Mater Domini. On the right pier is an early 18th-century statuette of St James by Bartolo Cabianca.

The old sacristy, with finely-carved wood panelling, is entirely decorated with a cycle of paintings celebrating the mystery of the Eucharist by Palma Giovane

(1575–81), one of the best works by this extremely prolific painter (he also painted the stories from the life of St Lawrence in the north transept, and the *Miracle of the Loaves and Fishes* in the south aisle). Outside the door into the sacristy is a good painting, *Sts Sebastian, Roch and Lawrence*, by Giovanni Buonconsiglio. There are two Crucifixes on the north side of the church, one dating from the 14th century in the porch, and the other (on the first altar) dating from the late 17th century.

To the south of the church (across a bridge), the name of Corte dell'Anatomia recalls the site of an anatomical theatre built here in 1671. The area north of the church, reached by Ramo dell'Isola, has boat-building yards and large warehouses, which until recently were surrounded on four sides by canals (now filled in except for Rio di San Zan Degolà).

San Giovanni Decollato

Map p. 410, C1. Open 10–12 except Sun and holidays.

From Calle Larga, just by two bridges, the tiny Calle del Spezier zigzags into the campo around the church of San Giovanni Decollato (San Zan Degolà; St John the Beheaded), founded in the early 11th century by the Venier family. A relief fragment of the Baptist's severed head has been built into the side wall. The basilican interior has Greek marble columns and Byzantine capitals and a lovely ship's keel roof. In the left apse chapel are 13th-century fresco fragments (remarkable because the damp lagoon climate makes fresco rare in Venice) of St Helen and the heads of four saints, and an *Annunciation*, as well as a frescoed vault with symbols of the Evangelists and a

17th-century carved Crucifix. In the right apse chapel there is a charming late 14th-century fragment of St Michael Archangel trampling the demon underfoot: notice the fearsome face incorporated into his armour: this was discovered behind the marble altarpiece which has been moved to the side wall.

Head of the Baptist, in the exterior wall of San Giovanni Decollato.

Fondaco dei Turchi

Map p. 411, D1.

Calle dei Preti leads to the Salizzada dei Fondaco dei Turchi which leads up to the Grand Canal and the Fondaco dei Turchi, which from 1621–1838 was the warehouse of the Turkish merchants. In 1381 it was given to the Dukes of Ferrara, and here, as their guests, stayed John Palaeologus, the Byzantine Emperor, in 1438, and the epic poet Torquato Tasso in 1562. Once the most characteristic Veneto-Byzantine palace (12th–13th century) in the city, it was virtually rebuilt after 1858 for the municipality by Federico Berchet—to the consternation of Ruskin, who found it in the process of its radical 'restoration' when he was in the city: '… its walls rent with a thousand chasms, are filled and refilled with fresh brickwork, and the seams and hollows are choked with clay and whitewash, oozing and trickling over the marble.' The courtyard has also lost all its character. The building contains a Natural History Museum (*open Sat and Sun 10–4*), which is much visited by Venetian children even though only a very few rooms are open. At present there is a tiny aquarium on the ground floor with a few sad fish from the lagoon, and a room upstairs has been imaginatively designed to exhibit the skeleton of a dinosaur, called an Ouranosaurus, over 3.5m high and 7m long, which was found, along with a giant crocodile nearly 12m long, in the Sahara in Niger in 1973. Both date from the Cretaceous period, the last age of the dinosaurs (144–65 million years ago). On the ground floor off the courtyard there is a film documenting its discovery.

WESTERN SANTA CROCE
Map p. 410, B1–A3

The churches of San Simeone

San Simeone Grande (*map p. 410, B1; open 8–12 & 5–7*) sits in a pretty little campo which opens directly onto the Grand Canal. The low interior has a wide nave with antique columns and statues above the arcade. In the chapel to the left of the sanctuary is a remarkable effigy of St Simeon, with an inscription of 1317 giving it as the work of Marco Romano. St Simeon the Prophet was an aged man of Jerusalem, who had been told that he would not die before beholding Christ. On seeing the infant in Bethlehem, he lifted the Child in his arms and pronounced the words now known as the *Nunc Dimittis*: Lord, now lettest thy servant depart in peace … For mine eyes have seen thy salvation.' (*Luke 2, 25–35*). This powerful sculpture, with extremely skilfully executed drapery, hair and beard, is a very unusual work, the only one signed and dated by Marco Romano, a Sienese sculptor who worked in Tuscany, Cremona, and Venice in the first two decades of the 14th century. It had an important influence on contemporary Venetian sculptors, but in the past some scholars have doubted the authenticity of the early date. Other 14th-century sculptures in the church include (south aisle) a figure of St Valentine, a relief of St Simeon and an abbot, a carved angel (above an arch), and (beneath the portico outside), a large relief of a saint. On the north wall, near the main door, is a large painting of the *Last Supper* by Jacopo Tintoretto. Over the high altar is a *Presentation in the Temple*, by Palma Giovane.

On Rio Marin stands the grand 18th-century **Palazzo Gradenigo** (*map p. 410, B2*), decorated with female heads on the two *piani nobili*. On the other side of its large garden is the smaller, buff-coloured **Palazzo Soranzo-Cappello**, dating from the previous century, with two rows of balconies and a tympanum on the top floor. Its lovely garden at the back can usually also be seen through the doorway. In the 19th century this was the residence of the American writer Constance Fletcher, a friend of Henry James; in 1887 the great writer took the palace as the setting for his wonderful short story *The Aspern Papers*.

Further west is the church of **San Simeone Piccolo** (*map p. 410, B2; open only Sun and holidays 10.30–12, and for concerts*). For the visitor to Venice arriving by train, this green-domed church is probably the first building that catches the eye. The church stands on a high stylobate with a pronaos of Corinthian columns. It is the best work of Giovanni Scalfarotto, who built it in 1718–38 on a circular plan derived from the Pantheon in Rome. It is in fact larger than San Simeone Grande, but the names do not refer to size: San Simeone Piccolo is dedicated to the Apostle Simon, while San Simeone Grande is named after Simeon the Prophet (*see above*).

Giardino Papadopoli and Piazzale Roma

Fondamenta San Simeon Piccolo follows the Grand Canal to Rio dei Tolentini, across which is the **Giardino Papadopoli**, a public garden which was laid out on the site of the church and monastery of Santa Croce after it was demolished in 1810. Important enough to give its name to an entire district of the city, only one solitary granite column (with a lovely 11th-century capital) survives from the buildings, inserted into the garden wall. Nearby is **Piazzale Roma** (*map p. 410, A2–A3*), the busy terminus of the road from the mainland, with its huge multi-storey car parks (when it was built in the 1930s, it was the largest multi-storey car park in Europe) and bus stations. A new bridge by the Spanish architect Santiago Calatrava (b. 1951) is under construction here across the Grand Canal, to connect the car park and bus terminus with the railway station. It will have a steel span of some 81m and a walkway built partly of glass and partly of Istrian stone with a bronze handrail.

San Nicola da Tolentino

Map p. 410, B3. Open 8–12 & 4–6.
From the Giardino Papadopoli, Fondamenta del Monastero follows the Rio dei Tolentini to a bridge which leads into the campo in front of the imposing church of San Nicola da Tolentino, often simply called 'I Tolentini'. The fine Corinthian portico by Andrea Tirali (1706–14) is an unexpected sight.

The monastic order of the Theatines, founded in Rome in 1524, escaped to Venice with their spiritual leader, Gaetano da Thiene, after the Sack of Rome three years later, knowing that Venice had supported Pope Clement VII rather than the Emperor Charles V, who was responsible for the sack. They built this church a few decades afterwards, on the site of an oratory dedicated to St Nicholas of Tolentino, which dedication they retained. The classical interior by Vincenzo Scamozzi (1591–1602) recalls Palladian models, despite the heavy decorations added in the 17th century. The cupola was demolished in the 18th century—only the drum remains. The tabernacle in the sanctuary by Baldassare Longhena has sculptures by Juste le Court (the two angels in the north transept are early works by the same artist). The tomb here of the patriarch Giovanni Francesco Morosini (d. 1678) is by Filippo Parodi. The painting of the *Annunciation* is by Luca Giordano. The organ was made by Nacchini in 1754.

In the first chapel on the south side are charming paintings by Padovanino with scenes from the life of St Andrea Avellino, helped by angels as he crosses a river and falls from his horse. The altarpiece by Sante Peranda shows the death of the saint. In the second chapel are three works by Camillo Procaccini, illustrating the life of St Charles Borromeo. In the third chapel, which has another altarpiece by Sante Peranda, the *Banquet of Herod* and *Beheading of St John the Baptist* are thought to be by Bonifacio Veronese. The south transept is the burial place of three doges from the Corner family, but it has no fewer than 12 busts of other members and a relief showing Caterina (Caterina Cornaro; *see p. 112*) giving the crown of Cyprus to Doge Agostino Barbarigo. The altarpiece of the *Virgin in Glory* is by Palma Giovane, and the *Ecstasy of St Francis* over the side door by Gerolamo Forabosco. There is also the pavement tomb of Paolo Renier, who was doge from 1779–89. In the north transept are two important works of their period: above one of the doors, the painting of *St Lawrence Distributing Alms* by Bernardo Strozzi and, close by, *St Jerome Visited by an Angel* by Johann Liss. On the north side are more works by Sante Peranda, and the third chapel has stories of St Cecilia and other saints by Palma Giovane. The convent of the church is now used by the University of Venice.

CANNAREGIO

This, the most northerly of the *sestieri*, takes its name from the *Canal Regio*, or Royal Canal (now the Canale di Cannaregio), once the main route into Venice from the mainland. Today it has a little row of shops and cafés, the lovely church of San Giobbe, and is also at the entrance to the old Ghetto. The bustling Rio Terrà San Leonardo, with its excellent daily food market, and the broad Strada Nuova both have quite a different character, with lots of local shops, and where life goes on apparently oblivious to the flow of visitors making their way from the station to Piazza San Marco. A few steps from the Strada Nuova is the Ca' d'Oro, perhaps the most beautiful of all the palaces on the Grand Canal. The lovely, remote area of northern Cannaregio, around the church of the Madonna dell'Orto, is described as a walk on p. 246. Other unexpected delights in this *sestiere* include the little church of the Madonna dei Miracoli.

CA' D'ORO
Map p. 402, A2

CA' D'ORO

Open 8.15–7.15, Mon 8.15–2. Entrance in the inconspicuous Calle della Ca' d'Oro, a few minutes' walk from the Rialto. It also has a landing-stage (vaporetto no. 1) on the Grand Canal. The rooms are not numbered, but the description below follows the plans given here.

The Ca' d'Oro is a splendid Gothic palace which houses one of the most important museums in the city, with a very fine collection of Venetian sculpture and small bronzes (15th and early 16th century), a masterpiece by Mantegna, and a large collection of paintings, detached frescoes and ceramics. The views of the Grand Canal from the palace windows are superb. The collection is very well displayed in modernised rooms, and there are ample places to sit.

History of the gallery

Famous as the most beautiful Gothic palace in Venice, the Ca' d'Oro was built between 1420 and 1434 for the procurator of St Mark's Marino Contarini, who preserved elements of the previous Veneto-Byzantine Palazzo Zeno on this site. It is the work of the little-known Matteo Raverti from Lombardy with collaborators, and of Giovanni and Bartolomeo Bon. It received its name (the 'Golden House') from the bright polychrome and gilded decoration carried out in 1431 by a French painter called Jean Charlier, which used to adorn the sculptural details of its façade (best seen from the Grand Canal). Having been poorly renovated in 1840, the palace was carefully restored by Baron Giorgio Franchetti in 1894, and he presented it to the state in 1916, together with his collection of paintings and antiquities which today constitute the Galleria Franchetti. It was first opened to the public in 1927, and some works from the Accademia and other state collections are also housed here. Palazzo Duodo, which adjoins the palace on the Grand Canal, has been restored to house part of the collection.

Ground floor

Beyond the ticket office is a charming little entrance court with a 15th-century well. Adjoining is the lovely portico (*closed in winter*), through which the house was approached from the canal, with the water-gate and an outside stair. The Greek marble columns have beautiful Veneto-Byzantine and Romanesque capitals. The mosaic pavement was added in Franchetti's time. The splendid well-head is the work of Bartolomeo Bon (1427) and is decorated with figures of *Charity*, *Justice* and *Fortitude*.

First floor

This consists of an anteroom with an alcove, and the *portego*, the characteristic feature of the *piano nobile* of Venetian palaces, extending the entire length of the building, and opening onto the *liagò* on the Grand Canal, with much smaller rooms on either side.

Room 1 (Anteroom): A miscellany of sculptural fragments made in the Veneto, some dating from the Byzantine period, and others from the 14th and 15th centuries, as well as a seated terracotta statue of the Madonna attributed to Andrea Briosco (Il Riccio). Non-Venetian works include alabaster scenes of English workmanship illustrating the life of St Catherine, and a Flemish tapestry, both dating from the 16th century.

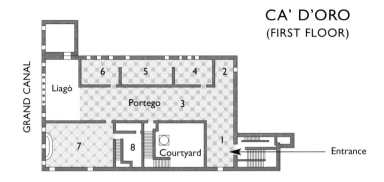

CA' D'ORO
(FIRST FLOOR)

Room 2 (Alcove, or Chapel): This room, with its richly decorated 15th-century ceiling (removed here from another building), was created by Franchetti for the most precious piece in his collection, the *St Sebastian* by **Mantegna** (*removed for restoration at the time of writing*), one of the last works by this famous painter of the Veneto school, dating from 1506. Although he was Giovanni Bellini's brother-in-law, and was very well known in his lifetime, he is now represented in Venice by just one other small painting in the Accademia. He spent most of his life working for the court of Mantua, where he painted the celebrated Camera degli Sposi. He is today one of the best known Italian painters of the Renaissance, also because many of the most important museums outside Italy contain very fine examples of his work.

Room 3 (Portego): Here is displayed a superb collection of **late 15th- and early 16th-century Venetian sculpture**. This was perhaps the period when the greatest works were produced in the city. It was the Lombardo family who introduced a new elegant Renaissance style of sculpture to Venice, and Tullio

Lombardo is splendidly represented here with his famous double portrait bust of a young couple. Also attributed to him is the unfinished relief of the *Last Supper* (formerly in the crypt of Santa Maria dei Miracoli), a copy of Leonardo's famous work in Milan. Antonio Rizzo came to Venice around the same time as Tullio's father Pietro. It is thought that the female statuette displayed here, called *Rhetoric* (but perhaps representing an angel), is by his hand.

Andrea Briosco (called 'Il Riccio'), from Padua, was one of the most original sculptors of the early Renaissance, and some of his very best bronze reliefs, made for the Venetian church of Santa Maria dei Servi, can be seen here: *St Martin and the Beggar*, four scenes of the legend of the True Cross, and a door of a tabernacle. His contemporary Vittore Gambello made the two battle scenes displayed close by for the same church. The charming bust of a boy (perhaps a member of the Gonzaga family), displayed on a pedestal, is attributed to Gian Cristoforo Romano.

In the early 16th century Giovanni Maria Mosca was at work in the city, and his is the marble relief of the *Death of Portia.* The life-like marble bust of a parish priest of San Gemignano called Matteo dai Letti (d. 1523) is attributed to his contemporary Bartolomeo di Francesco Bergamasco. The bronze andirons with *Venus* and *Adonis* are later 16th-century works by Girolamo Campagna. The *Assumption* and *Coronation of the Virgin*, from the funerary monument of the Doges Marco and Agostino Barbarigo in Santa Maria della Carità, dating from the same century, are by an unknown hand.

Room 4: In the case is displayed a very fine bronze **statuette of Apollo** by the artist nicknamed 'Antico' since he produced such very fine Classical works that they were sometimes confused with ancient Roman statues. Antico came from Mantua, where he also worked at the Gonzaga court. There is also a case of very fine **Renaissance medals**—double-sided small medallions in bronze, famous for their exquisite workmanship—which were usually cast to celebrate rulers, military leaders, Humanists, important buildings or events. Modelled on Roman coins, they often have a portrait head in profile. There are superb examples by Antico, and especially by the most skilled medallist of all, Antonio Pisanello, from Verona, who is known to have worked in Venice from 1415–20. There are others by Gentile Bellini, Vittore Gambello, Leone Leoni and Matteo de' Pasti.

There are a number of paintings of the Madonna around the walls, including works by Michele Giambono. The *Madonna 'dagli occhi belli'*, once attributed to Giovanni Bellini, is now thought to be by his follower Lazzaro Bastiani.

Room 5: More small bronzes, mostly Paduan and Florentine works, are exhibited here. The *Annunciation* by Carpaccio was one of six scenes from the life of the Virgin which once decorated the Scuola degli Albanesi.

Room 6: The display of small bronzes continues, and there are also andirons by Roccatagliata; two 16th-century *tondi* in bronze with portraits of Agostino Angeli da Pesaro and his son, the scientist Girolamo; and a striking bronze bust of Giampietro Mantova Benavides (d. 1520), by an unknown Paduan sculptor, based on his death mask.

Room 7: Here are displayed non-Venetian paintings of the 14th–16th centuries, including a *Madonna in Adoration of the Child* by Raffaellino del Garbo.

Room 8: The exquisite tiny painting of the *Flagellation* is by Luca Signorelli. There is a 15th-century carved wooden staircase.

Second floor

Room 10: This large room is hung with 16th-century Flemish tapestries. Here is displayed Jacopo Tintoretto's *Portrait of the Procurator Nicolò Priuli*. Other procurators (Giovanni Donà, Marino Grimani and Domenico Duodo) are commemorated with busts by Alessandro Vittoria, although his bust of Benedetto Manzini, the parish priest of San Gemignano, is the most striking of these portraits. A

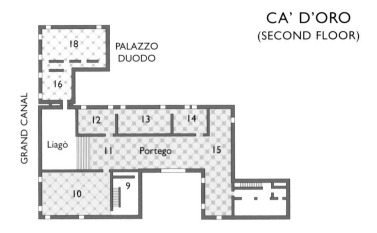

CA' D'ORO
(SECOND FLOOR)

PALAZZO DUODO

GRAND CANAL

18

16

12 13 14

Liagò 11 Portego 15

10 9

painting of *Venus* now generally attributed to Titian (but which has not always been considered by the master's hand, and which has part of the right side missing), is displayed near a *Sleeping Venus and Cupid* by Paris Bordone. There is a very fine portrait of an unknown gentleman, thought to have been painted by van Dyck when he was in Genoa between 1622 and 1627.

Room 11 (Portego): Here are detached and very damaged but beautiful frescoes from the cloister of Santo Stefano by Pordenone (c. 1532: *Expulsion from Paradise*, *Christ Appearing to Mary Magdalene*, and *Christ and the Samaritan*). Among the frescoes attributed to Domenico Campagnola, the three figures in niches of *Hope*, *Temperance* and *Charity*, and nudes and putti, are particularly interesting.

Room 12: German, Dutch and Flemish paintings are displayed here and in the

adjacent two rooms. Room 12 has works attributed to Antonio Mor, Jan van Scorel, and the circle of Dürer. The *Crucifixion* (with a view of Jerusalem in the background), attributed to a collaborator or follower of Jan van Eyck, was painted some time after 1430 and is known to have been in the Veneto by the mid-15th century.

Room 13: The display continues with *Jonah and the Whale* by Paul Brill, *The Alchemist* (1668) by Jan Steen, and a *Sleeping Woman* by Gabriel Metsu.

Room 15 (Anteroom): Here are interesting fragments of frescoes by Giorgione and Titian from the façade of the Fondaco dei Tedeschi, including a female nude by Giorgione, and, by Titian, two fragments with a battle between giants and monsters (from a frieze along the side façade), and the figure of *Judith* (or *?Justice*). Here are displayed terracotta models (*bozzetti*) by

Giacomo Piazzetta and Stefano Maderno. There is also a model by the great sculptor Gian Lorenzo Bernini for his fountain in Piazza Navona in Rome, and two marble busts by him of cardinals, both members of the Venetian Valier family. The two views of the Piazzetta and Molo are generally attributed to Francesco Guardi.

Palazzo Duodo

Two rooms in the palace (reached from the second-floor *liagò* of Ca' d'Oro) contain a well-displayed collection of ceramics. The first room (Room 16) has finds from recent excavations in the lagoon, including local ceramics of the 13th–14th centuries (the pieces from Malamocco are particularly interesting). The second room (Room 18) contains the Luigi Conton collection, with more ceramics (mostly 15th–17th century) from the lagoon, acquired in 1978. From the corner window there is a superb view down the Grand Canal.

THE STRADA NUOVA DISTRICT
Map p. 402, A2–B3

The Strada Nuova, opened in 1871, was the first of mercifully very few 19th-century interventions in the townscape, none of which was successful. Like the Calle Larga XXII Marzo and Via Garibaldi, it has no architectural distinction, and its dimensions—as can be seen at a glance on any map of Venice—are alien to the historic city. It is the only *strada* or 'street' in Venice, and even though exceptionally wide, it is always busy: Venetians come here to shop, and for tourists it is one of the most direct routes from the station to the Rialto and St Mark's. It has a great variety of simple shops selling clothes and hardware as well as food, and its bustling atmosphere provides a genuine glimpse into straightforward day-to-day Venetian life, with no pretensions to elegance.

More or less in the middle of the Strada Nuova (no. 4191), but hidden behind the housefronts, is the church of **Santa Sofia** (*open 9–12*), with a squat brick campanile. The light interior contains four statues of saints (on the west wall and on the high altar) by Antonio Rizzo. Many Venetians pop in here for a moment during the morning shop, and numerous candles are lit in front of the greatly venerated Crucifix displayed against the first nave column on the right. Apparently dating from the 15th century, with the Evangelists in the terminals (the bottom one is missing), it is rare to see such a precious work of art still serving as a devotional image. Campo Santa Sofia opens out onto the Grand Canal with the busy gondola ferry between here and the Rialto markets.

Just a little further up Strada Nuova is the narrow Calle della Ca' d'Oro, with the land entrance to the Ca' d'Oro.

Santi Apostoli

At the east end of the Strada Nuova, at the entrance to the pleasant Campo Santi Apostoli, is the former **Scuola dell'Angelo Custode** (now the Lutheran Evangelical

Church), with a façade by Andrea Tirali (1714). Opposite is the church of **Santi Apostoli** (*map p. 402, B2; open 8–12 & 5–7*), much rebuilt, which has a tall campanile of 1672, and the pretty domed exterior of the Cappella Corner. In the interior, the ceiling paintings date from 1748. The Cappella Corner on the south side is an interesting late 15th-century work attributed to Mauro Codussi, with the tombs of Marco and Giorgio Corner by the Lombardo family, including Tullio. The *Communion of St Lucy*, painted by Giambattista Tiepolo around 1748, was later placed on the altar. In the chapel to the right of the sanctuary are the remains of frescoes showing Byzantine influence (a *Deposition* and an *Entombment*), a rare survival in Venice from the early 14th century. The lovely marble relief of the head of St Sebastian is by Tullio Lombardo. In the chapel to the left of the sanctuary is a high relief of the *Madonna and Child*, a charming 15th-century work attributed to Niccolò di Pietro Lamberti, and a painting of the *Guardian Angel* by Francesco Maffei.

Opposite the church, a bridge from the campo crosses a rio to a calle which leads under the portico of **Palazzo Falier**, a Veneto-Byzantine palace dating from the end of the 13th century—a characteristic merchant's house of the period. It is traditionally thought to be the home of Doge Marin Falier, executed in 1355 for treason, by order of the Council of Ten. In the calle a huge stone has a long inscription set up in the 18th century by the Bakers' Guild, forbidding the making or selling of bread in the city by anyone who was not a guild member.

Behind the church, Calle Manganer leads out of the Campiello della Chiesa into the **Campiello della Cason**, which has a tree instead of a well and where Agnello Particiaco lived as doge in 811–27.

San Felice

At the other end of the Strada Nuova, a bridge leads over to Campo San Felice, where the church of **San Felice** (*map p. 402, A2; only open 4.30–7*) was founded in the 10th century, restored 1276 and rebuilt after 1531. Above the west door on the rio is a carved 14th-century angel. The pretty Fondamenta di San Felice can be seen following the rio, which is fronted by a portico for part of its length. Inside the church, on the altar to the right of the sanctuary, there is a painting by Jacopo Tintoretto of *St Demetrius* (dressed in shining armour with a red cloak and leggings and holding a red banner) together with the donor of the painting, against a mysterious backdrop of lightly sketched Classical ruins and mountain scenery.

The Strada Nuova continues across another bridge from which there is a view (right) of the splendid 15th-century façade (with ingenious corner windows) of **Palazzo Giovannelli**. This was a gift from the Republic to the *condottiere* Francesco Maria della Rovere, Duke of Urbino (for his services to Venice) in 1538. It later became the property of Prince Giovannelli, whose famous art collection included Giorgione's *Tempesta* (now in the Gallerie dell'Accademia). From the bridge in the other direction (left), there is a view of the façade of Ca' Pesaro across the Grand Canal. The Strada Nuova runs into Via Vittorio Emanuele, which continues to Campo Santa Fosca.

SANTA FOSCA & DISTRICT
Map p. 401, E3–D3

In Campo Santa Fosca is the fine, long 15th-century façade of Palazzo Correr (no. 2217), and a **monument to Fra' Paolo Sarpi**, commissioned from Emilio Marsili in 1892. Sarpi (1552–1623) was a Servite friar who became a great scientist (Galileo considered him his master) and historian (his history of the Council of Trent is of fundamental importance). But he is best remembered as the defender of the independence of the Venetian state against papal interference, advocating that the temporal power of secular rulers should remain separate from that of the Roman Church. In a famous dispute between Doge Leonardo Donà and Pope Paul V over the rights of temporal rulers, the pope, though he placed Venice under an interdict in 1606/7, was forced to give way, thanks largely to the able defence of the city's cause by Sarpi. His friend, the English ambassador Sir Henry Wotton (*see p. 135*), who was quick to support him in his conflict with the Jesuits and the pope, declared 'for learning, I think I may justly call him the most deep and general scholar of the world ... His power of speech consisteth rather in the soundness of reason than in any other natural ability'. Sarpi is buried in the church of San Michele in Isola.

Santa Fosca and San Marciliano

The church of **Santa Fosca** (*map p. 401, E3; open 9.30–11.30*) was founded in the 13th century, and the domed brick campanile was reconstructed after damage in 1410. The church was rebuilt in 1679, and restored in 1741 when the façade was constructed. It contains (over the door on the north side) a damaged *Holy Family* with a donor, by Domenico Tintoretto, and (on the altar on the right of the sanctuary) a fine Byzantine painting of the *Pietà and Two Saints* (recently restored).

From the bridge which leads across Rio di Santa Fosca, there is a good view (to the left) of the 17th-century Palazzo Diedo, attributed to Andrea Tirali, and across another canal, the ex-convent and church of **Santa Maria dei Servi**, founded in 1318 and consecrated in 1491, and once one of the most important Gothic buildings in Venice. Most of it was destroyed in 1812 and only a Gothic doorway, and a 15th-century statue of the Madonna on the wall survive. The view to the right takes in the noble Renaissance façade of Palazzo Vendramin on Fondamenta del Forner.

From here you can make a detour across the bridge to Calle Zancani, which leads across another rio to the church of **San Marciliano** or San Marziale; (*map p. 401, E3; open 4–7; Sun and holidays 8–1*). High up in the vault are circular paintings in pretty gilded frames, which are among the best works of Sebastiano Ricci (*see p. 215*). On the second south altar is *St Martial and Two Saints*, an over-restored painting by Jacopo Tintoretto, and on either side of the chancel the *Annunciatory Angel* and *Virgin Annunciate* by his son, Domenico. There is a lovely 15th-century wooden statue of the seated Madonna and Child on the second north altar. In the sanctuary there is a huge golden globe with the *Resurrection of Christ*, and the four side altars have twisted yellow columns.

The Maddalena and San Marcuola

From Santa Fosca Ponte Sant'Antonio leads to the little Campo della Maddalena, with a fine well-head, and surrounded by quaint old houses with tall chimney-pots. Palazzo Magno has a Gothic lunette over its doorway. The small round domed **church of the Maddalena** (*map p. 401, E3*) is attractively sited on its canal. A Neoclassical building by Tommaso Temanza (c. 1760), it is closed to worship.

Rio Terrà della Maddalena, dating from 1398, and now a crowded shopping street, continues past (right) the 17th-century Palazzo Donà delle Rose (no. 2343) and the 15th-century Palazzo Contin (no. 2347). Diverge left along Calle Larga Vendramin to reach the land entrance (no. 2079) of **Palazzo Vendramin-Calergi**, which since 1970 has been the winter home of the Casinò (the superb façade on the Grand Canal is by Mauro Codussi; *see p. 243*). In the courtyard a fine 11th-century Byzantine well-head can be seen. A plaque records Wagner's death here in 1883.

WAGNER IN VENICE

Richard Wagner, famous for his reform of opera, but also one of the most controversial figures in the history of music, came to Venice many times after his first visit in 1858, when he stayed at the Palazzo Giustinian on the Grand Canal and wrote the second act of *Tristan*. He found that the stillness of the city provided him with the peace he needed to compose, and he also spent much time in his later years in southern Italy and Sicily. Just after his last and perhaps his greatest opera, *Parsifal*, was staged in 1882, he returned to winter in Venice with his wife Cosima (Liszt's daughter) and their children. They decided to rent (on a long lease) a very large apartment (with some 20 rooms) on the mezzanine floor of Palazzo Vendramin from Count Bardi, nephew of Maria Carolina, Duchess of Berry, who had purchased the entire palace from the Vendramin-Calergi in 1844. Franz Liszt visited them here, but the great composer, already in poor health, died suddenly of a heart attack on 13th February 1883. A special train was sent from Bavaria to Venice so that his family could accompany his coffin back to Bayreuth, where he is buried in the town where the *Ring* cycle was first performed in 1876.

The Richard Wagner Association of Venice was given three of these rooms by the city of Venice in 1995, including the room in which the composer died. Although none of the original furnishings survive from Wagner's time, the rooms are now arranged as a small museum, with an important library, scores, programmes, autograph letters, and works of art relating to Wagner and his music, donated to the Association in 2003 by Josef Lienhart (*visits by appointment on Sat mornings; T: 041 276 0407 or 349 593 6990*). The Association also organises an annual programme of concerts dedicated to Wagner.

Ponte Storto (with a view of the end of the Fondaco dei Turchi over the Grand Canal) leads across Rio di San Marcuola.

The church of **San Marcuola**, or Santi Ermagora e Fortunato (*map p. 401, D3; open 8.30–12 & 5–7, except Sun*), by Giorgio Massari (1728–36), has an unfinished façade which faces the Grand Canal. From the campo, which has a landing-stage served by vaporetto no. 1, the view takes in the dome of San Geremia (right) and, in the distance by the station, the façade of the Scalzi. Directly across the Grand Canal stands the Fondaco dei Turchi, and to the left are the granaries of the Republic and Palazzo Belloni-Battagià with its two obelisks. The interior of the church has some unusual paintings around the two facing pulpits, including the *Christ Child Blessing between Sts Catherine and Andrew*, and the *Head of Christ* between two male portraits, thought to be by pupils of Titian (perhaps Francesco Vecellio). On the left wall of the chancel is a *Last Supper*, a good early work (1547) by Jacopo Tintoretto; on the right wall is a copy made in the 17th century of Tintoretto's *Washing of the Feet*; the original is now in Newcastle-upon-Tyne, England, and is almost identical to another painting by Tintoretto in the Prado, Madrid. The church also contains paintings—on the ceiling, in the presbytery, on the high altar and in the 18th-century sacristy—by Francesco Migliori, a little-known 18th-century Venetian artist. The statues in the church are by Giovanni Maria Morleiter and assistants. The Callido organ dates from 1775.

The façade of the Scuola del Cristo, founded in 1644, survives behind the church. Any one of the *calli* here leads up to Rio Terrà San Leonardo (*map p. 401, D3*), where there is a good daily street market much frequented by Venetians.

THE CANNAREGIO CANAL
Map p. 400, C3–A2

The Cannaregio Canal, after which the *sestiere* is named, is the widest waterway in Venice after the Grand Canal. It is lined with fine buildings, and at the beginning is a small group of local shops. The stone Ponte delle Guglie (1580; restored 1777) has a pretty balustrade, and masks on the arch. In 1987 a ramp for the disabled was carefully incorporated into the design of the steps. Here is an entrance to the Parco Savorgnan, public gardens with a children's playground, with two more entrances from Calle Riello and Campo San Geremia.

San Geremia and Palazzo Labia
On Campo San Geremia stands the church of **San Geremia** (*map p. 400, C3; open 8.30–12 & 4–6.30*). This is a clumsy building by Carlo Corbellini (1753–60), although the fine campanile is among the oldest in Venice. The interior (entrance by the south door) is more successful than the exterior, but it is very cluttered with mementoes of St Lucy. When the body of St Lucy (martyred in Syracuse in Sicily in 304) was stolen from Constantinople in 1204 by Venetian crusaders, the church of Santa Lucia was built for it (later redesigned by Palladio). When this church was demolished (in 1863)

to make way for the railway station (which was named after the saint), Lucy's body was moved here and can still be seen in her chapel (she has a sculpted head, but her skeletal hands and feet protrude from her rather hideous bright red robe). A portrait of her by Palma Giovane is preserved with relics and church vestments in a room where souvenirs are sold. Palma also painted *St Magnus Crowning Venice* on the second south altar.

Palazzo Labia (*map p. 400, C3*) has a façade in the campo by Alessandro (or Paolo) Tremignon (completed c. 1750). The main façade dating from the previous century, which faces the Cannaregio Canal is by Andrea Cominelli. The huge building is now the regional headquarters of RAI, the Italian radio and television corporation. In the ballroom the *trompe l'oeil* frescoes by Gerolamo Mengozzi-Colonna provide a setting for Giambattista Tiepolo's splendid frescoes of Antony and Cleopatra (*usually viewable by appointment, but at present being restored*).

The garish Lista di Spagna (with numerous souvenir shops) leads from San Geremia to the Scalzi church.

The Scalzi

Map p. 400, B4. Open 7–11.45 & 4–6.45.

The church of the Scalzi, built for the Discalced (Barefoot) Carmelites, is a fine Baroque building by Longhena (1670–80). The façade made of Carrara marble is by Giuseppe Sardi (1672–80). The impressive dark Baroque interior is profusely decorated with marbles and sculptures, and a huge elaborate tabernacle fills the apse. This is the work of the Carmelite friar Giuseppe Pozzo, who took over work on the interior decoration after Longhena retired from the project. Notice the monk peeping out from between the columns of the high altar. When the ceiling fresco by Giambattista Tiepolo was destroyed by a bomb in 1915, the Venetian painter Ettore Tito was called in to replace it with a painting of the Council of Ephesus. Two other vault frescoes painted for the church by Tiepolo survive, albeit in a damaged state (*St Teresa in Glory* in the second south chapel, and the *Agony in the Garden* in the first north chapel).

In a chapel on the south side dedicated to St Teresa of Avila, founder of the Carmelite Order, are large scenes from her life by Niccolò Bambini, and a sculpted altarpiece of her ecstasy by Lazzaro Baldi or Heinrich Meyring (clearly showing the influence of Bernini's famous work of the same subject in the church of Santa Maria della Vittoria, Rome). In the pavement is the tomb slab of Doge Carlo Ruzzini (d. 1735). In the third chapel is a statue of the *Redeemer* by Melchior Berthel and a vault fresco by Pietro Liberi.

The second north chapel was the burial place Lodovico Manin, the last doge of Venice (d. 1797), who paid for the elaborate Baroque decoration of the chapel. The sculpture of the *Holy Family* is by Giuseppe Torretti, and the vault fresco by Louis Dorigny. Two enormous turquoise-blue glass candlesticks made in Murano in the early 18th century have been placed here. In the adjoining chapel there is a bas-relief of *Christ Carrying the Cross* by Giovanni Maria Morleiter and an 18th-century wax *Ecce Homo*. The manual organ by B. Sona, dating from 1802, was restored in 2003.

Almost opposite the Scalzi church, the Ponte degli Scalzi, built in 1934 from Eugenio Miozzi's design, crosses the Grand Canal and links Cannaregio to Santa Croce. It replaced the original iron bridge of 1858, which had been built by the occupying Austrians. The **Santa Lucia railway station**, built on the site of the former church of St Lucy, hence its name, lies beyond the Scalzi church. The first station building was considered unsatisfactory, and a competition was held in the mid-1930s for the design of a new one. With no outright winner and the ensuing Second World War, construction of the present Rationalist-style building did not begin until the 1950s. The architect was the little-known Paolo Perilli, together with engineers from the Italian State Railways.

THE REMOTE NORTHWEST
Map p. 400, A2

Fondamenta Savorgnan leads along the Cannaregio Canal past the huge Palazzo Manfrin (no. 342), built in 1735 by Andrea Tirali. Next, at no. 349, is Palazzo Savorgnan, built c. 1663 to a design by Giuseppe Sardi. The fine garden façade behind can be seen from the public gardens here.

Beyond the terracotta-coloured 15th-century Palazzo Testa (no. 468), is the entrance to a housing development, next to an area formerly occupied by a factory (Saffa), where buildings designed by Vittorio Gregotti were erected in the 1990s. Further on, the canal is crossed by Ponte dei Tre Archi, designed in 1688 by Andrea Tirali (the brick parapet was added in the 18th century).

San Giobbe

Map p. 400, A2. Open Mon–Sat 10–5. In its secluded campo in the northwest corner of the city is the church of San Giobbe (St Job), built after 1450 by Antonio Gambello and enlarged by Pietro Lombardo, who was responsible (with assistants) for the fine doorway (the three statues are now exhibited in the sacristy). In the lunette is a relief of *St Francis and St Job*, the latter being the Old Testament prophet to whom the church is dedicated. The Gothic campanile can be seen from the

The entrance portal of San Giobbe, by Pietro Lombardo and assistants.

courtyard, which was once part of the convent which adjoined the church, and which preserves an attractive portico next to a pleasant little garden.

The interior is one of the earliest examples of a Franciscan Observant church plan; a single nave without aisles, with the monks' choir behind the presbytery. A carved triumphal arch flanked by two smaller semicircular chapels precedes the beautiful domed **sanctuary** with sculpted roundels, a masterpiece of Renaissance architecture and carving by Pietro Lombardo and assistants. It was built above the huge pavement tomb of Doge Cristoforo Moro when he died in 1471 (buried here with his wife Cristina Sanudo). The tomb is simply decorated with beautifully carved blackberries (*mori*; the family emblem) around the short inscription, and is devoid of all religious references. The doge is shown in a portrait which, most unusually, has been allowed to be hung on the right wall. He was the founder of the church, which he dedicated to his friend, St Bernardino of Siena, who stayed in the convent in 1443. He is also portrayed in a contemporary terracotta bust attributed to Bartolomeo Bellano, which was left to the church by the doge (and can now be seen in the sacristy). Behind the altar extends the long choir with 16th-century wood stalls.

The ante-sacristy was part of a late 14th-century oratory, and has a painting of the *Nativity* by Girolamo Savoldo. The **sacristy** has a 16th-century wooden ceiling and a charming little triptych of the *Annunciation between Sts Michael and Anthony* by Antonio Vivarini and Giovanni d'Alemagna (1440–50). Three statuettes from the main portal of the church are exhibited here. At the other end of the room is a small painting in a very beautiful frame of the *Marriage of St Catherine* by Andrea Previtali.

The second altar on the **south side** has a painting of the *Vision of God to Job* by Lattanzio Querena, in a beautiful marble frame which belonged to Giovanni Bellini's famous altarpiece, removed from here in the early 19th century and now in the Gallerie dell'Accademia (*see p. 145*). The monument to the French ambassador René d'Argenson by Claude Perrault (1651) is composed of black and white marble supported by two bizarre crowned lions and with a fat putto above the sarcophagus. The fourth altarpiece is by Paris Bordone (*Three Saints*).

The two chapels at the beginning of the **north side** are beautifully decorated: in the first is a statue of St Luke by Lorenzo Bregno; the second (Cappella Martini) was built by Tuscan artists in the early 1470s for a family of silk-workers from Lucca. The vault is lined with majolica tiles and contains five pretty della Robbian roundels in glazed terracotta, thought to be the work of Andrea, the most famous member (with his uncle Luca) of this remarkable family of Florentine sculptors. The marble altar with statuettes of St John the Baptist and other saints is by a follower of Antonio Rossellino; the relief of the *Madonna and Child* is missing, since it is now in the Fogg Museum in North America. The *Stations of the Cross* in the third chapel are attributed to Antonio Zucchi.

The lagoon end of the Cannaregio Canal

Beyond Ponte dei Tre Archi, the fondamenta continues to the edge of the lagoon past the huge **Macelli**, a slaughterhouse built in 1832 by Giuseppe Salvadori. It was one of the largest in Italy after its extension in 1915, and only ceased to function as such in 1972. Since 1990 it has been restored as premises for part of the University of Venice. The old brick buildings have been carefully preserved and the alterations made in red steel, in one of the most successful conservative restorations yet carried out in Venice. Another exemplary restoration project, if on a much simpler and small-er scale, can be seen close by at no. 792 in the Calle delle Beccarie, where in 2006 the municipality, in collaboration with the Venice in Peril Fund, restored an attractive small building to provide housing for a number of local families. On the opposite side of the canal, on the Sacca di San Girolamo overlooking the lagoon, new municipal housing was built in 1987–90.

Across Ponte dei Tre Archi (with a view out to the lagoon), Fondamenta di Cannaregio leads back down the other side of the canal, passing (no. 967) Palazzo Surian, almost certainly by Giuseppe Sardi. This was once the French Embassy, and the young Jean Jacques Rousseau was Secretary here in 1743–44, before he became famous as a political philosopher, educationist and essayist. A central figure of French Illuminism, his egalitarian writings were to inspire many thinkers, including Kant and Marx, and his political thought had a deep influence on post-Revolutionary France.

THE GHETTO
Map p. 400, C2–p. 401, D2

Admission to the museum and guided tour of the synagogues 10–4.30 or 5.30, Fri 10–sunset; closed Sat and Jewish holidays; T: 041 715 359. Tickets for the guided tour, in English and Italian, of the museum and (normally three) synagogues of the Ghetto can be bought from the museum in the campo of the Ghetto Nuovo.

The word 'ghetto' is derived from the Venetian word *geto*, indicating the place where metal was cast: there was an iron foundry here for making cannons until 1390, when it was transferred to the Arsenale. Although Jews from the East, northern Europe, Spain and Portugal had been coming to Venice for short periods (in which they were some-times tolerated and sometimes expelled), it was not until 1516 that the Great Council permitted Jews to live permanently in Venice, but compelled them to inhabit only this area. A curfew was enforced by guards, who had to be paid for by the Jews themselves. The word ghetto was subsequently used for segregated Jewish communities in other cities all over Europe. The first settlement was on the island of Ghetto Nuovo (named after a 'new' foundry); in 1541 it expanded to Ghetto Vecchio (the site of an 'old' foundry), and in 1633 to Ghetto Nuovissimo. It is estimated that as many as 5,000 Jews lived here in the 16th–17th centuries. Not until 1797 were Jews allowed (by Napoleon) to leave the Ghetto and live in other parts of the city. During the Austrian occupation, the Jews were asked to return to the Ghetto, and it was only definitively opened in 1866. There are now some 500 Jewish residents in Venice, only about 30 of whom have chosen to live in the Ghetto. The five main synagogues (or *scuole*) remain here, two of them still in use. Built for the first time in the 15th century, they are named after the various different communities who erected them, in their own distinctive styles of architecture, as meeting places and places of worship. The Jewish cemetery is on the Lido (*see p. 330*).

Tour of the Ghetto

At the beginning of Sottoportego del Ghetto (*map p. 400, C3*) are signs of the gate which closed the entrance at night. The dark calle leads past a stone (on no. 1131 on the left) with a long list of the rules for 'converted' Jews who wished to return to the Ghetto, inscribed in 1704. Beyond several carpenters' shops is Campiello delle Scuole with its two synagogues (on upper floors), still usually used for services, and a tall house with numerous windows, typical of this area (families were crowded into small flats with low ceilings). To the left as you enter the square, with an inconspicuous exterior, is the **Scuola Spagnola**, founded c. 1585 as the Scuola Ponentina, with an interior probably rebuilt by Longhena c. 1655. This is the largest of the Venetian synagogues. It has a fine elliptical women's gallery (today the women are permitted to sit below, but behind screens). The **Scuola Levantina**, opposite, probably founded around the same time as the Scuola Spagnola, and with a fine exterior, was erected by pupils of Longhena. The elaborate wood carving of the ceiling and pulpit is by Andrea Brustolon.

Ponte di Ghetto Vecchio leads over to the **island of Ghetto Nuovo**, the oldest area of the Ghetto, where large buildings were erected in the mid-15th century by a Venetian merchant around a huge courtyard with three wells. The campo (on the site of that courtyard), with its three wells and scattered trees, is now partly surrounded by tall 17th-century houses, with numerous windows: some have as many as seven floors. Here, on the upper floors, are three more synagogues. Above a 19th-century portico of four columns is the **Scuola Italiana** (1575); it has five windows on the top floor and a cupola. The interior dates mostly from 1739, but also has elements from other periods, from the early 17th to the mid-19th centuries. In the far corner of the campo is the **Scuola Canton** (1531), with its tiny wooden cupola just visible. This is the synagogue generally used by the Jewish community in Venice today. Its name may be derived from its corner position, or from the name of a family (Cantono des Juif). It was connected by a passageway with the Scuola Italiana. The **Scuola Grande Tedesca**, the oldest synagogue in Venice (1528), is now entered by a 19th-century staircase above the **Jewish Museum** (no. 2902b; *map p. 401, D2*), which has a well-labelled display of Jewish treasures (mostly 17th–18th century). It is in the process of renovation and expansion. The museum has a café and well-stocked bookshop (*for admission see opposite*).

On a wall in the campo, opposite the museum, bronze reliefs were set up in 1985 in memory of Jewish war victims, many of whom were deported to concentration camps in Germany; another memorial dates from 1993. A hospice for the poor here was founded in 1890, which later became an old people's home. At no. 2912, under a portico, is the site of a pawn shop, known as the Banco Rosso. This was one of three such shops here run by the Jews, along with banking and exchange offices, and the offices of money-lenders, all of which were busy during the day with Venetian clients. A passageway (where the doors which closed the Ghetto at night once stood) leads into the Ghetto Nuovissimo, added in 1633, with more tall houses.

An iron bridge (guarded by two old sentry boxes) with decorative wrought-iron railings (1865–66) leads out of the Ghetto to Fondamenta degli Ormesini.

MADONNA DELL'ORTO
Map p. 401, E2

Open Mon–Sat 10–5; Chorus Pass. The campo and adjoining area are described in a guided walk on pp. 246–54

The church of the Madonna dell'Orto was the parish church of Jacopo Tintoretto, who is buried here. It contains some of his most important works.

The first church on this site, dedicated to St Christopher, was founded around 1350 by Fra' Tiberio da Parma, general of the Umiliati order of Benedictines. After 1377 it became known as the Madonna dell'Orto from a miraculous statue of the Madonna and Child, which had been abandoned in a nearby orchard.

The façade is a fine example of 15th-century Venetian Gothic, with good tracery in the windows, and statues thought to be by some of the most important sculptors working in the city at that time, but which still await definitive attributions. In order of date they include: the Apostles in the niches (attributed to the dalle Masegne brothers), the Madonna and Annunciatory Angel flanking the doorway (attributed as early works to Antonio Rizzo), and St Christopher above (once attributed, as a late work, to Bartolomeo Bon, but now usually thought to be by the workshop of Niccolò di Giovanni Fiorentino). The campanile (1503), with its onion-shaped cupola, is a conspicuous feature of the skyline when seen from the lagoon towards Murano.

The interior

The nave and aisles of the spare interior are divided by columns of striped Turkish marble, and the semicircular apse is vaulted. The church organ by Pietro Bazzani (1878) has been restored. The colossal stone statue (radically restored) of the Madonna and Child by Giovanni de' Santi, which gave the church its name, is kept in a side chapel.

Choir and apse: This is adorned by two huge paintings by Jacopo Tintoretto, the *Last Judgement* and *Making of the Golden Calf.* Fourteen and a half metres high and nearly 6m wide, they were probably painted *in situ* around 1562–64 (they fit the Gothic vault of the ceiling). Apart from the paintings for the Scuola Grande di San Rocco, these were considered Tintoretto's most important commissions, and we know that he donated them as a gift to his parish church.

Flanking an *Annunciation* by Palma Giovane are the *Vision of the Cross to St Peter* and the *Beheading of St Paul*, also by Tintoretto, who painted the five *Virtues* in the vault, except for *Faith* in the centre, which was added in the 17th century.

Chapel on the right of the choir: A modest slab marks Jacopo Tintoretto's resting-place. A plaque on the wall on the left records Sir Ashley Clarke (1903–94), a former British Ambassador to Italy, who became an honorary citizen of Venice. He was founder of the Venice in Peril Fund, which has restored numerous monuments all over the city, including, in 1968–70, the fabric, sculptures and paintings of this church—the first Venetian building to be comprehensively restored after the flood of November 1966. This British Fund continues to contribute fundamental help to the city by funding restoration projects and the scientific investigations necessary before these can be initiated.

South aisle: This contains a masterpiece by Cima da Conegliano on the Renaissance altar at the beginning of the aisle. Still in its original frame, it depicts *St John the Baptist and Four Saints*, and was painted around 1493. In the distance you can see the castle of Conegliano, the artist's home. Also in this aisle is the Cavazza family monument, erected in 1657, richly decorated with polychrome marbles by Giuseppe Sardi, and commemorating in particular Girolamo Cavazza (1588–1681), a diplomat in the service of the Republic. Beside the fourth south altar is another famous work by Jacopo Tintoretto: the *Presentation of the Virgin in the Temple.* The inclusion of a grand staircase recalls Titian's painting of the same subject executed some 20 years earlier for the Scuola della Carità (now in the Accademia; *see p. 156*), although the risers of the steps in this painting are decorated in gold leaf. At the end of this aisle is the entrance to a devotional chapel where the original 14th-century statue of the *Madonna dell'Orto* is kept.

North aisle: The elegant Renaissance chapel at the beginning of the north aisle was completed for the Valier in 1526 by Andrea and Antonio Buora; it has a cupola and a semicircular apse. The charming sculpted tabernacle over the altar has remained sadly empty since 1993, when the very beautiful *Madonna*, painted by Giovanni Bellini around 1478, was stolen. The second chapel has Titian's *Tobias and the Archangel* from the church of San Marciliano, hung here since its restoration. The praying figure on the left is St John the Baptist (*for the*

story of Tobias, see p. 171). The Contarini are duly recorded in their chapel (the fourth), with a series of family busts, one (centre left) by Danese Cattaneo, and another (centre right) by Alessandro Vittoria. Over this altar is another notable work by Jacopo Tintoretto, *St Agnes Raising Licinius*. At the top of the aisle a narrow brick passage leads to the Sir Ashley Clarke Treasury, housed in a little barrel-vaulted room with massive walls which supports the base of the campanile. It displays liturgical objects typical of those kept in church sacristies, in an arrangement intended to illustrate their uses rather than their artistic value. These include vestments, monstrances, reliquaries, processional crosses and vessels for use at Mass. Among them is a precious 15th-century chalice and a reliquary also dating from that time.

EASTERN CANNAREGIO
Map p. 402

San Giovanni Crisostomo
Map p. 402, B3. Open 8.15–12.15 & 3–7; Sun and holidays 10–12.30 & 3.30–7.
This striking pink and white church almost fills its small campo. It was rebuilt after serious damage by fire and is dedicated to St John Chrysostom, a 4th-century preacher who became famous as the Patriarch of Constantinople and for his revision of the Greek Liturgy. A book which supposedly belonged to him was brought to Venice from Constantinople as a holy relic to be preserved in St Mark's. Built between 1497 and 1504, the church is a masterpiece of Venetian Renaissance architecture and the last work of Mauro Codussi (*see box opposite*).

The interior of the church is much visited by worshippers, especially since it became the Santuario della Madonna delle Grazie in 1977, dedicated to the highly venerated marble bust of the *Madonna delle Grazie* on the south side. The Greek-cross plan is of Byzantine inspiration. The superb high altarpiece of *St John Chrysostom with Six Saints* (1510–11), with the titular saint writing in his book for all to see and read, is by Sebastiano del Piombo. Above the south side door are four small paintings from the old organ, attributed to Girolamo da Santacroce: the present organ above the west door has its four doors painted by Giovanni Mansueti. The first south altarpiece of *Sts Christopher, Jerome and Louis of Toulouse* is a beautiful (late) painting by Giovanni Bellini. The *Death of St Joseph* above the second south altar is by Johann Carl Loth.

The second north altar bears a Classical bas-relief of the *Coronation of the Virgin* by Tullio Lombardo, and (above) a Veneto-Byzantine relief of the *Virgin Orans*. The first altar has a painting of *St Anthony of Padua* by a follower of Vivarini.

Mauro Codussi (c. 1440–1504)

Codussi was extremely important for introducing the Renaissance style to Venice in the late 15th century, and he designed numerous buildings in the city. He worked at the Scuola Grande of San Marco, and that of San Giovanni Evangelista, and made grand staircases part of the design of both buildings. Palazzo Vendramin-Calergi (*see p. 233*) is usually considered his masterpiece, and has his typical two-light windows beneath an oculus set within a larger rounded arch, a characteristic feature also seen in another palace by him on the Grand Canal, Palazzo Corner-Spinelli. Codussi also worked in Piazza San Marco on the Torre dell'Orologio, and provided the design for the reconstruction of the Procuratie Vecchie. He revived the use of centralised church plans, as can be seen in his lovely interiors, both here at San Giovanni Crisostomo and at Santa Maria Formosa. He produced the beautiful façade of San Michele in Isola, finished that of San Zaccaria, and designed the distinctive campanile of San Pietro in Castello, which also served as a lighthouse. His Classical style (and frequent use of the Corinthian order) owes much to Leon Battista Alberti, with whom he worked on the Tempio Malatestiano in Rimini.

Salizzada San Canciano leads right (across a bridge) from Salizzada San Giovanni Crisostomo to the church of **San Canciano**, of ancient foundation, rebuilt in the 18th century. Adjacent is Campiello Santa Maria Nova, where Palazzo Bembo-Boldù, with tall Gothic windows, bears a curious relief in a niche of a bearded figure holding a solar disc.

Santa Maria dei Miracoli

Map p. 402, C3. Open Mon–Sat 10–5; Chorus Pass.

On a small campo bordered by a canal stands the church of Santa Maria dei Miracoli, a delightful Renaissance work by Pietro Lombardo (1481–89), sumptuously decorated with splendid marble inlay both inside and out. It is thought that many of the Classical details may be derived from the Palace of Diocletian in Split, which Pietro is known to have visited on a journey to Dalmatia.

The church was built in this confined site, with its north side set directly on the water, because there was a shrine here in the 15th century with a painting of the Madonna, held to be miraculous. This is one of the few churches in Venice where you can see all four external walls. It has a single, unusually tall, nave, a barrel-vaulted roof, high domed apse and tiny attached campanile. A great variety of marble, including *pavon-*

azzetto, red Verona, white Carrara and *cipollino* was used in the elegant polychrome inlay in geometric designs. The exquisite carved friezes are decorated with shields, helmets, arms, griffins and marine creatures, as well as Classical motifs. The exterior is divided into two orders, with pilasters below and a blind arcade above. At the top is a semicircular gable which follows the curve of the roof and is decorated with a rose window, smaller *oculi*, and marble *tondi*. In the lunette above the door is a 16th-century *Madonna*.

SANTA MARIA DEI MIRACOLI

The decoration of the interior is as beautiful as the exterior, with marble walls and a raised choir and domed apse. The nuns' choir at the west end is supported by delicately carved pillars. The nave vault is adorned with 50 panels bearing heads of prophets and saints painted by Pier Maria Pennacchi (1528). The choir is preceded by a pretty marble balustrade, with fine half-length figures probably by Tullio Lombardo, who also carried out the rest of the exquisite carving together with his father Pietro. On the high altar is a charming *Madonna* (1409), the sacred image for which the church was built, by the little-known painter Niccolò di Pietro Paradisi.

Teatro Malibran and the area where Marco Polo lived

Calle Castelli (*map p. 402, C3*) leads away from the church and emerges on Fondamenta Sanudo (named after the 16th-century diarist Marino Sanudo or Sanuto). To the left is the fine Gothic doorway of **Palazzo Vanier-Sanudo-Van Axel**, with Gothic and Veneto-Byzantine elements on its handsome canal façade. One of the most important late Gothic palaces in the city, it was built for Marco and Agostino Soranzo in 1479, and was owned by the Van Axel in the 17th century, and restored in 1920. Ponte del Cristo stands at the junction of three canals. On the left is the white façade of Palazzo Marcello-Papadopoli, attributed to Longhena; and to the right is the 15th-century Gothic façade of Palazzo Pisani, with fine balconies.

Calle del Cristo leads into Campo Santa Marina, where a high archway connects the symmetrical wings of a former palace. From the end of the campo (right), Sottoportego and Calle Scaletta lead to Ponte Marco Polo. On the far side is the side entrance to the **Teatro Malibran** (*map p. 402, B3*), the successor to the theatre of San Giovanni Crisostomo, built in 1677, and the largest and most famous theatre in Europe for music in the 17th and early 18th centuries. In 1707 two operas by Alessandro Scarlatti were put on here, and in 1709 Handel's *Agrippina* had its première (in the presence of the composer); it was a major success. After restoration, the theatre was reopened in 1819 with Rossini's *La Gazza Ladra*. In 1835 Maria Malibran, the gifted Spanish mezzo-soprano, sang here in Bellini's *Sonnambula* in 1835, the year before her death (aged only 28); the theatre was subsequently named after her. It is still used for excellent concerts.

A *sottoportico* leads into two courtyards. They bear Marco Polo's nickname, earned because his contemporaries thought he always talked in 'millions' and exaggerated his description of his travels in the East. The **Corte Seconda del Milion** is surrounded by ancient houses which bear 12th–15th-century elements, and a beautiful Byzantine arch (possibly a survival from the 12th century), richly carved with animals and birds.

Marco Polo (1254–1324)

Marco Polo came from a merchant family; his father was one of three brothers who travelled regularly to the East. Marco accompanied his father and uncle in 1271 on a four-year overland journey, from Trebizond on the Black Sea through Persia, Tibet, and the Gobi Desert to Peking. He was employed for 17 years at the court of the Mongol ruler, Kublai Khan, grandson of Genghis Khan, and was sent as envoy throughout the Empire from Siberia to southern India and Japan. He returned to Venice by sea along the coast of China and India. In 1298 he was taken prisoner by the Genoese at the Battle of Cursola, and during a year's imprisonment he dictated to a fellow prisoner, Rusticello di Pisa, a superb description of the world he had seen on his travels. This was probably the first description of Asia ever to reach the West, and remained the most accurate for many centuries. His book was well known throughout Europe during the Middle Ages.

A WALK THROUGH CANNAREGIO

This walk covers a very quiet residential area of the city (characterised by its three parallel canals with single fondamente), from the remote church of Sant'Alvise to the Baroque church of the Gesuiti, with an important altarpiece by Titian. Between them is the beautiful church of the Madonna dell'Orto, which contains wonderful paintings by Tintoretto, who lived close by.

The walk begins just north of the Ghetto, on the Fondamenta degli Ormesini, which runs along the **Rio della Misericordia**, the first of the district's three parallel canals. By Sottoportego Alberagno, no. 2737 is a tiny bar (without a sign) seemingly in the back parlour of a delightfully chatty Venetian lady, where you can start out with an excellent and reasonably-priced coffee (especially recommended, since you will meet no more cafés along the way). The *fondamenta* has a number of pleasant small local shops, again the only ones you pass. Also here is a simple, family-run trattoria of good value, the Antica Mola, much beloved by Venetians (also with tables outside in a garden; *see p. 361*).

Calle Malvasia leads to **Rio della Sensa**, a quieter and even prettier canal. Calle del Capitello (or 'Capitolo') leads on up to another bridge, across which is one of the most remote parts of the city—since it is virtually an island with just two bridges connecting it to the rest of the city, it has a vaporetto landing-stage on the lagoon. Here a small campo surrounds the **church of Sant'Alvise**, which dates from the late 14th century. On its Gothic brick façade is an early 15th-century Tuscan statue of the titular saint, St Louis of Toulouse (Alvise in Venetian), in his bishop's mitre. Louis was the son of the King of Naples, Charles II of Anjou, and

became a Franciscan and then Bishop of Toulouse. He was canonised in 1317. The attractive little building in the campo, of the Scuola of Sant'Alvise, was reconstructed in 1608. The church interior (*open Mon–Sat 10–5; Chorus Pass*) has a 17th-century frescoed ceiling. Near the nuns' choir on the west wall are eight charming little 16th-century tempera paintings with pretty landscapes, apparently by different artists, showing the influence of Lazzaro Bastiani and Carpaccio. The subjects are *Rachel at the Well*, the *Finding of Joseph*, the *Golden Calf*, *Joshua Taking Jericho*, *Solomon and the Queen of Sheba*, the *Colossus with Feet of Clay*, the *Archangel Raphael with Tobias*, and the *Poverty of Job*. On the south altar is a seated 16th-century polychrome wood statue of St Alvise and two marble statuettes of St John the Baptist and St Anthony, perhaps early works by Girolamo Campagna.

Giambattista Tiepolo painted the three superb paintings of the *Passion*, probably towards the end of the 1730s. It is thought they were donated to the church by Alvise Corner, son of Doge Giovanni Corner, one of Tiepolo's earliest patrons. They were intended to form a huge triptych, but are now unfortunately displayed separately: the *Crown of Thorns* and *Flagellation* are on the right wall, and the magnificent central *Calvary* is hung on a wall of the sanctuary. The suffering

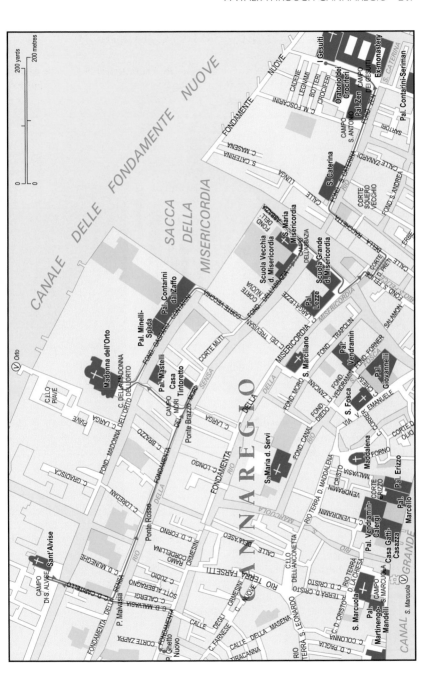

200 yards
200 metres

CANALE DELLE FONDAMENTE NUOVE

SACCA DELLA MISERICORDIA

Ⓥ Orto

Madonna dell'Orto

Pal. Minelli-Spada

Pal. Contarini dal Zaffo

FOND. GASPARO CONTARINI

CORTE VECCHIA

Pal. Mastelli

Casa Tintoretto

CAMPO DEI MORI

Ponte Brazzo

Scuola Vecchia d. Misericordia

S. Maria Misericordia

DELL'ABBAZIA

Scuola Grande di Misericordia

Pal. Lezze

FOND. DELL'ABBAZIA

CORTE NUOVA

FOND. MISERICORDIA

S. Marcilliano

S. Fosca

FOND. VENDRAMIN

Pal. Vendramin

Pal. Giovanelli

VIA. V. EMANUELE

FOND. TRAPOLIN

Pal. Contarini-Seriman

Ex-monastery

Gesuiti

Oratorio dei Crociferi

Pal. Zen

CAMPO DEI GESUITI

FONDAMENTE NUOVE

CADENE

LEGNAMI

BOTTER

C. M. FOSCARIN

CAMPO S. ANTONIO

SARTORI

CALLE ZANARDI

S. Caterina

CORTE SQUERO VECCHIO

FOND. S. ANDREA

ERBE

S. Maria Servi

S. Maria d. Servi

CANNAREGIO

DELLA

Maddalena

FORNO

Pal. Erizzo

Pal. Marcello

Pal. Vendramin-Calergi

Casa Gatti-Casazza

Sant'Alvise

CAMPO DI S. ALVISE

S. Marcuola

Pal. Martinengo Mandelli

CAMPO S. MARCUOLA

Ⓥ S. Marcuola

CANAL GRANDE

Ponte Rosso

Ponte dei Servi

of Christ is portrayed with extraordinary realism and pathos. The pulpit is surrounded by paintings from the old organ doors by Bonifacio Veronese.

Return now along Calle del Capitello to Rio della Sensa, and follow it left along the pretty fondamenta. Close to Ponte de la Malvasia, a demijohn on the pavement stands outside the Osteria Anice Stellato (*see p. 361*), a good place to eat, with a cosy little interior. On the opposite side of the canal is a house with a double façade on either side of a calle connected by an arch. A palace on this side (no. 3291) has a relief of *St George and the Dragon*. From Ponte Rosso, there is a view straight down a canal out to the lagoon, and from the next bridge, Ponte Brazzo, you can see the façade of the Madonna dell Orto.

Campo dei Mori has three quaint statues of Moors, popularly supposed to be the Levantine merchants of the Mastelli family, whose palace is close by (*see below*). Further along the fondamenta, a plaque at no. 3399 marks the charming **house where Jacopo Tintoretto lived** from 1574 until his death in 1594. Incorporated into the façade, along with several other ancient sculptural fragments, is a quaint turbanned figure, similar to those in Campo dei Mori (*pictured opposite*).

Walk through Campo dei Mori and cross another canal (with a view right of the statues crowning the facade of the Gesuiti) to reach the peaceful **Campo della Madonna dell'Orto**. The church (*open Mon–Sat 10–5; Chorus Pass*) was the parish church of Jacopo Tintoretto, who is buried here, and it contains some of his most important works (*described in full on pp. 240–42*). In the campo, which retains its old paving in stone and brick, the Scuola dei Mercanti was built in 1570, and the relief dates from that time.

The walk continues along Fondamenta Gasparo Contarini. On the opposite side of the canal is the fine **Palazzo Mastelli**, also called 'del Cammello', since it bears a charming relief of a man leading a camel (a reminder that Venetian merchants brought merchandise, and in particular spices, from the East by caravan), and then the double façade of a simple low house with symmetrical chimneys and water-gates. On this side is Palazzo Minelli-Spada with two obelisks, and the long façade of **Palazzo Contarini dal Zaffo** (no. 3539). This was built in 1530 for Cardinal Gasparo Contarini (1483–1542), who was also a scholar and diplomat and was well known in his time for the literary meetings he organised in a building (later known as the Casinò degli Spiriti) in the huge garden of this palace overlooking the lagoon. Restored at the beginning of the 20th century, it partly survives, and can be seen through the convent, called the Casa Cardinal Piazza, since it has been used partly as a conference centre and as a simple hotel.

The fondamenta ends at the **Sacca della Misericordia**, which opens onto the lagoon, and which in the last few years has been adapted for use as a mooring for private boats. There is a

Levantine merchant called Alfani, his huge turban made from the capital of a column, standing on a pedestal made in the 15th century in the style of an ancient Roman altar.

good view of the island of San Michele, with its dark cypresses and church façade, and of the larger island of Murano, with its lighthouse and bell-towers. A bridge leads to Corte Vecchia, which continues to Fondamenta dell'Abbazia, back on Rio della Sensa. Follow it left. The **Corte Nuova**, entered by a fine Gothic doorway with reliefs of the *Madonna della Misericordia* and saints, belongs to the almshouses built in 1506 by the Scuola della Misericordia. Continue along the fondamenta. At the end of an early 16th-century portico is Campo dell'Abbazia, with its old pave-ment and well-head. The worn Gothic façade of the **Scuola Vecchia della Misericordia**, founded in 1308 (and restored in the 15th century), stands next to the façade (1659) of the deconse-crated church of Santa Maria della Misericordia. On the wall is a precious 14th-century relief of the Madonna, Byzantine in style. The abbey buildings are now used as a restoration centre for works of art in stone and for paintings. If you follow the narrow fondamenta here towards the lagoon, it ends at a gate into Venice's only nursery, called the 'Laguna Fiorita' (*open Fri–Sat 8.30–12.30*), in a walled garden behind the abbey build-ings and beside its ancient campanile. With two greenhouses, it has a very fine collection of plants particularly adapted to the lagoon climate.

A wooden bridge crosses the rio to a fondamenta, where a little shrine has reliefs of the *Madonna della Misericordia* protecting two friars, and apparently providing them with two ships laden to the gunwales with supplies. It is set into the massive walls of the **Scuola Grande della Misericordia**, begun in 1532 by

Jacopo Sansovino, but left incomplete at his death because of lack of funds (and a subsequent project designed by Palladio in the 1570s was never carried out). The huge façade, which was to have been faced with marble, remains unfinished in brick. The building does, however, have a splendidly designed lower hall, with numerous columns, which was opened in 1589. At the fall of the Republic it was used as a military store, and then as an archive, builders' yard, and sports centre. There have been endless discussions in the last decade or so about how it could be used: one plan was to convert it into a concert hall, and another to make it into a museum of Venetian sculpture, but meanwhile it remains abandoned and empty.

Around the corner, on the Fondamenta della Misericordia, is the large Palazzo Lezze, by Longhena (1654). The walk takes Ramo della Misericordia, which leads across the wide canal to the Rio San Felice, here crossed by a private bridge with no parapet: most of the stone bridges in the city were originally built without parapets, but this is the only one to have so survived. In the distance there is a view of the lagoon and the island of Murano. The bridge beside it leads across the little canal to a passageway which continues through Corte dei Preti to Calle della Racchetta; follow it left. It passes several little walled gardens and the Sottoportego Molin, with a very worn angel holding a heraldic device above the archway, and lovely carved wooden eaves. One of the grandest buildings in the calle, **Palazzo Pesaro-Papafava** (no. 3764) became the prem-ises of The University of Warwick in

Fourteenth-century Byzantine-style relief of the *Virgin Orans*, on Santa Maria della Misericorida.

Venice in 2006. At the end a bridge leads across to the Fondamenta Santa Caterina, with the flank of the church of Santa Caterina, now deconsecrated and used as a store; the ship's keel roof, destroyed by fire in 1977, has been rebuilt. Part of the convent is used as a state school. Fondamenta Zen continues along the attractive Rio di Santa Caterina in another peaceful area of the city past the huge **Palazzo Zen** (nos 4922–4924) with its balconies (in poor repair), designed by Francesco Zen (d. 1538). The Zen family included Nicolò and Antonio, famous seafarers in the 15th century.

Across the canal, in the Salizzada Seriman, is the fine 15th-century **Palazzo Contarini-Seriman** (no. 4851), now a convent school. The interior (*admission on request*) contains a staircase with a fresco by the school of Giambattista Tiepolo and a lovely stuccoed alcove.

The long, stark Campo dei Gesuiti is usually empty. The huge ex-monastery of the Gesuiti has been awaiting restoration for years, and is partly used as a barracks. Opposite, with four tall chimneys, is a little chapel known as the **Oratorio dei Crociferi** (*open 1 April–31 Oct Thur, Fri, Sat 10–1*). The adjoining hospital was founded in the mid-12th century for crusaders, and received generous help from Doge Ranier Zeno in 1268: in the 14th century it became a hospice for women. The chapel, dating from 1582, with a relief of the *Madonna*

and Child Enthroned over the door, contains an interesting cycle of **paintings by Palma Giovane** (1583–92), illustrating the history of the hospital, and considered among the best works of this very prolific painter.

The monumental Baroque façade by Giovanni Battista Fattoretto of the **church of the Gesuiti** (Santa Maria Assunta; *open 10–12 & 4–6 or 5–7*) was rebuilt for the Jesuits in 1714–29 by Domenico Rossi. Both the façade and interior have recently been restored (and work is still in progress on the pavement and altar steps in the sanctuary). The highly elaborate Baroque interior has decorative grey and white marble intarsia imitating wall hangings. The frescoes on the ceiling of the nave are by Francesco Fontebasso. When the floor of Istrian stone and green marble was restored a few years ago, a Byzantine bas-relief was found beneath it: this is now displayed in the centre of the nave and represents the victory of Virtue over Vice (symbolised by an eagle killing a rabbit).

On the first north altar is a splendid painting of the *Martyrdom of St Lawrence*, commissioned from **Titian** in 1548 by Lorenzo Massolo, to decorate his tomb in the church. Finished in the following decade, Titian seems to have been inspired by the temples he had just seen on a trip to Rome for the architectural details in the background of the work, which is remarkable above all for its setting at night. The marty-

dom of this Roman saint, traditionally supposed to have been roasted alive on a gridiron in 258, has always been a favourite subject amongst painters and sculptors, and Titian himself painted another similar version of the same subject in later years for Philip II of Spain. It still hangs in the church of the Escorial.

On the west wall is the Lezze monument, attributed to Jacopo Sansovino. The first south altarpiece of the *Guardian Angel* is by Palma Giovane, who also carried out the entire pictorial decoration of the sacristy, in celebration of the Eucharist, in 1589–90. On the second south altar is a sculpture of St Barbara by Giovanni Maria Morleiter.

On the four piers of the dome are statues of archangels by Giuseppe Torretti; the *tondi* in the vault are by Louis Dorigny. The fantastic 18th-century high altar is by Fra' Giuseppe Pozzo, who also worked on the Scalzi. In the chapel to the right of the sanctuary is a painting of *St Francis Xavier*, by Pietro Liberi. Over the door into the sacristy, the monument to Doge Pasquale Cicogna has a fine effigy by Girolamo Campagna. In the north transept, the *Assumption* is an early work by Tintoretto.

A salizzada leads out onto the long Fondamente Nuove, which follows the waterfront along the northern lagoon.

CASTELLO

Castello, the largest *sestiere* of the city, occupies the area east of San Marco and Cannaregio. Its name is thought to come from the 8th-century fortress on the island of San Pietro, which is also where—as legend tells us—St Mark found shelter during a storm and his association with Venice began. It was for centuries the religious centre of the city, with San Pietro di Castello the cathedral of Venice until 1807. Castello was also the maritime heart of the Republic, with the shipyards of the Arsenale, from which her trading and naval fleets set sail. The area boasts some superb treasures: the magnificent church of Santi Giovanni e Paolo, that of San Zaccaria, and Carpaccio's delightful cycle of paintings in the little Scuola di San Giorgio degli Schiavoni. Beyond the Arsenale, away from the crush of tourists and souvenir stalls, Castello becomes an area where life goes on untrammelled by visitors, with washing strung out across the canals, and the delightful Via Garibaldi with its local shops and market stalls (*described on p. 296*).

THE RIVA DEGLI SCHIAVONI & SAN ZACCARIA
Map p. 404, A2–B2

Riva degli Schiavoni is a wide, busy quay on the Bacino di San Marco. Often over-crowded around its first few bridges, it becomes an increasingly attractive promenade as it approaches the Arsenale canal. It was called 'Schiavoni' from the inhabitants of *Schiavonia* (now Dalmatia), because the waterfront here was often used as a mooring for the trading vessels from Dalmatia and other Slavonic ports.

The **Hotel Danieli** was named after its first owner, a Swiss called Joseph da Niel, who opened it in 1822. It has always been one of Venice's most famous luxury-class hotels (*see p. 352*), and still retains its revolving door and an atmosphere from the days when it was patronised by great writers, musicians and artists, including George Sand and her lover Alfred de Musset, Charles Dickens, Ruskin, Wagner, Debussy and Proust. It occupies the neo-Gothic Palazzo Dandolo, with an ugly extension built in 1948. It was near here that Doge Vitale Michiel II was killed in 1172 as he tried to escape from the Doge's Palace to San Zaccaria. After a successful reign he became sud-denly unpopular because of diplomatic failures with Constantinople and his decision not to take the Venetian fleet into battle. By the time he decided to recall the ships from Greece, many of the crew had contracted the plague. After his assassin had been brought to trial and executed, the house on this site was razed to the ground and a decree was issued that no stone building should ever be built on the spot. This was, amazingly enough, observed right up until the 20th century.

Across Ponte del Vin (with pretty colonnades) towers a **monument to Vittorio Emanuele II**, first King of Italy, a typical rhetorical work by the Roman sculptor Ettore Ferrari (1887), showing the king on his prancing charger, holding his sword on high, with snarling lions around the base, one biting through the chains which shackle him. Ferrari erected a number of bronze monuments to Italy's heroes, but this is his only work in Venice. At a house on the quay here (no. 4161) Henry James finished *The Portrait of a Lady* in 1881, during one of the earliest of his many visits to the city—'Straight across, before my windows, rose the great pink mass of San Giorgio Maggiore ... Asked what may be the leading colour in the Venetian concert, we should inveterately say Pink ... It is a faint, shimmering, airy, watery pink; the bright sea-light seems to flush with it and the pale whiteish-green of lagoon and canal to drink it in'.

SAN ZACCARIA
Map p. 404, A1

Open 10–12 & 4–6, Sun and holidays only 4–6.
The church of San Zaccaria is built in a remarkably successful mixture of Gothic and Renaissance styles (1444–1515), begun by the little-known Antonio Gambello, but finished after 1483 by the important Renaissance architect Mauro Codussi (*see p. 243*). The church is dedicated to Zacharias, the father of St John the Baptist, whose

relics are preserved here. It was founded in the 9th century, at the same period as the Basilica of St Mark, and by the same doge, Giustiniano Particiaco. The Benedictine convent became one of the most famous in the city. The doge would make an annual visit to the convent at Eastertide in gratitude for the donation to the Signoria of part of the convent orchard in the 12th century, so that Piazza San Marco could be enlarged. During this ceremony he would be presented with the ducal cap (or *cornu*). No fewer than eight doges of the early Republic were buried in the first church.

The tall façade (*being restored at the time of writing*) is particularly handsome in a transitional style, with the lower part by Gambello and the upper storey by Codussi. Over the doorway, by Giovanni Buora (1483), is a statue of the patron saint, by Alessandro Vittoria. Behind the little garden with two elms and architectural fragments, is the brick façade of the earlier church which was used as an entrance to the Benedictine convent (with two fine cloisters, now a police station) and the 13th-century brick campanile. Along one side of the square, the 16th-century portico of the former cloister is incorporated into the house-fronts. Opposite the church a calle leads under an arch, the outer face of which is decorated with a large marble relief of the Madonna and Child between St John the Baptist and St Mark, dating from the first half of the 15th century.

The interior

The elegant interior has a high aisled nave; the columns on fine raised bases have good capitals. The multiple apse with an ambulatory and coronet of chapels lit by long windows, typical of northern European Gothic architecture, is unique in Venice. The aisle walls are entirely covered with 17th–18th-century paintings. The beautiful second south altarpiece, **Giovanni Bellini's *Madonna Enthroned and Four Saints*** is one of the artist's greatest works, signed and dated 1505, when he was perhaps 75 years old. It is the last of a series of altarpieces with similar subjects painted for the churches of Venice, which included the triptych still in the Frari and that painted for San Giobbe, now in the Gallerie dell'Accademia. The architectural setting is Classical, but incorporates an apse mosaic which recalls the interior of St Mark's. The monumental figures of St Peter, St Catherine, St Lucy and St Jerome are enveloped in a remarkable atmosphere of calm, while the angel plays a melody at the foot of the throne. Napoleon removed it to the Louvre, where it was transferred from its original panels onto canvas.

The chapels

Off the south aisle is the entrance (*small fee*) to the Chapels of St Anthanasius and St Tarasius. The **Chapel of St Athanasius** contains carved 15th-century wooden stalls by Francesco Cozzi and his brother Marco. There is an interesting little collection of paintings here, which includes an early work by Jacopo Tintoretto (the *Birth of St John the Baptist*) over the altar, a *Flight into Egypt* by Gian Domenico Tiepolo, and a small *Crucifixion* attributed to van Dyck (above the entrance). A *Madonna and Saints* attributed to Palma Vecchio is being restored by the Venice in Peril Fund. Beneath the pavement a fragment of an earlier pavement has recently been revealed—with beautiful marble inlay in a circular design reminiscent of the floor of St Mark's.

Central section of a Gothic polyptych in San Zaccaria: the *Madonna and Child* and St Blaise and St Martin are 14th-century; St Mark and St Elizabeth (1443) are by Antonio Vivarini and Giovanni d'Alemagna.

Beyond, a small room has a charming, old-fashioned display of the church treasury. The waterlogged **10th-century crypt**, with three aisles divided by low columns, can be visited: it is, amazingly enough, the only building in the city permanently flooded by water and is a remarkable sight.

The adjoining **Chapel of St Tarasius** has a predella recently attributed to Paolo Veneziano, painted some hundred years before the three fine altar paintings by Antonio Vivarini and his brother-in-law Giovanni d'Alemagna (executed in 1443), all of them with extraordinarily ornate gilded Gothic frames. The central polyptych incorporates an earlier *Madonna and Child and Two Saints*, signed by a certain 'Stefano from the parish of Sant'Agnese' in 1385. These polyptychs are typical of the florid late Gothic style of these painters from Murano, totally at odds with the new Renaissance art produced just the year before, which can be seen above in the fan vault (the early 15th-century chancel of the previous church). The frescoes by Andrea del Castagno and the less well-known Francesco da Faenza (signed and dated 1442; damaged) are one of the earliest-known works in Venice by the Tuscan Renaissance painters who were called to the city to work on the mosaics of St Mark's. Also here are two 15th-century wood statues of St Benedict and St Zacharias, and a fragment of mosaic pavement, thought to date from the 12th century (glass in the floor reveals another fragment which may survive from the earliest church). The five gilded chairs here (three of them dating from the 17th century) were used for the annual visit of the doge.

Other works of art in the church
At the end of the south aisle is the **tomb of Alessandro Vittoria** (1528–1608), with a bust of the sculptor and architect by himself (1595). The statues of the Baptist and of St Zacharias on the stoups at the church entrance are also by him. Other remarkable portrait busts by Vittoria of his Venetian contemporaries can be seen in the Ca' d'Oro and Seminario Patriarcale, and many Venetian churches have monuments, statues and altars by him.

The church also has paintings by Antonio Balestra and Angelo Trevisani, who both worked in the Veneto between the 17th and 18th centuries. The 16th-century *Saviour and Saints* (on the first north altar) is one of the paintings in Venice by Giuseppe Salviati which was important to the development of the Mannerist style in the city.

La Pietà
On Riva degli Schiavoni, beyond Rio dei Greci (the bridge, with a stone balustrade was first built in the 14th century), is the church of La Pietà (*map p. 404, A2; open in summer 10–1 & 3.30–7.30 except Tues; in winter it can usually only be seen from the doorway; concerts are held here regularly*). This belonged to an orphanage and hospital (*ospedale*) founded in 1346, and which was famous for its musical orphans (*see p. 289*). The institute of the Pietà still operates as an orphanage from a calle behind the church. Today's 18th-century façade by Giorgio Massari was only completed in 1906.

The bright interior was sumptuously rebuilt in the present oval plan (particularly suitable for musical performances) by Giorgio Massari (1745–60), with galleries for choir and musicians and an oblong vestibule. The contemporary decorations remain intact, with a fine ceiling fresco of the *Triumph of Faith* by Giambattista Tiepolo (1755), and a high altarpiece by Giovanni Battista Piazzetta. The other 18th-century altarpieces include one by Domenico Maggiotto, and another by Piazzetta's pupil Giuseppe Angeli. The 18th-century organ was built by Pietro Nacchini. Above the west door is a very fine painting of the *Supper in the House of Simon* by the Lombard artist Alessandro Buonvicino, usually called Moretto da Brescia (1548), who is known to have worked for a time in Venice under Titian. This is the only painting which survives by him in the city; most of his works are in his native town of Brescia.

Beyond the next bridge, with a stone balustrade (rebuilt in 1871), a plaque on no. 4145 records **Petrarch's house**. The great humanist and poet came to Venice in 1362 to escape the plague in Padua, and lived here with his daughter and her family until 1367. In 1363 he invited his close friend Giovanni Boccaccio to come up from Florence to stay with him here for three months, a few years after he had completed his famous *Decameron*. The house was given to Petrarch by the Republic in return for his promise to leave his library to the city of Venice (*see p. 82*).

SAN GIOVANNI IN BRAGORA
Map p. 404, B2

Open 9–11 & 3.30–7, Sun 9–12.
The church of San Giovanni in Bragora, founded possibly as early as the 9th century, was rebuilt in 1475. Dedicated to St John the Baptist, it is not known why it was called '*in Bragora*'; the name may derive from a word in Venetian dialect referring either to the marshy terrain here, or to a market-place, or even to the fishing which took place nearby. The interior of the church contains some remarkable works from various periods of Venetian art.

The campo, Bandiera e Moro, is named after three naval officers (the two Bandiera brothers lived here) who rebelled against Austrian rule and were executed by the Austrians in 1844.

The interior
In the sanctuary a great marble frame encloses the *Baptism of Christ*, one of the most beautiful works in Venice by **Cima da Conegliano**, painted in 1494. The figure of the Baptist is silhouetted against the evening sky as the fading light illuminates the river Jordan, which flows through a landscape reminiscent of the Veneto. Above, yellow, green, red and blue cherubim ride on a circle of clouds. Cima, a deeply religious painter, was born at Conegliano, in the Veneto, and many of his works can still be seen in that region, but he is also well represented in Venice with other superb altarpieces in the Carmini, Madonna dell'Orto, and the Gallerie dell'Accademia. He painted another work for this church eight years later (now hanging to the right of the sacristy door), of *Constantine and St Helen and the Finding of the True Cross*. It is known that **Alvise Vivarini** was Cima's master, so it is interesting to see a number of paintings by this artist in the church, including his *Risen Christ* (to the left of the above work), and in particular his small *Head of the Redeemer*, which now hangs in the north aisle and might even have provided the model for Cima's Christ in the *Baptism*. Alvise's skill in painting landscapes can also be seen in his otherwise damaged *Madonna and Child*, also in the north aisle. Alvise came from a Venetian family of painters: he was the son of Antonio, and the nephew of Bartolomeo, who painted the triptych in the south aisle of the *Madonna Enthroned between Sts John the Baptist and Andrew*, which is signed and dated 1478 and shows his skill in the use of bright colours, in particular the Madonna's striking red-and-black dress.

At the beginning of the south aisle is a wood Crucifix carved in 1491 by a sculptor known as Leonardo Tedesco (his generic last name—'German'—suggests he may have come from northern Europe); the painting and gilding was carried out by Leonardo Boldrini, a little-known artist who was born in Murano. The Crucifix has recently been moved here from a chapel in the church so that it is more accessible to worshippers. These artists worked together again in the second chapel in this aisle, which is dedicated to St John the Almsgiver, whose relics had been brought to the church from Alexandria in 1247. They made a new sarcophagus for the relics, the front of which, with an effigy of the saint, survives here. (The polychrome terracotta *Pietà* group in the chapel next door was once also attributed to Leonardo, but is now thought to be by a German master, since it is typical of northern European works of this subject.) The St John chapel was redecorated in the 18th century when Jacopo Marieschi provided the altarpiece showing *St John Dispensing Alms*, and the lunette illustrating the arrival in Venice of his relics. Marieschi is a typical Venetian painter of this period, whose works can also be seen in a few other churches in the city.

The church preserves two Byzantine Madonnas (over the side door and over the sacristy door). The latter, dating from the 12th or 13th century, is a very beautiful relief, which still has its polychrome decoration. Instead, in the second north chapel, there are three works in the Byzantine style which were carried out at least three centuries later by artists from Crete who set up a very successful workshop in Venice producing numerous such works for Venetian clients.

On the Baroque high altar are two statues of saints by Heinrich Meyring (c. 1688), and on the sanctuary walls are 16th-century works by Palma Giovane (*Washing of the Feet*—he also painted the *Christ before Caiaphas* on the west wall of the church) and Paris Bordone (*Last Supper*). Vivaldi, who was born in a house in the campo, was baptised in the lovely 15th-century font in 1678. Outside the church is a little 18th-century building, the Scoletta della Bragora, which used to house a confraternity.

Antonio Vivaldi (1678–1741)
Vivaldi, son of a barber and violinist, taught at the Pietà (*see p. 259 above*) on and off for most of his life. He was violin-master in 1704–18, and concert-master in 1735–38, and many of his best compositions were written for the hospital, including numerous concertos which were first performed here. Vivaldi took orders in 1703, but obtained permission not to serve as a priest, apparently because of ill-health. Goldoni, who praised him as a violinist but not as a composer, relates that he was nicknamed *Il Prete Rosso* (the red priest), either because of his red hair or from the red robes worn at La Pietà. Vivaldi also wrote some 50 operas and directed the opera house of Sant'Angelo in Venice from 1713–39. The *Quattro Stagioni* (*Four Seasons*) was published in Amsterdam in 1725. He travelled extensively in Italy and Europe, but died in poverty in Vienna, and was forgotten for many years after his death. Although Bach transcribed many of his concertos for keyboard, Vivaldi was not 'rediscovered' until the late 19th century.

THE GREEK DISTRICT
Map p. 404, A1–B1

Ponte dei Greci is named after the Greeks who settled in this area in the 15th century after the fall of Constantinople and subsequent invasion of Greece by the Turks.

Together with the Jewish community, this became the largest foreign settlement in the Renaissance city, and by the 16th century it numbered around 6,000 members. Venice represented the most important centre of Greek culture in the west, and the community is still active. Houses were built in the area for the Greek inhabitants, as well as a hospital, archive and cemetery.

At the end of the 15th century the Greeks were given permission to found the *scuola* and Greek Orthodox church on the canal here, in a charming courtyard planted with trees. Beside them is the Greek College, named after its 17th-century founder, Girolamo Flangini, and now the seat of the Hellenic Institute of Byzantine and post-Byzantine Studies. This building and the decorative wall of the court as well as the *scuola* itself (dating from 1678) are typical of the numerous 'minor' interventions in the townscape by the great Venetian architect Baldassare Longhena (architect of the Salute and Ca' Rezzonico).

San Giorgio dei Greci

The church of **San Giorgio dei Greci** (*map p. 404, A1; open 9–1 & 2.30–4.30, except Sun. Entrance along Rio dei Greci, off Calle Madonna*) was the most important outside Greece for the Greek Orthodox rite. Its construction was begun in 1539 to a design by Sante Lombardo, member of the large family of sculptors and architects who were at work in Venice in the 15th and 16th centuries. The cupola and graceful leaning campanile were added later in the century. The iconostasis is decorated with late Byzantine works.

The Scuola di San Nicolò dei Greci houses a **Museum of Icons** (*map p. 404, A1; open 9–12.30 & 1.30–4.30, Sun and holidays 10–5*), opened in 1959 in a room once used as a hospital by the confraternity. The well-labelled collection is arranged chronologically. The first two Byzantine icons are particularly precious: a *Madonna and Child with Apostles and Saints*, and *Christ in Glory with the Twelve Apostles*, both from churches in Constantinople and dating from around 1350. They were donated to the Greek confraternity by an aristocratic Greek woman (Anna Palaeologina Notara), who had come to Venice just before the fall of Byzantium in 1453 and who remained here for the rest of her life (she died in 1507). The rest of the collection has been formed by donations over the centuries and is interesting above all for the icons produced in Venice by artists from Crete (the island was under Venetian dominion from 1210 until 1669), whose workshop was known as that of the '*madoneri di Rialto*'. They combined Byzantine traditions with Venetian elements, and the most skilled artists of this school, particularly active from the 16th–17th centuries, included Georgios Klontzas, Michael Damaskinos and Emmanuel Tzanfournaris, all of whom are represented here with signed works. The most famous member of this group, Domenicos Theotokopoulos, came to Venice from Crete in 1567, and was greatly struck by the work of Titian and Tintoretto. He moved to Spain, to flourish under the name of El Greco. There is also a small room with a display of vestments and liturgical objects, and a 14th-century illuminated manuscript, an exquisite Byzantine work.

On the other side of Rio dei Greci is Fondamenta dell'Osmarin, crossed by two pretty bridges. The first one, Ponte del Diavolo, was well reconstructed in 1983, and the second one, Ponte dei Carmini, dates from 1793. **Palazzo Priuli**, on the corner of Rio de l'Osmarin, probably dates from the late 14th century, and as Ruskin noted is 'a most important and beautiful early Gothic palace'. It is well preserved and has a particularly attractive corner window with a balcony, although the frescoes on the façade by Palma Vecchio have totally disappeared. In contrast, another Gothic palace close by, the Ca' Zorzi on Rio dei Greci, has recently been over-restored as a hotel.

Calle della Madonna and Salizzada dei Greci connect Rio dei Greci and Rio della Pietà. Here is the church of **Sant'Antonin**. Traditionally thought to have been founded as early as the 7th century, its 13th-century building was reconstructed in the 17th century, around the same time as the buildings for the Greek community close by, under the direction of Baldassare Longhena (although his façade was left unfinished). The campanile dates from the following century. Although the exterior has been restored, the interior is still closed. A fondamenta follows the canal up to the little Scuola di San Giorgio degli Schiavoni.

THE SCUOLA DI SAN GIORGIO DEGLI SCHIAVONI
Map p. 404, B1

Open 9–1 & 3–6, Sun 10–12.30, closed Mon.
The Scuola di San Giorgio degli Schiavoni was founded in 1451 by the Dalmatians who came to live in the city (many of whom were sailors). The first (and closest) foreign territory to be conquered by the *Serenissima*, Dalmatia always enjoyed a special relationship with Venice, and its inhabitants are known to have rallied to the support of the Republic at its downfall at the hands of Napoleon. The façade of 1551 bears a relief of *St George and the Dragon* by Sansovino's pupil Pietro da Salò, and a 14th-century *Madonna and Child*.

The interior
A heavy red curtain hangs at the old-fashioned entrance to the dimly-lit interior, which is one of the most evocative places in the city, with an atmosphere that is redolent of old Venice. The walls of the famous little room are entirely decorated with a delightful series of **paintings by Vittore Carpaccio** (carried out between 1502 and 1508), relating to the lives of the three Dalmatian patron saints, Jerome, Tryphon and George, and bursting with detail, incident and symbolism.

Left wall: The *Duel of St George and the Dragon* is justly one of Carpaccio's best-known paintings. It shows St George wounding the dragon with his lance. Scattered all around are the bones and severed limbs of the dragon's victims; snakes and lizards hiss and spit at the spectacle. *The Triumph of St George* follows, showing the blond-haired knight, his sword raised and holding the dragon by the princess's girdle, about to kill the beast. The king, queen and princess look on, while exotic musicians celebrate. Although the dragon appears defeated, the horses pull their heads back and shy away, obviously still nervous.

Vittore Carpaccio: *Vision of St Augustine* (1502–08).

End wall: *St George Baptising the People of Silene* (the rescued king and princess kneel before St George, a white lurcher memorably in the foreground); and *The Miracle of St Tryphon* (the boy saint is freeing the daughter of the emperor from a demon, in the form of a basilisk).

Right wall: *Agony in the Garden*—Christ prays on the hillside, while the disciples lie stretched out and fast asleep—and the *Calling of St Matthew*. Another famous panel is the *Lion Led by St Jerome into the Monastery*, putting the terrified monks to flight, their habits streaming behind them, though the lion himself looks docile and bemused by all the fuss.

The *Funeral of St Jerome* is a touching depiction of the ceremony, with the lion throwing back his head in a final roar of grief. The last panel, the *Vision of St Augustine*, depicts the story of St Augustine writing a letter to St Jerome asking for his advice on a book he wanted to write about the saints in Paradise. St Jerome's death occurred at the same time, and Augustine's studio was suddenly filled with light and he heard a voice reproaching him for daring to describe Paradise before his own death. Carpaccio shows us in great detail the inside of a monk's study, with its neatly arranged bookcase and scientific instruments, and a little white dog looking up at its master. The six-winged seraph in the painting's mosaic altar-niche is reminiscent of that in Bellini's San Giobbe altarpiece (*see p. 145*).

The altarpiece of the *Madonna and Child* is attributed to Carpaccio's son, Benedetto.

Vittore Carpaccio (1460–1525/6)

Carpaccio, the greatest Venetian narrative painter of the 15th–16th centuries, produced his masterpiece for this *scuola*. He also worked for other *scuole* in the city, including that of Sant'Orsola (his nine paintings illustrating the *Legend of St Ursula* are now in the Gallerie dell'Accademia; *see p. 155*), and San Giovanni Evangelista (the *Miracle at the Rialto Bridge* or *Cure of a Lunatic by the Patriarch of Grado* is also now in the Accademia). Although influenced by the Bellini family (with whom he worked in the Doge's Palace on paintings subsequently lost in a fire), he had his own remarkable sense of colour and an eye for detail, and his works reflect an atmosphere of great calm. His famous painting of *Two Venetian Ladies* on a balcony is preserved in the Museo Correr. Carpaccio was the earliest Italian master of genre painting, and numerous details in his paintings give a particularly vivid picture of Venice and the Venetians at the end of the 15th century.

The room upstairs was decorated in the 17th century and has a prettily carved and gilded wood ceiling incorporating paintings attributed to Andrea Vicentino, and a 16th-century carved wood altarpiece of *St George*. The treasury of the guild (including a 15th-century processional Cross) is kept in the little sacristy on the ground floor.

San Lorenzo

Heading north along Rio Sant'Agostino, Calle San Lorenzo diverges left to the huge deconsecrated church of **San Lorenzo** (*map p. 403, E4*), which has been closed for many years. The first church, on a basilican plan, was founded by the Particiaco doges in the 9th century. Marco Polo (1256–1324) was buried here, but his sarcophagus was lost during the rebuilding in 1592. This was carried out by Simone Sorella, a little-known architect but who produced an interior on a grand scale, flooded with light (Sorella also worked on the much more famous church of San Giorgio Maggiore). San Lorenzo was damaged in the First World War, but is at last being restored. Excavations of the earlier buildings down to a depth of c. 1.60m below the level of the lagoon are in progress: three distinct periods will be visible: the earliest 9th-century foundations built directly on piles driven into the bed of the lagoon supporting a mosaic pavement in *opus sectile*; 10th–11th-century fragments; and remains of the 12th-century church of the Benedictine convent, part of the buildings of which are now used as a hospice. Roman fragments have also been found here. There are long-term plans to use the church as a museum illustrating the construction techniques of Venetian buildings.

Back on Rio della Pietà, the fondamenta passes beneath a portico before recrossing the canal into **Corte Nuova**, a typical old Venetian court, with its well and a bar which retains its characteristic sign painted in red. To the left is a street chapel which has two shrines and an old ceiling: walk through this along a passageway elaborately named 'Calle Zorzi va in [which leads into] Corte Nova'. An inscription records that it was built to commemorate the local inhabitants' gratitude to the Madonna '*della Salute*' for seeing them through a series of dangers, from the plagues in the 17th century to the air-raids in 1917–18. Some of the houses in this area, in *calli* which are exceptionally narrow, dark and dank, give a good idea of the hardships which face Venetian residents in their everyday life. Calle Zorzi continues to Salizzada Santa Giustina, brightened up with a few shops, and turns left and then right past some dilapidated but lovely old palaces across Ponte del Fontego into Campo Santa Giustina, with the 18th-century Palazzo Gradenigo and the former church of **Santa Giustina**. The façade of 1640 is a minor work by Longhena, although it was altered in the Neoclassical style by Giovanni Casoni in 1841, when it became a school for the education of sailors (the building is still used as a school). Follow the rio here (with a view out to the lagoon and the cypresses on the cemetery island of San Michele) and take Calle San Francesco, at the end of which can be seen the unexpectedly bright façade of San Francesco della Vigna.

SAN FRANCESCO DELLA VIGNA
Map p. 403, E3–F3

Open 8–12 & 3–7.
The name of this church recalls the vineyard bequeathed to the Franciscan order for a convent in 1253 by Marco Ziani, son of Doge Pietro Ziani. On this site, in 1534, Doge Andrea Gritti laid the foundation stone of the present church to be built by his friend Jacopo Sansovino. The humanist friar Francesco Zorzi was involved in the design, which is based on a complicated harmony of the progression of the number three. In 1562 Giovanni Grimani, Patriarch of Aquileia (*see p. 270 below*) paid for the façade to be added by Palladio. His design was entirely innovative in church architecture, using the Classical elements of columns and pediments derived from ancient temples, which were to be employed with even greater success in his other two churches in Venice, San Giorgio Maggiore and the Redentore. Although the high relief and brightness of the Istrian stone demand our attention, it is difficult fully to appreciate the splendid design, since the church is sighted in a rather cramped space. Above the door is one of the architect's typical Diocletian windows, which allows light into the nave. The medallion in the pediment bearing an eagle (symbol of Aquileia and of St John the Evangelist) and the inscriptions between the columns were ordered specifically by Grimani both to record the spiritual significance of the church and as a glorification of his own devotion. The two statues, *Moses* and *St Paul*, in contrasting dark bronze, added in 1592, stand out as the only colour on the façade. They are by Tiziano Aspetti, who is known principally for his works in bronze.

    The bell-tower, which rises behind the east end (and is thus difficult to see close to), is one of the highest and slenderest in Venice, recalling that of St Mark's. It served as an aid to navigators in the northern lagoon during the days of the Republic, and its bells were tolled to announce meetings of the Great Council in the Doge's Palace. Built in 1581, but repeatedly struck by lightning, it has been carefully restored over the centuries.

The interior

Sansovino's dignified interior has a broad nave with five side chapels between Doric pilasters on either side and a long chancel (with the monks' choir behind the altar). The church has numerous fine sculptures, many of them commissioned by doges, and a very lovely painting (in the south transept) by Antonio da Negroponte (*pictured overleaf*). This is the only work known by this artist.

SAN FRANCESCO DELLA VIGNA

A   Negroponte *Madonna*
B   Badoer-Giustiniani Chapel
C   Bellini *Madonna*
D   *Pala Giustiniani*
E   Sagredo Chapel
F   Contarini Chapel
G   Chapel of St Anthony Abbot
H   Grimani Chapel
I   West wall
J   Nave

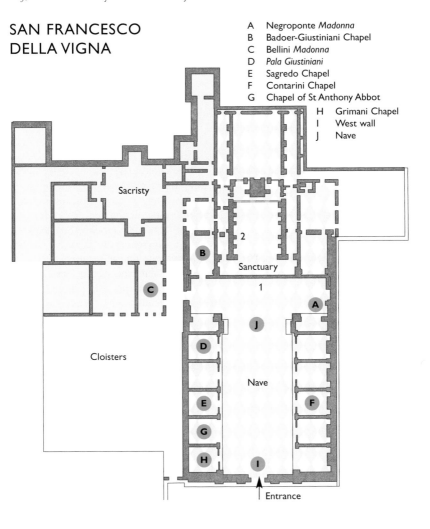

A Negroponte *Madonna*: This work (c. 1465) represents one of the last great paintings in the florid Gothic style which had persisted in Venice under the influence of Antonio Vivarini. It is an exceptionally large painting with a charming Madonna in a rich brocade robe sitting on an intricately carved throne beneath a garland of fruit and in front of a dark wood of pomegranate trees, with a great variety of birds on the lawn at her feet. Nothing is known of the artist, Antonio da Negroponte, except that he was a friar and a native of Euboea (known as Negroponte under the Venetians).

B Badoer-Giustiniani Chapel: This belonged to the procurator Lorenzo Giustiniani and his brother Antonio, and was designed in the 1530s by the architect of the church, Jacopo Sansovino. He decorated it with a series of very fine 15th-century sculpted reliefs by Pietro Lombardo and his two sons Antonio and Tullio, which had been removed from the earlier church where they were probably part of the choir screen. On the two side walls, rectangles bear reliefs of prophets and the four Evangelists, above which are scenes from the life of Christ. The same artists worked on the altarpiece.

C Bellini *Madonna*: From the north transept, a door leads out to a peaceful little chapel which has a charming small painting of the *Madonna and Saints* (*Sacra Conversazione*). Even though it is signed and dated 1507 by Giovanni Bellini, some scholars presume some of the figures were painted by assistants

(and the donor, Giacomo Dolfin, is certainly repainted). The figure of the Madonna, with her beautiful blue and gold-lined cloak, and that of St Sebastian, who calls us into the scene, as well as the charming landscape, all appear to be by the master's hand. Here you can sometimes visit two of the 15th-century cloisters of the convent, still in very good condition—the first has pavement tombs including that of a ship-builder, and the second has a lovely well decorated with large carved roses. Sansovino's sacristy (*marked on the plan*) also survives intact.

D Pala Giustiniani: This was painted by Veronese for the Giustiniani brothers Lorenzo and Antonio (*see B, above*). It was the great painter's first Venetian commission (1551), showing the Virgin and Child and shepherds with St Catherine and St Anthony Abbot. The Virgin is placed to one side, recalling Titian's *Pala Pesaro* in the Frari (*see p. 204*). Although charming, and even though the figure of St Catherine in the foreground is particularly graceful, this is clearly an early work: Veronese's skills progressed dramatically from here, and numerous later works are better painted and better composed.

E Sagredo Chapel: This beautifully decorated chapel was begun in 1675 by Doge Niccolò Sagredo, but most of the decoration was commissioned by his descendants in the late 17th and 18th centuries. Giovanni Gai carved the expressive bust of the doge, with his flowing hair, and that of his brother

Antonio da Negroponte: *Madonna Enthroned* (c. 1465).

Alvise, who was Patriarch of Venice. The statue of the most illustrious member of the family, St Gerard Sagredo, is by Gai's contemporary Andrea Cominelli. St Gerard is known as the 'Apostle of Hungary': he was influential in Christianising the Magyars and won the support of Hungary's saint-king, Stephen. In 1046, after Stephen's death, Gerard was seized by pagans and drowned in the Danube. The monochrome frescoes by Giambattista Tiepolo (including the four Evangelists and two medallions of the Virtues) and *trompe l'oeil* festoons fit well with the sombre sculpted decoration with its elaborate stucco garlands and angels flanking the Madonna in the lunette above the altar. The only colour is provided by the frescoes representing the *Apotheosis of St Gerard* in the cupola, by the Roman artist Girolamo Pellegrini (his only known work in Venice), and by the altar frontal in *pietre dure*.

F Contarini Chapel: Here are two more busts by Giovanni Gai's father, Antonio, which commemorate two Contarini doges, Francesco and Alvise, both buried here (Alvise, who died in 1684, was the last doge of the Contarini, a family who had supplied the Republic with no fewer than eight doges since the 11th century). The decorations of this chapel date from the 18th century except for the earlier altarpiece, a typical work by Palma Giovane.

G Chapel of St Anthony Abbot: The altar has three good statues of saints by Alessandro Vittoria. His *St Sebastian* recalls the pose of Michelangelo's *Dying Slave*, now in the Louvre.

H Grimani Chapel: The Patriarch of Aquileia Giovanni Grimani had this chapel decorated as his burial place. In 1559 he recalled from Rome the Venetian artist Franco Battista (also known as Semolei), who carried out the paintings in the pretty vault, including the *'Angelic'* and *'Human' Virtues*. (Some years before, Semolei had also painted the altarpiece of the *Baptism of Christ* in the fifth south chapel in this church for another Patriarch of Aquileia, Daniele Barbaro.) Federico Zuccari, who also worked mostly in Rome, took over on Semolei's death and finished the vault and painted the altarpiece of the *Adoration of the Magi*. Since Grimani was absolved by the Inquisition in 1563 of accusations of heresy for his views on predestination and pardon, the imagery in the chapel, including the two bronze statues of *Justice* and *Temperance* by Tiziano Aspetti (1592), can be seen as allusions to the virtues of this cultivated churchman, who, as mentioned above, also paid for Palladio's façade (where there are two more statues by Aspetti).

I West wall: The lovely 13th-century Byzantine relief of the *Madonna and Child* (to the right of the door as you face it) is known to have been brought to Venice from the East in 1341. The colourful triptych of *Three Saints* (to the left of the door) is attributed to Antonio Vivarini.

J Nave: Beneath the crossing is the large pavement tombstone of Doge Marcantonio Trevisan **(1)**, who died in 1554 having been doge for just one year. (There is a polychrome relief of him over the sacristy door, showing him kneeling before the Crucifix holding the standard of the Republic. This seems to have been made the year after his death.) On the left wall of the sanctuary is the tomb of Doge Andrea Gritti **(2)**, who founded the present church and built a palazzo in the campo for himself. The Palladian design of the funerary monument is in keeping with the architecture of the church, and it records with simple dignity this great doge—devoid of an effigy and with

inscriptions now too dusty to read. Gritti was a very cultivated man who could speak many languages, and although he was elected after his success as a military commander, his rule was distinguished by diplomatic skills which allowed the Republic to enjoy many years of peace. He died, aged 84, in 1538. He also set up the symmetrical monument opposite to commemorate his ancestors.

SANTA MARIA FORMOSA & DISTRICT

Map p. 402, C4

Campo Santa Maria Formosa, around the church of the same name, is one of the liveliest *camp*i near St Mark's. It has a few market stalls and lies in an area abounding in canals. Behind the church, at the end of the campo bordered by a canal with four small bridges (mostly private), is the 16th-century Ca' Malipiero-Trevisan (no. 5250), attributed to Sante Lombardo. On the side opposite the apse of the church, Palazzo Vitturi (no. 5246) has Veneto-Byzantine decorations. At the other end of the square, a plaque marks the small house (no. 6129) which was the home of Sebastiano Venier, commander of the victorious fleet at the battle of Lepanto in 1571, and later doge. Palazzo Donà next door (no. 6125–26) has a pretty doorway and Gothic windows, and at the far end of the campo, Palazzo Priuli is a classical work by Bartolomeo Monopola, dating from around 1580.

SANTA MARIA FORMOSA

Open Mon–Sat 10–5; Chorus Pass.

The church of Santa Maria Formosa is interesting for its unusual Renaissance interior and its very fine altarpiece by Palma Vecchio, as well as a charming triptych by Bartolomeo Vivarini. The name of the church is derived from the tradition that the Madonna appeared to its founder, St Magnus (in the 7th century), in the form of a buxom (*formosa*) matron. It was rebuilt by Mauro Codussi (*see p. 243*) in 1492, but only his dome can be seen from the exterior—the campanile and two façades were added later. The main front at the west entrance dating from 1542 overlooks a canal and bears a statue on a sarcophagus which commemorates Vincenzo Cappello, Captain of the Venetian fleet, who had died the previous year (his place here is justified by the fact that the Cappello family had paid for the construction of the façade). Ruskin complained bitterly about the total absence of religious elements here, declaring that this façade marked the beginning of the period 'when Venetian churches were first built to the glory of man instead of the glory of God'. The other façade on the campo dates from 1604 and has three busts of other members of the family, and five 17th-century statues on the summit.

The Baroque campanile, designed by the parish priest Francesco Zucconi in 1678, has a grotesque mask at its foot. Local lore suggests the priest put it here to scare away the devil in case he tried to enter the bell-tower and ring the bells at the wrong time.

The interior

The exterior in no way prepares you for the symmetry of the beautiful interior, particularly pleasing since it is so full of light (it is lit by some 30 windows). The Greek-cross plan of the original church, derived from Byzantine models, was preserved by Codussi when he gave it this lovely Renaissance form in the 15th century. Its complex design, which involves a most original spatial concept (and in which, interestingly, the visitor can feel somewhat disorientated), includes double open arches between the chapels, and domes over the bays in the aisles. It is the earliest purely Renaissance church in Venice, and set a model which was to be followed by other 15th-century architects who chose a centralised plan for their churches (Codussi repeated the design in San Giovanni Crisostomo).

The church contains two very lovely altarpieces in marble frames commissioned for their present positions. In the first south chapel is a charming **triptych by Bartolomeo Vivarini** of the *Madonna della Misericordia*, the *Meeting at the Golden Gate*, and *Birth of the Virgin* (signed and dated 1473). The artist's characteristic use of bright colours (in particular red) can be seen here, and the scene of the meeting of the elderly St Anne and Joachim is especially touching. Bartolomeo was a pupil of his more famous brother Antonio, whose son Alvise was another important Venetian artist, and they were all at work in the city at the same time as the Bellini family. In the south transept is the Chapel of the Bombardieri, really no more than a recess, which in 1509 was granted to the Scuola dei Bombardieri (bombadiers or artillery-men), who had their meeting hall close to the church. It contains a celebrated **altarpiece by Palma Vecchio**. In 1522 the *bombardieri* were wealthy enough to commission the great Venetian artist to paint the composite work showing saints and a *Pietà*, notable especially for the colourful and majestic figure of their patron saint St Barbara, in the centre, typical of the Giorgionesque style of Venetian beauty. Like Vivarini, Palma also makes ample use of wonderful shades of maroon and red. The marble frame was added by Giuseppe Torretti in 1719.

Palazzo Grimani and Palazzo Zorzi

Ruga Giuffa (*map p. 403, D4*), a busy street with a number of shops, leads out of the southeast side of Campo Santa Maria Formosa. In Ramo Grimani (left) is the monumental entrance (with three Roman busts) to the huge **Palazzo Grimani**, attributed to Michele Sanmicheli. The famous Grimani collection of antique sculpture, which now forms the nucleus of the Museo Archeologico (*see p. 80*), used to be housed here. The palace will be opened to the public when restoration work is completed. Some of the rooms are decorated by Giovanni da Udine and Francesco Salviati. Its Classical 16th-century façade, with its monumental water-gate on Rio di San Severo, can be seen by taking the next calle left (Calle di Mezzo) off Ruga Giuffa, and crossing a bridge to Fondamenta di San Severo.

Walking along Fondamenta di San Severo in the other direction, it leads past two Zorzi palaces: the Gothic Palazzo Zorzi-Bon, with two water-gates, and **Palazzo Zorzi**, by Mauro Codussi (c. 1480), with a beautiful façade on the water, and three water-gates. The palace has been restored as the seat of ROSTE, the UNESCO Regional Office for Science and Technology for Europe, and the lovely courtyard can sometimes be visited on request. A bridge crosses the canal beside the palace, which has an entrance on the salizzada beneath a long balcony. The tiny Campiello del Tagliapietra has a fine well-head.

Calle della Corona is filled with local shops. It leads to Calle Sagrestia (right), which in turn leads to a stark campo with the church of San Giovanni Nuovo (or San Giovanni in Oleo; *closed*). A church of ancient foundation, it was rebuilt in the 18th century by Matteo Lucchesi on a Palladian design (but the façade was left half-finished). Fondamenta di Remedio leads from here along a rio, which has interesting water-gates and a series of little private bridges with pretty iron balustrades. At the far end, a bridge leads into Campiello Querini.

PALAZZO QUERINI-STAMPALIA
Map p. 402, C4

Open 10–6, Fri and Sat 10–10; closed Mon.
The 16th-century Palazzo Querini-Stampalia is now occupied by the Museo Querini-Stampalia and the Fondazione Scientifico Querini-Stampalia. The Querini were among the earliest settlers in Venice, and by the 13th century one of the city's five richest families. They acquired their second name, Stampalia, from the Greek island where some members of the family chose to live after their exile from Venice in the 14th century for taking part in the Bajamonte Tiepolo conspiracy (*see p. 103*).

History of the building and its collection
The collection of paintings was begun by the family in the 16th century, when they built the present palace, which was used from 1807–50 as the residence of the patriarchs of Venice. In 1869 Count Giovanni Querini bequeathed the palace and its art collection to the city.

The Carlo Scarpa reconstruction of the ground floor (1961–63) is considered one of his most successful works. His elegant intervention includes the atrium of the main palace and the wood and metal bridge across the rio to the Campiello Querini; a lecture hall; and the little walled garden, in which water is a prominent feature. Scarpa redesigned the exhibition space in some of Italy's most important museums in the mid-20th century, including some rooms in the Uffizi, as well as part of the Museo Correr and Gallerie dell'Accademia in Venice.

The rest of the ground floor was radically restored and reconstructed in the 1990s by Scarpa's pupil, the Swiss architect Mario Botta: his work included covering the medieval courtyard and installing a huge new staircase, interventions which have altered the character of this historic palace. The third floor was totally modernised for exhibitions and lectures. Other innovations in questionable taste have included the installation of neon 'mottoes' on the façade. Contemporary art exhibitions, funded by the Consorzio Venezia Nuova and a fashion house, are held here every year.

The library has nearly 300,000 volumes and 1,300 manuscripts. It is extremely well run and has very long opening hours, so the palace is usually busy with students.

The museum is on the second floor (lift), displayed in the period rooms on the *piano nobile* once occupied by the Querini-Stampalia family. It has some important paintings and good Venetian furniture (mostly 18th and 19th century, including Pompeian-style furniture by Giuseppe Jappelli). The rooms are not numbered, and the arrangement is subject to change. A selection of highlights is given below.

The museum

The first room is the *portego*, the characteristic large central hall of the palace, which is decorated with stuccoes and frescoes by Jacopo and Vincenzo Guarana (1790), and has a colourful 19th-century Murano chandelier, and seven 17th-century marble busts. A room off the *portego* displays three allegorical ceiling paintings by Sebastiano Ricci, removed from another room in the palace, and two allegorical paintings by Padovanino.

In the room on the other side of the *portego* (on an easel designed by Scarpa) is the **Presentation of Christ in the Temple**, a very fine work usually attributed to Giovanni Bellini (apparently a copy made c. 1469 of a painting by his brother-in-law Andrea Mantegna, now in Berlin). The adjoining room has more paintings, including *Judith* by Vincenzo Catena; the *Coronation of the Virgin* by Catarino and Donato Veneziano (1372); and a *Sacra Conversazione* by Palma Vecchio. His great-nephew Palma Giovane's self-portrait is displayed in the next room, together with *St Sebastian* by Luca Giordano.

Some 30 **genre scenes by Pietro Longhi** (one of the most interesting of which is *The Geography Lesson*) are displayed together in a room with 18th-century Venetian furniture and 16th- and 17th-century musical instruments. There is more good furniture in the next room, which is hung with portraits by Sebastiano Bombelli (1635–1719). Two further rooms are filled with 67 charming 18th-century **views of Venetian life** by Gabriel Bella; the paintings provide a valuable document of the city at that period. The 18th-century bedroom has a tondo by Lorenzo di Credi, and in the Neoclassical boudoir there is an early portrait by Alessandro Longhi of Caterina Contarini-Querini.

The red drawing room has the two masterpieces of the collection, a pair of **portraits by Palma Vecchio** of Francesco Querini and Paola Priuli-Querini, commissioned by the family to celebrate the couple's engagement, but not finished in time for their marriage in 1528 since the artist died in the same year. Also here hangs a portrait of Andrea Querini by Bernardino Castelli. The green drawing room has four large portraits of officials of the Republic, including Giambattista Tiepolo's splendid **Procurator Daniele IV Dolfin**. Sèvres porcelain and biscuit ware is displayed in the dining room.

SAN LIO & SANTA MARIA DELLA FAVA

Arco del Paradiso

In front of the earlier (south) façade of Santa Maria Formosa, Fondamenta dei Preti runs right along the canal across a bridge (note on the right the Roman tabernacle with a Latin inscription, set into the corner of a house) to the short Fondamenta del Dose, where at no. 5878 Vivaldi lived in 1722–30 and wrote the *Four Seasons*. Ponte del Paradiso, a 17th-century bridge, was well reconstructed in 1901. Here the calle has a fine overhead arch, the Arco del Paradiso, with a 14th-century relief of the Madonna and a donor and the coats of arms of the Foscari and Mocenigo families. The calle preserves its wooden eaves for the whole of its length. The bridge, archway and calle were called '*Paradiso*' because in former days they were at the centre of a district which would be illuminated by hundreds of lanterns every year on Good Friday.

San Lio

Map p. 402, C4. Open 7.30–12 & 3–5.30, except Sun.

The church is dedicated to Pope St Leo IX (1049–54), who was born in Alsace and is remembered for his reforms of the Roman curia: he is shown in glory surrounded by angels and the Cardinal Virtues in the ceiling painting by Gian Domenico Tiepolo. The beautiful domed Gussoni Chapel (right of the high altar) is thought to be an early work by Pietro Lombardo (possibly with the help of his son Tullio). It has exquisite sculptural details including a marble relief of the *Pietà* (with the extraordinary stylised body of Christ), decorative carving on all the pilasters, and four gilded *tondi* of the Evangelists in the ceiling. Over the first north altar is a painting of *St James the Great* by Titian, one of his less known works, and next to it hangs a painted Byzantine *Madonna and Child*.

The organ (above the west door) bears paintings by the 18th-century Venetian school. High up at the end of the south wall (difficult to see) is a *Pietà*, attributed to Liberale da Verona, in an elaborate sculpted frame. On the left wall of the pretty sanctuary there is a large *Crucifixion* by Pietro Muttoni, which was an ex-voto for the plague of 1630. The silver high altar dates from the early 17th century, and the altarpiece of the *Deposition* above it is by Palma Giovane.

Santa Maria della Fava

Map p. 402, B4–C4. Open daily 7.30–12 & 4.30–7.30.

The church of Santa Maria della Fava (or Santa Maria della Consolazione) was begun in 1705 by Antonio Gaspari, and completed by Giorgio Massari. In the interior, the nave is decorated with statues in niches by Giuseppe Torretti, Canova's master, and the little high altar has exceptionally pretty marbles (the two angels on either side are by Morleiter). On the first altar on the south wall, Giambattista Tiepolo's *Education of the Virgin* is an early work (1732), and on the second altar on the north wall the very unusual painting in different tones of brown, the *Madonna Appearing to St Philip Neri*, is considered one of the best works by Giovanni Battista Piazzetta.

CAMPO SANTI GIOVANNI E PAOLO
Map p. 403, D3

Campo Santi Giovanni e Paolo is historically one of the most important *campi* in the city. Its simple houses, including a charming little old-fashioned café (Rosa Salva), are dominated by the flank of the Gothic brick church of the Dominican Order. Part of the original brick paving of the campo has been revealed close to the huge stained glass window of the south transept. The exterior of the Gothic apse of the church (seen from the calle behind) is particularly fine. The lovely 16th-century well-head is decorated with garlanded *putti*, and is thought to be the work of a Tuscan sculptor. It was moved here from the courtyard of Palazzo Corner in 1824, and is unfortunately now in very poor condition. On a high pedestal, silhouetted against the sky, rises the superb bronze equestrian statue of the *condottiere* Colleoni by Verrocchio.

THE STATUE OF BARTOLOMEO COLLEONI

This splendid monument, a masterpiece of the Renaissance, was designed by the great Florentine sculptor Andrea Verrocchio. He made a full-scale model for it which he sent to Venice in 1481, but by the time of his death in 1488 the statue had still not been cast. In 1490 the casting was eventually entrusted to a Venetian, Alessandro Leopardi, who signed his name prominently on the horse's girth. Leopardi also designed the pedestal (later, in 1505, he was also commissioned to cast the three bronze pedestals for the flagstaffs in Piazza San Marco).

The horse, which owes much to Classical works including the Horses of St Mark's and the Marcus Aurelius monument in Rome, is particularly fine, and technically more advanced than the charger which supports Donatello's famous equestrian statue of another *condottiere*, Gattamelata, in Padua, since its front hoof is raised off the ground, without the need for a support. The feeling of movement in the whole statue is further emphasised by the turn of the rider's body. Colleoni is portrayed as the embodiment of a great warrior, in an idealised portrait.

Colleoni (c. 1400–75), a native of Bergamo, was one of the most successful soldiers of fortune of his time. As a brilliant captain-general, he served both the Visconti and the Venetians at different periods, and he accumulated a huge personal fortune. When he died, he left a legacy to the Republic on condition that an equestrian monument be erected in his honour in front of St Mark's. Since this would have been extremely out of place in Piazza San Marco (and against the Venetian constitution, which forbade the erection of monuments to individuals in the city's most important public space), after four years of discussion the Signoria decided they were justified in interpreting the language of his will to mean the campo in front of the Scuola di San Marco instead. During the First World War the statue accompanied the Horses of St Mark's to Rome for safekeeping.

THE CHURCH OF SANTI GIOVANNI E PAOLO
Map p. 403, D3

Open 9.15–6.30, Sun and holidays 3–6.30.

The church of Santi Giovanni e Paolo, shortened in Venetian dialect to 'San Zanipolo', is the largest in Venice. Founded by the Dominicans in 1234, the present building was begun c. 1315, continued in 1373–85, and only completed in 1430 (and restored in 1921–26). It is the burial place of 25 doges, and from the 15th century onwards the funerals of all doges were held here.

The fine façade was never finished; against it are the tombs of three doges including (second on the left) the donor of the site, Jacopo Tiepolo. The delicately carved main portal, attributed to Bartolomeo Bon (1460), incorporates six Greek marble columns from Torcello. It is flanked by Byzantine reliefs of the Madonna and Angel Gabriel. On the corner facing the campo is an interesting early relief of *Daniel in the Lion's Den*, of unknown provenance.

The interior

The vast light interior, suffused with a pink glow when the sun shines, is 101m long and 46m across the transepts. It has tall aisles separated from the nave by ten columns of Istrian stone blocks, with slender arches and a beautiful luminous choir with a polygonal apse, lit by fine Gothic windows. The Baroque high altar, begun in 1619 (and attributed to Longhena) blends surprisingly well into the Gothic setting. Wooden tie-beams help to stabilise the structure of the building (an architectural feature of several Venetian churches). The organ was made in 1790 by Gaetano Callido.

Among the array of funerary monuments to doges and heroes of the Republic are some masterpieces of Renaissance sculpture by the Lombardo family, as well as earlier Gothic works. In 1851 Ruskin suggested in *The Stones of Venice* that this was the place to study Venetian sepulchral art and its significance in the history of the Republic: '… we find the early tombs at once simple and lovely in adornment, severe and solemn in their expression; confessing the power, and accepting the peace, of death, openly and joyfully … But the tombs of the later ages are a ghastly struggle of mean pride and miserable terror: the one mustering the statues of the Virtues about the tomb, disguising the sarcophagus with delicate sculpture, polishing the false periods of the elaborate epitaph, and filling with strained animation the features of the portrait statue …'.

The west end

(1) Monument to Doge Pietro Mocenigo: Pietro Lombardo's grand monument to this doge (d. 1476) is undoubtedly his masterpiece. With the help of Tullio and Antonio, he here produced a superbly designed tomb which set a standard for later commemorative sculpture. Inside a triumphal arch flanked with niches containing statues of warriors, the doge, depicted as a general, stands in triumph on his sarcophagus, borne by three warriors representing the three ages of man. The sarcophagus has two reliefs of his most famous victories at Scutari, and Famagusta in Cyprus, and the inscription is a reminder that the monument was funded by war booty: *Ex hostium Manibus*—from the hands of my enemies. In the lower part are two very fine reliefs, *Hercules and the Hydra* and *Hercules and the Nemean Lion*. The reli-

gious element is introduced only at the top of the monument with a relief of the Marys at the Sepulchre, and takes second place to the explicit intention to glorify the doge as a hero of the Republic.

(2) Monument to Doge Alvise Mocenigo: This enormous monument to the doge (d. 1577) and his wife was begun by Giovanni Grapiglia, but not completed until the mid-17th century. It was under this doge that Venice was victorious over the Ottomans at Lepanto.

(3) Monument to Doge Giovanni Mocenigo: This was the last monument to be designed for the church by Tullio Lombardo. The doge died in 1485. The very fine baptism reliefs (of Christ by St John and of Anianus by St Mark) were clearly inspired by ancient Roman art.

THE LOMBARDO FAMILY OF SCULPTORS

Pietro Lombardo and his sons Tullio and Antonio carried out numerous sculptural commissions in Venice in the late 15th and early 16th centuries, when they were considered the most important sculptors at work in the city. Pietro, who was born in Lombardy and worked in Padua before coming to Venice around 1467, was of fundamental importance to the development of the Venetian Renaissance. His early work reveals the influence of Tuscan sculptors such as Antonio Rossellino and Desiderio da Settignano, but, with the help of his talented sons, he went on to produce sculptures which are characterised by a clear Classicism even more pronounced than that which had been produced by earlier Florentine masters of the Renaissance. In 1498 he succeeded Antonio Rizzo as *proto* of the Doge's Palace—a post he held until his death in 1515.

His son Tullio, who also carried out many commissions elsewhere in the Veneto, came to be considered the greatest marble sculptor of his time (his skills can be examined especially in his remarkable Classical double bust, preserved in the Ca' d'Oro; *see p. 227*). The younger son Antonio carried out important works in the Cappella Zen in St Mark's and in the Basilica of Sant'Antonio in Padua. The family also worked together in Venice on the design and exquisite decoration of Santa Maria dei Miracoli, and in San Giobbe and the Frari. But it is here in Santi Giovanni e Paolo that their work can best be seen in no fewer than five doges' tombs erected between 1467 and the end of the century: that of Pasquale Malipiero (d. in 1462), and those of Nicolò Marcello (elected in 1473) and his four successors. Around the same time they were at work just outside the church on the lower façade of the Scuola Grande di San Marco.

North aisle

(4) St Jerome: The signed statue on the altar here, of the hermit saint with his lion slumbering at his feet, is by Alessandro Vittoria.

(5) Monument to Doge Nicolò Marcello: Marcello reigned for just one year in 1474. His monument is by Pietro Lombardo. This is a fine Renaissance work, and the statues of the four Virtues are clearly based on ancient Roman originals.

(6) Tomb of Doge Tommaso Mocenigo: This handsome sepulchre in a transitional style between the Gothic and Renaissance is by the Florentine sculptors who also worked on the façade of St Mark's, Pietro di Niccolò Lamberti and Giovanni di Martino da Fiesole. The doge died in 1423.

(7) Monument to Pompeo Giustiniani: This Classical monument with an equestrian statue is to the *condottiere* known as '*Braccio di Ferro*'

SANTI GIOVANNI E PAOLO

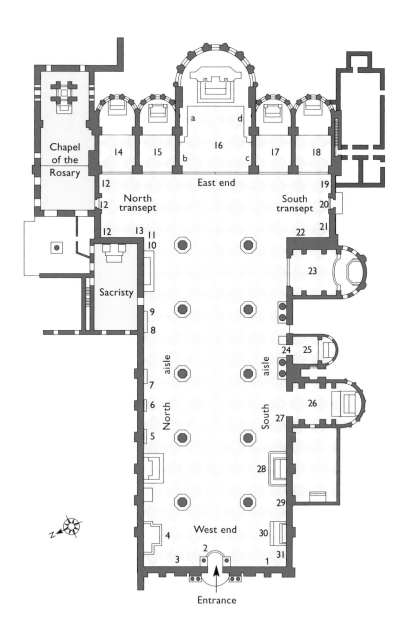

Chapel of the Rosary

14

15

16

a   d

b   c

17

18

East end

12

North transept

12

South transept

19

20

12

13

11

10

21

22

9

8

23

Sacristy

aisle

aisle

24   25

7

6

26

5

North

South

27

28

4

29

West end

30

2

3

1   31

Entrance

('iron-arm'), a play on this simile for strength, but also because he had a prosthetic limb, having lost an arm in battle. He died in 1616.

(8) Tomb of Doge Michele Steno: Ruskin considered this simple tomb the last to be fashioned in the pure Gothic style in Venice. The doge died in 1413 and his sarcophagus bears just two Crosses in quatrefoils, and an alabaster effigy.

(9) Tomb of Doge Pasquale Malipiero: By Pietro Lombardo, this is one of the earliest Renaissance monuments in Venice, and a masterpiece of delicate carving. The sarcophagus is protected by a baldacchino, and its design still shows the influence of Tuscan sculptors.

(10) Panels by Bartolomeo Vivarini: These three paintings of saints, once part of a larger altarpiece, show St Augustine flanked by St Dominic (on the left) and St Lawrence (on the right). They were painted for the church in 1473.

(11) Altar of St Joseph: The small altar is in the form of a marble aedicule. It contains a sentimentally sweet painting of St Joseph cradling the infant Jesus, by a follower of Guido Reni.

Sacristy

Palma Giovane's *Allegory of Fame* is fitted around three busts (of the artist himself, of his great-uncle Palma Vecchio, and of Titian) above the sacristy entrance. Palma died in 1628; this is his monument. The 16th-century interior has paintings by Andrea Vicentino, Palma Giovane, Alvise Vivarini (*Christ Carrying the Cross*; 1476), Leandro Bassano, and a ceiling painting by Marco Vecellio. Particularly striking is Bassano's scene of *Pope Honorius III Confirming the Rule of the Order of St Dominic* (1606; *pictured overleaf*). There are also fine carved benches.

North transept

(12) Venier tombs: There are two sumptuous tombs in the style of the dalle Masegne brothers above and to the left of the door of the Chapel of the Rosary: here are buried Doge Antonio Venier (d. 1400) and his wife and daughter Agnese and Orsola. The bronze statue of Doge Sebastiano Venier (d. 1578), who commanded the fleet at Lepanto, is by Antonio dal Zotto (1907).

(13) Tomb of Leonardo da Prato: The tomb of this *condottiere* (d. 1511) bears a gilded wood equestrian statue attributed to Lorenzo Bregno or Antonio Minello.

Chapel of the Rosary

This was erected at the end of the 16th century in memory of the Battle of Lepanto (fought on the feast day of the Madonna of the Rosary, 7th October), from the designs of Alessandro Vittoria. In 1867 it was gutted by fire. All its paintings were destroyed, including an important painting by Titian of *St Peter Martyr* (a copy of which, by

Dominicans and prelates busily discussing Pope Honorius III's confirmation of the rule of the Order of St Dominic. Detail from a painting of 1606 by Leandro Bassano.

Johann Carl Loth, can be seen on the second altar in the north aisle) and a *Madonna and Saints* by Giovanni Bellini, which had been placed here temporarily.

The ceiling was redecorated with paintings (coin light) by Paolo Veronese or his *bottega,* of the *Annunciation* (nearest the altar) *Assumption* (centre) and *Adoration of the Shepherds*, brought here from the ex-church of the Umiltà. In the choir is the *Adoration of the Magi*, certainly by the master's hand, and on the wall immediately on the left as you enter, another *Adoration of the Shepherds*, also an autograph work. The scenes in the ceiling have affinities with Paolo's *Esther and Ahasuerus* cycle in San Sebastiano, notably his use of architectural elements, and his fluted Solomonic columns. The wooden benches are finely carved by Giacomo Piazzetta (1698). In the choir the altar tabernacle is attributed to Alessandro Vittoria or Girolamo Campagna; it encloses a terracotta *Madonna and Child* by Carlo Lorenzetti. On the walls are statues of prophets and sibyls, also by Alessandro Vittoria. The 18th-century marble reliefs are by Morleiter, Giovanni and Antonio Bonazza, and Alvise and Carlo Tagliapietra.

Apsidal chapels at the east end

(14) Chapel of St Pius V: On the right-hand wall is the hanging sarcophagus of Jacopo Cavalli. The work of the dalle Masegne, it contains the remains of a captain of the Republic who had taken part (with Vettor Pisani; *see p. 284 below*) in the war against Genoa at Chioggia, when Venice came within an ace of destruction. The late 16th-century background scene by Lorenzino di Tiziano shows the battle. Cavalli died four years later, in 1384. His effigy, attributed to Paolo dalle Masegne, shows him in a suit of armour complete with helmet.

The hanging sarcophagus opposite is a modest tomb commemorating **Doge Giovanni Dolfin**, who died of the plague in 1361, after a reign of only four years. His election had come while he was defending Treviso against the territorial ambitions of Louis the Great of Hungary. The request for his safe deliverance to Venice for his coronation was turned down by Louis, who instead boasted that he now held the doge captive. Dolfin nevertheless managed to escape, and was met in triumph by the Senate when he finally reached safety at the edge of the lagoon.

(15) Chapel of the Trinity: The chapel contains a number of signed works by Leandro Bassano, including the altarpiece of the *Trinity*.

(16) Choir: John Ruskin felt that it was in the choir of Santi Giovanni e Paolo that one could see just how Venetian Gothic art deteriorated into a 'voluptuous and over-wrought' style which corrupted the simplicity of true Gothic.

The **tomb of Andrea Vendramin** (d. 1478) was given pride of place on the left wall **(a)** when it was moved here in the 19th century from the church of the Servi. This is a Renaissance masterpiece designed by Tullio Lombardo, with the help of his brother Antonio, and it is probably the most elaborate funerary

monument in the city. Similarly to the monument to Pietro Mocenigo **(1)**, it takes the form of a Roman triumphal arch above the effigy of the doge surrounded by allegorical figures and warriors, all beautifully carved, some from Classical models, others in the late-Gothic style. The figure of *Adam* made for this tomb was sold to the Metropolitan Museum of New York in 1937. It is known that Verrocchio also designed a tomb for this doge (it was never executed, but a drawing for it survives in the Victoria and Albert Museum in London).

Ruskin found the **tomb of Doge Marco Corner** (d. 1368) much to his taste **(b)**; it has a very beautiful *Madonna*, signed by Nino Pisano. Opposite is the **tomb of Doge Michele Morosini** (d. 1382) **(c)**. Barely 20 years later than the previous monument, it is considered the more important monument today, but Ruskin complained about it bitterly, objecting to its elaborate tabernacle with statuettes in niches flanking the effigy of the doge as being too richly decorated and riddled with those 'Renaissance errors' that he was to spend much of his life denouncing. It has a mosaic of the *Crucifixion* probably by 15th-century Tuscan artists, and the carving is attributed to the dalle Masegne workshop, run by the brothers Pier Paolo and Jacobello (and another Paolo, thought to be the son of Jacobello), who were busy in the city at the end of the 14th century (and who are best known for their work in St Mark's).

The **tomb of Doge Leonardo Loredan (d)** (d. 1520), in some ways bears out Ruskin's lament and illustrates how later Renaissance funerary sculpture became 'top heavy'. It is the work of the little-known artist Giovanni Grapiglia (who began the Mocenigo monument at the west end), but it incorporates good statues—that of the doge (in *cornu* hat) signed by Girolamo Campagna, and allegorical figures by Danese Cattaneo. It commemorates one of the most important doges in the history of the Republic, an extremely able diplomat at a time when Venice had few allies.

(17) Chapel of Mary Magdalene: The monument to Vettor Pisani is a modern reconstruction which incorporates the original framework and the statue. Pisani was the popular victor over the Genoese at the battle of Chioggia in 1380, decisive to the survival of the Republic. Also in this chapel is the sarcophagus of Marco Giustiniani della Bragora (d. 1346), and a plaque commemorating Marin Držić (d. 1567), the finest comic playwright of Ragusa (modern Dubrovnik), who died in Venice and is buried in the church.

(18) Chapel of the Crucifix: The figure on the 14th-century sarcophagus is thought to be Paolo Loredan, who took part in the conquest of Crete in 1365. Alessandro Vittoria made the two bronze statues for the *Crucifixion* group, and may also have designed the tomb of Edward, Duke of Windsor (d. 1574).

South transept

(19) *Christ between St Peter and St Andrew*: Painted in the early 16th century, this is one of the best works of Rocco Marconi.

(20) Stained glass window: The beautiful glass in the great window was made in Murano in 1473 from cartoons by Bartolomeo Vivarini. Some of the panels are signed by Girolamo Mocetto, but it is also thought that the much better-known artist Cima da Conegliano was involved in the work.

(21) *The Charity of St Antoninus*: This extraordinary painting of Antonio Pieruzzi, a Dominican friar who became Archbishop of Florence, is one of the last works of Lorenzo Lotto (1542). It shows the saint enthroned receiving the counsel of two eccentric angels, which are flying rather dangerously close to him, with his advisers below, behind a balcony spread with a rich rug, deeply involved in processing supplications from the poor people depicted at the bottom of the painting, some in attitudes of despair. We know that Lotto made studies of the poor in the city for this painting, and that he gave the Dominicans a discount on the price of the work in return for a place in the church cemetery (sadly, he died in a monastery in Loreto, and his body was never returned here).

Lotto was one of the most idiosyncratic painters of the early 16th century. Not very successful during his lifetime, he was largely forgotten after his death until Bernard Berenson published a monograph in 1895. Lotto worked in Treviso and Bergamo (where many of his paintings are now preserved) and then in Venice where he also produced another important altarpiece for the church of the Carmini. One of his most striking portraits (of a young man) is preserved in the Gallerie dell'Accademia.

(22) Coronation of the Virgin: This is attributed to Cima da Conegliano.

South aisle

(23) Chapel of St Dominic: The six large bronze reliefs (1716–35) are by the Bolognese sculptor Giuseppe Mazza. The fine ceiling painting of *St Dominic in Glory* is by Giovanni Battista Piazzetta (1727).

(24) Valier monument: The huge monument to Bertucci Valier (who became doge in 1656) and his son Silvestro (doge in 1694) is a splendid theatrical Baroque work designed by Andrea Tirali (1708; restored in 1999). A few years later Tirali designed the pavement which survives to this day in Piazza San Marco. In front of a huge yellow marble drape stand the figures of Bertucci Valier (by Pietro Baratta) flanked by his son Silvestro (by Antonio Tarsia), and his wife, Elisabetta Querini-Stampalia (the last doge's wife to be crowned as '*dogaressa*'), by Giovanni Bonazza.

(25) Chapel of the Madonna della Pace: The chapel (entrance beneath the Valier monument) has a Byzantine *Madonna* brought to Venice in 1349, and (on the right wall) a *Flagellation* by Aliense.

(26) Chapel of the Scuola del Santissimo Nome di Dio: This was given its Baroque decoration, with a richly-ornamented ceiling, around 1639 (*being restored at the time of writing*).

(27) Tomb of Alvise Diedo: This pavement slab, at the entrance to the chapel

of the Nome di Dio, is a masterpiece of *niello* work (black inlay using silver, lead and copper) by the hand of Pietro Lombardo.

(28) Polyptych of St Vincent Ferrer: This is perhaps the most beautiful painting in the church, with a *Pietà* and *Annunciation* above. It is usually attributed, as an early work, to Giovanni Bellini, with the possible help of assistants. The figure of St Christopher crossing a river is particularly remarkable. The predella appears to be by another hand. The fine frame dates from c. 1523.

(29) Bragadin monument: The monument with a bust above an urn is to Marcantonio Bragadin (d. 1571), the defender of Famagusta, flayed alive by the Turks.

(30) Virgin and Child altar: The altar surround in Istrian stone is by Pietro Lombardo. The painting itself, in rather bad condition, is by a follower of Bellini from the very early 16th century. The piece of paper pinned to the Virgin's throne is exquisitely executed.

(31) Tomb of Doge Ranier Zeno: This is the earliest doge's tomb in the church: Zeno died in 1268. It is without an inscription and is simply adorned with a Veneto-Byzantine relief of *Christ Enthroned in Glory* held aloft by two flying angels.

SCUOLA GRANDE DI SAN MARCO
Map p. 403, D3

The Scuola Grande di San Marco, founded in 1261, was one of the six great philanthropic confraternities of the Republic (*see box opposite*). The *scuola* moved to this site in 1437 and had to be rebuilt after a fire in 1485. The sumptuous façade (restored in 2005) was designed by Pietro Lombardo, assisted by Giovanni Buora (1489), but when half finished the brothers of the *scuola* decided to engage Lombardo's chief rival, Mauro Codussi, to complete it (1495). It seems, however, that the Lombardo workshop continued to supply many of the sculptural elements to Codussi (including the statues of St Mark, St John the Baptist, and the angels and Virtues crowning the façade). The whole façade is an original work of great charm, where coloured marbles (the details of which were originally gilded) are used in a combination of styles. It is interesting to study the linear perspective of the reliefs in relation to the architecture of the building. When work was being carried out on the façade, the head of the *scuola* was a rich jeweller named Domenico di Piero, who had a famous collection of superb jewels; he is thought to have influenced the design.

The lower part has four panels with unusual false perspectives (as if they were windows) by the Lombardo. Guarding the doors are two lions in Istrian stone, boldly foreshortened; and two other reliefs, attributed to Pietro's son Tullio, illustrate scenes from the life of St Mark in Alexandria (healing the cobbler Anianus, and baptising him; *for the story, see p. 197*). It seems that the fictive architecture surrounding these reliefs may have been added later. The main portal by Giovanni Buora incorporates a relief by Bartolomeo Bon in the lunette, which survives from before the fire, depicting St Mark with the brethren of the *scuola* (Bon also carved the statue of *Charity* above it).

The interior was first used as a hospital by the Austrians in 1809; since 1819 it has been occupied by the civic hospital of Venice, which extends all the way to the Fondamente Nuove on the lagoon. In typically Venetian good taste, and seemingly as a sign of respect for the magnificent architecture, there is no indication on the exterior that this is still one of Venice's busiest hospitals, and the main door leads straight into the columned ground-floor hall of the *scuola*, which has been remarkably well preserved (and is similar to those in the other main Venetian *scuole*).

THE VENETIAN SCUOLE

The *scuole* of Venice were lay confraternities dedicated to charitable works. Their members, elected mostly from the middle classes, attended to each other's needs and administered public charity throughout the city, as well as offering medical assistance and visiting prisoners. They were often associations of people in a particular trade or of a certain nationality. No priest or patrician could hold a position of responsibility in a *scuola*. The five most important *scuole*, known as the Scuole Grandi, were those of San Marco, San Rocco, Santa Maria della Carità, the Misericordia and San Giovanni Evangelista (San Teodoro also became a Scuola Grande in the 16th century). There were probably as many as a hundred other *scuole* in the city. Many of them became rich through legacies and donations, and were an important source of patronage as they commissioned numerous works of art for their headquarters. The *scuole* held a particularly prestigious place in Venetian life from the 14th–16th centuries, and would take part in full regalia in all state ceremonies and celebrations.

San Lazzaro dei Mendicanti

Map p. 403, D2. Open 8–12, but often in use for funerals.

The Fondamenta dei Mendicanti leads north past San Lazzaro dei Mendicanti, a

church built by Vincenzo Scamozzi (1601–31), and now used as the hospital chapel. The **Ospedale of San Lazzaro dei Mendicanti** was one of the four most important hospitals in Venice, transferred here from the island of San Lazzaro in 1595. It had been founded during the Crusades to help care for lepers, and later looked after the city's destitute. Attached to the Mendicanti was an orphanage for girls. The church façade was completed by Giuseppe Sardi in 1673 (to a design by his father Antonio). Between the vestibule and the interi-

Healing of Anianus (right) and relief of a lion (opposite); examples of the decorative panels by the Lombardo family on the Scuola Grande di San Marco.

or is the huge funerary monument in sumptuous marble (restored in 2004) of the procurator and admiral of the fleet Tommaso Alvise Mocenigo (d. 1654), also by Sardi, but carried out nearly 20 years earlier than the façade. It is one of the best Baroque monuments in Venice. On the side facing the church it has two Classical statues signed by Juste le Court, and reliefs of fortresses and battle scenes. Some of the sculptures here are attributed to an English artist named John Bushnell. This type of decoration was repeated by Sardi some 20 years later for another admiral (Antonio Barbaro), who commissioned him to erect a similar monument to commemorate his exploits on the façade of the church of Santa Maria del Giglio (*pictured on p. 118*). Antonio and Giuseppe Sardi were also at work at this time at the nearby Ospedaletto (*see below*).

The interesting architecture of the interior includes two singing galleries for the girls from the orphanage, where music was taught and performed (*see box*). Venetian society would frequently come here to attend recitals when Baldassare Galuppi was choir-master (1740–51). The organ is by Callido (1772). The paintings include a delightful early work, *St Ursula and the Eleven Thousand Virgins* (*for the story, see pp. 155–57*) by Jacopo Tintoretto, and a *Crucifixion with the Madonna and St John* by Paolo Veronese. On either side of the vestibule the two large cloisters of the hospital of San Lazzaro can be seen, both planted with trees and also designed by Scamozzi.

The fondamenta ends on the lagoon opposite the cemetery island of San Michele with its dark cypresses. Some way along the Fondamente Nuove, which skirt the waterfront, on the right behind a high wall, is the octagonal church of **Santa Maria del Pianto**, built by Francesco Contino in 1647–59. It has been abandoned and is closed indefinitely.

Ospedaletto

Map p. 403, D3. Open Thur, Fri, Sat; April–Sept 4–7; Oct–March 3–6.
Beyond the south side of Santi Giovanni e Paolo the salizzada continues to the church of the Ospedaletto, otherwise known as Santa Maria dei Derelitti, with an extremely elaborate façade by the great architect Baldassare Longhena (1674).

The church and Sala della Musica were part of the Ospedaletto, one of the four great Venetian hospitals (*see box opposite*). Founded in 1528, it included a hospice and orphanage, and is still an old peoples' home. The Palladian interior of the church (1575) contains a very fine organ by Pietro Nacchini (1751) above Palladio's high altar flanked by the *Birth of the Virgin*, the *Visitation* and small paintings of the *Annunciation*, attributed to Antonio Molinari. The fine painted 18th-century spandrels high up along the walls include (between the second and third south altars) a *Sacrifice of Isaac* by Giambattista Tiepolo. The two apostles in the spandrels above the first north altar are also now attributed to Tiepolo, as his earliest known works (1715–16). The first altarpiece on the south side is by Johann Carl Loth.

The **Sala della Musica** is shown on request (*open as the church*). It is reached by a beautiful spiral oval staircase by Antonio and Giuseppe Sardi. The elegant little oval music room, with four doors and a pretty pavement in the Venetian style, was designed by Matteo Lucchesi in 1777. The girls' orphanage here had a very high musical reputation, particularly in the 18th century, when its last director was Domenico Cimarosa (1749–1801). The children sang behind the three screens (those at the far end are *trompe l'oeil*). The charming frescoes are by Jacopo Guarana, with *quadrature* by Agostino Mengozzi-Colonna. On the end wall the depiction of *Apollo and the Muses* includes portraits of some of the girls of the Ospedaletto with their master of music at a concert; the *Triumph of Music* is painted on the ceiling. The room was beautifully restored in 1991, and it is sometimes possible to visit (on request) the charming gallery above, where the children sang. Concerts are still given here and in the church. The courtyard below was also designed by Longhena.

MUSIC AT THE HOSPITALS OF VENICE

There were four main hospitals in Venice (the Ospedaletto, the Incurabili, the Mendicanti and the Pietà) where music was taught and performed. These institutions attained a remarkably high reputation in the 18th century, overshadowing even the music school of St Mark's. The Pietà (*see p. 259*) had already achieved European fame for its music by the 17th century, through the choral and orchestral performances given by the orphans: the gifted *figlie di coro* were famed far beyond their cloisters. Vivaldi himself taught there, and sometimes even chose the instruments for his pupils. The hospitals were unique in that they were the only places in Italy where women were allowed to sing in church (although they were concealed behind grilles). Here they were even allowed to play instruments normally considered unsuitable for them (such as the oboe, bassoon, trumpet and horn). Some of the girls went on to become directors of the orchestra. In fact, the musical opportunities offered to orphan girls of talent often provided the greatest solace of their lives, as those who did not find husbands were often confined to the institution for the rest of their days.

THE ARSENALE
Map p. 404, C2

The Arsenale, the great shipyard constructed for the Venetian Republic's fleet and taken over by the Italian navy, is closed to the public, but its impressive land entrance can still be seen, guarded by ancient Greek lions. Close by is the well-kept Naval Museum (Museo Navale), with a superb display of boats, models and navigational instruments. The largest boats belonging to the museum are kept in an adjacent pavilion (*see p. 294 below*). The little church of San Martino, also in the vicinity, is well worth a visit.

Entrance to the Arsenale

At the end of Riva degli Schiavoni, Riva Ca' di Dio leads past the **Ca' di Dio**, a pilgrim hospital founded in the 13th century for Crusaders. In 1545 Jacopo Sansovino added a hospice wing along the rio (seen from the bridge, with its numerous chimney-stacks). Beyond it are the **Forni Pubblici** (1473), with an ornamental marble frieze. These were the bakeries of the Republic, which supplied ships as they set sail from the Arsenale. The monumental Ponte dell'Arsenale, built in 1936, crosses the Arsenale canal to Campo San Biagio (with the Museo Navale; *described on p. 292 below*), from which a fondamenta leads along the Canale dell'Arsenale past a Neoclassical guard-house built in 1829 by Giovanni Casoni during the Austrian occupation, and the six big windows of the Officina Remi, where the oars were made for the Arsenale, now part of the Museo Navale. At the end is a wooden bridge, which retains the form of previous bridges here, which up until 1938 were all drawbridges. The view embraces the oldest part of the Arsenale with the outlet onto the Fondamente Nuove.

On the other side of the bridge is the land entrance to the Arsenale, beside two massive towers (reconstructed in 1686) which protect the entrance from the lagoon. The great gateway, in the form of a triumphal arch, is one of the earliest Renaissance works in the city. It was begun in 1460 reusing Greek marble columns with Veneto-Byzantine capitals, by an unknown architect (it was formerly attributed to Antonio Gambello). Additions were made in the 16th–17th centuries. The statue of St Justina above it is by Girolamo Campagna.

The gate is flanked by two colossal lions sent from Piraeus by Admiral Francesco Morosini (*see p. 75*) as spoils of war after his conquest of the Peloponnese (1687), and placed here in 1692 after he had been elected doge. The one sitting upright on the left (which gave the name of *Porta Leone—Aslan Liman—* to Piraeus) bears a (worn) Runic inscription carved in 1040 by Varangian guards sent from Byzantium to Athens to put down an insurrection; its fellow possibly stood on the road from Athens to Eleusis. The two smaller lions, one of them also brought to Venice by Morosini and the other added in 1716 in celebration of the reconquest of Corfu, may have come originally from the Lion Terrace at

Ancient stone lion from Piraeus, guarding the land entrance to the Arsenale.

Delos. Beyond the door is a *Madonna and Child* signed by Jacopo Sansovino. In front of the doorway, a courtyard born on a little bridge designed in 1692–94 is surrounded by an elaborate railing with statues.

THE ARSENALE OF VENICE

The Arsenale was founded in 1104; it was enlarged between the 14th and 16th centuries, and now occupies 32 hectares (80 acres). It gave its name (from the Arabic *darsina'a*, meaning workshop) to subsequent dockyards all over the world. Here the Republic's ships were overhauled and repaired, and from the end of the 15th century onwards shipbuilding was also concentrated here. Specialised workers made ropes and armaments and everything necessary to equip the warships and merchant galleys before they set sail. The workers, known as *arsenalotti*, held a privileged position in Venetian society, as well as enjoying advantageous working conditions. At the height of Venetian prosperity they numbered some 16,000 (out of a population of some 130,000). They had the honour of carrying the doge in triumph in the procession immediately following his election. For centuries the Arsenale remained the symbol of the economic and military power of the Venetian Republic.

Dante visited the Arsenale in 1306, and again in 1321 when he was sent as emissary to Venice from Ravenna. He described it in the *Inferno* (*Canto XXI*).

The Arsenale is a fortress surrounded by crenellated walls with towers, enclosing huge monumental buildings. Some are attributed to Jacopo Sansovino (and are in urgent need of repair). Since it is still used by the armed forces, it can at present only be visited once a year on 4th November, but it will one day probably be opened to the public. Discussions have been underway for many years about plans to convert part of this vast area to civil use. In the northern zone, which is already demilitarised, a consortium for marine technology, research and development (called 'Thetis') operates, as well as the Italian Navy's Institute for Strategic Maritime Studies; and some of the docks are to be used by Venice's water transport company for the maintenance of their fleet. The Venice office of the Council for National Research is also to be transferred here. The *Corderie*, where the ropes were made, and the *Artiglierie*, where munitions were stored, have been restored and opened as temporary exhibition centres for the Biennale. Part of the northern area near the main canal of the Arsenale Vecchio, and the archway opened in 1964 in its walls on the Fondamente Nuove, can be seen from the Celestia and Bacini vaporetto stops (nos. 41 and 42), where the Thetis shipyard occupies the northern wharves. A huge crane built in Newcastle-upon-Tyne in 1883 and used by the Italian navy until the 1950s, still survives on the edge of the main basin, and is to be restored—appropriately enough—with the help of the (British) Venice in Peril Fund.

San Martino

Map p. 404, C2. Open 8–11 & 4.30–6.30; Sun only 8–12.
From the Arsenale gateway a short fondamenta leads along the side canal to the campo in front of the church of San Martino, founded by 932. The façade was remodelled in 1897. The interior was rebuilt in 1553 by Jacopo Sansovino on a Greek-cross plan. The ceiling has 17th-century *quadratura*, and *St Martin in Glory* by Jacopo Guarana. The very fine Nacchini organ was modified by Gaetano Callido in 1799 and has been carefully restored. On the organ case is a *Last Supper* by Girolamo da Santacroce (1549), who also painted the *Risen Christ* in the chapel to the right of the chancel.

Around the south door is a huge monument in coloured marbles to Doge Francesco Erizzo, dating from 1633, with the seated doge flanked by reliefs of trophies, and with an *Allegory of Faith* in the vault above painted by Jacopo Guarana. The doge's sombre black tomb-slab in the centre of the church bears the stark inscription stating that beneath it are the doge's bones. In the chancel are 18th-century frescoes by Fabio Canal and two paintings by Palma Giovane.

On the left of the north door is a late 15th-century altar by Lorenzo Bregno, supported by four charming kneeling angels by Tullio Lombardo—the curly locks flowing down to their shoulders are characteristic of Tullio's works. Completed by 1511, the altar was moved here from the Oratory of the Santo Sepolcro when it was demolished. The Crucifix was probably made in the mid-14th century, and there is a popular tradition that it was attached to the mast of a ship which took part in the Battle of Lepanto in 1571. In the sacristy the frescoed vault (with *quadratura*) by Antonio Zanchi was only rediscovered in 1960 (having been whitewashed in the 19th century). Zanchi also painted the altarpiece here, and the cupboards may have been designed by Baldassare Longhena. A Byzantine icon of the *Madonna and Child* (in an inappropriate bright red frame), a small 15th-century *Annunciation*, a 17th-century alabaster statuette of the *Immacolata* (with a ship beneath her feet), and three paintings of angels and a *Deposition* by Palma Giovane are all kept here. The little oratory next door has a 15th-century relief of *St Martin and the Beggar*. The porch on the north side has two Corinthian columns.

On Fondamenta del Piovan are some *barbacani*—the decorative wooden beams which support a projecting upper storey—which were once a characteristic feature of Venetian buildings.

MUSEO STORICO NAVALE
Map p. 404, C2

Open 8.45–1 or 1.30 except Sun; the admission fee goes to an orphanage for sailors' children.
The Museo Storico Navale or Maritime Museum is housed in the former Granary of the Republic. The exhibits are beautifully arranged on four floors, and the museum is superbly maintained. Since the labelling (in English) is extremely good, the following description has been kept to a minimum.

Ground floor

In Room 3 there is monument by Antonio Canova commemorating Angelo Emo (1731–92), last admiral of the Venetian Republic (he is buried in the church of San Biagio next door, *see overleaf*). Other highlights include cannon, one cast by Cosimo Cenni in 1643 (Room 5); models of the Fortezza di Sant'Andrea on the island of Le Vignole (*see p. 331*), and a fine display of arms with late 16th-century arquebuses, 18th-century muskets and blunderbusses, two cannon donated by the British to Garibaldi, 19th-century rifles, and 18th–19th-century swords (Room 6). Exhibits from the Second World War period include a torpedo, invented in 1935, which destroyed 16 ships (Room 2), as well as an electro-mechanical gunfire computer and diving gear for underwater assault operations (Room 7). Room 8 is devoted to models of boats, including an ancient Egyptian boat, Phoenician boats (7th century BC), material relating to the 1st-century AD Roman boats found at the bottom of Lake Nemi, a 17th-century Dutch whaler, 16th-century Venetian galleys, and the *Michelangelo*, the last large ocean-going liner to be built in Italy (1962).

First floor

At the top of the stairs is a wooden sculpture of two Turks in chains, from the galley sailed by Francesco Morosini in 1684. The rooms display nautical instruments and 17th-century charts, models of the Arsenale, and models of boats, including one of an ancient trireme; 16th-century Venetian galleys; elaborate 17th-century carvings from a Venetian galley; and 18th-century boats, including a vessel built in the Arsenale by order of Napoleon, which carried 80 cannon. Room 17 has a model of the last *bucintoro* (1728), the gala ship used for the ceremonial marriage of Venice with the sea, and a wooden statue of Venice as Justice.

Second floor

The displays here illustrate naval history, including navigational instruments, warships and torpedoes, and uniforms.

Third floor

The exhibits include plans of the Arsenale, and models of ocean-going liners, including the *Cristoforo Colombo*, and, in Room 33, the *Lusoria*, an 18th-century boat. The Turkish caique in the same room was used until 1920 by the Italian ambassador in Istanbul to cross the Bosphorus. Stairs lead up to a mezzanine floor where there are two rooms, both with splendid old roof beams, one illustrating the maritime relationship between Venice and Sweden, and the other displaying a collection of some 2,000 shells. The final rooms have models of boats, including fishing vessels and part of an old 19th-century fishing boat from Chioggia. There is also an exhibition devoted to gondolas (including the wooden shelter, or *felze*, used to protect passengers in bad weather; *see also box overleaf*), and a splendid collection of models of Far Eastern junks, and 18th-century Chinese embroidered panels.

THE GONDOLA

The gondolas of Venice are of ancient origin and peculiar build, and retain the form they had assumed by the 18th century. They have been painted black since 1562, when it was decided this was an effective way to minimise rivalry between noble Venetian families, each of which had its private gondola. Few noble Venetian families still maintain a gondola. The wooden shelter, or *felze*, which protected passengers in bad weather, is now no longer used. Although some 11m long, gondolas are particularly light and easy to manoeuvre by a single standing oarsman with just one oar. The asymmetrical shape compensates for the weight of the oarsman and the fact that the boat is rowed only at one side. Gondolas are able to transport a great number of passengers in respect of their weight and size. They are constructed with 280 pieces of seven different types of wood, and have a peculiarly shaped crutch (*forcola*), sculpted out of walnut, where the oar rests (it can be angled in three different positions). Another feature is the long prow: known as the *ferro*, it has six 'teeth' representing the six *sestiere*, and a seventh on the other side for the Giudecca. Until relatively recently, gondoliers operated as a closed guild, with the trade passed down from father to son. Nowadays, anyone wanting to take up the craft can train to do so. An association (*Ente Gondola*) for the protection of gondolas has been instituted (*for further information, T: 041 528 5075. For gondola ferries, see p. 349*).

Padiglioni delle Navi

Next to the museum stands the ex-naval church of **San Biagio** (*sometimes open to visitors, although closed to worship*). On the site of a 10th-century church, it was reconstructed in the 18th century. On the north altar there is an icon of St Spiridon painted in 1818 by a Greek artist named Karousos. The tomb of Angelo Emo, the last Captain of the Fleet, who died in Malta in 1792, has a good effigy by Giovanni Ferrari.

The 16th-century Officina Remi, part of the Arsenale where oars were made and wood stored, now called the **Padiglioni delle Navi** (entrance from the Arsenal canal; *map p. 404, C2*), is also part of the Museo Navale. The three huge halls still have their wooden roofs of 1546; they were large enough for the meetings of the Great Council to be held here for a time after the fire in the Doge's Palace in 1577. Displayed here is a miscellany of boats including an early 19th-century royal boat last used in 1959; a barge for divers built in the Arsenale; sailing boats used by the fishing fleet; a torpedo motor boat used in the last war, and part of Marconi's wrecked *Elettra*, recovered from the sea near Trieste, which was used for his first radio experiments.

In Campo della Tana, at the end of Calle S. Biasio, is the entrance to the **Corderia della Tana**, where the ropes were made for the Arsenale. The huge long warehouse was rebuilt in 1583 by Antonio da Ponte. It is now used for Biennale exhibitions.

Biennale exhibition ground

Map p. 405, F3–E4. Only open during the Biennale exhibitions, usually from June–early Oct. The art shows are held in odd years; architecture in even years.

The Biennale is Venice's famous biennial international modern art show. Since the late 20th century it has expanded its activities to include festivals of architecture, cinema, theatre, music and dance. The first exhibition took place in 1895, and during the 20th century various nations built permanent pavilions. The park is dominated by the Padiglione Italia, with a dome frescoed by Galileo Chini in 1909, and elements by Duilio Torres from 1932, though it has been altered over the years. In 1988 a competition for a new pavilion was won by Francesco Cellini (yet to be built). The Austrian pavilion, in an enclosed addition to the park across the Rio dei Giardini, is by Vienna Secessionist Josef Hoffmann (1934); the Swiss pavilion (1951) by Bruno Giacometti, brother of the sculptor. The Venezuelan pavilion is by Carlo Scarpa (1954), and the Dutch pavilion is by the de Stijl architect Gerrit Rietveld (1954); the cabin-like Icelandic pavilion is by modernist Alvar Aalto (1956). The British pavilion, by E.A. Rickards (1909), is one of the earliest buildings in the gardens. Among more recent additions have been the Australian pavilion by Philip Cox (1988) and the bookshop by James Stirling (1991).

Sant'Elena

Map p. 5. Served by vaporetto 1, 41 or 51.

The church of Sant'Elena stands in a very remote part of the city. Dedicated to St Helen, mother of Constantine, it was founded in the early 13th century by the Augustinians and rebuilt in 1435 when the Olivetan Benedictines moved here. They abandoned the church in 1807, but it was re-opened in 1928 and now belongs to the municipality and is run by four friars of the community of the Servi di Maria. Over the doorway is a very beautiful and unusual sculptured group dating from around 1467 representing Admiral Vittorio Cappello kneeling before St Helen. The sculptor is unknown, but the work is usually attributed to Antonio Rizzo, or to Niccolò di Giovanni Fiorentino. The fine vaulted interior (*for admission, ring at the convent next door*) is typical of an abbey church with a single nave and Gothic windows in the light chancel. The huge unattractive triptych which serves as the high altarpiece was painted in 1958 and hides the Gothic apse. The inappropriate lighting system was installed in the 1970s. The roof is leaking and the entire building is in urgent need of restoration—work is scheduled to begin soon. The paintings are at present kept in the sacristy, including an *Annunciation* attributed to Francesco Vecellio and a *Marriage of St Catherine* signed by Bernardo da Brescia (recently restored). The campanile dates from 1958.

Part of the convent, whose charming 15th-century cloister has an upper loggia on one side, is used by the University of Gorizia.

The Canale di Sant'Elena ends on the waterfront near the landing-stage (Sant'Elena) of *vaporetti* nos 1, 42, 52 which return to San Marco. The view encompasses many of the lagoon islands.

A WALK THROUGH CASTELLO

This walk covers part of the extreme eastern end of the city, through a characterful district where many Venetians still live. The solitary church of San Pietro di Castello, once the cathedral of Venice, preserves some interesting works of art.

Across the bridge on Fondamenta San Biagio, rebuilt in 1927, the long, broad **Via Garibaldi** leads away from the waterfront. The street was laid out by Napoleon in 1808 by filling in a canal (as the pavement, recently relaid, shows). This lively district of the city has a miscellany of local shops and stalls, selling everything from clothes to food, and including (at no. 1311) the very popular Bottegon, which boasts that it stocks over 20,000 household items—something very easy to believe once you penetrate its treasure-trove. The house at the beginning on the right (plaque) was the residence of the navigators John Cabot (1420–98) and his son Sebastian (1477–1537), who were the first to touch the American mainland and explore its coast, from Hudson's Bay to Florida.

Further on, Corte Nuova opens on the left with two well-heads and with a view of the Arsenale buildings in the distance across Rio della Tana. At Via Garibaldi no. 1791 are the little clubrooms of an association of carpenters and caulkers founded in 1867, just a few months after Venice was united to the Kingdom of Italy. The tools of their trades are exhibited in the window.

The church of **San Francesco da Paola** (*usually open 8–12 & 4–7*) was founded in the 16th century by the Neapolitan Carafa Caracciolo family, since they were astonished to find no church dedicated to the patron saint of

sailors when they visited the city. It was built in 1588 as a convent for the Minim Friars (the order founded by St Francesco da Paola), and the ceiling paintings were commissioned by the Carafa from Giovanni Contarini, who included the family arms four times to commemorate its four most illustrious members. There is an interesting series of paintings around the top of the walls, added in the 18th century by the leading artists of the day including Gian Domenico Tiepolo (the second on the right, depicting the *Liberation of a Soul Possessed*). The vault of the presbytery, has frescoes and paintings by Michelangelo Schiavone. The church contains three paintings by Palma Giovane (the best of which is in the chapel to the right of the presbytery), and the paintings in the right transept are by Antonio Zanchi.

Opposite the church, at no. 1310, the Gothic portal of the **Ospedale de le Pute** survives, dating from c. 1375. It has sculptures of the *Redeemer*, and, below, Sts Dominic, Andrew and Peter Martyr, perhaps by a pupil of Filippo Calendario, who is thought also to have worked on the Doge's Palace. The hospice for girls was founded by Doge Marino Zorzi in 1311, and only the façade remains. It stood next to the church and convent of San Domenico, used after 1560 as a residence for officials of the Inquisition, but which was destroyed by Napoleon when the public

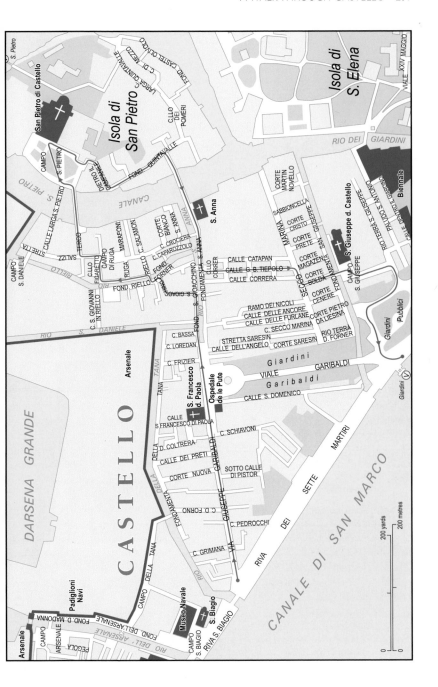

S. Pietro

San Pietro di Castello

Isola di San Pietro

FOND. CASTEL OLIVOLO
LARGA QUINTAVALLE
C. DI MEZZO
CLLO DEI POMERI

CAMPO S. PIETRO
CALLE LARGA S. PIETRO
DIETRO IL GARIBALDI
FOND. QUINTAVALLE

CAMPO S. PIETRO
STRETTA

CAMPO S. DANIELE
SALIZZ

RIELLO
CLLO FIGARETTO
CAMPO DI RUGA
RUGA
MARAFEONI
CORTE S. SALMON
CORTE BIANCO
S. ANNA
S. CROCIERA
C. CAPAROZZOLO

C. S. GIOVANNI IN RIELLO
FOND. RIELLO
RIO S. DANIELE
OVOIO
FOND. S. GIOACCHINO
FOND RIELLO
FOND FORNER
FONDAMENTA S. ANNA

Isola di S. Elena

VIALE XXIV MAGGIO

RIO DEI GIARDINI

CORTE MARTIN NOVELLO
SABBIONCELLA
CORTE CRISTO
MARINA
CORTE PRETE
CORTE MAGAZEN
CORTE SOLDA
CORTE CENERE
CORTE PIETRO DA LESINA
SECCO MARINA
S. Giuseppe d. Castello
CAMPO S. GIUSEPPE
FONDAMENTA SAN GIUSEPPE
RIO TERRA S. ANTONIO
CALLE DENTRO IL GIARDINO
Biennale

CLLO CORRER
CALLE CATAPAN
CALLE G. B. TIEPOLO
CALLE CORRERA
RAMO DEI NICOLI
CALLE DELLE ANCORE
CALLE DELLE FURLANE
C. SECCO MARINA
STRETTA SARESIN
CALLE DELL'ANGELO
CORTE SARESIN
RIO TERRA D. FORNER

Giardini Pubblici

Giardini

Giardini V

RIO S. DANIELE

CASTELLO

DARSENA GRANDE

Arsenale

TANA
FONDAMENTA DELLA TANA

C. BASSA
C. LOREDAN
C. FRIZIER
S. Francesco d. Paola
CALLE S FRANCESCO DI PAOLA
CALLE D. COLTRERA
CALLE DEI PRETI
CORTE NUOVA
C. D. FORNO

VIA GARIBALDI
Ospedale de le Pute
CALLE S. DOMENICO
C. SCHIAVONI
SOTTO CALLE DI PISTOR

Giardini
VIALE GARIBALDI
Garibaldi

SETTE MARTIRI

DEI

RIVA

C. PEDROCCHI
C. GRIMANA
VIA GIUSEPPE

CANALE DI SAN MARCO

Padiglioni Navi
CAMPO ARSENALE
PEGOLA
FOND. D. MADONNA
FOND. DELL'ARSENALE

Arsenale

Museo Navale
CAMPO S. BIAGIO
S. Biagio
RIVA S. BIAGIO

200 yards
200 metres

0

gardens (entrance just beyond the Ospedale) were laid out here in 1808–12. They were designed for Napoleon by his favourite architect, Giovanni Antonio Selva, and extend to the waterfront and adjoin the Biennale gardens. Today the gardens are called the **Giardini Garibaldi** (Garibaldi's statue by Augusto Benvenuti dates from 1885).

Via Garibaldi ends at the picturesque Rio di Sant'Anna, where a fruit and vegetable barge is moored. Number 1132 on the right is a Gothic house with Byzantine roundels. The fondamenta on the left leads over a bridge (with a view, left, down Rio di San Daniele, of the Arsenale wall and tower) to Calle San Gioacchino, which bears left at the end of the next bridge. As it turns the corner to the right, it passes (look up to the left) a mid-15th-century relief of the *Madonna and Child with Sts Peter and Paul*, and continues to the pretty **Rio Riello**, lined with the small houses that are typical of this area, with washing lines stretched across the canal. Across the bridge a fondamenta leads beneath a portico down the right side of the canal and, at the end, diverges right through **Campiello del Figaretto**, where there is a little votive chapel of 1842 (the wrought-iron doors were added in 1979). From here there is a good view of the campanile of San Pietro di Castello. From the adjoining Campo Ruga, which has two fine palaces with balconies, Salizzada Stretta leads out left towards the Arsenale wall. Calle del Terco diverges right for a long wooden bridge (recently built to replace one in

iron dating from 1883 close by) which leads over the wide Canale di San Pietro with its busy boatyards.

On the solitary Isola di San Pietro, formerly known as *Olivolo*, near the eastern limit of the city, the grass-grown Campo di San Pietro, with its line of plane trees and cluster of pretty houses, opens out before the church of **San Pietro di Castello** (*open Mon–Sat 10–5; Chorus Pass*). It was on this island that St Mark is said to have found shelter during a storm, and here it was that he had his dream, where the angel appeared to him and predicted that Venice would be his final resting place (*see also p. 43*). Probably founded in the 7th century, this church was the cathedral of Venice from the 11th century until 1807, when St Mark's assumed the role. The present church was built to a Palladian design of 1557.

The interior has Palladio's characteristic bright light. In the south aisle a venerable marble throne from Antioch is, incredibly enough, an Islamic work of the 13th century: the Arabic funerary stele is decorated with verses from the Koran. It may have been reworked when it came to Venice in the same century. The high altar, surmounted by rather too many statues, was designed by Longhena. Behind it is the organ by Nacchini (1754). On the right wall of the sanctuary is a large painting of *Doge Nicolò Contarini before the Blessed Lorenzo Giustinian during the Plague of 1630*. Giustinian became the first Patriarch of Venice in 1451, and this was commissioned shortly after his

Renaissance relief of the *Madonna and Child with St Peter*, on the Canale di San Pietro.

canonisation in 1690. In the chapel to the left of the high altar is a dark wooden relief of the Crucifix with terminals in beaten copper (14th century).

The Baroque Cappella Vendramin in the north aisle was designed by Longhena in the 1660s; it contains coloured marbles and reliefs by Michele Fabris Ongaro. The altarpiece of the *Madonna of the Carmelites* is by Luca Giordano. The Cappella Lando has some of the most interesting works in the church. Above the entrance is a painting by Paolo Veronese of *Sts John the Evangelist, Peter and Paul*. The altarfront is made from a pluteus which may date from as early as the 9th century, and, in the pavement in front, there is an unusual Roman mosaic probably dating from the late 5th century: monochrome except for the delightful little vase of pomegranates in the centre.

Above the altar is a mosaic (the pastelcoloured tesserae widely spaced) of a *Glory of Saints* by Arminio Zuccato (1580). Between two columns with lovely Veneto-Byzantine capitals (probably once part of the baptistery) is a half-figure of St Lorenzo Giustinian (*see above*), made during his lifetime and attributed to Antonio Rizzo. Also here is a 16th-century Crucifix. On the west wall (above the side door), is the sarcophagus of the procurator Filippo Correr (d. 1417).

The isolated **campanile**, in Istrian stone, by Mauro Codussi, dates from 1482–88, with a cupola of 1670. This was the first bell-tower in the city to be faced with Istrian stone, and also served as a lighthouse. Its design appears to have taken its inspiration from the Pharos of Alexandria. The cloisters (*being restored*) are now part of a private house. On the house behind the campanile are a 15th-century statue and relief.

The Calle dietro il Campaniel (the 'calle behind the campanile') soon rejoins Canale di San Pietro beside a fine (but damaged) Renaissance relief of the *Madonna and Child with St Peter*. The fondamenta continues to a bridge, first built in 1910 and one of the longest in the city (reconstructed in 1964), which re-crosses the canal near several busy boat-repair yards. At the foot of the bridge is the abandoned church of **Sant'Anna** founded c. 1240 and rebuilt in the 17th century, next to a former naval hospital. Opposite, the canal is lined by a quaint row of old houses with typical chimney-pots. Campiello Correr diverges left from Rio Sant'Anna to cross an area laid out with blocks of 19th-century tenement houses.

Beyond the more colourful Secco Marina, Corte del Soldà continues across a bridge to the campo and church of **San Giuseppe di Castello** (*usually open 10–12*). The façade bears a relief of the *Adoration of the Magi* by Giulio del Moro. In the interior, the perspective ceiling dates from the 17th century. The huge monument to Doge Marino Grimani, (d. 1605), was designed by Vincenzo Scamozzi, with two bronze reliefs by Girolamo Campagna. It is one of the grandest doge's tombs in the city, commissioned by the doge himself in 1601. His father,

the procurator Giovanni Grimani (d. 1570) is commemorated in a monument in the church sanctuary, which bears his portrait bust by Alessandro Vittoria. Over the high altar is an *Adoration of the Shepherds* by Paolo Veronese, and the second north altar bears a curious relief of the Battle of Lepanto.

From Campo San Giuseppe it is a short way through the public gardens out to the waterfront and the Giardini landing-stage. It is one stop on vaporetto no. 1, 41 or 51 from here to Sant'Elena (*see p. 295*). Between the Giardini landing-stages is the **Monumento alla Partigiana** (1970), a particularly moving monument to the women partisans of the Veneto killed in the Italian Resistance movement in the Second World War. Lying at the water's edge, her body lapped by the waters of the lagoon, is the poignant bronze figure of a woman, her hands covering her face, her hair dishevelled. It is the best known work of Augusto Murer, an artist from Belluno (d. 1985). Originally, the sculpture was to have been on a floating pontoon, so it would rise and fall with the tide, but it was decided instead to place it firmly at the water's edge, to be covered by the water. It is connected to the *riva* by separate stepping-stone blocks of Istrian limestone designed by Carlo Scarpa and Sergio Los.

THE ISLAND OF
SAN GIORGIO MAGGIORE

The small island of San Giorgio Maggiore, standing at the entrance to the city, across from the Bacino di San Marco and separated from the island of the Giudecca by the narrow Canale della Grazia, was given to the Benedictines in 982 by Giovanni Morosini, and the convent became the most important in the lagoon. In 1951 the Giorgio Cini Foundation was established here, and the buildings beautifully restored. In 1829 the island became a free port (open to boats from all countries and exempt from franchise duties). There are frequent vaporetto services to the island (no. 82) from San Zaccaria or the Giudecca.

THE CHURCH OF SAN GIORGIO MAGGIORE
Map p. 404, A3

Open 9.30–12.30 & 2–5.30 or dusk.

San Giorgio Maggiore is a masterpiece by Palladio, and one of the most conspicuous churches in Venice. The white façade, tall campanile, and brick main structure reflect the changing light of the lagoon, and are especially beautiful at sunset. The original church dedicated to St George was probably founded in the 10th century. In 1110 the body of St Stephen was brought to the church from Constantinople.

The present building was begun in 1565 by Palladio and is one of his most famous ecclesiastical works: it was completed after his death in the first years of the 17th century by Simone Sorella, who apparently finished the façade in 1610, almost certainly along the lines planned by Palladio. The front, with its four giant columns, is modelled on a temple portico, and was designed to have its greatest effect when seen from a distance across the water (and this is the way it is, indeed, most often viewed). The campanile was rebuilt in 1791 and is similar to that of St Mark's. Everything else about the façade reflects Palladio's interest in mathematical proportion. The triangle formed by extrapolating (in imagination) the lateral cornices of the lower pediment reaches its apex at the base of the upper pediment.

The interior

The interior reveals Palladio's constant concern with illumination: the clean architectural lines are emphasised through painted stucco surfaces which cover the brick structures, and the use of numerous apertures for natural light. In the absence of superfluous decoration, this produces an effect of brilliant reflected whiteness. The numerous Classical columns are raised on pedestals, repeating the design of the façade. The cruciform ground plan has side aisles in the nave, but the transepts are unusually wide. Divided by the dome, lit by windows above its circular balcony, each ends in a semicircular exedra (the shape is well seen from the outside). The chancel is a separate rectangular space illuminated by its own natural light. The longitudinal plan of the building receives further emphasis by the exceptionally deep monks' choir, which is a detached feature at the extreme east end of the church.

The **chancel** is entered between two candelabra by Niccolò Roccatagliata (1598). The high altar, designed by Aliense, has a fine bronze group by Girolamo Campagna of the Saviour on a globe borne by the Evangelists, and two bronze angels by Pietro Boselli (1644). On the walls are two beautiful late **works by Jacopo Tintoretto**, thought to be his very last, painted in the final year of his life (1594). The *Last Supper* (right wall) was the last of numerous paintings he produced of this subject, one which had fascinated him all his life. The row of disciples seems to take second place to the wonderful characteristic details of the food and the great variety of vessels, and the beautiful Venetian serving-girl kneeling in the foreground to unload a basket of sweetmeats for the banquet while a cat scrounges for a titbit. What is memorable above all is the disquieting presence of the ethereal spirits and angels which emerge from the dark background, perhaps harbingers of the death of this deeply religious painter. The *Shower of Manna* on the opposite wall is entirely different in atmosphere, seeming to portray a harmonious and joyous scene almost of domesticity. It is very different from Tintoretto's more dramatic rendering of the same subject on the ceiling of the Scuola di San Rocco.

Other paintings in the church attributed to Tintoretto or his school include, on the **north side**: the *Resurrection*, with portraits of the Morosini family (left of the high altar), and the *Martyrdom of St Stephen* (north transept); and on the **south side**: the *Martyrdom of Sts Cosmas and Damian*, a well-composed painting (third south altar), and the *Coronation of the Virgin* (south transept). The church also contains painted altarpieces by Jacopo Bassano (*Adoration of the Shepherds*, on the first south altar) and Sebastiano Ricci, and a Venetian wooden Crucifix dating from around 1470.

On the **west wall** is a monument by Alessandro Vittoria to Doge Leonardo Donà (d. 1612), who was a friend of Galileo. Another doge, Domenico Michiel (d. 1130), was commemorated centuries later in a monument attributed to Baldassare Longhena in a corridor (*at present locked*) off the monks' choir. (The corridor leads to the Chapel of the Dead, for which Jacopo Tintoretto painted a moving *Deposition* in 1592, but which has been inaccessible for a number of years.)

In the **monks' choir** the Baroque stalls and lectern are superb works made in the last decade of the 16th century by Albert van der Brulle and Gaspare Gatti, when the two small bronzes of St George and St Stephen on the balustrade were added by Niccolò Roccatagliata.

The campanile

A corridor leads to the lift for the campanile (*open as the church*). The original angel which crowned the campanile until 1993 is displayed here: it was replaced with a bronze copy after it was damaged by lightning.

From the summit there is one of the best views in Venice. The long island of the Giudecca can be seen on the right. Ahead is the lagoon with the islands of La Grazia and San Clemente and, just to the right, Sacca Sessola. In the distance a tower marks the island of Spirito Santo. To the left is the spit of the Lido and Malamocco, with the island of San Lazzaro degli Armeni on the extreme left and Lazzaretto Vecchio nearer the Lido.

Looking east you can see the little port of this island, with the Lido straight ahead (and the island of San Lazzaro degli Armeni on the right). Beyond the Giardini is the brick tower of Sant'Elena and further left the white tower of San Pietro di Castello and part of the Arsenale. To the north there is a good view of St Mark's and the Doge's Palace. Straight across the water is the façade of the Pietà, with the tall campanile of San Francesco della Vigna, and the end of the island of Murano visible behind. Farther left the huge church of Santi Giovanni e Paolo can be seen, with the campanile of the Gesuiti conspicuous to the left of that.

The monastery (Giorgio Cini Foundation)

Visits by appointment and when exhibitions are being held; T: 041 524 0119.

The Benedictine monastery was rebuilt in 1223, and again in 1433 when Cosimo de' Medici was briefly exiled here from Florence by his rivals, the Albizi family. At this time Cosimo's Florentine architect, Michelozzo, built the first library (later destroyed). After many years' use as barracks, it was restored in 1951–56 as the Giorgio Cini Foundation, set up as a memorial to Count Vittorio Cini's son, who was killed in an air crash in 1949. Now a study centre and an international conference centre, it is again in the process of restoration, with expanded accommodation, and a larger library. A school for the study of Italian language and civilization is also to be opened here. Outstanding art exhibitions are held in a 19th-century wing.

The first cloister (entered to the right of the church) was designed by Palladio (1579). It is separated from the second cloister by the library wing designed by Longhena, which contains 17th-century woodwork and ceiling paintings. The second cloister is by Andrea Buora (1516–40). Off it, and preceded by an anteroom with elaborate hand-basins (and a copy of Veronese's *Marriage at Cana*; *see below*), is the handsome refectory, another splendid work by Palladio (1560; now used as a conference hall). The *Marriage of the Virgin* by the school of Tintoretto hangs here in the place of Paolo Veronese's *Marriage at Cana* (now in the Louvre). From the first cloister a splendid double staircase by Baldassare Longhena (1643–45) leads up to the institute offices and exhibition rooms.

The dormitory was begun when Michelozzo was staying in the convent, and completed by Giovanni Buora (1494–1513). It closes the far wing of the second cloister and runs for 128 metres behind the church. It has a pretty gabled façade (with a relief of St George by Giovanni Battista Bregno; 1508) overlooking the little port. The two Istrian-stone lighthouses were designed by Giuseppe Mezzani in 1810–11.

In 1799, after the Pope (Pius VI) had died in exile in France and the French had occupied Rome, Venice was chosen as the most suitable place to hold the next Conclave. The numerous cardinals were housed in the monastery of San Giorgio Maggiore, and they took five long months in 1800 to elect Barnaba Chiaramonti who became Pope Pius VII, aged only 58. His solemn coronation was held in the church here.

THE GIUDECCA

The island of the Giudecca (*map pp. 412–413*) lies across the wide Giudecca canal, facing Dorsoduro. It was originally called *Spinalunga*, probably because of its elongated shape, but perhaps because thorn bushes used to grow here. Its present name could come from the fact that Jews (*Giudei*) established a colony here at the end of the 13th century, but it is more likely that it comes from *giudicato* (*zudecà*) or judgement, because in the 9th century allotments of land were conceded (by a judge) to families who were allowed to return to Venice from exile. Later on, grand villas and pleasure-gardens were built here by the aristocracy, and it is known that Michelangelo stayed here in 1529.

The Giudecca is home to many local families, and has an atmosphere all its own. Its most important building is Palladio's church of the Redentore, with a superb façade and bright white interior. The rest of the island is worth exploring, although some of the gardens, churches, and industrial buildings have now been abandoned. The southern edge of the island is mostly inaccessible, but there are wonderful views from the fondamenta along the Giudecca canal, always busy with boats.

Boat services

The Giudecca has three landing-stages: Palanca, Redentore and Zitelle. Vaporetto 82 stops at all of these (from San Zaccaria via the island of San Giorgio Maggiore), or from the railway station, Piazzale Roma, Sacca Fisola and San Basilio and the Zattere in the other direction. Vaporetto 42 also serves the Giudecca from San Zaccaria, and vaporetto 41 from the railway station, Piazzale Roma, Santa Marta and Sacca Fisola (for full details, see pp. 347–48). At night, there is a ferry service to the Zattere (landing-stage near Santa Maria della Visitazione), and this is also usually guaranteed in fog, during acqua alta or vaporetto strikes.

LE ZITELLE & THE EASTERN GIUDECCA

Near the eastern point of the island, on the Giudecca canal, is the church of **Le Zitelle** (*open April–Sept 9.30–12.30, and at 11 on Sun for a service*). This was designed c. 1570 by Palladio but built after his death in 1582–86. The interior follows the typical Palladian formula, brightly lit with a dome and on a central plan. The high altarpiece of the *Presentation of Mary in the Temple* is by Francesco Bassano. On the left altar is a *Madonna* by Aliense, and on the right altar, *Prayer in the Garden* by Palma Giovane. Around the upper part of the walls are mid-17th-century paintings. The statue of the *Madonna and Child* is by Giovanni Maria Morleiter.

Two wings of a hospice (part of it now the Bauer Palladio hotel) stand next to the church. It was originally founded in 1561 for young girls, who were taught the art of lace-making. Next to the convent the Antichi Granai, the old grain warehouses, have been restored and are used for exhibitions. To the left, the peaceful fondamenta continues up to the land entrance of the Hotel Cipriani (*see p. 354*), with its restaurant ('Cips') on the waterfront. The fondamenta ends at the headquarters of the customs police, whose grey launches are usually moored here. To the right of the Zitelle is the neo-Gothic Casa di Maria with an elaborate brick façade and three large windows, which takes its inspiration from the Doge's Palace. It was built by a painter called Mario de Maria as his studio in 1910–13, and is still in excellent condition.

Calle Michelangelo leads away from the waterfront through a stark modern district near a disappointing housing development, just opened, with tiny dwellings, to the other side of the island (one of the few points where this bank is accessible from land, since there is no fondamenta on this side). The calle ends beside the Villa Heriott, a mock Gothic building dating from 1929 now owned by the *comune* (and in very good condition). From here there is a view of the island of La Grazia. To the left, beyond the school and library, is the garden of the famous Hotel Cipriani, perhaps the most exclusive and invisible of Venice's luxury hotels, usually approached by water.

The Garden of Eden

Fondamenta della Croce continues along the Giudecca canal past warehouses and the Venice Youth Hostel, which must have the best position of all Italy's student hostels. Next to it a large red edifice has been restored to house part of the State Archives. On the left the huge church of **Santa Croce**, rebuilt in 1508–11 and now part of an institution for the elderly and under-privileged, with a garden, can be seen.

Across the canal, Calle della Croce leads inland past a house with a handsome lion's mask above the bell and out onto the pretty Rio della Croce, lined with quaint old houses with boats moored alongside. A bizarre small bridge, made partly of wood and partly of iron, leads over the rio to a cypress which marks the entrance to the walled 'Garden of Eden' (*no admission*), which was created between 1884 and 1900 by the wealthy Englishman Frederic Eden and his wife Caroline, with the advice of the great garden designer Gertrude Jekyll, who was Caroline's sister. On the site of an artichoke bed, it became one of the largest and finest private gardens in Venice, famous for its pergolas and lilies, with tubs of oranges and lemons decorating its paved courts, and pasture for a small herd of cows. Eden's diary, *A Garden in Venice*, published in 1903, describes the work they did on it. Frederic, who was an invalid, died in 1916 and it was later purchased by Princess Aspasia of Greece, who died in 1972. From 1979 to 2000 it was owned by the Austrian artist Hundertwasser. Best known for his eccentric 'Hundertwasserhaus' in Vienna, he was deeply committed to conservationism and the green movement. He considered Functionalist architects to be 'irresponsible vandals', and set himself up as the prophet of organic architecture, striving in his work to bring man and nature closer together (even to the extent of having vegetation sprouting from the walls of his buildings). It was his firm belief that nature should be unrestrained, and so this garden became a wilderness. He died in 2000, leaving the property to the Viennese charity Gemeinnützige Stiftung.

IL REDENTORE

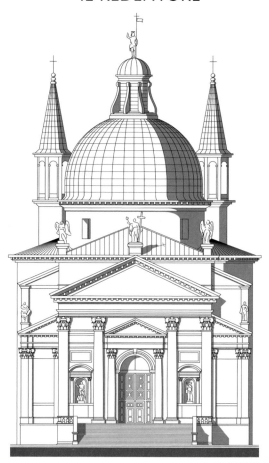

IL REDENTORE

Open Mon–Sat 10–5; Chorus Pass.

The Franciscan church of the Redeemer (Redentore) is the most complete and perhaps the most successful of Palladio's churches (1577–92), finished by Antonio da Ponte after Palladio's death in 1580. The very fine exterior includes a handsome façade on the Giudecca canal (carefully designed to have its maximum effect when approached across the water) and a lovely dome crowned by a statue of the Redeemer, and two little turreted spires. Its façade is a development of that of San Francesco della Vigna, which Palladio had designed some ten years earlier.

The church was built in thanksgiving for the deliverance of Venice from the plague in 1575–77 which left some 46,000 dead (25–30 per cent of the population). The doge vowed to visit the church annually across a bridge of boats which united the Zattere with the Giudecca. The feast of the Redentore (third Sunday in July) remains one of the most popular Venetian festivals, and a pontoon bridge is still usually constructed for the occasion. There are now some 20 Franciscan friars in the monastery attached to the church.

Andrea Palladio (1508–80)

The architect Andrea di Pietro della Gondola—by all accounts a pleasant, devout and modest man—was nicknamed Palladio, after Pallas Athene, the Greek goddess of wisdom. He was born in Padua and settled in Vicenza in 1523. His distinctive Classical style of architecture, with its harmonious proportions and bright illumination, was later imitated in domestic architecture all over the world, and he influenced both Vincenzo Scamozzi and Inigo Jones. His *Quattro Libri*, or *Four Books of Architecture*, became a manual for later architects, especially in England and the United States. In the engraved illustrations for this treatise, Palladio noted the significant dimensions of his buildings, linking together their plan, section and elevation in a series of proportional relationships. The seemingly easy elegance that distinguishes Palladio's designs was, in fact, the result of these careful calculations. In applying these systems of numerical progression, which were often associated with contemporary musical harmonic theory, to the spatial relationships of a building, Palladio succeeded in creating the pleasing visual harmonies that characterise his architecture.

After designing numerous country villas in the Veneto (on which he collaborated with Scamozzi) and rebuilding Vicenza, he planned the two conspicuous churches of San Giorgio Maggiore and the Redentore in Venice towards the end of his life. He also built the delightful suburban Villa Malcontenta on the Brenta canal, just before it enters the Venetian lagoon.

The interior

The wonderful interior, beautifully restored in 2000, is characteristic of Palladio's churches, always brightly lit by natural light. Its superb, clean architectural lines include elements derived from ancient Roman buildings, notably the Diocletian windows in each side chapel, above the cornice of the nave, and in the apse. The huge, centrally-planned chancel (designed specifically to provide ample room for the clergy who would attend the sumptuous church ceremonies held here) is separated from the nave by a high archway, and from the monks' choir beyond by a lovely semicircular screen of columns. Each area of the church receives its own particular illumination. The dome is especially beautiful.

On the Baroque high altar (by Giuseppe Mazza) are fine (but very un-Palladian) bronzes by Campagna of the Crucifix, St Francis and St Mark, with the *Risen Christ* placed high up in the dome. The altarpieces in the church are by painters from Venice and the Veneto, including Francesco Bassano (*Nativity* and *Resurrection*) and Palma Giovane (*Deposition*). The most interesting things to see are kept in the sacristy, which has unfortunately been closed since 2004. It contains paintings including a *Baptism of Christ* attributed to Paolo Veronese, and lovely Madonnas by Lazzaro Bastiani and Alvise Vivarini, as well as works by Jacopo Bassano, Francesco Bissolo, Rocco Marconi and Carlo Saraceni. There are also reliquaries, a Crucifix by Andrea Brustolon, and an unusual bronze statuette of the *Madonna and Child* attributed to Jacopo Sansovino. Under glass domes is a series of realistic wax heads (1710): they were all made from one mould, but the features, including glass eyes made in Murano, were altered to create supposed portraits of Franciscan saints of the 16th and 17th centuries.

Sant'Eufemia and Mulino Stucky

Fondamenta San Giacomo leads to a wide rio, just before which is a plaque set up in 1995 in memory of heroes of the Resistance movement in the Second World War. The rio is crossed by the Ponte Lungo, a long iron bridge constructed in 1895. Ingenious small lifts for the disabled have recently been installed at either end. The canal is filled with fishing boats. A brief detour inland (via Calle delle Erbe, Rio della Palada, and Corte Ferrando) leads through an area traditionally inhabited by fishermen.

The fondamenta from Ponte Piccolo as far as Sant'Eufemia has almost all the island's local shops, as well as simple cafés and *trattorie*, including the Osteria ae Botti, much frequented by locals. It is particularly lively around the Palanca landing-stage.

The church of **Sant'Eufemia** (*open 8–12 & 3–7, Sun and holidays only 8–12*) founded in the 9th century, has a 16th-century Doric portico (*at present covered for restoration*). On the exterior is an old relief of the *Crucifixion*, and a 16th-century lunette above the entrance with the *Madonna and Child with Sts Roch and Euphemia*. The Rococo interior has pretty stuccoes and paintings, some in grisaille. The Veneto-Byzantine capitals survive. The most precious work of art is a charming painting of *St Roch and the Angel* (with a *Madonna and Child* in the lunette above), signed by Bartolomeo Vivarini (1480; *at the time of writing removed for restoration*).

A bridge leads across to a pleasant waterfront with lawns and a few trees with benches in front of some handsome apartments. At the end is the large brick Fortuny factory building; at no. 805 is the shop (*open Mon–Fri 9–12 & 2–5*) selling the famous Fortuny fabrics (*see p. 125*). A bridge leads over to the huge brick **Mulino Stucky**, built in 1895 at the western extremity of the island by the German architect Ernst Wullekopf as a flour-mill complete with silos: when it was completed in 1920 it was considered the most modern such building in Italy. It still bears the name of its owner, Giovanni Stucky, who was part Swiss and part Venetian. Its neo-Gothic style is unusual for Italy, reminiscent of northern European industrial architecture. The mill ceased to function as such in the 1950s, and a long and complicated restoration is nearing completion, leaving the magnificent exterior almost exactly as it was. It now contains some 100 apartments and the huge 'Molino Stucky Hilton' hotel.

A long bridge connects the Giudecca to the island of Sacca Fisola, a 20th-century residential area.

THE ISLANDS OF THE LAGOON

No visit to Venice is complete without a trip across the lagoon, since this is the only way to understand the city's extraordinary setting. The most evocative island is that of Torcello, which was one of the first places of all to be settled: its cathedral is one of the most memorable sights in all Italy. The long sand-bars which protect the lagoon from the open sea, stretching all the way from the Lido to Pellestrina, with their sea wall and beaches a few metres from the settlements facing the lagoon in the other direction, are wonderful places to walk. (*For a map of the lagoon, see inside back cover.*)

SAN MICHELE

Vaporetti 42 and 41 every 20mins to San Michele (Cimitero), which then continue to the island of Murano. These are two circular routes: no. 42 calls at the station, and takes the Cannaregio canal to reach the Fondamente Nuove, while no. 41 runs from San Zaccaria via Giardini, Bacini and Celestia to the Fondamente Nuove. For full details, see pp. 347–48.

The walled island of San Michele is Venice's cemetery. The church is unfortunately in a site extremely vulnerable to flooding by the wash caused by motorboats: plans to move the navigation channel further away from the island have so far come to nothing. The paving in front of the church may have to be raised, but at present is protected by ugly metal breakwaters.

The cemetery
Open all day 7.30–dusk. Roman numerals refer to the labelled and signposted sections.
The cemetery, planted with magnificent cypresses, was designed in neo-Gothic style in 1871 by Annibale Forcellini. Near the west wall (VII; ask for directions from the custodian at the entrance) lies the writer Baron Corvo (Frederick Rolfe; d. 1913; *see p. 196*). The Protestant enclosure (XV) is on the far left. Here is buried G.P.R. James (1801–60), whose numerous historical romances are now forgotten, but who at the end of his life also served as British consul, first in Richmond, Virginia and then here in Venice, where he died. The historian Rawdon Brown (1806–83; *see p. 206*) and the poet Ezra Pound (1885–1972; *see p. 185*), both of whom lived in Venice for many years, are also buried here, as is the Venetian-born composer Ermanno Wolf-Ferrari (1876–1948): he is best remembered for his operas. Sir Ashley Clarke (1903–94), British Ambassador to Italy from 1953–62, founder of the Venice in Peril Fund (*see p. 241*), is also buried here.

In the adjacent Orthodox enclosure, Sergei Diaghilev (1872–1929; *see p. 329*), famous for his direction of the Ballets Russes, lies near his composer protégé, Igor Stravinsky (1882–1971), who died in New York but asked to be interred here.

San Michele in Isola

Usually open 7.30–12.15 & 3–4. Entrance by a side door from the cemetery.

The church of San Michele in Isola, built by Mauro Codussi in 1469–78, is the earliest Renaissance church in the city. The elegant and well-sited façade was the first church façade in Venice to be built in Istrian stone. The lovely doorway has a 15th-century statue of the Madonna and Child. The dome to the left belongs to the Cappella Emiliana (restored in 2006; *see below*). The campanile dates from 1460. The 15th-century cloister (*being restored*) has a gateway on the waterfront surrounded by a Gothic carving of *St Michael and the Dragon*.

In the interior the vestibule is separated from the rest of the church by the monks' choir, decorated with marble carving on the pilasters. In front of the west door, a marble lozenge in the floor marks the burial place of Fra' Paolo Sarpi (*see p. 232*). The monument around the west door to Cardinal Giovanni Dolfin (d. 1622) is by Pietro Bernini, but the bust of the cardinal is by his more famous son, Gian Lorenzo. The wooden sculptures of the Crucifix between the Madonna and St John date from the 16th century, and, beneath the monks' choir with its intarsia stalls, is a stone statue of St Jerome by Juste le Court.

The sacristy has an unusual ceiling—a painted vault in perspective. On the north wall of the church is an exquisitely carved Renaissance tablet (1501). At the beginning of the north side is the entrance, through a domed vestibule, to the charming little Renaissance Cappella Emiliana, built in 1528–43 by Guglielmo dei Grigi (Il Bergamasco). Ruskin rather grumpily described it as a 'summer house'. Hexagonal in form, it is beautifully designed with fine polychrome marble inlay and reliefs by Giovanni Antonio da Carona. The restoration of the chapel, complicated by the need for desalination and damp-proofing, was completed in 2006, financed by the Venice in Peril Fund. The Istrian stone cupola had to be restored and the rest of the stone re-pointed and the marble floor relaid.

The monastery

Originally (from 1212) San Michele was a monastery belonging to Camaldolensian monks, a strict Benedictine order founded in the early 11th century. The monastery was dissolved by Napoleon in 1819. At that time Venetians used the adjacent island of San Cristoforo della Pace as their cemetery, burials in the city itself having ceased because of the risk of contagion. Once San Cristoforo was full, the canal between the two islands was filled and the land on San Michele was used—and still is today—though because space is limited, bodies only remain there for ten years before being taken to a permanent resting place. In its heyday the monastery was famous as a centre of learning. The cartographer Fra' Mauro (1433–59) was a monk here, and in 1450–59, 40 years before the discovery of America, drew his map of the world (now in the Libreria Marciana; *see p. 83*). The writer Silvio Pellico (1789–1854) was imprisoned here by the Austrians before being sent to the Spielberg, a notorious prison near Brünn (modern Brno). The monastery's four remaining Franciscan friars are set to leave, and the complex is to be restored as a study centre.

MURANO

The circular vaporetto services nos. 41 and 42 serve the island every 20mins from the Fondamente Nuove. For full details of these services, see pp. 347–48. On Murano boats call at the landing-stages of Colonna, Faro, Navagero, Serenella, Museo and Venier. Boats leave Murano roughly every half hour from the Faro landing-stage, reached from Rio dei Vetrai via Viale Garibaldi for Mazzorbo and Burano (with the ferry for Torcello).

The pleasant island of Murano has 7,500 inhabitants. It was first settled by refugees from Altinum (on the mainland to the north) fleeing the Barbarian invasions. It had a considerable degree of independence from Venice as early as 1000, with its own governor, laws and mint. Since 1292 it has been the centre of the Venetian glass industry, and is now much visited by tourists for its numerous glass factories, in many of which the art of glass-blowing can be watched and objects in glass purchased. In 1441–50 Murano was the seat of a famous school of painters, headed by Antonio Vivarini and Giovanni d'Alemagna. At the beginning of the 16th century it is estimated that there were as many as 50,000 inhabitants, and it was a favourite retreat of Venetian noblemen, many of whom built villas here.

EXPLORING MURANO

From the landing-stage of Colonna, named after a column with a pretty base, the fondamenta along Rio dei Vetrai passes numerous glass factories (all of which welcome visitors). Palazzo dei Contarini (no. 27) is a Renaissance building which has suffered neglect and alterations. The name of Ponte Santa Chiara recalls the church and convent which once stood here. A few doors down from the Gothic no. 37, is a small 14th-century house with an overhanging upper storey above a portico. Ponte Ballarin (with a lion on its arch) marks the centre of the island; proclamations were read here beside the column with the symbolic lion. On the other side of the canal the Bressagio leads past a charming chapel of 1753 to the waterfront and the vaporetto stop of Faro (where the Burano boat also calls). The houses diminish in size on the last stretch of the canal, as it bends left. To the right of Ponte San Pietro Martire opens Campo Santo Stefano, with a bell-tower on the site of a church demolished in the 19th century.

San Pietro Martire

San Pietro Martire is a Dominican Gothic church, dedicated to St Peter Martyr, the first man to die in the Dominican cause. The church was partly rebuilt in 1511, restored in 1928, and again in the last few years. On the left of the façade, one side of the cloister survives, along with a well dated 1346.

The pretty interior (*open throughout the day*) is hung with chandeliers: these, together with the attractive dossals and confessionals, were made on the island at the beginning of the 20th century. Above the nave arches are quaint 16th-century frescoes of Dominican saints. On the south side, the lovely *Madonna with Angels and Saints, and*

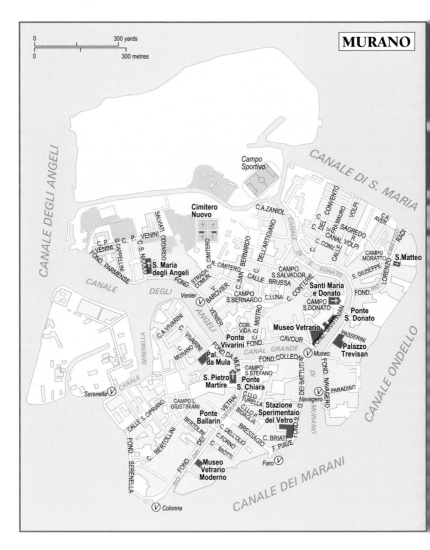

Doge Agostino Barbarigo is signed and dated 1488 by Giovanni Bellini. It was commissioned by the doge, who is represented kneeling before the Madonna to receive the blessing of Christ. St Mark is at his shoulder and his coat of arms is prominently displayed at the base of the Madonna's throne. The birds have a symbolic significance: the heron represents long life and the peacock eternal life. Barbarigo left the painting to the convent of Santa Maria degli Angeli on Murano—where two of his daughters were nuns—with the express wish that they pray before it for the salvation of his soul.

In a side chapel is the funerary monument of Giovanni Battista Ballarin, Grand Chancellor of the Republic, who died in 1666 in the war with Cyprus. The two interesting bas-reliefs show where he was imprisoned by the Turks, and his liberation from prison. The altarpieces on this side of the church are *St Nicholas and Saints* (by Palma Giovane), and the *Baptism of Christ* (attributed as a late work to Jacopo Tintoretto).

In the sanctuary are large paintings of the *Marriage at Cana* and the *Multiplication of the Loaves and Fishes* by Bartolomeo Letterini (1721–23). In the Gothic chapel to the left, there is a good collection of 16th–17th-century paintings, including works by Bernardino Licinio, Giovanni Contarini, Domenico Tintoretto and Gregorio Lazzarini. The Renaissance altar has a beautiful relief of the *Pietà* dated 1495.

On the north wall of the church there are two works, both in very poor condition, by Paolo Veronese (*St Jerome* and *St Agatha in Prison*); a huge *Deposition*, a very fine work by Giuseppe Salviati; and an altar decorated with luminous little *tondi* of the Rosary, charming 18th-century works. There is a fine red marble font on the west wall.

The **Parish Museum** (*usually open 9.30–12.30 & 1.30–5; Sun and holidays 12–5*) is beautifully kept, and includes the church sacristy, which has very finely carved panelling (1652–56), extremely well preserved, by Pietro Morando, as well as 18th-century church silver, reliquaries, vestments and lanterns.

Santa Maria degli Angeli

From the church Fondamenta dei Vetrai continues past a pharmacy with a ceiling painting by Francesco Fontebasso (1750–60; *shown on request*). Ponte Vivarini crosses the main Canale degli Angeli near Palazzo da Mula, one of the few grand palaces to have survived in Murano. It is partly Veneto-Byzantine, but was largely restored in the 16th century. Across the bridge, Fondamenta Venier leads left to Santa Maria degli Angeli in a remote part of the island (*usually closed except for a service at 10.30 on Sun*). Over the gate into the churchyard, planted with trees, is a beautiful bas-relief of the *Annunciation* (both it and the garden are in need of restoration). The interior has a ceiling with panels painted by Pier Maria Pennacchi (c. 1520; recently restored), and a high altarpiece of the *Annunciation* by Pordenone.

Museo Vetrario

Open 10–4 or 5, except Wed.

Palazzo Giustinian stands on a fondamenta of the same name. Since 1861, when the collection was founded by Vincenzo Zanetti, this has been the seat of the Museo Vetrario, the Glass Museum. It contains an excellent display of glass, from the oldest Roman period to the 19th century. The palace, built in the 15th century, was transformed by the Giustinian family in the 17th century, and in the 19th became the town hall. Beneath the loggia is a 14th-century well-head with a rim worn from use, and a damaged 10th–11th-century Byzantine sarcophagus. In the little walled garden are three 15th-century well-heads. Excavations in 1998 revealed traces of habitation from the 5th–17th centuries (since covered over).

VENETIAN GLASS

The ancient Romans, who had learned glass technology from their provinces in the East, and who valued it particularly for the brilliant colours and fluid abstract designs it afforded, had an important glass production centre at Aquileia. In the period after the collapse of the Roman Empire, when many of Aquileia's inhabitants took refuge in the Venetian islands, remnants of the tradition and technology must have moved with them to the lagoon. Fifth-century Christian art was the first to use glass extensively for the decoration of buildings, taking the art of mosaic-work— until then executed almost solely in stone tesserae on floors—and using the much lighter and brighter material of glass, thereby enabling its application to walls and ceilings. Demand for this in the earliest religious buildings to appear in the Venetian lagoon and on the mainland nearby must have kept the industry alive through the second half of the first millennium. The taking of Constantinople in 1204 added new impetus and new techniques to the production, as Venice availed herself of the ancient expertise and refinement of the glass-makers of the Byzantine capital and its oriental hinterland. The industry grew rapidly in Venice, and acquired European dominance: by 1291 it was important enough to the city's economy for it to be felt necessary to pass a law concentrating all the city's glass manufacturing in the enforced security of the island of Murano, ostensibly as a fire precaution, but more pragmatically for fear that the skills and secrets of the master glass-workers might be learnt by outside competitors in the market. The glass-makers were forbidden, on pain of death, to leave the island without the express permission of the Republic's council; although greatly privileged and often ennobled, they became, in effect, prisoners of the state. Murano's dominance of the European fine glass market was further secured by its mastery of the technique of using manganese dioxide for producing clear, transparent glass—an old and more complex technology which had been lost since Antiquity. Glass could now have the appearance of artefacts cut from rare and precious rock-crystal: for this reason, we still refer to 'crystal' glass today as a term for heavier, cut glass. There was also a growing market in clear glass for windows, since Venice, unlike other cities, was able to build unfortified houses without central courtyards, whose rooms needed and could afford large expanses of window. Later still, there was a new demand for the production of high-quality mirrors and lenses, which—after Galileo's visit to Venice to demonstrate his telescope—were keenly sought by the Republic's merchant and military navies. Most of all, though, Murano distinguished itself throughout the 15th and 16th centuries with its virtuoso and intricate designs for tableware, lamps, vases and objects in delicately coloured and often exaggeratedly worked glass, inspired by, and to some extent intended to replace, the designs of silverwork. The parabola of the trade's fortunes is well illustrated in the island's Museo Vetrario, which contains a wealth of superb examples of early glassware.

Sober at first, the designs become increasingly more flamboyant towards the middle of the 17th century: but competition, first from France and then from Bohemia in the 17th and 18th centuries, and the political demise of the Serene Republic, caused a severe dip in the fortunes of Venetian glass.

The industry was revived at the end of the 19th century under the impulse of Antonio Salviati (with the help of Henry Layard; *see p. 139*) and others, and since then there has been a resurgence in glass-making as art on the island. The name of one of the island's most celebrated, 15th-century master artists of glass-design, Angelo Barovier, who is cited by Filarete in his *Treatise on Architecture* (1464), is carried through in unbroken tradition by the Barovier descendants, whose business still flourishes today and now incorporates a museum and collaborates with an academy on Murano for the scholarship, dissemination and preservation of glass-making expertise and techniques. Once purveyors of fine glass to popes and kings, they now decorate and supply the *palazzi* of many of the celebrated residents of the city.

Today Murano is most widely known for the designs of its blown glass in translucent colour and intricate modelling, which manifestly follows in a long tradition from its ancient Roman predecessors. Always prized for its lightness, by comparison with French or English glass, and famous for its signature effects of *craquelure*, and *reticello* (in which threads of opaque white are used to form complex patterns of lines within the glass), Murano glass is now undergoing a renaissance, acquiring new terrain in the world of modern art, as sculpture, colour-collage and even fashion design.   N.McG.

Ground floor

Archaeological finds are shown here, including Roman glass from excavations carried out at the end of the 19th century in Dalmatia (1st–3rd centuries AD). Four glass cinerary urns date from the 1st century AD, and there is a fragment of a bowl engraved with the head of Isis (4th–5th century AD), and numerous bottles.

First floor

On the landing is a fine 14th-century relief of the *Baptism of Christ* from a demolished church in Murano. On the right is a room with an excellent display illustrating how glass is made. The *salone*, which survives from Palazzo Giustinian, is hung with three huge chandeliers, and has an allegorical ceiling fresco of the *Triumph of St Lorenzo Giustinian* by Francesco Zugno, and *quadratura*. In the centre is a remarkable 18th-century glass centrepiece, an intricate work reproducing an Italianate garden, acquired from Palazzo Morosini in 1894. Examples of 19th–20th-century glass are exhibited here, including pieces by Pietro Bigaglia (1842–45) and Art Nouveau works (1884–90).

In the room to the left of the windows the earliest Murano glass to survive (15th century) is displayed, including the famous dark blue Barovier marriage cup (1470–80). The little hanging lamp is of a type which often appears in Venetian paintings of the late 15th century (for instance in Giovanni Bellini's altarpiece in San Zaccaria, or Carpaccio's *Presentation of Christ in the Temple* in the Gallerie dell' Accademia). There is also enamelled and decorated glass from the Renaissance period. In two rooms off the other end of the *salone* is a good display of 16th- and 17th-century glass including crystal ware and filigree glass. In the room off the *salone*, opposite the windows is 18th-century glass, including examples from the Piratti workshops (showing the influence of Bohemian masters). The room at the end, with a 16th–17th-century wooden ceiling, is arranged as an 18th-century interior.

Opposite the Museo Vetrario is **Palazzo Trevisan**, attributed to Palladio. It contains frescoed landscapes by Paolo Veronese, the only works by him left in Venice in a private building, and reliefs by Alessandro Vittoria.

Santi Maria e Donato

Open all day 8–7.

The splendid Veneto-Byzantine basilica of Santi Maria e Donato stands on the former main square of the island (the war memorial is on the site of the town hall), and its magnificent **apse** faces the canal, once the entrance to Murano from the lagoon. It is beautifully decorated in an unusual and intricate design with two tiers of arches on twin marble columns, the upper arcade forming a balcony, and the lower arcade blind. It bears fine dog-tooth mouldings and carved and inlaid zigzag friezes, and carved Byzantine panels.

The church was founded in the 7th century by several wealthy families from the mainland settlement of Altinum, and restored in the 9th century. The present church was rebuilt around 1141 after the body of St Donatus, Bishop of Euroia in Epirus in the 4th century, had been brought here in 1125 from the Ionian island of Cephalonia, together with bones supposed to be those of the dragon he killed (four of its bones still hang behind the Baroque altar). In the early 18th century the wealthy Marco Giustinian became bishop and damaged the church, destroying many of its most beautiful possessions in the vain belief that he was improving things. During a thorough restoration of the church in 1973–79, the foundations were strengthened.

SANTI MARIA E DONATO: APSE FAÇADE

The simple **façade** was formerly preceded by the baptistery (destroyed in 1719). It bears a late 14th-century marble relief of St Donatus and a devotee, and two worn carved pilasters, good 2nd-century Veneto-Roman works. The entrance is to the left, through a chapel which has Roman and medieval sarcophagi. Above the door into the church is a lunette of the Madonna and Child with saints and donor (the canon of the church, Giovanni degli Angeli) by Lazzaro Bastiani (1484).

In the beautifully proportioned **interior**, with an early 15th-century ship's-keel roof, the columns of the nave with Corinthian capitals (dating from the late Roman period to the 6th century) support stilted arches. The most beautiful work of art in the church is the 12th-century apse mosaic of the Virgin, shown on a gold ground with her hands raised in prayer. Beneath are 15th-century frescoes of the Evangelists. The splendid pavement in mosaic *opus sectile* and *opus tessellatum* bears an inscription in the centre of the nave with the date 1141. In 1977 the entire pavement was taken up, restored and relaid on a concrete base, but it is now again in poor condition. The Byzantine-style pulpit survives from the 6th century, and the stoup is placed on a carved pillar (7th–8th century). A finely carved 9th-century sarcophagus in Greek marble, discovered in the 1979 restoration, now serves as the high altar. Above it have been placed a mid-14th-century polyptych with the *Dormition of the Virgin* and a large ancona of St Donatus in low relief, dated 1310 and commissioned by the *podestà* of Murano, Donato Memo, who is shown with his wife, kneeling.

The unusual square Roman sarcophagus from Altinum (2nd century), with an inscription saying that this was the gravestone of a Roman councillor called Lucus Acilius, is now used as the baptismal font (it has been given a modern glass top).

MAZZORBO

See Burano directions below for boat services.

The boat from Murano to Mazzorbo passes close to **San Giacomo in Palude**, an island abandoned in 1964, with a roofless building and overgrown gardens. Marco Polo airport can be seen in the distance, to the left. The boat skirts the abandoned island of the **Madonna del Monte** (right), and its dependent islet, where an ammunition factory operated up until the Second World War, which has more ruined buildings. Beyond, the canal forks left (the right branch goes on towards the conspicuous church of Santa Caterina with its leaning campanile; *see below*). The boat soon enters the pretty canal of Mazzorbo, lined with a few houses and a boatyard.

Near the landing-stage is a campanile, behind the churchyard wall and next to a lone cypress, which belonged to the destroyed convent of Santa Maria Valverde. The Trattoria alla Maddalena is on the waterfront here. The church of **Santa Caterina** dates from 1283–89. Above the door is a 14th-century bas-relief of the *Mystical Marriage of St Catherine*. The interesting Gothic interior has a ship's-keel roof, a 14th-century bas-relief of the Madonna and Child and a high altarpiece by Giuseppe Salviati. A long bridge connects Mazzorbo to Murano near a little settlement, where low-cost houses were built in 1979–86 by Giancarlo de Carlo, a well-known Italian architect who taught at Venice university, and carried out a lot of work in Urbino and elsewhere.

BURANO

Laguna Nord (LN) boats go c. every 30mins, from Fondamente Nuove via Murano (Faro) and Mazzorbo. Journey time c. 40mins. This is the quickest approach and also the most beautiful. A more leisurely approach (c. 70mins), also by LN boats, leaves from Pietà (Riva degli Schiavoni). It calls at Treporti, in a remote part of the lagoon, near the wide Canale di San Felice, then steers west along the Burano channel, through a particularly beautiful landscape with interesting bird life: buntings, curlew, sandpipers and warblers can sometimes be seen.

The private excursion launches which operate in summer from the Riva degli Schiavoni are much more expensive and make the round trip in 4hrs (including Murano, Burano, and Torcello), allowing only a very brief stay at Torcello.

Burano has a number of good trattorie and a simple hotel, see pp. 257 and 365.

Burano is a cheerful little fishing village (pop. 5,300) of immense charm, with brightly painted houses in a great variety of colours, and miniature canals (it has no cars). Most of the shops sell lace made on the island: curiously enough some of these shops open early to sell groceries to the islanders, and then turn into lace shops in time for the arrival of the first tourists around 9.30.

EXPLORING BURANO

Via Baldassare Galuppi (*see map overleaf*) is the wide main street of the island with a number of restaurants. Baldassare Galuppi (1706–85), known as *il Buranello*, the organist and composer of operatic and sacred music, was born here. He was music master at the Ospedale dei Mendicanti (1740–51) and later at the Incurabili (1768–76), and Maestro di Cappella at St Mark's. He wrote music for works by Goldoni and collaborated with him at several theatres in Venice. Robert Browning celebrated him in verse (*A Toccata of Galuppi's*). He is commemorated in a bronze half-figure (1989) in the piazza outside the parish church of San Martino.

San Martino

Open 7.30–12 & 3–6.

The traditional foundation date of the church is 959, and it was reconstructed several times up until 1645. The entrance is through a corridor to the right. In the north aisle is a splendid painting of the *Crucifixion* by Giambattista Tiepolo, commissioned by a pharmacist in 1722 (whose portrait, in an oval frame, is included in the painting). Christ is shown 'victorious' on the Cross, while one of the thieves (his nude figure superbly portrayed) lies rigid on the ground and the other writhes with pain on his cross. The Marys support the fainting Madonna, who has a deathly pallor, and the whole scene takes place beneath a threatening sky. The two (Venetian) bystanders are splendidly dressed: one, rather portly, in a grey and black striped costume and the other on horseback.

On the left wall of the sanctuary the painting of *St Mark Enthroned with Four Saints* is by Girolamo da Santacroce. At the end of the south aisle are three charming small paintings by Giovanni Mansueti. They illustrate the *Marriage of the Virgin*, the *Nativity* and the *Flight into Egypt*, and possibly once decorated a singing gallery. The seated figure on the left in the *Nativity* is probably the donor of all three paintings. The *Flight into Egypt* is full of charming naturalistic details with numerous animals, and all three works show the influence of Jacopo Bellini. A 19th-century Russian icon is also hung here.

Museo del Merletto

Open 10–4 or 5, except Tues.

Opposite the church is the former Scuola del Merletto, or lace-making school, now the Museo del Merletto, a lace museum. Burano has for long been celebrated as the centre of Venetian lace-making, and the school was founded in 1872 to revive the industry, which had decayed in the 18th century. Lace was first made in Venice in the

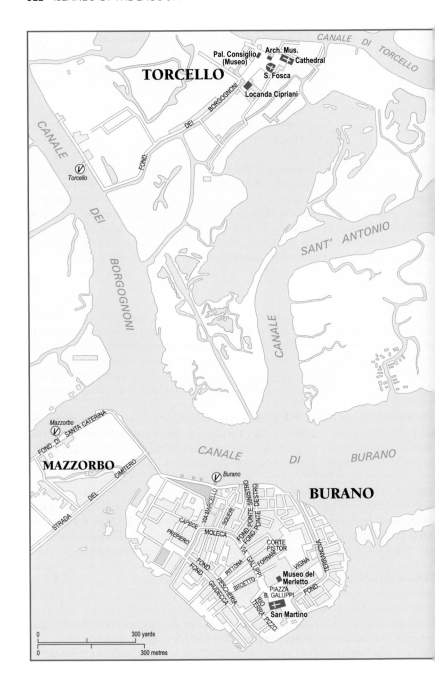

late 15th century, and spread to France, and in particular Flanders, in later centuries. In 1871–72, when the lagoon was frozen over and the fishermen out of work, the home industry of lace-making was reintroduced. Although the school has not taken students since 1991, it has a beautiful display of lace, and from Tuesday to Friday ladies from Burano still meet here to practise their art. Their products are sold (for very reasonable prices) all over the island.

SAN FRANCESCO DEL DESERTO

The island of San Francesco lies to the south of Burano, in a deserted part of the lagoon, identified by its clump of cypresses. It can be visited *(9–11 & 3–5.15 only)* by hiring a boat on Burano from the local fishermen (usually available on the waterfront near the church of San Martino). The journey takes about 20mins, and the boatman will wait for you while a friar conducts you round the island, which is said to have been a retreat of St Francis in 1220. In 1233, when it was known as the Isola delle Due Vigne, it was donated to the Franciscans by Jacopo Michiel. It took on its present name when it became a 'desert' after it was abandoned in the early 15th century.

The church was built in 1460 on the site of an earlier foundation. There are also two cloisters. The buildings and gardens are kept almost too immaculate by the ten friars who still live here. Recent excavations on the island have shown that it was settled in the 5th century AD, but was submerged by the waters of the lagoon at the end of the same century and only re-emerged at the beginning of the 6th century.

TORCELLO

Ferries leave Burano every half-hour on the hour and at half past, returning from Torcello at 15 and 45mins past the hour. Journey time 5mins; last boat from Torcello at 8.15pm. Torcello has a number of restaurants, but it is also a beautiful place to picnic (it has no shops, so food must be brought from Venice). For accommodation, see p. 357.

Torcello is the most beautiful and evocative place in the Venetian lagoon, inhabited before Venice itself. Though now only a remote small group of houses (and no cars), it still preserves some lovely relics of its days of splendour. From the 7th–13th centuries it was the island stronghold of the people of Altinum, who were driven from the mainland by Lombard invaders. They had already taken temporary shelter here by the 5th and 6th centuries. Bishop Paul moved the bishopric of Altinum to Torcello in 639, bringing with him the relics of St Heliodorus, Altinum's first bishop (still preserved in the cathedral). The foundation stone of the cathedral, dedicated by Bishop Paul in the same year, survives.

At one time Torcello is said to have had 20,000 inhabitants and was a thriving centre of wool manufacturing, but it had started to decline by the 15th century. The rivalry of Venice compounded by malaria—due to the marshes formed by the silting up

A view of the Italian Alps in the distance behind the cathedral of Torcello and its bell-tower.

of the river Sile—brought about its downfall. In the 17th century the population had already dwindled to a few hundred; in the 1950s it had 270 inhabitants, and in the 1970s just 70: it now has only a handful. However, during the day for most of the year it is populated by tourist groups.

In recent years there have been attempts to protect the island from flood tides and the force of the wash caused by speeding motorboats. This includes renewing the inner canal walls and raising the quay along the main canal, but since reinforced concrete and steel were being used (instead of the traditional wood, brick and mud) conservationists intervened because they feared the measures taken were too drastic and might alter the delicate ecology of the lagoon, as well as the appearance of the island. Cafés and lace shops have opened in the last few years; they threaten to alter irreparably the once extraordinarily peaceful atmosphere.

EXPLORING TORCELLO

From the landing-stage a charming brick path follows the peaceful canal, crossed by a picturesque old stone bridge without a parapet, to the centre of the island. The canal ends at Locanda Cipriani. Just beyond is the famous group of monuments. There is a combined ticket for all of them, but they all have slightly different opening times: details are given in the individual entries below.

The cathedral

Open March–Oct 10.30–5.30; winter 10–4.30; campanile March–Oct 10.30–5.

This superb Byzantine basilica is one of the most beautiful churches in Venice, famous for its mosaics. Dedicated to Santa Maria Assunta, it was founded in 639 and is a Veneto-Byzantine building, derived from the Ravenna-type basilicas. Altered in 864, it was rebuilt in 1008 by Bishop Otto (or Orso) Orseolo (later doge). In front of the façade are remains of the circular baptistery, which was built as a separate building in the late 7th or early 8th century, and joined to the basilica in the 11th (the foundations of the perimeter wall and bases of the columns are visible).

The interior

The dignified and cool aisled interior has 18 slender marble columns with well-carved capitals, and an atmosphere all its own. It is one of the highest achievements of Christian architecture. The stilted arches of the colonnades were rebuilt in the 12th century, and the vaulting is secured by wooden tie-beams. The superb pavement has a mosaic design in black, red and white marble. The splendid Byzantine mosaics were beautifully restored in 1977–84.

While at St Mark's the apse position is given to Christ Pantocrator, the cathedral of Torcello adheres to the usual rules of Byzantine iconography, showing the Mother of God in the curve of the central apse. Depicted on a bright gold ground, this **mosaic figure of the Virgin** is one of the most striking ever produced in Byzantine art (*illustrated overleaf*). We know that Greek craftsmen worked on the mosaics in the basilica, and this remarkable icon has no equal even in Constantinople itself. It is derived from a typical Byzantine image with Mary, as Mother of God (Theotokos), holding the Christ Child in her left arm and gesturing towards him, symbolising divine protection. Beneath are the Apostles (mid-11th century), and on the outer arch, the *Annunciation*, added in the second half of the 12th century.

An intricate Byzantine mosaic of the ***Last Judgement*** covers the west wall: it dates from the late 11th century, although the three upper registers were heavily restored in the 19th. At the very top are Christ on the Cross between the Virgin and St John the Evangelist. Below is the Descent into Limbo, with the huge figures of Christ and the archangels Michael and Gabriel on either side. The scene below shows a much smaller, stylised figure of Christ in Glory between the Virgin and St John the Baptist, with serried ranks of the apostles and saints on either side. Beneath can be seen the preparations for the Last Judgement, with the throne being set up and the angels awaken-

Gold-ground *Madonna and Child* by Byzantine mosaic artists, in the apse of Torcello cathedral.

ing the dead by blowing their trumpets. The lower register shows a number of scenes: in the centre above the lunette with the *Virgin Orans*, the archangel Michael and the Devil are weighing souls, and on the left is a crowd of the Blessed in Paradise (with the clergy conspicuously in the lead and the ladies very much in the rear) above Abraham in a garden receiving their souls, close to the Madonna standing beside the Good Thief, St Peter and an angel at the door of Paradise. In contrast, on the other side of the church door, are gruesome scenes of Hell against a background of fire, with two angels shovelling sinners towards the black devil surrounded by busy demons and monsters, and various compartments of the Devil's kingdom, one showing disembodied heads and limbs, one with worms at work on skulls, and one area almost totally black where one can only begin to imagine what is going on.

The **iconostasis** consists of four large marble *plutei* (11th century), elaborately carved with late Byzantine designs, and above the columns (with finely carved Corinthian capitals) are 15th-century local paintings of the Virgin and Apostles. Higher up is a wooden Gothic Crucifix. The **choir** has lovely marble panels (7th century) in the apse, beneath which fragments of frescoed decoration and figures have been revealed. In the centre of the brick benches reserved for the clergy, steps lead to the bishop's throne. Below the high altar is a pagan sarcophagus (3rd century) which contains the relics of St Heliodorus. On the left, set into the wall, is the foundation stone of the church, which has somehow survived intact from 639.

The marble pulpit and ambo on the north side are made up from fragments from the earliest church. In front of the north apse is the pavement tomb of Nicola Morosini, a bishop of Torcello, who died in 1305. In the south apse are more ancient mosaics: *Christ in Benediction with Saints and Angels*, and a delightful vault decoration of four angels with the mystic Lamb (11th century, possibly replacing an 8th- or even 7th-century mosaic), reminiscent of the mosaics in Ravenna. On the right wall of this chapel is a tiny 8th-century tabernacle, decorated with two dolphins.

The crypt, reached down steps behind the apse, and thought to date from the 9th century, is waterlogged at its lowest point. In the nave are two altars with gilded and painted wood tabernacles. Near the west door is a stoup carved with strange animals.

The campanile
The tall, square, detached campanile (11th–12th century) is a striking landmark in the lagoon, and has a wonderful peal of bells which ring out across the water. It is reached by a path along the south side of the basilica: the hinged stone slabs, installed in the 11th century to provide shutters for its windows, can still be seen *in situ*. A walkway provides a fine view of the east end of the basilica. The tower is ascended by a brick ramp, with a few steps: a very easy climb, and not at all claustrophobic. From the bell-chamber at the top there is a wonderful view of Torcello and of the entire lagoon with its islands and mudflats, and, on a clear day, of the mainland and Alps in the distance.

Santa Fosca
The church of Santa Fosca, a few steps from the cathedral, was built to house the body of St Fosca, brought to the island before 1011. The remarkable Byzantine design, on a Greek-cross plan, probably survives from the 11th-century building, although it has been drastically restored. It is surrounded by an octagonal portico on three sides (probably added in the 12th century). In the bare interior the beautiful marble columns have Byzantine capitals and support a circular drum, which once probably carried a dome. This may have been destroyed in an earthquake, and it has been replaced by a low conical wooden roof.

Museo di Torcello
Open 10.30–5; winter 10–4. Closed Mon and national holidays.
Palazzo del Consiglio houses the little museum of Torcello which contains archaeological material and an interesting collection of objects from the demolished churches on the island (which at one time numbered at least ten).

Ground floor
Mosaic fragments include late 12th-century works from the cathedral: the head of a (beardless) Christ and two angels formerly in the tympanum above the triumphal arch, and two pieces from the *Last Judgement*. The two heads of archangels come from a church in Ravenna and are sometimes dated as early as 545 or 546 (but may, instead, have been made in the 7th century). They found their way here after Frederick William IV of Prussia had the entire apse of the Ravenna church detached and moved to Venice for restoration. Most of it ended up in the Bode Museum in Berlin, but other fragments exist in London (V&A) and in St Petersburg (Hermitage).

A 6th-century stoup has a Greek inscription: 'Take this water with joy since the voice of God is on the waters' (*Isaiah 12, 3 and Psalm 29: 3*); and a medieval lance with astrological symbols and a runic inscription, thought to be an allusion to an ancient north German divinity. Among the architectural fragments are several plutei, and a 10th-century well-head. The very precious **Pala d'Oro** in gilded silver, just restored, consists of only 13 fragments, since the other 29 plaquettes were stolen in 1806. However, they are of exquisite workmanship dating from the 13th or 14th century, and showing the Madonna sitting on a very unusual throne in the shape of a lyre, and two archangels, two prophets, and six saints, all identified by engraved inscriptions, and two symbols of the Evangelists. The altarpiece, formerly decorated with precious stones and enamels, used to be above the iconostasis in the cathedral (as the painting of 1845 shows).

Upper floor
Material from the suppressed churches on the island, including the beautifully carved tomb of Santa Fosca as well as other 15th century Venetian wooden sculptures. Also here are an 11th-century Latin Cross in marble; *St Christopher*, an early 15th-century Venetian painting; ten small wooden panels (from a ceiling decoration) with biblical scenes, attributed to Bonifacio Bembo of Cremona (15th century); 16th-century paintings from the organ of Sant'Antonio; a case of 16th-century majolica found in recent excavations on the island; medallions, bronzes, doges' seals.

Archaeological Museum
Exhibits are well displayed in the former Palazzo dell'Archivio. In the open loggia below are some fine Roman sculptural fragments. The top floor has material from prehistory to the 6th century AD, including altars, funerary *cippi*, statues from the late Empire (from Torcello and Altinum), small Roman bronzes and Etruscan ceramics. On the grass outside you can sit in an ancient stone seat known as **Attila's Chair**, which has survived here over the centuries and has thankfully never been swept up into a museum.

THE LIDO

Vaporetto no. 1 (every 10mins) and no. 51 (every 20mins) both from San Zaccaria in c. 15mins via Giardini and Sant'Elena (no. 1 calls also at Arsenale). For full details of these services, see pp. 347–48. The return from the Lido is either by no. 1 or no. 52. An express weekday service (no. 61) runs from Piazzale Roma, Santa Marta, San Basilio, Zattere, Giardini and Sant'Elena to the Lido every 20mins in c. 30mins (no. 62 makes the return trip). In summer there is sometimes a direct service from Alberoni to the Zattere.

The best way of seeing the south part of the Lido island and Pellestrina is by bus no. 11 (from Piazzale Santa Maria Elisabetta (see p. 350).

The Lido (pop. 18,800), is a long narrow island (about 12km) between the lagoon and the open Adriatic sea. The first bathing establishments were opened here in 1857 and by the beginning of the 20th century it had become the most fashionable seaside resort in Italy. The name Lido was subsequently adopted by numerous seaside resorts all over the world. The Adriatic sea-front consists of a group of luxurious hotels and villas bordering the fine sandy beach, which is divided up into sections, each belonging to a particular hotel or bathing area, with deckchairs, beach huts and attendants (beach huts can often be hired by the day). At the extreme northern and southern ends of the island there are public beaches.

The rest of the northern part of the island has become a residential district, with fine trees and numerous gardens, crossed by several canals. The houses, mostly only a few storeys high, are spaciously laid out. The atmosphere on the Lido is very different from that in the city of Venice itself, as it does not have many canals, and cars and buses are the means of transport (although bicycles can sometimes be hired by the vaporetto landing-stage).

EXPLORING THE LIDO

The landing-stage of Santa Maria Elisabetta (SME), where the vaporetto services from Venice terminate, is named after the church of 1627. Buses to all destinations on the Lido pass through Piazzale Santa Maria Elisabetta. The Gran Viale Santa Maria Elisabetta, the main street crossing the widest part of the island, leads from here past the tourist office, the post office, and numerous hotels and shops, to Piazzale Bucintoro on the seafront. To the left, Lungomare d'Annunzio leads along the front to the public beaches of San Nicolò, while to the right Lungomare Marconi (with its numerous beach huts and private beaches) passes the **Grand Hotel des Bains**, built by Francesco Marsich in 1905 (*see box below*).

GRAND HOTEL DES BAINS

Shortly after the hotel opened in 1909, Diaghilev, Nijinsky and Leon Bakst all stayed together here, spending much time with Gabriele d'Annunzio and Isadora Duncan. Nijinsky's widow suggested that it was while the friends sat at Florian's watching the criss-cross movements of the pigeons and crowds in Piazza San Marco that the great dancer first thought of turning to choreography. Diaghilev and Nijinsky returned to Venice in 1916 for a charity performance of *tableaux vivants* after Italian masters, organised by Mrs William K. Vanderbilt to help the inhabitants of the Lido who had become homeless after a flood. Nijinsky played the part of one of Carpaccio's gondoliers. The hotel also provided the setting for Thomas Mann's *Death in Venice* (1913). The opera written by Benjamin Britten and the film by Luchino Visconti (1973) of the same name were both based on this celebrated example of a refined novel in the Age of Decadence.

Farther south is the Casinò, built in 1936–38 by Eugenio Miozzi, and the Palazzo del Cinema erected between 1937 and 1952 (to be rebuilt), where the international Venice Film Festival is usually held in summer. Just beyond is the famous Excelsior Palace Hotel (an elaborate building in Moorish style by Giovanni Sardi; 1898–1908) with its landing-stage on a canal (used by the hotel launches, and the Casinò boat).

The northern Lido

The northern end of the island is reached on foot or by bus A (from Lungomare Marconi, or Piazzale Santa Maria Elisabetta). The road skirts the lagoon past the conspicuous Tempio Votivo (or Santa Maria della Vittoria), a domed war memorial begun by Giuseppe Torres in 1925. Nearly 1km further on, Via Cipro leads to the **Catholic Cemetery**. In a corner of the newest part of the cemetery some 18th-century tombstones from the old Protestant Cemetery have recently been set up. This cemetery, in use from 1684–1810, was obliterated in the 1930s when the airport was extended. Here is preserved the tombstone of the collector and art dealer John Murray, who was appointed British Resident in Venice in 1754. In 1766 he left to take up the post of Ambassador to Constantinople. When he was granted leave to return to Venice, he was put in quarantine on the island of Lazzaretto Nuovo, and died there of a fever in 1775. The singer Catherine Tofts, the first wife of Consul Smith (*see p. 134*), is also buried here. Smith subsequently married John Murray's sister, Elizabeth.

Nearby is the **New Jewish Cemetery**, in use from 1774 onwards, where numerous older tombstones formerly in the Old Jewish Cemetery have recently been restored and set up in a corner by the gate.

On the main road, beside a row of seven cypresses, a small gate (signposted) precedes the **Old Jewish Cemetery** (*open Sun morning, guided tours at 2.30; T: 041 715 359*). The Jewish community was granted this land (which belonged to the Benedictine convent of San Niccolò, overlooking the lagoon) as a burial ground in 1386, the earliest recorded presence of the Jews in Venice. The cemetery, in use up until the 18th century, had to be enlarged over the years, and it grew to cover an area more than six times its present size. However, from the 17th century onwards it was encroached upon by military installations set up in this strategic part of the lagoon, and in the process many of the tombstones were moved, damaged or buried. Finally, in 1774, a new cemetery was opened a few hundred metres to the east. In the 19th century what remained of the old cemetery was cleared and the site 'arranged' with the tombstones placed haphazardly in rows, and the enclosure wall was built and the memorial obelisk erected, according to Romantic concepts. It was fondly described by both Byron and Shelley. In 1883–86, when the firing range (*see below*) was built close by, yet more tombstones came to light and were amassed in the new Jewish cemetery. In 1929 the area towards the lagoon (with the seven cypresses) was confiscated in order to widen the road, and the tombs were set up against the walls.

In 1997–99 the old cemetery was cleared of undergrowth, and the marshy area furthest from the gate reclaimed and many tombstones salvaged from below ground and carefully re-erected or set up around the walls. It is now well kept and includes about

1,200 tombstones, many of them decorated with beautifully-carved Hebrew symbols. The fourteen 17th-century tombstones in the unusual form of columns decorated with Samson and the lion belong to a family from Cividale del Friuli.

The main road continues past the **Tiro a Segno**, a huge building (in need of restoration) erected in 1883–86 as a firing range and still in use, to a pretty bridge over an inlet, at the end of which can be seen the Lido airport, opened after the First World War and enlarged in 1934. It is now used only for private planes.

San Nicolò al Lido

Usually open 9–12 & 4–7.

The monastery and church of San Nicolò al Lido, in the remote north of the island, were founded in 1044. The present convent was built in the 16th century. Its strategic position near the main entrance to the lagoon meant that the monastery was used by the doge as the official place to receive visitors. The emperor Barbarossa stayed here before his meeting with Pope Alexander III in St Mark's in 1177, and elaborate celebrations were held in honour of Henry III, King of France, in 1574. Domenico Selvo was elected doge here in 1071, while St Mark's basilica was being completed. Above the door of the church is a monument to Doge Domenico Contarini, the founder. The interior has an interesting narrow choir with huge capitals. In the sanctuary is a 14th-century wooden Crucifix, and a high altar in *pietre dure*. The choir stalls, in excellent condition, were finely carved by Giovanni da Crema in 1635.

On the right of the church, a paved lane leads down to the entrance (flanked by two 11th-century capitals) to the former Franciscan convent, which has a very grand staircase and a lovely cloister dating from 1530, with a wrought-iron well of 1710. Off the cloister, the abandoned remains of the Romanesque church have an interesting polychrome mosaic floor (1043) with a geometric and floral design (*removed for restoration*), the earliest so far found in the lagoon, apart from that of St Mark's. The convent is now used for a European Masters programme in Human Rights and Democratisation.

Outside the church there is a view across the lagoon to the campanile of St Mark's, and the dome and campanile of San Pietro di Castello. Near at hand is the green island of La Certosa. On the other side of the church stands the Palazzetto del Consiglio dei Dieci (1520), probably on the site of a 14th-century building.

Porto di Lido

The road continues past 16th-century military buildings to the northern tip of the island which overlooks the Porto di Lido, the main entrance to the lagoon and always strongly defended (at one time it was closed by huge chains to prevent the entrance of enemy ships). In November 1988 Mo.S.E. (Modolo sperimentale elettromeccanico), an experimental sluice gate, was laid on the bed of the sea as the first stage in the project, now underway, to install mobile flood barriers at all three entrances to the lagoon, in order to protect the city from flood tides (*see p. 36*).

Facing the Lido, on the island of Le Vignole, is the **Fortezza di Sant'Andrea**, the masterpiece of Michele Sanmicheli (1543), the architect and engineer appointed in 1534 to examine the defences of the lagoon. The Council of Ten finally gave their assent to the construction of a fortress here, despite the fact that Venice was renowned for the absence of heavily fortified buildings. It was one of the most important works of military architecture of its time, and a remarkable technical achievement since its foundations had to be laid on the lagoon bed. After years of neglect it has now been restored.

THE FESTA DELLA SENSA

In the Porto di Lido channel the doge performed the annual ceremony of the marriage with the sea, when he threw his ring to his watery 'bride'. By the 16th century this was one of the most important and elaborate state occasions, but it has complicated and confused origins. According to tradition, in 1177 Pope Alexander III gave Doge Sebastiano Ziani a golden ring and the right to 'wed' the sea with it, in gratitude for his support against the Emperor Frederick Barbarossa and his part in the reconciliation which took place between emperor and pope in St Mark's on Ascension Day in that year. Another tradition dates the gesture to Doge Pietro II Orseolo, the victor in 1000 over Slav pirates in Dalmatia, who is supposed to have blessed the sea here on Ascension Day every year. The legend of St Mark also incorporates an episode with a ring, when St Mark is said to have persuaded an old fisherman to placate a storm at the mouth of the lagoon by overturning a boatload of demons and afterwards present St Mark's ring to the doge (illustrated in Paris Bordone's painting in the Gallerie dell' Accademia; *see p. 152*).

Whatever its origins, the ritual, symbolising the Republic's dominion over the sea, took place every year on Ascension Day, when the doge was rowed out in the *Bucintoro* in a procession of thousands of boats, also welcoming on board the Patriarch of Venice. They then attended Mass at San Nicolò, and a state banquet was held. The ceremony also coincided with the first evening in the year when Venetian ships were able to set sail again after the winter months in port. The Festa della Sensa is still celebrated on the first Sunday after Ascension Day, when the mayor sadly has to take the place of the doge.

Across the channel is Punta Sabbioni on the mainland, connected by road with Lido di Jesolo, a popular seaside resort, between the old and new mouths of the Piave. The old village of Jesolo, formerly Cavazuccherina, perpetuates the name of an early medieval centre, known also as *Equilium* (since horses were bred on the marshes here), the rival of Heraclea in the affairs of the lagoon.

Malamocco and Alberoni

Via Malamocco runs south from Piazzale Santa Maria Elisabetta, a little inland from the lagoon, through a residential area with numerous gardens. The buildings become fewer as the island narrows.

Malamocco is a quiet fishing village on the water. The ancient *Metamauco* was one of the first places to be inhabited in the lagoon by people from Heraclea to the north-east, which had been an important episcopal and administrative centre in the 7th–8th centuries. Metamauco became the seat of the lagoon government in the 8th century. It was the scene of the famous defeat of Pepin, son of Charlemagne, who had laid siege to the city in 810. Submerged by a tidal wave c. 1107, the settlement was moved from the Adriatic seafront to this side of the island. It now consists of a colourful small group of pretty houses along the little paved main street called, as in Venice, the Merceria. The side *calli* have herring-bone paving, and one of them has a quaint little wayside shrine honouring the Madonna. In a campo with two wells, the church has a large painting by Gerolamo Forabosco, a carved polyptych of the *Dormition of the Virgin* (early 15th century), and an early 17th-century painting of the *Madonna and Saints*. The campanile is modelled on that of St Mark's. Opposite is a 15th-century palace, once the '*residenza della deputazione comunale*', which bears a high relief of the Venetian lion. The little Bishop's Palace is near the adjoining campo 'Maggiore', supplied with another well. Near the trattoria Scarso, with a large garden, in the public gardens with benches on the lagoon, the view takes in both Venice (on the extreme right), and (in front), the port of Marghera. Just offshore lies the island of Poveglia. At the other end of the Merceria, beyond a gateway, a path leads over two bridges near remains of the old moated fort (now built over), to the sea wall, which has a pleasant paved walkway parallel to the sea. For many years Malamocco was the home of the writer and cartoonist Hugo Pratt (1927–95), who came from a Venetian family and is best remembered as creator of 'Corto Maltese'.

At the southernmost tip of the island is **Alberoni**, a little bathing resort, with the Lido golf course (18 holes), entered through the tunnel of an old fortress, and an extensive public beach. Fine walks can be taken along the sea wall between Alberoni and Malamocco. The road continues to the end of the promontory where there is a car ferry (used by bus no. 11) for the island of Pellestrina.

PELLESTRINA

ACTV bus no. 11 from the Lido via a ferry c. every 45mins going on to Chioggia (a remarkable scenic journey, which can also be broken in order to visit San Pietro in Volta and Pellestrina on foot). The bus terminates beside the passenger ferry landing-stage for Chioggia (services in connection with the buses).

The thin island of Pellestrina (10km long, and only a few hundred metres wide) is separated from the sea by a wall known as the *Murazzi*, a remarkable work of engineering, undertaken in 1744–82 by an engineer from Brescia called Bernardino Zendrini following a project drawn up in 1716 by the cosmographer Vincenzo Coronelli. This great sea wall, which extends for the entire length of the island, was formerly some 20km long running all the way from the Porto di Lido as far as

Sottomarina. It was built of irregular blocks of Istrian stone and marble, and was later reinforced in places by huge blocks of concrete. The dyke is very well preserved and at intervals there are little flights of steps protected by ropes to the walkway along the top. There are numerous inscriptions recording the dates of the various stages in its construction and stones indicating distances. Since 1967 huge quantities of sand have been dredged from the sea and a fence erected to protect the seaward side of the wall.

The island is mostly well preserved and interesting for the colourful architecture of the two settlements of San Pietro in Volta and Pellestrina itself, which both face the lagoon. The houses, most of them in good repair (although the weather-proof doors, porches and windows detract from their appearance), are often connected with low porticoes, between the narrow *calli* and small *campi*. Despite the remoteness of the area, there is an air of well-being and the island does not appear to be suffering from depopulation, although the market gardens on which the local economy was partly based have now been abandoned. Many of the inhabitants are fishermen who work both in the lagoon (often at night) and the open sea, and their numerous fishing boats line the shore of the lagoon. The few shops are mostly in private houses without signs. Hardly any tourists come to this island, which is particularly peaceful (the only disturbing elements being the cars). In the last few years the *fondamente* along the lagoon have been carefully restored, and the low wall slightly raised so that the problem of flooding from high tides has been resolved.

San Pietro in Volta

San Pietro in Volta (pop. 1,600) is the first settlement on the island (with a request stop of bus no. 11, about 2km from the Porto di Malamocco). From the main road and bus stop, follow the lane which leads towards the lagoon along a moat which once surrounded a fortress, now in total ruin, where fishing boats are usually moored and nets spread out to dry. The road along the waterfront passes a house (no. 428) where Pope Pius VII sheltered from a violent storm in the year 1800. A passageway then leads past a bright red house in Art Nouveau style, near a water-tower. Beyond a little campo with pine trees and a public green used to hang out washing, are the post office, library, medical centre and kindergarten. The church of **San Pietro** was founded in the 10th century but was rebuilt in 1777–1813. It has a fine organ decorated with sculptures. The house beside the church has a bas-relief of St Peter. Nearby, slightly inland, a monument records the 1966 flood which miraculously reached only the ground floors of the houses, so that the island escaped serious damage. Near another mooring for boats there is a group of small produce shops, and a good seafood restaurant (Da Nane) at no. 276. The waterfront becomes even more picturesque, and, next to a café, a charming little yellow house which used to be a bakery, is built out over the pavement and has four prettily carved pilasters.

Pellestrina

Pellestrina, with some 3,600 inhabitants, is strung out for nearly 3km along the narrow sand-bar. The local industry of lace-making is disappearing, but most of the

View of the lagoon at Pellestrina.

inhabitants are still fishermen. The settlement is divided into four districts of Scarpa, Zennari, Vianello and Busetto, named after local families sent here from Chioggia on the mainland to settle the island after the sea battle with Genoa in 1381. The descendants of many of those families still live here. A huge shipyard right on the lagoon adjoins the district of Scarpa where there is a tiny votive chapel with a pretty campanile (1862). The wider lane here is one of a series on the island called 'carizzada' (each of them numbered): these were built from the lagoon to the seafront during the construction of the *Murazzi*: they were just wide enough for a cart (*carro*; hence 'carizzada') to pass with its load of heavy stones.

The **church of Sant'Antonio** was founded in 1612 but enlarged a century later. The third south altar by Baldassare Longhena has an altarpiece by a 16th-century painter called Lorenzino di Tiziano (he also painted a scene of the Battle of Chioggia in Santi Giovanni e Paolo; *see p. 283*). Beyond a playing field is the district of Zennari, with some bigger houses set back from the lagoon, with a well, school and water-tower. The town hall is in the district of Vianello, together with the octagonal church of **San Vito**. This was rebuilt by Andrea Tirali in 1723 in honour of the lovely 17th-century *Madonna and Child* on the high altar, of Spanish origin. As the ex-votos in the sanctuary show, this is greatly venerated since it is associated with a miracle in a chapel on this site in 1716 on the occasion of the defeat of the Turkish fleet at Corfu, and since 1923 the church has been named the *Madonna dell'Apparizione*. The large frescoes of four prophets on the vault and over the sanctuary date from 1950–52. In a side calle there is an interesting little tabernacle, with miniature antique columns and a bas-relief of the standing Madonna and Child, a rare survival. The last district, Busetto, has a few shops and a bar, and the very long church of Ognissanti, founded in the 12th century and rebuilt and extended in the 16th and 17th centuries. It contains a huge reliquary.

At the south end of the island is the cemetery and no. 11 bus terminus, next to the landing-stage for the passenger ferry to Chioggia. As the boat crosses the Porto di Chioggia, the third and last entrance to the lagoon, the Ca' Roman, a 16th-century fortification on the southern tip of the island, now inhabited by Canossian nuns, can be seen (some services call here on request). The boat takes a little under half an hour to reach Chioggia.

CHIOGGIA

Bus 11 operates from the Lido (Santa Maria Elisabetta) via Malamocco, Alberoni, San Pietro in Volta and Pellestrina. At Pellestrina (Cimitero) it connects with a boat which continues (25mins) to Chioggia. The whole journey, which is highly recommended, takes c. 1.5hrs. Chioggia and Sottomarina can also be reached from the mainland by bus from Piazzale Roma (no. 25) via Mestre in c. 1hr, but the approach from the Lido is much more interesting.

Chioggia (pop. 49,800), one of the main fishing ports on the Adriatic, is situated at the southern extremity of the Venetian lagoon, connected to the mainland by a bridge. The most important town after Venice in the lagoon, its unusual urban structure—dating from the late 14th century—survives, with numerous narrow straight *calli* very close to each other on either side of the the the Corso del Popolo and Canale Vena, with almost all the important churches and civic buildings in the centre.

HISTORY OF CHIOGGIA

Chioggia's history has been interwoven with that of Venice since it was first set-tled by inhabitants of Este, Monselice and Padua, in the 5th–7th centuries. Always loyal to Venice, Chioggia suffered destruction at the hands of the Genoese in 1380; but the Venetians under Vettor Pisani succeeded in shutting the Genoese fleet in the harbour immediately afterwards. Its subsequent surren-der marked the end of the struggle between the two rival maritime powers. The saltworks of Chioggia, first developed in the 12th century, were the most impor-tant in the lagoon and survived until the 20th century.

Famous natives include the hydraulic engineer of the Republic Cristoforo Sabbadino (1489–1560); the navigator John Cabot (1425–c. 1500); the musical theorist Giuseppe Zerlino (1517–90); the painter Rosalba Carriera (1675–1757); and the actress Eleonora Duse (1859–1924).

San Domenico

The boats from the Lido (and Venice) dock on the quay by Piazzetta Vigo, with its Greek marble column bearing the lion of St Mark. To the left Canale della Vena, used by the fishing fleet, is crossed by Ponte Vigo (1685), beyond which a calle leads to another bridge in front of the church of **San Domenico**. In the interior, on either side of the west door, are large historical canvases by Pietro Damini (1617–19). The first altarpiece on the south side of *Three Saints* is signed by Andrea Vicentino, who also painted the *Martyrdom of St Peter* on the altar opposite.

Beyond the second altar, *St Paul* is the last known work by Carpaccio (signed and dated 1520). On the right and left of the choir arch, *Deposition and Saints* by Leandro Bassano, and *Christ Crucified and Saints* attributed to Jacopo Tintoretto. On the high altar is a huge wooden Crucifix thought to date from the 15th century or earlier.

Corso del Popolo

The delightful Corso del Popolo, the lively main street, with porticoes and cafés, starts from Piazzetta Vigo. It crosses the town parallel to the picturesque Canale della Vena (with some interesting palaces including Palazzo Grassi at no. 742 and Palazzo Lisatti at no. 609). On the left of the corso stands the church of **Sant'Andrea**, rebuilt in 1743. In the interior, the second south altar has a polychrome wood statuette of St Nicholas (16th century), and in the apse is a small oval painting of *St Andrew*, by the local painter Antonio Marinetti, known as Il Chioggiotto. The sacristy contains a *Crucifix and Saints* by an unknown 16th-century artist, and ivory reliefs in Baroque frames. In the baptistery is an unusual 16th-century marble tabernacle. The detached 13th-century Veneto-Byzantine campanile contains a little museum arranged on its six floors, and the clock dating from 1384 has recently been restored.

A short way further on, on the corso, is the low red building of the **Granaio** probably first built in 1322 (it preserves part of its old carved wood portico with stone columns), but restored in 1864. In the centre of the façade is a little tabernacle with a *Madonna and Child* relief by Jacopo Sansovino. The fish market on the canal behind has specially designed marble slabs on which to display the fish. The large white town hall is a fine 19th-century building. At the far end is a flagstaff supported by three giants (1713). Here is the church of the **Santissima Trinità**, rebuilt by Andrea Tirali (1703). The well-designed interior has an oratory behind the high altar. The two organs bear paintings by Giovanni Battista Mariotti. On the north altar is the *Presentation in the Temple* by Matteo Ponzone. The oratory has a fine ceiling with paintings by the school of Tintoretto.

Across the canal can be seen the church of the **Filippini**. It contains (second south chapel) a *Visitation* by Francesco Fontebasso, and (second north chapel), *Madonna and Child with Saints* by Carlo Bevilacqua (1794).

In the church of **San Giacomo** the ceiling bears a fresco of St James, with remarkable perspective, by Il Chioggiotto. On the third south altar is a painting of *St Roch and St Sebastian* by the school of Bellini, incorporating a 15th-century fresco fragment. On the high altar, a *Pietà* by the 15th-century Venetian school is much venerated as the *Madonna della Navicella* (there are ex-votos all over the church, including some in silver, recently restored). Farther on is the family mansion of the painter Rosalba Carriera, later occupied by the playwright Goldoni (plaque).

The duomo and Museo Civico

The **duomo** has a detached campanile (1347–50). The interior (*usually open 9–12*) was reconstructed by Longhena in 1624. Beyond the third south altar is a small *Madonna and Child* by the school of Giovanni Bellini. The sacristy contains paintings (1593–98) of episodes in the history of Chioggia by Andrea Vicentino, Alvise dal Friso, Pietro Malombra and Benedetto Caliari. On the right of the sanctuary is a Baroque chapel decorated with marbles and stucco work by Giacomo Gaspari. The chapel also contains two oval paintings and a vault fresco by Michelangelo Schiavone. The chapel to the left of the sanctuary contains six fine paintings by Giovanni Battista Cignaroli, Gaspare Diziani, Giambattista Tiepolo (*Torture of Two Martyrs*), Giovanni Battista Piazzetta (attributed) and Pietro Liberi. On the north side is an 18th-century statue of St Agnes signed by Antonio Bonazza, and a polychrome wood statue of St Roch dating from the late 17th century. The marble baptistery contains three statues of *Virtues* by Alvise Tagliapietra.

The north side of the duomo flanks a canal with a pretty marble balustrade decorated with 18th-century statues, including a venerated *Madonna*. Here, at the end of the corso, is the little Torre di Santa Maria (or Porta Garibaldi), the old entrance to the town. The bridge leads over to the ex-church of San Francesco fuori le Mura, a large isolated building which houses the **Museo Civico della Laguna Sud** (*open Tues–Sat 9–1, Thur–Sun 3–6; T: 041 550 0911*). On the ground floor is archaeological material including amphorae (1st–6th-centuries AD) found offshore between Malamocco and Sottomarina; displays relating to the sea defences in the southern part of the lagoon and the changes in the coastline over the centuries; and the geology of the lagoon and its islands. Stairs lead up past a room with exhibits relating to Cristoforo Sabbadino, engineer of the Venetian Republic, and a display of ceramics dating from the 14th to the 18th century found in the district of Chioggia. On the top floor the splendid wooden roof of the former church can be seen.

THE MINOR ISLANDS

The small ACTV motorboat no. 20 from Riva degli Schiavoni runs about every 40mins to San Lazzaro degli Armeni (in just over 10mins) calling at San Servolo. Visitors are admitted to the island of San Lazzaro daily 3.20–5. With the present timetable, the 3.10 boat from Riva degli Schiavoni is the only one which coincides with the opening times of San Lazzaro. San Servolo is not officially open to visitors as it is occupied by various institutes and universities, and is used for international conferences.

San Servolo

The island of San Servolo is the site of one of the oldest and most important Benedictine convents in the lagoon, founded in the 9th century and dedicated to a Roman soldier martyred at the time of Diocletian. It became an important religious centre, and the buildings were transformed in the 18th century by Temanza. Later used as a hospital, it is now owned by the province, and some of the buildings are still being restored. A few palm trees grow on the island. Since 1980 it has been occupied by the workshops of the Venice European Centre for the Trades and Professions of the Conservation of Architectural Heritage (Associazione Europea Pro Venezia Viva). The Venice International University was opened here in 1997. In 2006 a museum opened here dedicated to the grim history of psychiatric hospitals.

San Lazzaro degli Armeni

The island of San Lazzaro degli Armeni, just off the Lido, is distinguished by its tall campanile amidst cypresses and pine trees, crowned by an oriental cupola. Formerly the property of the Benedictines, it was used from 1182 as a leper colony. After a period of abandon, it was given to the Armenians in 1717 as the seat of an Armenian Catholic monastery, founded by Peter of Manug, called Mekhitar (the Consoler). The island has increased in size fourfold since the 18th century, and is beautifully kept by the present community of about 20 Mekhitarian Fathers, some of whom are seminarists. The order is well known in academic and educational fields, and the island is a centre of Armenian culture. It used to be celebrated for its polyglot printing press, established here in 1789: the publishing house, which since 1994 has confined its activity to printing material for the Armenian Congregation, now operates on Punta Sabbioni, although the original presses have been kept on the island.

Visitors are shown the monastery by a father. Outside the entrance is a 14th-century Armenian memorial Cross, and a plaque commemorating Lord Byron.

BYRON IN VENICE

When in 1816 his wife left him and he was threatened with bankruptcy, George Gordon, Lord Byron, settled on this island for a few weeks admiring the monks as 'the priesthood of an oppressed and a noble nation'. He studied Armenian and he even helped publish an Armenian-English dictionary and grammar. The self-styled 'broken dandy' was to stay in Venice on and off for the next few years at the Palazzo Mocenigo on the Grand Canal, during which time he took daily rides on the Lido, and would often enjoy a swim in the lagoon as well as in the canals of the city. The eccentric lifestyle of this famous *milord inglese* caused considerable scandal amongst the Venetians, and it was here in 1819 that he met Contessa Teresa Guiccioli, his 'last attachment', at a reception given by the society hostess Contessa Marina Benzon in her palace on the Grand Canal. His devoted gondolier followed him to Greece in 1824, and attended him on his deathbed at Missolonghi.

In the attractive cloister are some archaeological fragments. The church has 18th- and 19th-century decorations, and stained glass made in Innsbruck in 1901. A fire in 1975 destroyed the sacristy and old library. In the refectory, where the fathers eat in silence while the Bible is read in classical Armenian, is a *Last Supper* by Pietro Novelli (1788). On the stairs are paintings by Palma Giovane, and ceiling frescoes by Francesco Zugno.

In the vestibule of the library is a fine ceiling painting of *Peace and Justice* by Giambattista Tiepolo, and a delightful small collection of antiquities, with an incredible miscellany of objects. The library, which houses some of the 150,000 volumes owned by the monastery in 18th-century carved pearwood cupboards with their original Murano glass, has more frescoes by Zugno. The typical Venetian mosaic floor survives. The Egyptian objects displayed here include a mummy of the 7th century BC, complete with its rare cover of glass and paste beads, donated to the monastery in 1825. Another room has been arranged as a small museum with Armenian books and porcelain and textiles. Steps lead down to Byron's room, where his portrait hangs. In 1980 some of his books, formerly belonging to the Casa Magni at Lerici, were donated to the monastery. The plaster sculpture of Napoleon's son (as the young St John the Baptist) is by Antonio Canova. The monastery also owns a rare 14th-century Indian throne.

A walkway leads across to the Library Rotunda, built in 1967 to house the very precious collection of some 4,000 Armenian manuscripts. Some of these are displayed, including the oldest known Armenian document (862), and an Evangelistery by Sarkis Pizak (1331), as well as rare bookbindings. A very fine Florentine polychrome terracotta relief (c. 1400) is also kept here.

Lazzaretto Vecchio

A hospice for pilgrims was founded on the island of Lazzaretto Vecchio in the 12th century. The island was occupied by the Augustinian monastery of St Mary of Nazareth when in 1423 a hospital was set up here by order of the Republic for plague victims. It was the first-known permanent isolation hospital in Europe, and the name *Lazzaretto* (a corruption of 'Nazareth', with a secondary etymology from Lazarus, patron saint of lepers) was later adopted for all leper hospitals. After a period of use as a military deposit it was abandoned in 1965, and is now a home for stray dogs and cats. There are plans to open a sports centre here.

San Clemente

The island of **La Grazia** was used until recently as an isolation hospital. The island of **San Clemente** lies one and a half kilometres to the south of the Giudecca. (*NB: Access to the island and the church is limited, and can only be arranged through the concierge of the San Clemente Palace Hotel; T: 041 244 5001.*) Originally a quarantine station for overseas visitors to the city, it became in 1645, after a series of outbreaks of the plague in Venice the home of a large Camaldolensian monastery, built around a pre-existing 14th-century church. In the 19th century the monastery was closed down and the buildings housed a hospital until 1992. In 2003 the whole complex opened as a luxury hotel. The island's principal interest lies in the fine monastery church. The dignified Renaissance facade (c. 1485) was restored in the 17th century (1653), at the time the monastery was being built. A number of interesting Baroque monuments to members of the Morosini family, who patronised the church, were added in the same period. (Giorgio Morosini, captain of the Venetian fleet between 1661 and 1663, is commemorated with a fine monument with a bust by Juste le Court.) The interior is dominated by an unusual and ornately decorated 'inner chapel' around the high altar. This chapel, which consciously replicates the proportions of the Holy House of Loreto, was added in 1643 as a votive offering to the Virgin of Loreto in thanks for the passing of a period of plague. Its exterior is embellished with fine marbles, and its eastern outside face bears a fine bronze bas-relief of the *Adoration of the Shepherds* by Giuseppe Mazza (1703).

To the south is the island of **Santo Spirito**, the site of a famous monastery destroyed in 1656. It was later used as an ammunition factory and was abandoned in 1965. It is destined to become a sports centre. **Sacca Sessola**, a large island to the west, was occupied by a hospital until 1980. In 1993 it was given to the United Nations Industrial Development Organisation as a marine research centre, but there are also plans to turn it into a hotel and conference centre.

LE VIGNOLE, LAZZARETTO NUOVO & SANT'ERASMO

Vaporetto no. 13 (about every hour) goes from Fondamente Nuove via Murano (Faro) to Le Vignole, Lazzaretto Nuovo (request stop) and Sant'Erasmo (which has three boat stops, Capannone, Chiesa and Punta Vela). The whole trip as far as Punta Vela takes c. 1hr. A few boats a day continue to Treporti.

Le Vignole

After leaving the lighthouse of Murano, the boat runs straight across the lagoon to the secluded island of **Le Vignole**, with a handful of houses, a few *trattorie* open in summer, and no cars. Most of the market gardens have now been abandoned, although some artichoke beds are still cultivated (and the interesting system of irrigation channels, with small locks to regulate the water, survives in places). Much of the island is now a wilderness, fenced off and inaccessible. A grassy path leads from the landing-stage to a group of pine trees and a public water pump outside the little chapel—with a miniature campanile—of Sant'Eurosia, whose pretty bust is above the door. A service is held here on holidays at 9.30 by the priest from Sant'Erasmo. The only bridge on the island leads over the canal, where an old boat-house on stilts can be seen. At the end of the canal there is a view of the lagoon, and a path leads to the other side of the island where there is a view towards Venice. On the extreme southern tip of Le Vignole is the Fortezza di Sant'Andrea (*described on pp. 331–32*) guarding the Porto di Lido; at present it is not accessible by land.

The island of **La Certosa**, between Le Vignole and Sant'Elena, used to be occupied by an explosives factory; it was abandoned in 1968, and is at present closed to the public, although it may become a public park.

Lazzaretto Nuovo

The Sant'Erasmo boat skirts the shore of Le Vignole and passes mud flats and marshes (known as *barene*), just above the level of the lagoon, with a view out to sea in the distance. At the beginning of the Sant'Erasmo channel is the landing stage on the island of Lazzaretto Nuovo, where the boats call on request. Visitors are met here and shown the island on Sat and Sun off the vaporetto which departs from Fondamente Nuove at 9 and 3.30 (*and at other times by appointment, T: 041 244 4011; or ekos@provincia.venezia.it*). An excellent system has been installed on the landing-stage by which you can activate a 'traffic light' to call the ACTV boats to return in either direction (for Sant'Erasmo or for Venice).

The island was first used as a quarantine hospital to prevent the spread of the plague in Venice in 1468, and was called the Lazzaretto Nuovo to distinguish it from the Lazzaretto Vecchio (*see p. 340 above*), the island just off the Lido, which was already functioning as a hospital for plague victims. It continued to be used as such for a number of centuries, and in the 19th century it was occupied by the Austrian armed forces and used as a deposit for arms in connection with their defence system on Sant'Erasmo, which at that time defended Venice from the open sea. The island was abandoned by the military in 1975, and restoration and excavations began here in the late 1980s with the cooperation of volunteers of a local branch of the Archeoclub d'Italia, who still look after the island.

In the centre of the island is the **Tezon Grande**, one of the largest public buildings in Venice, more than 100m long, although internally it is divided in half. This was used to decontaminate the merchandise from the ships which were made to dock at the island (the goods were then fumigated outside, using rosemary and juniper). The arches were blocked up when it was later used as a military store, but the splendid wood roof has recently been restored. On the walls are some interesting inscriptions made by sailors in the 16th century. The original brick herring-bone pavement survives (the Austrians inserted a wood floor above it, as can be seen from the raised stone blocks). Part of the building is now used as a deposit for the archaeological finds made in the lagoon (*open to scholars*), and there are long-term plans to use the building as a museum dedicated to the plague or to the natural history of the lagoon.

Some 200–300 sailors could be housed on the island in small cells, each with their own kitchen and fireplace and courtyard, built against the perimeter wall. These were demolished by the Austrians, but the floors of some of them have recently been excavated. The gunpowder and ammunition from the ships anchored here was stored in two little edifices which formerly had pyramidal roofs but were altered in the 19th century (one of them has been restored as a delightful little museum dedicated to the history of the island, which contains finds from excavations, including prehistoric flints, Greek and Roman coins, and ceramics from later centuries).

Two well-heads survive on the island, one decorated with the lion of St Mark. Excavations, still in progress, have also revealed remains of a church here (it is known that the Benedictines had a settlement on the island in the 12th century), and, most recently, a cemetery. A second line of walls built by the Austrians survives, and in one of the turrets a little observation platform has been built, which provides a good view of the lagoon.

A path outside the walls leads right round the island in about half an hour—from it there is a very good view of the lagoon and its islands, and you can see its typical vegetation and wildlife (which includes herons, cormorants, swamp hawks, kingfishers and egrets). A sea dyke has recently been constructed on the west side of the island in an attempt to protect it from *acqua alta*, and a pilot project has been carried out close to the landing-stage which demonstrates that water can be purified by plant biology.

Sant'Erasmo

Sant'Erasmo is a tongue of land formed by sediment from the sea, which became important to the defence of the lagoon. Artichokes and asparagus are now cultivated here. The inhabitants (about 800) use vespas or little vespa vans (called *ape*—'bees' rather than 'wasps') to get about. It is an exceptionally peaceful place, with narrow surfaced roads, very few fences, and a scattering of holiday houses. The vegetation includes aster, laurel, blackthorn and tamarisk, and white herons—some of them almost tame—abound at certain times of the year.

A road (built by the Austrians to connect the defences with the island of Lazzaretto Nuovo) leads straight from the Capannone landing-stage past market gardens to the other side of the island. Here the Torre di Massimiliano (*open at weekends, or by appointment; T: 041 523 0642*), a low circular fort built in 1813 and occupied by Daniele Manin in 1848, has been heavily restored and provided with an ugly stone entrance. A small exhibition and model attempts to illustrate its history.

Close by, a new landing-stage for private boats has been built, near a ramshackle trattoria-cum-café (known as 'I Tedeschi'), which is open all year and has lots of tables outside. There is a view straight out to sea through the Bocca di Lido, the northernmost channel which connects the lagoon to the sea: on the left can be seen Punta Sabbioni and on the right the end of the Lido (and the work in progress on the mobile flood barriers).

After the landing-stage of Capannone, the boat follows a channel between the low wall which protects the island and the marshes: the main settlement on the island is at the landing-stage of Chiesa (with a church and a shop), which can also be reached on foot (a pleasant walk) from Capannone. The restaurant called Ca' Vignotto is about 500m from here. From the last stop, Punta Vela, there is a good view of the island of San Francesco del Deserto with its cypresses, and Burano and Torcello in the distance. A few boats a day continue to Treporti.

PRACTICAL INFORMATION

PLANNING YOUR TRIP

When to go

Venice is one of the most visited places in the world, and is only relatively empty of tourists in late November, early December and January. This is the best time to see the major sights, even though the weather can be very cold and wet, and thick sea mists may shroud the city for days at a time. During the most crowded seasons—Easter, September, October, Christmas and New Year, and at Carnival (ten days around the beginning of February before Lent)—Venice often more than doubles its population; but even so it is always possible to escape from the crowds, which tend to congregate around Piazza San Marco and the Rialto Bridge. In July and August the city is crowded during the day, but most of the tourists do not stay overnight.

The climate of Venice is conditioned by its position on the sea; although it is subject to cold spells in winter and oppressive heat on some summer days, there is almost always a refreshing sea breeze. As everywhere in Italy, Venice is crowded with Italian school parties from March until early May.

Websites on Venice

Provincial tourist office (APT):	www.turismovenezia.it
Comune of Venice:	www.comune.venezia.it
ACTV transport system:	www.actv.it
Biennale cultural activities:	www.labiennale.org
Car parks:	www.asmvenezia.it

Disabled travellers

All new public buildings are obliged to provide disabled access and facilities. In the annual list of hotels published by the tourist board, hotels which have such facilities are indicated. Airports and railway stations provide assistance, and for rail travel the disabled are entitled to a *carta blu*, which allows a discount on the fare. Trains equipped to carry wheelchairs are listed in the railway timetable. Most museums and galleries have facilities for the disabled.

Wheelchairs can be wheeled straight onto *vaporetti* (but not *motoscafi*). The greatest obstacles in the city remain the bridges. Ponte delle Guglie over the Cannaregio canal has been equipped with a ramp. A mechanical lift is in operation on Rio dei Fuseri; the key is at present kept nearby at the shop of Testolini (with copies at the APT and *Municipio*). Other lifts have been installed on Riva del Carbon (Palazzo Dolfin-Manin), near San Lio, at Ponte Lunga on the Giudecca, on Murano at Ponte Santa Chiara, and on Burano. For further information contact Informahandicap at the Comune (www.comune.venezia.it; informahandicap@comune.venezia.it).

ARRIVING IN VENICE

By air

Venice airport—Marco Polo—is 9km north of the city (T: 041 260 6111; arrivals information, T: 041 260 9240; departures information; T: 041 260 9250; lost property office; T: 041 260 6436). The best way of reaching Venice from the airport is by water-taxi, which will take approx. 30mins, and cost around €100. A much cheaper option is the Alilaguna motorboat service (T: 041 523 5775) which runs at least every hour from 06.15 to 00.20. It approaches the city across the lagoon via Murano, and calls at the Lido, the Arsenale, San Marco and the Zattere (the entire trip takes 1hr 20mins). Alilaguna also runs an hourly service at peak hours from the airport direct to the Fondamente Nuove, going on to call at Santa Giustina, Riva degli Schiavoni and terminating at San Marco (the entire trip takes just 1hr).

A less pleasant (but cheaper and faster) approach to the city is by ACTV bus to Piazzale Roma, which has services about every 15mins (from 04.40 to 00.40). There is also an excellent bus service which takes 20mins run by ATVO (blue coaches) in conjunction with flight arrivals and departures between the airport and Piazzale Roma (departures from the airport between 08.50 and 23.20). From Piazzale Roma there are 24-hour vaporetto services to all destinations.

By train

The railway station—Stazione Santa Lucia—is right on the Grand Canal, near its west end (T: 892021), and water-taxis, *vaporetti* and gondolas all operate from the quay outside. Some trains terminate at Venezia Mestre on the mainland. Connecting trains continue to Santa Lucia in 5mins. The Santa Lucia left luggage office is open 24 hours a day.

By car

Venice was connected to the mainland by a causeway (Ponte della Libertà) in 1933, and you have to leave your car at one of the garages or open-air car parks (unless you are going on to the Lido, in which case you board the car ferry at Tronchetto). Parking space is very limited (the garages are used also by Venetian residents). At the most crowded times of year automatic signs on the motorway approaches indicate the space available at the time of arrival in the various car parks and garages.

Car parks

Piazzale Roma. This is the most convenient car park (multi-storey garages), with a landing-stage (served by water-bus nos 1, 52, and 82, and an all-night service) on the Grand Canal, and a taxi-stand. The garage at the end of the bridge is the Autorimessa Comunale di Venezia (municipal car park), used almost exclusively by Venetian residents. Other garages here charge considerably more. For information T: 041 272 7211. It is forbidden to park outside in Piazzale Roma; cars are towed away by the police to Via Torino, Mestre.

Isola del Tronchetto. Garage parking for 3,500 cars (open 24hrs); T: 041 520 7555. Also served by vaporetto services to San Marco (no. 82, and an all-night service).

Open-air car parks (cheaper than the garages) are also open at certain times of the year (Carnival time, Easter and summer) at **San Giuliano**, and at **Fusina**. When open (T: 041 272 7211), these are also connected to Venice by vaporetto.

If the car parks are full, cars have to be left on the mainland in **Mestre** or **Marghera**, both connected by frequent bus and train services to Venice. One of the cheapest car parks is in front of Mestre station (trains to Venice every 10mins). There are also car parks on the far (east) side of the lagoon at **Punta Sabbioni**, **Treporti** and **Cavallino**. These are much further away from Venice, but are sometimes less full. They are also connected to Venice by vaporetto (less frequent than the main services).

Information offices and hotel booking offices

The official Venice tourist office, the Azienda di Promozione Turistica della Provincia di Venezia (APT; T: 041 529 8711) has lists of opening times of museums and churches, a list of hotels, details of festivals, and they also sell an excellent map and brief city guide. Their offices are at the Venice Pavilion, Giardinetti Reali (*map p. 407, D3*. Open daily 10–6; T: 041 529 8730); and, nearby, at 71f San Marco (usually open 9–4). Their head office is on Fondamenta San Lorenzo, 5050 Castello (*map p. 403, D4*).

Smaller APT branches at the railway station (*open 8–7*), Piazzale Roma car park, and the airport. There is usually an office open also at the Marghera exit from the Milan *autostrada*. In summer there is an office on the Lido in Viale Santa Maria Elisabetta.

Hotel booking facilities are run by the Associazione Veneziana Albergatori (AVA) at the airport and the car parks at Piazzale Roma (in the Autorimessa Comunale garage). T: 041 522 2264 (from abroad); last-minute booking in Italy: T: 19 917 3309.

GETTING AROUND

Water-buses (*vaporetti*)

ACTV (Azienda del Consorzio Trasporti Veneziano) runs an excellent service. A map of vaporetto routes is given on p. 414. Transport information; T: 041 2424, www.actv.it

Tickets can be bought at tobacconists (*tabacchi*), newsagents, and most landing-stages, although since some landing-stages are not manned, and at others there can be long queues, it is always best to buy a number of tickets at one time. If you board without a ticket, you can buy one from the conductor. Tickets must be stamped at automatic machines on the landing-stages before each journey.

Travelcards. 24-hour or 72-hour tickets (which are stamped just once when the time period starts) give unlimited travel on all the lines . Return tickets and 90-min tickets are also available.

Student and youth fares. Visitors under 29 with a *Rolling Venice* card (*see p. 373*) are entitled to a cheap ACTV ticket which allows unlimited use of the system for 72hrs, and is sold at the manned landing-stages.

The *vaporetti* (nos 1 and 82) which serve the centre of the city can carry up to 220 people, and are more comfortable and provide better views for the visitor than the smaller and quicker *motoscafi* (nos 41, 42, 51 and 52), which make two circular routes of the city and carry around 130 people. Most of the services run at frequent intervals (every 10mins).

Timetables are usually available on request, free of charge, at the manned landing-stages. All the services stick to a rigid timetable and are extremely reliable. Some of the services (including no. 52) are suspended or modified during fog, although the Giudecca ferry, and the services to the Lido, and between Fondamente Nuove and Murano are kept open whatever the weather conditions (using radar). *Motoscafi* nos 41, 42, 51 and 52 can be suspended during *acqua alta*.

Vaporetto routes serving the Grand Canal and the Giudecca

1 (every 10mins by day, from 05.00–23.43): A comfortable vaporetto which runs slowly up and down the Grand Canal stopping at all landing stages on both banks, and providing superb views of the city. It takes just under an hour with 20 stops between Piazzale Roma and the Lido:
Piazzale Roma (car park)–Ferrovia (railway station)–Riva di Biasio–S. Marcuola –S. Stae (Ca' Pesaro)–Ca' d'Oro–Rialto– S. Silvestro–S. Angelo–S. Tomà (Frari)– Ca' Rezzonico–Accademia–S. Maria del Giglio–S. Maria della Salute–S. Marco (Vallaresso)–S. Zaccaria– Arsenale–Giardini–S. Elena–Lido.

82 (every 10mins, from 04.49 to 23.00): S. Zaccaria–S. Giorgio Maggiore– Zitelle–Redentore–Palanca–Zattere– S. Basilio–Sacca Fisola–Tronchetto –Piazzale Roma–Ferrovia (Scalzi)–S.

Marcuola– Rialto–-S. Tomà– S. Samuele–Accademia–San Marco (Vallaresso). It follows the same route on the return journey

N The above two routes are substituted at night by this service, which runs every 20mins: San Zaccaria–S. Giorgio Maggiore–Zitelle–Redentore–Palanca–Zattere–Palanca–S. Basilio–Sacca Fisola–Tronchetto–Piazzale Roma–Ferrovia–S. Marcuola–S. Stae–Ca' d'Oro–Rialto–S. Tomà–S. Samuele–Accademia–Vallaresso–S. Zaccaria– Giardini–Lido. It follows the same route on the return journey

Traghetto The ferry across the Giudecca canal from Zattere to Giudecca (Palanca) comes into operation at certain times of day.

Circular motoscafo routes for the Giudecca, Fondamente Nuove, Murano, Lido

41 (every 20mins, circular route of the city in an anti-clockwise direction): Murano (Museo, Venier, Serenella, Colonna stops)–Cimitero–Fondamente Nuove–Madonna dell'Orto–S. Alvise–

Cannaregio canal (Crea and Guglie stops)–Ferrovia– Piazzale Roma– S. Marta–Sacca Fisola–Palanca– Redentore–Zitelle–S. Zaccaria– Arsenale–Giardini–S. Elena–Bacini–

Celestia–Ospedale–Fondamente Nuove–Cimitero–Murano (Colonna, Faro, Navagero, Museo and Venier stops)

42 (every 20mins, circular route of the city in a clockwise direction): Murano (Venier, Museo, Navagero, Faro and Colonna stops)–Cimitero–Fondamente Nuove–Ospedale–Celestia–Bacini–S. Elena–Giardini–Arsenale–S. Zaccaria–Zitelle–Redentore–Palanca–Sacca Fisola–S. Marta–Piazzale Roma–Ferrovia–Cannaregio canal (Guglie and Crea stops)–S. Alvise–Madonna dell' Orto–Fondamente Nuove–Cimitero–Murano (Colonna, Serenella, Venier and Museo stops)

51 (every 20mins, circular route of the city in an anti-clockwise direction): Lido–S. Pietro di Castello–Bacini–Celestia–Ospedale–Fondamente

Nuove–Madonna dell'Orto–S. Alvise–Cannaregio canal (Crea and Guglie stops)–Riva di Biasio–Ferrovia–Piazzale Roma–S. Marta–Zattere–S. Zaccaria–Giardini–S. Elena–Lido

52 (every 20mins, circular route of the city in a clockwise direction): Lido–S. Elena–Giardini–S. Zaccaria–Zattere–S. Marta–Piazzale Roma–Ferrovia–Cannaregio canal (Crea and Tre Archi stops)–S. Alvise–Madonna dell'Orto–Fondamente Nuove–Ospedale–Celestia–Bacini–S. Pietro di Castello–Lido

61 (every 20mins from Piazzale Roma): Piazzale Roma–S. Marta–S. Basilio–Zattere–S. Zaccaria–Giardini–S. Elena–Lido

62 (every 20mins from Lido): Lido–S. Elena–Giardini–Zattere–S. Basilio–S. Marta–Piazzale Roma

Lagoon services

DM (diretto Murano) direct service to and from Murano every 30mins: Piazzale Roma–Ferrovia–Murano (Colonna, Faro, Navagero, Serenella, Venier and Museo stops)–Ferrovia–Piazzale Roma

LN (Laguna Nord), the service which serves the northern lagoon (and is the quickest approach to Burano, where the ferry for Torcello operates) about every half hour from Fondamenta Nuove: Fondamente Nuove–Murano (Faro)–Mazzorbo–Burano–Treporti–Punta Sabbioni–Lido–Riva degli Schiavone (Pietà); it also runs in the opposite direction from Riva degli Schiavoni (Pietà)–Lido–Punta Sabbioni–Treporti–Burano–Mazzorbo–Murano (Faro)–Fondamente Nuove

T (Traghetto), the ferry between Burano

and Torcello runs every half hour

11 (runs c. every hour, with bus connections for part of the journey). The service between the Lido, Pellestrina and Chioggia, calling at Lido–Alberoni–Santa Maria del Mare–Pellestrina–Chioggia. The trip takes about 1.5 hrs

13 (c. every hour): Fondamente Nuove–Murano (Faro)–Vignole–S. Erasmo (Capannone)–Lazzaretto Nuovo (on request)–S. Erasmo (Chiesa and Punta Vela stops). Some services continue to Treporti

Car ferry (no. 17; c. every hour) from Tronchetto non-stop via the Giudecca canal to the Lido in 30mins (the boat docks near S. Nicolò, north of S.M. Elisabetta)

20 (service by small motorboat) Riva
degli Schiavoni–San Servolo–Isola di

San Lazzaro degli Armeni

Summer services

There are frequent variations in the services which operate in summer. There is normally a direct vaporetto service from Tronchetto to San Marco via the Grand Canal, and from the station via the Giudecca to San Zaccaria. The latest services and timetables have to be checked on the spot.

By water-taxi

Water-taxis (motor-boats) charge by distance, and tariffs are officially fixed. However, it is always wise to establish the fare before hiring a taxi. It is also possible to hire a taxi for sightseeing (hourly tariff). Taxi-stands are on the quays in front of the station (T: 041 716 286), Piazzale Roma (T: 041 716 922), Rialto (T: 041 523 0575), San Marco (T: 041 522 9750), the Lido (T: 041 522 2303) and the airport (T: 041 541 5084). For **Radio taxis** (cars) on the mainland: T: 041 936 137.

By gondola

The famous gondolas of Venice still decorate her canals and manage to keep majestically afloat amidst the many other boats needed to keep the city functioning. Indeed, they proudly take precedence in the busy traffic on the Grand Canal. The gondolier stands above and behind the passenger, and it is fascinating to watch how skilfully he navigates his vessel. They are, however, now used almost exclusively by tourists, except for the excellent gondola ferries across the Grand Canal, which are a quick way of getting from one side to the other. Those who hire a private gondola are supplied with luxurious cushioned armchairs and travelling rugs, and the cost of the memorable, leisurely trip is understandably high; those who take the ferry, each manned by two gondoliers, are usually expected to stand for the short journey, and the very small fare is traditionally placed on the gunwale of the boat. They are a cheap and delightful way of getting about, and provide the opportunity to board a gondola for those who cannot afford to hire one. There have been gondola ferries across the Grand Canal for centuries, and up until the 16th century each ferry had its own guild. Today the gondoliers, all of whom own their boat, take it in turns to man the ferries to ensure some sort of stable income. To hire a private gondola, it is best to agree the fare at the start of the journey. They can be hired for 45-min periods and the tariffs are fixed (information from APT offices), with a night surcharge (after 8pm). There are gondola stands at the Station, Piazzale Roma, Calle Vallaresso (San Marco), Riva degli Schiavoni and Rialto, among other places.

Gondola ferries or *traghetti* cross the Grand Canal in several places (usually marked by green signs on the waterfront, and yellow signs in the nearest calle), either straight (*diretto*) or diagonally (*trasversale*). At present they run at Calle Vallaresso to the Punta della Dogana; Campo Santa Maria del Giglio to the Salute area; San Barnaba (near Ca' Rezzonico) to San Samuele; San Tomà (near the Frari) to Santo Stefano and Sant'Angelo; Riva del Carbon to Riva del Vin in the Rialto area; Santa Sofia (near Ca' d'Oro) to the Rialto markets, San Marcuola to the Fondaco dei Turchi; and at the railway station. They normally operate from 6 or 8am–6 or 7pm including holidays, but some of them close at lunch time. Those at San Barnaba, Riva del Carbon and the railway station operate on a reduced timetable (mostly only in the morning), and the Santa Sofia ferry operates from 7am–8.55pm (holidays 7.30am–6.55pm), and that at San Tomà until 8.30 or 9pm. Services are suspended in bad weather.

An association (*Ente Gondola*) exists for the protection of gondolas. For further information, T: 041 528 5075.

Buses on the Lido

These are run by ACTV. Tickets are stamped on board. From Piazzale Santa Maria Elisabetta (at the vaporetto landing-stage), service A goes to San Nicolò al Lido and, via Lungomare Marconi, to the Casinò and Excelsior Hotel; service B to Alberoni via Malamocco. Bus no. 11 runs the entire length of the Lido (via Malamocco and Alberoni) and has a connecting ferry from Alberoni (Santa Maria del Mare) to San Pietro in Volta and Pellestrina.

ACCOMMODATION

Hotels

Hotels are all listed with their rates and 'star' ratings, from the most expensive 5-star hotels down to the cheapest 1-star establishments in the annual (free) publication of the APT, *Venezia, Where to Stay* (available from tourist information offices). But since these categories do not always reflect quality, we have chosen to list our selection of hotels by location, and loosely by price range.

As Venice has a great number of visitors, it is essential to book well in advance. To confirm the booking you are usually asked for a credit card number. If you have to cancel the booking, you should do so at least 72hrs in advance, but each hotel has its own cancellation policy which you should check when making a reservation. Contact hotels directly for seasonal changes or special offers.

In addition to its famous luxury-class hotels, Venice also has a number of good new middle-range hotels in some of the city's historic small palaces. At the other end of the scale, a number of convents or former convents have recently been transformed into excellent hostel-type accommodation. Rooms are very simple but often have their own modern bathrooms. Rooms in Venetian hotels tend to be particularly small because of the way the city is built.

Dorsoduro has perhaps the best choice of moderately priced hotels away from the most crowded areas. The hotels near Piazzale Roma and the station are good value, but in a much less attractive part of town. Rooms and apartments for rent are also listed in the annual APT hotel list under '*Unità abitative*'.

A selection of hotels, according to location and price range, is given below. Prices are a guideline only for a double room in high season:

€€€€   €1,000+   €€   €150–€300
€€€   €400+   €   €60–€120

BLUE GUIDES RECOMMENDED

Hotels, restaurants and cafés that are particularly good choices in their category—in terms of location, charm, value for money or the quality of the experience they provide—carry the **Blue Guides Recommended** sign: ■. These have been selected by our authors, editors or contributors as places they have particularly enjoyed and would be happy to recommend to others. We only recommend establishments that we have visited. To keep our entries up-to-date, reader feedback is essential: please do not hesitate to contact us (www.blueguides.com) with any views, corrections or suggestions.

Cannaregio

€€€€ **Boscolo Grand Hotel dei Dogi**. *3500 Cannaregio (Fondamenta Madonna dell'Orto), T: 041 220 8111, www.boscolohotels.com. 70 rooms. Map p. 401, E2.*
The special attraction of this hotel is that it is in an exceptionally peaceful and picturesque area of the city, a long way from the tourists, and therefore highly recommended for those who wish to have a quiet holiday. It has a long, walled, shady garden, with fine trees, which stretches all the way to the lagoon (looking towards the island of San Michele), with its own private water-gate (close to the Madonna dell'Orto landing-stage), and a delightful terrace on the waterfront. The 70 bedrooms are pleasantly furnished, although the bathrooms are a little bit small. There are seven particularly grand rooms (more expensive) with high ceilings and chandeliers, and two 'presidential suites' at the bottom of the garden on the lagoon. The restaurant is tastefully decorated and there are lovely

marble floors. It is part of the Boscolo group of hotels, and the service could be more friendly.
€€ **Locanda ai Santi Apostoli**. ■
4391 Cannaregio (Strada Nuova), T: 041 521 2612, www.locandasantiapostoli.com. 11 rooms. Map p. 402, B3.
A charming little hotel on the third floor of Palazzo Bianchi-Michiel dal Brusà on the Grand Canal, with an inconspicuous entrance portal on the busy Strada Nuova (you ring the bell to enter the pretty courtyard and ancient columned *androne* with its well-head and water-gate on the Grand Canal). It is run by the family who still occupies the first two floors of the palace. The rooms (reached by the old staircase or a lift), with wooden ceilings and Venetian marble floors, are particularly spacious, and prettily decorated with colourful matching fabrics, and have excellent bathrooms. They have views over the roofs and are especially quiet. The two splendid rooms on the Grand Canal, each with three windows (includ-

ing a corner window which provides a magnificent view straight down the Grand Canal) are the best (but a bit more expensive). The *portego* has comfortable chairs by the windows overlooking the Grand Canal and Rialto markets. With very friendly service, this is one of the best hotels in its category.

Castello

€€€€ **Danieli**. *4196 Castello (Riva degli Schiavoni), T: 041 522 6480, www. starwoodhotels.com/luxury. 200 rooms. Map p. 407, F2.*
One of the most famous hotels in Venice, frequented since the 19th century by the city's most illustrious visitors, it occupies a neo-Gothic palace and its modern extension (built in 1948), a few steps from the Doge's Palace. Now owned by the Starwood hotel group, the best and most expensive rooms overlook the lagoon. There is an elegant bar. The luxury-class restaurant and bar on the roof has a superlative view. Between 3.30 and 6.30pm this bar is open to the public, and is a splendid place to relax with a bird's eye view of the city. Extremely professional and friendly service.

€€€ **Colombina**. ■ *4416 Castello (Calle del Remedio), T: 041 277 0525, www.hotel-colombina.com. 35 rooms. Map p. 402, C4.*
Opened in 1999, in a pretty palace on the Rio di Palazzo in a very quiet position despite its proximity to San Marco (the Bridge of Sighs is at the end of its canal), with its own water-gate. Three rooms have balconies on the canal and two on the fourth floor have roof terraces with splendid views. The marble floors are 'alla veneziana' and there are nice marble bathrooms. The rooms on the inside overlooking a courtyard cost less (but are larger). No groups, no restaurant.

€€€ **Londra Palace**. ■ *4171 Castello (Riva d. Schiavoni), T: 041 520 0533, www.*

hotelondra.it. 53 rooms. Map p. 407, F2.
Excellent waterfront location for this comfortable boutique hotel, noted for quality of service. Unusually for Venice, it was purpose-built as a hotel (in 1860), giving well-proportioned rooms, with lagoon views or views across the rooftops to San Zaccaria. Some rooms have rooftop terraces. Pleasant bar.

€€€ **Metropole**.■ *4149 Castello (Riva degli Schiavoni), T: 041 520 5044, www.hotelmetropole.com. 63 rooms. Map p. 404, A2.*
An old-established hotel,very well renovated. Its small restaurant (*see p. 362*) is considered one of the best places to eat in Venice. It has a lovely little garden, nice bar, and a series of intimate reception rooms on the ground floor, where there is an eclectic collection (from Crucifixes to nut crackers) displayed in old showcases. The bedrooms are beautifully furnished, and include more expensive suites and penthouses with roof terraces. Water-gate on the side canal. No groups. Rates are reduced off season. Excellent service.

€€ **Locanda Remedio**. *4412 Castello (Calle del Remedio), T: 041 520 6232. 12 rooms. Map p. 402, C4.*
A *dépendence* of the Colombina next door, reached directly across an inner courtyard. This was restructured in 2003 (when the main room received its slightly gloomy décor), but the twelve bedrooms are very pleasant (especially

hose with wooden floors), some of which have disabled facilities.

€€ La Residenza. ■ *3608 Castello (Campo Bandiera e Moro), T: 041 528 5315, www.venicelaresidenza.com. 14 rooms. Map p. 404, B1.*
A small hotel in a lovely old Gothic palace in the peaceful campo beside the church of San Giovanni in Bragora. It has a splendid old frescoed *portego* on the *piano nobile* with a piano and comfortable chairs, where breakfast is served. The rooms are pleasant, and the bathrooms have been modernised. No groups. Cheaper rates Jan–March, July and Aug, and Nov–Christmas.

Dorsoduro

€€ Accademia Villa Maravege. *1058 Dorsoduro (Fondamenta Bollani), T: 041 521 0188, www. pensioneaccademia.it. 30 rooms. Map p. 409, D3.*
An old-established hotel, which has for long been a favourite place to stay with the British and Americans. In an old palace with a *portego* hung with chandeliers, and spacious reception rooms, its special feature is its secluded courtyard (where breakfast is served in warm weather), with a little terrace close to the Grand Canal, and its garden at the back (where four of the most expensive rooms are situated). The rooms have marble Venetian floors or parquet, but some of them are extremely small, and the bathrooms are not large. Sometimes closed in Jan. Book well in advance. The service is sometimes not as friendly as it might be.

€€ La Calcina. *780 Dorsoduro (Zattere), T: 041 520 6466, www. lacalcina.com. 29 rooms. Map p. 409, E4.*
In a delightful position on the Zattere overlooking the Giudecca canal. Ruskin stayed here in 1877. The rooms on the waterfront are more expensive. Parquet floors and modernised bathrooms. It was taken over a few years ago by the niece and nephew of the former proprietor and they have restored it and turned the ground floor into a restaurant (La Piscina), which has tables on the terrace built out onto the water. No groups. The cheapest rates are on weekdays for part of Jan and Feb and from late Nov–21 Dec. Since 2003 the hotel also rents apartments nearby (daily rates).

€€ Locanda San Barnaba. ■ *2785 Dorsoduro (Calle del Traghetto), T: 041 241 1233, www.locanda-sanbarnaba.com. 14 rooms. Map p. 409, D2.*
A delightful little hotel in a 16th-century palace, a few steps from the Ca' Rezzonico vaporetto stop on the Grand Canal. Reopened in 2000, the rooms are simply furnished with parquet floors (no lift). Some of those off the *portego* on the *piano nobile* have 18th-century ceiling frescoes, and the ones on the top floor have a little terrace. There is a pretty garden courtyard (where breakfast is served in warm weather), and a charming little bar and breakfast room. The family who lived here up until the last war still run it and give it its extremely cordial and attentive atmosphere.

€€ Tiziano. ■ *1873 Dorsoduro (Calle Riello), T: 041 275 0071, www. hoteltizianovenezia.com. 14 rooms. Map p. 408, A2.*
A charming hotel opened in 2004 in a small palace in a delightful, peaceful

position far away from the crowds, at the extreme western end of Dorsoduro. The rooms (three of them single) have pleasant wood ceilings and marble floors, and painted furniture, although the bathrooms are rather small. Most of the rooms are on the front, where the window-boxes are always full of flowers, but two of them, which are particularly spacious, overlook the canal. Run by a delightful family, who bake bread and cakes for breakfast. The nearest vaporetto stop is San Basilio on the Giudecca canal.

€€ **Messner**. *216 Dorsoduro (Fondamenta di Ca' Bala), T: 041 522 7443, www.hotelmessner.it. 13 rooms. Map p. 409, F3.*

First opened in 1942, this is still run by a family, and has been renovated over the years. It is on the Rio della Fornace, one of the prettiest and most peaceful canals in the whole of Dorsoduro. It has a tiny garden. Cordial service. It has two *dépendences* on the same canal.

€€ **Seguso**. ■ *779 Dorsoduro (Zattere), T: 041 528 6858, www.pensioneseguso.it. 36 rooms. Map p. 409, E4.*

A charming *pensione* in an historic little house on the Zattere overlooking the wide Giudecca canal. Run by the same family for many years, it retains a delightful old-world atmosphere, with all its furnishings intact. The bedrooms are simply furnished, with marble floors. It has a restaurant with a fixed menu, and the half-board terms are extremely advantageous. Picnic lunch available. The rooms on the front are without bathrooms, but never more than two rooms have to share a bathroom. There are a few tables on the rio outside where you can sit and enjoy the scene. No groups.

Giudecca

€€€€ **Cipriani**. *Giudecca 10, T: 041 520 7744, www.hotelcipriani.com. 104 rooms. Map p. 413, F2.*

The hotel is in a secluded part of the city, on the island of the Giudecca (private motor-boat service), with a large swimming pool, a tennis court, and a renowned restaurant, surrounded by lovely gardens. Favoured by the rich and famous, it was founded by Giuseppe Cipriani of Harry's Bar fame. Open from end March–Nov, with a small *dépendence* in the handsome Palazzo Vendramin, open all year. The luxury-class restaurant called 'Cips' overlooks the Giudecca canal.

San Marco

€€€€ **Gritti Palace**. ■ *2467 San Marco (Campo S. Maria del Giglio), T: 041 794 611, www.hotelgrittivenice.com. 90 rooms. Map p. 406, C3.*

A famous old-established hotel in a 16th-century palace at the beginning of the Grand Canal, furnished with great taste in Venetian style. Less grand than the Danieli, although also owned by the Starwood group, it is one of the smaller luxury-class hotels in the city, in a quiet position near San Marco, with a particularly friendly atmosphere. One of the loveliest rooms is no. 310 on the corner, with a superlative view of the Grand Canal. Terrace restaurant and a renowned foyer bar. Private motor-boat service to the Excelsior and Des Bains hotels on the Lido (with swimming pools and sea bathing). John and Effie Ruskin stayed here in 1851.

€€€ **Europa & Regina**. *2159 San Marco (Corte Barozzi, off Calle Larga XXII Marzo), T: 041 240 0001, res075.europa&regina@westin.com. 192 rooms. Map p. 406, C3.*

In three palaces (including the 17th-century Palazzo Tiepolo) on the Grand Canal opposite the church of Santa Maria della Salute. The most attractive and largest rooms are those with cool marble floors and Neoclassical furniture, others are much simpler and carpeted. Owned by the Starwood hotel group, it has friendly and efficient staff, and most of its clients are American or Japanese. Approached on foot through a very secluded campo. Luxury-class restaurant.

€€€ **Kette**. ■ *2053 San Marco (Piscina S. Moisè), T: 041 520 7766, www.hotelkette.com. 61 rooms. Map p. 406, C2.*

In a very peaceful position in a side calle which ends on a small canal, but also extremely central. A well-run hotel, with a very friendly atmosphere. The spacious rooms, on five floors are pleasantly furnished, with good bathrooms, and overlook either the front or the small canal.

€€ **Al Gambero**. *San Marco 4687 (Calle dei Fabbri), T: 041 522 4384, www. locandaalgambero.com. 27 rooms. Map p. 407, D2.*

A pleasant small hotel with rooms on three floors (no lift), with good marble bathrooms. The pleasantest rooms are on the first floor with pretty windows overlooking the side canal. Charming breakfast room. Restaurant (independently run).

€€ **Flora**. *2283a San Marco (Calle dei Bergamaschi), T: 041 520 5844, www.hotelflora.it. 43 rooms. Map p. 406, C3.*

A hotel with an extremely friendly atmosphere, lovely little garden and comfortable reception rooms. The bedrooms, all very different (no. 23 on the second floor is particularly pleasant), are well furnished, although a little old fashioned and very slightly shabby. Some of the bathrooms are small. No groups.

Santa Croce

€€€ **San Cassiano** (**Ca' Favretto**). ■ *2232 Santa Croce (Calle della Rosa), T: 041 524 1768, www.sancassiano.it. 36 rooms. Map p. 411, E1.*

Entered from the narrow and dark calle between Ca' Pesaro and the church of San Cassiano, this occupies a spacious old palace on the Grand Canal with a lovely ground floor, splendidly fur-

nished with tapestries and chandeliers. The rooms on the floors above (there is no lift) have high ceilings, some rather too heavily furnished (the best are the seven on the Grand Canal). There is a tiny terrace on the waterfront and a little entrance court with tables outside. A number of other pleasant reception rooms. No groups.

Hostels and cheaper accommodation

€ **Venice Youth Hostel** (Ostello per la Gioventù). *Giudecca 86 (Fondamenta Zitelle), T: 041 523 8211, vehostel@tin.it. 260 beds. Map p. 413, p. E2.*
In a splendid position on the Giudecca canal. Closed last two weeks in Jan. Book in advance in writing.

€ **Casa Cardinal Piazza**. *3539a Cannaregio (Fondamenta G. Contarini), T: 041 721 388. 24 rooms. Map p. 401, F2.*
A convent in the splendid Palazzo Contarini-Minelli, in a very peaceful area with a large garden, close to the Madonna dell'Orto vaporetto stop. Run also as a conference centre, and as a home for retired priests. All the rooms have bathrooms. Breakfast is available, and there is a little bar, but otherwise the restaurant is reserved for groups. Curfew at 11pm.

€ **Casa Querini**. ■ *4388 Castello (Campo San Giovanni Nuovo), T: 041 241 1294, www.locandaquerini.com. 11 rooms. Map p. 407, E1.*
A simple hotel in a central but extremely quiet position. Run by a friendly lady, the spacious, air-conditioned rooms, well furnished and with high wooden ceilings, overlook a quiet campo and are kept spotless. In summer you can sit outside in the campo for breakfast.

€ **Centro Culturale Don Orione Artigianelli**. *909a Dorsoduro (Campo Sant'Agnese), T: 041 522 4077, www. donorione-venezia.it. 76 rooms. Map p. 409, E3.*
A 'religious guest house'. Most of the rooms (single, double and triple, all with bathrooms) overlook the two somewhat severe cloisters. In a lovely position in Dorsoduro just off the Zattere. Very peaceful and friendly atmosphere. Breakfast available.

€ **Domus Ciliota**. *2976 San Marco (Calle delle Muneghe, off Calle de le Botteghe), T: 041 520 4888, www.ciliota.it. 60 rooms. Map p. 406, B2.*
Formerly an Augustinian monastery, in a very quiet position, close to Campo Santo Stefano. It was restored in 1999 and all of the rooms (single and double) have bathrooms: the most pleasant are those on the upper floors overlooking the cloister. Breakfast is available. No curfew. (Since it is also used as accommodation for university students, it is easiest to find rooms here from mid-July through August, but there is limited space at other times.)

€ **Istituto Canossiano**. *1323 Dorsoduro (Fondamenta degli Eremite), T: 041 240 9713, cvenezia@fdcc.org. 30 rooms. Map p. 408, C2.*
This convent is on one of the prettiest and most peaceful canals in the Dorsoduro district. Since it also offers accommodation to university students, less than 30 places are available during the academic year (it is much easier to find a room in summer). All rooms (whether single, double or triple) have bathrooms, and some have facilities for the disabled. Most of the rooms are on the interior courtyard, and those on the third floor are the most pleasant. No breakfast. Curfew at midnight unless you make prior arrangements.

€ **Locanda al Leon**. ■ *4270 Castello (Calle Albanesi), T: 041 277 0393, www. hotelalleon.com. 6 rooms. Map p. 407, E2.*
In a very central location, just off Campo San Filippo e Giacomo in a fam-

ily house. Opened in 1998, it has a delightful atmosphere, and is particularly popular with Americans. The door on the street leads straight into a pretty little hall with the staircase. All the rooms (including a family room which sleeps four), simply furnished with great taste, have bathrooms with showers, and overlook the campo, campiello, or calle.

€ **Villa Rosa**. ■ *389 Cannaregio (Calle Misericordia), T: 041 716 569, www. villarosahotel.com. 34 rooms. Map p. 400, B3.*

A pleasant little hotel in an attractive house with a walled courtyard where you can sit or have breakfast in the summer. Although very close to the station and off the busy Lista di Spagna, it is in a surprisingly peaceful position. The rooms, most of them well lit and recently renovated, with air conditioning, are all very different, but the best are those on the upper floors with views over the roofs and balconies. One single room, and a number of family rooms also available. Friendly atmosphere and good value.

Accommodation in the lagoon

The **Lido** is still a famous resort; its two oldest and best-known luxury-class hotels, the Excelsior and Des Bains, are now owned by the Starwood group. There are numerous other pleasant hotels, some with tennis-courts and swimming pools. A delightful family-run hotel (ideal for visitors with children as it has a large garden and is a short walk from the beach) is the €€€ **Villa Mabapa** (*16 Riviera San Nicolò, T: 041 526 0590, www.villamabapa.com, 61 rooms*). In a very quiet position, it also has a good restaurant.

The €€€€ **San Clemente Palace** ■ (*T: 041 244 5001, www.sanclementepalace.com, 200 rooms*) occupies the entire island of **San Clemente**. Palatially restored, its rooms are superbly spacious and well-appointed. Private launch to San Marco.

On the island of **Torcello** is the €€€ **Locanda Cipriani** (*Isola di Torcello 29, T: 041 730 150, www.locandacipriani.com, 6 rooms*). It was opened by Giuseppe Cipriani in 1935 and is now run by his grandson. Its guests have included Ernest Hemingway, Charlie Chaplin, and the British royal family. The rooms (three doubles and three singles), were renovated in 2000. Famous for its luxury class restaurant (half-board terms available), this is one of the most delightful and peaceful places to stay near Venice in winter (*closed Jan; boat takes about 1hr from Venice*). Lovely garden.

On **Burano** is € **Raspo de ua** (*Piazza Galuppi, 560 Burano, T: 041 730 095, www.alraspodeua.it, 7 rooms; map p. 322*). It is the only one-star hotel on an island in the lagoon. Reached by regular boats from the Fondamente Nuove in 40mins. Garden.

FOOD & DRINK

VENETIAN SPECIALITIES

First courses

Risotto is a favourite Venetian first course. The rice is often cooked with fish (*risotto di pesce*), or with squid in their ink (*risotto nero* or *risotto di seppie*). *Risotto primavera* is a vegetable risotto, while *risi e bisi* is a risotto served in spring cooked with fresh peas, celery and ham. As in the rest of Italy, pasta is served in numerous ways in Venice, fish sauces (such as *pasta alle vongole*, spaghetti with clams) being the most common. A winter dish is *pasta e fagioli*, a bean soup made from haricot beans and short pasta seasoned with bay leaves and dressed with olive oil. Polenta in Venice is made from a particularly fine grained maize from the Friuli region and tends to be white, and served in a more liquid form than the yellow polenta popular in the rest of Italy.

A delicate first course, only available in season, is baby grey shrimps (*schie*) served with polenta. Cold hors d'oeuvres include *sarde in saor*, fried sardines, marinated in vinegar and onions, and *granseola*, dressed crab in its shell. Mussels (*cozze*) in their shells are also often served in Venice: if they are *in bianco* they are lightly cooked with parsley and garlic, whereas *cozze al pomodoro* is a richer, spicier dish.

In summer raw (cured) ham (*prosciutto crudo*) is particularly good (the best come from San Daniele in Friuli, or from Parma) served with melon or green figs.

Second courses

Meat Probably the most famous meat dish of Venice is the *fegato alla veneziana*, calf's liver thinly sliced and fried with onions. *Carpaccio*, raw beef sliced very thinly and sometimes served with bitter green salad and parmesan cheese, was invented in Venice, although Venetians now tend to prefer poultry to red meat.

Fish The chief speciality of Venetian cooking is fish, which is always the most expensive item on the menu, and unfortunately only about 20 per cent is now caught locally. Especially good is *dentice* (dentex) or *orata* (gilthead bream), often best served grilled. Much of it, sadly, is not caught in the open sea, but is farmed (*di allevamento*). The cheapest fish dish is usually *fritto misto*, small fried fish, including octopus, squid, cuttlefish and prawns. Crustaceans include *scampi* (the Venetian word for shrimp), which are often served grilled, or boiled and dressed with olive oil, lemon, salt and pepper.

A particularly Venetian dish is *seppie*, cuttlefish (or squid), usually cooked in their own ink and served with polenta. Eel (*anguilla* or *bisato*) is also often served: sometimes grilled, or *alla Veneziana*, cooked in lemon with tuna fish, or marinated in oil and vinegar (with a bay leaf) and then fried with wine and tomato. Crab is also a favourite Venetian dish: *granseola* is dressed crab served cold in its shell; *molecche* (or *moeche*) are soft shelled tender baby crabs, stuffed with egg and fried and served hot (they are only available in early spring); *mezancolle* are also a variety of crab. Scallops are called *capesante*, and clams are *caparozzoli*. *Baccalà* is salt cod: when called *baccalà mantecato* it is cooked in milk, oil and garlic, and blended into a creamy mixture, and when simmered in milk it is called *baccalà alla vicentina*. *Stoccafisso* is unsalted cod. *Sampiero* is John Dory and *Coda di rospo* is angler fish (served grilled or baked). *Zuppa di pesce*, fish stew made with a variety of fish, is a meal in itself.

Vegetables which are particularly good in spring include locally grown asparagus and artichokes. A vegetable found almost exclusively in Venice and the Veneto is *radicchio rosso*, bitter red chicory usually served grilled.

It is worth spending time looking (if not buying) at the splendid Rialto markets, open every morning except Sunday (*see pp. 191–92*), where the local fish and vegetables can be seen in all their splendour.

Desserts

Although Venice has numerous cake shops (*pasticcerie*) which sell delicious confectionery, the city is not famous for its desserts. However, the rich *zabaione*, made with beaten egg yolk and Marsala, and *tiramisù*, made with biscuits, coffee, mascarpone and eggs, are sometimes served in restaurants here, as they are all over Italy.

A great variety of delicious biscuits are baked in Venice, and sold at cake-shops, bakeries or grocery stores. They include *zaeti*, made partly from cornmeal, and *Bussai buranei*, made in Burano. The Venetians are very fond of the simple biscuits (rather similar to rusks) known as *baicoli*, made from wheat flour, sugar, salt and yeast. Fritters (*frittelle*) are often served in bars in winter (especially at Carnival time), flavoured with raisins, pine nuts or lemon peel. Charming biscuits in the form of St Martin on horseback, decorated with sugar and chocolate, are widely available all over the city around the feast of San Martino (11th Nov). At this time *cotognata* (or *persegada*), a sweet jelly made from quinces, is also sold. After Christmas, for Epiphany, *pinsa* is made from cornmeal, fennel seeds, raisins, candied fruit and dried figs.

Drinks

A tradition persists in Venice and the Veneto of taking an *ombra* or *ombreta* (usually before dinner): a glass of white or red wine (or sparkling white wine, *prosecco*) in a *bacaro* or *osteria* (*a selection of these is given on pp. 365–67*). The word *ombra* means shadow, and comes from the stall selling wine by the glass which used to be in Piazza San Marco in the shadow of the campanile. Some people prefer a cocktail: *spritz* is a typical Venetian aperitif made from white wine, bitters and lemon soda, and the *Bellini* is a famous cocktail invented at Harry's Bar, the ingredients of which include champagne and peach juice. *Mimosa* is a cocktail made with orange juice. *Ombre* or cocktails are served with delicious savoury snacks (*cicchetti*), a great Venetian speciality, which may include fried fish, cooked or raw vegetables, a piece of tasty cheese, a creamy mixture of salt cod, olives, *sarde in saor*, amongst many other possibilities.

Wine

In restaurants the house wine (*vino della casa* or *vino sfuso*) varies a great deal, but is normally of average standard and reasonable price. The best wines produced in the Veneto are described in the box overleaf. Other wines readily available in Venice include those from the Collio hills in the Friuli region, where white varieties such as Pinot Bianco, Pinot Grigio, Verduzzo, Tocai and Chardonnay are produced. On the Friuli plain, the dominant variety is Merlot. Picolit is a medium-sweet white wine, also from the Friuli, which was drunk with enthusiasm during the days of the *Serenissima*, and exported to the courts of Europe in the 18th century (and much appreciated by Goldoni). Another indigenous grape is Terrano, producing an intense wine with an unusual acidic taste.

WINE OF THE VENETO

Viticulture in the modern sense of the word has been practised in the Veneto since the 7th century BC. In the Middle Ages the land under vine increased dramatically with plantations made by the monastic orders, mainly the Benedictines. The wine regions of Verona, Vicenza and Treviso developed as a result of this. The whole area around Venice, including the islands of the lagoon (though not the parts facing the open sea) were all covered in vineyards. Indigenous grape varieties include Corvina, Garganega, Raboso and Rondinella (grown chiefly around Verona) and Barbera, Riesling Italica and Renana. Cabernet and all three Pinots (Bianco, Nero and Grigio) are also popular. The best known wines of the Verona region are Valpolicella, Bardolino (red), Soave (white) and Recioto (*passito*).

Recioto is perhaps the region's most important wine, largely because of the unique way in which it is made. *Appassimento* is the most characteristic wine-making technique of the Veneto, and involves naturally drying the grapes before pressing, either on straw or by leaving them to hand and shrivel on the vine. This latter method was widespread throughout the Mediterranean, from Spain to the Greek islands. One of the most refined examples of this ancient technique survives in the Veneto, in the hills that border Verona to the north. The results are the red Amarone (where the wine ferments to dryness) or sweet Recioto (where some residual sugar remains).

The origins of the name Recioto are not documented, though it may derive from a word denoting the 'ears' of a bunch of grapes: a protruding cluster which caught more sun and thus developed more sweetness. What is certain is that the wine known to the ancient Romans as *Retico* was one and the same. Virgil considered it one of the finest wines known to man, second only to the Neapolitan Falernian. Cassiodorus, minister of the Gothic emperor Theodoric, has left a description of *Retico* to posterity. Several centuries later, red and white wines from Verona, white Recioto from Vicenza, and Passito from Treviso, were being apostrophised as the Wine of Doges. Among the best such wines made today are Moscato and Passito di Bagnoli, Recioto di Gamberella, Torcolato Breganze and—the two most important—Recioto di Soave and Amarone della Valpolicella.

Another characteristic wine of the Veneto is the sparkling Prosecco, whose heartlands lie among the hills of Conegliano-Valdobbiadene. Prosecco is a grape variety which has given its name to the wine from which it is made. It is quite a sight hanging on the vine: enormous bunches of huge, round, yellow berries, whose intoxicating, muscat-like scent fills the air at harvest time. Bottled Prosecco comes in two types: the gently fizzing *frizzante*, and the *spumante* bubble-bath. The fresh, playful, flowery character of the grape is present in both. Its qualities of youthfulness and optimism and its low alcohol content make it a drink which can be taken quite harmlessly at any time of the day or night.

RESTAURANTS

A selection of a few restaurants—divided into five categories according to price per person for dinner (bottled wine excluded)—is given below. Those in the lower categories are almost invariably the best value, particularly those in the €€ range, but they can be crowded and are usually much less comfortable than the *trattorie* and restaurants in the higher price ranges.

The restaurants below have generally been chosen first and foremost for the excellence of their food—in all categories and with prices which match—and those in quiet, sometimes out-of-the-way, spots have usually been preferred. Blue Guide recommended restaurants are marked: ■. (*For information on Blue Guides Recommended, see p. 351.*)

€€€€	€80 a head or over
€€€	€50–80 a head
€€	€20–40 a head
€	€20 a head, or less

Cannaregio

€€€ Anice Stellato. ■ *3272 Fondamenta della Sensa at Ponte de la Malvasia, T: 041 720 744. Closed Mon and Tues. Map p. 401, D2.*
Opened in the last few years by two enterprising young Venetian couples, and offering traditional Venetian fare, with an interesting menu which changes frequently. Dishes include pasta with filletted sardines, tomato, olives, pine nuts and orange, and swordfish steak. The bread and desserts are home-made. The simple low interior supported by an old column is very pleasant with bare wood tables, and in warm weather four tables are put out on the fondamenta. Very small; essential to book. During the morning local people frequently call in for a glass of wine.
€€ Alla Vedova (Ca' d'Oro). ■ *3912 Calle del Pistor, directly across the Strada Nuova from the Calle di Ca' d'Oro, T: 041 528 5324. Closed Thur and Sun lunch. Map p. 402, A2.*
This has been an excellent place to eat cheaply for many years, and has a delightful atmosphere—used by the Venetians both as a *bacaro* for a quick drink with excellent *cicchetti* at the counter, and as a trattoria, where you can also order a plate of *cicchetti*, or one of the 5 or 6 first courses and 5 or 6 second courses, all of them extremely good (usually including *spaghetti alle vongole*, *fritto misto di pesce*, and *polpette* (meat balls). Very reasonably priced. Professional friendly service.
€€ Antica Mola. *2800 Fondamenta degli Ormesini, T: 041 717 492, just by the Ghetto Nuovo bridge. Map p. 401, D2.*
A very simple trattoria frequented mostly by Venetians. It is particularly pleasant in summer when tables are put outside on the canal front. The *antipasto laguna* is substantial enough to have as a main course. Down-to-earth menu, mostly fish, and reasonably priced.

Castello

€€€ **Al Covo**. *3968 Campiello della Pescaria, off Riva degli Schiavoni near San Giovanni in Bragora, T: 041 522 3812. Closed Wed and Thur. Map p. 404, B2.*
Run by a professional chef, Cesare Benelli, and his charming wife Diane. It has a few tables outside in the quiet little campiello. Excellent fresh fish exclusively from the lagoon or the Adriatic, and seasonal locally-grown vegetables. Very imaginative menu with specialities including raw, fried and grilled fish, shellfish, home-made pasta, and also meat dishes. Home-made desserts by Diane.

€€€ **Corte Sconta**. *3886 Calle del Pestrin, T: 041 522 7024. Closed Sun and Mon. Map p. 404, B1.*
Very inconspicuous in a narrow calle, a few steps from San Giovanni in Bragora, off Calle del Forno which runs into the Riva degli Schiavoni. This is famous amongst Venetians for its good fish. Excellent hors d'oeuvres. Unassuming old-style restaurant which retains its old red painted sign.

€€€ **Da Remigio**. ■ *3416 Salizzada dei Greci, T: 041 523 0089. Closed Mon evening and Tues. Map p. 404, B1.*
Run by a delightful family, with excellent fish, caught locally. Specialities include raw fish soaked in grapefruit juice. On a busy calle, frequented by Venetians, with a bustling (sometimes almost too noisy) atmosphere.

€€€ **L'Osteria di Santa Marina**. *5911 Campo Santa Marina, T: 041 528 5239. Closed Sun and Mon lunch. Map p. 402, C3.*
A traditional Venetian trattoria with good food. Comfortable interior.

Besides à la carte, it offers several different fixed menus, with particularly interesting dishes such as *mantecato d'orzo al nero di seppia, su crema di zucca e scampi* (puréed barley with squid in their ink, with pumpkin and scampi sauce), raw fish.

€€€ **Metropole**. *4149 Riva degli Schiavoni, in the 4-star hotel of the same name, T: 041 520 544. Map p. 404, A2.*
Known simply as the 'Met', this tiny restaurant has become famous in recent years because it is run by the brilliant young chef Corrado Fasolato, who has enjoyed international recognition. It operates in a room on the front overlooking the Riva, or in the garden behind in warm weather. Very unusual dishes include *ravioli a torre*, served in a pile, with a rabbit and apple filling, and *capriolo cotta al vapore di erbe con tortino di castagne e salsa al miele e caffè* (venison steamed with herbs accompanied by a chestnut mousse with a honey and coffee sauce): more ordinary fare includes *baccalà* (salt cod) cooked in a great variety of ways.

€€ **Mascaron**. *Calle Lunga Santa Maria Formosa, T: 041 522 5995. Closed Sun. Map p. 403, D4.*
Next to the **Mascheretta** (*T: 041 523 0744*), which has been a well known *bacaro* for many years, this is a simple trattoria typical of Venice with a pleasant atmosphere, which serves good fish as well as standard fare. The hors d'oeuvres and first courses are especially good, including *spaghetti alla scogliera* (pasta with shell fish). You can also have just a simple snack, instead of a full meal.

Dorsoduro

€€€ **Antica Locanda Montin**. *1147 Fondamenta di Borgo, T: 041 522 7151. Closed Wed. Map p. 409, D3.*
An old-established restaurant on one of the most picturesque and quiet canals in the Dorsoduro district. Long popular with the British. Its great feature is its very large shady garden with a lovely pergola: a delightful, peaceful place to eat outside in warm weather. It usually has good fish, and a speciality are the *tortelli ripieni di zucca* (pasta stuffed with pumpkin), and there is a wide range of desserts. It also operates as a reasonably-priced hotel, with just 12 very spartan rooms, not all of them with bathrooms, on the floor above.

€€€ **Ai Gondolieri**. *366 Fondamenta Ospedaletto (very close to the Peggy Guggenheim Collection), T: 041 528 6396. Closed Tues. Map p. 409, E3.*
A very pleasant place to have a reasonably-priced meal. The little old-world interior retains its old furnishings. Specialises in meat and vegetables, rather than fish, but serves good risotto.

€€€ **Lineadombra**. *Fondamenta delle Zattere (Ponte dell'Umiltà), T: 041 241 1881. Closed Wed. Map p. 406, C4.*
Recently opened, with a very imaginative menu, and friendly staff. It has modern décor in the three little rooms, one of which is upstairs, but it is particularly pleasant when it is warm enough to eat out at one of the tables on the Giudecca canal. Its view must be one of the best from any restaurant in Venice.

€€€ **Oniga**. *Campo San Barnaba, T: 041 522 4410. Closed Tues. Map p. 409, D2.*
Opened quite recently, this is considered a sound, if perhaps a little pretentious, restaurant. It has a comfortable interior, and tables also outside in the campo.

€€€ **Riviera**. ■ *1473 Zattere, T: 041 522 7621. Closed Mon and Wed. Map p. 408, B3.*
In the little building of the ex-Scuola dei Luganegheri, the grocers' confraternity. It has a charming statue of St Anthony Abbot, appropriately with his pig, on the façade. No frills, no fusion, just good home cooking from a Venetian woman's kitchen. Monica cooks; her brother takes care of customers on the other side of the hatch. Good value set menus; brisk, friendly service.

€€ **L'Incontro**. *3062 Rio Terrà Canal, Campo Santa Margherita, T: 041 522 2404. Closed Mon and Tues morning. Map p. 408, C2.*
Run by Sardinians, this offers particularly good meat, including pork, cooked in the traditional Sardinian way. It has two small rooms, but in warm weather it has tables outside on the wide *rio terrà*. Conveniently placed in the centre of the lovely district of Dorsoduro. It offers a lunch menu.

Giudecca

€€€ **Altanella**. *Calle delle Erbe, T: 041 522 7780. Closed Tues evening and Wed. Map p. 412, B3.*
In a very inconspicuous position halfway down a narrow calle which leads away from the waterfront at the Ponte Lungo. An old-established family-run restaurant with a devoted clientèle, mostly

foreigners. It can be stuffy in the winter, so it is at its best in the summer when you can eat outside on the simple terrace on a side canal. Specialities include *polenta al nero di seppia* (polenta with cuttlefish cooked in their ink), *bigoli in salsa* (spaghetti with an onion and anchovy sauce), bean soup, and the white grappa with raisins served at the end of the meal.

San Marco

€€€€ **Harry's Bar**. *Calle Vallaresso, T: 041 528 5777. Map p. 407, D3.*
Probably the most famous restaurant and cocktail bar in Venice. It has had a devoted international clientèle since it was opened by the Cipriani in the 1920s.
€€€€ **Quadri**. *120 Piazza San Marco, T: 041 528 9299. Map p. 407, D2.*
Above the famous café of the same name (*see p. 70*), this was opened in 1844. With just two extremely elegant rooms hung with chandeliers overlooking the Piazza, it has for long been considered one of the best luxury-class places to eat in Venice. The charming old-fashioned atmosphere and highly professional service recalls the very best French restaurants. There is also a set menu.
€€€ **Da Arturo**. *3656 Calle degli Assassini, between Calle della Mandola and Campo San Fantin, T: 041 528 6974. No credit cards. Map p. 406, C2.*
A tiny restaurant (booking essential) but extremely good. One of the few restaurants in Venice which does not specialise in fish, it is especially renowned for its excellent vegetables, imaginatively cooked, and meat dishes.

San Polo

€€€€ **Osteria Da Fiore**. ■ *2202 Calle del Scaleter, T: 041 721 308. Closed Sun and Mon. Map p. 411, D2.*
In a very narrow out-of-the-way calle by Ponte Bernardo, still with its old red and yellow sign. A tiny terrace on the canal, just large enough for a table for two, has a view of the superb Gothic Ca' Bernardo. Run by Mara and Maurizio Martin, this is considered by many to be the best restaurant in Venice in its class. The menu consists exclusively of fish and vegetables. It can serve just 50, and the interior, devoid of all fussy decoration, has a club atmosphere (with one table filling a room all on its own).
€€€ **Antiche Carampane**. ■ *1911 Rio Terrà Rampani, T: 041 524 0165. Closed Sun and Mon. Map p. 411, E2.*
Tucked away in a very quiet spot near Campo Sant'Aponal (the nearest vaporetto stop is San Silvestro). Its name recalls the Ca' Rampana, which in the 16th century was rented by prostitutes from the Rampana family. Round the corner is Ponte delle Tette (where 'topless' courtesans could be found in Republican days), and Fondamenta della Stua, named after one of the numerous 'bathhouses' which used to exist in the city. Opened some 25 years ago by the same cordial family who still runs it, this is a very small restaurant with a simple little interior, and tables outside in summer on the narrow calle. Popular and well-known for the excellence of its food,

including fish served in a great variety of ways—as an hors d'oeuvre, with pasta, baked, or fried—as well as meat dishes including Angus steaks, and an excellent wine list. Home-made desserts and sweet white wine served with Venetian biscuits. €€€ **Alla Madonna**. *594 Calle della Madonna, T: 041 522 3824. Closed Weds. Map p. 411, F2.* Off Riva del Vin, very near the Rialto.

According to some Venetians this famous old trattoria still serves the best fish in the city, and it has a faithful local and foreign clientèle. Its size (it can serve up to 250 people at a time) and its numerous rooms mean that it can be chaotically busy, and so it is sometimes difficult to enjoy your meal in peace. However, the service is professional and the atmosphere is that of old Venice.

Restaurants in the lagoon

Murano has a number of simple *trattorie*, including the **Osteria al Duomo**, at the foot of Ponte San Donato on Fondamenta Maschio (*T: 041 527 4303; map p. 314*). There is also a good bakery on this fondamenta.

    Burano has a number of fish restaurants, notably **Da Romano** (*221 Piazza Galuppi, T: 041 730 030; map p. 322*). On Mazzorbo there is **Trattoria alla Maddalena** (*T: 041 730 151, closed Thur*), a simple little restaurant on the waterfront by the landing-stage, which serves fish and game.

    Torcello has the famous luxury restaurant **Locanda Cipriani** ■, (*T: 041 730 150, closed Jan; map p. 322*) and a number of others.

    Good places to eat on the **Lido** include **Trattoria Andri** (*21 Via Lepanto, T: 041 526 5482*), **Al Porticciolo**, **Da Valentino**, and **Favorita** (all at Malamocco). **Trattoria Scarso**, also at Malamocco (*T: 041 770 834, closed Tues*) is a pleasant, family-run fish restaurant with a large garden. **Da Nane al Canton** and **Da Memo** are pleasant places at **San Pietro in Volta**.

    Chioggia has good fish restaurants including **El Gato** (*Campo S. Andrea, T: 041 401 806*) and **Garibaldi** (*T: 041 554 0042*). A cheaper trattoria (and pizzeria) is **Vecio Foghero** (*91 Via Scopici, T: 041 404 679*).

    On **Sant'Erasmo** there is **Vignotto** (*agriturismo*) in Via Forti; **Le Vignole** has only one trattoria, **All'Oasi** (*T: 041 520 4207, open May–Sept*).

Bacari

Osterie, or *bacari* as they are known in Venice, are cheap eating places which sell wine by the glass and good simple food (usually crowded and often less comfortable than normal *trattorie*). Many of these are open only at lunch time and closed at weekends.

Da Mario. *Fondamenta della Malvasia (Rio Malatin), near Santa Maria del Giglio, San Marco, Open 12–2.30 & 7.30–9.30. Map p. 406, C3.* Outside it vaunts its old red-painted sign, and the cosy interior is crammed full of every kind of decoration. In the hands of the efficient *padrona*, Anna Lisa Masiero, with a character all her own, this is a very popular traditional eating place. Apart from the simple gen-uine food, you will eat in the company of Venetians from all walks of life: the clientèle changes dramatically from the earliest customers at 12 (a notice in the window declares that for the first hour only *operai*, in other words, workmen who only get a one-hour lunch break between 12 and 1, will be served) to the businessmen who arrive around 1.30. You have the impression that the prices are thought up on the spot according to sympathy, and that only a happy few are allowed to chose their meal by a visit to the kitchen. However, 'tourists' are offered an excellent set menu (which includes fish).

Do Mori. ■ *Off Ruga Vecchia S. Giovanni Elemosinario, between 429 Sottoportego dei Do Mori and the parallel Ramo Prima Gallazza, with an entrance on each, San Polo, T: 041 522 5401. Open 8.30am–8.30pm except Sun. Map p. 411, E2.*
A tiny *bacaro* without tables, but with one or two seats at a counter, and the ceiling hung with pewter pots. Although just a few steps from the busy Rialto markets, it is in a quiet corner. This is a favourite place for Venetians to have an aperitif before lunch or dinner, and it is one of the most genuine such places left in the city. Good wine sold by the glass from large demijohns, and a wide selection of excellent *cicchetti*.

Osteria ai Canottieri. *690 Fondamenta San Giobbe, Cannaregio, T: 041 717 999. Closed Sun and Mon. Map p. 400, A2.*
A straightforward little restaurant, with tables outside on the canal in summer.

Osteria al Ponte. *(often called 'Bacaro della Patata' or 'Patatina'), Calle dei Saoneri near San Polo church, T: 041 523 7238. Map p. 411, D3.*
This has seating and is usually busy with Venetians at lunch time.

Specialising in potatoes, and in particular uniquely good fried potatoes, which are always hot and sizzling around 12 and 6pm. The nickname comes from the fact that if you eat just potatoes, you are charged for '*una patata*'.

Osteria Antico Dolo. *778 Ruga Vecchia S. Giovanni Elemosinario (opposite the end of Sottoportego and Calle dei Cinque), San Polo, T: 041 522 6546. Map p. 411, E2.*
Good *cicchetti* are served as hors-d'oeuvres, and other dishes include *zuppa di fagioli* (bean soup), *minestra di trippa* (tripe), and *polenta*.

Pane e Vino. ■ *Campo Angelo Raffaele, Dorsoduro, T: 041 523 7456. Closed Wed. Map p. 408, B2.*
In a delightful position away from the crowds, behind the church of the Angelo Raffaele. Reasonably priced and nicely run, with a warm interior and tables out in the campo. *Cicchetti* served at lunch time, as well as more substantial dishes (the first courses are particularly good). A popular place to eat for Venetians, its clientèle includes staff and students from the nearby university architecture faculty.

Quattro Ferri. *Calle Lunga San Barnaba, 2754a Dorsoduro, T: 041 520 6978. Closed Sun. Map p. 409, D2.*
At present considered one of the best and most reasonably priced simple *trattorie* in town. Air conditioning in summer. Specialities include *spaghetti alla scogliera* (spaghetti with seafood) and *schie con polenta caldo* (baby grey shrimps with polenta).

San Bartolomeo, *5424 Calle della Bissa, San Marco. T: 041 522 3569. Map p. 407, D1.*
Above Venice's most famous *rosticceria*, specialities include fish risotto, cuttlefish and *baccalà* (salt cod).

Schiavi (or **Vini al Bottegon**). ■ *Rio San Trovaso, Dorsoduro. T: 041 523 0034. Closed Sun afternoon. Map p. 409, D3.* Known simply as *Il Bottegon*, this is one of the most typical of all the Venetian *bacari*, run by a cordial and indefatigable Venetian and his sons, who are always busy serving drinks and excellent, imaginative *cicchetti*. Wide selection of wines, but no seating.

Vecio Fritolin. *2262 Calle della Regina, at the end of Sottoportego de Siora Bettina, Santa Croce, T: 041 522 2881. Open midday–11pm. Closed Mon. Map p. 411, E2.* A very simple small restaurant with good fresh fish (they are proud not to own a freezer). It is said that in the old days the fried fish was served together with forks chained to the counter.

Food for picnics

Bars sell ready-made sandwiches (*tramezzini*), which can be very good (one of the best places to find them is the **Bar dei Nomboli**, *2717c Rio Terrà dei Nomboli, San Polo; map p. 411, D3*). Sandwiches (*panini*) can also be made up on request at grocery shops. There are excellent food markets open in the mornings (except Sunday) at the Rialto and in Rio Terrà San Leonardo (Cannaregio; *map p. 401, D3*), and supermarkets Rio Terrà della Scoazzera (Dorsoduro; *map p. 408, C2*), on the Zattere (Dorsoduro; *map p. 408, B3*), in Salizzada San Lio (Castello; *map p. 402, C4*), and at Piazzale Roma (*map p. 410, A2*).

Cafés

Cafés and bars which are open from early morning to 8 or 9pm (those with tables outside remain open longer on summer evenings), serve numerous varieties of excellent refreshments which are usually eaten standing up. You should pay the cashier first, and show the receipt to the barman in order to get served. Italians sometimes leave a small tip for the barman, but this is certainly not expected. If you sit at a table you are charged considerably more (at least double) and given waiter service (you should not pay first).

The two most famous cafés in the city are **Florian** and **Quadri** in Piazza San Marco, with tables outside and orchestras—you are charged extra for your magnificent surroundings. They are described on pp. 70–71. **Harry's Bar** (*map p. 407, D3*) is the most celebrated cocktail bar, but the **Danieli** and **Gritti** hotels (*map p. 407, F2 and p. 406, C3*) also have foyer bars, renowned for their cocktails, décor and atmosphere.

Among the best cafés for ice-cream (*gelaterie*) are **Nico**, on the Zattere (*map p. 409, D3*), and **Causin** in Campo Santa Margherita (*map p. 408, C2*).

Cake-shops (pasticcerie)

Many Venetians consider **Tonolo**, on the corner of Calle dei Preti and Calle San Pantalon (Dorsoduro; *map p. 409, D1*) the best *pasticceria* in the city. **Colussi** in Calle Lunga San Barnaba (Dorsoduro; *map p. 408, C2*) has been run for many years by a delightful Venetian couple, and it still survives (though it has very erratic opening hours and can be closed for long periods). Others include **Bonifacio**, 4237 Calle degli Albanesi, off Salizzada San Provolo, between St Mark's and San Zaccaria (*map p. 407, E2*); **Marchini** in Calle del Spezier (San Marco; *map p. 406, C2*). **Rosa Salva** has three shops, in Merceria San Salvador (5020 San Marco; *map p. 407, D1*), Calle Fiubera (951 San Marco; *map p. 407, D2*) and Campo Santi Giovanni e Paolo (Castello; *map p. 402, C3*). **Dal Cò**, Calle dei Fabbri (San Marco; *map p. 407, D2*); **Canonica**, Campo Santi Filippo e Giacomo (Castello; *map p. 407, E2*); **Rizzardini**, Campiello dei Meloni (San Polo; *map p. 411, E3*); **Didovich** in Campo Santa Marina (Castello; *map p. 402, C3*); and **Boscolo** in Campiello dell'Anconetta, near San Marcuola (Cannaregio; *map p. 401, D3*).

MUSEUMS & CHURCHES

Museum opening times vary and often change without warning; those given in the text should therefore be accepted with reserve (it is sometimes a good idea to telephone in advance to make sure of the times). A current list of opening times is always available at the APT offices. Ticket offices close one hour before the museum. Opening hours for Sundays apply also to public holidays (*giorni festivi*).

At certain times of the year the opening hours of some museums may be prolonged (when financed by sponsor companies). Some museums are closed on the main public holidays: 1st January, Easter, 1st May, 15th August, and Christmas Day, although there is now a policy all over Italy to keep at least some of them open on these days: information can be obtained about these from the APT offices.

Admission charges vary between about €2 and €7. There is a combined ticket for the Doge's Palace, Museo Correr and Museo Archeologico; and for the 18th-century museums (Ca' Rezzonico, Palazzo Mocenigo and Casa Goldoni); and for the island museums (Murano and Burano). EU citizens under 18 and over 65 are entitled to free admission to state museums and monuments in Italy (on production of an identity card proving your age). EU students between the ages of 18 and 26 are also entitled to a reduction (usually 50%) to state museums, and some other museums have special student tickets.

For one week during the year (the *Settimana per i Beni Culturali e Ambientali*), usually in March, there is free entrance to all state-owned museums in Italy, and others are opened specially.

Churches

Where possible, opening times have been given in the text. For some years now there have been various projects to open as many churches as possible for certain hours of each day. The association called Chorus provides access to the following 16 churches with a single admission ticket (or, much cheaper, combined ticket for them all): Santa Maria del Giglio, Santo Stefano, Santa Maria Formosa, Santa Maria dei Miracoli, San Giovanni Elemosinario, the Frari, San Polo, San Giacomo dell'Orio, San Stae, Sant'Alvise, the Madonna dell'Orto, San Pietro di Castello, the Redentore, Gesuati, San Sebastiano, and San Giobbe. These are open Mon–Sat 10–5; except for the Frari which is open Mon–Sat 9–6; Sun, including July and Aug, 1–6.

Six other churches are kept open free of charge by an association called Imago: the Carmini (Mon–Sat 2.30–5); San Trovaso (Mon–Sat 2.30 or 3–5.30 or 6); San

Giovanni in Bragora (Mon–Sat 9–11 & 3.30–5.30); San Salvatore (Mon–Sat 9–12 & 3–6); San Barnaba (9.30–12.30), and San Moisè (11.30–2.30). This association also keeps open the basilica and bell-tower of Torcello (entrance fee).

Lights (coin-operated) have now been installed in almost every church to illuminate frescoes and altarpieces. As a result it is essential to carry a great deal of change (if you run out, the sacristan or custodian can usually help). Some churches now ask that sightseers do not enter during a service, but normally visitors not in a tour group may do so, provided you are silent and do not approach the altar in use. If you are wearing shorts or have bare shoulders, you can sometimes be stopped from entering. Churches in Venice are very often not orientated. In the text, the terms north and south refer to the liturgical north (left) and south (right), with the high altar at the east end.

GENERAL INFORMATION

Acqua alta

Acqua alta, a high tide above 110cm, occurs frequently throughout the year (especially between Sept and April). Sirens are sounded when an *acqua alta* is imminent. The flood tide usually lasts 2 or 3 hours, and *passarelle* or duck-boards are laid out in Piazza San Marco, by the landing-stages and in some of the *calli*. This raised thoroughfare throughout the city totals about 4km. A map showing the *calli* which do not usually get flooded, and where the duckboards are set up, is provided in the ACTV timetable and posted up in the ACTV landing-stages. However, it is not possible to get about the city on these occasions without wellington boots. Some of the ACTV water-buses (including nos 41, 42, 51 and 52) are suspended during an *acqua alta* because they are unable to pass below the road and rail bridges near the station. The Centro Previsioni e Segnalazioni Maree (Palazzo Cavalli, San Marco 4090, T: 041 274 3787 or 041 241 1996) gives information on tides. For a 24hr recorded message, T: 041 520 6344 or 041 520 7722.

Banking services

Banks are usually open Mon–Fri 8.30am–1.30pm, and for one hour in the afternoon (usually 2.45–3.45pm or 3.15–4.15pm); some banks also stay open on Sat morning but are always closed on holidays. They close early (about 11am) on days preceding national holidays.

Church services

Roman Catholic services: On Sunday and, in the principal churches, often on weekdays, Mass is celebrated from the early morning up to midday and from 5.30–7pm. High Mass, with music, is celebrated in St Mark's at 10am on Sun. At 11am Gregorian chant is sung at San Giorgio Maggiore. Mass in English is also held at San Giuliano.
Religious festivals: On saints' days Mass and vespers with music are celebrated in the churches dedicated to the saints concerned. On the Feast of St Mark (25th April) spe-

cial services are held and the Pala d'Oro exposed on the high altar (also displayed a Christmas and Easter). For the Feasts of the Redentore (3rd Sunday in July) and o Santa Maria della Salute (21st November; *see opposite*).

Non-Catholic churches: Anglican: St George's, Campo San Vio (Dorsoduro; *map p 409, E3*); Lutheran: Campo Santi Apostoli (Cannaregio; *map p. 402, B3*); Greek Orthodox: Ponte dei Greci (Castello; *map p. 404, A1*); Waldensian Evangelical and Methodist: 5170 Calle Lunga Santa Maria Formosa (Castello; *map p. 403, D4*).

Synagogues: Scuola Spagnola and Scuola Levantina, Ghetto Vecchio (*map p. 400, C2*)

Organisations for the safeguarding and restoration of Venice

The Association of International Private Committees for the Safeguarding of Venice operates in conjunction with UNESCO from the UNESCO Liaison office at Palazzo Zorzi, 4930 Castello, T: 041 520 7050. Among the 30 members of the Association are the British Venice in Peril Fund (www.veniceinperil.org; *see p. 30*). The two North American organisations are Save Venice Inc., New York (www.savevenice.org), and Venetian Heritage Inc. (www.venetianheritage.org). The Associazione Amici dei Muse e Monumenti Veneziani has its headquarters in Palazzo Mocenigo at San Stae, and Italia Nostra is at 1260 San Marco.

Emergencies

For all emergencies, T: 113: the switchboard will coordinate the help you need.

First aid services (*Pronto Soccorso*) are available at hospitals, railway stations and air ports. The most central hospital is Ospedale Civile, Santi Giovanni e Paolo, T: 04 529 4111, where first aid services are available. For emergency first aid and ambu lance service, T: 041 523 0000; for the 24-hr service, T: 118.

Fire brigade T: 115

Lost property: For the municipal police office, T: 041 522 4576. For the railway los property, T: 041 785 238; and for objects lost on ACTV water-buses, T: 041 272 2179

Festivals

The Venetian **Carnival** was famous throughout the Republic, when it lasted from 26th December to the first day of Lent. Parties and pageants were organised by special soci eties, and it was a time when the authority of Church and State was ignored and the masked inhabitants enjoyed a period of freedom and anarchy. In the 20th century the spirit of Carnival died out, but since 1980 the week or ten days in February before Len has been celebrated by ever-increasing numbers, and it has become the most crowded (and expensive) time of year. The city is invaded by merry-makers in fancy dress and masks, and numerous theatrical and musical events take place, both indoors and out On some days during Carnival week the city more than doubles its population. The festivities end on Shrove Tuesday, when a huge ball is usually held in Piazza San Marco For information, contact the Consorzio Carnevale di Venezia, T: 041 717 065.

The **Vogalonga** (literally 'long row') takes place on a Sunday in May. First held in 1975, it has become a very popular Venetian event. It is open to anyone prepared to row from the mouth of the Giudecca canal around the east end of Venice (Sant' Elena) up past Murano, through the Mazzorbo canal, around Burano, past San Francesco del Deserto and back down past the islands of Sant' Erasmo and Le Vignole, through the main canal of Murano, and back to Venice via the Cannaregio canal and the Grand Canal to the Punta della Dogana; a course of 32km. Any type or size of boat may participate, with any number of oarsmen in each boat. Rowing crews from London and Oxford also take part. A small participation fee is paid on enrolment. The departure is at 9am (best seen from the Zattere or Riva degli Schiavoni and the Giardini) and the first boats usually arrive back in the city at 11 or 11.30am (seen from the Cannaregio canal and the Grand Canal). It is a non-competitive course, and the last oarsmen usually return around 3pm. Normally, some 1,500 boats and over 5,000 people take part in the event in a remarkable variety of boats, some of them elaborately decorated.

On the **Festa del Redentore** (3rd Sat and Sun in July) a bridge of boats is constructed across the Giudecca canal; its vigil is celebrated with aquatic concerts and splendid fireworks (best seen from the Giudecca, the Zattere, or from a boat). Motorboats are excluded from the Bacino di San Marco after 9pm.

The **Festa della Salute** (21st Nov) is also celebrated by a bridge of boats across the Grand Canal at the Dogana.

The **Regata Storica** (first Sun in Sept) starts with a procession on the Grand Canal of the historic *bissone*, boats of a unique shape with their high prows richly decorated. This is followed by the most famous of the Venetian regattas with four different races, culminating in that of the two-oar *gondolini*, rowed by expert Venetian oarsmen. Other *Regate* are held from June–Sept in the lagoon near Sant'Erasmo, Murano, Pellestrina and Burano.

The **Festa della Sensa** takes place on the Sunday after Ascension Day (usually in May). This was celebrated throughout the Republic when the Doge ceremonially cast a ring into the lagoon at San Nicolò al Lido (*see p. 332*) symbolising the marriage of Venice with the sea. For the occasion, the doge was transported from Venice in the elaborate *Bucintoro*. It is now celebrated by the Mayor and Patriarch and other Venetian authorities. They depart from the Bacino di San Marco and proceed to San Nicolò al Lido.

Opening hours

Shops are normally open from 8 or 9am–1pm & 3 or 3.30pm–7.30 or 8pm, although recently the local authority has allowed shops to adopt whatever opening hours they wish. Most of the year, some food shops are closed on Wed afternoon (in July and August they are closed instead on Sat afternoon); although now many of them only close on Sun. Clothes shops, hairdressers, etc. are usually closed on Mon morning. For banking hours, see p. 369.

Pharmacies

Pharmacies or chemists (*farmacie*) are identified by their street signs, which show a luminous green cross. They are usually open Mon–Fri 9am–1pm & 4–7.30 or 8pm. Some are open 24hrs a day. A few are open on Sat, Sun (and holidays), and at night:

these are listed on the door of every chemist. Five or six chemists remain open all night in various parts of the city (daily information in the local newspapers, *Un ospite di Venezia*, or T: 041 523 0573).

Porters

Porters in Venice are distinguished by their hats (with *portabagaglio* on the badge) and are available in various parts of the city to help with heavy luggage (they will also accompany you on *vaporetti*). Although tariffs are fixed, you should establish the price for each piece of luggage before hiring a porter.

Public holidays

The main holidays in Italy, when offices, shops and schools are closed, are as follows:

1st January	New Year's Day
25th April	Liberation Day and the Festival of St Mark
Easter Monday	
1st May	Labour Day
15th August	Assumption
1st November	All Saints' Day
21st November	Festa della Salute
8th December	Immaculate Conception
25th December	Christmas Day
26th December	St Stephen

The festival of the Redentore (third weekend in July) is also usually considered a public holiday in Venice.

Museums are usually closed on Easter Sunday and 15th Aug, although some state museums stay open. There is usually no public transport on 1st May and the afternoon of Christmas Day.

Shopping

Fine **hand-made paper and stationery** is sold at the Antica Legatoria Piazzesi, near Santa Maria del Giglio, 2511 San Marco (*map p. 406, C3*) and at Alberto Valese-Ebrù, Campo Santo Stefano, 3471 San Marco (*map p. 406, B2*). **Venetian glass** is sold in numerous glass factories and shops on the island of Murano and all over Venice, including Paolorossi, Campo San Zaccaria, 4685 Castello (*map p. 404, A2*) and Amadi, Calle Saoneri, 2747 San Polo (*map p. 411, D3*). Beautiful **silk** furnishings, scarves, etc, modelled on the Fortuny silks, are sold at Venetian Studium, Calle Larga XXII Marzo, 2403 San Marco (*map p. 406, C3*). Models of **boats and nautical curiosities** are made by Gilberto Penzo, Calle 2 dei Saoneri, 2681 San Polo (*map p. 411, D3*), and another interesting shop is Anticlea Antiquariato, Calle San Provolo, 4719 Castello (*map p. 407, F2*).

Bookshops Among the best stocked are Sansovino, Bacino Orseolo, 84 San Marco (*map p. 407, D2*); Goldoni, Calle dei Fabbri, 4742 San Marco (*map p. 407, D1*); Fantoni, near Campo San Luca, 4121 San Marco (*map p. 406, C1*); and Alla Toletta, Calle della Toletta, 1213 Dorsoduro, also with a large selection of discount books (*map p. 409, D3*). Filippi, near Santa Maria Formosa, in Calle del Paradiso, 5763 Castello (*map p. 402, C4*), and in the Casselleria, 5284 Castello (*map p. 402, C4*) specialises in books on Venice. Another good place for books on Venice (as well as second-hand books and prints) is Lineadacqua, Calle della Mandola, 3717 San Marco (*map p. 406, C2*). An excellent bookshop, which also carries books in English, is Tarantola, at Campo San Luca (4268 San Marco; *map p. 406, C1*). English antiquarian books are sold at Old World Books, Ponte di Ghetto Vecchio, 1190 Cannaregio (*map p. 400, C2*). The Italian publisher Mondadori has a bookshop in Salizzada San Moisè, 1345 San Marco (*map p. 407, D2*).

Open-air markets The most important food market in Venice is the Rialto market, which sells a superb variety of produce every morning except Sun. The colourful vegetables include locally grown asparagus and artichokes, and the wholesale market is particularly lively in the early morning when boats put in laden with food. The large fish market here has excellent fresh fish. There is a small daily produce market in Campo Santa Margherita (Dorsoduro; *map p. 408, C2*), and, nearby, on Rio di San Barnaba, fruit and vegetables are sold from a picturesque boat (*map p. 408, C2*). In Rio Terrà San Leonardo (Cannaregio; *map p. 401, D3*) there is a large street market on weekdays. Another small local market is in Castello at the end of Via Garibaldi (*map p. 405, E2*).

There are some small supermarkets in various parts of Venice, including Billa, on Fondamenta delle Zattere (*map p. 408, B3*), which is also open all day on Sun.

Students and young visitors

Visitors between the ages of 14 and 29 can buy a *Rolling Venice* card at the Comune office (Assessorato alla Gioventù), Corte Contarina 1529, San Marco, which entitles you to a ticket valid on nearly all ACTV services for 72hrs, as well as discounts in certain restaurants, hotels, hostels, shops and museums. It also gives access to the university canteen in Palazzo Badoer, Calle del Magazen, 2840 San Polo (closed in Aug). For student reductions in museums, see p. 368.

Telephones

Telephone numbers in Italy require the area code, whether you are making a local call or a call from outside Venice. The Venice area code is 041.

dialling UK from Italy (00 44) + number.
dialling US from Italy (001) + number.

Tipping

Tipping is less widespread in Italy than in North America. Most prices in restaurants include service: always check whether this has been added to the bill before leaving a tip. It is customary to leave a euro or two on the table to convey appreciation. Even taxi-drivers rarely expect more than a euro added to the charge (which officially includes service). In hotels, porters who show you to your room and help with your luggage, or find you a taxi, usually expect a euro or two.

FURTHER READING

The number of books that have been written about Venice is enormous. Ever since the first published descriptions of the city appeared in the 16th century, writers have been exploring her history, analysing her art and architecture, and using her as the backdrop for works of fiction. The list below gives some of the most recent publications, as well as seminal works of scholarship, or works of unique charm and vision, though these may be less readily available. Where relevant, first editions are given in square brackets, latest editions in rounded brackets.

General background

Paolo Barbaro, *Venice Revealed*, Souvenir Press (2002)
John Freely, *Strolling Through Venice*, Penguin (1994).
Christopher Hibbert, *Venice: Biography of a City*, [1988], Grafton (1990)
Hugh Honour, *Companion Guide to Venice* [1965], Companion Guides (2001)
Joe Links, *Venice for Pleasure* [1962], (2003)
Jan Morris, *Venice* [1960], Faber & Faber (1993)

History and Social history

David Chambers and Brian Pullan, *Venice: a Documentary History* 1450–1630, Blackwell (1992)
Charles Freeman, *The Horses of St Mark's*, [2004], Abacus (2005)
Ralph A. Griffiths and John E. Law (ed.), *Rawdon Brown and the Anglo-Venetian Relationship*, Nonsuch Publishing (2005)
Jonathan Keates, *The Siege of Venice*, Vintage (2006)
Frederic C. Lane, *Venice: A Maritime Republic*, Johns Hopkins University Press (1973)
Mary MacCarthy, *Venice Observed* [1963]; *The Stones of Florence and Venice Observed*, Penguin (2006)
Jan Morris, *The Venetian Empire: A Sea Voyage*, Penguin (1990)
Francesco da Mosto, *Francesco's Italy*, BBC Books (2004)
Jane da Mosto and Caroline Fletcher, *The Science of Saving Venice*, Umberto Allemandi & Co (2004)
John Julius Norwich, Venice: *The Rise to Empire*, Alan Lane [1977], and Venice: *The Greatness and the Fall*, Viking [1981]; reissued as a single volume in paperback as *The History of Venice*, Penguin (2003)
John Julius Norwich, *Paradise of Cities: Venice and its Nineteenth-century Visitors*, Penguin (2004)
John Pemble, *Venice Rediscovered*, Oxford University Press (1996)
Bruce Redford, *Venice and the Grand Tour*, 1670–1830, Yale University Press (1996)
Margaret Plant, *Venice: Fragile City 1797–1997*, Yale University Press (2002).

Art history

J. Clegg, *Ruskin and Venice*, Junction Books (1981)

Ennio Concina, *A History of Venetian Architecture*, Cambridge University Press (1998)

Patricia Fortini Brown, *The Renaissance in Venice* (1997); *Venice and Antiquity*, Yale University Press (1997).

Richard Goy, *Venice: the City and its Architecture*, Phaidon (1999)

Julian Halsby, *Venice. The Artist's Vision* [1990], UnicornPress (2002)

Robert Hewison, *Ruskin and Venice*, La Stamperia di Venezia (1983)

Paul Hills, *Venetian Colour—marble, mosaic, and glass 1250–1550*, Yale University Press (1999)

Deborah Howard, *Venice and the East: The Impact of the Islamic World on Venetian Architecture*, Yale University Press (2000); *The Architectural History of Venice* [1980], Yale University Press (2005)

Peter Humfrey, *Painting in Renaissance Venice*, Yale University Press [1995], (2001)

Ralph Lieberman, *Renaissance Architecture in Venice*, Frederick Muller (1982)

Mary Lutyens (ed.) *Effie in Venice: Effie Ruskin's Letters Home 1849–1852* [1965], Pallas Athene (2003)

Margaret F. MacDonald, *Palaces in the Night: Whistler in Venice*, University of California Press (2001)

Sarah Quill, *Ruskin's Venice. The Stones Revisited*, Lund Humphries (2003)

John Ruskin, *The Stones of Venice* (3 vols) [1851], Pallas Athene (2003)

John Steer, *Venetian Painting*, Thames & Hudson [1970], (1991)

Arnold Whittick, *Ruskin's Venice* (1976)

Literary works and poetry

Robert Browning, 'A Toccata of Galuppi's'

Lord Byron, 'Childe Harold's Pilgrimage', 'Marino Faliero', 'The Two Foscari'

Henry James, *The Princess Casamassima* [1886], *The Aspern Papers* [1888], *The Wings of the Dove* [1902]

Thomas Mann, *Death in Venice* [1913]

Hetty Meyric Hughes (ed.), *Venice: Poetry of Place*, Eland (2006)

Marcel Proust, *Albertine Disparue* [1925]

William Wordsworth, 'On the Extinction of the Venetian Republic'

Modern fiction

Michael Dibdin, *Dead Lagoon,* Faber & Faber (1995)

L.P. Hartley, *Eustace and Hilda* [1947]

Donna Leon, crime novels set in Venice. The most recent include *Through a Glass Darkly*, (2006); *Doctored Evidence*, (2005); *Wilful Behaviour*, (2003); *Death at La Fenice* (2004)

Daphne du Maurier, 'Don't Look Now' (short story in the collection *Not After Midnight* [1971], famous as the basis for the Nicholas Roeg film of the same name)

Frederick Rolfe (Baron Corvo), *The Desire and Pursuit of the Whole* (1934)

Muriel Spark, *Territorial Rights*, Penguin [1979]
Emma Tennant, *Felony*, Vintage (2003)
Barry Unsworth, *Stone Virgin* [1985]
Salley Vickers, *Miss Garnet's Angel*, HarperCollins (2001)

Modern non-fiction and anthologies

Milton Grundy, *Venice. An Anthology Guide*, Giles de la Mare Publishers (1998)
Ian Littlewood, *A Literary Companion to Venice*, St Martin's Press (1995)
David C. McPherson, *Shakespeare, Jonson and the Myth of Venice*, University of
  Delaware Press (1990)
Michael Marqusee, Venice. *An Illustrated Anthology*, HarperCollins (1989)
Paula Weideger, *Venetian Dreaming*, Pocket Books (2004). A memoir of a year spent
  living in the Palazzo Donà delle Rose.

Some older histories and descriptions

Horatio Brown, *Life on the Lagoons* [1884]; *Venice: An Historical Sketch* [1895]; *In and
  Around Venice* [1905], *Studies in Venetian History* [1907]
Shirley Guiton, *No Magic Eden*, Hamish Hamilton [1972], on Torcello, Burano, and
  Murano in particular, and *A World by Itself:Tradition and Change in the Venetian
  Lagoon*, Hamish Hamilton [1977], the sequel
William Dean Howells, *Venetian Life* [1866], Northwestern University Press (2001)
Edward Hutton, *Venice and Venetia* [1911]
Henry James, *Italian Hours* [1909], Kessinger (2004)
Logan Pearsall Smith (ed.), *Life and Letters of Sir Henry Wotton*, (2 vols); a vivid insight
  into life in Venice in the early 17th century [1907]
E.V. Lucas, *A Wanderer in Venice* [1914], Indypublish (2005)
Pompeo Molmenti, *Venice* [1906]
Thomas Okey, *Venice and its Story* [1910]
Margaret Oliphant, *The Makers of Venice* [1898]
Lonsdale and Laura Ragg, *Things Seen in Venice* [1912]; *Venice* [1916]
Alexander Robertson, *Venetian Sermons* [1905], Kessinger (2004)
Margaret Symonds, *Days Spent on a Doge's Farm* [1893]
Alethea Wiel, *Venice* [1894], Kessinger (2005)

GLOSSARY OF SPECIAL TERMS

Albergo, small room used for committee meetings on the upper floor of a *scuola*

Altana (pl. *altane*), terrace made of wood, on the roof of a Venetian house

Ambo (pl. *ambones*), pulpit in a Christian basilica; two pulpits on opposite sides of a church from which the gospel and epistle were read

Ancona, retable or large altarpiece (painted or sculpted) in an architectural frame

Androne, principal ground-floor hall behind the water entrance of a Venetian palace

Architrave, the lowest part of an entablature, the horizontal frame over a door

Archivolt, moulded architrave carried round an arch

Atlantes (or *telamones*), male figures used as supporting columns

Atrium, forecourt, usually part of a Byzantine church or a classical Roman house

Attic, topmost storey of a classical building, hiding the spring of the roof

Baldacchino, canopy supported by columns, usually over an altar

Bardiglio, marble streaked with blue and white

Basilica, originally a Roman building used for public administration; in Christian architecture, an aisled church with a clerestory and apse

Bas-relief, sculpture in low relief

Bottega, the studio of an artist; or the pupils who worked under his direction

Bozzetto, sketch, often used to describe a small model for a piece of sculpture

Campanile (pl. *campanili*) bell-tower, often detached from the building to which it belongs

Ca' (*casa*), Venetian term for palace (or important residence)

Calle (pl. *calli*) narrow Venetian street

Campiello, small Venetian piazza

Campo (pl. *campi*), Venetian term for piazza (or square)

Chiaroscuro, distribution of light and shade, apart from colour, in a painting

Ciborium, casket or tabernacle containing the Host (Communion bread)

Cipollino, greyish marble with streaks of white or green

Cippus (pl. *cippae*), sepulchral monument in the form of an altar

Cloisonné, type of enamel decoration, where areas of colour are partitioned by narrow strips of metal

Condottiere, captain-general of a city militia; soldier of fortune at the head of an army

Corbel, a projecting block, usually of stone, to support a beam or other roof structure

Cornu (or *berretta*), peaked doge's beret in red velvet, worn over a white linen skull cap

Corte, courtyard

Diocletian window, also known as a thermal window, the term refers to a (usually large) semicircular window derived from those used in ancient Roman public baths (notably those of Diocletian). A characteristic feature of Palladian architecture

Diptych, painting or ivory tablet in two sections

Dossal, altarpiece

Duomo, cathedral

Exedra, semi-circular recess

Ex-voto, tablet or small painting expressing gratitude to a saint

Fondaco (*fontego*), trading post

Fondamenta (pl. *fondamente*), street alongside a canal

Forno (pl. *forni*), bakery

Fruttarol, greengrocer, hence 'Calle del Fruttarol', of which Venice has many

Greek cross, cross with vertical and transverse arms of equal length

Herm, quadrangular pillar decreasing in girth towards the ground, surmounted by a head

Iconostasis, high balustrade hung with icons of saints, separating the sanctuary of a Byzantine church from the nave

Intarsia, inlay of wood, marble or metal

Latin cross, cross where the vertical arm is longer than the transverse arm

Liagò, upper-floor loggia which protrudes from a Venetian palace façade

Lista, a lane which led up to an ambassador's palace

Loggia, covered upper-floor gallery

Lunette, semi-circular space in a vault or above a window or doorway, often decorated with a painting or relief

Magazen (*magazzino*), warehouse

Merceria, market

Matroneum, gallery reserved for women in early Christian churches

Monstrance, a vessel for displaying the Host (Communion bread)

Narthex, vestibule of a Christian basilica

Niello, a black inlay into stone, using silver, lead, copper, sulphur and borax

Ogee, of an arch, shaped in a double curve, convex above and concave below

Opus alexandrinum, mosaic design of black and red geometric figures on a white ground

Opus sectile, mosaic or paving of thin slabs of coloured marble cut in geometrical shapes

Palazzo, palace; any dignified and important building

Pali, wood piles used as foundations for buildings in Venice; and the mooring posts in front of palaces showing the livery colours of their proprietors

Pantocrator, in Byzantine iconography the Almighty, the ruler of the Universe

Paten, flat dish on which the Host (Communion bread) is placed

Patera (pl. *paterae*), small circular carved ornament (often Byzantine), sometimes used as a decorative feature on façades in Venice

Pavonazzetto, yellow marble blotched with blue

Pax, sacred object used by a priest for the blessing of peace, and offered for the kiss of the faithful, usually circular, engraved, enamelled or painted in a rich gold or silver frame

Pendentive, one of four concave spandrels formed when a dome attaches to quadrilateral walls; often they are decorated with images of the Evangelists

Piano nobile, the main floor of a house, where the grandest apartments are to be found

Pier, a square or compound pillar used as a support in architecture

Pietà, group of the Virgin, sometimes with saints and angels, mourning the dead Christ

Pietre dure, hard or semi-precious stones, often used in the form of mosaics to decorate cabinets, tabletops, etc.

Piscina, place where a basin of water connected to a canal formerly existed

Pistor, a baker, hence 'Calle del Pistor', of which Venice has several

Pluteus (pl. *plutei*), marble panel, usually decorated; a series of them are often used to form a parapet to precede the altar of a church

Polyptych, painting or panel divided into multiple sections

Porphyry, an extremely hard purplish rock quarried in Egypt, often used for sculpture by the Romans

Portego, the central hall of a Venetian house, usually running the whole depth of the building

Predella, small painting (usually a panel) attached below a large altarpiece

Pronaos, vestibule in front of the inner room of a temple

Proto, 'protomagister', chief architect

Pulvin, cushion-shaped block between the capital and the arch surmounting it

Putto (pl. *putti*), sculpted or painted figure, usually nude, of a baby boy

Quadratura (pl. *quadrature*) painted architectural perspectives

Quatrefoil, four-lobed cusp (on an arch)

Ramo, offshoot of a canal

Reredos, decorated screen rising behind an altar

Rio terrà, street along the course of a filled-in rio

Riva, wharf

Rood-screen, a screen below the Rood or Crucifix, dividing the nave from the chancel in a church

Ruga, street

Rustication, denotes the grooves or channels cut at the joints between huge blocks of facing masonry (ashlar) on grand buildings

Sacca, stretch of water where canals meet

Salizzada, name given to the first paved streets of Venice in the 17th century; now simply denotes a paved street

Sandalo, flat-bottomed Venetian rowing boat, used on the lagoon

Scuola (pl. *scuole*), lay confraternity, dedicated to charitable works

Sestiere (pl. *sestieri*), district of Venice

Situla, a water-bucket, for ceremonial use

Soffit, underside (or intrados) of an arch

Sottoportico, Venetian term for a street which passes beneath a building, or a street entered under arches

Spandrel, surface between two arches in an arcade or the triangular space on either side of an arch

Spezier, spicer or apothecary, hence 'Calle del Spezier', of which Venice has a number

Stilted arch, round arch that rises vertically (on a 'stilt') before it springs

Stoup, vessel for Holy Water, usually near the entrance of a church

Stylobate, basement of a columned temple or other building

Telamones, see Atlantes

Tessera, small cube of marble, glass, etc. used in mosaic work

Tondo (pl. *tondi*), roundel

Transenna, open grille or screen, usually of marble, in an early Christian church

Trefoil, three-lobed cusp (on an arch)

Tricuspid, having three points or cusps

Triptych, painting or tablet in three sections

Vera da pozzo, well-head

Verde antico, dark green marble from Thessaly, Greece

Virgin orans, Byzantine style of depicting the Madonna, with her two arms raised in supplication

Volute, tightly curled spiral scroll

THE DOGES OF VENICE

1.	697–717	Paoluccio Anafesto
2.	717–726	Marcello Tegalliano
3.	726–737	Orso Ipato
	737–742	*Interregnum*
4.	742–755	Teodato Ipato
5.	755–756	Galla Gaulo
6.	756–764	Domenico Monegario
7.	764–775	Maurizio Galbaio
8.	787–804	Giovanni Galbaio
9.	804–811	Obelario d. Antenori
10.	811–827	Agnello Particiaco
11.	827–829	Giustiniano Particiaco
12.	829–836	Giovanni Particiaco I
13.	836–864	Pietro Tradonico
14.	864–881	Orso Particiaco I
15.	881–887	Giovanni Particiaco II
16.	887	Pietro Candiano I
17.	888–912	Pietro Tribuno
18.	912–932	Orso Particiaco II
19.	932–939	Pietro Candiano II
20.	939–942	Pietro Particiaco
21.	942–959	Pietro Candiano III
22.	959–976	Pietro Candiano IV
23.	976–978	Pietro Orseolo I
24.	978–979	Vitale Candiano
25.	979–991	Tribuno Memmo
26.	991–1008	Pietro Orseolo II
27.	1008–1026	Otto (Orso) Orseolo
28.	1026–1032	Pietro Centranico
29.	1032–1043	Domenico Flabanico
30.	1043–1071	Domenico Contarini
31.	1071–1084	Domenico Selvo
32.	1084–1096	Vitale Falier
33.	1096–1102	Vitale Michiel I
34.	1102–1118	Ordelafo Falier
35.	1118–1130	Domenico Michiel
36.	1130–1148	Pietro Polani
37.	1148–1156	Domenico Morosini
38.	1156–1172	Vitale Michiel II
39.	1172–1178	Sebastiano Ziani
40.	1178–1192	Orio Mastropiero
41.	1192–1205	Enrico Dandolo
42.	1205–1229	Pietro Ziani
43.	1229–1249	Giacomo Tiepolo
44.	1249–1253	Marin Morosini
45.	1253–1268	Ranier Zeno
46.	1268–1275	Lorenzo Tiepolo
47.	1275–1280	Jacopo Contarini
48.	1280–1289	Giovanni Dandolo
49.	1289–1311	Pietro Gradenigo
50.	1311–1312	Marino Zorzi
51.	1312–1328	Giovanni Soranzo
52.	1329–1339	Francesco Dandolo
53.	1339–1342	Bartolomeo Gradenigo
54.	1343–1354	Andrea Dandolo
55.	1354–1355	Marin Falier
56.	1355–1356	Giovanni Gradenigo
57.	1356–1361	Giovanni Dolfin
58.	1361–1365	Lorenzo Celsi
59.	1365–1368	Marco Corner
60.	1368–1382	Andrea Contarini
61.	1382	Michele Morosini
62.	1382–1400	Antonio Venier
63.	1400–1413	Michele Steno
64.	1414–1423	Tommaso Mocenigo
65.	1423–1457	Francesco Foscari
66.	1457–1462	Pasquale Malipiero
67.	1462–1471	Cristoforo Moro
68.	1471–1473	Nicolò Tron
69.	1473–1474	Nicolò Marcello
70.	1474–1476	Pietro Mocenigo
71.	1476–1478	Andrea Vendramin
72.	1478–1485	Giovanni Mocenigo
73.	1485–1486	Marco Barbarigo
74.	1486–1501	Agostino Barbarigo
75.	1501–1521	Leonardo Loredan
76.	1521–1523	Antonio Grimani
77.	1523–1538	Andrea Gritti

78.	1539–1545	Pietro Lando
79.	1545–1553	Francesco Donà
80.	1553–1554	Marcantonio Trevisan
81.	1554–1556	Francesco Venier
82.	1556–1559	Lorenzo Priuli
83.	1559–1567	Girolamo Priuli
84.	1567–1570	Pietro Loredan
85.	1570–1577	Alvise Mocenigo I
86.	1577–1578	Sebastiano Venier
87.	1578–1585	Nicolò da Ponte
88.	1585–1595	Pasquale Cicogna
89.	1595–1605	Marino Grimani
90.	1606–1612	Leonardo Donà
91.	1612–1615	Marcantonio Memmo
92.	1615–1618	Giovanni Bembo
93.	1618	Nicolò Donà
94.	1618–1623	Antonio Priuli
95.	1623–1624	Francesco Contarini
96.	1625–1629	Giovanni Corner I
97.	1630–1631	Nicolò Contarini
98.	1631–1646	Francesco Erizzo
99.	1646–1655	Francesco Molin
100.	1655–1656	Carlo Contarini
101.	1656	Francesco Corner
102.	1656–1658	Bertucci Valier
103.	1658–1659	Giovanni Pesaro
104.	1659–1675	Domenico Contarini
105.	1675–1676	Nicolò Sagredo
106.	1676–1684	Alvise Contarini
107.	1684–1688	Marcantonio Giustinian
108.	1688–1694	Francesco Morosini
109.	1694–1700	Silvestro Valier
110.	1700–1709	Alvise Mocenigo II
111.	1709–1722	Giovanni Corner II
112.	1722–1732	Alvise Mocenigo III
113.	1732–1735	Carlo Ruzzini
114.	1735–1741	Alvise Pisani
115.	1741–1752	Pietro Grimani
116.	1752–1762	Francesco Loredan
117.	1762–1763	Marco Foscarini
118.	1763–1778	Alvise Mocenigo IV
119.	1779–1789	Paolo Renier
120.	1789–1797	Lodovico Manin

INDEX

Explanatory or more detailed references (where there are many), or references to places where an artist's work is best represented, are given in bold. Dates are given for all artists, architects and sculptors. Numbers in italics are picture references.

A

Aalto, Alvar (1898–1976) 295
Accademia Bridge (*see Ponte dell'Accademia*)
Accademia di Belle Arti 152, 188
Accademia galleries 143–58
Acqua alta 36, 67
Ala Napoleonica 71
Albanian community in Venice 120
Alberegno, Jacobello (d. before 1397) 144
Alberoni (Lido) 333
Albertinelli, Mariotto (1474–1515) 165
Aldine Press 195
Alechinsky, Pierre (b.1927) 161
Alexander III, Pope 48, 331, 332
Alexius IV, emperor 60
Aliense, (Antonio Vassilacchi; c.1556–1629) 104, 106, 164, 285, 304, 306; (works from cartoons by) 55, 56, 63
Altinum 313, 318, 323
Alvise dal Friso (nephew of Veronese; c.1544–1609) 171, 172, 338
Amigoni, Jacopo (1675–1752) 184, 216
Ammannati, Bartolomeo (1511–92) 84
Ando, Tadao (b.1941) 126
Andrea da Murano (d.1512) 154
Andrea del Castagno (c.1420–57) 20, 52, 258–59; (works from cartoons by) 56
Angeli, Giuseppe (pupil of Piazzetta; 1712–98) 115, 123, 180, 210, 213, 215, 259
Angelo Raffaele, church of 171–72
Anianus, legend of 197
Antico (Pier Jacopo Alari Bonacolsi; 1460–1528) 228
Antonello da Messina (c.1430–79) 24, **77**, 78
Antonello da Saliba (nephew of Antonello da Messina; 1466–1535) 109, 154
Antonio da Negroponte (15C) 268, 269
Antonio da Ponte (1512–97) 87, 102, 108, 133, 186, 308
Antonio Palma (1511–75) 170
Appel, Karel (b.1921) 161

Archivio di Stato 188, 206
Arco del Paradiso 275
Aretino, Pietro 125, 193
Armenian, Armenians 111, 173, 339–40
Arp, Jean (1886–1966) 159, 160, 219
Arsenale 289–91
Aspetti, Tiziano (c.1559–1606) 82, 101, 139, 266, 270
Attila's Chair 328
Austria, Austrians 14, **15–16**, 70, 71, 109, 117, 120, 124, 138, 141, 236, 238, 260, 286, 312, 342, 343

B

Bacari 365–67
Baccio da Montelupo (Bartolomeo di Giovanni d'Astore dei Sinibaldi; 1469–1535) 200
Bachiacca (Francesco Ubertini; 1494–1557) 165, 184
Bacino Orseolo 114
Bacon, Francis (1909–92) 161
Baldassare d'Este (Baldassare Estense; 1440–1504) 76, 159
Balestra, Antonio (1666–1740) 175, 214, 259
Balla, Giacomo (1871–1958) 160, 162, 218
Ballarin, Giovanni Battista 315
Balzac, Honoré de 71
Bambini, Niccolò (1651–1736) 123, 164, 168, 174, 176, 215, 235
Bandiera e Moro, rebels 260
Bandini, Giovanni (1540–99) 95, 105
Baratta, Pietro (1668–1729) 176, 216, 285
Barbari, Jacopo de' (d.1511/16) 76
Barbarigo, Doge Agostino 164, 314; (tomb sculpture of) 164; (pieces from tomb of) 228
Barbarigo, Doge Marco 94; (pieces from tomb of) 228
Barbaro family 118, *118*
Barbarossa, emperor Frederick 48, 331, 332
Bardi, Count Enrico di 219–20, 233
Barovier, Angelo (1405–60) 317, 318
Barzaghi, Francesco (1839–92) 120

Basaiti, Marco (active 1496–1530) 24, 145, 154, 158, 204

Bassano, Francesco (1549–92) 104, 220, 306, 310

Bassano, Jacopo (Jacopo da Ponte; c.1510–92) 101, 151, 304, 310

Bassano, Leandro (1557–1622) 104, 108, 110, 151, 193, 281, 282, 283, 337; (works from cartoons by) 55

Bastiani, Lazzaro (?1425–1512) 73, 154, 158, 246, 310, 319

Baziotes, William (1912–1963) 161

Beccafumi, Domenico (c.1485–1551) 165

Bella, Gabriel (1730–99) 274

Bellano, Bartolomeo (1434–96) 75

Bellini, Gentile (brother of Giovanni; c.1429–1507) **21**, 62, 69, 79, 152, 165, 228; (*Procession in Piazza San Marco*) 68–69, 154–55; (True Cross painting cycle) 154–55; (works attributed to) 162, 165

Bellini, Giovanni (son of Jacopo; c.1433–1516) 21, **24**, 77, 99, **145–46**, 146, 152, 165, 237, 243, 268, 285, 314; (Frari triptych) 200, *205*; (S. Giobbe) 145; (S. Zaccaria *Madonna*) 24, 257; (works attributed to) 113, 274

Bellini, Jacopo (father of Gentile and Giovanni; c.1400–70/71) 20–21, 146

Bellini, Vincenzo 117, 245

Belliniano, Vittore (1456–1529) 152

Bello, Francesco (16C) 101

Bellotto, Bernardo (nephew of Canaletto; 1721–80) 152, 181

Bembo, Pietro 82, 112, 132, 195, **196**

Benato, Jacopo di Marco (14C) 55

Benoni, Giuseppe (1618–84) 142, 165

Benvenuti, Augusto (1838–99) 299

Benzon, Countess Marina 132, 339

Berchet, Federico (1831–1909) 222

Bergamasco, Bartolomeo di Francesco (early 16C) 208

Bergamasco, Il (Guglielmo dei Grigi; fl. 1515–30) 70, 138, 312

Bernini, Gian Lorenzo (1598–1680) 165, 230, 312

Bernini, Pietro (father of Gian Lorenzo; 1562–1629) 312

Berthel, Melchior (1625–72) 205, 235

Bessarion, Cardinal 13, 82; (reliquary of) 158

Bevilacqua, Giovanni Carlo (1775–1849) 73, 337

Biennale exhibition ground 295

Bigaglia, Pietro (1786–1876) 318

Bissolo, Francesco (c.1475–1554) 158, 217, 310

Boccaccino, Boccaccio (c.1466–1524) 109, 111

Boccioni, Umberto (1882–1916) 160, 162, 219

Boito, Camillo (1836–1914) 16, 121

Boldrini, Leonardo (active 1452–93) 260

Bombelli, Sebastiano (1635–1716) 274

Bon family 95

Bon, Bartolomeo the Elder (c.1405–64/65) 23, 56, 70, **89**, 93, 131, 140, 226; (works attributed to) 93, 194, 277

Bon, Bartolomeo the Younger (active late 15C/early 16C) 66, 204, 208

Bon, Giovanni (father of Bartolomeo the Elder; c.1360–c.1443) 23, 226, 286; (works attributed to) 55, 194

Bonazza, Antonio (1698–c.1763) 282, 338

Bonazza, Giovanni (1654–1763) 86, 176, 282, 285

Bonifacio Veronese (Bonifacio de' Pitati; 1487–c.1557) 123, 149, **151**, 171, 184, 217, 249

Boninsegna, Gian Paolo (14C) 59

Bordone, Paris (1500–71) 152, 158, 229, 237, 261

Borro, Luigi (1826–86) 47, 124

Borsato, Giuseppe (1771–1849) 73

Bosch, Hieronymus (c.1450–1516) 107

Boselli, Pietro (c. 1590–1659) 304

Botta, Mario (b.1943) 274

Botticelli, Sandro (Alessandro Filipepi; 1445–1510) 159

Bouts, Dieric (c.1420–75) 77

Bragadin, Marcantonio 285

Brancusi, Constantin (1876–1957) 162

Braque, Georges (1881–1963) 159

Brauner, Victor (1903–66) 160

Bregno, Antonio (active 1425–57) 95

Bregno, Giovanni Battista (late 15C) 305

Bregno, Lorenzo (nephew of Antonio Rizzo; fl.early 16C) 58, 200, **217**, 237, 292

Bresciano, Andrea (Il Brescianino; 1530–69) 164

Bridge of Sighs 91, 107

Brill, Paul (16C–17C) 229

Briosco, Andrea (*see Riccio*)

Britten, Sir Benjamin 117

Bronson, Edith 128

Bronson, Katherine 128

Brown, Horatio 188
Brown, Rawdon 135, 142, **206**; (grave of) 311
Browning, Pen 140, 179
Browning, Robert 128, 140, 179, 184
Brueghel, Pieter the Elder (c.1525–69) 77
Brulle, Albert van der (16C) 304
Bruno, Giordano 131, 132
Brusaferro, Girolamo (c.1677–1745) 115
Brustolon, Andrea (1660–1732) 179, 180, 200, 239, 310
Bucintoro 15, 79–80, 293, 332
Buonconsiglio, Giovanni (Il Marescalco; c. 1465–1536) 158, 186, 221
Buonvicino, Alessandro (*see Moretto*)
Buora, Andrea (son of Giovanni; early 16C) 242, 305
Buora, Antonio (son of Giovanni; d.1538) 242
Buora, Giovanni (c.1450–1513) 173, 209, 257, 286, 305
Burano 320–23
Bushnell, John (c.1630–1701)
Byron, Lord 16, 131, 132, 147, **339**; (portrait of) 340
Byzantine, Byzantium 8, 9, 60; (*see also Constantinople*)
Byzantine art and architecture, major examples of (Museum of Icons) 262; (Pala d'Oro) 19, 59; (SS. Maria e Donato) 318–20; (St Mark's) 41–65; (Torcello) 325–27, *326*

C
Ca' Dario 141–42, *142*
Ca' di Dio 289
Ca' del Duca 131
Ca' Foscari 12, 140
Ca' Grande 130
Ca' Lioni 133
Ca' Malipiero-Trevisan 271
Ca' Michiel 168
Ca' da Mosto 133
Ca' d'Oro 11, 21, 135, 225–30
Ca' Pesaro 138, 217–20
Ca' Rezzonico 140, 178–84
Ca' Roman 336
Ca' Zorzi 263
Cabianca, Bartolo (early 18C) 200, 220
Cabot, John 296, 336
Cadorin, Lodovico (19C) 71
Caffi, Ippolito (1809–66) 184, 218
Calatrava, Santiago (b.1951) 137, 223
Calder, Alexander (1898–1976) *161*, 162, 219

Calendario, Filippo (14C) 87; (works attributed to) 296
Caliari, Benedetto (brother of Veronese; 1538–98) 83, 170, 338
Caliari, Carletto (son of Veronese; c.1567–92/6) 101
Caliari, Gabriele (son of Veronese; 1568–1631) 101, 103
Callas, Maria 117
Calle dell'Ascension 114
Calle Larga XXII Marzo 116
Calle Querini 185
Callido, Gaetano (organ-maker; 1727–1813) 58, 111, 113, 115, 168, 195, 204, 216, 234, 278, 288, 292
Calvetti, Alberto (17C) 111
Cambi, Giovanni (late 16C) 101
Campagna, Girolamo (c.1549–1625) 101, 102, 110, 112, 174, 199, 209, 212, 228, 254, 284, 290, 301, 304, 309
Campo Manin 124
Campo dei Mori 249
Campo Morosini (*see Campo S. Stefano*)
Campo Sant'Angelo 123
Campo Sant'Aponal 194
Campo San Bartolomeo 113
Campo San Giacomo 191
Campo Santi Giovanni e Paolo 276
Campo Santa Margherita 175–76
Campo Santa Maria Formosa 271
Campo San Polo 194
Campo Santo Stefano 120–22
Campo San Tomà 197
Campo San Vio 141
Canal, Fabio (1703–67) 292
Canal, Giambattista (1745–1825) 115, 216
Canale della Giudecca (*see Giudecca canal*)
Canaletto (Giovanni Antonio Canal; 1697–1768) 29, 121, 134, 152, 180, **181**, 207
Candi, Giovanni (active late 15C) 125
Candiano IV, Doge Pietro 42
Cannaregio canal 234
Cannaregio, *sestiere* of 225ff
Canova, Antonio (1757–1822) 15, **73**, 123, 130, 132, 165, 293, 340; (mausoleum of) 206
Canozzi, Cristoforo and Lorenzo (15C) 204
Cappello, Bianca 194
Cappello, Vincenzo, Captain of the Fleet, statue of 271
Cappello, Admiral Vittorio, sculpture of 295

Cariani, Giovanni (Giovanni Busi; 1485/90–after 1547) 148
Carlini, Giulio (c.1830–87) 141
Carlo, Giancarlo de (1919–2005) 320
Carmini, church of 173–74
Carnevalis, Luca (1663–1730) 180, 181
Carnival 370
Carpaccio, Benedetto (son of Vittore; c.1500–60) 184
Carpaccio, Vittore (c.1460–1525/6) **23–24**, 79, 95, 121, *121*, 145, 155, 158, 228, **265**, 337; (*Legend of St Ursula*) 23, 155–57; (Schiavoni) 23, 263–65, *264*; (*Two Venetian Ladies*) 79
Carrà, Carlo (1881–1966) 162, 219
Carracci, Annibale (1560–1609) 151
Carriera, Rosalba (1675–1757) 134, 152, 168, 179, 182, 184, 336; (house of) 338; (house where died) 141
Casa Biondetti 141
Casa Bragadin-Favretto 138
Casa Civran-Badoer 131
Casa Corner-Martinengo-Ravà 132
Casa Corner-Valmarana 132
Casa Correr 137
Casa Gatti-Casazza 136
Casa Goldoni 196–97
Casanova, Giacomo 14, 109
Casetta delle Rose 130
Casinò 136, 233, 330
Casoni, Giovanni (19C) 266, 290
Casorati, Felice (1886–1963) 219
Castelli, Bernardino (1750–1810) 179, 274
Castello, *sestiere* of 255ff
Catarino Veneziano (active 1362–82) 274
Catena, Vincenzo (c.1478–1531) 217, 274
Cattaneo, Danese (c.1509–73) 84, 109, 112, 218, 242, 284
Cavalli, Jacopo 282–83
Cavalli, Pier Francesco 57
Celesti, Andrea (1637–1712) 111
Cemeteries (Catholic) 330; (Jewish) 330–31; (San Michele) 311
Certosa, La, island of 341
Chagall, Marc (1887–1985) 160, 219
Charlier, Jean (early 15C) 226
Chini, Galileo (1873–1956) 295
Chioggia 335, 336–38; (battle of) 10, 283, 284
Chioggiotto, Il (Antonio Marinetti; 1719–90) 337
Chirico, Giorgio de (1880–1978) 160, 219

Chrysogonus, St 166
Chrysostom, St John 242
Ciardi, Emma (1879–1933) 184
Ciardi, Guglielmo (1842–1917) 218
Cignaroli, Giovanni Battista (1679–1770) 213, 338
Cima da Conegliano (Giovanni Battista Cima; c.1459–1518) 24, 145, 158, 165, 174, 184, 241, **260**; (works attributed to) 284, 285
Cimarosa, Domenico 117, 123, 289
Cini Collection 158–59
Cini Foundation 158, 305
Cini, Vittorio 141, 158
Cipriani hotel 307, 354
Cipriani, Giuseppe 85
Civetta, Il (*see Herri*)
Clarke, Sir Ashley 241; (grave of) 311
Codussi, Mauro (c.1440–1504) **22**, 132, 136, 213, 233, 242, **243**, 256, 271, 272, 273, 286, 300, 312; (works attributed to) 231
Collegio of Venice 96
Colleoni, Bartolomeo, *condottiere* 74, 276
Cominelli, Andrea (17C–18C) 173, 235, 270
Comnenus, Emperor Alexius 48
Constantinople 8, 9, 10, 12, 20, 22, 59, **60**, 65, 262, 316
Contarini family 242, 270
Contarini, Doge Andrea 213
Contarini, Doge Domenico 42, 74
Contarini, Cardinal Gasparo 11, 12, 249
Contarini, Giovanni (c.1549–1605) 101, 102, 296, 315
Contarini, Marino 226
Contino, Antonio (1566–1600) 91, 108
Contino, Bernardino (c.1568–c.1597) 112
Contino, Francesco (brother of Antonio; c.1590–before 1675) 171, 288
Contino, Tommaso (early 17C) 108
Cooper, James Fenimore 132
Corbellini, Carlo (18C) 234
Corderia 291; (Corderia della Tana) 294
Cornaro, Queen Caterina 112, 138; (images of) 155, 224; (tomb of) 112
Cornell, Joseph (1903–1972) 160
Corner family 224, 231
Corner, Alvise 246
Corner, Caterina (*see Cornaro*)
Corner, Federico 204
Corner, Doge Marco, tomb of 283
Corner Piscopia, Elena 132
Corona, Leonardo (1561–1605) 173, 192

Coronelli, Vincenzo, cartographer (1650–1718) 75, 333
Corradini, Antonio (1668–1752) 80, 168, 174, 179, 180
Correr, Teodoro 73, 137–38
Corte Nuova (Cannaregio) 250; (Castello) 265
Corte Seconda del Milion 245
Corvo, Baron (*see Rolfe*)
Council of Ten 10, 14, **97**, 103, 114, 168, 231, 332
Cox, Philip (b.1938) 295
Cozzi, Francesco (15C) 123, 257
Cozzi, Marco (brother of Francesco 15C) 123, 144, 204, 257
Crivelli, Carlo (1430/35–94/5) 20, 152
Crosato, Giovanni Battista (c.1685–1758) 179
Crusades, Fourth 9, 47, **60**, 65
Curtis family 130

D

D'Annunzio, Gabriele 130, 329
Daddi, Bernardo (active 1317–50) 159
Dalí, Salvador (1904–89) 160
Dalmatia, Dalmatian community in Venice 255, 263
Damaskinos, Michael (16C) 262
Damini, Pietro (1592–1631) 337
Dandolo, Doge Andrea 56, 59, 62; (sarcophagus of) 62
Dandolo, Doge Enrico 9, 60, 132
Dandolo, Doge Francesco 200
Dandolo, Marco 114
Danieli, hotel 255, 352
Dante (Dante Alighieri) 291
Dario, Giovanni 141
Daru, Pierre 15
David, Gerard (c.1460–1523) 165
Davie, Alan (b.1920) 161
Death in Venice 15, 329
Delaunay, Robert (1885–1941) 159
Delvaux, Paul (1897–1994) 160
Demus, Otto 52
Depero, Fortunato (1892–1960) 162
Desiderio da Firenze (16C) 61
Diaghilev, Sergei 329; (grave of) 311
Diamantini, Giuseppe (1621–1705) 115
Diana, Benedetto (Benedetto Rusconi; 1460–1525) 155, 184
Dickens, Charles 255
Diedo, Antonio (18C) 120
Diziani, Gaspare (1689–1767) 119, 123, 174, 213, 338

Doesburg, Theo van (1883–1931) 160
Dogana di Mare 142, 165
Doge of Venice 96–97
Doge's Palace 13, 21, 86–109, *86*
Dolfin, Doge Giovanni 283
Donà, Doge Leonardo 66, 232; (monument to) 304
Donatello (Donato di Niccolò; ?1386–1466) 20, 201
Donato Veneziano (active 1344–88) 95, 274
Donatus, St 318
Donizetti 117
Dorigny, Louis (1654–1742) 235, 254
Dorsoduro, *sestiere* of 143ff
Dossi, Battista (Giovanni Battista Luteri; active 1517–48) 159
Dossi, Dosso (1480–1542) 159
Dragonetti, Domenico 57, 63
Dubuffet, Jean (1901–85) 161
Duchamp, Marcel (1887–1968) 159
Dufy, Raoul (1877–1953) 219
Duodo, Francesco 119
Dürer, Albrecht (1471–1528) 94, 113

E

Eden, Frederic and Caroline 307
Emo, Admiral Angelo 293; (tomb of) 294
Erasmus, Desiderius 195
Erberia 138, 192
Eremite, church of 168
Ernst, Max (1891–1976) 159, 160, 161, 219
Eyck, Jan van (fl.1422–41) 77

F

Fabbriche Nuove di Rialto 138, 192
Fabbriche Vecchie di Rialto 138, 191
Falier, Giovanni, stele of 123
Falier, Doge Marin 10, 103, 106, 231; (sarcophagus of) 138
Falier, Doge Ordelafo 59
Falier, Doge Vitale 42, 43, 48; (portrait of) 54
Fattoretto, Giovanni Battista (fl.1715–30) 252
Fattori, Giovanni (1825/28–1908) 218
Favretto, Giacomo (1849–87) 138, 218
Fenice theatre 116–17
Ferrari, Ettore (1849–1929) 255–56
Ferrari, Giovanni (1744–1826) 294
Festa della Sensa 332, 371
Festivals: Redentore 309, 371; Salute 162, 371
Fetti, Domenico (1589–1624) 151

Filippini, church of (Chioggia) 337
Flangini, Girolamo 262
Fletcher, Constance 223
Florian, café 14, 16, 67, **70–71**
Fondaco dei Tedeschi 113–14, 133
Fondaco dei Turchi 16, 138, 222
Fondamenta degli Ormesini 246
Fondamenta Ospedaletto 185
Fondamente Nuove 288
Fondazione Angelo Masieri 140
Fondazione Cini (*see* Cini)
Fontana, Lucio (1899–1968) 161
Fontebasso, Francesco (1709–59) 119, 172, 186, 252, 315, 337
Forabosco, Gerolamo (c.1604–79) 224, 333
Forcellini, Annibale (1827–91) 311
Forni Pubblici 290
Fortezza di Sant'Andrea 331–32
Fortuny factory 310
Fortuny, Mariano (1871–1949) 125
Foscari, Doge Francesco 11, 73–74, 140; (portrait head of) 93; (statue of) 89; (tomb of) 203
Foscarini, Jacopo 174
Foscarini, Doge Marco 138
France, French 15, 71, 89, 305
Francesco da Faenza (15C) 258
Francesconi, Francesco (19C) 61
Franchetti, Baron Giorgio 226, 227
Francis, St 323
Franco, Battista (*see Semolei*)
Frangipane, Niccolò (1555–1600) 220
Frari, church of 198–206, *198*
Fratina, Il (Giovanni de Mio; 16C) 83
Frigimelica, Girolamo (1653–1732) 122
Fumiani, Gian Antonio (1643–1704) 176

G

Gabrieli, Andrea and Giovanni 57
Gaddi, Taddeo (d.1366) 159
Gaetano da Thiene, St 186, 223
Gai, Antonio (1686–1769) 66, 270
Gai, Giovanni (son of Antonio; active 1734–77) 268
Galileo (Galileo Galilei) 66, 132, 316
Galleria Franchetti (*see Ca' d'Oro*)
Galleria Internazionale d'Arte Moderna (*see Ca' Pesaro*)
Gallerie dell'Accademia 143–58
Galuppi, Baldassare 57, 288, 321
Gambello, Antonio (1451–81) 236, 256, 257
Gambello, Vittore (c.1460–1537) 227, 228

Gandolfi, Ubaldo (1728–81) 184
Gardella, Ignazio (1905–99) 186
'Garden of Eden' 307
Gardner, Isabella Stewart 130
Gaspari, Antonio (pupil of Baldassare Longhena; 1793–after 1823) 107, 133, 138, 173, 174, 217, 275
Gaspari, Giacomo (mid-18C) 338
Gattamelata, *condottiere* 74, 104
Gatti, Gaspare (fl.1594) 304
Gemito, Vincenzo (1852–1929) 126
Genoa, Genoese 10, 65, 283, 336; (*see also* Chioggia, battle of*)
German community in Venice 11, 113
Gesuati, church of 190
Gesuiti, church of 252–54
Ghetto 238–39
Ghislandi, Vittore (Fra' Galgario; 1655–1743) 152
Ghisoni, Fermo (pupil of Giulio Romano; 1505–75) 113
Giacometti Alberto (1901–66) 159, 162
Giacometti, Bruno (brother of Alberto; b.1907) 295
Giambono, Michele (c.1400–62) 56, 76, 144, 166, 228
Giardini Pubblici (Giardini Garibaldi) 15, 299
Giardino Papadopoli 223
Giolfino, Bartolomeo (c.1410–86) 152
Giordano, Luca (1632–1705) 158, 163, 224, 274, 300
Giorgione (Giorgio Barbarelli; c.1476–1510) **25**, 114, 145, **146–48**, 212; (frescoes from Fondaco dei Tedeschi) 229; (house where died) 194
Giovanni Antonio da Carona (1477–1534) 312
Giovanni d'Alemagna (brother-in-law of Antonio Vivarini; mid-15C) 158, 176, 237, *258*, 258, 313
Giovanni da Crema (17C) 331
Giovanni da Udine (1487–1564) 273
Giovanni di Martino da Fiesole (15C) 89, 279
Giovanni Veneziano (son of Paolo; 14C) 64
Girolamo da Santacroce (1480–1556) 110, 193, 292, 321
Girolamo da Treviso (Girolamo Pennacchi; 1498–1544) 164
Giudecca 306–10
Giudecca canal 186
Giulio del Moro (1566–1618) 112, 119, 301
Giustinian (Giustiniani) family 12, 268, 315

Giustinian, St Lorenzo 299; (paintings and sculptures of) 151, 152, 165, 300, 318
Giustinian, Marco 319
Giustiniani, Pompeo 279
Glass-making 13, 19, 316–17
Gleizes, Albert (1881–1953) 159
Gobbo di Rialto 192
Goes, Hugo van der (?c.1440–82) 77
Goethe, Johann Wolfgang von 8
Goldoni, Carlo 14, 134, 196–97, 261; (statue of) 113; house of (Chioggia) 338
Gondolas 188, 294, 349
González, Julio (1876–1942) 162
Gorky, Arshile (Vosdanig Manoog Adoian; 1904–48) 161
Government of Venice 96–97
Gradenigo, Doge Bartolomeo 49
Gradenigo, Doge Pietro 10, 103
Granaries of the Republic 138
Grand Canal 127ff
Grand Hotel des Bains 329
Grapiglia, Giovanni (1572–1621) 20, 278, 284
Grassi, Angelo 126
Grazia, La, island of 340
Great Council 15, **96**, 114, 238, 294
Greco, El (Domenicos Theotokopoulos; 1541–1614) 27, 262
Greeks, Greek community in Venice 261–63
Gregotti, Vittorio (b.1927) 236
Grigi, Gian Giacomo dei (d.1572) 132, 139
Grigi, Guglielmo (*see* Bergamasco)
Grimani, Cardinal Domenico 80, 107
Grimani, Giovanni, Patriarch of Aquileia 80, 83, 266, 270
Grimani, Giovanni, procurator, tomb of 301
Grimani, Doge Marino 95, 301
Gris, Juan (1887–1927) 159
Gritti, Doge Andrea 84, 266, 271; (relief of) 57
Gritti Palace Hotel 128, 354
Guarana, Jacopo (1720–1808) 63, 176, **179**, 182, 213, 216, 220, 274, 289, 292
Guarana, Vincenzo (c. 1735–1815) 115, 176, 274
Guardi, Francesco (1712–93) **29**, 152, 181, **182**, 184; (works attributed to) 230
Guardi, Giovanni Antonio (brother of Francesco; c.1699–1760) 171, 180, 182
Guariento (active 1338–68) 105, 159
Guercino (Giovanni Francesco Barbieri; 1591–1666) 184

Guggenheim Collection 159–62
Guggenheim, Peggy 159, 161
Guidi, Virgilio (1891–1984) 219

H
Handel, George Frideric 245
Harry's Bar 85, 359, 364
Hayez, Francesco (1791–1881) 73
Heliodorus, St 323, 326
Hélion, Jean (1904–87) 160
Heraclea 332, 333
Herri met de Bles (Il Civetta; c.1510–50) 107
Hoffmann, Josef (1870–1956) 295
Hospitals of Venice 289 (*see also Incurabili, Mendicanti, Ospedaletto, Ospedale de le Pute, Pietà*)
Hundertwasser, Friedensreich (1928–2000) 307

I
Incurabili, hospital of 186, 289

J
Jacobello del Fiore (1370–1439) 76, 95, 144
Jacopo della Quercia (1371/4–1438) 47, 64, 89, 200
James, G.P.R. 311
James, Henry 67, 128, 130, 142, 223, 256
Jappelli, Giuseppe (1783–1852) 274
Jews, Jewish community in Venice 238–39, 330
John XXIII, pope 49, 86
Jorn, Asger (Asger Oluf Jørgensen; 1914–73) 161

K
Kandinsky, Wassily (1866–1944) 160, 219
Karousos (early 19C) 294
Klee, Paul (1879–1940) 160
Klimt, Gustav (1862–1918) 219
Klontzas, Georgios (c.1540–1608) 262
Kupka, Frantisek (1871–1957) 160

L
Lace-making 321–23
Lagoon of Venice 34–35
Lama, Giulia (pupil of Piazzetta; 1681–1774) 121
Lamberti, Niccolò di Pietro (father of Pietro; 1370–1456) 46, 47
Lamberti, Pietro di Niccolò (son of Niccolò; 1393–1435) 47, 64, 89, 279

Laudis, Giovanni (c.1583–1631) 164
Law, John 115
Layard, Enid 140
Layard, Sir Henry 139, 141, 317
Lazzaretto Nuovo, island of 342–43
Lazzaretto Vecchio, island of 340
Lazzarini, Gregorio (1655–1730) 111, 175, 176, 180, 215, 315
Le Court, Juste (17C) 118, *118*, 163, 164, 179, 206, 224, 288, 312, 341
Legend of St Ursula, cycle of paintings, 155–57
Léger, Fernand (1881–1955) 159
Leoni, Leone (Il Cavalier Aretino; 1510–92) 228
Leopardi, Alessandro (1450–c.1523) 62, 276
Lepanto, battle of 12, 108, 119, 292
Letterini, Bartolomeo (1669–1745) 315
Liberale da Verona (1451–1536) 275
Liberi, Pietro (1614–87) 111, 115, 163, 235, 254, 338
Libreria Marciana 82–83, 84
Libro d'Oro 15, 96, 108
Licinio, Bernardino (c.1489–d. before 1565) 148, 184, 204, 315
Licinio, Giulio (1527–91/3) 82
Lido 328–33
Lippi, Filippino (son of Filippo; c.1457–1504) 165
Lippi, Fra' Filippo (1406/7–69) 159
Liss, Johann (c.1590–1631) 151, 224
Lissitzky, El (Eliezer Markowich; 1890–1941) 160
Lombardo family 23, 89, 94, 227, 231, **279**, 286, 287
Lombardo, Antonio (son of Pietro; c.1458–1516) 62, 95, 99, 268; (SS. Giovanni e Paolo) 278, 283
Lombardo, Pietro (Pietro Solari, father of Antonio and Tullio; c.1438–1515) **22–23**, 87, 95, 123, 165, 204, 212, 236, *236*, 237, 268, 286; (SS. Giovanni e Paolo) 278, 279, 285; (S. Maria dei Miracoli) 22–23, 243–44; (works attributed to) 275
Lombardo, Sante (son of Tullio; 16C) 262, 270; (works attributed to) 271
Lombardo, Tommaso (Tommaso da Lugano; 16C) 84, 112
Lombardo, Tullio (son of Pietro; 1455–1532) 23, 62, 95, 99, 111, 123, 162, 200, **227**, 231, 243, 268, 292; (SS. Giovanni e Paolo) 278, 283; (S. Maria dei Miracoli) 244; (works attributed to) 286

Lombards, Lombard League 8, 48, 323
Longhena, Baldassare (1604–82) **28**, 70, 86, 131, 138, 140, 164, 174, **179**, 206, 217, 224, 235, 250, 262, 263, 266, 288, 289, 299, 300, 305, 335, 338; (Salute) 28, 162–64; (works attributed to) 205, 239, 245, 278, 292, 304
Longhi, Alessandro (son of Pietro; 1733–1813) 75, 152, 176, 184, 274
Longhi, Pietro (1701–85) 29, 152, **182**, 274
Loredan, Andrea 136
Loredan, Doge Leonardo, tomb of 283–84
Lorenzetti, Carlo (1858–1945) 282
Lorenzo di Credi (c.1459–1537) 274
Lorenzino di Tiziano (16C) 283, 335
Lorenzo Veneziano (active 1356–72) 19, 75, 144
Los, Sergio (b.1934) 301
Loth, Johann Carl (1632–98) 119, 193, 243, 282, 288
Lotto, Lorenzo (1480–1556) 79, 148, 174, 220, **284–85**; (works from cartoons attributed to) 48
Louis of Toulouse, St 246
Loyola, St Ignatius 186
Luca Veneziano (son of Paolo; 14C) 64
Lucchesi, Matteo (1705–76) 273, 288
Lucy, St 234–35
Lutheran Church 230

M
Maccaruzzi, Bernardino (c.1728–1800) 208
Macchiaioli School (fl.1855–65) 218
Macelli 237–38
Maddalena, church of 233
Maderno, Stefano (1576–1636) 230
Madonna del Monte, island of 320
Madonna dell'Orto 240–42, *240*
Maestro del Crocifisso dei Frari (13C) 203
Maestro dell'Osservanza (14C–15C) 159
Maestro di Badia a Isola (active late 13C) 159
Maestro di San Trovaso (15C) 168
Maffei, Francesco (1605–60) 180, 231
Maffeo da Verona (1576–1618) 64, 215; (works from cartoons by) 63
Magazzini del Sale 186
Maggior Consiglio (*see* Great Council)
Maggiotto, Domenico (1713–94) 259
Magister Bertuccio (early 14C) 44
Magritte, René (1898–1967) 160
Malamocco 333
Malevich, Kasimir (1878–1935) 160

Malibran, Maria 245
Malipiero, Gian Francesco 117
Malipiero, Doge Pasquale 281
Malombra, Pietro (late 16C) 338
Mancini, Antonio (1852–1930) 184
Manfrediniana Picture Gallery 164
Manin, Daniele 16, 117, 120, **124**, 343; (sarcophagus of) 47
Manin, Doge Lodovico 15, 124, 235
Mann, Thomas 15
Mansueti, Giovanni (c.1485–1526/7) 152, 158, 243, 321
Mantegna, Andrea (brother-in-law of Giovanni Bellini; 1431–1506) 21, 24, 146, **227**
Manutius, Aldus 13, 147, **195**, 196
Manzù, Giacomo (1908–81) 49, 218
Maratta, Carlo (1625–1713) 126
Marcello, Benedetto 136
Marcello, Jacopo, monument to 199
Marcello, Doge Nicolò, monument to 279
Marchiori, Giovanni (1696–1778) 208, 212
Marconi, Rocco (active 1504–29) 284, 310
Marescalco, Il (*see Buonconsiglio*)
Marghera 35
Marieschi, Jacopo (1711–94) 119, 123, 213, 261
Marieschi, Michele (1710–1743) 158
Marinetti, Antonio (*see Chioggiotto*)
Marini, Marino (1901–80) 159
Mariotti, Giovanni Battista (c.1685–1765) 215, 337
Mark, St 8, 62; (legend of) **43**, 49, 152–54, 197, 299, 332; (sarcophagus of) 58
Marsich, Francesco (early 20C) 329
Marsili, Emilio (1841–1926) 232
Martini, Arturo (1889–1947) 219
Martini, Francesco di Giorgio (1439–c.1501) 174
Marziale, Marco (active c.1492–1507) 154
Masegne, dalle, brothers 57, 59, 165, 282, 283; (works attributed to) 241
Masegne, Jacobello dalle (d. ?1409) 55, 64, 75, 88, 123
Masegne, Paolo dalle (son of Jacobello; 15C) 283
Masegne, Pier Paolo dalle (brother of Jacobello; d. ?1403) 55, 64, 88, 123
Massari, Giorgio (1687–1766) 126, 131, 140, 141, 143, **179**, **190**, 213, 234, 259, 275
Master of the Horne Triptych (13C–14C) 159
Matas, Juan (late 14C) 165
Matisse, Henri (1869–1954) 219

Matta (Roberto Matta Echaurren; 1911–2002) 160
Mauro, Fra', cartographer (15C) 83, 312
Mazza, Giuseppe Maria (1653–1741) 285, 309, 341
Mazzolino, Ludovico (c. 1478–1528) 159
Mazzorbo, island of 320
Medici, Cosimo de' 305
Meduna, Giambattista (1800–80) 116, 121, 136
Memling, Hans (c. 1440–94) 146
Mendicanti, hospital of 287, 289
Menescardi, Giustino (1720–76) 175
Mengozzi-Colonna, Agostino (18C) 289
Mengozzi-Colonna, Gerolamo (1688–1772) 179, 235
Merceria 110–11
Messina, Francesco (1900–95) 218
Mestrovich Collection 184
Metamauco 333
Metsu, Gabriel (1629–67) 229
Metsys, Quentin (1465/6–1530) 107
Metzinger, Jean (1883–1956) 159
Meyring, Heinrich (1628–1723) 113, **115**, 119, 193, 261
Mezzani, Giuseppe (active early 19C) 305
Michaelangelo (Michaelangelo Buonarroti; 1475–1564) 306
Michelozzo (di Bartolomeo Michelozzi; c.1396–1472) 305
Michiel, Doge Vitale II 83, 255
Migliori, Francesco (1684–1734) 216, 234
Minio, Tiziano (pupil of Jacopo Sansovino; 1511–52) 61, 84
Miozzi, Eugenio (1898–1969) 131, 137, 176, 236, 330
Miró, Joan (1893–1983) 160
Mocenigo family 131, 214
Mocenigo, Doge Alvise I (monument to) 278; (portrait of) 151
Mocenigo, Doge Alvise II 214
Mocenigo, Doge Giovanni 77–78; (monument to) 23, 278
Mocenigo, Doge Pietro, monument to 278
Mocenigo, Doge Tommaso 11, 87; (tomb of) 279
Mocenigo, Tommaso Alvise, monument to 288
Mocetto, Girolamo (1458–1531) 284
Modigliani, Amedeo (1884–1920) 162, 169
Molinari, Antonio (1655–1705) 180, 288
Molmenti, Pompeo 14

Molo 85
Mondrian, Piet (1872–1944) 160
Monet, Claude (1840–1926) 130, 141
Monopola, Bartolomeo (17C) 63, 87, 89, 94, 95, 122, 271
Montagna, Bartolomeo (1450–c.1523) 79, 154, 158
Montemezzano, Francesco (c. 1540–after 1602) 173
Monteverdi, Claudio 57, 116; (tomb of) 204
Monumento alla Partigiana 301
Moore, Henry (1898–1986) 159, 219
Moore, Thomas 132
Morandi, Giorgio (1890–1964) 162, 219
Morando, Pietro (late 17C) 315
Moretta da Brescia (Alessandro Buonvicino; c.1498–1554) 259
Morleiter, Giovanni Maria (c. 1699–1781) 119, 190, 234, 235, 254, 275, 282, 306
Morleiter, Michelangelo (son of Giovanni; 1729–1806) 115, 172
Moro, Doge Cristoforo (bust of) 93; (tomb of) 237
Morosini family 132, 303, 304, 341
Morosini, Doge Francesco **75**, 164, 290, 293; (bust of) 105; (home of) 120; (sepulchral seal of) 122; (sword of) 61, 75
Morosini, Giorgio, monument to 341
Morosini, Doge Marin 49
Morosini, Doge Michele, tomb of 283
Mosca, Giovanni Maria (1493–c.1573) 123, 208, 227
Mo.S.E. project 30, 36, 331
Mosto, Alvise da 133
Motherwell, Robert (1915–91) 160
Mulino Stucky 310
Murano 19, 313–20
Murazzi (Pellestrina) 35, 333–34
Murer, August (1922–85) 301
Murray, Elizabeth 134
Murray, John 330
Museums:
 Archeologico 80–82
 Ca' d'Oro 225–30
 Ca' Pesaro 217–20
 Ca' Rezzonico (Settecento Veneziano) 178–84
 Chioggia 338
 Cini 158–59
 Correr 72–80
 Diocesan Art 86
 Doge's Palace 91–93

Museums contd.
 Fortuny 125–26
 Glass 315–18
 Icons 262
 Jewish 239
 Lace 321–23
 Merletto (*see Lace*)
 Natural History 222
 Naval 292–94
 Oriental 219
 Palazzo Mocenigo 216–17
 Parish Museum, Murano 315
 Querini-Stampalia 273–74
 San Marco 63–64
 Torcello 327–28
 Vetrario (*see Glass*)
Muttoni, Pietro (della Vecchia; c.1603/5–78) 119, 215, 275; (works from cartoons by) 54

N
Nacchini, Pietro, organ-maker (1700–c.1770) 192, 224, 259, 288, 292, 299
Nanni di Bartolo (1419–51) 199
Napoleon **14–15**, 65, 70, 71, 89, 97, 104, 117, 124, 238, 293, 296, 299
Negri, Pietro (1628–79) 210
Nervi, Pier Luigi (1891–1979) 124
Niccolò di Pietro (active 1394–1427) 144, 158
Nicholson, Ben (1894–1982) 161, 219
Nino Pisano (active c.1349–60) 283
Nittis, Guiseppe de (1846–84) 218
Nogari, Giuseppe (1699–1763) 152
Nono, Luigi (1850–1918) 218
Nono, Luigi, composer 117
Novecento art movement 219
Novelli, Pietro (1603–47) 340

O
Ognissanti, church and hospital 168; (Pellestrina) 336
Ongaro, Michele (Michele Fabris; 1644–84) 163, 300
Oratorio dei Crociferi 252
Orseolo, Doge Pietro I 42, 59
Orseolo, Doge Pietro II 114, 332
Ospedale (*see Hospitals*)
Ospedale de le Pute 296
Ospedaletto 288–89
Ottomans 12, 14

P

Padiglioni delle Navi 294
Padovanino (Alessandro Varotari;
  1588–1648/9) 82, 158, 164, 174, 175,
  190, 220, 224, 274; (works from cartoons
  by) 56
Pagan, Matteo (active 1538–62) 74
Paisiello, Giovanni 116
Pala d'Oro 19, 59; (Torcello) 328
Pala Pesaro 204–05
Palaeologus, Emperor John 222
Palaeologus, Emperor Michael 10, 60
Palazzi and Palazzetti
  Palazzo dell'Ambasciatore 141
  Palazzo Arian-Cicogna 173
  Palazzo Balbi 140
  Palazzo Barbarigo (Cannaregio) 135
  Palazzo Barbarigo (Dorsoduro) 141
  Palazzo Barbarigo (S. Marco) 130
  Palazzo Barbarigo della Terrazza 140
  Palazzo Barbaro 130
  Palazzo Barbaro (Wolkoff) 142
  Palazzo Barzizza 139
  Palazzo Belloni-Battagià 138
  Palazzo Bembo 132
  Palazzo Bembo-Boldù 243
  Palazzo Benzon 132
  Palazzo Bernardo 139
  Palazzo Boldù 135
  Palazzo Businello 139
  Palazzo dei Camerlenghi 138, 191
  Palazzo Cappello-Layard 139
  Palazzo Cappello-Malipiero 131
  Palazzo Cavalli-Franchetti 121, 131
  Palazzo Centani (*see Casa Goldoni*)
  Palazzo Civran 133
  Palazzo Civran-Grimani 140
  Palazzo Coccina-Tiepolo-Papadopoli 139
  Palazzo Contarini del Bovolo 124
  Palazzo Contarini delle Figure 131
  Palazzo Contarini degli Scrigni 141
  Palazzo Contarini dal Zaffo (Cannaregio)
    249, 253, 356
  Palazzo Contarini dal Zaffo (Polignac) 141
  Palazzo Contarini-Corfù 141
  Palazzo Contarini-Fasan 128, *128*
  Palazzo Contarini-Michiel 141
  Palazzo Contarini-Pisani 135
  Palazzo Contarini-Seriman 252
  Palazzo Contin 233
  Palazzo Corner (*see Ca' Grande*)
  Palazzo Corner della Regina 138

Palazzi contd.
  Palazzo Corner-Contarini dei Cavalli 132
  Palazzo Corner-Gheltof 132
  Palazzo Corner-Mocenigo 196
  Palazzo Corner-Spinelli 22
  Palazzo Correr 232
  Palazzo Correr-Contarini 137
  Palazzetto Dandolo 132
  Palazzo dei Dieci Savi 139
  Palazzo Diedo 232
  Palazzo Dolfin-Manin 132
  Palazzo Donà (Campo S. Maria Formosa)
    271
  Palazzo Donà (Grand Canal) 139
  Palazzo Donà della Madonnetta 139
  Palazzo Donà delle Rose 233
  Palazzo Duodo (Campo S. Angelo) 123
  Palazzo Duodo (Gall. Franchetti) 135, 230
  Palazzo Duodo (San Stae) 138
  Palazzo Emo 135
  Palazzo Erizzo alla Maddalena 135
  Palazzo Erizzo-Nani-Mocenigo 131
  Palazzo Falier 231
  Palazzetto Falier 131
  Palazzo Farsetti 132
  Palazzo Flangini 137
  Palazzo Flangini-Fini 128
  Palazzo Fontana 135
  Palazzo Foscari 133
  Palazzo Foscari-Contarini 137
  Palazzo Foscarini-Giovannelli 138
  Palazzo Gaggia 128
  Palazzo Garzoni 132
  Palazzo Genovese 142
  Palazzo Giovannelli (Cannaregio) 231
  Palazzo Giovannelli (Grand Canal) 137
  Palazzi Giustinian 140
  Palazzo Giustinian 127
  Palazzo Giustinian (Murano) 315, 318
  Palazzo Giustinian-Persico 140
  Palazzo Giustiniani-Lolin 131
  Palazzo Gradenigo 223
  Palazzo Grassi 126, 131
  Palazzo Grimani 272
  Palazzo Grimani (Court of Appeal) 132
  Palazzo Grimani (Sorlini) 139
  Palazzo Gussoni-Grimani della Vida 135
  Palazzo Labia 29, 235
  Palazzo Lando-Corner-Spinelli 132
  Palazzo da Lezze (Rio di Noale) 135
  Palazzo Lezze 250
  Palazzo Loredan (Cini) 141

Palazzi contd.
Palazzo Loredan (Grand Canal) 132
Palazzo Loredan (S. Stefano) 120
Palazzetto di Madame Stern 141
Palazzo Magno 233
Palazzo Manfrin 236
Palazzo Mangilli-Valmarana 133
Palazzo Manolesso-Ferro 128
Palazzo Marcello 135
Palazzo Marcello-Papadopoli 245
Palazzo Martinengo 132
Palazzo Martinengo-Mandelli 137
Palazzo Mastelli 249
Palazzo Michiel dal Brusà 133, 351
Palazzo Michiel dalle Colonne 133
Palazzo Minelli-Spada 249, 253
Palazzo Minotto 130
Palazzo Mocenigo 131
Palazzo Mocenigo (S. Stae) 216–17
Palazzo Molin 135
Palazzo Molin-Balbi-Valier 141
Palazzo Moro 141
Palazzo Moro-Lin 131
Palazzo Morosini 120
Palazzo Morosini-Brandolin 138
Palazzo Morosini-Sagredo 133
Palazzo da Mula 141
Palazzo da Mula (Murano) 315
Palazzo Orio-Semitecolo 142
Palazzo Pesaro degli Orfei 125–26
Palazzo Pesaro-Papafava 250
Palazzo Pesaro-Ravà 133
Palazzo Pisani 122
Palazzo Pisani (Cannaregio) 245
Palazzo Pisani (Gritti Palace) 128, 354
Palazzo Pisani della Moretta 140, 196
Palazzo Priuli 263
Palazzo Priuli (S.M. Formosa) 271
Palazzo Priuli-Bon 138, 214
Palazzo Querini 141
Palazzo Querini-Stampalia 273–74
Palazzo Ravà 139
Palazzo Salviati 142
Palazzo Savorgnan 236
Palazzo Sernagiotto 133
Palazzo Soranzo (Grand Canal) 135
Palazzo Soranzo (S. Polo) 194
Palazzo Soranzo-Calbo-Crotta 137
Palazzo Soranzo-Cappello 223
Palazzo Surian 238
Palazzo Testa 236
Palazzo Tiepoletto 140

Palazzi contd.
Palazzo Tiepolo (Europa & Regina Hotel) 128
Palazzo Tiepolo (Campo S. Polo) 194
Palazzo Tiepolo (Grand Canal) 140
Palazzo Treves de' Bonfili 128
Palazzo Trevisan (Murano) 318
Palazzo Trevisan-Cappello 86
Palazzetto Tron 132
Palazzo Tron (S. Marco) 132
Palazzo Tron (S. Croce) 138, 216
Palazzo Tron (S. Stae) 138
Palazzo Valier 194
Palazzo Vanier-Sanudo-Van Axel 245
Palazzo Vendramin 232
Palazzo Vendramin-Calergi 136, 233
Palazzo Venier dei Leoni 141, 159
Palazzo Venier-Contarini 130
Palazzetto Viaro 217
Palazzo Vitturi 271
Palazzo Zen 252
Palazzo Zenobio 173
Palazzo Zorzi 273
Palazzo Zorzi-Bon 273
Palladio (Andrea di Pietro della Gondola; 1508–80) **27–28**, 84, 101, 158, 234, 266, 288, 305, 306, **309**; (Redentore) 308–09; (S. Giorgio Maggiore) 303–04; (works attributed to) 318
Palma Giovane (Giacomo Negretti; great-nephew of Palma Vecchio; 1548–1628) 27, **102**, 106, 107, 110, 166, 174, 186, 192, 195, 199, 213, **220**, 223, 224, 235, 241, 252, 254, 261, 270, 275, 281, 292, 296, 306, 310, 315, 340; (monument to) 281; (self-portrait) 274; (works from cartoons by) 52, 55, 56
Palma Vecchio (Giacomo Negretti; great-uncle of Palma Giovane; c.1480–1528) 150, 152, **272**, 274; (works attributed to) 257
Paolo Uccello (Paolo Doni; 1397–1475) 52
Paolo Veneziano (active 1335–60) 19, 64, 75, 126, 144, 176, **200**, *201*; (works attributed to) 220, 258
Paradisi, Niccolò di Pietro (fl.1394–1430) 244
Parodi, Filippo (1630–1702) 122, 224
Particiaco family 265
Particiaco, Doge Agnello 231
Particiaco, Doge Giustiniano 42, 43, 257
Pasti, Matteo de' (15C) 228

Paul V, pope 14, 232
Paul, bishop of Torcello 323
Pellegrini, Giovanni Antonio (1675–1741)
    180, 214
Pellegrini, Girolamo (c.1624–after 1700) 270
Pellestrina, island of 333–36; (village of)
    334–36
Pellico, Silvio 109, 312
Pennacchi, Pier Maria (1464–1514/5) 158,
    164, 244, 315
Pepin, son of Charlemagne 333
Peranda, Sante (1566–1638) 111, 123, 213,
    224
Perilli, Paolo (20C) 236
Perrault, Claude (1613–88) 237
Pesaro family 200, 204
Pesaro, Admiral Benedetto, tomb of 200
Pesaro, Doge Giovanni, 217; (mausoleum of)
    205–06
Pesaro, Bishop Jacopo 204–05
Pescheria 138, 192
Petrarch (Francesco Petrarca) 82, 83, 196,
    259
Petrus F. (early 16C) 58
Pevsner, Antoine (1886–1962) 160, 162
Piaggia, Giovanni Battista (organ-maker; early
    18C) 204, 213
Pianta, Francesco il Giovane (c. 1632–72)
    200, 210
Piatti, Sante (17C) 115, 174
Piazza, Paolo (1557–1621) 195
Piazza San Marco (*see S. Mark's*)
Piazzale Roma 223
Piazzetta Giovanni XXIII 86
Piazzetta, Giacomo (c.1640–1705) 230, 282
Piazzetta, Giovanni Battista (son of Giacomo;
    1683–1754) 121, *122*, 52, *153*, 158, 175,
    180, 184, 188, 190, 259, **275**, 285; (works
    attributed to) 338
Piazzetta di San Marco (*see S. Mark's*)
Picabia, Francis (1879–1953) 160
Picasso, Pablo (1881–1973) 159
Piero della Francesca (1416–92) 146, 159
Piero di Cosimo (?1461–?1521) 159
Pietà, church and music school of 259, 261,
    289
Pietro da Cortona (Pietro Berrettini;
    1596–1669) 158
Pietro da Saliba (active 1497–1530) 154
Pietro da Salò (pupil of Jacopo Sansovino;
    fl.1535–61) 109, 192, 263
Pinault, François 126, 131, 165

Pisanello (Antonio Pisano; 1377–1455) 228
Pisani, Vettor 284, 336
Pisano, Giunta (1202–55) 159
Pisis, Filippo de (1896–1956) 219
Pitati, Bonifacio de' (*see Bonifacio Veronese*)
Pittoni, Giovanni Battista (1687–1767) 152,
    193, 215
Pius VII, pope 305, 334
Plague in Venice 12, 162, 207, 308
Pollock, Jackson (1912–56) 160, 161
Polo, Marco 83, 245, 265
Ponte dell'Accademia 131
Ponte dei Pugni 176
Ponte delle Tette 364
Pontormo (Jacopo Carucci; 1494–1556) 159
Ponzone, Matteo (1586–1675) 193, 337
Pordenone (Giovanni Antonio de' Sacchis;
    c.1483–1539) 151, 192, 208, 229, 315
Porta della Carta 23, 89
Porto di Chioggia 336
Porto di Lido 331, 332
Pound, Ezra 185–86; (grave of) 311
Pozzo, Giuseppe (1645–1721) 235, 254
Pozzo, Leopoldo dal (early 18C) 44, 52
Pratt, Hugo 333
Previtali, Andrea (c.1480–1528) 237
Procaccini, Camillo (c.1546–1627) 224
Procuratie Nuove 70–71
Procuratie Vecchie 70
Proust, Marcel 127, 129, 255
Punta della Dogana 165

Q
Quadri, café 14, 67, **70**, 364
Querena, Lattanzio (1768–1853) 189, 237
Querini family 103, 273

R
Raffaellino del Garbo (1466–1524) 228
Rangone, Tommaso 79, 110, 118, 150
Ravenna 8, 325, 327
Raverti, Matteo (fl.1389–1434) 226
Redentore, church of 28, 307–10, *308*
Rezzonico family 14
Rezzonico, Carlo (Pope Clement XIII) 135,
    179
Rialto 191–93; (bridge) 133, 139, 191;
    (markets) 138
Ricci, Marco (nephew of Sebastiano;
    1679–1729) 134, 151, 184, 215
Ricci, Sebastiano (1659–1734) 121, 134, 151,
    152, 164, 174, 190, 208, 214, **215**, 232,

274; (works from cartoons by) 44
Riccio, Il (Andrea Brisoco; 1470–1532) 75, 226, 227
Rickards, E.A. (1872–1920) 295
Ridotto 114, 182
Ridotto Venier 111
Rietveld, Gerrit (1888–1964) 295
Rio delle Fornace 185
Rio della Misericordia 246
Rio Riello *298*, 299
Rio di Sant'Anna 299
Rio della Sensa 249
Rio Terrà San Leonardo 234
Riva degli Schiavoni 255–56
Rizzo, Antonio (uncle of Lorenzo Bregno; c.1430–99) 54, 55, 57, 87, 89, **94**, 95, 105, 164, 203, 227, 230; (works attributed to) 241, 295, 300
Robbia, Andrea della (works attributed to) 237
Roberti, Ercole de' (c.1456–96) 159
Roccatagliata, Niccolò (17C) 115, 228, 304
Roccatagliata, Sebastiano (17C) 115
Roch, St 207
Rolfe, Frederick (Baron Corvo) 196; (grave of) 311
Romano, Marco (active early 14C) 222
Rosa, Cristoforo (16C) 83
Rossellino, Antonio (Antonio Gamberelli; 1427–79) 165
Rossi, Aldo (1931–97) 116
Rossi, Davide (c.1744–after 1815) 194
Rossi, Domenico (1657–1737) 138, 214, 252
Rossini, Gioacchino 116, 117, 245
Rosso, Medardo (1858–1928) 218
Rost, Giovanni (16C) 64
Rothko, Mark (1903–70) 161
Rouault, Georges (1871–1958) 219
Rousseau, Jean Jacques 14, 238
Rovetta, Giovanni 57
Rubens, Sir Peter Paul (1577–1640) 119
Rubini, Agostino (1560–95) 133
Rudge, Olga 185, 186
Ruer, Tommaso (d.1696) 163, 168
Ruga degli Orefici 191
Rusconi, Giovanni Antonio (d.1599) 101, 108
Ruskin, John 9, 16, 27, 63, 79, 92, 127, 128, **129**, 189, 200, 206, 209, 222, 255, 263, 271, 278, 281, 283, 312
Russolo, Luigi (1885–1947) 162

S
Sabbadino, Cristoforo 336, 338
Sacca della Misericordia 249–50
Sacca Fisola 310
Sacca Sessola, island of 341
Saetti, Bruno (1902–84) 219
Sagredo, St Gerard 270
Salute (*see S. Maria della Salute*)
Salvadori, Giuseppe (19C) 237
Salviati glassworks 139, 142, 317
Salviati, Francesco (1510–63) 273
Salviati, Giuseppe (c.1520–c.1575) 82, 83, 119, 164, 199, **259**, 315, 320; (works from cartoons by) 52, 63
S. Agnese 189
S. Alvise 246–49
S. Andrea (Chioggia) 337
S. Angelo Raffaele (*see Angelo Raffaele*)
S. Anna 301
S. Antonin 263
S. Antonio (Pellestrina) 335
S. Apollonia, cloister of 86
S. Aponal 194
SS. Apostoli 231
S. Barnaba 178
S. Bartolomeo 113
S. Basso 86
S. Benedetto 126
S. Biagio 294
S. Canciano 243
S. Cassiano 193
S. Caterina 252
S. Caterina (Mazzorbo) 320
S. Croce, church of 307
S. Croce, monastery of 223
S. Croce degli Armeni 111
S. Domenico (Chioggia) 336
S. Elena 295
SS. Ermagora e Fortunato (*see S. Marcuola*)
S. Eufemia 310
S. Eurosia (Le Vignole) 341
S. Eustachio (*see S. Stae*)
S. Fantin 117–18
S. Felice 231
S. Fosca 232
S. Fosca (Torcello) 327
S. Francesco della Vigna 266–71
S. Francesco da Paola 296
S. Gemignano 15, 71
S. George (Anglican Church) 140, 141
S. Geremia 234
S. Giacomo (Chioggia) 337

S. Giacomo dell'Orio 220–21
S. Giacomo di Rialto 10, 191–92
S. Giobbe 236–37, *236*
S. Giorgio dei Greci 262
S. Giorgio Maggiore 27, 28, *302*, 303–05
S. Giovanni in Bragora 260–61
S. Giovanni Crisostomo 242–43
S. Giovanni Decollato 221
S. Giovanni Elemosinario 192
S. Giovanni Evangelista 213
S. Giovanni Nuovo 273
SS. Giovanni e Paolo 277–85, *277*
S. Giuliano 110–11
S. Giuseppe di Castello 301
S. Giustina 266
S. Gregorio 142, 185
S. Lazzaro dei Mendicanti 287–88
S. Lio 275
S. Lorenzo 265
S. Luca 125
S. Marciliano 232
S. Marcuola 234
S. Margherita 175
S. Maria degli Angeli (Murano) 315
S. Maria Assunta (Cannaregio; *see Gesuiti*)
S. Maria Assunta (Torcello) 325–27
S. Maria della Carità 141, 143, 152, 158
S. Maria dei Carmini 173–74
S. Maria della Consolazione (*see S. Maria della Fava*)
S. Maria dei Derelitti (*see Ospedaletto*)
S. Maria della Fava 275
S. Maria Formosa 271–72
S. Maria del Giglio 118–19, *118*
S. Maria Gloriosa dei Frari *198*, 198–206
S. Maria Mater Domini 217
S. Maria dei Miracoli 22–23, 243–44, *244*
S. Maria della Misericordia 250
S. Maria del Pianto 288
S. Maria del Rosario (*see Gesuati*)
S. Maria della Salute 28, 162–64, *163*
S. Maria dei Servi 232
S. Maria della Visitazione *189*, 190
SS. Maria e Donato (Murano) 318–20, *319*
S. Mark's:
    Basilica of 9, 18–19, 22, **41–62**, *53*
    Campanile of 66
    Horses of 64, 65
    Loggetta 66
    Museum of 63–64
    Piazzetta of 22, 83–84
    Procurators of 70
    Square 9, 10, 15, 67–72

S. Martino 292
S. Martino (Burano) 321
S. Maurizio 120
S. Michele in Isola 15, 22, 312
S. Moisè 114–15
S. Nicola da Tolentino 223–24
S. Nicolò al Lido 331
S. Nicolò dei Mendicoli 172–73
S. Pantalon 176
S. Pietro (Pellestrina) 334
S. Pietro di Castello 13, 299–300
S. Pietro Martire (Murano) 313–15
S. Polo 194–95
S. Rocco 207–08
S. Salvatore 111–13
S. Samuele 126
S. Sebastiano 169–71
S. Silvestro 193
S. Simeone Grande 222–23
S. Simeone Piccolo 137, 223
S. Sofia 136, 230
S. Stae 138, 214–16
S. Stefano 122–23; (frescoes from) 229
SS. Trinità (Chioggia) 337
S. Trovaso 166–68
S. Vitale 120–21
S. Vito (Pellestrina) 335
S. Zaccaria 20, 22, 24, 256–59, *256*
S. Zan Degolà (*see S. Giovanni Decollato*)
S. Zanipolo (*see SS. Giovanni e Paolo*)
S. Zulian (*see S. Giuliano*)
San Clemente, island of 340–41
San Francesco del Deserto, island of 323
San Giacomo in Palude, island of 320
San Giorgio Maggiore, island of 303–05
San Lazzaro degli Armeni, island of 339–40
San Marco, *sestiere* of 41ff
San Michele, island of 311–12
San Pietro in Volta (Pellestrina) 334
San Polo, *sestiere* of 191ff
San Servolo, island of 338–39
Sanmicheli, Michele (1484–1559) 32, 132, 331–32; (works attributed to) 272
Sansovino, Jacopo (1486–1570) 13, 42, 57–58, 61, 63, 66, 70, 71, **84**, 85, 94, 109, 110, 112, 130, 132, 138, 171, 186–88, 192, 204, 250, 266, 267, 268, 290, 292, 337; (Libreria Marciana) 82, 84; (tomb of) 62; (works attributed to) 254, 291, 310
Sant'Erasmo, island of 342, 343
Santa Croce, *sestiere* of 216ff
Santa Lucia Station 236
Santi, Giovanni de' (late 14C) 62, 241

Santi, Lorenzo (19C) 73, 85, 86, 193, 206

Santo Spirito, island of 341

Saraceni, Carlo (1579–1620) 310

Sardi, Antonio (father of Giuseppe; 17C) 119, 287, 288

Sardi, Giovanni (1863–1913) 330

Sardi, Giuseppe (son of Antonio; 1624–99) 110, 111, 118, **119**, 137, 176, 235, 236, 241, 287, 288; (works attributed to) 238

Sargent, John Singer (1856–1925) 130, 179

Sarpi, Fra' Paolo 13–14, 132, 135, **232**; (tomb of) 312

Sassetta (Stefano di Giovanni; 1392–1450) 159

Sassoferrato (Giovanni Battista Salvi; 1609–85) 164

Savelli, Paolo, tomb of 200

Savoldo, Girolamo (15C–16C) 237

Scalfarotto, Giovanni (c.1690–1764) 13, 223

Scalzi, church of 137, 235

Scamozzi, Vincenzo (pupil of Palladio; 1552–1616) 70, **84–85**, 101, 111, 136, 141, 224, 287, 288, 301, 309

Scarlatti, Alessandro 245

Scarpa, Carlo (1906–78) 70, 73, 143, **273**, 274, 295, 301

Scarpagnino (Antonio Abbondi; 16C) 87, 89, 94, 108, 114, 120, 131, 138, 139, 169, 191, 192, **208**, 210

Scattolin, Angelo (20C) 124

Schiavone, Lo (Andrea Meldolla; ?1500–1563) 82, 83, 119, 174, 220

Schiavone, Michelangelo (1712–72) 296, 338

Schütz, Heinrich 57

Schwitters, Kurt (1887–1948) 160

Scolari, Massimo (20C) 173

Scuole and Scuole Grandi, general 10–11, 23, 287

Scuola degli Albanesi 120; (painting from) 228

Scuola dell'Angelo Custode 230

Scuola dei Battiloro e Tiraoro 138, 216

Scoletta della Bragora 261

Scuola dei Calegheri 197

Scuola Canton, synagogue 239

Scuola Grande della Carità 141, 143, 144

Scuola Grande dei Carmini 174–75

Scuola del Cristo 234

Scuola Italiana, synagogue) 239

Scuola Levantina, synagogue 239

Scuola dei Luganegheri 363

Scuola della Misericordia 250; (original floor from) 84

Scuole contd.

Scuola dei Morti 137

Scuola di S. Alvise 246

Scuola di S. Fantin 118

Scuola di S. Giorgio degli Schiavoni 23–24, 263

Scuola Grande di S. Giovanni Evangelista 212–13; (paintings from) 21, 154–55, 158

Scuola Grande di San Marco 286; (paintings from) 150–51, 152

Scuola di S. Nicolò dei Greci 262

Scuola di S. Orsola, paintings from 23, 155–57

Scuola Grande di S. Rocco 27, 207, 208–12

Scuola di S. Teodoro 111

Scuola Spagnola, synagogue 239

Scuola del Spirito Santo 186

Scuola Grande Tedesca 239

Scuola dei Varotari 176

Sebastiano del Piombo (Sebastiano Luciani; 1485–1547) 145, 242

Segala, Francesco (active 1558–92) 62

Selva, Giovanni Antonio (c.1753–c.1819) 116, 117, 120, 152, 158, 299

Selvo, Doge Domenico 42

Seminario Patriarcale 164

Semolei, Il (Battista Franco; c.1498–1561) 82, 83, 112, 270

Senate of Venice 96, 102

Severini, Gino (1883–1966) 160, 162

Signorelli, Luca (c.1441–1523) 228

Signorini, Telemaco (1835–1901) 218

Simeon, St 222

Sironi, Mario (1885–1961) 162, 219

Smeraldi, Francesco (16C) 110

Smith, Consul Joseph 133, **134**, 181, 215; (tomb of) 141

Soffici, Ardengo (1879–1964) 162

Solari, Cristoforo (1460–1527) 176

Soli, Giuseppe (1745–1823) 71

Soranzo, Doge Giovanni 62

Sorella, Simone (fl.1587–1610) 265, 303

Sottoportico del Ghetto 239

Spavento, Giorgio (15C) 62, 87, 108, 111, 114

Spirito Santo, church of 186

Sposalizio (*see Festa della Sensa*)

Squero (Rio della Avogaria) 168; (S. Trovaso) 190

State Archives (*see Archivio di Stato*)

Steen, Jan (1626–79) 229

Stefano di Sant'Agnese (14C) 258
Steno, Doge Michele, tomb of 281
Stephen, St 303
Still, Clyfford (1904–80) 160
Stirling, James (1926–92) 295
Stom, Antonio (1688–1734) 216
Stones of Venice, The 129
Strada Nuova 230
Stravinsky, Igor 117; (grave of) 311
Strozzi, Bernardo (1581–1644) 82, 126, 151, 224
Sustris, Lambert (c.1515–84) 83
Synagogues 239

T
Tagliapietra, Alvise (1670–1747) 282, 338
Tagliapietra, Carlo (17C–18C) 282
Tancredi (1927–64) 161
Tanguy, Yves (1900–55) 160, 219
Tarsia, Antonio (1663–1739) 216, 285
Tasso, Torquato 222
Teatro Malibran 245
Tedesco, Girolamo (active early 16C) 114
Tedesco, Leonardo (15C) 260
Temanza, Tommaso (1705–89) 233, 339
Temporello (15C) 165
Terese, church of 173
Tetrarchs, the 46, 47
Tezon Grande 342
Theatines, order of 223
Theodore, St 8
Theotokopoulos (*see El Greco*)
Tiepolo, Bajamonte 103, 110, 133
Tiepolo, Doge Giacomo 97
Tiepolo, Giambattista (1696–1770) **28–29**, 102, 126, 151, 152, **175**, 181, 188, 195, 212, 231, 246, 259, 270, 274, 288, 338, 340; (*Antony and Cleopatra*) 29, 235; (Ca' Rezzonico) 179, 180, 182; (Carmini) 174–75; (Gesuati) 190; (*St Bartholomew*) 214–15
Tiepolo, Gian Domenico (son of Giambattista; 1727–1804) 158, 175, **195**, 213, 257, 275, 296; (Ca' Rezzonico) 179, 181–82, *183*,
Tiepolo, Lorenzo (son of Giambattista; 1736–76) 179
Tiepolo, Doge Lorenzo 47
Tintoretto, Domenico (son of Jacopo; c.1560–1635) 74, 99, 105, **106**, 108, 135, 151, 166, 192, 193, 209, 210, 213, 232, 315
Tintoretto, Jacopo (Jacopo Robusti; 1519–94) **27**, 74, 83, 99, 101, 102, 109, 119, 148,

151, 158, 166, 184, 190, 193, **210**, 217, 228, 231, 232, 249, 254, 257, 288, 304; (paintings of *Crucifixion*) 193, 212; (paintings of *Last Supper*) 27, 166, 194, 223, 234, 304; (Madonna dell'Orto) 241; (*Miracles of St Mark*) 150–51; (S. Rocco) 27, *207*, 208–10; (S. Stefano) 123; (*Wedding at Cana*) 164; (self-portrait) 210; (house of) 249; (tomb of) 241; (works attributed to) 315, 337; (works from cartoons by) 52, 55, 58, 63
Tirali, Andrea (c.1660–1737) 86, 121, 223, 231, 236, **285**, 335, 337
Titian (Tiziano Vecellio; c.1485–1576) **25–27**, 82, 83, 99, 101, 114, 125, 148, 150, 158, 163, 164, 165, 171, 192, **203**, 210, 212, 242, 252, 275; (*Assumption*) 26, 199, 201, 203; (frescoes from Fondaco dei Tedeschi) 229; (*Pala Pesaro*) 204–05; (*Pietà*) 26, 151; (*Presentation of the Virgin*) 156, 157–58; (S. Salvatore) 112; (monument to) 199; (portrait of) 220; (copy of painting by) 281; (works from cartoons by) 52; (works attributed to) 229
Tito, Ettore (1859–1941) 235
Tofts, Catherine 134, 330
Tommaseo, Niccolò 120
Torcello 8, 323–28, *324*
Torlioni, Fra' Bernardo 169
Torre dell'Orologio 13, 72
Torre di Massimiliano 343
Torres, Duilio (20C) 295
Torres, Giuseppe (1872–1935) 330
Torretti, Giuseppe (1661–1743) 174, 216, 235, 254, 272
Torretti, Giuseppe (Giuseppe Bernardi, nephew of Giuseppe Torretti, teacher of Canova; 1694–1774) 275
Tremignon, Alessandro (late 17C) 114, 128, 186, 235
Trevisani, Angelo (1669–1753) 214, 259
Triva, Antonio (1626–99) 123
Tron, Doge Niccolò, tomb of 203
True Cross, painting cycle 21, 154–55; (relic of) 213
Tura, Cosmè (1429–95) 46, 76, 159
Turks, Turkish community in Venice 11, 138, 222; (*see also Ottomans*)
Turner, J.M.W. (1775–1851) 127
Tuscan artists in Venice 52, 64, 199–200, 258; (*see also Andrea del Castagno, Donatello, Jacopo della Quercia, Michelozzo*)
Tzanfournaris, Emmanuel (1573–1631) 262

V

Vaporetto routes 347–49
Vecchietta (Lorenzo di Pietro; 1410–80) 159
Vecellio, Francesco (brother of Titian; c.1490–c.1560) 112
Vecellio, Marco (nephew of Titian; 1545–1611) 101, 104, 192, 281
Vedova, Emilio (b.1919) 161, 218
Vendramin, Doge Andrea (monument to) 23; (tomb of) 283
Vendramin, Gabriele 147
Venice in Peril Fund 30–31, 241
Venier family 116, 221, 281
Venier, Doge Antonio (portrait of) 75–76; (tomb of) 281
Venier, Elena 111
Venier, Doge Francesco, monument to 112
Venier, Doge Sebastiano (home of) 271; (monument to) 281
Verdi, Giuseppe 117, 127
Veronese (Paolo Caliari; 1528–88) 82, 83, 101, 102, 104, 106, 109, 110, 118, 125, 148, 150, 165, **169**, 174, 176, 195, 268, 282, 288, 300, 301, 305, 315, 318; (*Christ in the House of Levi*) 148–49, 150; (San Sebastiano) 169–70; (house where died) 126; (tomb of) 170; (works from cartoons by) 55; (works attributed to) 310
Verrocchio, Andrea del (1435–88) 276
Via Garibaldi 296
Viani, Alberto (1906–86) 218
Viani, Lorenzo (1882–1936) 218
Vicentino, Andrea (c.1542–c.1617) 95, 101, 106, 107, 168, 213, 281, 337, 338
Vicentino, Marco (17C) 174
Vignole, Le, island of 331, 341
Villa Heriott 307
Visconti, Pietro (active mid-18C) 179
Visentini, Antonio (1688–1782) 133, 134
Vittoria, Alessandro (1525–1608) 75, 79, 83, 84, 95, 101, 110, 112, 118, 165, 170, 180, 192, 199, 228, 242, 257, **259**, 270, 279, 281, 282, 284, 301, 304, 318; (tomb of) 259
Vivaldi, Antonio 136, **261**, 275, 289
Vivarini family 20
Vivarini, Alvise (son of Antonio; 1445/6–1503/4) 79, 152, 184, 204, **260**, 281, 310
Vivarini, Antonio (brother-in-law of Giovanni d'Alemagna; c.1415–84) 144, 158, 165, 176, 237, 258, *258*, 313; (works attributed to) 270

Vivarini, Bartolomeo (brother of Antonio; active 1450–99) 76, 123, 152, 201, 204, 260, **272**, 281; (works from cartoons by) 284

W

Wagner, Richard 117, 136, 140, **233**, 255
Wells, Venetian 33–34
Whistler, James McNeill (1834–1903) 130, 179
Wildt, Adolfo (1868–1931) 219
Willaert, Adrian 57
Wolf-Ferrari, Ermanno 176; (grave of) 311
Woolson, Constance Fenimore 142
Wotton, Sir Henry **135**, 232
Wright, Frank Lloyd (1869–1959) 140
Wullekopf, Ernst (late 19C) 310

Z

Zais, Guiseppe (1709–81) 151, 180, 182
Zanchi, Antonio (1631–1722) 110, 119, 164, 175, 210, 292, 296
Zanchi, Francesco (1734–72) 63
Zandomeneghi, Luigi (1778–1850) 199, 206
Zandomeneghi, Pietro (son of Luigi; 1806–66) 206
Zara (Zadar) 166
Zattere, Fondamenta delle 186–90
Zecca 13, 85
Zelotti, Giovanni Battista (1526–78) 82, 109
Zen family 252; (Cappella Zen) 62
Zen, Francesco 252
Zen, Cardinal Giovanni Battista 62, 63
Zen, Doge Ranier (*see* Zeno)
Zendrini, Bernardino (1679–1747) 333
Zeno, Doge Ranier 9, 252; (portrait of) 54; (tomb of) 285
Ziani, Doge Pietro 59
Ziani, Doge Sebastiano 9, 48, 87, 332
Zitelle, church of 306
Zoppo, Marco (Marco Antonio di Ruggero; c.1433–78) 158
Zorzi, Fra' Francesco 266
Zotto, Antonio dal (1841–1918) 113, 281
Zuccarelli, Francesco (1702–88/9) 151
Zuccari, Federico (?1540–1609) 106, 270
Zuccato, Arminio (son of Valerio; d.1606) 300
Zuccato brothers (Francesco and Valerio; d.1577 and 1576) 52, 63
Zucconi, Francesco 272
Zugno, Francesco (1709–87) 318, 340

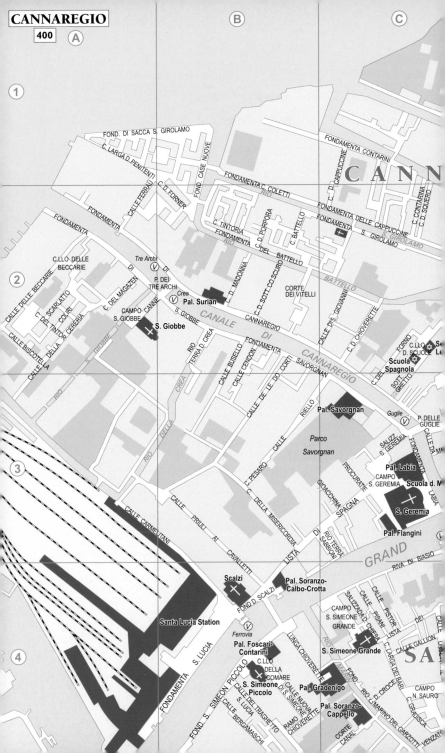

CANNAREGIO

400 (A)

(B)

(C)

1

FOND. DI SACCA S. GIROLAMO

C. LARGA D. PENITENTI

FONDAMENTA

FONDAMENTA CONTARINI

C A N N

C. D. CAPPUCCINE

C. CONTARINA

C. D. SQUERO

FOND. CASE NUOVE

FONDAMENTA C. COLETTI

FONDAMENTA DELLE CAPPUCCINE

FONDAMENTA S. GIROLAMO

CALLE FERRAU

C. D. FORNER

C. TINTORIA

C. DI PORPORA

C. BATTELLO

C. D. SOTT. CO. SCURO

FONDAMENTA

C. DEL BATTELLO

C. DEL MAGAZEN

Tre Archi

P. DEI TRE ARCHI (V)

Crea

Pal. Surian

S. GIOBBE

CANALE

CANNAREGIO

CORTE DEI VITELLI

BATTELLO

C.LLO DELLE BECCARIE

C. DELLE BECCARIE

CALLE DEL SCARLATTO

C. DEI TINTOR

COLORI

CERERIA

DELLA

2

CAMPO S. GIOBBE

CANNE

S. Giobbe

S. GIOBBE

RIO DI

DI

C. DI S. GIOVANNI

C. D. CHIOVERETTE

FORNO

C.LLO D. SCUOLE

S

Le

CALLE BISCOTELLA

DI

S. GIOBBE

RIO

DELLA

TERRA D. CREA

FONDAMENTA

DI

CANNAREGIO

Scuola Spagnola

SOTT.

DEL GHETTO

RIO

CALLE BUSELLO

CALLE CENDON

CALLE DE LE DO. CORTI

SAVORGNAN

RIELLO

Pal. Savorgnan

Guglie

P. DELLE GUGLIE (V)

3

CALLE CARMELITANI

CALLE PRIULI AL CAVALLETTI

C. PESARO

CALLE

C. DELLA MISERICORDIA

Parco Savorgnan

PROCURATI

GIOACCHINA

SPAGNA

DI

RIO TERRA

SABBION

SALIZZ. S. GEREMIA

CAMPO S. GEREMIA

Pal. Labia

Scuola d. M

S. Geremia

LABIA

CALLE DA

Pal. Flangini

GRAND

RIVA DI BIASIO

LISTA

4

Scalzi

FOND. D. SCALZI

Pal. Soranzo-Calbo-Crotta

CAMPO S. SIMEONE GRANDE

SALIZZADA D. CHIESA

CALLE PISANI

CALLE PISTOR

DEL

LISTA

SA

Santa Lucia Station

Ferrovia (V)

Pal. Foscari-Contarini

C.LLO DELLA COMARE

S. Simeone Piccolo

LUNGA CHIOVERETTE

S. Simeone Grande

CALLE GALLION

FONDAMENTA S. LUCIA

FOND. S. SIMEON PICCOLO

CALLE BERGAMASCHI

S. LUCIA

CALLE DEL TRAGHETTO

CALLE NUOVA DI S. SIMEONE

RAMO CHIOVERETTE

Pal. Gradenigo

Pal. Soranzo-Cappello

FOND. C. MARINO DEL GARZOTTI

RIO C. MARINO DEL GARZOTTI

CAMPO N. SAURO

CALLE GRADISCA

VENZATO

CORTE CANAL

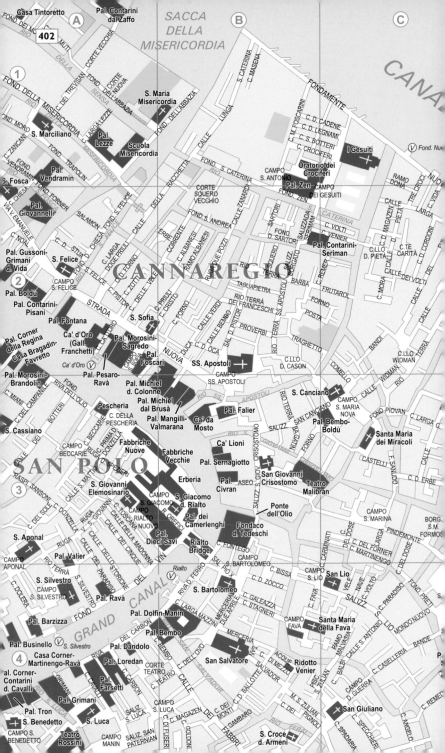

D

E

F

1

0   300 yards

0   300 metres

2

DELLE

FONDAMENTE

NUOVE

Ⓥ Ospedale

S. Lazzaro d. Mendicanti

NUOVE

Ⓥ S. Giustina

Celestia Ⓥ

3

rande
larco

vanni e Paolo

Ospedaletto

C. TORRELLI

OV. E PAOLO

OSPED.

BARBARIA DELLE TOLE C. DEL CAFFETTIER

MUAZZO

MOSCHETTE

CALLE D.

CALLE DELLE CAPPUCCINE

FONDAMENTA DI S. GIUSTINA

S. FRANCESCO

CALLE
TEDEUM

C. D.

San Francesco della Vigna

CAMPO
D. CONFRATERNITA

CALLE

CIMITERO

CALLE D' ORATORIO

CALLE SAGREDO

C. D. ORTI

FOND

CASE NUOVE

CAMPO
D. CELESTIA

CORTE
D. MUNEGHE

CASTELLO

S. Giustina

CAMPO
S. GIUSTINA

C. DEL
FONTEGO

SALIZZ. S. GIUSTINA

DEL MORION

CAMPO
S. TERNITÀ

MADONNETTA

C. LARGA S. LORENZO

BORGOLOCO S. LORENZO

CALLE
CAPPELLO

S. Lorenzo

CAMPO
S. LORENZO

CALLE

S. LORENZO

RIO S. LORENZO

SALIZZ. S. GIUSTINA

C. ZORZI

CORTE NUOVA

CALLE
FRANCESCO

SALIZZ S. GATTE

SALIZZ.
D. GATTE

C. D. VIDA

VIDA

CALLE DRAZZI

C. DEL'OLIO

C. DONA

C. MAGNO

C. CESI

4

RIOSA

METZO

FONDAM. S. SEVERO

CORTE D.
PARADISO

Zorzi-Bon

Pal. Zorzi

Questura

FONDAM.
GIORGIO D. SCHIAVONI

SALIZZ. S. AGOSTINO

Scuola di San Giorgio
degli Schiavoni

CAMPO
D. GATTE

CALLE DEI FURLANI

C.LLO
DUE POZZI

C. D. SCUDI

C. DONA

MUNEGHETTE

GORNE

al.
ani

CORONA

SALIZZ. ZORZI

CORTE

ROTTA

Pal. Priuli

PRETI

FOND.
OSMARIN

FOND. DELL'OSMARIN

LION

Ponte
d. Greci

MADONNA

SALIZZ. D. GRECI

MAGAZEN

FOND. D. FURLANI

S. Antonin

C. DELL'ARCO

PISC. S. MARTIN

Arsenale

REMEDIO

Museum
of Icons

San Giorgio dei Greci

D E F

DARSENA

GRANDE

1

S. Pietro Ⓥ

CAMPO
S. DANIELE

RIO

RIELLO

STRETTA

CALLE LARGA S. PIETRO

S. PIETRO

CAMPO
S. PIETRO

San Pietro di Castello

TERCO

C. S. GIOVANNI
IN RIELLO

C.LLO
FIGARETTO

CAMPO
DI RUGA

RUGA

MARAFONI

DIETRO IL
CAMPANILE

CANALE

Isola di
San Pietro

Arsenale

S. DANIELE

TANA

FOND. RIELLO

RIELLO

C. SALAMON

FOND. QUINTAVALLE

LARGA QUINTAVALLE

C. DI MEZZO

2

DELLA

DELLA

TANA

C. FRIZIER

C. BASSA

C. LOREDAN

CHINOTTO

FOND. FORNER

C. CAPROZOLO

CORTE
BIANCO

CROCIERA

S. ANNA

S. ANNA

FOND. QUINTAVALLE

C.LLO
DEI
POMERI

FOND. CASTEL QUINO

CALLE DEI PRETI

CALLE S. FRANCESCO DI PAOLA

S. Francesco
d. Paola

FOND. S. GIOACCHINO

FONDAMENTA S. ANNA

ANNA

S. Anna

C.LLO
CORRER

Ospedale
de le Pute

CALLE S. DOMENICO

CALLE S. SCHIAVONI

CORTE
NUOVA

GARIBALDI

SOTTO CALLE
DI PISTOR

CALLE DELL'ANGELO

STRETTA SARESIN

C. SECCO MARINA

CALLE DELLE ANCORE

RAMO DEI NICOLI

CORTE SARESIN

CALLE FURLANE

CORTE MAGAZEN

CALLE CORRERA

CALLE G. B. TIEPOLO

CALLE CATAPAN

CALLE
CORRERA

MARINA

CORTE
CRISTO

SABBIONERA

CORTE
MARTIN
NOVELLO

Viale Garibaldi

Giardini Garibaldi

VIALE GARIBALDI

RIO TERRA D. FORNER

SECCO

CORTE
CENERE

CORTE
SOLDA

FONDAMENTA SAN GIUSEPPE

CORTE
PIETRO

CORTE
PRETE

CALLE S. GIUSEPPE

3

Isola di

S. Elena

CAMPO
S. GIUSEPPE

S. Giuseppe d. Castello

RIO TERRÀ S. GIUSEPPE

PALUDO S. ANTONIO

CALLE DENTRO IL GIARDINO

GIARDINI

VIALE
XXIV MAGG.

RAMO DI
MONTELLO

NERVESA

SETTE

MARTIRI

RIVA

Giardini Ⓥ

Giardini

Pubblici

V.LE
TRIESTE

DEI

Biennale

TRENTO

NOVEMBRE

CAMPO
D. GRAPPA

C. D. MONTELLO

IV

4

PARTIGIANI

CALLE DEL
CARSO

VIALE

GEN. CHINOTTO

CALLE
BAINSIZZA

GORIZIA

M A R C O

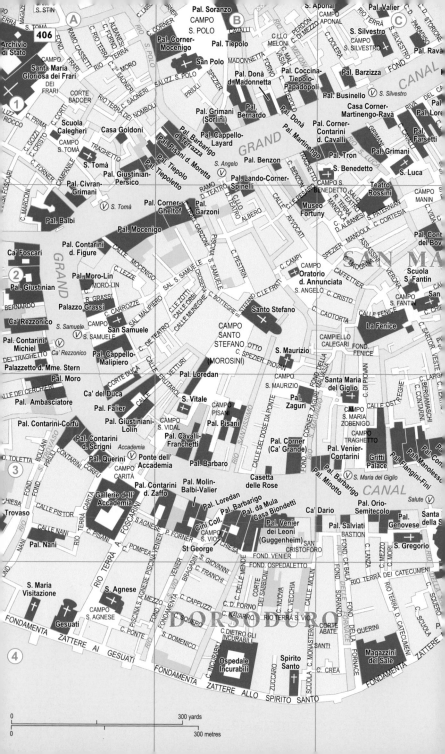

SAN MARCO & EAST DORSODURO

BACINO DI S. MARCO

Isola di San Giorgio Maggiore

San Lio
CAMPO S. LIO
C. BISSA
C. D. ZOCCO
C. FAVA
C. PARADISO
FOND. PRETI
CAMPO SANTA MARIA FORMOSA
C. LUNGA S. M. FORMOSA
MADONNETTA
BORGOLOCO S. LORENZO
C. LARGA S. LORENZO
Pal. Grimani
Questura
C. D. GALEAZZA
C. STAGNERI
MERCERIA DUE APRILE
CAMPO FAVA
Santa Maria della Fava
RAMO MALVASIA
CALLE S. ANTONIO
C. M. NUOVO
BANDE
Santa Maria Formosa
RUGA GIUFFA
C. DEGLI
C. DEL MEZZO
FOND. S. SEVERO

San Salvatore
MERCERIA
C. C. DI MEZZO
Ridotto Venier
C. BALBI
PISC. ZULIAN
ACQUE DI MEZZO
C. D. BALLOTTE
SALVADOR
CAMPO D. GUERRA
C. QUERINI
FOND. REMEDIO
Pal. Querini-Stampalia
CORTE D. PARADISO
Pal. Zorzi-Bon
Pal. Zorzi
SALIZZ. ZORZI
PRETI
Ponte d. Greci

M. S. ZULIAN
C. DEI MONTI
C. DEI PIGNOLI
San Giuliano
C. ANGELO
FOND. REMEDIO
S. Giovanni Nuovo
SAGRESTIA
MERCANTI
CALLE CORONA
CORTE ROTTA
Pal. Priuli
FOND. OSMARIN
FOND. DELL'OSMARIN
Museum of Icons

GAMBARO
RIO FERAL
C. DEI FERALI
C. SPADARIA
C. SPECHIERI
S. MARCO
C. FIGHER
C. DEL CHIESA
CAMPO SS. FILIPPO E GIACOMO
SALIZZ. S. PROVOLO
FOND. DELL'OSMARIN

STRAZZE
TERRA D. COLONNE
S. Croce d. Armeni
MERC. D'OROLOGIO
C. CANONICA
RUGA GIUFFA
CAMPO S. PROVOLO
San Zaccaria

GRIGOLINI
RAMO S. GALLO
C. FIUBERA
CALLE
PTTA GIOVANNI XXIII
Pal. Patriarcale
ALBANESI
CAMPO S. ZACCARIA
RIO D. GRECI

C. GALLO
FABBRI
Torre d'Orologio
Mus. Diocesan Art
FOND. D. VIN
SOTT. S. ZACCARIA

CRON DORSODURO
BAC. ORSEOLO
Procuratie Vecchie
St Mark's Basilica
Bridge of Sighs
CALLE D. RASSE
Hotel Danieli
C. D. VIN

B. DI PIAZZA
SALVADEGO
CALLE DELL'ASCENSION
PIAZZA SAN MARCO
Campanile
Doge's Palace
Prisons
Ponte d. Vin
DEGLI
SCHIAVONI

Museo Correr
Procuratie Nuove
Museo Archeologico
PIAZZETTA S. MARCO
RIVA
P. DELLA PAGLIA
V S. Zaccaria

S. MOISE
Ridotto
Zecca
Libreria Marciana
Giardinetti

Moisè
BAROZZI
C. 13 MARTIRI
FOND. DEL RIDOTTO
C. VALLARESSO
FOND. D. FARINE
Pal. Giustinian
Cap. Porto
Harry's Bar
V San Marco Vallaresso

Treves onfili
OGANA ALLA SALUTE
gana di Mare
Punta della Dogana

CAMPO S. GIORGIO
S. Giorgio V
San Giorgio Maggiore
Cini Foundation

① ② ③ ④
D E F

SAN POLO & SANTA CROCE

A · B · C

1

300 yards
300 metres

CALLE BRULI AI CAVALLETTI

CALLE CARMELITAN

CALLE DI SPAGNA

LISTA DI SPAGNA

CAMPO S. GEREMIA

Scuola d. Morti

S. Geremia

Pal. Flangini

GIOACCHINA

ROCCHRATE

CANNA

LABIA

PONTE EDUIA

 C. ANTONIO

C. QUERINI

Pal. Correr-Co

Pal. Giovan

R. d. Biasio

RIVA DI BIASIO

GRAND

RIO TERRA SABBION

Scalzi

FOND. D. SCALZI

Pal. Soranzo-Calbo-Crotta

Santa Lucia Station

Ferrovia

Pal. Foscari-Contarini

C.LLO DELLA COMARE

S. Simeone Piccolo

CALLE BERGAMASCHI

CALLE S. LUCIA

FONDAMENTA S. LUCIA

FOND. S. SIMEON PICCOLO

FOND. RIO MONASTERO

FOND. DEI TOLENTINI

Piazzale Roma

Giardino Papadopoli

CAMPO S. SIMEONE GRANDE

SALIZADA D. SIMEONE

CALLE PISANI

CALLE PISTOR

CALLE LISTA

DEI BARI

CALLE LARGA DEI BARI

CALLE GALLION

RUGA VECCHIA

SANTA

S. D

C. BEMBO

CORTE CAZZA

SALIZ. GIUSTO

RAMO CAZZA

CALLE SAVIO

RUGA BELLA

San de

S. Simeone Grande

Pal. Gradenigo

CALLE NUOVA DI S. SIMEONE

RAMO CHIOVERETTE

Pal. Soranzo-Cappello

LUNGA CHIOVERETTE

CALLE DEL TRAGHETTO

CAMPO N. SAURO

CAMPO D. STROPE

CORTE ANATOMIA

CALLE D.

C.LLO DEL CRISTO

C. S. ZUANE

RIO MARIN

FOND. RIO D. CROCE

CORTE CANAL

CALLE CANAL

CALLE VISCIGA

CALLE LARGA CONTARINA

MARINO DEL GARZOTT

DEL VENZATO

CORTE CASE NUOVE

CAMPO DELLA LANA

SACCHERE

CALLE DELLA

CALLE

Scuola Grande S. G. Evangelista

CALLE ZANE

CAMPO S. STIN

S. Giovanni Evangelista

LACCA

MAGAZEN

S. TOMA

TERRA

CON

CALLE AMAI

SACCHERE

CALLE MEZZO

C. CAMPAZO

FONDERIA

RIO

C. D. CHIOVERE

PIAZZALE ROMA

CAMPO TOLENTINI

S. Nicola d. Tolentino

C. LAVADORI

C. CONDULMER

FOND. MAGAZEN

FOND. MINOTTO

FOND. DEL GAFFARO

RAMO CIMESIN

CORTE D. SPIRITI

CALLE SPIRITI

CALLE FALIER

C. D. FORNO

RAMO S.

C.LLO DELLETRO

PIETRO TINTORETTO S. ROCCO

C. DIETRO

C.LLO CASTELFORTE

Archivio di Stato

San Rocco

Santa Maria Gloriosa dei Fr

DEI FRARI

CAMPO

C. PRIMA

S. Ca

S. Cal

C. CRISTO

C. FORNER

COSSETTI

CALLE

CAMPAZZO TRE PONTI

FOND. ELLE BURCHIELLE

FONDAMENTA TRE PONTI

FOND. PIGAN

FOND. CAZZIOLA

FOND. CREMONESE

RIO TERRA DEI PENSIERI

FONDAMENTA DEL RIO NUOVO

FONDAMENTA

C. CERERIA

C. SBIACCA

FOND. GALLO

CORTE GALLO

CALLE E CORTE BASEGO

SALIZ. S. PANTALON

C. MOLIN

C. D. FORNO

C.TE NUOVA

C. VINANTI

C.LLO MOSCA

CORTE BARBO

S. Pantalon

CAMPO S. PANTALON

CALLE DEI PRETI CROSERA

SAONERIA

Scuola Grande di San Rocco

SALIZ. S. ROCCO

CAMPO

C. SCALATER

FONDAMENTA RIZZI

FOND. DELLE PROCURATIE

RIO TERRA DEI PENSIERI

FONDAMENTA ROSSA

CALLE DEI GUARDIANI

CAPPELLO

FONDAMENTA DEL

CERERI

SFORCA

CALLE LARGA RAGUSEI

CALLE RAGUSEI

DEL RIO

RIO NUOVO

RIO NUOVO

CALLE RENIER

C. DELLA CHIESA

C.LLO S. PANTALON

MAGARAN

DELL'ASEO

SAONERIA

CALLE LARGA FOSCARI

CAMPO MAGAZEN

SANTA MARGHERITA

CALLE LARGA FOSCARI

RIO

FOSCARI

D. CA'

Pal. Ba

Ca' Foscari

Pal. Giustinian

C. MARCONI

FORNO

FOSCARINI

C. CAPPELLER

C.LLO SQUELLINI

Scuola Varotari

Scuola Grande dei Carmini

CAMPO CARMINI

S. Maria dei Carmini

Pal. Arian

Pal. Zenobio

FONDAMENTA BRIATI

FONDAMENTA

SOCCORSO

RIO TERRA DELLA SCOAZZERA

RIO TERRA SCOAZZERA

RIO TERRA CANAL

C. D. VIDA

C.LLO SQUELLINI

BARNABA

Ca' Rezzonico

Pal. Contarini Michiel

S. Barnaba

Palazzetto d. Mme S

CALLE BERNARDO

Pala

FOND. ALBERTI FOND. REZZONICO

FOND. SQUERO

RIO GHERARDINI

Ponte d. Pugni

CAMPO S. BARNABA

Ca' Re

C. DEL TRAGHETTO

DORSODURO

2

3

4

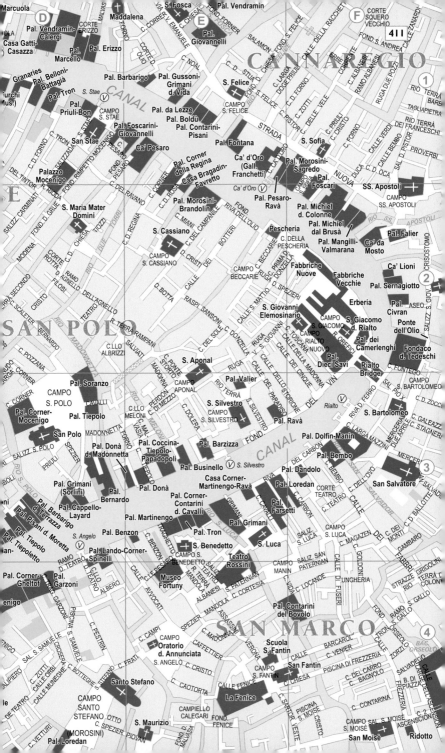

NAL

D Ⓥ Salute

o-
olo

Pal.
Genovese

Santa Maria
della Salute

CAMPO
SALUTE

FOND. DOGANA ALLA SALUTE

E

Dogana di Mare

Punta della
Dogana

GIUDECCA

F 413

C. MEZZO

C. MORI

+
S. Gregorio

DEI CATECUMENI

Seminario
Patriarcale

1

RIO TERRA D. CATECUMENI

C. SQUERO

SCUOLA

ZATTERE AI

C. SALONI

P. dell'Umiltà

RIO DELLA SALUTE

azzini
Sale

DAMENTA

CAMPO
NANI E BARBARO

FOND. S. GIOVANNI

2

DECCA

Zitelle Ⓥ

FOND. D. ZITELLE

+

Zitelle

Hotel Cipriani

CROCE

DELLA

FONDAMENTA

CALLE   DELLA

CROCE

C. DRIO LA CROCE

CALLE

CALLE

C. DEL GRAN

C. D. ASILO MASON

3

MICHELANGELO

CALLE DELLO OSPIZIO

FOND. AL RIO DELLA CROCE

CALLE DELLO SQUERO

C. D. FONDERIA

4

Map

**Pianta generale
e avvertenze**

*General map
and notes*

Linee centrocittà

in entrambi i sensi
two ways

Linee giracittà

in senso antiorario
anticlockwise

in senso orario
clockwise

Linee lagunari

in entrambi i sensi
two ways

Linee stagionali

monodirezionali
one way

Legenda

Effettua la fermata
Does stop here

Non effettua la fermata
Does not stop here

Autobus actv
Actv bus

Ospedale
Hospital

Ferrovia
Railway

Parcheggio
Park

Taxi

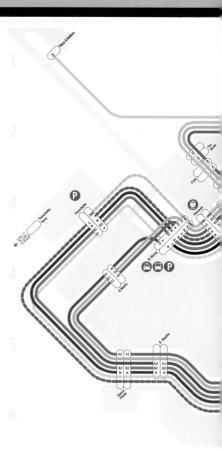

Avvertenze

Per valigie o colli il cui alto supera i 50 cm il passeggero è tenuto al pagamento di un regolare biglietto di corsa semplice.

Nessuna responsabilità può essere attribuita agli agenti addetti alla vendita se i reclami non vengono presentati tempestivamente (Ministero dei Trasporti, n.11246 del 15.10.1957 e n.4273 del 17.05.1961).

I biglietti in corso di validità non sono rimborsabili e non possono essere sostituiti.

In caso di chiusura della biglietteria il passeggero può acquistare il biglietto a bordo richiedendolo al marinaio subito dopo l'imbarco evitando così le sanzioni per mancanza di titolo di viaggio.

La mancanza del biglietto o il suo uso irregolare comporta l'applicazione delle sanzioni della Legge Regionale n.25 del 30.10.1998 che prevedono il pagamento della tariffa ordinaria più una sanzione.

Notes

Please try to prepare the right change before buying your ticket.
Important: you must check both your ticket and change as our ticket staff cannot be held responsible for complaints that are not made immediately (Ministry of Transport regulations No. 11246 of 15.10.1957 and No. 4273 of 17.05.1961).

Once you have stamped your ticket, it cannot be refunded or replaced.

If the ticket offices are closed, you can buy your ticket on board by asking the boat attendant immediately after getting on otherwise you will have to pay a fine.

If you travel without a proper ticket or are using a ticket improperly, you will be liable for a fine (as per Regional Law No. 25 of 30.10.1998) plus the cost of the ticket.

If you have a bag, case or other item having one side longer than 50 cm, you must pay the price of a full oneway ticket.

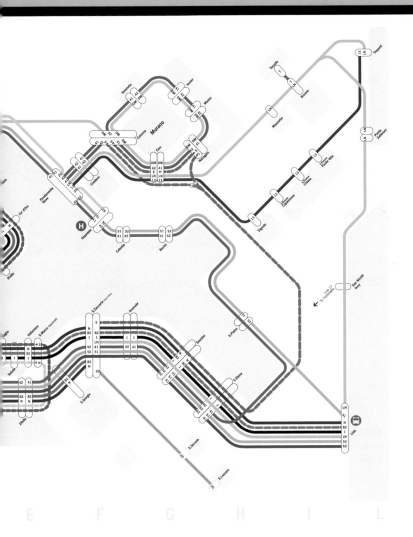

contd. from p. 6

Editor-in-chief: Annabel Barber
Assistant editor: Judy Tither; Editorial assistant: Sophie Livall
Editorial board: Charles Freeman, Nigel McGilchrist

With additional contributions to the text from Joseph Kling (wine);
and special thanks to Jonathan Brown, Rowley Leigh and Richard Robinson

Layout and design: Anikó Kuzmich
Maps: Dimap Bt
Floor plans and watercolours: Imre Bába
Architectural line drawings: Michael Mansell RIBA & Gabriella Juhász

Photo editor: Hadley Kincade
Photographs by Sarah Quill ©: pp. 128, 142, 167, 236, 248, 286, 287, 324, 335;
Phil Robinson: pp. 45, 46, 53, 92, 93, 118, 177, 189, 302;
Annabel Barber: pp. 3, 121, 122, 172, 197, 221, 251, 253, 258, 290, 298, 300; Imre Baric: p. 317
Alinari Archives/Bridgeman: pp. 78, 183, 201, 282; Alinari Archives, Florence: pp. 205, 264;
Uliano Lucas ©/Alinari: p. 161; © Cameraphoto Arte, Venezia: pp. 207, 269, 326;
Courtesy of the Ministero per i Beni e le Attività Culturali: pp. 68–69, 148–49, 153, 156–57.

Cover images
Top: View of Piazza San Marco and San Giorgio Maggiore (©Navin Mistry/Alamy);
Bottom: Door of Sant'Alipio (detail), St Mark's basilica (photo: Phil Robinson);
Spine: Detail from Vittore Carpaccio's San Vitale altarpiece.

Author's acknowledgements
The author is indebted in the first instance to Frances Clarke, who, as for all the previous
editions of this guide, provided generous help in countless ways. She was always at hand to
share her profound knowledge of Venice, from its works of art to the problems it faces. Laura
Corti provided hospitality on several visits during work on the guide. Helpful information on
restaurants was kindly supplied by Gabriela Torzo Comunello. At the Azienda di Promozione
Turistica della Provincia di Venezia, Roberta Valmarana checked part of the practical information.

Printed in Hungary by Dürer Nyomda Kft, Gyula

ISBN 978–1–905131–17–4

About the contributors
Nigel McGilchrist (N.McG.) is an art historian who has lived in the Mediterranean—Italy, Greece
and Turkey—for over twenty-five years, working for a period for the Italian Ministry of Arts and
then for six years as Director of the Anglo-Italian Institute in Rome. He has taught at the
University of Rome, for the University of Massachusetts, and was for seven years Dean of
European Studies for a consortium of American universities. He lectures widely in art and
archaeology at museums and institutions in Europe and the United States, and lives near Orvieto.

Charles Freeman (C.F.) is a freelance academic historian with a long-standing interest in Italy and
the Mediterranean. His *Egypt, Greece and Rome, Civilizations of the Ancient Mediterranean* (second
edition, Oxford University Press, 2004) is widely used as an introductory textbook to the ancient
world. His most recent book, *The Horses of St Mark's* (Little Brown, 2004), is a study of the famous
horses through their history in Constantinople and Venice. He leads study tours of Italy for the
Historical Association and has recently been elected a Fellow of the Royal Society of Arts.